Soft Computing
in Financial Engineering

Studies in Fuzziness and Soft Computing

Editor-in-chief

Prof. Janusz Kacprzyk
Systems Research Institute
Polish Academy of Sciences
ul. Newelska 6
01-447 Warsaw, Poland
E-mail: kacprzyk@ibspan.waw.pl

continued on page 507

R. A. Ribeiro · H.-J. Zimmermann
R. R. Yager · J. Kacprzyk (Eds.)

Soft Computing
in Financial Engineering

With 160 Figures
and 73 Tables

Physica-Verlag

A Springer-Verlag Company

Dr. Rita Almeida Ribeiro
Department of Informatics
Faculty of Sciences and Technology
Universidade Nova de Lisboa
2825 Monte Caparica
Portugal
E-mail: rr@di.fct.unl.pt

Prof. Dr. Dr. h.c. Hans-Jürgen Zimmermann
Lehrstuhl für Unternehmensforschung
Rheinisch-Westfälische Technische Hochschule (RWTH)
Templergraben 64
52062 Aachen
Germany
E-mail: zi@or.rwth-aachen.de

Prof. Ronald R. Yager
Machine Intelligence Institute
Iona College
New Rochelle, NY 10801
USA
E-mail: Yager@panix.com

Prof. Janusz Kacprzyk
Systems Research Institute
Polish Academy of Sciences
ul. Newelska 6
01-447 Warsaw
Poland
E-mail: kacprzyk@ibspan.waw.pl

ISBN 3-7908-1173-4 Physica-Verlag Heidelberg New York

Cataloging-in-Publication Data applied for
Die Deutsche Bibliothek – CIP-Einheitsaufnahme
Soft computing in financial engineering / Rita A. Ribeiro ... ed. – Heidelberg; New York:
Physica-Verl., 1999
   (Studies in fuzziness and soft computing; Vol. 28)
   ISBN 3-7908-1173-4

© Physica-Verlag Heidelberg 1999
Printed in Germany

Hardcover Design: Erich Kirchner, Heidelberg

SPIN 10697003   88/2202-5 4 3 2 1 0 – Printed on acid-free paper

Preface

Soft computing, a term coined by L. A. Zadeh of the University of California at Berkeley, consists of a number of interrelated disciplines which include: fuzzy sets theory, neural networks, genetic computing, and probabilistic methods. However, more important then the constituents of this field is the underlying philosophy of soft computing.

The basic agenda of soft computing is to bring to bear to the complex problems we are trying to solve with computers some of the effective tools that humans use in solving problems. Particularly important is the idea that precision in terms both of our available information and our rules of action is neither possible nor often desirable.

A second important idea in soft computing is the use of generalization based upon an the assumption of local continuity. This view allows practitioners of soft computing to use well know prototypical situations to provide guidelines for actions in novel situations. This idea is in the spirit of case based reasoning.

In the 1960's and 1970's the functioning of the computer as an information processing device served as an inspiration for the construction of systems models in a number of disciplines. However, especially in the cognitive and biological sciences, soft computing can be seen as the reversal of this process: here human biological and cognitive processes are being used as the inspiration for computer models, i.e. *hard science* is imitating *soft science*.

In this book we focus on the application of soft computing to a new emerging discipline called *financial engineering*. Financial engineering can be seen as a field emerging out of an attempt to address the issues of concern in finance with the tools and perspectives of engineering, especially electrical and systems engineering.

The ability to measure almost all financial variables in quantifiable terms, the strong emphasis on optimization, and the centrality of time dependency provide for a strong overlap of those disciplines. This all provides a synergistic effect, and makes it possible to more effectively and efficiently deal with a variety of problems related to broadly perceived financial analyses.

In the first part of the volume a discussion of more general issues related to fuzziness, verbal variables and decision making is provided.

M. Mareš and R. Mesiar (*Vagueness of Verbal Variables*) discuss the representation and processing of vague, verbal expressions (variables and relations) which are often used by humans in virtually all analyses of economic and financial problems, in addition to precise, quantitative expressions employed in conventional models.

R.R. Yager and M.T. Lamata (*Decision Making under Uncertainty with Nonnumeric Payoffs*) present a general model of decision making under uncertainty using the Dempster-Shafer belief structure, and the ordered weighted avaraging (OWA) operators. Nonnumeric payoffs are assumed, and the linear and nonlinear scale is assumed to represent that nonnumeric information.

S. Greco (*Fuzzy Measures and Equilibrium Conditions on the Financial Market*) discusses a generalization of a well known equilibrium condition on the financial market. Situations are considered in which the representation of uncertainty in terms of a probabilistic measure is inappropriate. Uncertainty is modeled by using a fuzzy measure of events.

M. Mareš (*Sharing Vague Profit in Fuzzy Cooperation*) considers economic cooperation using tools and techniques of coalition game theory. He assumes that agents may have a vague idea about the expected coalitional profits, and employs fuzzy sets and fuzzy numbers to represent that vague knowledge, and then to derive vague output distributions of individual payoffs.

In the second part of the volume issues related to the use of soft computing techniques, mainly of fuzzy sets theory and neural networks, to financial time series analyses and prediction are dealt with.

S. Giove and P. Pellizzari (*Time Series Filtering and Reconstruction Using Fuzzy Weighted Local Regression*) discuss an important problem in the detection of outliers in time series analysis. They propose a fuzzy weighted index to select suspicious values and then describe a procedure for the replacement of those anmalous points based on fuzzy linear local approximation. An application to the Italian COMIT stock index in presented.

O. Castillo and P. Melin (*Automated Mathematical Modelling for Financial Time Series Prediction Combining Fuzzy Logic and Fractal Theory*) present a new method for time series prediction using a combination of techniques in fuzzy logic, dynamic systems and fractal theory. Basically, this synergistic combination of soft computing tools can help better simulate and automate the human reasoning process in financial time series prediction. The method proposed can be implemented as a intelligent decision support system.

P.L. Belcaro and M. Corazza (A 2-Stage Artificial Neural Network Predictor with Application to Financial Time Series) develop a neural network forecasting system using a two-stage approach. At the first stage some networks are implemented to consider different specifications of forecasting models, for each forecasting scenario. At the second stage, different predictions obtained from the particular first stage forecasting models are combined to generate a final output whose quality is improved.

R. Kozma and N.K. Kasabov (*Generic Neuro-Fuzzy Chaos Methdology for Time-Series Analysis and Building Intelligent Adaptive Systems*) propose a general methodology for chaotic time series analysis. The prediction is implemented as a hierarchical process in which higher level trends are predicted first. Then a corresponding hierarchical multimodular structure is built to model the time series at different levels. This is done by using a fuzzy neural network, *FuNN*, which allows for structural learning with forgetting, rules insertion and extraxtion, etc. Fuzzy rules for explaining chaotic time series are extracted. An application for the analysis of a stock index time series is presented.

M. Krawczak (*Dynamic Programming and Fuzzy Reinforcement of Back-propagation for Interest Rate Prediction*) shows that the use of dynamic programming for the learning of a feedforward neural network elucidates the very nature of the backpropagation algorithm. It is shown that some features of the learning process can be converted into fuzzy linguistic rules for the reinforcement of the backpropagation algorithm.

The third part of the volume is concerned with various issues relevant for the stock and currency markets.

H. Tanaka and P. Guo (*Portfolio Selection Based on Possibility Theory*) discuss possibilistic models of portfolio selection of fuzzy mathematical programming type. First, possibilistic models based on aspiration levels of the decisionmaker, possibility and necessity measures, and fuzzy probabilities are discussed. Then, possibilistic models based on lower and upper exponential possibility distributions are dealt with. A numerical example of selecting a portfolio of American stocks is shown.

S. Siekmann, R. Neuneier, H.G. Zimmermann and R. Kruse (*Neuro-Fuzzy Methods Applied to the German Stock Index DAX*) develop a neuro-fuzzy system, combined with a semantic preserving learning algorithm, which can make an effective and efficient use of expert knowledge and historical data. The method proposed is implemented in SENN (Simulation Environment for Neural Networks), a product of Siemens AG. Encouraging prediction results of daily returns of the German Stock Index DAX are reported.

M.A. Soares Machado, L.A. Rodrigues Gaspar, A. Aradjo de Freitas Jr. and R. Castro Souza (*IBOVESPA Neuro-Fuzzy Forecasting: A Case Study in Brazilian Capital Markets*) present two neuro-fuzzy adaptive inference systems, using the ANFIS (Adaptive Neuro-Fuzzy Inference System) model, for time series prediction. A mechanism for the inclusion of empirical knowledge is included. The model is used for the prediction of the highly liquid Brazilian IBOVESPA nominal spot index. A comparison with the Box-Jenkins algorithm is presented.

K.K. Yen and S. Ghoshray (*Application of Fuzzy Regression Models to Predict Exchange Rates for Composite Curencies*) concern issues related to the prediction of exchange rates for composite currencies characterized by an inherent volatility, and uncertain and vague knowledge. They propose a new fuzzy regression analysis model based on fuzzy statistics, assuming that the relationship between the independent and dependent variables is not sharply defined, and that the deviations between the estimated values and the corresponding real values of the output variable is due to imprecisely known system parameters.

S. Ghoshray and K.K. Yen (*A Fuzzy Inferencing Approach Towards the*

Chaotic Nature of Foreign Currency Interactions) analyze the very nature of time series data from the viewpoint of a dynamic system, and explore its deterministic chaotic nature. They present a corresponding method of predicting time series data built around the concepts of embedding and fuzzy reconstruction. The proposed fuzzy reconstruction method based on fuzzy multiple regression analysis is employed to predict foreign currency rates.

S. Tano (*Application of Fuzzy Methodologies to Financial Fields: FOREX, Case Studies and Generalizations*) presents, first, FOREX (Foreign Exchange Trade Support Expert System), one of the biggest fuzzy expert systems developed at LIFE Laboratory in Japan which contins ca. 300 fuzzy frames and 5000 fuzzy rules. Then, he describes a fuzzy system development tool, FINEST (Fuzzy Inference Environment Software with Tuning), which is a knowledge based system shell developed on the basis of experience gained from the use of FOREX.

The fourth part of the volume is concerned with the use of soft computing methods for various corporate financial analyses.

S. Benferhat, H. Farreny and II. Prade (*Possibilistic Rule-Based Inference: A Case Study in Financial Analysis*) present an inference engine based on a possibilistic ATMS (Assumption Based Truth Maintenance System) which can deal with uncertain propositions and imprecisely known numerical variables. Moreover, it can correctly handle exceptions. A financial knowledge base containg ca. 40 rules and ca. 20 propositional symbols is used to test the inference engine developed.

R.A. Ribeiro and F. Moura-Pires (*Financial Analysis of Non-Financial Companies with Neural Networks*) present a neural network for the classification of 500 biggest Portuguese companies with the main purpose to find relations and correlations between relevant economic and financial attributes which characterize those companies. Moreover, information relevant from the viewpoint of the most important market players exemplified by banks, stockholders, managers, and government is elicited.

P. Hofmeister (*Customer Segmentation with Fuzzy Clustering*) discusses the use of intelligent data analysis, exemplified by the fuzzy c-means clustering algorithm and non-dichotomous assignment, to represent a fuzzy segmentation of costomers. This is a relevant problem due to an increased competition on financial markets where banks need to better know their customers to be able to more efficiently compete on the market. An example of ca. 300 bank customers described by demographic and socio-economic attributes is presented.

N. Vojdani and M. Bellmann (*A Rejects Management Information System by Means of Fuzzy Logic*) present R-MIS (Rejects Management Information System) which is based on fuzzy logic and uses linguistic variables, fuzzy queries, etc. The system is meant to detect problems and irregularities in the manufacturing of goods. R-MIS is implemented using the pcExpress database and the graphical tool Express/EIS from ORACLE, and applied in the manufacturing of automotive parts.

The fifth part of the volume is devoted to the use of soft computing techniques for the calculation and analyses of risk and value, mainly in the sense of credit solvency, risk of business failure, insurance risk, valuation of real estate properties, etc.

H.J. Rommelfanger (*Fuzzy Logic Based Systems for Checking Credit Solvency of Small Business Firms*) proposes the use of fuzzy control related tools and techniques – mainly the representation of experts' testimonies by linguistic expressions and fuzzy numbers, fuzzy inference, etc. – in expert systems meant for non-engineering field. More specifically, these ideas are used to develop a system for checking the credit solvency of small firms.

R. Weber (it Applications of Fuzzy Logic for Creditworthiness Evaluation) presents the use of fuzzy rule-based and connectionist techniques for a hierarchical aggregation of different criteria with subjective evaluations. These are employed for creditworthiness evaluation of bank customers.

R. Slowinski, C. Zapounodis, A.I. Dimitras and R. Susmaga (*Rough Set Predictor of Business Failure*) propose the use of Pawlak's rough sets theory to the prediction of business failure. They consider 80 Greek companies, divided into "healthy" and bankrupt, and described by 12 financial attributes, and look for a minimal set of attributes providing a satisfactory approximation of the above two classes. The results are compared with those obtained by using an indutive learning technique.

M.R. Simonelli (*Fuzzy Insurance Premium Principles*) considers the premium principle for insurance contracts as a decision theoretic problem, and shown that its relevant part boils down to fuzzy integration. Then, she devises premium functionals using Choquet's and Sugeno's integrals. The variance principle is finally generalized yielding a so-called variance-fuzziness premium principle.

G. Gim and Th. Whalen (*Second Order Data Mining: Fire Risk Classification in a Newly-Developed Country*) examine first the fire risk classification system in South Korea. Mainly, they compare the current manual-based fire insurance rate classification system with statistical loss-based rates. Then, they develop two fire risk assessment models for individual properties. The first is based on linear additive discriminant analysis, and the second on a supervised backpropagation neural network. Linguistic versions of those models are devised.

P.P. Bonissone, W. Cheetham, D.C. Golibersuch and P. Khedkar (*Automated Residential Property Valuation: An Accurate and Reliable Approach Based on Soft Computing*) present a soft computing system which uses multiple fuzzy logic algorithms to determine an estimate of residential property values. The system combines multiple estimates into a single value for the real estate value and an estimate of the reliability of that value. The system is built using enhanced neural networks and case-based reasoning techniques with aspects of fuzzy logic.

The sixth part of the volume is concerned with various issues related to auditing and analysis of financial reports.

S.K. Dutta and R.P. Srivastava (*Theoretical Investigation of Belief Revi-*

sion in Auditing) provide an analysis of the use of belief revision, in both the Bayesian and Dempster-Shafer frameworks, to model the behavior of auditors, mainly in the sense of changing their beliefs based on additional evidence. The concept of a discounted belief function is employed to model the auditors' behavior in the aggregation of evidence.

E.H. Feroz and T.M. Kwon (*Self-Organizing Fuzzy and MLP Approaches to Detecting Fraudulent Financial Reporting*) compare a class of neural network, a multi-layered perceptron, and a self-organizing fuzzy controller to determine the efficacy of some selected redflags of Statement of Auditing Standard No. 53 in predicting targets of the Securities and Exchange Commission (SEC). An analysis of data from 70 companies is presented. A comparison with conventional statistical methods is provided.

June, 1998

Lisbon, Portugal	R. Ribeiro
Aachen, Germany	H.-J. Zimmermann
New Rochelle, NY, USA	R.R. Yager
Warsaw, Poland	J. Kacprzyk

Contents

3. STOCK AND CURRENCY MARKETS

4. CORPORATE FINANCIAL ANALYSES

5. ANALYSES AND CALCULATION OF RISK AND VALUE

6. AUDITING AND REPORTING

1

INTRODUCTORY SECTIONS: IMPRECISE DATA, AND DECISION MAKING UNDER FUZZINESS

Vagueness of Verbal Variables[3]

Milan Mareš[1] and Radko Mesiar[2]

[1] Institute of Information Theory and Automation
   Academy of Sciences of the Czech Republic
   P. O. Box 18, 182 08 Praha 8, Czech Republic
   e–mail: mares@utia.cas.cz

[2] Faculty of Civil Engineering, Slovak Technical University
   Radlinského 11, 813 68 Bratislava, Slovak Republic
   e–mail: mesiar@cvt.stuba.sk

Abstract. Quantitative data and relations are typical for economic thinking. Some of them, namely those ones regarding the expectations of future development, are vague and their evaluation is connected with some uncertainty. The verbal variables and verbally described relations among them represent a specific type of vagueness also frequently appearing in the economic analysis. The representation of verbal variables by fuzzy quantities (and, generally, by fuzzy sets) is natural, and it was already presented in the existing literature. In this paper, we suggest a formal model of verbal variables, consisting of two basic components – a source of the vague data reflecting their typical structure of vagueness, and a generator of the shape of membership functions reflecting the uncertainty of particular fuzzy quantities. Manipulations (compositions, computations, etc.) of verbal expressions can be transformed into analogous handling the two components of their generators. The main purpose of this paper is to suggest corresponding formal operations and to derive their properties. The paper prevailably summarizes and further develops the approach suggested in [9, 10]. Special attention is paid to the interpretations and discussions of its basic concepts.

Key–words: fuzzy set, fuzzy quantity, verbal variable, generating function of fuzzy data, shape generator, vagueness.

1 Introduction

The economic thinking is based on quantitative concepts. In the economic reality, some of them are exactly known, their numerical values and functional

---

[3]Particular parts of the research the results of which are summarized in this paper were partly supported by the Key Project of the Academy of Sciences of the Czech Republic No. 1, by the Grant Agency of the Czech Republic grant No. 402/96/0414, by the EU PHARE Project No. P 95–2014–R, and by the Ministry of Education, Youth and Sports of the Czech Republic project No. VS 96063.

relations are explicitely given. Some other quantities and relations are statistically estimated and they can be processed by means of the classical probabilistic methods. Nevertheless, there still exist economic concepts which are formulated in vague terms. Their vagueness does usually follow either from uncertain knowledge of exact values or from the tendentionally non-exact verbal expressions appearing optimal for their adequate representation. It concerns vague words like *"big"*, *"small"*, *"adequate to situation"*, and additional relativization of numerical values like *"approximately..."*, *"rather more than..."*, *"near to..."* and others. Vague verbal expressions can describe also functional phenomena like *"rather increasing"*, *"with stabilized trend"*, *"irregular development"* of *"almost constant"*. In many cases the vagueness of verbal terms expresses inherent vagueness of the concepts. For example, the verbal formulation *"balanced budget"* does not (and cannot) mean absolute equality of relevant quantities but their approximate similarity where differences of some extent are fully negligible and some others are percepted but regarded as unimportant.

The vagueness can be modelled by fuzzy set theoretical concepts, as shown in well known literature. The quantitative vagueness is well modelled by fuzzy numbers and fuzzy quantities [3, 6, 12]. The mathematical model of vague quantities would be of very little use if we are not able to compute with them. The computation with fuzzy quantities was thoroughly investigated and its properties were derived. It does not exactly repeat the properties of the deterministic algebra, as shown, e. g., in [3, 6, 8].

However, managing the differences between fuzzy and crisp computations led to several interesting questions. Some of them and theoretical approach to their analysis are briefly summarized in this paper.

Evidently, the set of all fuzzy quantities (i. e., membership functions mapping the real line on the closed interval $[0, 1]$) is much richer than the set of verbal quantitative expressions. It means, each such expression can be represented by a whole (and relatively large) class of fuzzy quantities which should be in some sense "similar" or "analogously generated". The process of generation of fuzzy quantities seems to be crucial for understanding their structure and for advanced manipulation with them.

In the following sections we suggest a general model of the structure of components generating particular fuzzy quantities. These elements can be used to specify the classes of fuzzy quantities corresponding to verbal values. The structure generating fuzzy quantitative representatives of words generally includes three basic components:

— a *crisp number* which is to be extended into vague value in verbal expressions (like "approximately x", "rather less than y"); this component may be empty in some cases (like "big", "several", "enormous");

— a source of vague data characterized by specific distribution of uncertainty (or, on the other hand, exactness) over the real line and referring about it for fuzzy extensions of verbal data;

— a "normalized" shape (or shapes) of membership functions which are to reflect the form of vagueness connected with particular words like ("almost", "near to", "rather more than", "about", etc.)

The generating structures can be used for characterization of classes of fuzzy quantities determined by their crisp "core", by their source, by their "shape" or by combinations of these components. But they may be used also in the following way.

In usual applications, the actual fuzzy data input standard algorithms and are processed due to them. This processing by means of the usual arithmetic or functional operations over fuzzy quantities can be computationally complicated and it almost always leads to formal growth of the uncertainty (of the extent of the supports of resulting membership functions). It can be useful to extend the algorithms from fuzzy quantities to analogous processing of their generators. Each fuzzy quantity entering an algorithm is produced by some generator, and these generators can be combined due to the steps of that algorithm. The result of this combination is a new generating structure. This generating structure can be used to produce the resulting fuzzy quantities. Moreover, proper formalism of the combinations can limit the extent of the resulting quantities without loss of their natural structure.

The following sections and subsections can be divided into three groups. The introductory ones present the auxiliary concepts. Then, the main part of this paper deals with particular components of the generating structure. The conclusive section completes the model and discusses its adequacy to processing verbal quantities.

2   Auxiliary Concepts

Here, we briefly remember the basic notions of the algebra of fuzzy quantities.

2.1   Fuzzy Quantity

The *fuzzy quantities* are dealt in numerous papers. Let us remember, e. g. [6, 8, 3, 12]. In this paper we use the term for any fuzzy subset a of the real line R with membership function $\mu_a : R \to [0,1]$ such that

$$(1) \qquad \exists\, x_a \in R : \mu_a(x_a) = 1.$$

The real number x_a fulfilling (1) is called *modal value* of the fuzzy quantity a. We denote by $I\!R$ the class of all fuzzy quantities.

The second definitoric assumption used in some works on fuzzy quantities, namely the limitedness of their supports

$$(2) \qquad \exists\, x_1,\, x_2 \in R,\ x_1 < x_2,\ \forall\, x \notin [x_1, x_2] : \mu_a(x) = 0$$

is not respected in this paper. It could exclude the fuzzy set theoretical counterparts of some vague expressions like "very bid number" or "unlimited amount" (even if in real economic also "very big" and "unlimited" quantities have their practical limits). Moreover, assumption (2) was necessary for consistent definition of some concepts of algebra of the fuzzy quantities (cf. [6, 8]) which are not essential for the theoretical model suggested in this paper.

2.2 Extension Principle–Operations

The definitions of algebraic operations with fuzzy quantities usually respect the *extension principle* (cf., [3, 6]) which can be formulated in several levels of generality. For our purpose we use the following one.

Let $f : R \times R \to R$ be a binary operation. Then it can be extended to the set $I\!R$ in such way that for any a, b, $c \in I\!R$, $c = f(a, b)$, the membership function μ_c fulfills for any $z \in R$

$$(3) \qquad \mu_c(z) = \sup \left[\min(\mu_a(x), \mu_b(y)) : x, y \in R, z = f(x, y) \right].$$

Remark 1. The previous formula evidently implies that for modal values x_a, x_b of a, b, respectively, $x_c = f(x_a, x_b)$ is a modal value of c, and, vice versa, if x_c is a modal value of c then there exist modal values x_a, x_b of a, b, such that $x_c = f(x_a, x_b)$.

The extension principle, for example, means that addition and multiplication of fuzzy quantities are defined, for a, $b \in I\!R$ as fuzzy quantities $a \oplus b$ or $a \odot b$ where

$$
\begin{aligned}
(4) \qquad \mu_{a \oplus b}(z) &= \sup_{y \in R} \left[\min(\mu(y), \mu_b(z - y)) \right], & z \in R, \\
(5) \qquad \mu_{a \odot b}(z) &= \sup_{y \in R, \, y \neq 0} \left[\min(\mu_a(y), \mu_b(z/y)) \right], & z \neq 0, \\
&= \max(\mu_a(0), \mu_b(0)) \quad \text{for } z = 0.
\end{aligned}
$$

To simplify the notations, we denote for any $y \in R$ the degenerated fuzzy quantity $\langle y \rangle \in I\!R$

$$(6) \qquad \mu_{\langle y \rangle}(y) = 1, \quad \mu_{\langle y \rangle}(x) = 0 \quad \text{for } x \neq y,$$

and then we may define the product of deterministic and fuzzy quantity $y \cdot a$, $y \in R$, $a \in I\!R$ as $y \cdot a = \langle y \rangle \odot a$ and, consequently,

$$
\begin{aligned}
\mu_{y \cdot a}(x) &= \mu_a(x/y) \quad \text{for } y \neq 0, \\
&= \mu_{\langle 0 \rangle}(x) \quad \text{for } y = 0.
\end{aligned}
$$

The operations with fuzzy quantities generally fulfill only some of the group properties of linear space properties as shown, e.g., in [3, 6]. The overview of the validity of the algebraic axioms for fuzzy quantities is presented in [8] where also their limited validity in a weaker form or for special fuzzy quantities is summarized.

For this paper, it is significant to note only that the operations based on the extension principle do not possess some classical algebraic properties which fact makes their applications rather uncomfortable.

2.3 Warning Properties

The operations defined via the extension principle are well known and their definitions reflect the natural logical patterns used in the fuzzy set theory. Anyhow, three of their features are worth mentioning.

As already remembered above, these operations do not fully repeat the algebraic properties which are selfevident in the deterministic case. Namely, there are some problems with the concepts of the opposite elements (and fuzzy zero) or the inverted element (and fuzzy unit), and the distributivity is also connected with some problems, as shown, e. g., in [6, 8].

Further, the computing due to the extension principle is not very simple, and its multiple repetitions in some applied algorithms need certain endeavor.

Last but not least, the extension principle means that the result of computation is more "uncertain" than the input quantities in the sense that the difference

(7) $$\sup\{x \in R : \mu_a(x) > 0\} - \inf\{x \in R : \mu_a(x) > 0\}$$

increases. If a practical algorithm demands several computational steps then the extent of possible values of the outputs is enormously large. It is possible to reduce this vagueness by eliminating some 0-symmetric components of fuzzy quantities, as shown in [6, 8]. Nevertheless this general property contradicts the everyday practical experience where manipulation with vague data brings relatively stabilized results. It seems that practical handling of vagueness is realized with respect to procedures which cannot be mathematically reflected by the extension principle. Their formal representation is the main subject of the next sections.

3 Elementary Formulation of Model

Let us briefly introduce the basic concepts of the model of verbal quantity whose particular components are delt in the following sections. The presentation offered here is rather heuristic one and its main purpose is to determine the frame of the next, more detailed, explanations.

Generally, each vague verbal quantity can be in some way described by a fuzzy quantity (or class of fuzzy quantities). In the following sections we suppose that a verbal quantity V is represented by a triple consisting of:

— crisps "core value" $x_V \in R$ to which the verbal expression is regarded (e. g., "approximately x_V", "near to x_V ", "rather more than x_V ", etc.),

— a real valued function f_V (or, briefly, f) characterizing the reliability (or vagueness) of the *source of the verbal expression*,

— a mapping φ_V or φ from R to $[0, 1]$ representing the *shape of the vagueness* and characterizing the actual verbal expression (its symmetry or asymmetry, extension of possible values, etc.).

These three components can be interpreted and more formally defined as follows.

The crisp "core value" is interpreted as shown above, i.e., as a real value $x_V \in R$ to which the verbal quantity is regarded. In some cases, this component keeps unspecified, it might happen in some representations of general verbal quantities like "many", "several", "a few", etc. In the cases where the relative crisp value x_V is specified (e.g. "near to 8", for $x_V = 8$, "approximately 1", for $x_V = 1$) and where the verbal quantity is connected with a fuzzy quantity $a \in \mathbb{R}$, the "crisp core" is either identical with the modal value x_a of a (e.g. in somehow "symmetrical" verbal expressions like "approximately", "not very different from", etc.), or it can be different from the modal values of a (e.g., if the verbal expressions is asymmetric like "rather less than", "much greater than", "nearing to x_V from below", and others). In the latter case the value x_V may be not only different from the modal values of a, but it need not be even an element of the support of the membership function μ_a.

It can be easily seen that the computation with verbal variables almost always starts with deterministic numerical operation with their crisp cores ("approximately 3 plus approximately 5" is naturally "approximately 8"). The operations and manipulations with the vague expressions related to the "crisp cores" are the main objects of interest of this paper.

The source of vague quantities is represented by the *generating function* which is an increasing continuous mapping $f : R \to R$ with $f(0) = 0$.

More detailed analysis of operations with the generating functions are presented in Section 4. Here we briefly introduce their interpretation. Each generating function represents the distribution of vagueness typical for a source of vague verbal data. There exist operators $\varphi : R \to [0, 1]$ called shape generators (see more in Section 5 or in [10]) which generate individual fuzzy quantities with respect to the structure of the generating function f. For example,

$$(8) \qquad \varphi(x) = \max\left(0, 1 - |f(y) - f(x)|\right), \quad x \in R,$$

where $y \in R$ is a fixed real number, is one of possible shape generators. For each y, (8) defines the membership function of a fuzzy quantity with modal value y. The analytic form of $f(x)$ for x from a neighborhood of y influences the membership function derived from (8). Generally, the higher the gradient of f near y is, the narrower the support of the membership function follows from (8). In another formulation, higher gradient of the generating function f in some area of its domain indicates lower vagueness of quantitative data with modal values situated there. Variability of the gradient indicates the changing reliability of the data source in various areas of the values of data.

The "shape" of the vagueness is characterized by the operator which for particular "crisp cores" and for given source generates the actual membership function. An example of such *shape generator* is introduced by (8), others are suggested in Section 5. The shape generators can be considered for "normalized" forms of the membership functions corresponding to actual verbal expressions.

Some shape of membership function is expected for the formal representation of "approximately equal to...", another one can represent "rather more than...", etc. The actual shape of any concrete membership function results from the application of the normalized shape generator to specific area of the generating function.

There exist qualitatively different relations between the "crisp core" and the shape generator to be applied. In the first case the shape generator is connected with a crisp value which represents its modal value. It concerns such verbal quantitative expressions which fuzzify the referred crisp value ("approximately...", "very near to...", "about...", etc.). In the second case the shape generator reflects rather a vague (fuzzy) relation of the verbally described quantity to a crisp value ("a bit more than...", "value nearing to...", "almost..."). In such case the referred crisp value is not the modal value of the generated fuzzy quantities but there exists an objective relation between both concepts. Finally, some verbal quantitative expressions are not explicitely related to some concrete numerical value (e. g., "many", "large number", "suffuciently many", and, may be, also "very small", "negligible", etc.). Their independence of some real value is rather discutable. The terms like "very small" are evidently linked to crisp zero. On the other hand, terms like "many", "large number" or "sufficiently many" are only seemingly free. In real applications "many" has well interpretable meaning ("many" can be very different in different situations). It concerns not only the lower values which can be considered for possible "many" but also the upper ones. However "many" is theoretically unlimited, in all real applications it has its upper bounds given by practical reasons. It means that also those verbal quantities which seemingly are not connected with some crisp core can be in the applications realistically understood as "very approximately...", "something between...and..." or "in broad sense about...". In such case the shape generators modelling those verbal variables behave quite analogously to the previous types.

Formal model of verbal quantity can be, after introducing the above concepts, represented by a structure

$$(9) \qquad\qquad (x_a, (f, \varphi)),$$

where x_a is the *crisp core* of the verbal quantity and the pair

$$(10) \qquad\qquad (f, \varphi)$$

is its *generator*, with the generating function f and the shape generator φ. All three components are interpreted as show above.

If $(f_1, \varphi_1), \ldots, (f_n, \varphi_n)$ are generators of verbal variables then an algorithm calculating with them results into new verbal variable (e. g., their algebraic mean) then this output verbal variable is also connected with some generator (f, φ) which respects $(f_1, \varphi_1), \ldots, (f_n, \varphi_n)$ and the structure of the applied algorithm. Then any new application means the input of a vector of crisp cores

$x_1, \ldots, x_n$ to the model. The traditional approach means to put $x_1, \ldots, x_n$ to $(f_1, \varphi_1), \ldots, (f_n, \varphi_n)$, respectively, to calculate fuzzy quantities $a_1, \ldots, a_n \in \mathbb{R}$ with membership functions $\mu_1, \ldots, \mu_n$, and (using operations (4), (5) and others) to calculate the output fuzzy quantity a with membership function μ_a, where all the discrepancies mentioned in Section 2.3 take place.

It is also possible to proceed in another way. To apply the algorithm to the crisp cores (which is regularly much simpler) and then to put the achieved result $x \in R$ (in our example the mean of $x_1, \ldots, x_n$) to (f, φ). The output fuzzy quantity is the representative of the verbal variable following from the application of the algorithm. This procedure avoids some of the problems mentioned in Section 2.3. It not only significantly simplifies the calculations but it can also, in case of reasonably defined combinations of the shape generators $\varphi_1, \ldots, \varphi_n$ into φ, eliminate the enormous extension of the uncertainty of the output quantities. The effectivity of such alternative approach depends on managing the methods of transformation of the input generating functions $f_1, \ldots, f_n$ into f and input shape generators $\varphi_1, \ldots, \varphi_n$ into φ. The first theoretical attempt to this problem was introduced in [9] and [10]. In the following sections we remember the main results and, namely, discuss their meaning in the specific case of computing with verbal variables.

4 Generation Functions

In this section we briefly recollect the methods of manipulations with the first components of generators of verbal quantities (cf. [9]).

The *generating functions* of verbal variables were introduced as mappings $f : R \rightarrow R$ such that

(11) f is continuous and strictly increasing,

(12) $f(0) = 0$.

We denote the set of all generating functions by $\mathcal{F}$.

4.1 Operations With Generating Functions

The processing of generators includes also processing of the generating functions. In their case, the algebraic operations with verbal quantities are reflected by in certain sense analogous (i.e., similar to the algebraic operations) processing.

If $f, g \in \mathcal{F}$ and $r \in R$, $r \neq 0$ then we define the operations $r \cdot f$, $f \boxplus g$, $f \boxdot g$ as follows

$$
\begin{aligned}
(13) \qquad (r \cdot f)(x) &= f(x/r) \quad \text{for } r > 0, \\
&= -f(x/r) \quad \text{for } r < 0, \\
(14) \qquad (r \boxplus f)(x) &= (f^{-1} + g^{-1})^{-1}(x), \\
(15) \qquad (r \boxdot f)(x) &= \text{sign}(x) \cdot (f^{-1} \cdot g^{-1})(x),
\end{aligned}
$$

for any $x \in R$, where $\text{sign}(x) = 1$ for $x > 0$, $\text{sign}(x) = -1$ for $x < 0$ and $\text{sign}(0) = 0$.

Remark 2. Definitions $(13), (14)$ and (15) are correct as follows from the continuity and strict monotonicity of the generating functions.

Lemma 1. For any $x \in R$

(16) $$(r \cdot f) = \text{sign}(r) \cdot (r \cdot f^{-1})^{-1}(x).$$

P r o o f. Equality (16) follows from (13) immediately.

Lemma 2. Mappings $r \cdot f$, $f \boxplus g$ and $f \boxdot g$ resulting from definitions $(13), (14)$ and (15) are also generating functions from $\mathcal{F}$.

P r o o f. The statement follows from $(13), (14), (15)$ and from the continuity and strict monotonicity of the generating functions, immediately.

Theorem 1. The set of generating functions $\mathcal{F}$ is closed regarding operations $(13), (14), (15)$ and, moreover, for $f, g, h \in \mathcal{F}$, $r_1, r_2 \in R$, $r_1 \cdot r_2 \neq 0$,

$$
\begin{array}{lll}
(17) & f \boxplus g = g \boxplus f, & f \boxdot g = g \boxdot f, , \\
(18) & f \boxplus (g \boxplus h) = (f \boxplus g) \boxplus h, & f \boxdot (g \boxdot h) = (f \boxdot g) \boxdot h, , \\
(19) & r \cdot (f \boxplus g) = (r \cdot f) \boxplus (r \cdot g), \\
(20) & (r_1 + r_2) \cdot f = (r_1 \cdot f) \boxplus (r_2 \cdot f), & \text{for } r_1 \cdot r_2 > 0, \\
(21) & (r_1 \cdot r_2) \cdot f = r_1 \cdot (r_2 \cdot f), \\
(22) & f \boxdot (g \boxplus h) = (f \boxdot g) \boxplus (f \boxdot h).
\end{array}
$$

P r o o f. The statements of this theorem follow from the definitions of the relevant operations. (17) is obvious, (18) for the additive case follows from

$$
\begin{aligned}
(f \boxplus (g \boxplus h))(x) &= (f^{-1} + (g \boxplus h)^{-1})^{-1}(x) = \\
&= (f^{-1} + ((g^{-1} + h^{-1})^{-1})^{-1})^{-1}(x) = (f^{-1} + g^{-1} + h^{-1})^{-1}(x) = \\
&= ((f \boxplus g) \boxplus h)(x)
\end{aligned}
$$

for any $x \in R$. The proof for the multiplicative case is analogous. Proving (19), we use Lemma 1 and then for any $x \in R$

$$
\begin{aligned}
(r \cdot (f \boxplus g))(x) &= \\
&= \text{sign}(r) \cdot (r \cdot (f \boxplus g)^{-1})^{-1}(x) = \\
&= \text{sign}(r) \cdot (r \cdot ((f^{-1} + g^{-1})^{-1})^{-1})^{-1}(x) = \\
&= \text{sign}(r) ((r \cdot f^{-1}) + (r \cdot g^{-1}))^{-1}(x) = \\
&= \text{sign}(r) \cdot ((rf)^{-1} + (rg)^{-1})^{-1}(x) = ((rf) \boxplus (rg))(x).
\end{aligned}
$$

Similarly (20) is evident,

$$((r_1 + r_2) \cdot f)(x) = (r_1 \cdot f)(x) + (r_2 \cdot f)(x)$$

for any $x \in R$, if $r_1 \neq 0$, $r_2 \neq 0$. Equality (21) follows from

$$((r_1 \cdot r_2) \cdot f)(x) = \text{sign}(r_1 \cdot r_2) \cdot (r_1 \cdot r_1 \cdot f^{-1})^{-1}(x) =$$
$$= \text{sign}(r_1) \cdot \text{sign}(r_2) \cdot (r_1 \cdot (r_2 \cdot f^{-1}))^{-1}(x) =$$
$$= (r_1 \cdot (r_2 \, f))(x).$$

Finally, equality (22) follows from

$$(f \, \square \, (g \, \boxplus \, h))(x) = (f^{-1} \cdot (g \, \boxplus \, h)^{-1})^{-1}(x) =$$
$$= (f^{-1}((g^{-1} + h^{-1})^{-1})^{-1})^{-1}(x) =$$
$$= (f^{-1} \cdot g^{-1} + f^{-1} \cdot h^{-1})^{-1}(x) =$$
$$= ((f \, \square \, g)^{-1} + (f \, \square \, h)^{-1})^{-1}(x) =$$
$$= ((f \, \square \, g) \, \square \, (f \, \square \, h))(x).$$

Remark 3. If $f \in \mathcal{F}$ and $g = f \boxplus (-1 \cdot f) \in \mathcal{F}$ then for any $x \in R$ $g(-x) = -g(x)$.

The previous remark corresponds in an interesting way with the concept of fuzzy zero. If the shape generator φ respecting (8) (or any other symmetric one) is used then the realization of verbal quantity $(0, (g, \varphi))$ with generator (g, φ) leads to a fuzzy quantity with modal value equal to 0, and symmetric membership function for any original generating function f. It corresponds with the concept of fuzzy zero suggested, e.g., in [6] or [8]. The approach based on the generating functions, moreover, allows to distinguish proper fuzzy zeros obtained due to Remark 3 from the fuzzy quantities with modal value equal to 0 but derived from general generating function not resulting from the substraction like in Remark 3.

Another comment which is worth mentioning regards the extension of vagueness resulting from algebraic operations with them. If f, $g \in \mathcal{F}$, $r \in R$, $r \neq 0$, then the gradient of $f \boxplus g$ is lower (in corresponding areas) than the gradients of f and g. Analogous conclusion for $r \cdot f$ is valid only for $r > 1$ and for $g \, \square \, g$ only for those domains on which $f(x) > 1$ and $g(x) > 1$. In the following section we show that the vagueness of results of operations over generators can be reduced by proper combinations of the shape generators.

4.2 Examples of Generating Functions

The simplest type of generating functions is the *linear* one, $f(x) = x$ or, more generally, $f(x) = k \cdot x$, $k > 0$, where the degree of vagueness of the referred source of data is uniform for all parts of the real line and its determinism is proportional to the value of k (its vagueness is the greater the smaller is the parameter k).

The *partwise linear* generating function reflect the changing vagueness of the source. For example,

$$f(x) \quad = \quad x \qquad\qquad \text{for } x \leq 10,$$
$$= \quad 2x - 10 \qquad \text{for } 10 < x < 20,$$
$$= \quad 0.2x + 26 \quad \text{for } x \geq 20,$$

where the source offers relatively well determined data with values in the segment $[10, 20]$, and their vagueness rapidly increases for higher values.

The changes of vagueness can be much more fluent, for example expressed by the generating function

$$f(x) = \text{sign}(x) \cdot \sqrt{x}$$

where the vagueness of the produced data gradually increases. Such generating function is quite natural. The larger values of the crisp core x are considered the "wider" the range of possible values "approximately x" is.

Similarly, the generating function

$$f(x) \quad = \quad \ln(x + 1), \qquad\quad \text{for } x \geq 0,$$
$$= \quad -\exp(-x) + 1, \quad \text{for } x < 0,$$

reflects other rates of the decrease of vagueness.

Of course, these and other generating functions can be partwise combined to reflect changing character of the reliability of the produced data.

5   Shape Generators

The second component of the generator, heuristically introduced in Section 3, is the *shape generator*. Formally, it is a mapping $\varphi : R \to [0, 1]$ such that

(23) $\qquad\qquad \varphi(0) = 1$

(24) $\qquad\qquad \varphi(x)$ is increasing for $x < 0$ and decreasing for $x > 0$.

5.1   Shapes of Membership Functions

The shape generator φ connects the generated membership function μ_a of fuzzy quantity $a \in \mathbb{R}$ with generating function $f \in \mathcal{F}$ by means of the relation

(25) $\qquad\qquad \mu_a(x) = \varphi(f(x) - f(k_a \cdot (x_a + m_a))),$

where x_a is the crisp core as presented in Section 3, $m_a \in R$, $k_a > 0$ are coefficients with the following meaning. If $m_a = 0$ and $k_a = 1$ then x_a is not only the crisp core but also a modal value of μ_a. This situation, as mentioned in Section 3, represents the typical case of verbal variables like "approximately x_a", "near x_a", "about x_a or rather more", etc. If $k_a = 1$ and $m_a \neq 0$ then the modal value of the generated membership function is different from the crisp core and the difference is constant for all fuzzy quantities generated by (f, φ) for various crisp cores. They correspond to the verbal variables like "add one handful of...to x_a", "about one inch shorter than x_a" and similar, where m_a can be positive or negative. Finally, if $k_a \neq 1$, $m_a \neq 0$ (usually $k_a > 1$) then the difference between the modal value of the generated fuzzy quantity and the referred core differs for different crisp cores. It corresponds with verbal variables like "much more than x_a", "a bit less than x_a", etc., as, evidently, "much more than 10" refers to completely different relation between the crisp core x_a and possible values of the generated fuzzy quantity than "much more than 10 000".

In Section 3 we have also discussed verbal variables seemingly not being connected with any actual crisp core, e. g., "many", "" few, "enormous", etc. We have noted that these verbal variables are regarded to some actual numerical crisp core intuitively following from the modelled situations. Expressions like "enormous expenses" or "negligible costs" mean something completely different when being regarded to the family budget or state economy, e. g. The relatively big vagueness of those expressions in actual situations can be reflected by sufficiently "wide" shape generators.

The formalism of some further samples will be simplified if we denote (in some cases) a shape generator φ as a pair

$$(26) \qquad \varphi = (\varphi_L, \varphi_R), \quad \varphi_L : R_- \to [0, 1], \quad \varphi_R : R_+ \to [0, 1]$$
$$\varphi_L(x) = \varphi(x) \text{ for } x < 0, \quad \varphi_R(x) = \varphi(x) \text{ for } x > 0.$$

By Φ, Φ_L, Φ_R, $\Phi = \Phi_L \times \Phi_R$ we denote the sets of the shape generators φ and their left and right components, respectively.

Remark 4. If the membership function μ_a is defined by (25) then, evidently

$$\begin{aligned} \mu_a(x) &= \varphi\left(f(x) - k_a^{-1} \cdot f(x_a + m_a)\right) = \\ &= \varphi\left(k_a^{-1}\left[f(k_a^{-1} \cdot x) - f(x_a + m_a)\right]\right), \quad x \in R. \end{aligned}$$

Especially for $m_a = 0$ these formulas imply

$$\varphi\left(f(x) - f(k_a \cdot x_a)\right) = \varphi\left(k_a^{-1}(f(k_a^{-1}(x) - f(x_a))))\right)$$

as follows from Lemma 1.

5.2 Composition of Shape Generators

As explained above, we aim to compose an output generator (f, φ) based on input generators $(f_1, \varphi_1), \ldots, (f_k, \varphi_k)$ connected with the verbal or vague variables entering an algorithm. The combinations of generating functions were suggested and discussed in Section 4. Here we deal with combinations of the shape generators. It is to be stressed that, meanwhile the combinations of the generating functions reflect mainly the algebraic operations with the verbal variables, the combination of their shapes would rather characterize their logical or merital relations. Consequently, the combinations of the shape generators can be mostly defined by means of logical operators and their systems even if other forms of these combinations are not excluded, as well. The actually chosen form of the combination of the shape generators depends on the specific demands of the considered vague situation. The properties of the combinations of the shape generators were briefly investigated in [10], as well.

Remark 5. The class Φ of all shape generators is partly ordered, its minimal element is

$$\varphi^{(0)}; \quad \varphi^{(0)}(0) = 1, \quad \varphi^{(0)}(x) = 0 \quad \text{for } x \in R,$$

its maximal element is

$$\varphi^*; \quad \varphi^*(x) = 1 \quad \text{for all } x \in R$$

and generally

$$\varphi^{(1)} \succeq \varphi^{(2)} \quad \text{iff } \varphi^{(1)}(x) \geq \varphi^{(2)}(x) \quad \text{for all } r \in R.$$

A *composition of shape generators* is any non-decreasing commutative binary operation $C : \Phi \times \Phi \to \Phi$. It means that for any $\varphi^{(1)}, \varphi^{(2)} \in \Phi$

$$(27) \qquad C(\varphi^{(1)}, \varphi^{(2)}) = C(\varphi^{(2)}, \varphi^{(1)}) = \varphi \in \Phi,$$

and for $\varphi^{(3)} \in \Phi$ such that $\varphi^{(3)}(x) \geq \varphi^{(1)}(x)$ for all x,

$$(28) \quad \varphi = C(\varphi^{(1)}, \varphi^{(2)}), \quad \varphi' = C(\varphi^{(3)}, \varphi^{(2)}) \Longrightarrow \varphi'(x) \succeq \varphi(x) \quad \text{for all } x \in R.$$

We say that a composition of shape generators C is contractive iff for any $\varphi^{(1)}, \varphi^{(2)} \in \Phi$, $\varphi = C(\varphi^{(1)}, \varphi^{(2)})$ implies

$$\varphi^{(1)} \succeq \varphi \quad \text{and} \quad \varphi^{(2)} \succeq \varphi.$$

Remark 6. If C is contractive $\varphi^{(1)}, \varphi^{(2)} \in \Phi$, $\varphi = C(\varphi^{(1)}, \varphi^{(2)})$ then evidently

$$\varphi(x) \leq \min(\varphi^{(1)}(x), \varphi^{(2)}(x)), \quad x \in R.$$

Theorem 2. If the composition of shape generators C is contractive, if $\varphi^{(1)}, \varphi^{(2)}, \ldots, \varphi^{(n)}, \ldots \in \Phi$, and if we denote by $\psi^{(1)}, \psi^{(2)}, \ldots \in \Phi$ the composed shape generators

$$\psi^{(1)} = C(\varphi^{(1)}, \varphi^{(2)}), \quad \psi^{(k)} = C(\psi^{(k-1)}, \varphi^{(k+1)}), \quad k = 2, 3, \ldots,$$

then the sequence $\{\psi^{(k)}\}_{k=1}^{\infty}$ is convergent.

P r o o f . The statement immediately follows from Remark 6 and from the non-negativeness of the shape generators.

5.3 Examples of Shape Generators and Their Compositions

The first example of the shape generator was shown in Section 3, formula (8). It is one of possible representations of the verbal expressions like "*approximately* x_a". Of course, its linearity can be rather modified, e. g., as

$$\varphi(y) = \max(0,\, 1 - r \cdot |y|), \quad y \in R,\; r > 0$$

which, with coefficients $k_a = 1$, $m_a = 0$ in (25), defines for any crisp $x_a \in R$ the membership function

$$\mu_a(x) = \varphi(f(x) - f(x_a)) = \max(0,\, 1 - r \cdot |f(x) - f(x_a)|),$$

where r influences the "width" of the generated membership functions.

As already mentioned above, the shape generator φ representing verbal expressions like "rather more than x_a" can be defined, e. g., by (for $m > 0$)

$$\varphi_L(x) \quad - \quad \max(0,\, 1 - |y|) \qquad \text{for } y < 0,$$

$$\varphi_R(x) \quad = \quad 1 \qquad\qquad\qquad \text{for } y \in [0, m],$$

$$\qquad\qquad = \quad \max(0,\, 1 - (y - m)) \quad \text{for } y > m.$$

Using (25) for $k_a = 1$, and $m_a \in R$ is such that

$$f(x_a + m_a) - f(x_a) = m + 1$$

we derive

$$\mu_a(x) \quad = \quad 0 \qquad\qquad\qquad\qquad\qquad\qquad \text{for } x < 0,$$

$$= \quad \max\left(0,\, 1 - (|f(x) - f(x_a + m_a)| - m)\right) \quad \text{for } x \in [0, m_a],$$

$$= \quad 1 \qquad\qquad\qquad\qquad\qquad\qquad \text{for } x \in (m_a,\, m_a + m],$$

$$= \quad 0 \qquad\qquad\qquad\qquad\qquad\qquad \text{for } x > m_a + m.$$

An analogous procedure can be used for modelling verbal expression "much less than" where the corresponding shape generator may be, e. g., for some $r \in R$, $r > 0$

$$\varphi_L(y) \quad = \quad 1$$

$$\varphi_R(y) \quad = \quad -y/r + 1 \quad \text{for } y \in [0, r],\; r > 0,$$

$$\qquad\quad = \quad 0 \qquad\qquad \text{for } y > r$$

where the membership functions can be derived using (25) for $k_a = 1$, $m_a > r$.

The compositions of the shape generators can also reflect a wide scale of logical relations between them. If $\varphi^{(1)}$, $\varphi^{(2)} \in \Phi$ and $\varphi = C(\varphi^{(1)}, \varphi^{(2)})$ then this composition can express the logical conjunction of both verbal patterns modelled by $\varphi^{(1)}$ and $\varphi^{(2)}$, i. e.

$$(29) \qquad\qquad \varphi(x) = \min(\varphi^{(1)}(x), \varphi^{(2)}(x)), \quad x \in R,$$

or their logical disjunction

$$\varphi(x) = \max(\varphi^{(1)}(x), \varphi^{(2)}(x)), \quad x \in R.$$

These two composition operators very well fit to situations in which one quantity is described by two sources using verbal expressions. For example, "*the quantity a is approximately x_a*" and/or "*it is rather bigger than x'_a*".

The classical extension principle can be generated to the compositions of shape generators

$$(30) \qquad \varphi(x) = \sup_{y \in R} \left(\max(\varphi^{(1)}(y), \varphi^{(1)}(x-y)) \right), \quad x \in R$$

in the additive case or, analogously, for the product of vague quantities, due to (5).

It is also possible to express certain type of independence of the considered quantities by a product composition

$$(31) \qquad \varphi(x) = \varphi^{(1)}(x) \cdot \varphi^{(2)}(x), \quad x \in R$$

and other relation between them can be modelled by the combined sum

$$\varphi(x) = \varphi^{(1)}(x) + \varphi^{(2)}(x) - \varphi^{(1)}(x) \cdot \varphi^{(2)}(x), \quad x \in R.$$

It is not difficult to see that all the compositions defined above really result into shape generators. Moreover, the minimum operator (29) and the product operator (31) are evidently contractive. It is also easy to verify the following statements.

Remark 7. Under the notations of Theorem 2, if all shape generators $\varphi^{(k)}$, $k = 1, \ldots, n, \ldots$ are unimodal ($\varphi^{(k)}(x) = 1$ if and only if $x = 0$) and if the product composition (31) is used then the limit shape generator

$$\psi = \lim_{k \to \infty} \psi^{(k)}$$

is the minimal shape generator, i.e., $\psi(0) = 1$, $\psi(x) = 0$ for $x \neq 0$.

Remark 8. Under the assumptions of Remark 7, with the minimum composition (29) considered instead of the product, the limit shape operator ψ fulfills

$$\psi(x) = \inf \left(\varphi^{(n)}(x) : n = 1, 2, \ldots \right), \quad x \in R.$$

6 Representation of Verbal Variables

In the preceding sections the tools were prepared to describe the formal representations of verbal variables and their processing.

General quantitative verbal expressions are, in the suggested model, represented by *generators*, i.e. pairs formed by a generating function and shape generators. These general verbal expressions are related to specific numerical values, called *crisp cores*. Application of a shape generator to the considered generating function in the actual crisp point which is formally described by (25), defines the membership function of fuzzy quantity representing the concrete fuzzy value of the considered verbal variable.

For example, let us consider a source of verbal data (for example an expert) whose vagueness is represented by a generating function $f \in \mathcal{F}$

$$
\begin{aligned}
f(x) \;&=\; x && \text{for } x \in (-\infty, 8), \\
&=\; x/2 + 4 && \text{for } x \in [8, \infty).
\end{aligned}
$$

Let us represent the verbal expression $V = $ "approximately" by shape generator

$$
\varphi_V(y) = \max(0,\, 1 - |y|), \quad y \in R,
$$

(it is useful to remember (8)). Then for any actual crisp value x_V, for example $x_V = 9$, the fuzzy quantity a representing the verbal variable $V(9) = $ "approximately 9" will be defined by its membership function

$$
\mu_a(x) = \varphi(f(x) - f(9)) = \max\left(0,\, 1 - |f(x) - f(9)|\right), \quad x \in R,
$$

i.e.

$$
\begin{aligned}
\mu_a(x) \;&=\; x - 7.5 && \text{for } x \in [7.5, 8], \\
&=\; x/2 - 3.5 && \text{for } x \in [8, 9], \\
&=\; -x/2 + 5.5 && \text{for } x \in [9, 11], \\
&=\; 0 && \text{for } x \notin [7.5, 11].
\end{aligned}
$$

The main goal of the suggested model of verbal variables was formulated in Section 3 in the paragraphs headed *"Formal Model of Verbal Quantity"*. If an algorithm with input verbal fuzzy quantities is dealt then it appears useful to combine their generators, to construct a new one corresponding to the output of the algorithm, and then to realize that algorithm with the crisp values (crisp cores) only. The resulting crisp value will be processed by the output generator, and the resulting fuzzy quantity describing the verbal result of the algorithm can be computed. This procedure has certain advantages among which the computational simplification can be considered. Moreover, application of contracting compositions of the shape generators helps to keep the extent of the resulting fuzzy values in acceptable limits.

Here we illustrate the described procedure on the linear algebraic operations with verbal variables.

Let us consider verbal expressions V_1 and V_2 whose sources and uncertainty shapes are characterized by generators $(f^{(1)}, \varphi^{(1)})$ and $(f^{(2)}, \varphi^{(2)})$, respectively.

If the considered algorithm supposes the sum of these verbal variables "V_1 plus V_2" then it is connected with a generator (f, φ), where $f = f^{(1)} \boxplus f^{(2)}$ and

$\varphi = C(\varphi^{(1)}, \varphi^{(2)})$ where C is a composition rule reflecting the logical relations between the vagueness of both expressions (e.g. $C(\varphi^{(1)}, \varphi^{(2)})$ is the product composition (31)). Then, whenever the verbal expression V_1 regards a numerical value x_1 and expression V_2 regards $x_2 \in R$, the membership function μ_{a+b} of the fuzzy quantity characterizing "V_1 plus V_2" is generated from (f, φ) by means of (25), namely

$$(32) \quad \mu_{a \oplus b}(x) = \varphi\left(f(x) - f(k_a \cdot (x_1 + m_a) + k_b \cdot (x_2 + m_b))\right), \quad x \in R,$$

usually (for $k_a = k_b = 1$, $m_a = m_b = 0$)

$$(33) \quad \mu_{a \oplus b}(x) = \varphi(f(x) - f(x_1 + x_2)), \quad x \in R.$$

The latter formula is typical if both verbal expressions are like "near to", "approximately", "about", "similar", etc.

Analogously, if the verbal quantities a and b are to be multiplied then $f = f^{(1)} \boxdot f^{(2)}$ and $\mu_{a \cdot b}$ is derived by means

$$(34) \quad \mu_{u \odot b}(r) = \varphi\left(f(x) - f(k_a \cdot k_b \cdot (x_1 + m_a) \cdot (x_2 + m_b))\right), \quad x \in R.$$

If the verbal quantity a is multiplied by a crisp number $r \in R$ then $f = r \cdot f^{(1)}$, and

$$(35) \quad \mu_{r \cdot a}(x) = \varphi\left(f(x) - f(r \cdot k_a \cdot (x_1 + m_a))\right), \quad x \in R.$$

Here, we have denoted by a and b the fuzzy quantities generated by $(f^{(1)}, \varphi^{(1)})$ and $(f^{(2)}, \varphi^{(2)})$ for x_1, x_2, respectively. In all cases the choice of adequate composition procedure $C(\varphi^{(1)}, \varphi^{(2)})$ or, in the last case, $C(\varphi^{(1)}, \varphi^{(1)})$ keeps rather free. Generally, it would reflect the logical or merital relations between the vagueness connected with mutual superposition of the verbal expressions V_1 and V_2. This reflection still represents an interesting topic for investigation.

The main motivation for studying the relation between the composition rules and the logical structures being typical for verbal expressions and their interactions in algorithms follows from the practical applications of vagueness. There exist many traditional algorithms dealing with verbal quantities (they exist in traditional technologies, pharmacology, also geography, etc.). Instructions like *"Mix two handfuls of... and one glass of..."* or *"Sail... weeks along the river and then ride... days to the North"* are quite typical for the historical sources. The usual processing of the corresponding fuzzy quantities by means of the extension principle leads to very wide extent of possible values of the resulting quantities (let us remember Section 2.3). On the other hand, the results of the practical applications of such instructions were usually quite stabilized and their vagueness, usually, did not exceed acceptable limits. It allows us to assume that the practical handling of vague verbal quantities does not fully respect the extension principle (3) but that the composition of the corresponding shape generators can be based on other operations than those like (30) (and its analogies). Namely, if at least some of them are contractive (like the product or minimum) or if they at least do not extend the domain of the resulting shape generator $\varphi = C(\varphi^{(1)}, \varphi^{(2)})$ like the maximum operator. In this sense the model suggested above seems to be more adequate to the reality than the traditional extension principle.

References

[1] B. De Baetz, M. Mareš, R. Mesiar: T-partition of the real line generated by idempotent shapes. Fuzzy Sets and Systems (special volume on fuzzy numbers), to appear.

[2] B. De Baetz, R. Mesiar: T-partitions. Fuzzy Sets and Systems, to appear.

[3] D. Dubois, H. Prade: Fuzzy numbers: an overview. In: J. Bezdek (Ed.): Analysis of Fuzzy Information. CRC–Press, Boca Raton 1987, Vol. I, 3–39.

[4] J. Jacas, M. Mareš, J. Recasens: Homogeneous classes of fuzzy quantities. Mathware, to appear.

[5] J. Jacas, J. Recasens: Fuzzy numbers and equality relations. In: Proceedings of the Second IEEE'93 International Conference on Fuzzy Systems – San Francisco. IEEE 1993, 1298–1301.

[6] M. Mareš: Computation Over Fuzzy Quantities. CRC–Press, Boca Raton 1994.

[7] M. Mareš: How much is "many" minus "several"? In: Proceedings of International Conference SIC'96 – Budapest. Technical University of Budapest 1996, 187–192.

[8] M. Mareš: Weak arithmetics of fuzzy numbers. Fuzzy Sets and Systems (special volume on fuzzy numbers), to appear.

[9] M. Mareš, R. Mesiar: Processing of sources of fuzzy quantities. In: IPMU'96 – Granada, Universidad de Granada 1996, Vol. I, 359–363.

[10] M. Mareš, R. Mesiar: Composition of shape generators. Acta Mathematica et Informatica Universitatis Ostraviensis 4 (1996), 1, 37–45.

[11] R. Mesiar: LR–fuzzy numbers. In: IPMU'96 – Granada, Universidad de Granada 1996, Vol. I, 337–342.

[12] R. Mesiar: A note to the T–sum of $L - R$ fuzzy numbers. Fuzzy Sets and Systems 79 (1996), 259–261.

Decision Making Under Uncertainty with Nonnumeric Payoffs

Ronald R. Yager
Machine Intelligence Institute, Iona College
New Rochelle, NY 10801, USA

and

Maria T. Lamata
Department of Computer Sciences and Artificial Intelligence
University of Granada
18071 Granada, Spain

Abstract. We consider the problem of decision making in environments in which there exists some uncertainty about the state of nature. A general approach to the representation of uncertainty using the Dempster-Shafer belief structure is presented. A comprehensive methodology for evaluating the worth of each of the alternatives using the OWA operators to model the decision makers attitude is described. It is noted that central to this approach is the use of a weighted average operation. We then consider the situation in which the payoffs are nonnumeric values. Two scales for representing nonnumeric information are introduced. One scale assumes only the existence of a linear ordering on the allowable values a second scale, called a uniform scale, assumes in addition to a linear ordering the scale values are uniformly spaced. It is noted out that in these nonnumeric environments a need arises for an operation to replace the weighted average. We show that in the case of only a linear ordering on the payoffs we can use a weighted median operation to replace the weighted average. In the case in which the payoffs come from a uniform scale an operation called the weighted average on a uniform scale is used to replace the weighted average.

1. Introduction

Decision making in environments in which there exists some uncertainty with respect to a factor affecting the decision, generically called the state of nature, have been long considered in the literature [1, 2]. The methodologies for solving these problems have been strongly dependent upon the assumption of the type of uncertainty associated with the state of nature. Two assumptions about the knowledge of the uncertainty have dominated the literature. The first case is where one assumes a probabilistic knowledge and the second is where one assumes a set of values which includes the actual value, however no probabilistic information is assumed. In the case of probabilistic knowledge considerable use is made of the expected value as a tool for obtaining the optimal alternative. In the second case, sometimes called decision making under ignorance [2], the introduction of a decision making attitude, optimistic, pessimistic etc, is used to help provide an optimal answer. In [3, 4] the authors suggested that by using the Dempster-Shafer belief structure we can provide a framework which unifies these two assumptions about our knowledge of the uncertainty and in addition provides a structure for representing other more sophisticated types of information about the uncertainty in the environment. Strat [5, 6] and Nguyen and Walker [7] have also investigated decision making in the Dempster-Shafer environment. In [4] he also suggested that with the aid of the Ordered Weighted Averaging (OWA) operators we can provide a unification of types of decision making attitude used in solving these problems. In [4] it was assumed that the payoffs associated with the problem were numeric values. In many real problems the requirement of specific numeric values for the payoffs is not realistic. In this work we consider a relaxation of this restriction by allowing the the nonnumeric values for the payoffs such as those carried by linguistic values [8], *big, small, about thirty thousand.* Considerations of nonnumeric values in decision making have also been considered in other works [9-14] The relaxation of this requirement, however, comes at the price of not allowing the use of some operations, particularly the weighted average, needed to implement the process of determining the optimal solution. In the following we suggest two operations which can be used in place of the weighted average in the decision making technique. The first operation, called the weighted median [15, 16], only requires that the payoffs can be ordered. The second operation, called the weighted average on a uniform scale based on work in [12], requires a slightly more sophisticate scale but still doesn't require numbers.

2. Decision Under Various Kinds of Uncertainty

A classic paradigm of decision making can be captured by the following matrix.

	S_1	S_2	S_j	S_n
A_1	C_{11}	C_{12}		C_{1n}
A_2				
A_i			C_{ij}	
A_m	C_{m1}			C_{mn}

In this matrix the A_i indicate alternative actions that are possible for a decision maker to take. The S_j indicate possible states of nature and the C_{ij} indicate the payoff to the decision maker for selecting alternative i when the state of nature is S_j. The problem of concern is to select one of the alternatives as being the optimal. The solution to this problem can be decomposed into a two step process:

(1) For each alternative evaluate the effective value of selecting that alternative, we shall denote this as V_i

(2) Select the alternative with the highest V_i value.

The interest and difficulty associated with this problem arises because in many cases we don't know the state of nature and thus the calculation of the valuation of each alternative, V_i, is not straight forward. In the classic literature three different situations with respect to our knowledge of state of nature have been considered and means for finding V_i in these cases have been suggested.

1. Decision Making Under Certainty

In this case the state of nature is exactly known. If we know that the state of nature is S_j, for example, we then simply calculate

$$V_i = C_{ij}$$

2. Decision Making Under Risk

In this case it is assumed that we have a probability distribution on the set $S = \{S_1, ..., S_n\}$ such that P_j is the probability associated with state S_j. The valuation of any alternative A_i is obtained by taking the expected value, hence

$$V_i = \sum_{j=1}^{n} P_j C_{ij}$$

We should note that the decision making under certainty can be considered as a special case in which $P_j = 1$ for some alternative S_j.

3. Decision Making Under Ignorance

In this case we have no information about the state of nature except that its some element in the set S. In this environment the decision maker replaces knowledge about the state of nature by assuming some particular decision making attitude. Among the attitudes considered in the literature are the following:

i.) Pessimistic Attitude - Using this attitude the decision maker selects as their valuation for an alternative the worst possible outcome under that alternative.

ii) Optimistic Attitude - Under this strategy the decision maker selects as their valuation for an alternative the best possible outcome under that alternative.

iii.) Hurwicz Approach - In this approach the decision maker selects some value degree of optimism, $\alpha \in [0, 1]$, and then for each alternative calculates V_i as the weighted average of the pessimistic and optimistic value,

$$V_i = \alpha * Opt + (1 - \alpha)Pess$$

iv.) Normative Approach - In this approach the decision maker uses the average of the possible payoffs under an alternative,

$$V_i = \frac{1}{n} \sum_{j=1}^{n} C_{ij}.$$

More generally we can express the strategy for decision making under ignorance as

$$V_i = F(C_{i1}, C_{i2}, ..., C_{im})$$

where the function F depends upon the attitude selected. The following table expresses the function F for the four attitudes discussed above.

Attitude	Valuation Function
Pessimistic	$V_i = Min_{j \in s} C_{ij}$
Optimistic	$V_i = Max_{j \in s} C_{ij}$
Hurwicz	$V_i = \propto Max_{j \in s} C_{ij} + (1 - \propto)Min_{j \in s} C_{ij}$
Normative	$V_i = \frac{1}{n} \sum_{j=1}^{n} C_{ij}.$

In [3, 4] the authors extended and generalized the possible representation for our knowledge about the state of nature with the use of the Dempster-Shafer belief structure [17, 18]. Assume S is a set of elements, in this environment the set of possible states of nature, a belief structure has associated with it a collection of non-null subsets of S, $B_1, B_2, ...B_q$, called the focal elements and a function m, called the probability density function, defined on the collection of focal elements such that

$$m(B_i) \in [0, 1]$$

$$\sum_{k=1}^{q} m(B_k) = 1$$

Essentially $m(B_k)$ is a probability associated with each of the focal elements.

Example: Assume S = {4%, 5%, 6%, 7%, 8%, 9%, 10%} are a collection of possible interest rates. Assume our knowledge about the state of nature is that there is a 0.5 probability that interest rates will be low, a 0.3 probability that interest rates will be high, and 0.2 probability that the interest rates can be anything. We represent this as a belief structure with

$$B_1 = \{4\%, 5\%, 6\%\}$$
$$B_2 = \{8\%, 9\%, 10\%\}$$
$$B_3 = S = \{4\%, 5\%, 6\%, 7\%, 8\%, 9\%, 10\%\}$$

As the preceding example illustrates the focal elements don't have to be disjoint.

Using the concept of a belief structure the classic situations with respect to our knowledge about the state of nature can be easily represented in this framework.

1) Certainty about the state of nature:

Assume we know the state of nature is S_j. In this case we have just one focal element $B_1 = \{S_j\}$ and $m(B_1) = 1$.

2) Probabilistic knowledge about the state of nature:

Assume we have P_j is the probability of S_j. In this case we have n focal elements $B_j = \{S_j\}$ for j = 1, ..., n and $m(B_j) = P_j$.

3) Ignorance about the state of nature:

Here we have one focal element B = S where m(B) = 1.

In addition to unifying our representation regarding our knowledge of the state the use of belief structures allows for the representation of many other different kinds of knowledge about the state on nature as illustrated in the preceding example.

In [4] an approach to finding the valuation for an alternative under the situation in which our knowledge about the state of nature is known in terms of a belief structure was suggested. Assume our knowledge about the state of nature is captured by the belief structure with focal elements $B_1, B_2, ...B_q$ and probability density function m. To obtain the valuation of alternative A_i we proceed as follows:

1. For each focal element obtain the collection of associated payoffs, denote these as $E_K, k = 1 ... q$.

2. Using a selected decision making attitude find the evaluation of each of the E_K, we shall denote these as $V_i(E_K)$

3. Calculate overall evaluation associated with A_i, V_i, as

$$V_i = \sum_{K=1}^{q} m(B_K) V_i(E_K).$$

Example: Consider the following abbreviated decision making matrix

	S_1	S_2	S_3	S_4	S_5
A_1	10	15	25	6	13

Assume our knowledge about the state of nature is

$$B_1 = \{S_1, S_2, S_3\}$$
$$B_2 = \{S_5\}$$
$$B_3 = \{S_1, S_2, S_3, S_4, S_5\}$$

where $m(B_1) = 0.5$, $m(B_2) = 0.3$ and $m(B_3) = 0.2$. Furthermore assume our decision attitude is a pessimistic one. We first calculate the E_K,

$$E_1 = \{10, 15, 25\}$$
$$E_2 = \{13\}$$
$$E_3 = \{10, 15, 25, 6, 13\}$$

Using the pessimistic attitude we calculate

$$V_1(E_K) = Min (E_K)$$

hence $V_1(E_1) = 10$, $V_2(E_2) = 13$ and $V_3(E_3) = 6$. Finally our overall valuation for this alternative is

$$V_1 = (0.5)10 + (0.3)13 + (0.2)6 = 10.1$$

In the above we have suggested a very general approach to decision making under uncertainty. This approach, with the aid of the belief structure, allows for the inclusion very sophisticated information about the knowledge of the state of nature.

3. Generalization of Attitudinal Evaluation

In the preceding when face with a collection $E = \{C_1, ..., C_n\}$ of possible payoffs and no information about the probabilities associated with these we selected a decision making attitude and used this to obtain the valuation of E. The decision making attitude was selected from among the four previously described attitudes. In [4] Yager suggested a generalization of this process. This generalization is based upon the use of the ordinal weighted averaging (OWA) operators introduced in [19]. In addition to providing a generalization of the process of decision making under ignorance this extension will provide a very useful semantics for the problem. We first introduce the OWA operator.

Definition: An OWA operator of dimension n is a function

$$F_W: R^n \to R$$

that has an associated weighting vector W,

$$W = \begin{bmatrix} w_1 \\ w_2 \\ \vdots \\ w_n \end{bmatrix}$$

such that: 1) $w_i \in [0, 1]$

$$2)\ \sum_{i=1}^{n} w_i = 1$$

and where for any collection $a_1, ..., a_n$ of values

$$F_W(a_1, ..., a_n) = \sum_{i=1}^{n} w_i * b_i$$

where b_i is the ith largest element of the collection $a_1, ..., a_n$.

In [19] Yager showed that we can use this OWA aggregation to provide a methodology for finding the valuation associated with a collection of values. In this framework W was called the *attitudinal vector*. We first note that the four classic attitudes can be captured in this framework. For

$$W = W_* = \begin{bmatrix} 0 \\ 0 \\ 0 \\ \vdots \\ 1 \end{bmatrix}$$

we obtain the pessimistic approach. For

$$W = W^* = \begin{bmatrix} 1 \\ 0 \\ 0 \\ \vdots \\ 0 \end{bmatrix}$$

we obtain the optimistic approach. For

$$W = W_H = \begin{bmatrix} \alpha \\ 0 \\ \vdots \\ 0 \\ 1 - \alpha \end{bmatrix}$$

we obtain the Hurwicz method. Finally for

$$W = W_A = \begin{bmatrix} 1/n \\ 1/n \\ \vdots \\ 1/n \end{bmatrix}$$

we obtain the normative approach.

However by introducing this OWA approach we see that we can implement many different types of attitudinal valuation by simply choosing a particular attitudinal vector W. In this spirit in [19] it was suggested using

$$\alpha = \frac{1}{n-1} \sum_{j=1}^{n} w_j \, (n-j)$$

for measuring the degree of optimism associated with a particular selection of W. We note that

$$\alpha(W_*) = 0, \; \alpha(W^*) = 1, \; \alpha(W_H) = \alpha \text{ and } \alpha(W_A) - 0.5.$$

It is also to be noted that by assigning most of the total weight of one to elements near the top of W we essentially assuming a kind of optimistic attitude. Assigning most of total to elements near the bottom of W provides a kind of pessimistic attitude.

In [4] a semantics was suggested that can be used with this OWA approach to valuation of decisions under ignorance. Noticing that the w_i's have the properties of a probability distribution, $w_i \in [0, 1]$ and $\sum_i w_i = 1$, it was suggested that we can view the vector W as a probability distribution. In this probability distribution w_i corresponds to the *probability that the ith best thing will occur*. Thus the pure optimist, with $w_1 = 1$, is saying that the probability is one that the best thing will happen. On the other hand the pessimist, with $w_n = 1$, is saying that the worst possible outcome will happen will probably one. Viewed in this way the OWA aggregation

$$F_w(a_1, ..., a_n) = \sum_i w_i \, b_i,$$

where b_i is the ith best outcome of the a_j's, can be seen as an expected value.

In [4, 19] Yager introduced a measure of entropy that can be associated with a particular attitudinal vector W,

$$H(W) = - \sum_i w_i \ln (w_i).$$

The introduction of these OWA operators provides us with a vast array of possible means for finding these valuations. Using a method suggested by O'Hagan [20] we can greatly ease the burden of obtaining W. All that is required is that the decision maker select a value α indicating their degree of optimism. O'Hagan then suggested solving the following mathematical programming problem for determining the weights in W based upon a given value α.

$$\text{Max: } H(W) = - \sum_i w_i \ln (w_i)$$

such that:

$$\alpha = \frac{1}{n-1} \sum_i w_i (n-i)$$
$$\sum_i w_i = 1$$
$$0 \le w_i \le 1$$

We see that this approach is very much in the spirt of maximal entropy methods.

In the above we have suggested a very general approach to finding the valuation of a collection of potential payoffs in environments in which we have no information about the probabilities of each of the potential payoffs. As described above this approach involves the introduction of an attitudinal vector and an aggregation process based upon the use of the OWA operator.

4. Decision with Ordinal Payoffs

In the preceding we have suggested a very general approach to decision making under uncertainty. This approach allows the representation of our knowledge about the state of nature in terms of a belief structure and uses the OWA operator to find valuations of collections of potential payoffs. Let us now summarize this method.

Assume we have a belief structure on the state of nature with focal elements B_1, ..., B_q and m. Let α be our degree of optimism. In order to find the valuation of a given alternative, A_i, we proceed as follows:

1. For each B_k calculate the associated possible payoffs under alternative A_i, denote these as E_k, $k = 1 \dots q$.

2. For each E_k, using α and the method suggested by O'Hagan calculate an associated weighting vector W_k. (We note the dimension of W_k depends upon the dimension of E_k.)

3. For each E_k calculate

$$V_i(E_k) = F_{W_k}(E_k) = \sum_{j=1}^{Dim(k)} w_{jk} \, b_{jk} \qquad \textbf{(I)}$$

b_{jk} is the jth largest element in E_k and Dim(k) is the dimension of W_k.

4. Calculate

$$V_i = \sum_{k=1}^{q} m(B_k) \, V_i(E_k) \qquad \textbf{(II)}$$

In the preceding we have implicitly assumed that the payoff, the C_{ij}'s, where numeric values. One can easily envision situations in which there may exist some difficulty in obtaining such crisp information regarding these payoffs. For example, we may have payoff values such as: *very high, low, about $30,000*, etc. These can be seen as kinds of linguistic payoffs. In this environment, at best, one can associated with such payoff values a linear ordering indicating the decision makers preference among the various potential payoffs. Thus, in the following we shall assume that the payoff values are drawn from the following linear scale,

$$L = \{L_1, L_2, ..., L_m\}$$

such that $L_i > L_j$ if $i > j$, hence $C_{ij} \in L$.

In attempting to use our general approach to finding the valuation of alternatives in this environment we are faced with a problem in attempting to implement the operations (I) and (II). As we see these operations, which are essentially weighted averages, require that we perform operations not available to us in this environment where the payoffs are drawn from an ordinal scale. For example, in trying to implement (I) even though we have numeric values for the weights, the w_{jk}, the b_K are just drawn from L and thus we can't implement this operation.

In the following sections we shall present two approaches for extending our decision making methodology to this less precise environment. The first approach is based upon the use of a weighted median operator introduced in [15, 16, 21]. As we shall see this approach only requires the payoffs be drawn from a scale having only a linear ordering. The second approach is based upon the work of Delgado, Verdegay, and Vila [12]. As we shall see this approach requires a slightly more sophisticated scale but still doesn't require crisp numeric values. The scale we shall require we shall call a uniform scale and requires addition structure than a simple linear ordering.

5. Weighted Median Decision Making

The operations performed in (I) and (II) can be easily seen to be a weighted average. Let us now consider the basic weighted average operation,

$$T = \sum_{i=1}^{n} w_i x_i \qquad \text{(III)}$$

We shall denote this aggregation as

$$T = WA((w_1, x_1), (w_2, x_2), ..., (w_n, x_n)) \qquad \text{(III)'}$$

In (III) the w_i are the weights, numbers that satisfy (**a**). $w_i \in [0, 1]$ and (**b**). $\sum_i w_i = 1$. The x_i are the values that are aggregated, we shall denote the x_i's as the arguments of this aggregation. As we see from (III) the performance of this weighted average operation requires that the arguments, the x_i, be numbers drawn from the real line. The weighted average has a number of well known properties [22]:

1. **Idempotency:** If all the arguments, the x_i, are equal to some value a then the aggregation must equal this value.

2. **Commutativity/Symmetry:** Each of the pairs (w_i, x_i) are treated in the same manner

3. **Monotonicity with respect to arguments:** If any of the x_i increase, then the weighted average can't decrease.

4. **Monotonicity with respect to weights:** If $x_i > x_j$ then if we move some of the weights associated with the pair (w_j, x_j) to the pair (w_i, x_i) then the value of weighted average can't decrease.

5. **Bounded by Max and Min:** $\text{Min}_i \, x_i \leq \sum_i w_i x_i \leq \text{Max}_i \, x_i$

In order to be able to apply our general approach to decision maker under uncertainty to environments in which the payoffs are drawn from a linear ordering we must provide some operation to replace the weighted average. In [15, 16] Yager introduced the idea of the weighted median. In the following we shall assume that the

w_i are still numbers corresponding to weights, satisfying *a* and *b*. On the other hand we shall only require that the arguments are drawn from a scale which allows us to order the arguments, a linear ordering.

Definition: The weighted median aggregation denoted,

$$WM((w_1, x_1), (w_2, x_2), ..., (w_n, x_n)),$$

is defined as follows:

1. Reindex the arguments so that (y_j) corresponds to the argument which has the jth largest value (y_j is the jth largest of the x_i).

2. Consider the reindexed pairs (u_j, y_j) where u_j is the weight associate with the x_i that is the jth largest.

3. Let $T_k = \sum_{j=1}^{k} u_j$, be the sum of the weights associated with k largest arguments.

4. The weighted median is the value y_k* such that

$$T_{k*-1} < 0.5$$
$$T_{k*} \geq 0.5$$

Example: Consider the calculation of the weighted median of the following
$$((0.2, L_6), (0.4, L_3), (0.2, L_2), (0.1, L_7), (0.1, L_1)).$$
To calculate the weighted median we provide the following table:

k	u_k	y_k	T_k	
1	0.1	L_7	0.1	
2	0.2	L_6	0.3	
3	0.4	L_3	0.7	⇐
4	0.2	L_2	0.9	
5	0.1	L_1	1	

In this case we get that the weighted median is L_3.

In [16] it is shown that the weighted median satisfies the five conditions previously listed for the weighted average. He suggested that the weighted median provides an alternative operation to the weighted and thus can be used to implement (I) and (II) in the general approach to decision making under uncertainty in environments where the payoffs are drawn from a simple linear ordering. The following example illustrates the use of the weighted median in the decision making problem.

Example: Consider the following decision problem where we assume that the payoffs are drawn from the following scale:

Extremely High	EH
Very High	VH
High	H
Medium	M
Low	L
Very Low	VL

Extremely Low   EL

Consider the following payoff matrix:

	S_1	S_2	S_3	S_4	S_5
A_1	VL	VH	EH	EL	L
A_2	M	L	VH	M	EH

We shall assume our knowledge about the state of nature is known in terms of the belief structure in which

$B_1 = \{S_1, S_2, S_3\}$, $B_2 = \{S_5\}$ and $B_3 = \{S_1, S_2, S_3, S_4, S_5\}$ where $m(B_1) = 0.4$, $m(B_2) = 0.4$ and $m(B_3) = 0.2$.

We shall further assume the decision making attitude is captured by a degree of optimism of $\alpha = 0.25$. We first consider the alternative A_1.

1. For each B_i we calculate the associated possible payoffs:

$E_1 = (VL, VH, EH)$

$E_2 = (L)$

$E_3 = (VL, VH, EH, EL, L)$

2. With $\alpha = 0.25$, we must solve the mathematical programming problem described earlier to obtain the OWA weights associated with each of the focal elements. Solving this problem we get:

For n = 3 $W_3 = \begin{bmatrix} 0.11 \\ 0.27 \\ 0.62 \end{bmatrix}$

For n = 1 $W_1 = [1]$

For n = 5 $W_5 = \begin{bmatrix} 0.05 \\ 0.08 \\ 0.15 \\ 0.26 \\ 0.46 \end{bmatrix}$

3. To calculate the effective value of each E_i we calculate

i. $V_1(E_1) = WM((0.11, EH), (0.27, VH), (0.62, VL)) = VL$

ii. $V_1(E_2) = WM((1, L)) = L$

iii. $V_1(E_3) = WM((0.05, EH), (0.08, VH), (0.15, L), (0.26, VL), (0.46, EL))$
       $= VL$

4. Next we calculate the overall valuation of alternative A_1

$V_1 = WM((m(B_i), V_1(E_i)) = WM((0.4, VL), (0.4, L), (0.2, VL)) = VL$.

Let us now consider A_2:

1. For each B_i we calculate the associated possible payoffs:

$E_1 = (M, L, VH)$, $E_2 = (EH)$ and $E_3 = (M, L, VH, M, EH)$

2. With $\alpha = 0.25$ we set the same weight vectors as in the case of A_2.

3. Next we calculate the valuation for each of the E_i using the weighted median

    i. $V_2(E_1) = WM((0.62, L), (0.27, M), (0.11, VH)) = L$

    ii. $V_2(E_2) = WM((1, EH)) = EH$

    ii. $V_2(E_3) = WM((0.46, L), (0.26, M), (0.15, M), (0.08, VH), 0.05, EH))$

           = M

4. Finally we calculate the overall valuation of alternative A_2

    $V_2 = WM((0.4, L), (0.4, EH), (0.2, M)) = M$

Thus we see A_2 is preferred to A_1.

In the above we have introduced an approach to solving decision problems in the payoffs are drawn from a scale which has only the structure of a linear ordering. The key to handling this type of problem is the use of the weighted median as the primary aggregation operation.

6. Payoffs Drawn from a Uniform Scale

In this section we shall consider an alternative approach to decision making under risk in environments in which the payoffs are non-numeric. The approach we shall use is based upon a method introduced by Delgado, Verdegay, and Vila [12] which here we shall call the **Weighted Index (WI)** method. In the preceding we indicated that when the payoffs are expressed in some scale with less structure than a purely numeric scale we need to find some operation to replace the weighted average used in (I) and (II). Furthermore, we showed that if the scale used to measure the payoffs only possess a linear ordering then we can use a weighted median to perform the necessary weighted aggregation operation. In this section we consider the measurement of the payoffs, while still not on a numeric scale, are drawn from a scale with slightly more structure than a simple linear ordering. The scale we shall use we shall call a *uniform* scale. It is very much in the spirit of an equal spaced difference measurement structure [23].

Informally by a uniform scale we mean one in which the scale values, the allowable values for indicating the payoffs, are assumed to be equally spaced through the range of possible values for the payoffs. In the following we shall provide a more formal discussion of this scale with special emphasis on understating the allowable operations on this scale. A more through discussion of this type of scale can be found in [23, 24].

Let U be a set of elements constituting the scale on which we measure the payoffs in the decision problem, $U = \{U_1, U_2, ..., U_m\}$. We shall assume that U has a linear ordering where $U_i > U_j$ if $i > j$.

As is will established in preference theory [25] the possession of a linear ordering means there exists some function

    $f: U \rightarrow \mathbb{R}$ (real line)

such that $U_i > U_j$ implies $f(U_i) > f(U_j)$. Furthermore, we shall assume that U has a uniform property, U is a uniform scale, in particular f is such that for all i and j

    $f(U_{i+1}) - f(U_i) = f(U_{j+1}) - f(U_j) > 0$ for all i, j

We shall now introduce a operation which we call the *weighted index (WI) method*, which is based on the ideas introduced in [12]. This operation will be used as a surrogate for the weighted average. Let $w_1, ..., w_n$ be a collection of weights drawn such that

$$w_i \in [0, 1]$$

$$\sum_{i=1}^{n} w_i = 1.$$

Let $a_1, ..., a_n$ be a collection of arguments such that $a_i \in U$. Furthermore if $a_i = U_p$ we shall let $Index(a_i) = p$. We now define

$$WI((w_1, a_1), (w_2, a_2), ..., (w_n, a_n)) = U_s$$

where

$$S = Round(\sum_{i=1}^{n} w_i * Index(a_i))$$

We note the operation Round means to round off to the nearest integer.

Example: Find U_s such that $WI((0.2, U_5), (0.5, U_3), (0.3, U_2)) = U_s$. In this case

$$s = Round((0.2)(5) + (0.5)(3) + (0.3)(2)]$$
$$s = Round [3.1] = 3.$$

In order to justify the use of this operator in our problem of decision making we need to show the appropriateness of using this type of aggregation as a surrogate for the weighted median as well as to justify the meaningfulness of the operation of WI with respect to the uniform scale.

Consider the weighted average of

$$WA((w_1, a_1), (w_2, a_2), ..., (w_n, a_n)).$$

If the a_i are drawn from the scale U we can't directly implement this operation because the a_i are not numbers, however we can consider using a function f to transform the a_i into numbers and then take an inverse of f, $\hat{f}$, to obtain a value in the scale U. Thus we calculate for some choice of

$$WA((w_1, f(a_1)), (w_2, f(a_2)), ..., (w_n, f(a_n))) = T$$

and then take $u = \hat{f}(T)$.

In order to prove the meaningfulness of the weighted index operation we must show that the results obtained are independent of any particular choice of function f. We recall that we assume for a uniform scale that we can use any function f that satisfies

1. $f(U_j) > f(U_i)$ for $j > i$
2. $f(U_{i+1}) - f(U_i) = K$ for all i.

In addition we must define $\hat{f}$. We define this as follows

$$\hat{f}: \mathbb{R} \rightarrow U$$

such that $\hat{f}(r) = U_s$ where U_s minimizes $|r - f(U_j)|$ over all $U_j \in U$.

From the properties of f we see that whatever f we choose we have

$$f(U_{i+1}) = f(U_i) + K$$

and therefore

$$f(U_2) = K + f(U_1)$$
$$f(U_3) = 2K + f(U_1)$$
$$f(U_i) = (i - 1)K + f(U_1)$$

Consider now the aggregation $\sum_{i=1}^{n} w_i f(a_i)$ where $a_i \in U$. From the above we can express $f(a_i) = (Index(a_i) - 1) K + f(U_1)$ and then

$$\sum_{i=1}^{n} w_i f(a_i) = \sum_{i=1}^{n} w_i((Index(a_i) - 1) K + f(U_1))$$

since $\sum_{i=1}^{n} W_i = 1$ we get

$$\sum_{i=1}^{n} w_i f(a_i) = \sum_{i=1}^{n} (w_i (Index(a_i) - 1)) K) + f(U_1).$$

Since for any U_j in U we have $f(U_j) = (j - 1) K + f(U_1)$ and thus

$$\Delta = |f(U_j) - \Sigma w_i f(a_i)| = |(j - 1) K - \sum_{i=1}^{n} (w_i (Index(a_i) - 1)) K)|$$

$$\Delta = |j - \sum_{i=1}^{n} (w_i Index(a_i))|.$$

From this we see that the minimum of this value occurs for $j = Round(\sum_{i=1}^{n} (w_i Index(a_i)))$. Hence we get our aggregated value U_s where

$$s = Round [\sum_{i=1}^{n} w_i Index(a_i)].$$

We see that this approach in addition to emulating the weighted average is independent of any choice of the function f and thus is meaningful with respect to the scale U.

We shall now further show that the weighted index operation has the basic properties associated with the weighted average and as such can be used as a surrogate for the weighted average in steps (I) and (II) of the decision process. We first note WI is idempotent. If

$$WI(w_1, x_1), (w_2, x_2), ..., (w_n, x_n)) = U_s$$

where $x_i = U_p$ for all i then

$$s = Round(\sum_{i=1}^{n} w_i Index(x_i)) = Round(\sum_{i=1}^{n} w_i Index(U_p)) = p$$

and hence idempotency is satisfied.

It is also seen that each of the pairs (w_i, x_i) are treated in the same and hence WI is commutative. The monotonicity with respect to the arguments and the weights can be easily shown and we leave this to the reader. It also can be easily seen that

$$Min_i[a_i] \le U_s \le Max_i[a_i].$$

Thus we see that the weighted index method has the fundamental properties of weighted average.

We use the example of the preceding section to illustrate the approach suggested in this section.

Example: Assume the payoffs are drawn from the following scale which we now assume is a <u>uniform</u> scale on the space of payoffs.

Extremely High	U_7
Very High	U_6
High	U_5
Medium	U_4
Low	U_3
Very Low	U_2
Extremely Low	U_1

In this case we consider the payoff matrix.

	S_1	S_2	S_3	S_4	S_5
A_1	U_2	U_6	U_7	U_1	U_3
A_2	U_4	U_3	U_6	U_4	U_7

Assuming the knowledge of state of nature is again carried by the belief structure

$$B_1 = \{S_1, S_2, S_3\}$$
$$B_2 = \{S_5\}$$
$$B_3 = \{S_1, S_2, S_3, S_4, S_5\}$$

where $m(B_1) = 0.4$, $m(B_2) = 0.4$, and $m(B_3) = 0.2$. Again we assume $\alpha = 0.25$.

Consider alternative A_1, in this case we get

1. $E_1 = \{U_2, U_6, U_7\}$
    $E_2 = \{U_3\}$
    $E_3 = \{U_2, U_6, U_7, U_1, U_3\}$

2. With $\alpha = 0.25$ the attitudinal vectors are the same as before

$$W_3 = \begin{bmatrix} 0.11 \\ 0.27 \\ 0.62 \end{bmatrix} \qquad W_1 = [1] \qquad W_5 = \begin{bmatrix} 0.05 \\ 0.08 \\ 0.15 \\ 0.26 \\ 0.46 \end{bmatrix}$$

3. To calculate the effective value of each of the E_i we proceed as follows

i. $V_1(E_1) = WI((0.11, U_7), (0.27, U_6), (0.62, U_1)) = U_s$

where

$s = \text{Round}[(0.11)(7) + (0.27)(6) + (0.62)(2)] = \text{Round } [3.63] = 4$

hence $V_1(E_1) = U_4$.

ii. $V_1(E_2) = WI[(1, U_3)] = U_3$

ii. $V_1(E_3) = WI[(0.05, U_7), (0.08, U_6), (0.15, U_3), (0.26, U_2), (0.46, U_1)] =$
$V_1(E_3) = U_s$

where

s = Round[(0.05)(7) + (0.08)(6) + (0.15)(3) + (0.26)(2) + (0.46)(1)]

s = Round(2.26) = 2

hence $V_1(E_3) = U_2$.

4. Finally we calculate V_1

$$V_1 = WI[(0.4, U_4), (0.4, U_3), (0.2, U_2)] = U_s$$

where

s = Round[(0.4)(4) + (0.4)(3) + (0.2)(2)] = Round [3.2] = 3

hence $V_1 = U_3$.

We now calculate V_2.

In this case

$$E_1 = (U_4, U_3, U_6)$$
$$E_2 = (U_7)$$
$$E_3 = (U_4, U_3, U_6, U_4, U_7)$$

i. $V_2(E_1) = WI[(0.11, U_6), (0.27, U_4), (0.62, U_3)] = U_s$

where s = Round [(0.11(6) + (0.27)(4) + (0.62)(3)] = Round [3.6] = 4. Hence $V_2(E_1)$ = U_4.

ii. $V_2(E_2) = WI[1, U_7)] = U_7$

iii. $V_2(E_3) = WI [(0.05, U_7), (0.08, U_6), (0.15, U_4), (0.26, U_4), (0.46, U_3)]$

$$= U_s$$

where s = Round [3.85] = 4. Hence $V_2(E_3) = U_4$

Finally

$$V_2 = WI[(0.4, U_4), (0.4, U_7), (0.2, U_4)] = U_5$$

Thus we see that A_2 is the preferred alternative.

It should be noted that since the uniform scale assumes a linear ordering among the scale values it is also possible to use the weighted median in the case in which the payoffs are drawn from a uniform scale. However, since the WI operation is more sensitive to the value of the arguments it appears to be the more preferred operation in this environment. Informally, we see this increased sensitivity as follows. If we use WM then any transformation g, on our arguments, which preserves the linear ordering can be used and we still get the same result. If we use WI then any transformation f, on the arguments, which preserves both the linear ordering and the keeps the differences constant can be used. Since every f must also be a g we see that the WI is more sensitive than WM.

7. Conclusion

In the preceding we have looked at the problem of decision making in environments in which there exists some uncertainty about the state of nature. We discussed a general approach to the representation of this uncertainty using the Dempster-Shafer belief structure. A general methodology for representing the decision makers attitude was described using the OWA operators. We presented a general methodology for evaluating the worth of each of the alternatives, central to this approach was the use of a weighted average operation. We then considered the situation in which the payoffs associated with a problem are nonnumeric values. We discussed two scales for representing nonnumeric information. The first scale, L, assumes only the existence of a linear ordering on the allowable values. The second scale, U, called a uniform scale assumes that in addition to a linear ordering the scale values are uniformly spaced. It was noted that in these nonnumeric environments a need arises for an operation to replace the weighted average. We showed that in the case of only a linear ordering on the payoffs we can use a weighted median operation to replace the weighted average. In the case in which the payoffs come from a uniform scale an operation called the weighted average on a uniform scale can be used to replace the weighted average.

8. References

[1]. Luce, R. D. and Raiffa, H., Games and Decisions: Introduction and Critical Survey, John Wiley & Sons: New York, 1967.

[2]. Richmond, S. B., Operations Research for Management Decisions, Ronald Press: New York, 1968.

[3]. Bolanos, M. J., Lamata, M. T. and Moral, S., "Decision making problems in a general environment," Fuzzy Sets and Systems 25, 135-144, 1988.

[4]. Yager, R. R., "Decision making under Dempster-Shafer uncertainties," International Journal of General Systems 20, 233-245, 1992.

[5]. Strat, T. M., "Making decisions with belief functions," in Proceedings Fifth Workshop on Uncertainty in Artificial Intelligence, Windsor, Ont., 351-360, 1989.

[6]. Strat, T. M., "Decision analysis using belief functions," in Advances in the Dempster-Shafer Theory of Evidence, edited by Yager, R. R., Kacprzyk, J. and Fedrizzi, M., John Wiley & Sons: New York, 275-310, 1994.

[7]. Nguyen, H. T. and Walker, E. A., "On decision making using belief functions," in Advances in the Dempster-Shafer Theory of Evidence, edited by Yager, R. R., Kacprzyk, J. and Fedrizzi, M., John Wiley & Sons: New York, 311-330, 1994.

[8]. Zadeh, L., "The concept of a linguistic variable and its application to approximate reasoning: Part 1," Information Sciences 8, 199-249, 1975.

[9]. Yager, R. R., "A new methodology for ordinal multiple aspect decisions based on fuzzy sets," Decision Sciences 12, 589-600, 1981.

[10]. Lamata, M. T., "Problemas de decision con informacion general," Tesis doctoral, Universidad de Granada, 1986.

[11]. Lamata, M. T. and Moral, S., "Decision: Utilidades Linguisticas," Proceedings III Spanish Congress on Fuzzy Technologies and Logic, Santiago de Compostela, Spain, 1993.

[12]. Delgado, M., Verdegay, J. L. and Vila, A., "On aggregation operations of linguistic labels," International Journal of Intelligent Systems 8, 351-370, 1993.

[13]. Lamata, M. T. and Moral, S., "Calculus with linguistic probabilities and belief," in Advances in the Dempster-Shafer Theory of Evidence, edited by Yager, R. R., Fedrizzi, M. and Kacprzyk, J., John Wiley & Sons: New York, 133-152, 1994.

[14]. Yager, R. R., "An approach to ordinal decision making," International Journal of Approximate Reasoning 12, 237-261, 1995.

[15]. Yager, R. R. and Rybalov, A., "Understanding the median as a fusion operator," International Journal of General Systems 26, 239-263, 1997.

[16].Yager, R. R., "Fusion of ordinal information using weighted median aggregation," International Journal of Approximate Reasoning, (To Appear).

[17]. Dempster, A. P., "A generalization of Bayesian inference," Journal of the Royal Statistical Society, 205-247, 1968.

[18]. Shafer, G., A Mathematical Theory of Evidence, Princeton University Press: Princeton, N.J., 1976.

[19]. Yager, R. R., "On ordered weighted averaging aggregation operators in multi-criteria decision making," IEEE Transactions on Systems, Man and Cybernetics 18, 183-190, 1988.

[20]. O'Hagan, M., "Aggregating template or rule antecedents in real-time expert systems with fuzzy set logic," Proceedings 22nd Annual IEEE Asilomar Conf. on Signals, Systems and Computers, Pacific Grove, Ca., 681-689, 1988.

[21]. Yager, R. R., "Fuzzy logic control with discrete outputs," Proceedings of World Congress on Neural Networks, Washington, DC, II:595-601, 1995.

[22]. Yager, R. R., "On mean type aggregation," IEEE Transactions on Systems, Man and Cybernetics 26, 209-221, 1996.

[23]. Roberts, F. S., Measurement Theory, Addison-Wesley: Reading, MA, 1979.

[24]. Krantz, D. H., Luce, R. D., Suppes, P. and Tversky, A., Foundations of Measurement, Academic Press: New York, 1971.

[25]. Roubens, M. and Vincke, P., Preference Modeling, Springer-Verlag: Berlin, 1989.

Fuzzy Measures and Equilibrium Conditions on the Financial Market

Salvatore Greco
Facoltá di Economia
Universitá di Catania
Corso Italia, 55
95129 Catania
Italy
E-mail: salgreco@vm.unict.it

Abstract. The formal generalization of a well-known equilibrium condition on the financial market is considered. This extension is based on the concept of fuzzy measure of events. The aim is the useful modelling of an uncertainty which cannot be covered by a probability measure.

Keywords. Fuzzy financial laws, uncertainty, fuzzy logic, splitting property

1 Introduction

The fuzzy formulation of financial mathematics, proposed by Buckley (1987) is based on the extension principle (Zadeh, 1975) which makes it possible to generalize the habitual functions considered in classic financial mathematics in order to operate on typical financial dimensions (capital, terms, rates, timing) expressed as fuzzy numbers. This approach has been studied by a number of authors (Li Calzi, 1990, Biacino and Simonelli, 1991, Buckley, 1992, Giove, 1993).

In this article an alternative approach is introduced: while the usual financial dimensions are considered "crisp", fuzzy calculation instruments are used to model the uncertainty of financial operations. Uncertainty is defined here as a situation in which it proves appropriate to use the fuzzy measure of an event (Sugeno, 1974, Zadeh, 1978, Grabisch et al., 1992), that is, a generalization of the concept of probability obtained by weakening the additive property and substituting it with a weaker hypothesis, that of monotony.

The concept of uncertainty defined by Knight (1937) can also be connected to the fuzzy measure of events. It is referred to the case of aleatory variables whose probability distribution is not known. As Keynes suggested (1937) the concept of uncertainty can prove very useful in explaining some events occurring on the financial market. The implications of this concept of uncertainty have become very clear as a result of the paradox proposed by Ellsberg (1961). Recently, many authors have defined suitable models for describing the behaviour of individuals in situations of uncertainty (Gilboa, 1987, Schmeidler, 1989, Gilboa and Schmeidler, 1989, Sarin and Wakker, 1992, Cardin and Ferretti, 1993 and 1995). These models are based on a definition of "non-additive probability" (capacity measure of events) which coincides with the concept of fuzzy measure of events. It is necessary to point out, however, that while in the studies mentioned the attention is focused on the union of disjoint events, in this article the intersection of events is the object of modelling. More precisely, with reference to Ellsberg's paradox, the idea is that the credibility of obtaining a return from a specific investment A and from a specific reinvestment B may be compared to lots drawn from two urns, A and B, the contents of which however are not exactly known. E.g. if urn A contains *at least* ten red balls on a total of twenty and urn B contains *at most* ten black balls on a total of twenty, what is the credibility of the event "extraction of a red ball from A and a black ball from B"? As a result of the insufficient level of knowledge in this case the classic instruments for calculating probability cannot be used, while fuzzy measures and the instruments of fuzzy logic (for a rather complete survey on this subject see Chapter 1 of Fodor and Roubens, 1994), prove to be particularly useful. Some theoretical justifications of this approach have been developed: Dubois (1985) gives a generalization of the usual notion of independent events useful outside a purely frequentist approach to the probability theory; on the same lines Dubois et al. (1996) outline an extension of the Von Neumann-Morgestern utility theory.

The structure of the present article is as follows. Section 2 presents the concept of fuzzy measure of events and a specific definition of independent events. Section 3 introduces the concept of fuzzy financial laws. In section 4 the splitting property of fuzzy financial laws is obtained as consequence of two simple axioms on specific form of lotteries. The splitting property of fuzzy financial law generalizes a well-known equilibrium condition of the financial markets to a fuzzy environment. Section 5 gives a characterization of the splitting property with respect to the fuzzy financial laws. Section 6 contains the conclusions.

2 Fuzzy measures of events

Let I be the finite set $\{1,...,n\}$ and 2^I the set of all the subset of I. A function $g:2^I \rightarrow [0,1]$ is a fuzzy measure if

1) $g(\emptyset)=0,$
2) $g(I)=1,$
3) $A \subseteq B \subseteq I \Rightarrow g(A) \leq g(B)$

(Sugeno, 1974, Grabisch et al., 1992). 3) is a monotony property which weakens the classical probabilistic additivity property, i.e. if $A \subseteq I$, $B \subseteq I$ and $A \cap B = \emptyset$ then

$$g(A \cup B) = g(A) + g(B).$$

More generally fuzzy measures can be defined on a σ-algebra of sets.

The concept of fuzzy measure admits as specific cases the measures of probability and possibility, Shafer's credibility functions and Shackle's consonant credibility functions (Dubois and Prade, 1980, Grabisch et al. 1992). We observe that the fuzzy measures coincide with the capacity measures (Choquet, 1953-54, Wakker, 1989). We define credibility a fuzzy measure of an event E.

We use the concept of t-norm for modelling the credibility of the intersection of two independent events. A triangular norm T (t-norm for short) (Menger, 1979, Schweizer and Sklar, 1983) is a conjunction operator in the field of fuzzy logic (Weber, 1982). In particular a t-norm is a function from $[0,1]^2$ to $[0,1]$ which satisfies the following conditions:

$$T(1,\alpha) = \alpha \quad \forall \alpha \in [0, 1],$$
$$T(\alpha,\beta) = T(\beta,\alpha) \ \forall \alpha, \ \beta \in [0, 1],$$
$$T(\alpha,\beta) \leq T(\mu,v) \ \forall \ \alpha \leq \mu \text{ and } \beta \leq v,$$
$$T(\alpha,T(\beta,\gamma)) = T(T(\alpha,\beta),\gamma) \ \forall \alpha,\beta,\gamma \in [0, 1].$$

The following are some well-known t-norms:

$$1) \ T(x,y)=\min\{x,y\};$$
$$2) \ T(x,y)=xy;$$
$$3) \ T(x,y)=\max\{x+y-1,0\}.$$

The powers of the function T are defined by setting

$$T^1(\alpha_1, \alpha_2) = T(\alpha_1, \alpha_2)$$

and

$$T^n(\alpha_1, ...,\alpha_{n+1})=T(T^{n-1}(\alpha_1, ...,\alpha_n), \alpha_{n+1}) \ \forall n \geq 2.$$

A t-norm is considered strict if it is strictly increasing in each place on $]0,1[^2$.

Let E_1 and E_2 be two events whose probabilities are respectively $P(E_1)$ and $P(E_2)$. Usually the two events E_1 and E_2 are defined independent if

$$P(E_1 \cap E_2)=P(E_1)P(E_2) \quad (2.1)$$

where $E_1 \cap E_2$ is the event that both E_1 and E_2 occur (e.g. Feller, 1962). However this definition may be too restrictive outside a frequentist framework. With respect to a more general approach a good extension of the independence between events can be obtained considering a t-norm T in (2.1) instead of the multiplication (Dubois, 1985). Let g(E) be the measure of the generic event E. Then E_1 and E_2 are independent with respect to T if

$$g(E_1 \cap E_2)=T(g(E_1), g(E_2)).$$

In the same line Weber (1987) proposed the following definition for the conditional measure of events. Let T a strict t-norm and let E_2 an event such that $g(E_2)>0$. Then $g(E_1| E_2)$ is the T-conditional measure of the event E_1 given the event E_2, if it is a solution of the following equation in the unknown variable x

$$g(E_1 \cap E_2)=T(x, g(E_2)).$$

3 Fuzzy financial laws

Let t_0 represents the current time. It is possible to define as fuzzy financial law a function $\psi: R_0^+ \times [t_0,+\infty[\times [t_0,+\infty[\times]0,1] \to R_0^+$, with the following characteristics:

$\psi 1) \ \psi(x,t,t,1)=x, \ \forall x \in R_0^+ \text{ and } \forall t \in [t_0,+\infty[,$

$\psi 2) \ \psi(0,t_1,t_2,\alpha)=0, \ \forall t_1, t_2 \in [\ t_0,+\infty[\text{ and } \forall \alpha \in]0,1],$

$\psi3)$ $x_1 > x_2 \Rightarrow \psi(x_1,t_1,t_2,\alpha) > \psi(x_2,t_1,t_2,\alpha),$ $\forall x_1, x_2 \in R_0^+,$ $\forall t_1, t_2 \in [t_0, +\infty[$ and $\forall \alpha \in]0,1],$

$\psi4)$ $t_1 > t_2 \Rightarrow \psi(x,t_1,t_3,\alpha) \le \psi(x,t_2,t_3,\alpha),$ $\forall x \in R_0^+,$ $\forall t_1, t_2, t_3 \in [t_0, +\infty[$ and $\forall \alpha \in]0,1],$

$\psi5)$ $t_2 > t_3 \Rightarrow \psi(x,t_1,t_2,\alpha) \ge \psi(x,t_1,t_3,\alpha),$ $\forall x \in R_0^+,$ $\forall t_1, t_2, t_3 \in [t_0, +\infty[,$ $\forall \alpha \in]0,1],$

$\psi6)$ $\alpha > \beta \Rightarrow \psi(x,t_1,t_2,\alpha) < \psi(x,t_1,t_2,\beta),$ $\forall x \in R_0^+,$ $\forall t_1, t_2 \in [t_0, +\infty[$ and $\forall \alpha, \beta \in]0,1].$

A fuzzy financial law may be given the following interpretations: investing a capital x at the term t_1 you can obtain an amount $\psi(x,t_1,t_2,\alpha)$ at the term t_2 with credibility α.

Conditions from $\psi1)$ to $\psi5)$ are quite usual and admit the following interpretation:

$\psi1)$ says that the final amount at time t of the investment of a capital x at the same time t is equal to x with credibility 1;

$\psi2)$ says that, in any case, investing a capital 0, the final amount shall be 0;

$\psi3)$ says that, all other conditions being equal, greater is the invested capital greater is its final amount;

$\psi4)$ says that, all other conditions being equal, the final amount is not increasing with the investment time;

$\psi5)$ says that, all other conditions being equal, the final amount is not decreasing with the disinvestment time.

Let us explain condition $\psi6)$. An investment is riskier than another if it pays its final amount with a smaller credibility. $\psi6)$ simply states that the riskier investments should yield a greater final amount, all other conditions being equal.

The function ψ can be interpreted in terms of some lotteries similar to those proposed in the utility theory of von Neumann and Morgenstern (1944) (see also Hersteirn and Milnor, 1953 and for a generalization to a fuzzy context Dubois et al. 1996). Let $B[x,y;t,\alpha]$ be the lottery in which you can receive a win x at time $t \in [t_0, +\infty[$ if the event E(B) which has a credibility α is verified or y otherwise. Furthermore let be p(B,s) the price at time $s \in [t_0, +\infty[$ of the lottery B. Let us remark that the win of a lottery can be a fixed amount of money but also another lottery. In the following we consider lotteries in which the win is a fixed amount of money if it is not explicitly said differently. In this context a fuzzy financial law must satisfies the following expression with respect to each lottery $B[y,0;t_2,\alpha],$ $\forall y \in R_0^+,$ $\forall t_1, t_2 \in [t_0, +\infty[$ and $\forall \alpha \in]0,1],$

$$\psi(p(B,t_1),t_1,t_2,\alpha)=y. \qquad (3.1)$$

When we consider events with a credibility 1 practically we are considering situations in a condition of certainty. Let us observe that by means of function ψ in this case we can describe several concepts well known in finance. If $\forall\, t_1, t_2 \in [t_0, +\infty[$ and $\forall x \in R_0^+$

$$\psi(x, t_1, t_2, 1)= x\,\psi(1, t_1, t_2, 1), \qquad (3.2)$$

then x is called the present value at time t_1 of the amount $\psi(x, t_1, t_2, 1)$ available at time t_2 and $\psi(1, t_1, t_2, 1)$ is the amount which can be obtained in time t_2 for the investment of one unit in time t_1. In this case, if $P(t_1, t_2)$ is the unitary price at t_1 of a pure discount bond which gives the right to obtain a monetary unit at time t_2, we have

$$P(t_1, t_2)\,\psi(1, t_1, t_2, 1) = 1$$

and then

$$P(t_1, t_2)=1/\,\psi(1, t_1, t_2, 1).$$

Furthermore if the following widely accepted condition is considered

$$\psi(1, t_1, t_3, 1) = \psi(1, t_1, t_2, 1) \; \psi(1, t_2, t_3, 1), \quad (3.3)$$

then we have also

$$1 = \psi(1, t_1, t_1, 1) = \psi(1, t_1, t_2, 1) \; \psi(1, t_2, t_1, 1)$$

and lastly

$$\psi(1, t_2, t_1, 1) = 1/ \psi(1, t_1, t_2, 1) = P(t_1, t_2). \quad (3.4)$$

From (3.3) and (3.4) we can obtain

$$P(t_1, t_3) = P(t_1, t_2) \; P(t_2, t_3) \quad (3.5)$$

which is the no arbitrage condition usually considered for determining the implied forward rates. Effectively the forward rate between t_1 and t_2, $f(t_1, t_2)$, can be computed as

$$f(t_1, t_2) = 1/ P(t_1, t_2) - 1 = \psi(1, t_1, t_2, 1) - 1.$$

(3.5) also states that having fixed $t \in [t_0, +\infty[$ it is possible to compute any price $P(x,y)$ from the prices $P(t,s)$, $x,y,s \in [t_0, +\infty[$. In fact from (3.5) we have

$$P(x,y) = P(t,y)/ P(t,x) \quad (3.7)$$

$\forall t,x,y \in [t_0, +\infty[$.

We observe that the function ψ is quite general to describe some other specific phenomena as explained by the following examples.

a) If condition (3.2) is not satisfied the unitary price of a pure discount bond depends on its face value: in this case we can model some price pressure phenomena. E. g. the investment policy of a large investor can influence the behaviour of the prices and therefore in this case the prices depend on the quantity treated.

b) If condition (3.3) is not satisfied but condition (3.2) holds then we can consider some phenomena of different passive and active interest rates. In fact in this case $\psi(1, t_2, t_1, 1) \neq 1/ \psi(1, t_1, t_2, 1)$. More precisely, considering $t_1 < t_2$, we have:

b1) $\psi(1, t_2, t_1, 1)$ can be interpreted as the amount you can obtain in t_1 against your engagement to pay the amount of one unit at time t_2 and

$$f^-(t_1, t_2) = 1/ \psi(1, t_2, t_1, 1) - 1$$

is the passive forward rate between t_1 and t_2,

b2) $1/ \psi(1, t_1, t_2, 1)$ can be interpreted as the amount you must pay in t_1 in order to obtain an amount of one unit in time t_2 and

$$f^+(t_1, t_2) = \psi(1, t_1, t_2, 1) - 1$$

is the active forward rate between t_1 and t_2.

The problems illustrated by points a) and b) have recently been considered within financial mathematics (e.g. Cvitanic and Ma, 1996, Cvitanic and Karatzas, 1993).

4 The splitting property

In this section we introduce two axioms and obtain an equilibrium condition for the lotteries of the type $B[x,0;t,\gamma]$ and $B[A,0;t,\gamma]$ where A is another lottery.

Let us consider the following lotteries:

a) $B_1 = B[z,0;t_3,\beta]$, i.e. the lottery giving a win z if the event $E(B_1)$, having credibility β is verified, and nothing otherwise,

b) $B_2 = B[B_1,0;t_2,\alpha]$, i.e. the lottery giving as win the lottery B_1 if the event $E(B_2)$, having credibility α is verified, and nothing otherwise,

c) $B_3 = B[z,0;t_1,T(\alpha,\beta)]$, i.e. the lottery giving a win z if the event $E(B_3)$, having credibility $T(\alpha,\beta)$, is verified, and nothing otherwise,

d) $B_4 = B[y,0;t_2,\alpha]$, i.e. the lottery giving a win y if the event $E(B_4)$, having credibility α, is verified, and nothing otherwise,

where $z,y \in R_0^+$, $t_2,t_3 \in [t_0,+\infty[$ and $\alpha,\beta \in]0,1]$.

The two axioms are the following:

1) $p(B_2,t) = p(B_3,t) \ \forall t \in [t_0,+\infty[$;

2) $p(B_2,t) = p(B_4,t) \Leftrightarrow y = p(B_1,t_2), \ \forall t \in [t_0,+\infty[$.

Let us observe that B_2 is a compound lottery, i.e. a lottery where an outcome is another lottery, in the specific case B_1. From the compound lottery B_2 we obtain a win of z at time t_3 if $E(B_1) \cap E(B_2)$ is verified. Since the credibility of $E(B_1) \cap E(B_2)$ is $T(\alpha,\beta)$, then the win of the composition of B_1 and B_2 gives the same win of B_3 , y, at the same time, t_3, and with the same credibility, $T(\alpha,\beta)$. Therefore axiom 1) says that if a compound lottery gives the same win of another lottery at the same time and with the same credibility, then the price of the two lotteries should be equal. Furthermore let us remark that the win of lotteries B_2 and B_4 are delivered at the same time, t_2, and with the same credibility, α. However the win of B_2 is another lottery, B_1, while the win of B_4 is a fixed amount, y. Thus the interpretation of the axioms 2) is that these two lotteries have the same price if and only if the value of the two wins is the same, i.e. the price of B_1 at the delivery time t_2 is equal to y.

THEOREM 4.1. Axioms 1) and 2) hold if and only if there exists a fuzzy financial law ψ such that

$$\psi(\psi(x,t_1,t_2,\alpha),t_2,t_3,\beta) = \psi(x,t_1,t_3,T(\alpha,\beta)) \quad (4.1)$$

$\forall x \in R_0^+$, $\forall t_1,t_2,t_3 \in [t_0,+\infty[$ and $\forall \alpha,\beta \in]0,1]$.

Proof. Let us consider the lotteries B_1, B_2, B_3 and B_4 already introduced. Let us suppose that $\forall t \in [t_0,+\infty[$

$$p(B_2,t) = p(B_4,t), \quad (4.2)$$

and therefore, for axiom 2), we have also that

$$y = p(B_1,t_2). \quad (4.3)$$

For axiom 1), (4.2) implies that

$$p(B_2,t_1) = p(B_3,t_1) = p(B_4,t_1) \quad (4.4)$$

with $t_1 \in [t_0,+\infty[$.

Applying (3.1) to the lotteries B_1 and B_4 we obtain

$$\psi(p(B_1,t_2), t_2, t_3,\beta) = z \quad (4.5)$$
$$\psi(p(B_4,t_1), t_1, t_2,\alpha) = y. \quad (4.6)$$

From (4.3), (4.5) and (4.6) we obtain

$$\psi(p(B_1,t_2), t_2, t_3,\beta) = \psi(y, t_2, t_3,\beta) = \psi(\psi(p(B_4,t_1), t_1, t_2,\alpha), t_2, t_3,\beta) = z. \quad (4.7)$$

Applying (3.1) to B_3 we have

$$\psi(p(B_3,t_1),t_1,t_3,T(\alpha,\beta)) = z$$

from which, on the basis of (4.4) we obtain

$$\psi(p(B_4,t_1), t_1,t_3,T(\alpha,\beta)) = z. \quad (4.8)$$

Thus if we state $p(B_4,t_1) = x$ and compare (4.7) and (4.8) we obtain the thesis. ˆ

Let us point out that (3.3) can be viewed as a particular case of (4.1) when $\alpha=\beta=1$ and condition (3.2) holds. We call condition (3.3) splitting property because whenever satisfied it states that whatever we split an investment into two subsequent investments the final result is the same. Cantelli (1914) was the first to analyze the splitting property (3.3). (4.1) takes into consideration and generalizes in a fuzzy context a formulation of the splitting property introduced by Manca (1969, 1978) and studied also by Lisei (1979, 1980, 1988), Benvenuti and Geronimo (1982) and Mulazzani (1993).

We call splitting property also condition (4.1), because whenever satisfied it allows us to split a specific lottery into the composition of two lotteries of the same type. However the splitting property of fuzzy financial laws may be given a slightly different interpretation from the one attributed to the habitual splitting property (3.2), which is seen as a condition of equilibrium of the whole financial market (Cacciafesta, 1990). With reference to the splitting property of fuzzy financial laws it is necessary in fact to bear in mind that this depends on the specific formulation of the t-norm, i.e. from the way by which the investors evaluate the credibility of intersection of events. The splitting property (4.1) could therefore be interpreted as a general condition of equilibrium on the financial market, if the hypothesis that the same t-norm may be applied to all the investors is accepted. If on the other hand, this hypothesis proves too restrictive, then the splitting property may be interpreted as a condition of subjective equilibrium of each single investor. In fact the individual investor would draw no advantage from splitting his investment.

THEOREM 4.2. If ψ is a fuzzy financial law satisfying the splitting property with respect to the t-norm $T(\alpha,\beta)$ then T is strict.

Proof. Let us suppose that T is not strict, so that $\exists \alpha_1,\alpha_2,\beta \in]0,1]$ such that $\alpha_1<\alpha_2$ but $T(\alpha_1, \beta)=T(\alpha_2, \beta)$.

Because of the splitting property of ψ we obtain

$$\psi(\psi(x,t_1,t_2,\alpha_1),t_2,t_3, \beta)= \psi(x,t_1,t_3 ,T(\alpha_1, \beta))$$

and

$$\psi(\psi(x,t_1,t_2,\alpha_2),t_2,t_3, \beta)= \psi(x,t_1,t_3 ,T(\alpha_2, \beta)).$$

Since $T(\alpha_1, \beta)=T(\alpha_2, \beta)$ we have

$$\psi(x,t_1,t_3,T(\alpha_1,\beta))= \psi(x,t_1,t_3,T(\alpha_2, \beta)). \quad (4.9)$$

Since $\alpha_1<\alpha_2$, because of the property $\psi 6$), we have

$$\psi(x,t_1,t_2,\alpha_1)> \psi(x,t_1,t_2,\alpha_2),$$

so that for $\psi 3$) we should obtain

$$\psi(\psi(x,t_1,t_2,\alpha_1),t_2,t_3,\beta)> \psi(\psi(x,t_1,t_2,\alpha_2),t_2,t_3, \beta)$$

and therefore, for the splitting property,

$$\psi(x,t_1,t_3,T(\alpha_1,\beta))> \psi(x,t_1,t_3,T(\alpha_2, \beta)). \quad (4.10)$$

The contradiction between (4.9) and (4.10) proves the thesis. ˆ

5 A characterization

Let be $h: R_0^1 \times [t_0,+\infty[\times]0,1] \to R_0^+$ a function satisfying the following properties:

h1) $h(0, t, \alpha)=0$, $\forall t \in [t_0,+\infty[$ and $\forall \alpha \in]0,1]$,

h2) $x_1 > x_2 \Rightarrow h(x_1, t, \alpha) > h(x_2, t, \alpha)$, $\forall x_1, x_2 \in R_0^+$, $\forall t \in [t_0,+\infty[$ and $\forall \alpha \in]0,1]$,

h3) $t_1 > t_2 \Rightarrow h(x, t_1, \alpha) \leq h(x, t_2, \alpha)$, $\forall x \in R_0^+$, $\forall t_1, t_2 \in [t_0,+\infty[$ and $\forall \alpha \in]0,1]$,

h4) $\alpha > \beta \Rightarrow h(x, t, \alpha) < h(x, t, \beta)$, $\forall x \in R_0^+$, $\forall t \in [t_0,+\infty[$ and $\forall \beta \in]0,1]$.

For each fuzzy financial law ψ and each $k \in [t_0,+\infty[$, a function $\eta: R_0^+ \times [t_0,+\infty[\times]0,1] \to R_0^+$ can be defined as

$$\eta(x, t, \alpha)= \psi(x, t, k, \alpha).$$

Let us observe that, due to properties $\psi 2)$, $\psi 3)$, $\psi 4)$ and $\psi 6)$ of ψ, η satisfies properties h1), h2), h3) and h4).

THEOREM 5.1. If ψ is a fuzzy financial law satisfying the splitting property then there exists a function $h: R_0^+ \times [t_0,+\infty[\times]0,1] \to R_0^+$ satisfying properties from h1) to h4), such that for every x,y,z and β with $x \geq 0$, y, $z \in [t_0,+\infty[$ and $\beta \in]0, 1]$, $(\psi(x,y,z,\alpha),\alpha)$ is the solution of the equation in the unknown quantities u and ξ

$$h(u,z, \beta)=h[x,y,T(\xi,\beta)].$$

Proof. Let us establish $k \in [t_0,+\infty[$ and suppose $h(v,w,\chi)= \psi(v,w,k,\chi)$ $\forall v \in R_0^+$ and $\forall w \in [t_0,+\infty[$. h therefore satisfies properties from h1) to h4). Moreover we obtain

$$h(\psi(x,y,z,\alpha),z,\beta)= \psi[\psi(x,y,z,\alpha),z,k,\beta]= \psi[x,y,k,T(\alpha,\beta)]=h[x,y,T(\alpha,\beta)]$$

from which, by comparing the first and the last element, we obtain the thesis. ˆ

THEOREM 5.2. If there exists one function $h: R_0^+ \times [t_0,+\infty[\times]0,1] \to R_0^+$ satisfying properties from h1) to h4) and a function $\psi: R_0^+ \times [t_0,+\infty[\times [t_0,+\infty[\times]0,1] \to R_0^+$ such that for every x, y, z and β with $x \geq 0$, $y,z \in [t_0,+\infty[$ and $\beta \in]0,1]$ $((\psi(x,y,z,\alpha), \alpha)$ is the solution of the equation in the unknown quantities u and ξ

$$h[x,y,T(\xi,\beta)]=h(u,z, \beta),$$

then $\psi(x,y,z,\beta)$ is a fuzzy financial law satisfying the splitting property.

Proof. The assumption means that

$$h[x,y,T(\alpha,\beta)]=h[\psi(x,y,z,\alpha),z, \beta]. \quad (5.1)$$

Observe that $x_1 > x_2 \Rightarrow h[x_1,y,T(\alpha,\beta)] > h[x_2,y,T(\alpha,\beta)]$. Since (5.1) must be satisfied, we obtain

$$h[\psi(x_1,y,z,\alpha),z, \beta] > h[\psi(x_2,y,z,\alpha),z, \beta],$$

from which for h2)

$$\psi(x_1,y,z,\alpha) > \psi(x_2,y,z,\alpha).$$

Therefore $x_1 > x_2 \Rightarrow \psi(x_1,y,z,\alpha) > \psi(x_2,y,z,\alpha)$ and in conclusion if ψ satisfies (5.1) then ψ also satisfies $\psi 3)$. Analogously it is possible to prove that if (5.1) is valid then ψ verifies also $\psi 1)$, $\psi 2)$, $\psi 4)$, $\psi 5)$ and $\psi 6)$ and therefore 5.1 implies that ψ is a fuzzy financial law.

Applying the above equality (5.1) three times, we find

$$h[\psi(\psi(x,y,t,\alpha),t,z,\beta),z,\chi]=h[\psi(x,y,t,\alpha),t,T(\beta,\chi)]=$$
$$=h[x,y,T(\alpha,\beta,\chi)]=h\{[\psi(x,y,z,T(\alpha,\beta)],z,\chi\}$$

from which, comparing the first and last members, we obtain

$$\psi(\psi(x,y,t,\alpha),t,z,\beta)=\psi(x,y,z,T(\alpha,\beta))$$

which is the thesis. ˆ

Theorems 5.1 and 5.2 state that a fuzzy financial law satisfies the splitting property if and only if it proves to be entirely determined, through condition (5.1), by a function

$$h(x,t,\alpha)=\psi(x,t,k,\alpha)$$

where $k\in[t_0,+\infty[$. From this viewpoint condition (5.1) can be seen as an extension of condition (3.7).

Some other expressive results can be obtained if a quite usual hypothesis which is a generalization of (3.2) is introduced. Suppose that $\forall x\in R_0^+$, $\forall t_1,t_2\in[t_0,+\infty[$ and $\forall\alpha\in]0,1]$, the following condition holds

$$\psi(x,t_1,t_2,\alpha)=x\,\psi(1,t_1,t_2,\alpha). \quad (5.2)$$

In this case we have that, if $P^*(t_1,t_2,\alpha)=1/\psi(1,t_1,t_2,\alpha)$ is the price at time t_1 of the lottery $B[1,0;t_2,\alpha]$, then $x\,P^*(t_1,t_2,\alpha)$ is the price at time t_1 of the lottery $B[x,0;t_2,\alpha]$.

Furthermore, if the splitting property (4.1) is satisfied, then we obtain

$$\psi(1,t_1,t_3,T(\alpha,\beta))=\psi(1,t_1,t_2,\alpha)\,\psi(1,t_2,t_3,\beta), \quad (5.3)$$
$$P^*(t_1,t_3,T(\alpha,\beta))=P^*(t_1,t_2,\alpha)\,P^*(t_2,t_3,\beta). \quad (5.4)$$

Conditions (5.3) and (5.4) are straightforward generalizations of conditions (3.3) and (3.5) in a fuzzy environment.

THEOREM 5.3. If the fuzzy financial law ψ satisfies conditions (4.1) and (5.2) then there exists one increasing function $\pi:]0,1]\rightarrow]0,1]$, satisfying the property $\pi(1)=1$, such that $\forall x\in R_0^+$, $\forall t_1,t_2\in[t_0,+\infty[$ and $\forall\alpha\in]0,1]$ we have

$$\psi(x,t_1,t_2,\alpha)P(t_1,t_2)\pi(\alpha)=x. \quad (5.5)$$

Proof. Since $\forall\chi\in[0,1]$ we have $T(1,\chi)=\chi$, for condition (4.1) and (5.2), according to (5.3), we can write

$$\psi(x,t_1,t_2,\alpha)=x\,\psi(1,t_1,t_2,1)\,\psi(1,t_2,t_2,\alpha), \quad (5.6)$$
$$\psi(x,t_1,t_2,\alpha)=x\,\psi(1,t_1,t_1,\alpha)\,\psi(1,t_1,t_2,1). \quad (5.7)$$

$\forall x\in R_0^+$, $\forall t_1,t_2\in[t_0,+\infty[$ and $\forall\alpha\in]0,1]$. From the comparison of (5.6) and (5.7) we obtain that $\psi(1,t_1,t_1,\alpha)=\psi(1,t_2,t_2,\alpha)$. Therefore $\psi(1,t,t,\alpha)$ does not depend on $t\in[t_0,+\infty[$ and we can state $\pi(\alpha)=1/\psi(1,t,t,\alpha)$. Furthermore, for property $\psi6)$, $\pi(\alpha)$ is an increasing function of the credibility α and for property $\psi1)$ we have $\pi(1)=1/\psi(1,t,t,1)=1$. Finally, remembering that $P(t_1,t_2)=1/\psi(1,t_1,t_2,1)$, from (5.6) we obtain (5.5). ˆ

Theorem 5.3 admits the following interpretation. Let us consider a financial operation giving a final amount $\psi(x,t_1,t_2,\alpha)$ at time t_2 if an event E, which has a credibility α, is verified, upon the investment of capital x at time t_1. Since $\pi(\alpha)$ is an increasing transformation of the credibility α having value in $]0,1]$, it can be compared to a probability. Therefore the product $\psi(x,t_1,t_2,\alpha)\pi(\alpha)$ can be viewed as the "expected value" of the final amount of the considered investment and $\psi(x,t_1,t_2,\alpha)\pi(\alpha)P(t_1,t_2)$ as the present value of this expected value. Thus, if the conditions of theorem 5.3 are satisfied, then capital x invested in the considered financial operation equals the present value of the expected value of the final amount. In other words, in this case the proposed general model of evaluation of uncertain investments collapses to the classical model, well known e.g. in economics, in finance and in insurance theory.

6 Conclusions

The concept of fuzzy financial law has been introduced. This instrument proves useful in representing some financial phenomena in situations of uncertainty. The concept of splitting property of a fuzzy financial law has also been examined. It has been interpreted as a condition of subjective equilibrium of a single investor. Finally, a characterization has been given to the fuzzy financial laws which satisfy the splitting property.

References

Benvenuti, P., Geronimo, S., "Sulla scindibilità delle leggi finanziarie", *Giornale dell'Istituto Italiano degli Attuari*, 1982, 51-58.

Biacino, L., Simonelli, M. R., "The internal rate of return of fuzzy cash flow", *Rivista di matematica per le scienze economiche e sociali*, 14(2), 1991, 3-13.

Buckley, J. J., "The fuzzy mathematics of finance", *Fuzzy Sets and Systems*, 21, 1987, 257-273.

Buckley, J. J., "Solving fuzzy equations in economics and finance", *Fuzzy Sets and Systems*, 50(1), 1992, 289-296.

Cacciafesta, F., "Una luce nuova su una vecchia storia: la "scindibilità" di Cantelli-Insolera e la struttura a termine dei tassi d'interesse", *Rivista di matematica per le scienze economiche e sociali*, 1 - 2, 1990, 65-72.

Cantelli, F. P., *Genesi e costruzione delle tavole di mortalità*, Bollettino di Notizie sul Credito e sulla Previdenza, Ministero dell'Agricoltura, Industria e Commercio, Roma, 1914.

Cardin, M., Ferretti, P., "Certo equivalente, avversione al rischio e avversione all'incertezza", in *Atti del XVII Convegno A.M.A.S.E.S.*, 1993, 315-332.

Cardin, M., Ferretti, P., "Attitudine verso l'incertezza nei modelli con capacità", in *Atti del XIX Convegno A.M.A.S.E.S.*, 1995, 208-221.

Choquet, G., "Theory of Capacities", *Annales de l'Institut Fourier*, 1953-54, 131-195.

Cvitanic, J., Karatzas, I., "Hedging contingent claims with constrained portfolios", *Annals of Applied Probability*, 3, 1993, 652-681.

Cvitanic, J., Ma, J., "Hedging options for a large investor and Forward-Backward SDE's", *Annals of Applied Probability*, 6, 1996, 370-398.

Dubois, D., "Generalized probabilistic independence and utility functions", *BUSEFAL*, 23, 1985, 83-91.

Dubois, D., Fodor, J. C., Prade, H., Roubens, M., "Aggregation of decomposable measures with application to utility theory", *Theory and Decision*, 41, 1996, 59-95.

Dubois, D., Prade, H., *Fuzzy Sets and Systems. Theory and Applications*, Academic Press, New York, 1980.

Ellsberg, D., "Risk, ambiguity and Savage axioms", *Quarterly Journal of Economics*, 75, 1961, 643-669.

Feller, W., An Introduction to Probability Theory and its Application, vol. 1, Wiley, New York, 1962.

Fodor, J., Roubens, M., Fuzzy preference modelling and multicriteria decision support, Kluwer, Dordrecht, 1994.

Gilboa, I., "Expected utility with purely subjective non-additive probabilities", *Journal of Mathematical Economics*, 16, 1987, 65-88.

Gilboa, I., Schmeidler, D., "Maxmin expected utility with non unique prior", *Journal of Mathematical Economics*, 16, 1987, 141-153.

Giove, S., "Funzioni ed equazioni a coefficienti fuzzy: un'applicazione al tasso interno di rendimento", *Rendiconti del Comitato per gli Studi Economici*, 30-31, 1993, 227-239.

Grabisch, M., Murofushi, T., Sugeno, M., "Fuzzy measure of fuzzy events defined by fuzzy integrals", *Fuzzy Sets and Systems*, 50, 1992, 293-313.

Hersteirn, I.N, Milnor, J., "An axiomatic approach to measurable utility", *Econometrica*, 21, 1953, 291-297.

Keynes, J. M., "The General Theory of Employment", *Quarterly Journal of Economics*, 1937, 209-223.

Knight, F. H., *Risk, Uncertainty and Profit,* London School of Economics, Londra, 1937.

Li Calzi, M., "Towards a general setting for the fuzzy mathematics of finance", *Fuzzy Sets and Systems*, 35, 1990, 265-280.

Lisei, G., "Su un'equazione funzionale collegata alla scindibilità delle leggi finanziarie", *Giornale dell'Istituto Italiano degli Attuari,* 1979, 1-6.

Lisei, G., "Ancora su un'equazione funzionale collegata alla scindibilità delle leggi finanziarie", *Giornale dell'Istituto Italiano degli Attuari*, 1980, 1-5.

Lisei, G., "On the functional equation $\varphi(x,y,z) = \varphi(\varphi(x,y,t)t,z)$", *Rivista di matematica per le scienze economiche e sociali*, 1-2, 1988, 3-9.

Manca, P., "Equazioni funzionali e leggi di interesse finanziario", *Giornale dell'Istituto Italiano degli Attuari*, 1969, 1-5.

Manca, P., "Funzioni di utilità e leggi finanziarie", *Giornale dell'Istituto Italiano degli Attuari*, 1978, 49-57.

Menger, K., "Probabilistic theories of relations", *Proc. Nat. Acad., Sci. (Math.)*, 37, 1951, 178-180.

Mulazzani, M., "Aspetti dinamici di leggi finanziarie scindibili", *Rivista di matematica per le scienze economiche e sociali*, 16(1), 1993, 87-97.

von Neumann, J., Morgenstern, O., *Theory of Games and Economic Behavior*, Princeton Universiry Press, Princeton, NJ, 1944.

Sarin, R., Wakker, P., "A simple axiomatization of nonadditive expected utility", *Econometrica*, 60, 1992, 1255-1272.

Schmeidler, D., "Subjective probability and expected utility without additivity", *Econometrica*, 57, 1989, 571-587.

Schweizer, B., Sklar, A., *Probabilistic Metric Spaces*, North-Holland, Amsterdam, 1983.

Sugeno, M., *Theory of fuzzy integrals and its application*, Doct. Thesis, Tokio Institute of Technology, 1974.

Wakker, P., *Additive representations of preferences*, Kluwer, Dordrecht, 1989.

Weber, S., "A general concept of fuzzy connectives, negations and implications based on t-norms and t-conorms", *Fuzzy Sets and Systems*, 11, 1983, 115-134.

Weber , S., "Conditional measures and their application to fuzzy sets", 2nd IFSA Congress, Tokyo, July 20-25, 1987, 412-415.

Zadeh, L. A., "The concept of a linguistic variable and its application to approximate reasoning", parts 1, 2 and 3, *Information Sciences*, 8, 1975, 199-249; 8, 1975, 301-357; 9, 1975, 43-80.

Zadeh, L. A., "Fuzzy sets as a basis for a theory of possibility", *Fuzzy sets and Systems*, 1, 1978, 3-38.

Sharing Vague Profit in Fuzzy Cooperation[1]

Milan Mareš

Institute of Information Theory and Automation
Academy of Sciences of the Czech Republic
P. O. Box 18, 182 08 Praha 8, Czech Republic
e–mail: mares@utia.cas.cz

Abstract: The economic cooperation is motivated by the endeavour of its participants to increase their individual profits by means of coordinated activities. The coalition game theory offers results showing the general form of possible cooperation and conditions under which it is achievable. In many cases there exists a relatively wide class of achievable cooperation patterns and of the distributions of final profits, and it is desirable to suggest exactly one of them as the best, or most unbiased one. Also this problem was investigated by the coalition game theory and its approach was represented by the concept of the values of coalition games.

The real bargaining usually takes part before the application of the coordinated strategies and the agents have only a vague idea about the expected coalitional profits. It means that also the results of the bargaining including the distribution of the profit can be only vague. Using the theory of fuzzy sets and fuzzy numbers it is possible to study this vagueness and to follow the path from the vague input idea about the expected profits via the bargaining process to the possibilities of vague output distributions of individual pay-offs.

Key words: Coalition game, fuzzy coalition game, coalition, characteristic function of coalition game, core of coalition game, value of coalition game, Shapley value, fuzzy number, fuzzy quantity.

1 Introduction

The coalition game theory offers a useful model of cooperation which can be applied also to the behaviour of economic subjects. Nevertheless, the classical

---

[1]Particular parts of the research the results of which are summarized in this paper were partly supported by the Key Project of the Academy of Sciences of the Czech Republic No. 1, by the Grant Agency of the Academy of Sciences of ČR grant No. A 1075503, by the Grant Agency of the Czech Republic grant No. 402/96/0414, by the EU PHARE Project No. P 95–2014–R, and by the Ministry of Education, Youth and Sports of the Czech Republic project No. VS 96063.

game theoretical description of cooperation is fully deterministic. Its basic data – the coalitional pay-offs – are supposed to be exactly known and the bargaining process dealing with them reflects this determinism. In the contrary, the real bargaining situations, namely in practical economic cooperation, are full of uncertainties. These uncertainties are of several different types.

First, the expected income of any coalition is usually defined as the guaranteed one (maximizing the minima of possible outcomes due to the least favourable behaviour of the anticoalition) and in this sense it seems to be determined. In practical situations the sets of possible strategies are not completely known and, consequently, the guaranteed pay-offs are guaranteed in some degree, only.

Second, the "two-person" game between coalition and anti-coalition need not be fully antagonistic. Then the "min-max" strategies and following "guaranteed" profits need not be realistic. The proper course of the game can be quite different from the antagonistic prevention of the least favourable behaviour of the anti-players, which fact makes the realistic expectations of the coalition incomes even more uncertain.

Third, the results of games and the following utilities need not be the monetary ones. They include also such phenomena like ownership of shares (or machines, land, etc.), or even more abstract utilities like copyrights, know-how or licenses. All of them are usually transformed into the terms of some financial equivalent. But it is necessary to note that this transformation is usually found as a result of subjective evaluations and it is connected with some degree of vagueness. Exactly, also the utility of money is not quite deterministic in several senses. It means that the utilities being the objects of bargaining are vague and the utility functions are fuzzy.

The theory of fuzzy coalition games attempts to reflect this fuzziness of utilities (e. g., in [5, 7]) or other types of vagueness being connected with cooperative behaviour (e. g. [2]). In the following sections we briefly recollect the concepts of the results of bargaining based on the vague expected coalitional incomes, and try to suggest a model of the "true" or "justified" distribution of the common vague profit of a coalition into vague individual pay-offs of players.

The game model considered below generalizes coalition games with side payments (see [1, 11, 12, 13]) whose fuzzification was partly investigated in [7], already. This coalition game model is simpler than the one without side-payments (see [8, 12]) which was considered, e. g. in [5, 10] and which demands rather more complex approach to the vagueness of bargaining.

The present paper is divided into six sections. After the Introduction, the next two sections are devoted to the introductory concepts of the deterministic coalition game with side payments, and of fuzzy quantities. Following two sections deal with the fuzzification of the coalition game model, namely with the concept of the fuzzy coalition game with side payments, its core and related properties, of the values of such games, and of the effectivity (possibility of realization) of particular coalitions and coalition structures. The last section includes brief conclusive remarks.

The results derived in this work are denoted as *lemmas* and *theorems*. Results known from other works are referred as *statements*.

2 Coalition Game With Side Payments

In the deterministic game theory the *coalition game with side payments* is defined as a pair (I, v) where I is a non-empty and finite *set of players*, subsets of I are called *coalitions*, and v, which is called a *characteristic function* of the game, is a mapping, $v : 2^I \to R$, prescribing to every coalition $K \subset I$ a real number $v(K)$. For the formal completeness of the definition we put $v(\emptyset) = 0$ for the empty coalition, and $v(K) \geq 0$ for any $K \subset I$.

In this paper we suppose that the considered game (I, v) is *superadditive*, i.e., for any disjoint K, $L \subset I$, $K \cap L = \emptyset$, the inequality

$$(1) \qquad v(K \cup L) \geq v(K) + v(L)$$

holds. The supearadditivity assumption can be easily fulfilled if the values $v(K)$ are interpreted as the guaranteed "min-max" pay-offs of coalitions in the two-players game coalition-anticoalition.

Each real-valued vector

$$(2) \qquad x = (x_i)_{i \in I} \in R^I$$

is called an *imputation*, and it is *accessible* for a coalition $K \subset I$ iff

$$(3) \qquad \sum_{i \in K} x_i \leq v(K).$$

A set of imputations

$$(4) \qquad C = \left\{ x = (x_i)_{i \in I} : \sum_{i \in I} x_i \leq v(I), \ \forall K \subset I : \sum_{i \in I} x_i \geq v(K) \right\}$$

is called *core* of the game (I, v). The core, if it is non-empty, represents the set of possible distributions of the total profit achievable by the coalition of all players I and in this sense it is the set of natural solutions of bargaining in the considered game. It is accessible for the coalition of all players and none of coalitions can offer to its members uniformly more than what they obtain accepting some imputation from the core.

The game theory offers conditions under which the core is non-empty.

Statement 1 (cf. [12]). Let for any pair of coalitions K, $L \subset I$ the following inequality holds
$$(5) \qquad v(K \cup L) + v(K \cap L) \geq v(K) + v(L).$$

Then the core of the game is non-empty.

The game fulfilling (5) is called *convex*.

Let $K_1, \ldots, K_n \subset I$ be a set of coalitions. We say that it is *balanced* iff there exist real numbers $\alpha_1, \ldots, \alpha_n > 0$ such that for any $i \in I$

$$(6) \quad \beta_1 + \cdots + \beta_n = 1, \quad \text{where} \quad \beta_j = \alpha_j \quad \text{if} \quad i \in K_j, \ \beta_j = 0 \quad \text{if} \quad i \notin K_j.$$

We say that (I, v) is a *balanced game* if for any balanced set of coalitions $\{K_1, \ldots, K_n\}$

(7)
$$\sum_{j=1}^{n} \alpha_j \cdot v(K_j) \le v(I).$$

Statement 2 (Bondareva) (cf. [1, 12]). The core of a coalition game (I, v) is non-empty if and only if the game is balanced.

The core of a coalition game may be empty and then it is difficult to model the possible bargaining results. On the other hand, the core can be a more element class of imputations – exactly, it is a closed convex polyhedron in the hyperplane

(8)
$$\sum_{i \in I} x_i = v(I)$$

in R^I. In such case it is possible to suggest a choice of exactly one imputation in the core which in the "best" or "most justified" way reflects the individual contributions of players to the total income of the coalition I. Such imputation is called the *value* of the considered game.

There exists a special branch of the coalition game theory dealing with the value concept and its axiomatization. For the relatively simple case of the coalition games with side payments the widely accepted value concept is the *Shapley value* which for every player $i \in I$ defines the element x_i^* of the values x^* by the formula

(9)
$$x_i^* = \sum_{K \subset I} c(K) \cdot (v(K) - v(K - \{i\})),$$

where, denoting by k the number of players in K,

(10)
$$c(K) = (k - 1)! \, (n - k)!/n!.$$

There are more possibilities how to define the value of a coalition game, and (9) is the most popular one. It is, generally a functional joining the characteristic function v with a real-valued vector $(x_i^*)_{i \in I} \in R^I$. Shapley has formulated (cf. [13]) general conditions which should be fulfilled by any actual vector of values:

- The values x_i^* are independent of the ordering of indices of the vector $(x_i^*)_{i \in I}$.
- The values are achievable by the coalition of all players,

$$\sum_{i \in I} x_i^* = v(I).$$

- If (I, v_1) and (I, v_2) are coalition games with vectors of values $(x_i^*)_{i \in I}$, $(y_i^*)_{i \in I}$, respectively, then the values of the game $(I, v_1 + v_2)$ are $(x_i^* + y_i^*)_{i \in I}$.

When considering the applications of the theory to economic problems it is useful to mention two brief comments regarding the Shapley value. First, even if the formal definition (9) aloves the computation of the Shapley value in any coalition game, only for the games with non-empty core containing the Shapley value this value has real sense and fulfils the second condition. In any other case it can be eliminated by more profitable offer of some subcoalition, unless very high level of discipline among players is assumed. Such situations farely exceed the limits of the mathematical game theory. Second, meanwhile the concept of core is fully intensional, based only on the properties of the considered game model and on the natural preferences of players and coalitions, the concept of value is extensional – some new concept is to be included into the original game model. Namely, the concept of "justice" or "proportionality between pay-offs and contributions of players". This extensionality can be interpreted also in such way that the "justice" is less natural component of the bargaining process than "profit" or rationality. Each cooperation leading to some imputation from the core is for all participants evidently better than "non-cooperation" meanwhile the condition of "justice" is something "above" the elementary rationality, added to the game model by some "judge" being out of the game and needing some kind of additional acceptance by players.

3   Fuzzy Quantities

Let us briefly recollect some properties of fuzzy quantities (cf. [3, 4, 9], e. g.), the main fuzzy set theoretical tool used below to the modelling of vagueness in the bargaining process. Each *fuzzy quantity* a is a fuzzy subset of R with membership function $\mu_a : R \to [0, 1]$ such that

(11) $\exists\, x_a \in R : \mu_a(x_a) = 1,$

(12) $\exists\, x_1, x_2 \in R,\ x_1 < x_2,\ \forall\, x \notin [x_1, x_2] : \mu_a(x) = 0.$

The set of all fuzzy quantities is denoted by $I\!\!R$, and we also denote by $I\!\!R^+$ the subset of $I\!\!R$ defined by

(13) $I\!\!R^+ = \{a \in I\!\!R : \forall\, x < 0,\ \mu_a(x) = 0\}.$

Fuzzy quantity degenerated into one value $y \in R$ is denoted by $\langle y \rangle \in I\!\!R$, where

(14) $\mu_{\langle y \rangle}(y) = 1, \quad \mu_{\langle y \rangle}(x) = 0 \quad \text{for } x \neq y,$

and it is called a *crisp quantity*. The real number x_a in (11) is called the *modal value* of the fuzzy quantity a. The definitions of elementary arithmetic operations over $I\!\!R$ are usually based on a more general *extension principle* (cf. [3, 4], e. g.) due to which the *sum* of fuzzy quantities $a \oplus b \in I\!\!R$, where $a,\ b \in I\!\!R$, has membership function

(15) $\mu_{a \oplus b}(x) = \sup_{y \in R}(\min(\mu_a(y), \mu_b(x - y))), \quad x \in R,$

and their *product* $a \odot b \in I\!\!R$ has

(16) $\mu_{a \odot b}(x) \;=\; \sup_{y \in R,\, y \neq 0} (\min(\mu_a(y), \mu_b(x/y))), \quad x \in R,\ x \neq 0,$

$\qquad\qquad\quad =\; \max(\mu_a(0), \mu_b(0)) \quad \text{for } x = 0.$

It is easy to define, for $y \in R$, $a \in I\!\!R$, $y + a = \langle y \rangle \oplus a$ and $y \cdot a = \langle y \rangle \odot a$, i.e.

$$(17) \qquad \begin{aligned} \mu_{y+a}(x) &= \mu_a(x - y), \quad x \in R, \\ \mu_{y \cdot a}(x) &= \mu_a(x/y) \quad \text{for } y \neq 0, \\ &= \mu_{\langle 0 \rangle}(x) \quad \text{for } y = 0. \end{aligned}$$

The essential operations for the fuzzification of some game theoretical concepts are the fuzzy addition $a \oplus b$ and multiplication by a crisp number $y \cdot a = \langle y \rangle \odot a$, where $a, b \in I\!\!R$, $y \in R$. It is known, e.g., from [4, 6] or [9], that the algebraic properties of those operations are rather poor. Obviously,

$$a \oplus b = b \oplus a, \quad (a \oplus b) \oplus c = a \oplus (b \oplus c), a \oplus \langle 0 \rangle = a,$$
$$(18) \qquad y \cdot (a \oplus b) = (y \cdot a) \oplus (y \cdot b),$$

for $a, b \in I\!\!R$, $y \in R$, but the remaining group property (the existence of opposite element) and the complementary distributivity are not generally fulfilled. That type of distributivity (cf. [9], for example) is not the crucial one for the topic of this paper. The natural concept of opposite fuzzy quantity to $a \in I\!\!R$ is $-a \in I\!\!R$, where for all $x \in R$

$$(19) \qquad \mu_{-a}(x) = \mu_a(-x).$$

Then $a \oplus (-a)$ is not equal to $\langle 0 \rangle$. As show, e.g., in [4, 9] or [6], it is crucial to understand the meaning of "fuzzy zero". Due to the works referred above, it can be any fuzzy quantity with possibilities symmetrically distributed around the crisp 0. This implies also rather modified concept of "equality" or "similarity" of fuzzy quantities which are considered to be "additively equivalent" if they differ in fuzzy zeros.

In formulas, fuzzy quantity $s \in I\!\!R$ is called 0-*symmetric* iff

$$(20) \qquad \mu_s(x) = \mu_s(-x) \quad \text{for all } x \in R,$$

and two fuzzy quantities $a, b \in I\!\!R$ are *additively equivalent*, denoted by $a \sim_\oplus b$, iff there exist 0-symmetric fuzzy quantities s_1, s_2 such that

$$(21) \qquad a \oplus s_1 = b \oplus s_2.$$

Then it can be easily seen that for any $a \in I\!\!R$

$$(22) \qquad a \oplus (-a) \sim_\oplus \langle 0 \rangle \quad \text{and} \quad a \oplus (-a) \text{ is 0-symmetric.}$$

The concepts of 0-symmetry and additive equivalence guarantee the classical properties of the addition $\oplus$ at least in this weakened form. More precisely, the following statements are valid (see [4] and [9]).

Statement 3. The set $I\!\!R$ forms a commutative group with the addition operation $\oplus$, opposite elements defined by (19) and the zero-element is identified with the equivalence class of elements fulfilling (20) if the additive equivalence (21) is used instead of the equality.

Statement 4. Operations of addition $\oplus$ and multiplication by crisp number are distributive in the sense of (18) in the weaker form as 0-equivalence if $a \in \mathbb{R}$ is trapezoidal, i.e.,

$$
\begin{aligned}
\mu_a(x) &= (x - \alpha_1)/(\alpha_0 - \alpha_1) && \text{for } x \in [\alpha_1, \alpha_0], \\
&= 1 && \text{for } x \in [\alpha_0, \alpha_0'], \\
&= (x - \alpha_0')/(\alpha_2 - \alpha_0') && \text{for } x \in [\alpha_0', \alpha_2],
\end{aligned}
$$

where $\alpha_1 < \alpha_0 \le \alpha_0' < \alpha_2$, $\alpha_1, \alpha_0, \alpha_0', \alpha_2 \in R$. Then also for $y, z \in R$

(23) $$(y + z) \cdot a \sim_\oplus (y \cdot a) \oplus (z \cdot a)$$

and turns into strict equality if $y \cdot z \ge 0$.

The fuzzy quantities can be also "ordered" in some sense. There exist various definitions of the ordering-like relations over $\mathbb{R}$ (cf. [3, 9]) among which the following one seems to be adequate to the purpose of this contribution. Even here the general paradigm of the extension principle is respected. If $a, b \in \mathbb{R}$ then the validity of the preference relation $a \succeq b$ is also vague, and it is true with some possibility being dependent on the possibilities of actual values of a and b. It means that the *preference* $\succeq$ *is a fuzzy relation* with membership function $\nu_\succeq : \mathbb{R} \times \mathbb{R} \to [0, 1]$ where for any ordered pair $(a, b) \in \mathbb{R} \times \mathbb{R}$ the real value $\nu_\succeq(a, b)$ denotes the possibility of $a \succeq b$, and

(24) $$\nu_\succeq(a, b) = \sup_{x, y \in R} (\min(\mu_a(x), \mu_b(y))).$$

Analogously, it is possible to define *strict preference relation* $\succ$ and *similarly relation* $\sim$ as fuzzy relations with membership functions

(25) $$\nu_\succ(a, b) = \sup_{x, y \in R,\, x > y} (\min(\mu_a(x), \mu_b(y))),$$

(26) $$\nu_\sim(a, b) = \sup_{x \in R} (\min(\mu_a(x), \mu_b(x))),$$

for $a, b \in \mathbb{R}$.

Remark 1. It can be easily seen that for $x, y \in R$, $a, b \in \mathbb{R}$,

(27) $$\nu_\succeq(\langle x \rangle, b) = \sup_{y \in R,\, y \le x} (\mu_b(y)), \quad \nu_\succeq(a, \langle y \rangle) = \sup_{x \in R,\, x \ge y} (\mu_a(x)),$$

and analogously

$$\nu_\succ(\langle x \rangle, b) = \sup_{y \in R,\, y < x}(\mu_b(y)), \quad \nu_\succ(a, \langle y \rangle) = \sup_{x \in R,\, x > y}(\mu_a(x)),$$
$$\nu_\sim(\langle x \rangle, b) = \mu_b(x), \quad \nu_\sim(a, \langle y \rangle) = \mu_a(y).$$

Remark 2. Even if there is none conceptual relation between the similarity $\sim$ and 0-equivalence $\sim_\oplus$, the implication $a \sim_\oplus b \Rightarrow a \sim b$ follows from (26), (21) and from the fact that due to (15) addition $a \oplus s$ does not change the modal value of a.

Lemma 1. Let $a, b, c \in \mathbb{R}$, and let there exist $x_a, x_b, x_c \in R$ such that $\mu_a(x) = 1$ or $\mu_b(x) = 1$ or $\mu_c(x) = 1$ if and only if $x = x_a$ or $x = x_b$ or $x = x_c$, respectively. Then $\nu_\succeq(a, b) = 1$ iff $\nu_\succeq(a \oplus c, b \oplus c) = 1$, $\nu_\sim(a, b) = 1$ iff $\nu_\sim(a \oplus c, b \oplus c) = 1$ and $\nu_\succ(a, b) = 1$ iff $\nu_\succ(a \oplus c, b \oplus c) = 1$.

Proof. Due to (15)

$$\mu_{a \oplus c}(x) = 1 \quad \text{iff} \quad x = x_a + x_c, \qquad \mu_{b \oplus c}(x) = 1 \quad \text{iff} \quad x = x_b + x_c.$$

The desired implications follow from definitions $(24), (25), (26)$, immediately.

Fuzzy relations $\succeq, \succ, \sim$ respect many (but not all) properties known for the analogous inequality, strict inequality and equality relations between real numbers. The main inconsistency is connected with the lack of transitivity (cf. [9]). The bargaining models, luckily, do not demand the processing of transitive chains of preferences, and the isolated application of the preferences (and similarity) does not contradict the naturally separate steps of the bargaining procedure.

4 Fuzzy Coalition Game With Side Payments

Let (I, v) be a (deterministic) coalition game and let $w : 2^I \to \mathbb{R}^+$ be a mapping connecting every coalition $K \subset I$ with a fuzzy quantity $w(K) \in \mathbb{R}^+$ with membership function $\lambda_K : R \to [0, 1]$ where $v(K)$ is the modal value of $w(K)$. Then the pair (I, w) is called a *fuzzy coalition game* and we also say that (I, w) is a *fuzzy extension* of (I, v). To complete the formal properties, we put $w(\emptyset) = \langle 0 \rangle$ for the empty coalition.

4.1 Fuzzy Superadditivity

As the expected incomes of coalitions are fuzzy numbers, many properties derived from them become fuzzy, as well. This is true also for the superadditivity, where the fuzzy coalition game is said to be *superadditive* iff for any pair of disjoint coalitions

$$w(K \cup L) \succeq w(K) \oplus w(L)$$

which relation is fulfilled with the possibility

$$\nu_\succeq(w(K \cup L), (w(K) \oplus w(L))),$$

and the possibility that the game (I, w) is superadditive is equal to

$$(28) \qquad \sigma = \min\left(\nu_\succeq(w(K \cup L), (w(K) \oplus w(L))) : K, L \subset I, K \cap L = \emptyset\right).$$

Lemma 2. If (I, w) is a fuzzy extension of (I, v) and (I, v) is superadditive then the (I, w) is certainly superadditive, $\sigma = 1$.

Proof. The statement follows from (24) and from the fact that $v(K) + v(L)$ is the modal value of $w(K) \oplus w(L)$, immediately.

Theorem 1. If (I, w) is a fuzzy extension of (I, v) and for every coalition $K \subset I$, $\lambda_K(x) \neq 1$ for $x \neq v(K)$ then (I, w) is certainly superadditive ($\sigma = 1$) if and only if (I, v) is superadditive.

Proof. The statement follows from Lemma 1, formula (28) and (24), and from the definition of deterministic superadditivity, immediately.

4.2 Fuzzy Core

Also the core of fuzzy coalition game becomes a fuzzy set and being accessible for a coalition becomes a fuzzy property for any imputation. The fact that the core may be (and really is) a fuzzy set brings a new dimension into the considerations about the outcomes of the bargaining process. In the deterministic case, the class of coalition games is divided into two strictly separated groups. Into the games of non-empty core where a stabile agreement of all players is possible, and the others where any global agreement can be successfully endangered by some coalitions. In the first case the bargaining process aims to a generally acceptable imputation, in the second one it is more dynamic process without a circumspectable terminal state and any discussion about the justice of the final distribution of profiles is very limited.

On the other hand, the fuzzy core means that the class of games with non-empty core is also a fuzzy subset of the class of coalition games. Moreover, in some of them, the core (stabile agreement) is certainly achievable, in others it is connected with some degree of possibility, and in a (perhaps rare) group of games the possibility of such agreement is fully excluded. Also the core itself is a fuzzy subset of R^I. This degree of possibility that an imputation may belong to the core of the game evidently influences the consequent considerations about such qualities like "fainess" or "proportionality" to the contribution of the player's activities to the coalitional profit.

The *fuzzy core* of (I, w) is defined as a fuzzy subset C of R^I with the membership function $\mu_C : R^I \to [0, 1]$, where for any $x = (x_i)_{i \in I} \in R^I$

$$(29)\, \mu_C(x) = \min\left[\nu_{\succeq}\left(w(I), \left\langle \sum\nolimits_{i \in I} x_i \right\rangle\right), \min_{K \subset I}\left(\nu_{\succeq}\left(\left\langle \sum\nolimits_{i \in K} x_i \right\rangle, w(K)\right)\right)\right].$$

Remark 3. Definition (29) obviously implies

$$(30)\, \mu_C(x) = \min\left[\nu_{\sim}\left(w(I), \left\langle \sum\nolimits_{i \in I} x_i \right\rangle\right), \min_{K \subset I}\left(\nu_{\succeq}\left(\left\langle \sum\nolimits_{i \in K} x_i \right\rangle, w(K)\right)\right)\right]$$

and

$$\mu_C(\boldsymbol{x}) \quad = \quad \min\left[\sup\left\{\lambda_I(y) : y \in R,\ y \geq \sum_{i \in I} x_i\right\},\right.$$

$$(31) \qquad \left.\min\left(\sup\left\{\lambda_K(z) : z \in R,\ z \leq \sum_{i \in K} x_i\right\}\right)\right],$$

as follows from (29) and (27) in Remark 1.

It is not difficult to verify natural relations between the deterministic core of a coalition game and the fuzzy core of its fuzzy extension.

Lemma 3. If (I, w) is a fuzzy extension of a game (I, v), and if $C \neq \emptyset$ is the core of (I, v), then for any $\boldsymbol{x} \in C$ $\mu_C(\boldsymbol{x}) = 1$.

Proof. The statement follows from (29) immediately as

$$\sum_{i \in I} x_i \leq v(I) \quad \Longrightarrow \quad \nu_{\succeq}\left(w(I), \left\langle \sum_{i \in I} x_i\right\rangle\right) = 1$$

$$\sum_{i \in K} x_i \geq v(K) \quad \Longrightarrow \quad \nu_{\succeq}\left(\left\langle \sum_{i \in K} x_i\right\rangle, w(K)\right) = 1.$$

Theorem 2. Let (I, w) be a fuzzy extension of a coalition game (I, v). Let for all $K \subset I$ $\lambda_K(\boldsymbol{x}) < 1$ iff $\boldsymbol{x} \neq v(K)$. Then there exists $\boldsymbol{x} \in R^I$ such that $\mu_C(\boldsymbol{x}) = 1$ if and only if the deterministic core C of (I, v) is non-empty. In such case

$$\{\boldsymbol{x} \in R^I : \mu_C(\boldsymbol{x}) = 1\} = C.$$

Proof. One implication follows from Lemma 2. Proving the latter one, we consider $\boldsymbol{x} \in R^I - C$. Then either

$$\sum_{i \in I} x_i > v(I)$$

and, due to the assumption, $\lambda_I(\boldsymbol{y}) < 1$ for all $\boldsymbol{y} \in R^I$ such that

$$\sum_{i \in I} y_i > v(I).$$

It means that

$$\nu_{\succeq}\left(w(I), \left\langle \sum_{i \in I} x_i\right\rangle\right) < 1.$$

Or, for some $K \subset I$,

$$\sum_{i \in K} x_i < v(K)$$

and then, analogously,

$$\nu_{\succeq} \left(\left\langle \sum_{i \in K} x_i \right\rangle, w(K) \right) < 1.$$

In both cases, $\mu_C(x) < 1$.

It is worth mentioning that for more general fuzzy coalition games, where the fuzzy sets of possible payments are described by generalized membership functions λ_K, the relation between fuzzy and deterministic core becomes more structured as shown, e.g. in [10].

4.3 Fuzzy Convexity

Conditions for the existence of non-empty core in deterministic coalition games (see Statement 1 and 2 in Section 2) can be transformed into their fuzzy analogies. First, the concept of convexity (5) of a fuzzy coalition game is to be formulated. Analogously to the superadditivity also the convexity of fuzzy coalition game is a fuzzy property and the membership function determining the possibility that a game belongs to the fuzzy subclass of convex games can be defined by the following procedure.

The possibility that (I, w) is convex is the possibility that (5) in Statement 1 is fulfilled. For $K, L \subset I$ is equal to

$$(32) \qquad \nu_{\succeq}((w(K \cup L) \oplus w(K \cap L)), (w(K) \oplus w(L))).$$

Remark 4. If $K, L \subset I$ then the possibility (32) is equal to

$$\sup_{x,y \in R,\, x \geq y} \left[\min \left(\sup_{z_1 \in R} [\min(\lambda_{K \cup L}(z_1), \lambda_{K \cap L}(x - z_1))], \right. \right.$$
$$\left. \left. \sup_{z_2 \in R} [\min(\lambda_K(z_2), \lambda_L(y - z_2))] \right) \right]$$

as follows from (32), (24) and (15).

In the deterministic case (5) is equivalent to $v(K \cup L) \geq v(K) + v(L) - v(K \cap L)$. The fuzzy case is not as clear as the deterministic one. Nevertheless, the following statements can be proven.

Lemma 4. Let (I, w) be a fuzzy extension of (I, v), let $K, L \subset I$, and let $\lambda_K(x) = 1$, $\lambda_L(y) = 1$ if and only if $x = v(K)$ or $y = v(L)$, respectively. Then the possibility (32) is equal to 1 if and only if

$$(33) \qquad \nu_{\succeq}(w(K \cup L), [w(K) \oplus w(L) \oplus (\langle -1 \rangle \odot w(K \cap L))]) = 1.$$

Proof. Due to Remark 3, (32) is equal to 1 iff $v(K \cup L) + v(K \cap L) \geq v(K) + v(L)$ under the assumptions of this lemma. It is equivalent to $v(K \cup L) \geq v(K) + v(L) - v(K \cap L)$ and this is, due to (24) and (27), equivalent to the equality of (33) to 1.

Lemma 4. Let (I, w) be fuzzy extension of (I, v), let K, $L \subset I$, let there exist x_K, x_L, $x_{K \cup L}$, $x_{K \cap L} \in R$ such that $\lambda_K(x) = 1$ or $\lambda_L(x) = 1$ or $\lambda_{K \cup L}(x) = 1$ or $\lambda_{K \cap L}(x) = 1$ iff $x = x_K$ or $x - x_L$ or $x - x_{K \cup L}$ or $x = x_{K \cap L}$, respectively. Then the possibility (32) is equal to 1 if and only if there exists a fuzzy number $\overline{w}(K \cup L) \in \mathbb{R}$ and 0-symmetric fuzzy quantity $s \in \mathbb{R}$ such that $\overline{w}(K \cup L) = w(K \cup L) \oplus s$ (i. e., $\overline{w}(K \cup L) \sim_\oplus w(K \cup L)$) and such that $\overline{w}(K \cup L)$ fulfills (33).

Proof. Possibility (32) is the possibility that fuzzy relation

$$w(K \cup L) \oplus w(K \cap L) \succeq w(K) \oplus w(L)$$

holds. Due to Lemma 1,

$$w(K \cup L) \oplus w(K \cap L) \oplus (-w(K \cap L)) \succeq w(K) \oplus w(L) \oplus (-w(K \cap L)),$$

Putting $s = w(K \cap L) \oplus (-w(K \cap L))$ we get $\overline{w}(K \cup L) = w(K \cup L) \oplus s$ and the statement holds.

The *possibility that the considered fuzzy coalition game* (I, w) *is convex is* equal to

$$(34) \qquad \gamma = \min_{K, L \subset I} [\nu_\succeq((w(K \cup L) \oplus w(K \cap L)), (w(K) \oplus w(L)))].$$

Under the condition of unimodality of all membership functions, the following conditions holds.

Theorem 3. Let (I, w) be fuzzy extension of a coalition game (I, v). Let, for any $K \subset I$, $\lambda_K(x) = 1$ iff $x = v(K)$. Then $\gamma = 1$ if and only if

$$\min_{K, L \cup I} (\nu_\succeq(w(K \cup L), [w(K) \oplus w(L) \oplus (-w(K \cap L))])).$$

Proof. The theorem follows from Lemma 3 and from (34), immediately.

Theorem 4. Let (I, w) be fuzzy extension of (I, v), let, for any $K \subset I$, $\lambda_K(x) = 1$ iff $x = v(K)$. The game (I, w) is convex with possibility $\gamma = 1$ if and only if there exists a fuzzy coalition game $(I, \overline{w})$ and 0-symmetric fuzzy numbers $s_K \in \mathbb{R}$, $K \subset I$, such that for any $K \subset I$,

$$\overline{w}(K) = w(K) + s_K$$

and for any K, $L \subset I$

$$\nu_\succeq (\overline{w}(K \cup L), [\overline{w}(K) \oplus \overline{w}(L) \oplus (-\overline{w}(K \cap L))]) = 1.$$

Proof. The theorem follows from Lemma 4, where for any $K \subset I$ $s_K = w(K) \oplus (-w(K))$ and any K, $L \subset I$, $\overline{w}(K \cup L) = w(K \cup L) \oplus s_{K \cap L}$.

The fuzzy convexity is an extension of the deterministic one as shown by the following statement.

Lemma 5. Let (I, w) be a fuzzy extension of a convex game (I, v). Then the possibility of (I, w) being convex is

$$\gamma = 1.$$

Proof. The statement of the lemma follows from definition (32). Let K, $L \subset I$. Then the convexity of (I, v) means that

$$v(K \cup L) + v(K \cap L) \geq v(K) + v(L).$$

It means that possibility (32) for K, L, is equal to 1. As this is true for any K, $L \subset I$, definition (34) implies that (I, w) is certainly fuzzy convex.

The fuzzification of the convexity concept allows to extend Statement 1 for the fuzzy coalition games.

Theorem 5. Let (I, w) be fuzzy coalition game, $\mathcal{C}$ be its fuzzy core with membership function $\mu_{\mathcal{C}}$ and γ be possibility (34) of the convexity of (I, w). Then

$$\sup(\mu_{\mathcal{C}}(\boldsymbol{x}) : \boldsymbol{x} \in R^I) \geq \gamma.$$

Proof. Number γ denotes the possibility that (I, w) is fuzzy convex. It means, due to Statement 1, that there exists $\boldsymbol{x} \in R^I$ belonging to the (fuzzy) core with at least the same possibility, which proves the statement of the theorem.

4.4 Fuzzy Balancedness

The necessary and sufficient condition for the existence of deterministic core in deterministic coalition game (see Statement 2) can be in certain degree extended to fuzzy games. The concept of balanced set of coalitions (6) need not be modified.

Let us consider a fuzzy extension (I, w) of a coalition game (I, v). Let $\{K_1, \ldots, K_n\} \subset 2^I$ be a balanced set of coalitions with vector of coefficients $\boldsymbol{\alpha} = (\alpha_1, \ldots, \alpha_n) \in R^n$. Let us calculate the fuzzy quantity

$$(35) \qquad w(K_1, \ldots, K_n, \boldsymbol{\alpha}) = \alpha_1 \cdot w(K_1) \oplus \cdots \oplus \alpha_n \cdot w(K_n) \in \mathbb{R}^+$$

with membership function $\mu_{K, \boldsymbol{\alpha}} : R \to [0, 1]$, the *fuzzy balancedness* of the fuzzy coalition game (I, w) is a vague, i.e. fuzzy, property with possibility defined, for (I, w), by

$$(36)\, \beta(I, w) = \min \nu_{\succeq}[w(I), w(K_1, \ldots, K_n, \boldsymbol{\alpha})) : n\text{-natural}, K_1, \ldots, K_n \subset I,$$
$$\boldsymbol{\alpha} = (\alpha_1, \ldots, \alpha_n) \in R^n, K_1, \ldots, K_n, \boldsymbol{\alpha} \text{ fulfil } (6)],$$

where (24) and evident analogy to (7) were exerted. The following statements are analoguous to several ones formulated in previous paragraphs.

Lemma 6. Let (I, w) be a fuzzy extension of a balanced coalition game (I, v). Then it is certainly fuzzy balanced, i. e.

$$\beta(I, w) = 1.$$

Proof. If (I, v) is balanced then for any balanced set of coalitions $K_1, \ldots, K_n$ with the vector of coefficients $\boldsymbol{\alpha} = (\alpha_1, \ldots, \alpha_n)$ there exist numbers $x, y \in R$ such that

$$\mu_I(x) = 1, \quad \mu_{K, \boldsymbol{\alpha}}(y) = 1, \quad x \geq y.$$

Consequently,

$$\nu_{\succeq}(w(I), w(K_1, \ldots, K_n, \alpha)) = 1$$

for any balanced set of coalitions. It means that $\beta(I, w) = 1$.

Theorem 6. Let (I, w) be fuzzy coalition game. Then it is certainly balanced if and only if its core is certainly non-empty; in symbols

$$\beta(I, w) = 1 \iff \sup(\mu_C(\boldsymbol{x}) : \boldsymbol{x} \in R^I) = 1.$$

Proof. Let us denote by (I, v) the deterministic coalition game whose extension (I, w) is, it means that for any $K \subset I$

$$\mu_K(v(K)) = 1.$$

Due to Lemma 6, $\beta(I, w) = 1$ if and only if (I, v) is balanced. This is true if and only if its core C is non-empty and this is true if and only if $\sup(\mu_C(\boldsymbol{x}) : \boldsymbol{x} \in R^I) = 1$, as follows from Lemma 2.

5 Fuzzy Values

The vagueness connected with the possible (or expected) utility distributed among the players leads to the vagueness of the concept of the *value*, in the deterministic form mentioned in Section 2. It can be fuzzified in several ways. Regarding the Shapley value, which is the most significant one in the case of the side payments games, we briefly present the following method. It exceeds the calculation method (9), (10) and uses operations (15) and (17).

If (I, w) is a fuzzy coalition game then its *fuzzy Shapley value* is a vector $s = (s_i)_{i \in I}$ of fuzzy quantities $s_i \in R$ with membership functions $\xi_i : R \to [0, 1]$ defined for any particular $i \in I$ as follows.

First we denote the set of all coalitions

(37) $$\{K_1, K_2, \ldots, K_m\} = 2^I$$

and the set of coalitions K such that $i \in K$

(38) $$\mathcal{K}_i = \{K_{i1}, K_{i2}, \ldots, K_{ir}\}.$$

Then we denote, for any $K \subset I$,

$$(39) \qquad d(K) = c(K) \cdot [w(K) \oplus (\langle -1 \rangle \odot w(K - \{i\}))] \in \mathbb{R}$$

where $c(K)$ is defined by (10), and calculate

$$(40) \qquad s_i = d(K_1) \oplus \cdots \oplus d(K_m).$$

Remark 5. If (I, w) is a fuzzy extension of (I, v) and $\boldsymbol{x}^* = (x_i^*)$ is the Shapley value of (I, v) then for any $i \in I$, $\xi_i(x_i^*) = 1$, as follows from (9) and (40).

Lemma 7. Let (I, w) be fuzzy coalition game, let us denote for any $i \in I$ and any $K \in \mathcal{K}_i$ the fuzzy quantity $d_i^*(K) \in \mathbb{R}$, where

$$d_i^*(\{i\}) = w(\{i\}),$$
$$d_i^*(K) = c(K) \cdot [w(K) \oplus (\langle -1 \rangle \oplus (K - \{i\}))], \text{ for } K - \{i\} \neq \emptyset,$$

and $c(K)$ is defined by (10). If we denote by $\boldsymbol{s}^* = (s_i^*)_{i \in I}$ the vector of fuzzy quantities $s_i^* \in \mathbb{R}$ with membership functions $\xi_i^* : R \to [0, 1]$ such that

$$(41) \qquad s_i^* = d^*(K_{i1}) \oplus \cdots \oplus d^*(K_{ir}),$$

then for any $i \in I$ $s_i^* = s_i + o$, where $o \in \mathbb{R}$ is 0-symmetric (see (20)).

Proof. Due to (39) and assumptions of this lemma,

$$d_i(\{i\}) = w(\{i\}) - w(\emptyset) = w(\{i\}) = d_i^*(\{i\})$$

and for $K \in \mathcal{K}_i$, $K \neq \{\{i\}\}$

$$d_i(K) = d_i^*(K) \quad \text{for } K \in \mathcal{K}_i, \ K \neq \{i\},$$
$$d_i(K) = c(K) \cdot [w(K) \oplus (\langle -1 \rangle \oplus w(K))] = c(K) \cdot o_1 = o_2 \quad \text{for } K \in 2^I - \mathcal{K}_i,$$

as o_1, o_2 are 0-symmetric (see (20) and [4]). It means that, substituting each $d_i(K)$ in (40) either by $d_i^*(K)$ (if $K \in \mathcal{K}_i$) or by some 0-symmetric fuzzy quantity (if $i \notin K$), we get $s_i = s_i^* \oplus o$ with o being 0-symmetric, as it is sum of 0-symmetric fuzzy quantities.

Theorem 7. Let (I, w) be fuzzy extension of (I, v), let $\boldsymbol{x}^* = (x_i^*)_{i \in I}$ be Shapley value of (I, v) and let $\boldsymbol{s} = (s_i)_{i \in I}$ and $\boldsymbol{s}^* = (s_i^*)_{i \in I}$, be vectors of fuzzy quantities, $s_i \in \mathbb{R}$, $s_i^* \in \mathbb{R}$, $i \in I$, defined by (40) and (41), respectively. Then

$$\xi_i(x_i^*) = \xi^*(x_i^*) = 1 \quad \text{and}$$

$$s_i \text{ is additively equivalent to } s_i^*, \ s_i \sim_\oplus s_i^*.$$

Proof. The statement follows from Remark 5, Lemma 7, and (40), (41), immediately, where (21) was used.

5.1 Fuzzy Game Values — Shapley Postulates

It is interesting to verify how does the fuzzy Shapley value (40) – or its additive equivalent (41) – fulfil the Shapleys general postulates remembered in Section 2.

It is easy to see that the membership functions ξ_i and ξ_i^* do not depend on the ordering of additions in (40) and (41), as all the operations with fuzzy quantities, used here, are commutative.

The second condition – achievability of the Shapley value for the coalition of all players (in a superadditive game with non-empty core) is also quite well verifiable. It follows from Theorem 7. As $\xi_i(x_i^*) = \xi_i(x_i^*) = 1$, for all $i \in I$, and $\mu_I(v(I)) = 1$, then the validity of the deterministic condition

$$\sum_{i \in I} x_i^* = v(I)$$

means, due to (26), that for z, $z^* \in \mathbb{R}$,

$$z = x_1 \oplus x_2 \oplus \cdots \oplus x_n, \quad z^* = x_1^* \oplus x_2^* \oplus \cdots \oplus x_n^*,$$

(42)
$$\nu_\sim(w(I), z) = \nu_\sim(w(I), z^*) = 1.$$

It is useful to remember Theorem 2, regarding the non-emptness of the cores.

The last condition is also fulfilled in satisfactory degree. Let us consider games (I, w_1), (I, w_2), $(I, w_1 \oplus w_2)$ and denote by $d_1(K)$, $d_2(K)$ and $d_{12}(K)$, $K \in 2^I$, the fuzzy quantities (39) for the considered games, respectively. Then

$$d_{12}(K) = c(K) \cdot [(w_1(K) \oplus w_2(K)) \oplus (\langle-1\rangle \oplus (w_1(K-\{i\})) \oplus w_2(K-i))]$$
$$= c(K) \cdot [(w_1(K) \oplus w_2(K)) \oplus (\langle-1\rangle \oplus (w_1(K-\{i\})) \oplus (\langle-1\rangle \odot w_2(K-\{i\})))]$$
$$= c(K) \cdot [w_1(K) \oplus (\langle-1\rangle \odot (w_1(K-\{i\})))] \oplus$$
$$\oplus c(K) \cdot [w_2(K) \oplus (\langle-1\rangle \odot (w_2(K-\{i\})))] = d_1(K) \oplus d_2(K).$$

Let us denote, for any $i \in I$, $s_i^{(1)}$, $s_i^{(2)}$ and $s_i^{(1,2)}$ the components of fuzzy Shapley values in (I, w_1), (I, w_2) and $(I, w_1 \oplus w_2)$. Then the previous relation between d_1, d_2 and d_{12} immediately implies

$$s_i^{(1,2)} = s_i^{(1)} \oplus s_i^{(2)},$$

and quite analogous equality can be proved for s_i^* defined by (41).

5.2 Values and Effectivity – Comment

Up to now, we have simply copied the concept of coalition games and their solutions with fuzzy inputs being used instead of the crisp ones. It means that we were interested in the coalitional profits and their distributions. In fact, the vagueness of the utilities which is transmitted to the overall vagueness of the bargaining process and its results offers a qualitatively new view at the role of players in the bargaining process. The participation of a player in a coalition does influence not only its total income but also the possibility of its stabile existence. This is true, especially, for the coalition of all players whose stability is a necessary condition for the negotiations about the "fair" distribution of the total income among the players.

The concept of the effectiveness of coalitions was mentioned, e. g. in [7]. In the case of superadditive game (let us remember Lemma 1 and Theorem 1), its definition ca be simplified as follows.

Let us consider a non-empty coalition $K \subset I$ and a game (K, w) where w is reduced to the subcoalitions of K. If the original game (I, w) was a fuzzy extension of some (I, v) then, of course, (K, w) is a fuzzy extension of the reduced deterministic game (K, v). If C_K is the deterministic core of (K, v) then we say that K is *effective* iff $C_K \neq \emptyset$. If we consider fuzzy core $\mathcal{C}_K$ of the fuzzy game (I, w) with membership function $\mu_{\mathcal{C}_K} : R^I \to [0, 1]$ then the numbers

$$(43) \qquad \sup(\mu_{\mathcal{C}_K}(\boldsymbol{x}) : \boldsymbol{x} \in R^I)$$

denote the *possibility that the coalition K is effective* in the fuzzy game (I, w). If a player $i \in I - K$ joins K, it means that K is transformed into $L = K \cup \{i\}$, then this act influences the possible effectiveness of L related to K. The ability of a player to increase the effectivity of an agreement by joining it, of course, depends on the relations between $v(K)$ and $v(L)$ (in the notation used above), and, consequently, on the relation between $w(K)$ and $w(L)$. This influence is also reflected in the calculation of Shapley value, and it should be reflected by any rational determination of the game value. But its consequences are larger than the increasing of utility to be distributed. They concern the proper ability of the coalition to find an effective and stable agreement. It seems that in the fuzzy coalition games theory the value should be a functional, reflecting not only differences between $v(L)$ and $v(K)$ or $w(L)$ and $w(K)$ but also the differences (or their relations) between the possibilities (43) for L and K. The actual analytical formulas for such construction of fuzzy values may be an interesting subject of further investigation.

6   Conclusive Comments

It was shown and discussed above that the vague total utilities of coalitions make vague all results of bargaining and also other properties of the game like its superadditivity (also subadditivity and additivity not being mentioned here but being significant in some economic applications). The vagueness does not avoid the existence of core and its formal shape which is crucial for the bare possibility of cooperation on the level of all players. In the concept of effectiveness, this phenomenon is extended to the possibility of the coalitional agreements on the level of particular "smaller" coalitions. This can be, among other consequences, used for finding the possible terminal structure of cooperation in the coalition structures, as it was done in [7].

The distribution of the total profit among the participants of the bargaining situation under the existence of only vague promises can lead to vague agreements, only. The rates of the profit distribution and their possibilities are generally characterized by the fuzzy core. The maximal possibility of its elements also defines the possibility of agreement of all players in the principle. Moreover, the choice of a most "fair" imputation in the core necessarily depends on the possibility of its realization (on the value of the membership function of the core) and on the negotiated sharings whose "fairness" is expressed by the concept of the game value. Also this value depends on the variable coalitional profits and can be, of course, only vague. This fact, the dependence of the fuzzy value of a game on the effectiveness of coalitions, the fuzziness (and, consequently, richer formal structure) of the core which deeply influences the rationality of the value, and the generally vague character of arguments and contraarguments in the bargaining process, that all probably decreases the real importance of the value concept in fuzzy games. If the fuzzy value is not a one-point-set but a fuzzy subset of R^I with structured possibilities then it looses an important part of its justification. The more significant seems to be the concept of fuzzy core (a quite natural one) with its interesantly structured possibilities.

It is worth mentioning, as well, that the limitation to the games with side payments (however it simplifies the formal theory) limits the interpretations and applications of the theoretical model. Some attempts that were done to generalize the concept of fuzzy cooperation to the games without side payments [8] (let us remember [5]) have shown the formal difficulties connected with such extension of the model. These difficulties concern even such basic notions like the domination of imputations and the core. Nevertheless, it is possible to expect some development even in this direction.

References

[1] O. Bondareva: Yadro igr N lic (in Russian: Core of N-person games). Viestnik Leningradskovo Universiteta 13 (1962), 141–142.

[2] D. Butnariu, E. P. Klement: Triangular Norm–Based Measures and Games With Fuzzy Coalitions. Kluver, Dordrecht 1993.

[3] D. Dubois, H. Prade: Fuzzy numbers: An overview. In: Analysis of Fuzzy Information (Ed.: Bezdek, J. C.), CRC–Press, Boca Raton 1988, 3–39.

[4] M. Mareš: Computation Over Fuzzy Quantities. CRC–Press, Boca Raton 1994.

[5] M. Mareš: Coalition forming motivated by vague profits. In: Transactions "Mathematical methods in Economy", Ostrava'95. Technical University of Ostrava, Ostrava 1995, 114–119.

[6] M. Mareš: Fuzzy zero, algebraic equivalence: yes or no? Kybernetika 32 (1996), 4, 343–351.

[7] M. Mareš: Fuzzy coalition forming. In: Transactions "7th World IFSA Congress", Prague 1997. Submitted.

[8] M. Mareš: General coalition games. Kybernetika 14 (1978), 5, 350–368.

[9] M. Mareš: Weak arithmetics of fuzzy numbers. Fuzzy Sets and Systems. To appear.

[10] M. Mareš: Fuzzy coalition structures. Fuzzy Sets and Systems. Submitted.

[11] J. Rosenmüller: Kooperative Spiese and Märkte. Springer–Verlag, Heidelberg–Berlin 1971.

[12] J. Rosenmüller: The Theory of Games and Markets. North–Holand, Amsterdam 1982.

[13] L. S. Shapley: The value of n-person games. In: Contribution to the Theory of Games II. Annals of Math. Studies, 28 (1953), 307–317.

2

TIME SERIES
ANALYSES AND PREDICTION

Time Series Filtering and Reconstruction Using Fuzzy Weighted Local Regression

Silvio Giove and Paolo Pellizzari

Dept. of Applied Mathematics and Computer Science
University of Venice, Dorsoduro, 3825/E, Venice (ITALY)
E-mail: sgiove@unive.it

Abstract. The problem of outliers detection in time series is addressed. We propose a fuzzy weighted index to select suspicious values, and next we outline a procedure based on fuzzy linear local approximation to replace the anomalous points. We tested the above method on synthetic noised chaotic series (Mackey-Glass map) showing that we can effectively deal with such points. Finally we detect the most outlying prices in the Italian COMIT stock index.

Keywords. Fuzzy logic, time series filtering, outliers detection.

Introduction

This paper deals with financial time series analysis. It is now well recognized that such processes contain, at least partially, some non-linear part, that can be identified and reconstructed by suitable identification algorithms. In particular, we suggest a two-phase algorithm, using the concept of *fuzzy similarity* between patterns [16]. At first, in the *outliers detection* phase, we *filter* the series, trying to recognize possible anomalous values; to this purpose, a measure of the *outlying* character for the value at time t is introduced. From simulation and from theoretical point of view we verified that the procedure is remarkably robust. Our method is related to non parametric estimation of a conditional probability density [13], thus extending and generalizing the well known Nadaraya-Watson approach [12]. In the second phase we use the Fuzzy Linear Local Approximation algorithm (*FLLA*) to modify the previously identified outliers [4]. When the two-phase procedure terminates, a new *filtered* series is produced, in which hopefully the most significative erroneous values are removed and replaced. This corrected dataset can be used to fit other models like Neural Network [1], [2]. It is shown in

Section 4 that better modeling results are obtained using the filtered time series in the learning phase.

We tested the procedure over two data sets: the synthetic Mackey-Glass chaotic series [11], and the Italian Comit stock index. In both cases, good performances were obtained, showing the advantages of our filtering procedure.

1. Fuzzy similarity and time series analysis

Despite the strengh of the *Efficient Market Hypothesis* [15], there is a substantial body of evidence that some typical patterns exist, leading to weak short-term predictability of financial time series [7].

In some sense, we could adfirm that, despite the obvious sources of noise and the unpredictable occurrence of exogenous *shocks*, the average behaviour of the investors modifies the future price movements, and this behaviour depends mainly upon psychologic conditionings, like, for istance, panic or imitation effects.

The same basic idea, that is identification of typical structures in the data can be used to recognize *spurious* values, usually called *outliers* [4].

Let us observe that the identification of such suspicious values, and the consequent substitution with some more *realistic* ones, can be very useful if other automatic tools are used, using a *learning* approach, like Neural Nets or Neural Fuzzy Systems [3], [9], [10]. Note that the filtering phase is usually a difficult problem, since, in fact, it not easy to decide if an anomalous value occurs, expecially without assumptions on the Data Generating Process (DGP).

In what follows, we deal with a real time series $\{X_t, t = 1,...,N\}$. Let us now consider the following definitions [13]:

DEFINITION 1.1 The *(uncomplete) pattern* (of lenght P), or *P-pattern*, at time t is the vector $\underline{x}_t^P = \left[X_{t-P}, X_{t-P+1}, ..., X_{t-1} \right]^T$, where P is an integer, $P \ll N$.

This vector is the collection of all the consecutive P past values in the series. If the value X_t is also included in the vector, we refer to the complete *P-pattern*:

DEFINITION 1.2 The *complete P-pattern* about X_t is the vector

$$\underline{\tilde{x}}_t^P = \left[\underline{x}_t^P \ X_t \right]^T = \left[X_{t-P}, X_{t-P+1}, ..., X_{t-1}, X_t \right]^T \tag{1.1}$$

Similar definitions of delay patterns are used in *chaotic* systems analysis, see [6].

DEFINITION 1.3 A *similarity* measure [16] between the two *P*-patterns $\underline{x}_t^P$, $\underline{x}_\tau^P$, $t \neq \tau$, is a symmetric and monotone operator φ, such that:

$$\varphi(\underline{x}, \underline{y}) = \varphi(\underline{y}, \underline{x}), \quad \forall \underline{x}, \underline{y} \in U$$

$$\varphi(\underline{x}, \underline{x}) \geq \varphi(\underline{x}, \underline{y}), \quad \forall \underline{x}, \underline{y} \in U$$

With obvious modifications, we can define a similarity measure for *complete* patterns.

DEFINITION 1.4 A *fuzzy* similarity relation is a particularization of the Def. 1.3 to the fuzzy case, that is $U = [0,1]$.

Usually, a fuzzy similarity relation is identified by a *membership* function [8] that measures the similarities between the ordered components of the two patterns, and by an *aggregation* operator G. In what follows, we shall write $\mu_i(x_t^P, y_t^P)$ to indicate the membership degree of the absolute difference between the $i - th$ components of the two patterns $\underline{x}_t^P$ and $\underline{y}_t^P$. The similarity between the two *P*-patterns, denoted by $w(x_t^P, y_\tau^P)$ is:

$$w(\underline{x}_t^P, \underline{x}_\tau^P) = G\left[\mu_1(\underline{x}_t^P, \underline{x}_\tau^P), \mu_2(\underline{x}_t^P, \underline{x}_\tau^P), \dots, \mu_P(\underline{x}_t^P, \underline{x}_\tau^P)\right] \tag{1.2}$$

where we suppose that the aggregation operator G is a *MICA* operator[1], see [8].

Naturally, if the two patterns are similar, all their ordered components are close, and this intuitive observation justifies the previous definition of the measure $w(\underline{x}_t^P, \underline{y}_t^P)$.

Among others, we recall that the most popular membership functions are the so called *triangular*, $tri_h(x)$, and *trapezoidal*, $tra_h(x)$, functions defined respectively as:

---

[1] MICA means Monotonic, Identity, Commutative, Aggregative.

$$ttri_h(x) = \begin{cases} 1 - \left|\dfrac{x}{h}\right|, & |x| \le h \\ 0, & |x| > h \end{cases}$$

$$ra_{h,\varepsilon}(x) = \begin{cases} 1, & |x| \le \varepsilon \\ 1 - \dfrac{x - \varepsilon}{h - \varepsilon}, & \varepsilon < |x| \le h \\ 0, & |x| > h \end{cases} \tag{1.3}$$

where $0 < \varepsilon \le h$.

The *similarities degrees* between uncomplete and complete P-patterns are denoted by:

$$w_{t,\tau} = \varphi(\underline{x}_t^P, \underline{x}_\tau^P), \quad \tilde{w}_{t,\tau} = \varphi(\underline{\tilde{x}}_t^P, \underline{\tilde{x}}_\tau^P) \tag{1.4}$$

It is easy to verify [13] that, under the stated assumptions on G those index are two fuzzy similarity measures between the two P-patterns considered.

To give an example of the previous definitions, let $P = 3$, consider the two patterns $\underline{x} = (0.6, 0.1, -0.1)$, $\underline{y} = (0.4, 0.2, 0.3)$ and let $h = 0.5$ in the membership function (1.3). Then the similarity $w(\underline{x}, \underline{y})$ is:

$$w(\underline{x}, \underline{y}) = \left(1 - \left|\frac{0.6 - 0.4}{0.5}\right|\right)\left(1 - \left|\frac{0.1 - 0.2}{0.5}\right|\right)\left(1 - \left|\frac{-0.1 - 0.3}{0.5}\right|\right) = 0.096$$

Note that the above similarity (which is always in [0,1]) is very low, mainly because of the relative difference in the third components of patterns $\underline{x}, \underline{y}$. In the present context, this might imply that an unlikely observation occured in the third components of one of the two patterns.

Now we describe a fuzzy similarity index η_t able to signal potential outliers. See [13] for a rational explanation of such a definition.

DEFINITION 1.6 Let us consider the following *similarities ratio* index:

$$\zeta_t = \frac{\tilde{W}_t}{W_t} = \frac{\displaystyle\sum_{k=P+1}^{t-1} \tilde{w}_{t,k}}{\displaystyle\sum_{k=P+1}^{t-1} w_{t,k}} \tag{1.5}$$

The use of η_t is justified by the following intuitive consideration: when η_t is small, being $\tilde{W}_t \ll W_t$, the sum of the similarities of the complete P-patterns with the current one is only a fraction of the sum of the uncomplete similarities, reinforcing the suspect for X_t to be an outlier. The converse holds if $\zeta_t \cong 1$: then X_t is, in some sense, a *regular* value in the series.

For what concerns the index ζ_t, the following result can be proved [13]:

THEOREM 1.1 Let G be a *MICA* operator, as a *triangular-norm* [8]. Then:

1.1) $0 \le \zeta_t \le 1$

1.2) If we use a triangular membership function $tri_h(x)$, then the condition $\zeta_t = 1$, $\forall h \in [0,1]$ implies that the time serie is costant, i.e. $X_t = \bar{x}$, $\forall t = 1,..,N$, $\bar{x} \in R$. If we deal with a trapezoidal membership function like $tra_h(x)$, then the following is true $|X_t - X_\tau| \le \varepsilon$, $\forall \tau = P+1,...,t-1$.

Limiting our interest to forecasting purposes, and following partially what proposed in [14], observe that we can forecast the future value of the series at the actual time $(t-1)$, say $\hat{X}(t)$, comparing $\underline{p}_t$ with all the other past patterns in the series, $\underline{p}_\tau$, $P+1 < \tau < t$; on the basis of such similarity degrees, the value $\hat{X}(t)$ is computed taking the weighted average values of $X_{\tau+1}$ into account, see [5].

2. The Fuzzy Linear Local Approximation algorithm (*FLLA*)

In what follows, a brief explanation of the *FLLA* algorithm will be given, see [14] for details.

Consider the following least squares problem:

$$\underline{\beta}_t := \arg \min_{\beta \in R^{P+1}} \sum_{i = P+1, i \neq t}^{t-1} \left[X_i - \underline{\beta}_t^T \cdot (\underline{x}_i^P, 1)^T \right]^2 \cdot w(\underline{x}_t^P, \underline{x}_i^P) \qquad (2.1)$$

The components of $\underline{\beta}_t$ are the coefficients of the regressors that, in the mean square sense, best forecast $X(t)$, where the weights $w(x_t^P, x_i^P)$ are the similarities degrees between patterns. It is natural to define the *predictor* $\hat{X}(t)$, as:

$$\hat{X}(t) \equiv FLLA_t(\underline{x}_t^P) = \underline{\beta}^T{}_t \cdot (\underline{x}_t^P, 1)^T \tag{2.2}$$

Hence the previous predictor is a linear combination of regressed values plus a constant. Assume for exemplification that, $\underline{x}_t^3 = (0.6, 0.1, -0.1)$ and suppose we estimate $\underline{\beta}_t = (0.1, 0.2, 0.3, -0.1)$ by minimization of (2.1). Then the forecast (2.2) is

$$\hat{X}(t) \equiv FLLA_t(\underline{x}_t^3) = (0.1, 0.2, 0.3, -0.1) \cdot (0.6, 0.1, -0.1, 1) = -0.05$$

The forecast is *local* and highly adaptive, being tailored to each observation $X(t)$. It is immediate to note that this method can be used to provide a better value of the outliers detected with the procedure proposed in Section 1.

In the following section the global filtering procedure (outliers detection and modification) is presented.

3. Filtering: *outliers* detection and time serie reconstruction

The filtering procedure consists of two subsequently phases; first, we look for suspicious values in the series (*outliers*), and next we replay them by other reconstructed values. We use in the first phase the *similarities ratio* index ζ_t (1.5) to select the suspected outliers, and in the second phase we use the *FLLA* predictor (2.2) to compute the modified values.

It is difficult to provide an unambiguous definition of *outlier* and this problem is still debated. We only provided an operational procedure to detect patterns that appear to have low similarity with respect to all the other patterns in the series.

Recall that the index ζ_t depends upon the window width h and in what follows we shall write $\zeta_t(h)$ instead that ζ_t to underline this dependency.

Moreover, the results depend even upon the choices of parameter P, the lenght of the considered pattern, and we can try to optimize the performances, as suggested in [14], repeating the procedure varying the values of P and h. We first detect the outlying observations by examination of $\zeta(h)$. Next, in the second phase, the *FLLA* is used to substitute the outliers found in the first phase.

The main steps of the two-phases procedure are listed below:

First phase:

1.1) Select a value $h > 0$, a pattern lengh P, a threshold value $\zeta^* \in (0,1)$. Set $L = \varnothing$ (list that will contain the time indices of the outliers).

1.2) For $\tau = P+1,........,N$, compute $\zeta_\tau(h)$; if $\zeta_\tau(h) < \zeta^*$ then X_τ is classified as an outlier: $L = L \cup \tau$.

Note that the list L depends on h and on the threshold ζ^*. It is not wise to take further actions only examining the results provided by a single h and ζ^* values; repeating the previous algorithm with various values of h gives a more accurate portrait of the outliers possibly occuring. The pictures in the next section will clarify this point.

Second phase:

2.1) $\forall \tau \in L$: substitute X_τ with the *reconstructed* value $\hat{X}_\tau = FLLA_\tau(\underline{x}_\tau^P)$.

We observe that, despite the robustness in the first phase, the reconstruction strongly depends upon the choices of h; thus we select an *optimal* value h^* such that:

$$h^* = \min_h \sum_{t=P+1}^{N} \left[X_t - \hat{X}_t\right]^2 \qquad (3.1)$$

minimizing the sum of squared forecasting errors.

Then, the values X_t, $t \in L$ are replaced by $FLLA_t(\underline{x}_t^P, h^*)$, where the argument h^* stresses the dependence on the value computed in (3.1).

In the first phase, for any considered value of h, it is possible to compute the list of the suspected outliers, and the decision maker is free to decide, on the basis of the visual ispection of *histogram*-like graphs if such values are or not suspicious (see Fig. 3, for an example). Obviously, if an observation is signalled for many h values, there is more confidence in its outlying character.

We feel that a significative advantage of our method is the fact that the procedure is completely *model-free*, that is, no assumptions on the DGP are required.

4. Computational experience

This section presents some examples and applications of the methodology previously outlined. We filter and correct the suspicious observations of the synthetic Mackey-Glass non linear time series, which exhibits chaotic behaviour. Next we test the filtering procedure on a real financial time series, namely the COMIT index of the Italian stock Exchange.

4.1 The Mackey-Glass time series

The time series we analyze is generated by the following non linear deterministic map:

$$X(t) = a \cdot X(t-1) + \frac{b \cdot X(t-\tau)}{1 + X(t-\tau)^c}$$

where $a = 0.4, b = -5, c = 10, \tau = 5$. We discarded the first 1000 data to reduce the effect of initial transients and kept observations 1001-st to 1300-th.

We feel that the assumption of deterministic DGP, even if chaotic, is rather optimistic and rarely occurring in pratice, especially when financial time series are examined. A substantial level of noise is generally aknowledged in financial series. We disturbed the original data in two different ways, *observationally* and *dynamically*. In the first case we consider the series:

$$Y(t) = X(t) + \varepsilon_t$$

where ε_t is a sequence of zero-mean i.i.d. random variables with given variance σ_Y. In the latter we use the series:

$$Y(t) = a \cdot Y(t-1) + \frac{b \cdot Y(t-\tau)}{1 + Y(t-\tau)^c} + \varepsilon_t$$

Loosely speaking, observational noise affects the precision of the observed value of the time series. Note that the observational noise in $Y(t)$ has no effect in subsequent observations. On the other hand, dynamical noise affects the following observations, being incorporated in the DGP. As a consequence, dynamical noise has more complex effect on data.

Although it would be interesting, we do not intend to examine which kind of noise is possibly present in financial time series. However we stress the importance of testing computational methods on noisy time series, which are more likely to provide better insight on real time series. This is in our opinion even more important when detecting outlying data which are quite often embedded in a noisy environment.

We considered three different noise sources, contaminating the raw series using:

$$\varepsilon_t \approx U[-a,a]$$

where $a = \dfrac{1}{4}, \dfrac{1}{2}, 1$, and $U[-a,a]$ means "uniformly distributed in $[-a,a]$".

For easier reference we denote by MK the raw Mackey Glass time series, by MKO1/4, MKO1/2, MKO1, the observationally noised series, and by MKD1/4, MKD1/2, MKD1 the dynamically noised datasets. Each serie is labelled by 1/4, 1/2, 1, depending on the amplitude of the noise artificially introduced. The series MK and MKD1 are shown in Fig.1, 2.

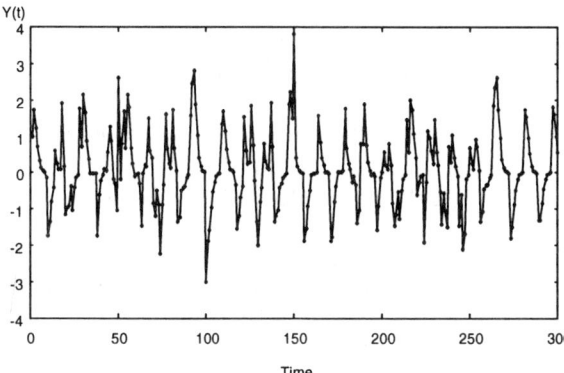

Fig. 1 - MK series

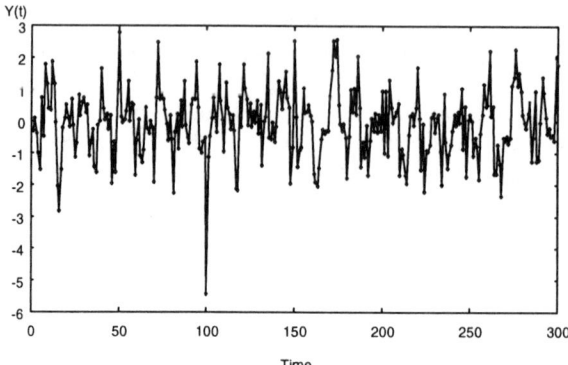

Fig. 2 - MKD1 series

All the series we tested were additively contaminated setting:

$$Y(50) = Y(50) + 3\sigma_Y$$
$$Y(100) = Y(100) - 3\sigma_Y$$
$$Y(150) = Y(150) + 3\sigma_Y$$

and were then normalized by the standard deviation σ_Y.

Setting $P = 2$, we can scrutiny ζ_t for various values of $h \geq 0.5$ to assess the strangeness of observations. We consider ζ_t small when it is smaller than $\zeta^* = 0.1$. We will see in the following that this choice is not critical, and that a proper application of the method is quite robust to different specification parameters. The following Fig. 3, 4, 5, 6 show the values of h such that we have $\zeta_t(h) < \zeta^*$ for the time series MK, MKO1/4, MKO1/2, MKO1. The pictures are to be interpreted in the following way: consider Fig. 3 and $t = 150$. The graph shows that $Y(150)$ is outlying for h in the range $[0.5, 3.25]$. On the other hand, $Y(175)$ is recognized as outliers only if $h \in [0.5, 1]$.

Some remarks are in order:

1) The outliers artificially induced are clearly visible in all the graphs, showing remarkable peaks. $Y(100)$ is not very strongly visible in time series MKO1, which is the most disturbed dataset, although it is still more persistent than other outliers.

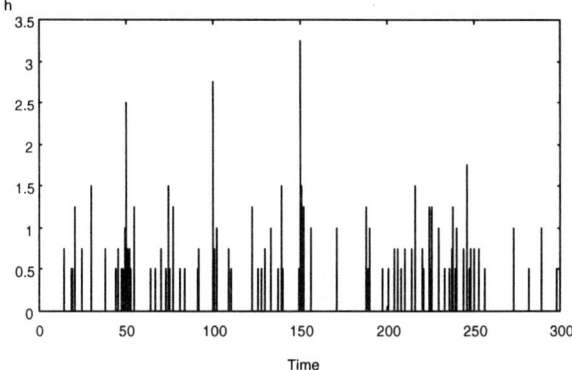

Fig. 3 - $h{:}\zeta \leq \zeta^*$ for MK

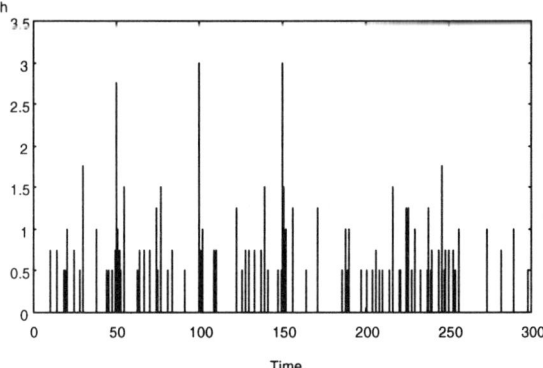

Fig. 4 - $h{:}\zeta \leq \zeta^*$ for MKO1/4

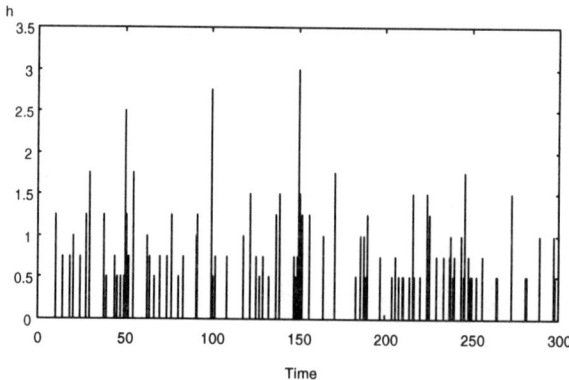

Fig. 5 - $h:\zeta \leq \zeta^*$ for MKO1/2

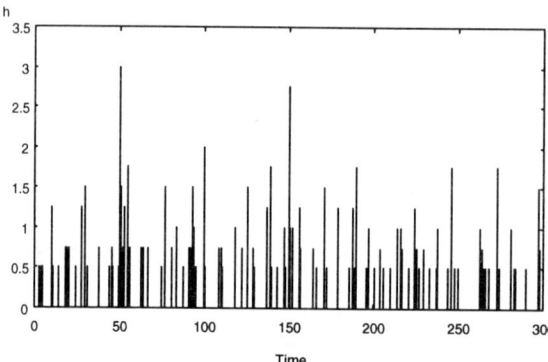

Fig. 6 - $h:\zeta \leq \zeta^*$ for MKO1

2) The cleanest results are obtained when low noised time series are considered. As the noise level is increased, the peaks of $Y(50)$, $Y(100)$ and $Y(150)$ are lower with respect to other data and there are other observations exhibiting potential outlying behaviour (see Fig. 6). Note that this is to be expected, being the detection of outliers difficult in very noisy time series. Let us turn to the examination of dynamically perturbed Mackey-Glass time series. A look at the data of MKD1 depicted in Fig. 2 shows that $Y(100)$ is an eyeballer, but that the other induced outliers are quite difficult to detect. The results of the analysis of the MKD1/2 and MKD1 are shown in Fig.7, 8. All the outliers have been clearly detected, even in the noisest case (MKD1) when the structure of the original Mackey-Glass series is hardly detectable.

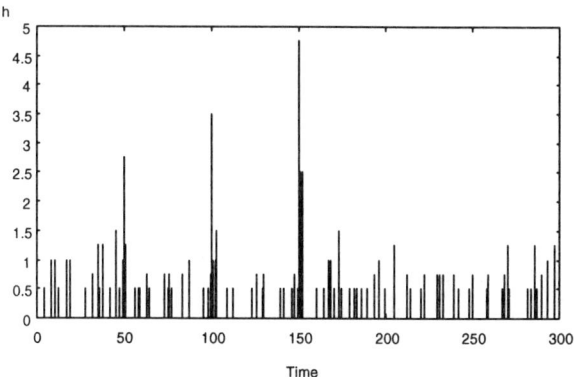

Fig. 7 - $h{:}\zeta \leq \zeta^{*}$ for MKD1/2

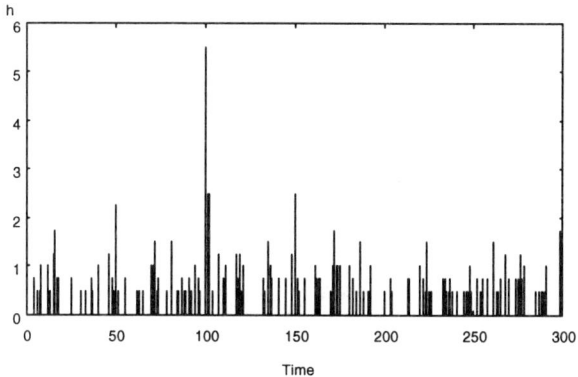

Fig. 8 - $h{:}\zeta \leq \zeta^{*}$ for MKD1

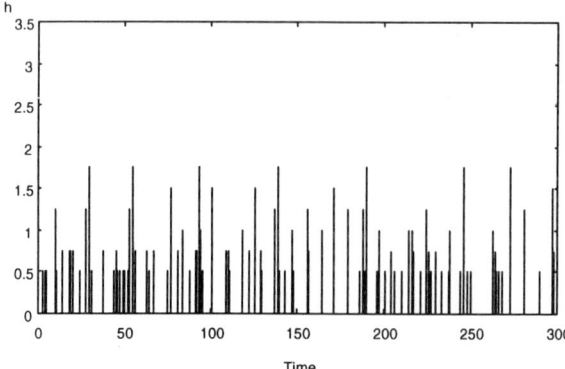

Fig. 9 - $h: \zeta \leq \zeta^*$ for MKO1 (corrected)

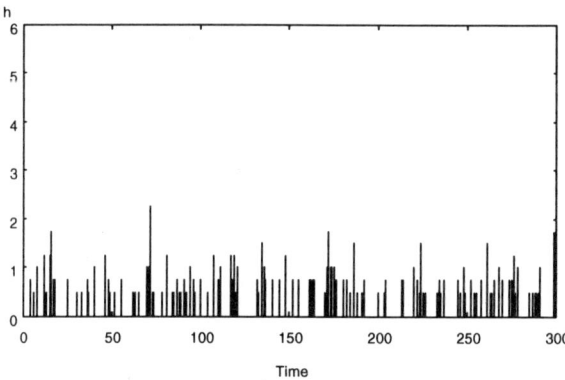

Fig. 10 - $h: \zeta \leq \zeta^*$ for MKD1 (corrected)

It is interesting to examine the recostruction of some detected outliers. We report only the results for series MKO1 and MKD1, that are the noisest datasets. The minimization of (2.1) for the *observationally* noised time series (MKO1) occurs when $P = 5$, X_{t-1}, X_{t-5} are used for prediction and $h^* = 0.9$. In this case the ratio of RMSE (Root mean Square Error) to standard deviation of the series is 0.78. On the basis of the previous findings, using (2.2), we replace the observations $Y(50)$, $Y(100)$ and $Y(150)$ according to the following Table 1:

Table 1

n.	Corrected	Outliers	Original
50	-0.337	3.012	0.013
100	-0.325	-2.541	0.471
150	1.174	3.596	0.611

Note that the corrected values are quite close to the original ones, if the presence of noise is taken into account. The outliers detection algorithm does not signal any more the observations $Y(50), Y(100), Y(150)$, after correction, showing that the suggested replacements appear to be a proper way to deal with ouliers.

The effect of replacement can be seen in Fig. 9, which is to be compared with Fig. 6.

The same analysis was performed on the *dynamically* noised time series (MKD1) and produced the result of Table 2 and the diagnostic graph in Fig. 10, obtained after correction of observations $Y(50), Y(100), Y(150)$. The outliers of Fig. 8 disappeared.

Table 2

n.	Corrected	Outliers	Original
50	-0.747	2.783	-0.201
100	-1.626	-5.441	-2.261
150	0.047	2.502	-0.460

The correction is based on a local model of order 5 (that is, $P = 5$), using only the predictor X_{t-5} with $h^* = 0.2$. The ratio of RMSE to standard deviation for the model used for correction is 0.580.

Finally we tested the positive effects that filtering can have on model performance before its estimation. We consider a simple feed-forward Neural Network model for the noisest datasets MKO1 and MKD1. We use 5 regressed variables as inputs, 3 hidden units with sigmoidal transfer function and 1 linear output unit. The Networks were fully connected (layer by layer) and were trained using only the first 250 observation, keeping the last 50 points to obtain out of sample predictions. The training algorithm is standard backpropagation (with *learning rate* $\mu = 0.1$), repeated for 300 complete cycles by the computer software tool SNNS [17]. The results are reported in Table 3, where some out-of-sample forecasting indicators are shown for the models fitted to contaminated and corrected data. The latter were obtained by detection and substitution of the bad values, namely observations 50,100, 150.

Table 3

	no correction			with correction		
	sse	*rsq*	*aic*	*sse*	*rsq*	*aic*
dynamic noise	14.46	0.75	-18.05	9.59	0.84	-38.57
obs. noise	24.74	0.54	8.82	23.97	0.56	7.23

In the previous table, *sse*, *rsq* and *aic* stand for the sum of square errors, Pearson's R^2 and Akaike's information criterion [17].

An impressive deterioration of out-of-sample forecasting performances is apparent for dinamically noisy data if no filtering is performed. The presence of 3 non-extreme outliers out of 250 data increases the MSE of predictions of roughly 35%. Note also that this poor fit is not due to the three outliers, but that it is sparse on the whole out-of-sample forecasting set, which is clean from malicious data.

The effect is much smaller if observationally noised data are examined. The main reason for this behaviour is the fact that $E[F(X_t) + \varepsilon_t] = F(X_t)$ while, in general, we have for nonlinear functions F that $E[F(X_t) + \varepsilon_t] \neq F(X_t)$. Hence the effect of dynamic noise can severely bias the obtained forecasts.

We stress that the previous models are by no means the best neural networks one can fit to data. However, given the other parameters (number and type of units, learning rate, training cycles,...), this experiment shows that outliers can have a profound impact on the results of the models, showing the great advantage to pre-process the data.

4.2 The COMIT time series.

We applied the previous method to a real time series, namely the italian Stock Index COMIT. The 357 observations were recorded daily from 2-nd January 1995 to 31-st May 1996. A plot of the index is in Fig.11. The data were not preprocessed and we perform analysis with $P = 4,5,10$ and h ranging from 10 to 40. The results appears to be very similar for different P, pointing to some data that are strongly and persistently signalled for outlying behaviour. In particolar, observations 10, 205 and 330 are quite evident altough, especially when $P = 10$, there are some doubts also on point 265, 286 and 306. The use of large P is apparently able to detect finer structures in data, allowing further examination of observations not clearly detected with lower P. However, note that the relative strangeness of the outliers is smaller than for $P = 4,5$.

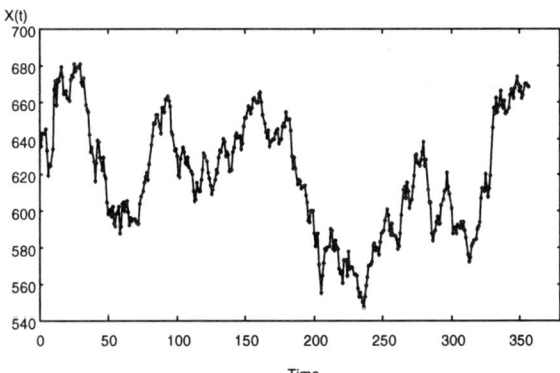

Fig. 11- COMIT time series

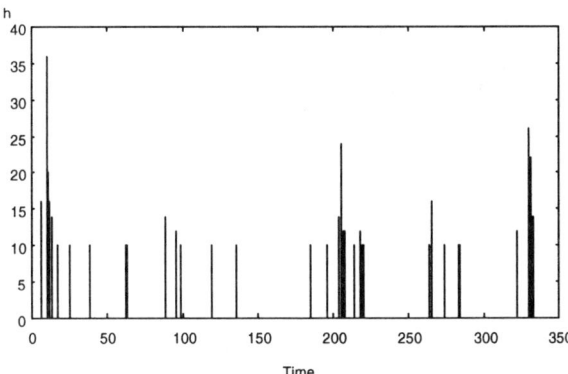

Fig. 12- $h : \zeta \leq \zeta^*$ for COMIT ($P = 4$)

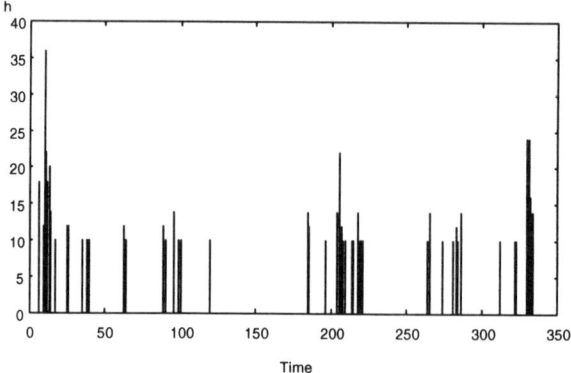

Fig. 13- $h:\zeta \leq \zeta^*$ for COMIT ($P=5$)

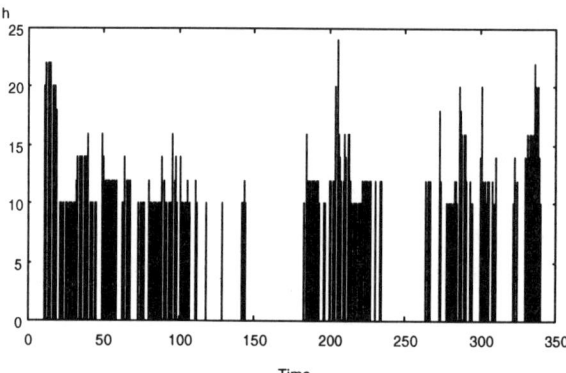

Fig. 14- $h:\zeta \leq \zeta^*$ for COMIT ($P=10$)

The previous results show that the method is very robust to the choice of P. The same finding was obtained also for the Mackey Glass datasets, but we did not report the results for brevity. As far as choice of ζ^* and h are concerned, note that the same robustness is obtained for a fair range of ζ^* values: graphs like the ones in Figs. 3,..,10 are shifted along the y-axis but the same qualitative results about outliers are obtained. On the contrary, the parameter h must be choosen with some care, examining the results for many h to assess their stability, as we do. This is important as any prefixed observation can be forced to be signalled as outlying by choosing h small enough (of course, in general such procedure would produce a huge number of outliers).

5. Discussion

We propose a broad-applicable method to detect outliers. The same ideas used in the detection phase can be adapted to obtain hopefully better values for bad observations in the data. The assumptions on the time series are minimal, and encouraging results have been obtained even on COMIT time series which is almost surely non stationary. The procedure relies on the definition of the parameters P, h, ζ^*. The case-studies show the remarkable robustness of the algorithm with respect to the choice of P. Note that the analysis of the Mackey-Glass series was performed with $P = 2$ when the true order was obviulsy 5.

More work is needed to understand fully the impact of ζ^* and h on the detection and correction of outliers. Some ideas on "optimal" estimation of h is in [13]. We feel that the better way to cope with this problem is the consideration of various h values.

There is a certain amount of subjective judgement in the detection of outliers, due to the choice of the parameters. We think that this is not necessarily a drawback of the method, as the concept of outlier is still tricky and not completely unambigous. The method appears to detect outliers that do not lie in the tails of distribution and are very difficult to detect visually (see observations 50 and 150 of Fig. 2 for an example).

Even if a more complete simulation study would be needed to strength this conclusion, the detection and correction of outliers is likely to give a substantial improvement in modelization and forecasting results, as some Neural Networks-based forecasting examples show.

References

1) Apostolos Refenes P., ed., *Neural Networks in the Capital Markets*, John Wiley & Sons, Chichester, England, 1995.
2) Azoff E., *Neural Networks Time Series Forecasting of Financial Markets*, Wiley & Sons, Chichester, 1994.
3) Baestaens D.E., et al., *Neural Networks Solutions for Trading in Financial Markets*, Pitman Publishing, London, 1994.

4) Barnett V., Lewis T., *Outliers in Statistical Data*, Wiley & Sons, Chichester, 1994.

5) Canestrelli E., Giove S., Sogliani A., Time series forecasting: a fuzzy approach, *Badania Operacyjne i Decyzyjne*, n. 3, 1996.

6) Casdagli M., et al., State space reconstruction in the presence of noise, *Physica D*, **51**, pp. 52-98, 1991.

7) Deboek G. J., *Trading on the Edge*, John Wiley & Sons, Chichester, England, 1994.

8) Fuller R., *Neural Fuzzy Systems*, Abo Akademi, Ser. A:443, 1995.

9) Goonatilake S., Treleaven P., ed., *Intelligence Systems for Finance and Business*, Wiley & Sons, Chichester, 1995.

10) Kosko B., *Neural Networks and Fuzzy Systems*, Prentice Hall, USA, 1992.

11) Mackey M., Glass L., Oscillation and chais in physiological control systems, *Science*, **197**, pp. 287-289, 1977.

12) Nadaraya E., On estimating regression, *Th. Prob. Appl.*, **9**, pp. 141-142, 1964.

13) Pellizzari P., Pizzi C., Fuzzy-like conditional density estimation in time series outliers detection, submitted to *Technometrics*, 1996.

14) Pellizzari P., Pizzi C., Linear local approximation for financial time series forecasting, *Rendiconti per gli Studi Economici Quantitativi*, University of Venice, 1997, available at URL:http:\\pluto.dma.unive.it\~paolop\rendi.ps.Z.

15) Scheinkman, LeBaron B., Nonlinear dynamics and stock returns, *J. of Business*, **62**, pp. 311-337, 1989.

16) Sneath P., Sokal R., *Numerical Taxonomy*, Freeman, San Francisco, 1973.

17) Zell A., et al. *SNNS User Manual Version 4.0*, Report No. 6, 1995.

Automated Mathematical Modelling for Financial Time Series Prediction Combining Fuzzy Logic and Fractal Theory

Oscar Castillo[*]   and   Patricia Melin[**]

[*] Department of Economics, UABC University, P.O. Box 4207
Chula Vista, CA 91909, USA
E-mail: ocastillo@mail.tij.cetys.mx

[**] School of Engineering, CETYS University, P.O. Box 4207
Chula Vista, CA 91909, USA
E-mail: emelin@mail.tij.cctys.mx

Abstract. We describe in this paper a new method to perform automated mathematical modelling for financial time series prediction using Fuzzy Logic Techniques, Dynamical Systems and Fractal Theory. The main idea in this paper is that using Fuzzy Logic techniques we can simulate and automate the reasoning process of the human experts in mathematical modelling for financial time series prediction. Our new method for automated modelling consists of three main parts: Time Series Analysis, Developing a set of Admissible Models and Selecting the "Best" model. Our method for Time Series Analysis consists in the use of the fractal dimension of a set of points as a measure of the geometrical complexity of the time series. Our method for developing a set of admissible dynamical systems models is based on the use of Fuzzy Logic techniques to simulate the decision process of the human experts in modelling financial problems. The selection of the "best" model for Financial Time Series Prediction (FTSP) is done using heuristics from the experts and statistical calculations. This new method can be implemented as a computer program and can be considered an intelligent system for automated mathematical modelling for FTSP.

Keywords: Fuzzy Logic, Finance, Economics, Fractal Theory

1. Introduction

We describe in this paper a new method to perform automated mathematical modelling for FTSP using Fuzzy Logic techniques, Dynamical Systems and Fractal theory. The idea of using Dynamical Systems Theory and Fractal Theory as alternative approaches for prediction can be justified if we consider that traditional statistical methods only have limited success in real world complex financial applications, and this is mainly because many financial problems show very complicated dynamics in time. Traditional statistical methods assume that the erratic behavior of a time series is mainly due to a external random error (that can not be explained). However, a Dynamical Systems approach, using non-linear mathematical models, can explain this erratic behavior because "chaos" is an intrinsic part of this type of models. It is a well known fact from Dynamical Systems, see Devaney [10], that even very simple non-linear mathematical models can exhibit the behavior known as "chaos" for certain parameter values, and therefore are good candidates to use as equations for prediction in complex financial situations. Fractal Theory, see Mandelbrot [13], also offers a way to explain the erratic behavior of a time series, but the method is geometrical in the sense that the fractal dimension is used to describe the complexity of the distribution of the data points.

We describe a prototype implementation of our new method for Automated Mathematical Modelling (AMM) as a computer program written in the PROLOG programming language. This computer program can be considered an intelligent system for the domain of FTSP because it uses Artificial Intelligence (AI) techniques to obtain the "best" mathematical model for a given financial problem. The use of AI techniques is to achieve the goal of automated modelling of financial problems by simulating (in the computer) how human experts in this domain obtain the "best" model for a given problem. Given a financial time series the intelligent system develops mathematical models based on the geometry of the data. The method for AMM consists of three main parts: Time Series Analysis, Developing a Set of Admissible Models and Selecting the Best Model. First, the computer program uses the fractal dimension to classify the components of the time series over a set of qualitative values, then the program uses this information to decide (using a fuzzy rule base) which dynamical models are the most appropriate for the data, and finally the program decides which model is the "best" one for prediction using heuristics and statistical calculations. In a prior prototype intelligent system developed by the authors [7] the method used didn't consider using the fractal dimension as a measure of classification and also didn't consider a fuzzy rule base for the simulation of the decision process.

The use of Fuzzy logic in financial applications has been now well recognized and many applications have been developed [8, 9]. In this case we came to the conclusion that the best way to convey the information of financial modelling problems was using fuzzy sets [1]. Also, we think that the best way to reason with uncertainty in this case is using Fuzzy Logic.

The intelligent system develops only the kind of mathematical models that are more likely to give a "good' prediction based on the knowledge that human experts have about this matter. This knowledge is contained in the knowledge base of the intelligent system, and is the main factor in limiting the number of models that the system explores. The intelligent system also has some generalized knowledge about the mathematical models that we expect to discover in the financial domain. This knowledge is expressed as families of parameterized mathematical models.

2. Description of the Financial Modelling Problem

Financial forecasting systems are necessarily limited by the data presented to them. After all, it is the data upon which they make decisions or estimates. Therefore, for any given market of interest, one must determine which data is relevant to the overall requirements. In the case of financial forecasting systems, such data is often derived from various time series, usually represented as prices and volumes, but also as open interest, dividends, etc. Sufficient "historical" data is needed for developing software tools intended to extract characteristics of previous market behavior in an effort to apply this knowledge to trading or investing in the "future" market [4].

Many financial time series are composed of relatively long-term trends plus some degree of periodic and noise-like components. Periodic components may include those related to seasonalities or limit-cycles in the data. The linearities and periodicities of the series can be removed, leaving the random or noise-like components. Such noise-like components may truly be random and be describable by a probability distribution function. On the other hand, they may only appear to be random and/or non-periodic, while actually representing an underlying deterministic non-linear dynamic time series. In fact, our hypothesis is that in many financial problems this is the case, and that "chaotic" time series are present in different scales and for different kinds of data. Some evidence on the correctness of this hypothesis has been found over the years by several researchers. Brock [3] has found evidence of complex dynamics in stock returns and strong evidence of "chaotic" behavior on T-bill returns. Eckmann et. al. [11] also found evidence of non-linear dynamics in time series of weekly stock returns. Castillo [5] also found evidence of non-linear dynamics in time series of world oil prices. Jurik [12] described a method potentially useful for determining the forecast horizon for T-Bonds using "Chaos Analysis". This evidence is the main reason why we are considering non-linear dynamical systems models in our space of mathematical models for the computer system.

With all of this in mind our goal in this paper is to show how AI techniques can be used to automate the process of discovering the best model for a financial problem. The human financial experts usually try several (in some cases many) mathematical models before they are satisfied with the "goodness" of one model. The experts use their knowledge about modelling financial problems to limit their search of models, in this way obtaining the "best" results as quickly as possible. The "goal" of our work is to capture this knowledge of modelling in a computer program, in this way obtaining a software tool capable of emulating intelligent behavior in this domain. In the remaining sections of this paper we describe the basic algorithm for discovering mathematical models, then the implementation of the algorithm as a computer program and finally the validation of the system using real financial data.

Our new method for solving the financial modelling problem is based on several novel ideas. We consider that the financial modelling problem can be divided in three main parts: Time Series Analysis, Selection of Appropriate Models and Selection of the Best Model. The first part of the problem consists in obtaining the time series components from the data. Our solution to this part of the problem is a new classification scheme based on the notion of the fractal dimension . This classification scheme is a one to one map between the fractal dimension of the data set and the qualitative values for the components of the time series. Once this part of the problem is solved, the second part consists in simulating an expert decision process that gives us the set of Mathematical Models appropriate for the geometry of the time series. This expert decision process is simulated using AI techniques and is the main part of the intelligent system. The third part of the problem consists in designing a method to compare all the models obtained in the second part, to obtain which one is the "best" model for predicting the time series. Our method to compare all the models has to consider statistical measures of goodness between non-linear dynamical systems and linear statistical models, to decide which model fits best the data set (time series).

3. Mathematical Modelling for Time Series Prediction

The problem of achieving automated mathematical modelling can be defined as follows:

Given: A data set (time series) with n data points, $D = \{d_1, d_2, ..., dm\}$ where $di \in R^n$, $i = 1,...,m$, and $n = 1, 2,...$.

Goal: From the data set D, discover automatically the "best" mathematical model for the time series.

This problem is not a simple one, because in theory there can be an infinite number of mathematical models that can be build for a given data set [16]. So the problem lies in knowing which models to try for a data set and then to select the "best" one. We can state the problem more formally in the following way:

Let M be the space of mathematical models defined for a given data set D. Let $MA = \{M_1, ..., Mq\}$ be the set of admissible models that are considered to be appropriate for the geometry of the data set D. The problem is to find automatically the "best" model Mb for time series prediction.

We consider mathematical statistical models of the following form:

$$Y = F(X) + \varepsilon (0,\sigma) \qquad (1)$$

where $\varepsilon (0,\sigma)$ represents a 0-mean Gaussian noise-process with standard deviation σ. F(X) is a polynomial equation in X, where the p predictor variables are in the vector $X = (X_1, X_2, ..., Xp)$.

We consider mathematical models as the following "dynamical systems":

$$dY/dt = F(Y) \qquad (2)$$

where Y is a vector of variables of the form (p is the number of variables):

$$Y = (Y_1, Y_2, ..., Yp)$$

and F(Y) is a non-linear function of Y. Other kind of mathematical models are the discrete "dynamical systems" of the following form:

$$Y_t = F(X) \tag{3}$$

where $X = (Y_{t-1}, Y_{t-2}, ..., Y_{t-p})$ and F(X) is a non-linear function of X. Note that in this case we have deterministic models expressed as differential or difference equations.

We consider the use of the fractal dimension as a mathematical model of the time series in the following form:

$$d = [\log(N)/\log(1/r)] \tag{4}$$

where d is the fractal dimension for an object of N parts, each scaled down by a ratio r. For an estimation of this dimension we can use the following equation:

$$N(r) = \beta[\ 1/r^d\ ] \tag{5}$$

where N(r) = number of boxes contained in a piece of object and r = size of the box.

We can obtain the box dimension of a geometrical object [13] counting the number of boxes for different sizes and performing a linear logarithmic regression on this data. For our particular case the geometrical object consists of the curve constructed using the set of points from the time series.

The models for the statistical methods can be linear as well as non-linear equations. We show below some sample statistical models [14] that the intelligent system explores:

a) linear regression: $\qquad\qquad\qquad Y_t = a + bt \qquad\qquad\qquad$ (6)

b) quadratic regression: $\qquad\qquad\quad Y_t = a + bt + ct^2 \qquad\qquad$ (7)

c) logarithmic regression: $\qquad\qquad \ln Y_t = a + b\ln t \qquad\qquad\quad$ (8)

d) semi-log regression: $\qquad\qquad\quad Y_t = a + b\ln t \qquad\qquad\quad$ (9)

e) first order autoregression: $\qquad\quad Y_t = a + bY_{t-1} \qquad\qquad\quad$ (10)

f) second order autoregression: $\qquad Y_t = a + bY_{t-1} + cY_{t-2} \qquad$ (11)

g) third order autoregression: $\qquad Y_t = a + bY_{t-1} + cY_{t-2} + dY_{t-3} \qquad$ (12)

The mathematical models for continuous dynamical systems can be one-dimensional, two-dimensional or three-dimensional. We show below some sample models [17] that the intelligent system explores:

a) logistic differential equation: $dY_1/dt = a\,Y_1(1 - Y_1)$ (13)

b) Lotka-Volterra two dimensional:

$$dY_1/dt = aY_1 - bY_1Y_2$$
$$dY_2/dt = bY_1Y_2 - cY_2$$
(14)

c) Lotka-Volterra three dimensional:

$$dY_1/dt = Y_1(1 - Y_1 - aY_2 - bY_3)$$
$$dY_2/dt = Y_2(1 - bY_1 - Y_2 - aY_3)$$
$$dY_3/dt = Y_3(1 - aY_1 - bY_2 - Y_3)$$
(15)

d) Lorenz three dimensional:

$$dY_1/dt = aY_2 - aY_1$$
$$dY_2/dt = -Y_1Y_3 + bY_1 - Y_2$$
$$dY_3/dt = Y_1Y_2 - cY_3$$
(16)

The mathematical models for discrete dynamical systems can also be one, two or three dimensional. We show below some sample models [17] that the intelligent system explores:

a) logistic difference equation: $Y_{t+1} = aY_t(1 - Y_t)$ (17)

b) logistic two dimensional difference equation:

$$Y_{t+1} = X_t$$
$$X_{t+1} = aX_t(1 - X_t)$$
(18)

c) Lotka-Volterra two dimensional:

$$Y_{t+1} = aY_t - bY_tX_t$$
$$X_{t+1} = bY_tX_t - cX_t$$
(19)

d) Henon map two dimensional:

$$Y_{t+1} = X_t$$
$$X_{t+1} = a - X_t^2 + bY_t$$
(20)

In all of the above mathematical models a, b and c are parameters that need to be estimated using the corresponding numerical methods. For example, for the regression models we can use the least squares method for parameter estimation, but for the differential equations we need to use a Gauss-Newton type method.

The algorithm for automated mathematical modelling for prediction is shown in Figure 1.

STEP 1 Read the data set D = {d_1, d_2, ..., dm}.
STEP 2 Time Series Analysis of the set D to find the components.
STEP 3 Find the set of Admissible models MA = {M_1, M_2, ..., Mq}, using the qualitative values of the time series components.
STEP 4 Find the "Best" mathematical model Mb from the set MA using the measures of "goodness" of each of the models from the set MA.

Figure 1. Algorithm for automated mathematical modelling

We call this algorithm IDIMM (for Intelligent Discovery of Mathematical Models) and is an integration of Artificial Intelligence techniques with Dynamical Systems Theory, Fractal Theory and Statistical Methods, to obtain mathematical models for prediction of time series in the financial domain.

In the following section we will show how this algorithm can be implemented to achieve the goal of AMM for FTSP.

4. Implementation of the Method for Automated Modelling

The implementation of the method for AMM as a computer program was done using the PROLOG programming language. The choice of PROLOG is because of its symbolic manipulation features and also because it is an excellent language for developing Prototypes [2]. The computer program was developed using an architecture very similar to that of an intelligent system (knowledge base, inference engine and user interface) with the addition of a numerical module for parameter estimation. We will focus our description of implementation details only to the knowledge base of the intelligent system. In the computer program, the knowledge base is the part that simulates the process of model discovery described by step 1 to 4 in the algorithm of the last section. Accordingly, the knowledge base consists of three Expert Modules: Time Series Analysis, Expert Selection and Best Model Selection. In the following lines we will describe briefly each of these modules.

4.1 Description of the Time Series Analysis Module

This module is the implementation of Step 2 of the algorithm and contains the knowledge necessary for time series analysis, i.e., the knowledge to extract from the data the time series components. Our method for time series analysis consist in the use of the fractal dimension of the set of points D as a measure of the geometrical complexity of the time series. We use the value of the fractal dimension to classify the time series components over a set of qualitative values. Our classification scheme was obtained by a combination of expert knowledge and mathematical modelling for several samples of data. To give an idea of this scheme we show in Table 1 some sample rules of this module.

Table 1. Sample rules for time series analysis

IF	THEN
Fractal_dimension(D)$\in(0.8,1.2)$	Trend = linear, Time_series = smooth
Fractal_dimension(D)$\in[1.2,1.5)$	Trend = non_linear, Time_series = cyclic
Fractal_dimension(D)$\in[1.5,1.8)$	Time_series = erratic
Fractal_dimension(D)$\in[1.2,1.4)$	Periodic_part = simple
Fractal_dimension(D)$\in[1.4,1.6)$	Periodic_part = regular
Fractal_dimension(D)$\in[1.6,1.7)$	Periodic_part = difficult
Fractal_dimension(D)$\in[1.7,1.8)$	Periodic_part = very_difficult
Fractal_dimension(D)>1.8	Periodic_part = chaotic

We performed several experiments with real data sets to decide on the classification needed for this "Time Series Analysis Module" and we found that for the moment classifying the periodic components in "simple", "regular", "difficult" and "chaotic" was sufficient. Also, we only classify the "trend" component in two kinds: "linear" and "non-linear". Of course, it is possible that we may need a better classification in the future, for a more accurate implementation of this Module, but now we are only showing how the method can be implemented.

In conclusion our method for time series analysis consists of a one to one mapping between the fractal dimension of the set D and the qualitative values of the time series components. This set of qualitative values for the components is the information needed as input for the "Expert Selection Module" (implementing Step 3 of the algorithm).

4.2 Description of the Expert Selection Module

This module is the implementation of the step 3 of the algorithm and contains the knowledge necessary to select the kind of mathematical models more appropriate for the type of data given, i.e., given the qualitative values of the time series components decide which models are more likely to give a good prediction. Our method for selecting the models consists of a set of fuzzy rules (heuristics) that simulates the human expert decision process of model selection. In our approach the qualitative values of the time series components are viewed as fuzzy sets (using the fractal dimension as a classification variable). We have membership functions for each of the qualitative values of the time series components. Also, the qualitative values of the "Type_Model" variable are considered as fuzzy sets and we have membership functions for each of this values. To give and idea of the way this Expert knowledge is structured, we show in Table 2 some sample rules of this module.

The rules in Table 2 show how this expert module selects the appropriate models for a given financial problem, using as information the dimensionality of the problem (number of variables, which are the "Dim" values in Table 2) and the qualitative values of the time series components. Each rule of this expert module contains a piece of knowledge about the problem of model selection.

We have to mention here that the role of Fuzzy Logic is very important for this application, because it enables the simulation of the expert reasoning process under uncertainty. We came to the conclusion that the rules, for deciding which models are appropriate for a given time series, can't be categorical because the complexity of financial modelling problems is very high. Since, it is well known that fuzzy logic has been applied successfully to problems in Finance and Economics [1], and our modelling problem required reasoning under uncertainty, we decided to use fuzzy logic techniques. In the following lines we will explain how the knowledge of the experts is contained in the fuzzy rules of this module with an example.

Suppose that a Time Series Analysis on a particular data set (time series) for a one-dimensional problem results in a Trend component valued as "non-linear" with a fractal dimension of 1.37, and a Periodic component valued as "simple" with the same fractal dimension, then the logical conclusion is that the "Logistic Map" is the best model for this problem with a 90% degree of certainty. Of course, other mathematical models have a lower degree of certainty for this particular example. The reasoning behind this rule is that a time series that exhibits a non-linear trend and simple periodicity can be modeled by a logistic map with relatively good accuracy.

Table 2. Sample fuzzy rules for model selection

IF			THEN
Dim	Trend	Periodic_part	Type_Model
one	non_linear	simple	logistic_differential_equation
two	non_linear	simple	lotka_volterra_differential_equation
three	non_linear	regular	lorenz_differential_equation
one	non_linear	simple	logistic_difference_equation
two	non_linear	regular	lotka_volterra_difference_equation

4.3 Description of the Best Model Selection Module

This module is the implementation of step 4 of the algorithm and contains the knowledge to select the "best" mathematical model for prediction, i.e., given the set of selected models generated by step 3, decide which model is the "best" one to predict the time series. Our method for selecting the "best" model consists of comparing the Sum of Squares of Errors (SSE) for all the models and selecting the one that minimizes SSE. This criteria has the advantage of been valid for all the types of models that we consider for the intelligent system (statistical models and non-linear dynamical systems models). The reasoning behind this criteria is that the value of the SSE is a measure of how well a particular mathematical model fits the data (time series) for a given problem. To give an idea of our method, we show in Table 3 a sample case where the set of selected models is:

$$MS=\{M_1, M_2, M_3, M_4, M_5, M_6\}$$

and the model with the lowest SSE is M_4.

Table 3. Method for best model selection using the SSE

MODEL	TYPE	SQUARES SUM	BEST MODEL
$M_1: Y = a_1 + b_1 t$	Statistical	SSE_1	no
$M_2: Y = a_2 + b_2 t + c_2 t^2$	Statistical	SSE_2	no
$M_3: \ln Y = \ln a_3 + b_3 \ln t$	Statistical	SSE_3	no
$M_4: \text{logistic\_differential\_eq}$	Dynamical	SSE_4	yes
$M_5: \text{lotka\_volterra\_difference\_eq}$	Dynamical	SSE_5	no
$M_6: \text{lorenz\_differential\_eq}$	Dynamical	SSE_6	no

In Table 3 the best model is M_4 because:

$$SSE_4 = \min \{SSE_1, SSE_2, SSE_3, SSE_4, SSE_5, SSE_6\}$$

The implementation of this minimization procedure is easy once the numerical values of the Sum of the Squares (SSE) are calculated by the numerical module.

We have to say here that this method for selecting the "best" model for a given problem can be improved in several ways to consider other factors that relate to this decision process. For example, one may like to consider the "type" of the model or the "simplicity" of the model as other factors of importance in the process of "best" model selection. In this case, a set of if-then rules would be required to make the decision and the module would be then considered a real "knowledge base". For the moment, we have only a method for "best" model selection that uses statistical measures and "knowledge" about the process of mathematical modelling.

5. Validation of the Intelligent System and Experimental Results

The process of validation for the prototype intelligent system consists of comparing the results of the computer program against the known results by the human experts, for a set of financial problems. The results of this validation are encouraging, the computer program has a 90% accuracy with respect to the human experts in this domain. However, there is still much work to be done, because we are only considering a relatively small variety of mathematical models for this kind of financial problems.

We have to say that the results of the validation of the intelligent system can be considered good evidence that the algorithms presented in this paper are "sound" and that our work as a whole can be considered a promising line of future research in the area of Mathematical Modelling using AI techniques.

We are now going to show some of the results of the validation process performed on the intelligent system. In Table 4 we show the comparison between the Mathematical models selected by the computer program and the Models given by the human experts for a set of examples from the areas of Finance and Economics. In this table, AR (2) means an autorregresive second order statistical model and DS (2) means a Dynamical Systems difference equation (model) of second order.

Table 4. Sample validation of the system

Problem (time series)	Model by the System	Model by the Experts	Result
Prices Color Vision Co.	AR (2) linear	AR (2) linear	equal
Sales of Electrical Co.	AR (2) linear	AR (2) linear	equal
World Oil prices 84-89	DS (2) non-linear	DS (2) non-linear	equal
Mexico's real exchange rate 84-94	AR (2) linear	AR (2) linear	equal
Mexico's GNP 82-90	DS (2) non-linear	AR (2) linear	not equal

From the results of the validation we can see that the intelligent system predicts very well the right model for many problems in Finance and Economics.

However, the are still some cases where the system runs into trouble, i.e., the problem for Mexico's GNP where the computer program predicts a Non-linear (Dynamical System) model and the human experts predict an Autorregresive model. The reason why this happens is that both of these models are very similar and the computer program can't distinguish very well, for this case, the level of complexity of the problem. We still have to do some work in the knowledge base of the intelligent system to refine the process of selection of the mathematical models.

6. Comparison with Related Work

There has been some work recently in the area of numerical law discovery, but much of the research in Machine Learning is in other areas such as induction [18]. We think that this is mainly because "discovery" is a more difficult kind of "learning". However, we can state that automated mathematical modelling is very important for many domains of application for obvious reasons. For example in the engineering and financial domains is critical to obtain mathematical models for the problems, to be able to understand them and also to be able to predict their future behavior. This is why we consider that more research in this area is very important.

Similar work with respect to Machine Learning can be found in a paper by Moulet [15], however the approach to model discovery is different to ours (this can be seen from the heuristic method by Moulet). Also in a paper by Rao and Lu [16] we can see a method for model discovery for engineering domains, but also with a different approach to ours (his approach is similar to "clustering"). Also, there is another very important difference with other authors, in the kind of mathematical models that we are considering for our intelligent system. We are considering non-linear mathematical models from the theory of Dynamical Systems and not only linear regression models like other authors. This is because non-linear dynamical models offer the possibility of explaining the erratic behavior of financial time series with "chaos theory" [10]. In this paper we have successfully generalized our previous work on this matter [6, 7], by considering this type of non-linear models.

7. Conclusions

We described in this paper a new method to perform automated mathematical modelling for financial time series prediction. Also, we described the implementation of this new method as a prototype intelligent system for the domain of financial problems. We have tested this computer program with real financial data with encouraging results. In this paper we have successfully generalized our previous work on this matter [6] by using non-linear dynamical systems models. Also, we have improved our work [7] by using the fractal dimension for time series analysis and by using Fuzzy Logic techniques for the simulation of the expert reasoning process [8]. The importance of our work can be measured if we consider that accurate prediction is critical in the areas of Finance,

Economics, Management and Accounting. We think that our work can help in making more easy the job of mathematical modelling and prediction in all of these areas.

The implementation of our new method for AMM can be improved in several ways. First of all, the Time Series Analysis Module can be improved by designing a better classification scheme using the fractal dimension (with this making it more accurate). Second of all, in the Expert Selection Module we can increase the number of different mathematical models that can be used for the financial domain, in this way making the intelligent system capable of solving a bigger variety of problems. Also, in the Module for Selection of the Best Model, we can refine our selection method by using heuristics related to other factors that can be considered important for the decision process. Finally, we think that other AI techniques can be tested for the implementation of our method for AMM with the idea of possibly improving efficiency. We are planning to follow this lines of research in the near future.

Acknowledgments

The authors would like to thank the Research Grant Committee of UABC University for supporting this project, and the School of Engineering of CETYS University for providing the Computing facilities needed for this research work.

References

[1] Badiru, A.B. (1992). "Expert Systems Applications in Engineering and Manufacturing", Prentice-Hall.

[2] Bratko, I. (1990). "Prolog Programming for Artificial Intelligence", Addison Wesley.

[3] Brock, W.A., (1988). "NonLinearity and Complex Dynamics in Economics and Finance", The Economy as an Evolving Complex System, Edited by Anderson, P.W., Arrow, K.J., Pines, D, Addisson Wesley, 5, pp. 77-97.

[4] Caldwell, R.B. (1994). "Design of Neural Network-based Financial Forecasting Systems: Data Selection and Data Processing", Neurovest Journal, 2 (5), pp. 12-20.

[5] Castillo, O. (1991). "Una Introducción al Estudio del Caos en Sistemas Dinámicos. Su Aplicación en Economía Matemática", Cuadernos de Economía, No.4, Editorial UABC.

[6] Castillo, O. and P. Melin (1994). "An Intelligent System for Discovering Mathematical Models for financial time Series Prediction", Proceedings of the IEEE Region 10's Ninth Annual International Conference, IEEE Computer Society of Singapore, pp. 217-221.

[7] Castillo, O. and P. Melin (1995). "An Intelligent System for Financial time Series Prediction Combining Dynamical Systems Theory, Fractal Theory and

Statistical methods", Proceedings of the IEEE/IAFE 1995 Conference on Computational Intelligence for Financial Engineering (CIFER), pp. 151-155.

[8] Castillo, O. and P. Melin (1996). "Automated Mathematical Modelling for Financial Time Series Prediction using Fuzzy Logic, Dynamical Systems and Fractal Theory", Proceedings of the IEEE/IAFE 1996 Conference on Computational Intelligence for Financial Engineering (CIFER), pp. 120-126.

[9] Derry, J. (1994). " A Fuzzy Expert System and Market Psychology", NeuroVest Journal, Vol. 2, No. 1, pp. 20-22.

[10] Devaney, R. (1989). "An Introduction to Chaotic Dynamical Systems", Addison Wesley Publishing Company.

[11] Eckmann, J.P.,Kamphorst, S.O., Ruelle D. and Scheinkman J., (1988). "Lyapunov Exponents for Stock Returns", The Economy as an Evolving Complex System, Edited by Anderson, P.W., Arrow, K.J., Pines, D, Addisson Wesley, 5, pp. 301-304.

[12] Jurik, M., (1994). "Estimating Optimal Forecast Distance using Chaos Analysis", Neurovest Journal, 2(1), pp. 14-19.

[13] Mandelbrot, B. (1983). "The Fractal Geometry of Nature", W. H. Freeman and Company.

[14] Mendenhall, W. and J.E. Reinmuth (1981). "Statistics for management and Economics", Wadsworth International.

[15] Moulet, M. (1992). "A symbolic Algorithm for Computing Coefficients Accuracy in Regression", Proceedings of the Ninth International Workshop on Machine Learning, Morgan Kauffman Publishers, pp. 332-337.

[16] Rao, R. B. and S. Lu (1993). "An Knowledge-Based Equation Discovery System for engineering Domains, IEEE Expert, pp. 37-42.

[17] Rasband, S. (1990). "Chaotic Dynamics of Non-Linear Systems", John Wiley & Sons.

[18] Sleeman, D. and Edwards P. (1992). Proceedings of the Ninth International Workshop on Machine Learning, Morgan Kauffman Publishers.

A 2-Stage Artificial Neural Network Predictor with Application to Financial Time Series[*]

PierLuigi Belcaro[1] and Marco Corazza[2]

[1] Department of Applied Mathematics and Computer Science, University *Ca' Foscari* of Venice, Dorsoduro 3825/E, 30123 Venice, ITALY - E-Mail: belcaro@unive.it
[2] Department of Applied Mathematics and Computer Science, University *Ca' Foscari* of Venice, Dorsoduro 3825/E, 30123 Venice, ITALY - E-Mail: corazza@unive.it
Department of Economics, *Loyola* University of Chicago, 820 North Michigan Avenue, Chicago, ILLINOIS (U.S.A.) 60611 - E-mail: mcorazz@wpo.it.luc.edu

Abstract. Artificial Neural Networks are quantitative non-parametric tools able to model financial time series in which stochastic and, possibly, non-linear underlying processes may be supposed.

The purpose of this work is to develop a neural network forecasting system by using a 2-stage approach. In the first stage some networks are realized in order to consider different forecasting model specifications, each being referred to a particular forecasting scenario. In the second stage the different outputs (predictions) coming from each first stage forecasting model are suitably combined to generate a final output, whose quality level is expected to be higher.

Different time series are used and the corresponding results critically analyzed and compared.

Keywords. Artificial neural network, multi-layer perceptron, forecasting scenario, financial time series.

1 Introduction

In literature there is a growing interest about the predictability of the financial stock markets. The classical hypothesis according to which variations of stock prices are independently log-normally distributed, that is

$$r(t + \Delta t) = \ln[P(t + \Delta t)] - \ln[P(t)] \sim N(\mu \Delta t, \sigma^2 \Delta t), \ \Delta t > 0, \tag{1.1}$$

has not been settled in an increasing number of empirical works. In particular, several studies show the inadequacy of such hypothesis because the empirical distributions of the stock price logarithmic variations are generally characterized by many outliers, non-stationarity in the variance level and asymmetry (see, for example [Mandelbrot, 1963], [Fielitz *et al.*, 1972a], [Fielitz *et al.*, 1972b], [Blattberg *et al.*, 1974], [Hsu *et*

---

[*] Although the general ideas on which this work is based have been jointly developed by the two authors, sections 1, 5, 6 and 7 have been written by both the authors and sections 2, 3, 4 and data computation have been realized by Marco Corazza.

al., 1974], [Simkowitz *et al.*, 1980] and [Bollerslev, 1987]) and by short-term and long-term dependence (see, for example [Greene *et al.*, 1977], [Helms *et al.*, 1984], [Lo, 1991], [Peters, 1991], [Ding *et al.*, 1993] [Peters, 1994], [Corazza *et al.*, 1996] and [Corazza, 1996]).

Because of that, some authors conjecture that such stock price logarithmic variations could be, further than stochastic, highly non-linearly dependent (see, for example [Scheinkman *et al.*, 1989], [Hinich *et al.*, 1989], [Hsieh, 1989], [Hsieh, 1991], [Peters, 1991], [Booth *et al.*, 1992], [Malliaris *et al.*, 1992], [Peters, 1994] and [Campbell *et al.*, 1997]). Notice that, in general, few *a priori* assumptions can be made about the form of such conjectured highly non-linear dependence and, therefore, a significant role in financial time series forecasting can be played by the class of both non-linear and non-parametric models. In particular, in recent works some authors analyze different stock markets by using non-linear and non-parametric models coming from the soft Artificial Intelligence (sAI) approach, the so called (supervised feedforward) Multy-Layer Perceptron (MLP) Artificial Neural Networks (ANNs), finding evidence of predictability (see, for example [Azoff, 1994], [Baestaens *et al.*, 1994], [Refenes, 1995], [Belcaro *et al.*, 1996], [Gately, 1996] and [Turban *et al.*, 1996]).

Generally, because of such few *a priori* assumptions that can be made in a financial context, one must consider different forecasting model specifications, each being referred to a particular forecasting scenario[1]. Consequently, one must face in a whole measure the following "difficulties":

(1.a) managing the (relative) shortage of data due to the use of several scenarios;

(1.b) ordering the adopted scenarios on the basis of their capability to explain the analyzed (financial) phenomenon;

(1.c) extracting from each adopted scenario its (implicit) information about the analyzed phenomenon in order to combine all such information in a new scenario more explicative than the previous ones.

The purpose of this work consists in developing a 2-stage MLP ANN forecasting system able to effectively manage the "difficulties" listed above and, consequently, to improve the "quality" of the predictions which could be obtained by using a "classical" 1-stage approach. In particular, we analyze two different time series by using such a forecasting system: a benchmark time series which is generated by the deterministic chaotic[2] McKey-Glass map and a financial time series consisting of the logarithmic daily returns of the Italian Polyannual Treasury Bond (or BTP) Future.

The rest of this paper is structured as follows. In section 2 we synthetically introduce the definitions and the tools used in the successive sections; in section 3 we detail the approach to the 2-stage MLP ANN predictor; in section 4 we describe the data sets to be used in the applications; in section 5 we synthetically illustrate the framework adopted to evaluate the results obtained in the analysis; in section 6 we report the results of the implemented applications and, finally, in section 7 we set forth some concluding remarks.

---

[1] The sense in which "forecasting scenario" is meant here is defined in section 2.

[2] The sense in which "deterministic chaos" is meant here is explained in section 4.

2 Preliminary Aspects: Definitions and Tools

In this section we synthetically introduce definitions and tools that are required to develop our 2-stage MLP ANN forecasting methodology.

Firstly, because of its significant role played in this work, we set the definitions below, related to the sense in which "forecasting scenario" is meant in the following sections.

Definition 2.1 *Let* $x_i(t)$ *and* $y_j(t)$, *with* $i = 1,\ldots,I$, $I \in N_0$, $j = 1,\ldots,J$ *and* $J \in N_0$, *be* $I + J$ *real variables at time* t *and let* $x(t) = (x_i(t - N_i\Delta),\ldots,x_i(t); i = 1,\ldots,I)$ *and* $y(t) = (y_j(t + \Delta),\ldots,y_j(t + M_j\Delta); j = 1,\ldots,J)$, *with* $N_1,\ldots,N_I,M_1,\ldots,M_J \in N_0$ *and* $\Delta \in R_0^+$, *be two real vectors; let* $e_1(t)$, *with* $1 = 1,\ldots,L$ *and* $L \in N$ *be* L *random variables at time* t *which can be, or not, independently and identically distributed and let* $e(t) = (e_1(t); 1 = 1,\ldots,L)$ *be a real random vector; let* p_k, *with* $k = 1,\ldots,K$ *and* $K \in N_0$ *be* K *real parameters and let* $p = (p_k; k = 1,\ldots,K)$ *be a real vector; let* $f(,;) \subseteq R^N \times R^L \times R^K \to R^M$, *where* $N = I + \sum_{i=1}^I N_i$ *and* $M = \sum_{j=1}^J M_j$ *be a function such that* $y = f(x(t),y(t);p)$.

One defines (t) *-forecasting scenario for the phenomenon* $y(t)$ *the set* $FS_{y(t)} = \{x(t),e(t),p,f(\cdot,;\cdot)\}$.

Notice that this definition includes both the absence of random variables ($L = 0$ and, consequently, $e(t) = \varnothing$) and their presence ($L \neq 0$).

Definition 2.2 *Let* $y(\tau)$, *with* $\tau = t,\ldots,t + T\Delta$ *and* $T \in N_0$, *be* $(T\Delta - t)/\Delta$ *phenomena and let* $y(t, t + T\Delta) = (y(\tau); \tau = t,\ldots,t + T\Delta)$ *be a real matrix.*

One defines $(t, t + T\Delta)$ *-forecasting scenario for the matrix* $y(t, t + T\Delta)$ *of phenomenona the vector of set* $FS_{y(t,t+T\Delta)} = \{FS_{y(\tau)}; \tau = t,\ldots,t + T\Delta\}$.

From a qualitative point of view, the **Definition 2.1** states that one can forecast[3] J variables which describe a (financial) phenomenon, each of them for a pre-fixed number of steps-ahead, by using I variables which "explain" the analyzed phenomenon, each of them for a pre-fixed number of lagged values, then L random variables which represent the error terms, one previously defined forecasting model $f(\cdot,;\cdot)$ and K properly pre-determined parameters. In particular, notice that such a definition includes both the univariate approach ($I = 1$ and $J = 1$) and the multivariate one ($I \neq 1$ or $J \neq 1$). Furthermore, the **Definition 2.2** states that one can use the same previously defined forecasting model and the same properly pre-determined parameters in order to predict the considered (financial) phenomenon in successive time istants.

Of course, from an operative point of view, one must define both the functional

---

[3] Actually, it does not matter here if in a bad or (better) in a good way.

form of the forecasting model and, consequently, the methodology by which to determine the K parameters. In particular, in this work, in order to develop the 2-stage ANN predictor, we adopt the (supervised feedforward) MLPs as forecasting models. Because of that, secondly, we simply introduce the class of such ANN models.

In general, such ANN models show the same structure of direct arch weighted graphs whose nodes are arranged in one (so-called) input layer (N nodes, with $N \in N_0$), O (so-called) hidden layers, with $O \in N_0$, (respectively, $H_1, ..., H_O$, with $H_1, ..., H_O \in N_0$) and one (so-called) output layer (M nodes, with $M \in N_0$). Each of these layers is fully connected with the adjacent ones (if any) without inner (that is, intra-layer) connections[4] (see, for more details [Hecht-Nielsen, 1990], [Hertz et al., 1994] and [Campbell et al., 1997]). Notice that in such an approach the role of the variables $x_i(t)$, with $i = 1,...,I$, and $y_j(t)$, $j = 1,...,J$, are, respectively, played by the input and the output nodes. In the remainder of this work, we indicate these ANN models by the notation

$$MLP(N + 1; H_1 + 1,..., H_O + 1; M) \tag{2.1}$$

where +1 indicates the presence, in the considered layer, of an additional node due to "technical reasons". Each of these nodes, except the input ones, is endowed with local memory and able to perform data computation. In fact, each non-input node is characterized by two functions. The first one determines the node input by computing a weighted "aggregation" of the values incoming in the node itself and the second one, the so-called activation, or transfer, function, determines the node output by properly trasforming such a previously determined node input (see again, for more details [Hecht-Nielsen, 1990], [Hertz et al., 1994] and [Campbell et al., 1997]). The "aggregation" function and the activation one which are adopted in this work are, respectively, the classical weighted summation and the logistic ones.

Once the functional form of the forecasting model is defined, one can choose a consequent methodology by which to determine the (free) parameters of the model itself, that is, in such an ANN approach, the so-called weights[5]. The "optimal" values of such weights are determined by using an iterative estimation procedure, the so-called training (or learning) algorithm which, in this work, is based on the Levenberg-Marquardt optimization method (see, for more details [Press et al., 1986]) instead of on the "classical" Error Back Propagation one. This estimation procedure, by using the input-output vectors $(x(p), y(p); p = 1,...,P)$, with $P \in N_0$, belonging to a pre-determined data set D, iteratively updates the MLP model weights in order to reach the (absolute) minimum of the following cost function, the well known Mean Square Error (MSE),

---

[4] Because of that, the values of the input nodes are feedforwardly propagated from the input layer through the hidden ones to the output layer.

[5] Notice that, without loss of generality, in this work the threshold parameters, the so-called biases, are considered as weights associated to a (fictitious) arch incoming in the node, arch propagating a costant signal equal to -1.

$$\text{MSE} = \frac{1}{P}\sum_{p=1}^{P}\left(\left\|y(p) - y^*(p)\right\|\right)^2 \qquad (2.3)$$

where $\|\cdot\|$ indicates the Euclidean norm, $y(p)$ and $y^*(p)$, with $p = 1,\dots,P$, are, respectively, the observed and the forecasted phenomena.

Notice that in such a training algorithm a crucial role is played by the so-called stop-learning criterion. In particular, in order to avoid the biasing possibility that this algorithm can detect some unexisting relationships between the "input" sub-vector $x(p)$ and the corresponding "output" one $y(p)$, with $p = 1,\dots,P$, we adopt a stop-learning criterion based on the so-called Concurrent Descent Methodology (CDM). In this approach, firstly, the data set D is suitably split up into two not-overlapping subsets, the training set D_T and the validation one D_V. Secondly, the training algorithm is iterated on the training subset as long as the (possibly absolute) minimum of the pre-fixed cost function on the validation subset is reached.

3 The 2-Stage MLP ANN Approach

In this section we detail the approach to the 2-stage MLP ANN forecasting system. In particular, firstly, we describe such a 2-stage approach and, secondly, we give some remarks about it.

In the first stage, we consider a pre-fixed number of Q $(t, t + T\Delta)$-forecasting scenarios $FS_{q,y(t,t+T\Delta)}$, with $Q \in N_0$, $T \in N$ and $q = 1,\dots,Q$, for the same pre-determined (financial) phenomenon $y(t, t + T\Delta)$. Of course, each of such Q $(t, t + T\Delta)$-forecasting scenarios is characterized by different "explanatory" variables $x_{q,i}(\cdot)$, with $q = 1,\dots,Q$ and $i = 1,\dots,I$, different ANN forecasting models $MLP_q(N_q + 1; H_{q,1} + 1,\dots,H_{q,O_q} + 1; M_q)$, with $q = 1,\dots,Q$, and different vectors of parameters that is, weights) p_q, with $q = 1,\dots,Q$. Notice that also each of the Q vectors of parameters is determined by using Q different data sets $D_q = (x_q(p), y(p); p = 1,\dots,P)$, with $q = 1,\dots,Q$, being each of them properly split up into a training set $D_{q,T}$ and a validation set $D_{q,V}$, with $q = 1,\dots,Q$.

For each of such Q "forecasting frameworks" we firstly determine the corresponding predictions for the (financial) phenomenon (that is, $y_q^*(t, t + T\Delta)$, with $q = 1,\dots,Q$) and, secondly, the (different) predictions for all the (known) "output" sub-vector belonging to the corresponding validation data sets (that is, $y_q^*(p)$, with $q = 1,\dots,Q$ and $p = 1,\dots,P_V$). In particular, each of these Q validation set must be referred to the same "output" sub-vectors (that is, $y_q(p) = y(p)$, with $p = 1,\dots,P_V$).

In the second stage, we consider a new $(t, t + T\Delta)$-forecasting scenario $FS_{II,y(t,t+T\Delta)}$ for the (financial) phenomenon $y(t, t + T\Delta)$ in which the Q previously obtained (different) predictions play, this time, the role of "explanatory" variables. In particular, the vector of parameters of this latter "forecasting framework" is determined by using a data set whose "input" sub-vectors are formed by the Q (different) predictions of the corresponding (known) "output" sub-vector coming from each of the 1st-stage scenarios.

This 2-stage ANN MLP forecasting methodology can be summarized as follows:

Remark *1st STAGE.*
Step 1 *Consider a (financial) phenomenon* $y(t, t + T\Delta)$.

Step 2 *Consider* Q *data sets* $D_q = (x_q(p), y(p); p = 1, ..., P)$, *with* $q = 1, ..., Q$ *and* $P < t - \Delta$, *and suitably split up each of them in the corresponding training set* $D_{q,T}$ *and validation set* $D_{q,V}$.

Step 3 *Determine* Q $(t, t + T\Delta)$ *-forecasting scenarios by properly defining the corresponding* Q *ANN forecasting models* $MLP_q(N_q + 1; H_{q,1} + 1, ..., H_{q,O_q} + 1; M_q)$, *with* $q = 1, ..., Q$, *and by suitably estimating the corresponding* Q *vectors of weights* p_q, *with* $q = 1, ..., Q$.

Step 4 *Determine, for each of these* Q *"forecasting structures", the corresponding predictions* $y_q^*(t, t + T\Delta)$, *with* $q = 1, ..., Q$, *of the (financial) phenomenon.*

Step 5 *Determine, for each of these* Q *"forecasting structures", the predictions* $y_q^*(p)$, *with* $q = 1, ..., Q$ *and* $p = 1, ..., P$, *for all the "output" sub-vectors of the corresponding validation data sets.*

Remark *2nd STAGE.*
Step 6 *Consider a data set* $D_{II} = ((x_q(p); q = 1, ..., Q), y(p); p = 1, ..., P)$ *and split it up into a training set* $D_{II,T}$ *and a validation set* $D_{II,V}$.

Step 7 *Determine the* 2nd *-stage* $(t, t + T\Delta)$ *-forecasting scenario by properly defining the corresponding ANN forecasting model* $MLP_{II}(N_{II} + 1; H_{II,1} + 1, ..., H_{II,O} + 1; M_{II})$ *and by suitably estimating the corresponding vector of weights* p_{II}.

Step 8 *Determine, by using such a* 2nd *-stage* $(t, t + T\Delta)$ *-forecasting scenario, the* 2nd *-stage predictions* $y_{II}^*(t, t + T\Delta)$ *of the (financial) phenomenon.*

With regard to this 2 -stage ANN MLP forecasting methodology, one can notice the following.

In general, in providing to an ANN model some really "explanatory" or "generalizing" capability, a crucial role is played by the correct "sizing" of the model itself, that is by the choice of the proper number of layers and the proper number of nodes within. In particular, in order to size in such a proper way an ANN model, there exist both empirical and theoretical results giving lower bounds for the ratio $N_T / N \cdot H_1 \cdot ... \cdot N_O \cdot M$, where N_T is the cardinality of the training data set D_T (see, for more details [Baum et al., 1989], the references therein and [Azoff, 1994]). Because of that, the functional forms of a really "explanatory" ANN models is conditioned on the number of the "input-output" training vectors available.

Of course, from this particular standpoint, to analyze the considered (financial) phenomenon by adopting a "classical" 1-stage approach characterized by an ANN forecasting model $\text{MLP}(1 + \sum_{q=1}^{Q} N_q; H_1 + 1, \ldots, H_O + 1; M)$ could request a larger number of such "input-output" training vectors than by using the proposed 2-stage one. In particular, it is possible to (simply) prove that the 2-stage approach requests a lower or equal number of "input-output" training vectors than the "classical" 1-stage one if and only if

$$\frac{\left(1 + \sum_{q=1}^{Q} N_q\right)H_1 + \sum_{o=1}^{O-1}(H_o + 1)H_{o+1} + (H_O + 1)M}{\max_{1 \leq q \leq Q}\left\{(N_q + 1)H_{q,1} + \sum_{o=1}^{O_q - 1}(H_{q,o} + 1)H_{q,o+1} + (H_{q,O_q} + 1)M\right\}} \geq 1. \quad (3.1)$$

Secondly, let us recall that because of the few *a priori* assumptions that can be made in a financial context, in the first stage, *ex ante*, one should consider all the "reasonably explanatory" forecasting scenarios for the analyzed phenomenon and, *ex post*, one should must face the "difficulty" of ordering the implemented forecasting scenarios on the basis of their capability to (implicitly) explain such an analyzed (financial) phenomenon.

In order to cope with the "difficulty" above we propose an ordering criterion based on the following *ad hoc* developed index

$$\text{IEC}_q = 100\left(1 - \frac{\text{MSE}_q}{\max_{1 \leq q \leq Q}\{\text{MSE}_q\}}\right) \in [0, 100], \quad q = 1, \ldots, Q, \quad (3.2)$$

where IEC_q, with $q = 1, \ldots, Q$, is the "measure" of the "(implicit) explanatory capability" of the qth $(t, t + T\Delta)$-forecasting scenario and MSE_q, with $q = 1, \ldots, Q$, is the value reached at the "optimal" training iteration by the MSE cost function associated to the MLP forecasting model in the qth $(t, t + T\Delta)$-forecasting scenario.

On the basis of this criterion the "(implicit) explanatory capability" of each of the Q $(t, t + T\Delta)$-forecasting scenarios increases/decreases as IEC_q approaches $0/100$. Notice that the value assumed by the "(implicit) explanatory capability" index associated to the $(t, t + T\Delta)$-forecasting scenario which is characterized by the highest MSE is equal to 0. Of course, this occurrence simply means that such a $(t, t + T\Delta)$-forecasting scenario shows, among the Q ones introduced, the lowest "(implicit) explanatory capability".

4 Data and Forecasting Scenarios

In this section we describe the data and the forecasting scenarios that are utilized in the applications. In particular, firstly, we consider the benchmark time series and, secondly, we consider the financial time series.

The benchmark time series is generated by using the nonlinear deterministic

McKey-Glass map

$$z(t+1) - \alpha z(t) + \beta \frac{z(t-\tau)}{1+z^{\gamma}(t-\tau)}. \tag{4.1}$$

Such a map, for particular values of its parameters, that is $\alpha = -0.4$, $\beta = -5$, $\gamma = 10$ and $\tau = 5$, is characterized by a so-called (deterministic) chaotic behaviour (see, for more details [McKey *et al.*, 19..]). In correspondence of these parameter values, the MacKey-Glass map generates a so difficultly predictable time series to be mistaken for a purely random one. Because of it, this map is a highly diffused benchmark time series generator.

In order to analyze this first time series, we consider the following three 1st- stage data sets ($Q_B = 3$):

$$D_{B;1} = \left(z(t-p), z(t+1-p); \ p = 1,\ldots,506 \right), \tag{4.2.1}$$

$$D_{B;2} = \left(z(t-3-p), z(t+1-p); \ p = 1,\ldots,506 \right) \text{ and} \tag{4.2.2}$$

$$D_{B;3} = \left(z(t-5-p), z(t+1-p); \ p = 1,\ldots,506 \right) \tag{4.2.3}$$

($I_{B;1} = I_{B;2} = I_{B;3} = 1$, $\qquad J_B = 1$, $\qquad x_{B;1}(t) = (z(t-p); \ p = 1,\ldots,506)$, $x_{B;2}(t) = (z(t-3-p); \ p = 1,\ldots,506)$, $\quad x_{B;3}(t) = (z(t-5-p); \ p = 1,\ldots,506)$ and $P_B = 506$), and we report the following (corresponding) three 1st- stage $(t, t+15)$ - forecasting scenarios ($T_B = 15$ and $\Delta_B = 1$):

$$FS_{B;i,z(t,t+15)} = FS_{B;i} = \left\{ z_{B;i}(t), e_{B;i}(t), p_{B;i}, MLP_{B;i}(1+1;3+1;1) \right\},$$
$$i = 1,2,3 \tag{4.3.i}$$

($N_{B;1} = N_{B;2} = N_{B;3} = 1$, $H_{B;1,O_1} = H_{B;2,O_2} = H_{B;3,O_3} = 3$ and $M_B = 1$).

Notice that only the first and the third one among the three $(t, t+15)$ -forecasting scenarios described above are characterized by a sub-set of the really "explanatory" variable set (respectively, the 1 step-lagged variable set and the 5 step-lagged variable set). Because of that, only or, at least, mainly these "forecasting frameworks" are expected to explain (at a some degree) the analyzed phenomenon.

Moreover, notice that, being *a priori* known the analytical properties of the underlying generator process (the McKey-Glass map), the definition of the functional forms of the ANN forecasting models involved are based on the following A. N. Kolmogorov's theorem (see, for more details [Hecht-Nielsen, 1990] and [Belcaro, Canestrelli and Corazza, 1997]).

Theorem 4.1 *Let* $x \in [0,1]^N$ *and* $y \in R^M$ *be two vectors and let* $f:[0,1]^N \rightarrow R^M$ *be a continuos function such that* $y = f(x)$. *Then* $f(\cdot)$ *can be implemented exactly by a* 3 *-layer feedforward ANN having* N *fanout processing elements in the first (* x *input) layer,* $2N+1$ *processing elements in the middle layer and* M *processing elements in the top (* y *output) layer.*

The financial time series consist of the logarithmic daily returns of the Italian Polyannual Treasury Bond (or BTP)

$$r(t+1) = \ln[P(t+1)] - \ln[P(t)].$$ (4.4)

In order to analyze this second time series, we consider the following two 1st- stage data sets ($Q = 2$):

$$D_{F;1} = \left(\left(r(t+4-p), \ldots, r(t-p) \right), r(t+1-p); \ p = 1, \ldots, 506 \right) \text{ and} \quad (4.5.1)$$

$$D_{F;2} = \left(\left(v(t+4-p), \ldots, v(t-p) \right), r(t+1-p); \ p = 1, \ldots, 506 \right) \quad (4.5.2)$$

where $v(\cdot)$ is the daily traded volume[6] ($I_{F;1} = I_{F;2} = 1$, $J_F = 1$, , $M_F = 1$, $x_{F;1} = (r(t+4-p), \ldots, r(t-p))$, $x_{F;2} = (v(t+4-p), \ldots, v(t-p))$ and $P_F = 506$), and we consider the following (corresponding) two 1st- stage $(t, t+15)$ -forecasting scenarios ($T_F = 15$ and $\Delta_F = 1$):

$$FS_{F;i,r(t,t+15)} = FS_{F;i} - \left\{ x_{F;i}(t), e(t)_{F;i}, p_{F;i}, MLP_{F;i}(5+1;3+1;1) \right\},$$
$$i = 1,2$$ (4.6.i)

($H_{F;1,O_1} = H_{F;2,O_2} = 3$ and $M = 1$). In particular, with regard to these phenomenon predictions we consider the sample time period from November 25, 1996 to December 13, 1996.

Notice that the definitions of the functional forms of the ANN forecasting models are based on a one-hidden-layer "bottleneck" architectural structure because of its strength in facing several financial forecasting problems (see, for more details [Refenes, 1995] and [Belcaro et al., 1996]).

5 Evaluating Framework

In this section we synthetically illustrate the framework we use to evaluate the results obtained in both applications. A preliminary question we must face in order to determine how effectively the phenomenon predictions "match" the corresponding observed values, is to set up a proper evaluating framework. In order to define that, we consider the dynamic behaviour of each different index from a set of both statistical and operative ones, each index being referred to a particular performance aspect.

Firstly, we consider a statistical index giving a measure of the "distance" between the phenomenon predictions and the corresponding observed values, the Mean Absolute Percentage Error (MAPE), whose analytical definition is the following one

---

[6] The choice of this second "explanatory" variable set is due to its operative utilization in several trading rules (see, for example [Brock et al.,]).

$$MAPE(T) = \frac{1}{T}\sum_{\tau=1}^{T}\left|\frac{y_1(t+\tau)-y_1^*(t+\tau)}{y_1(t+\tau)}\right| \in [0,+\infty) , \quad T = 1,\dots,15 \qquad (5.1)$$

We adopt an absolute value based error measure (instead of a "classical" root square based one) because of its wide dffusion in operative financial evaluations. Moreover, we state it in a percentage form in order to ensure the comparability among its values coming from different time series characterized by different dimentional scales.

Notice that it is simple to "generalize" the previous quantity (and the following ones) when one forecasts more variables, each of them for more number of steps-ahead (see, for example, [4]).

Secondly, we consider a statistical index giving a measure of the linear correlation between the phenomenon predictions and the corresponding observed values, the Bravais-Pearson index R, whose analytical definition is the following

$$R(T) = \frac{Cov[y_1(t+\tau), y_1^*(t+\tau)]}{\sqrt{Var[y_1(t+\tau)]Var[y_1^*(t+\tau)]}} \in [-1,1], \quad T = 2,\dots,15. \qquad (5.2)$$

For this statistical index, the desiderable values are higher than zero and best values are close or equal to one.

Thirdly, we consider a statistical index giving a measure on how worse/better the considered phenomenon predictions are performing with respect to the (trivial) Random Walk ones, the Theil's coefficient of inequality, whose analytical definition is the following one

$$T_r(T) = \sqrt{\frac{\sum_{\tau=2}^{T}(y_1(t+\tau)-y_1^*(t+\tau))^2}{\sum_{\tau=2}^{T}(y_1(t+\tau)-y_1(t+\tau-1))^2}} \in [0,+\infty), \quad T = 2,\dots,15. \qquad (5.3)$$

For this statistical index, desiderable values are lower than one and best values are close or equal to zero.

Fourthly, we consider an operative index giving a measure of the considered forecasting methodology "ability" to catch the turning points correctly, the Correct Signum (CS), whose analytical definition is the following one

$$CS(T) = \frac{100}{T}\sum_{\tau=1}^{T}\beta(\tau) \in [-100,100]\% ,$$

$$\beta(\tau) = \begin{cases} 1 & \text{if} \quad y_1(t+\tau)y_1^*(t+\tau) > 0 \\ 1 & \text{if} \quad y_1(t+\tau) = y_1^*(t+\tau) = 0 , \\ 0 & \text{otherwise} \end{cases} \qquad (5.4)$$

$$T = 1,\dots,15.$$

For this operative index, the desiderable values are higher than fifty and best values are close or equal to one hundred.

Finally, we consider an operative index giving a measure of the net (that is, gain-and-loss balanced) profitability "ability" of the considered forecasting methodology, the Average Relative Net Profitability (ARNP). This index is developed on the basis of a simple trading strategy, according to which a stock is bought, held or sold depending on its rise-stay-and-fall time evolution. Its analytical definition is the following one

$$\text{ARNP}(T) = \frac{\sum_{\tau=1}^{T} \gamma(\tau) y_1(t+\tau)}{\sum_{\tau=1}^{T} |y_1(t+\tau)|} \in [-100,100]\%, \ \gamma(\tau) = \begin{cases} 1 & \text{if } \beta(\tau) > 0 \\ 0 & \text{if } \beta(\tau) = 0, \\ -1 & \text{if } \beta(\tau) < 0 \end{cases} \ (5.5)$$

$$T = 1,\ldots,15 .$$

For this operative index, the desiderable values are higher than one and best values are close or equal to one-hundred.

Of course, notice that such a choice of indexes and indicators is nor univocal nor exhaustive.

6 Experimentation Results

In this section we report the results of the implemented experimentations. In particular, firstly, we present the 1st-stage experimentation results and, secondly, we present the 2nd-stage ones.

6.1 1st-Stage Results

From **Table 6.1** we can deduce the following about the (implicit) explanatory capabilities of the utilized 1st-stage forecasting scenarios.

Table 6.1: IEC of the 1st-stage forecasting scenarios

	$FS_{B;1}$	$FS_{B;2}$	$FS_{B;3}$		$FS_{F;1}$	$FS_{F;2}$
$\text{IEC}_{B;q}$	3.06141	0.00000	42.90821	$\text{IEC}_{F;q}$	2.75993	0.0000

With regard to the benchmark time series, the second $(t,15+t)$-forecasting scenario is distinguished by the lowest "(implicit) explanatory capability", that is by the highest MSE. This occurrence is in accordance with the fact that only the first and third forecasting scenarios are characterized by the really "explanatory" variables.

Moreover, the third of such "forecasting frameworks", that is the one distinguished by the sub-set of the nonlinear really "explanatory" variables, shows an higher "(implicit) explanatory capability" than the first "forecasting frameworks", that is the one characterized by the sub-set of the linear really "explanatory" variables. This evidence is well in conformity with the theory of the deterministic chaotic dynamics. In fact, for proper values of their parameters, the corresponding deterministic chaotic behaviours are exclusively due to the nonlinear relationships.

Finally, notice that, of course, the considered benchmark time series could be analyzed using a "classical" 1-stage approach. The functional form of the corresponding forecasting ANN model, being *a priori* known the analytical properties of the underlying process (see map (4.1)), should be (see **Theorem 4.1**)

$$MLP(2 + 1; 5 + 1; 1) \,. \tag{6.1.1}$$

In this case, the ratio (3.1) should be equal to 2.1. Because of that, to ensure to the 1-stage MLP forecasting model involved a proper sizing (in the sense in which that is meant in the section 3) a higher number of "input-output" training vectors would be needed than in the case of the 2-stage approach.

Table 6.2: Dynamic behaviour of the index MAPE

#	$FS_{B;1}$	$FS_{B;2}$	$FS_{B;3}$	$FS_{B;II}$	#	$FS_{F;1}$	$FS_{F;2}$	$FS_{F;II}$
1	1.003	0.927	2.063	*1.142*	1	6.034	7.457	*3.172*
2	1.996	3.626	2.561	*1.254*	2	3.495	4.045	*2.024*
3	5.691	16.706	3.073	*4.437*	3	2.984	2.942	*1.429*
4	4.488	12.675	2.318	*3.355*	4	2.989	2.393	*2.635*
5	3.712	10.284	1.879	*2.701*	5	2.825	2.180	*2.604*
6	3.130	8.669	1.598	*2.258*	6	2.809	2.000	*2.779*
7	2.692	7.597	1.428	*1.943*	7	2.531	1.860	*2.490*
8	2.420	6.727	1.338	*1.721*	8	2.410	1.700	*2.289*
9	2.393	6.175	1.295	*1.540*	9	2.222	1.646	*2.064*
10	2.547	6.358	1.217	*1.474*	10	2.134	1.614	*1.982*
11	16.957	43.978	13.236	*12.334*	11	2.051	1.502	*2.036*
12	15.636	40.366	12.133	*11.307*	12	1.974	1.474	*1.954*
13	14.491	37.320	11.205	*10.450*	13	1.925	1.443	*1.863*
14	13.463	34.752	10.426	*9.720*	14	2.274	2.051	*1.868*
15	12.583	32.500	9.763	*9.072*	15	2.204	1.981	*1.835*

As far as the financial time series is concerned, the first $(t, 15 + t)$-forecasting scenario shows a higher "(implicit) explanatory capability", that is a lower MSE, than the second one. This evidence is consistent with other empirical results to be found in literature (see, for example [Brock, 1992]). Notice that, in general, the benchmark 1st-stage forecasting scenarios are characterized by a higher (implicit) explanatory capability than the financial ones. Such a feature can be reasonably connected to the bigger "difficulties" that the ANN models must face in forecasting a real economic and (possibly) highly noisy time series rather than a deterministic (although chaotic) one.

In **Table**s **6.2**, **6.3**, **6.4**, **6.5** and **6.6** we, respectively, report the dynamic behaviour of the indexes MAPE, R, T_r, CS and ARNP (see section 4) for both the analyzed time series. In particular, for both 1st-stage forecasting scenarios and 2nd-stage ones, we use the bold typeset style to indicate that the considered index value belongs to its "desirability" interval (notice that such an interval does not exist for the index MAPE) and, for the 2nd-stage forecasting scenarios, we use the italic/underlined typeset style to indicate that the considered index value is better or, at least, equal to the corresponding worst/best 1st-stage forecasting scenario one.

With regard to the benchmark time series, the third column index values of each table are, in general, worse than the corresponding second and fourth column ones. Again, this is in accordance with the fact that only the first and third $(t, 15 + t)$-forecasting scenarios are characterized by the really "explanatory" variables.

Moreover, the second and fourth column index values of each table, in general, belong to their corresponding "desirability" interval. In particular, the values of the indexes R, CS and ARNP are especially satisfactory.

Table 6.3: Dynamic behaviour of the index R

#	$FS_{B;1}$	$FS_{B;2}$	$FS_{B;3}$	$FS_{B;II}$	#	$FS_{F;1}$	$FS_{F;2}$	$FS_{F;II}$
1	--	--	--	--	1	--	--	--
2	**1.000**	**1.000**	-1.000	**1.000**	2	-1.000	**1.000**	*1.000*
3	**0.998**	**0.993**	-0.847	*-0.757*	3	-0.163	0.452	*0.007*
4	**0.619**	**0.661**	**0.983**	**0.985**	4	-0.383	0.635	-0.504
5	**0.856**	**0.725**	**0.993**	*0.990*	5	-0.486	0.618	-0.498
6	**0.774**	**0.761**	**0.977**	**0.990**	6	-0.525	0.637	*-0.521*
7	**0.719**	**0.537**	**0.961**	**0.990**	7	-0.150	0.153	*-0.123*
8	**0.686**	**0.555**	**0.957**	**0.990**	8	-0.122	0.152	*-0.108*
9	**0.684**	**0.596**	**0.960**	**0.990**	9	-0.083	0.046	*-0.006*
10	**0.698**	**0.621**	**0.962**	**0.991**	10	-0.149	-0.073	**0.107**
11	**0.712**	**0.636**	**0.960**	**0.990**	11	-0.174	0.266	-0.326
12	**0.657**	**0.745**	**0.977**	**0.994**	12	-0.247	-0.028	*-0.086*
13	**0.802**	**0.790**	**0.987**	**0.995**	13	-0.514	-0.111	*-0.051*
14	**0.777**	**0.568**	**0.983**	**0.995**	14	-0.491	-0.127	-0.035
15	**0.782**	**0.568**	**0.980**	**0.995**	15	-0.499	-0.093	-0.045

Table 6.4: Dynamic behaviour of the index T_r

#	$FS_{B;1}$	$FS_{B;2}$	$FS_{B;3}$	$FS_{B;II}$	#	$FS_{F;1}$	$FS_{F;2}$	$FS_{F;II}$
1	--	--	--	--	1	--	--	--
2	1.984	4.197	2.030	**0.906**	2	**0.915**	0.604	*0.838*
3	2.509	6.932	1.892	1.678	3	**0.830**	0.510	*0.681*
4	**0.885**	**0.723**	**0.130**	*0.152*	4	**0.844**	0.495	0.869
5	**1.124**	**1.162**	**0.199**	**0.175**	5	**0.911**	0.537	0.954
6	**1.058**	**1.194**	**0.250**	**0.166**	6	**0.952**	0.548	1.023
7	**0.990**	**1.243**	**0.303**	**0.157**	7	**0.857**	0.821	*0.831*
8	**0.968**	**1.214**	**0.330**	**0.157**	8	**0.767**	0.713	*0.726*
9	**0.967**	**1.206**	**0.332**	**0.155**	9	**0.785**	0.782	**0.722**
10	**0.971**	**1.221**	**0.332**	**0.157**	10	**0.752**	0.749	**0.693**
11	**0.976**	**1.248**	**0.342**	**0.174**	11	**0.820**	0.755	0.980
12	**1.032**	**1.027**	**0.257**	**0.131**	12	1.020	0.991	1.113
13	1.210	1.213	**0.248**	**0.206**	13	**0.829**	0.757	*0.782*
14	1.136	1.382	**0.288**	**0.233**	14	**0.783**	0.729	*0.730*
15	1.102	1.368	**0.313**	**0.225**	15	**0.808**	0.743	*0.768*

As far as the financial time series is concerned, it appears again more difficultly predictable than the benchmark one. In fact, the index values of each tables, although, in general, belonging to their corresponding "desirability" intervals, are less satisfactory than those of the benchmark study-case. Notice that this can be also due to the plain determination we work out as to the "optimal" 1st-stage forecasting scenario frameworks (this is not the main purpose of our work).

Moreover, the eighth column index values of each table are, generally, a little better than the corresponding seventh column ones. This occurrence is, partially, in disaccordance with the results reported in **Table 6.1**, according to which the first $(t, t+15)$-forecasting scenario, instead of the second one, should show a higher "(implicit) explanatory capability". Nevertheless, this same matter is in accordance with other empirical results to be found in literature (see, for example [Brock *et al.*, 1992]).

Table 6.5: Dynamic behaviour of the index CS

#	$FS_{B;1}$	$FS_{B;2}$	$FS_{B;3}$	$FS_{B;II}$	#	$FS_{F;1}$	$FS_{F;2}$	$FS_{F;II}$
1	0.000	**100.000**	0.000	*0.000*	1	0.000	0.000	0.000
2	0.000	50.000	0.000	*0.000*	2	50.000	50.000	50.000
3	0.000	33.333	33.333	33.333	3	33.333	**66.667**	**66.667**
4	25.000	50.000	50.000	50.000	4	25.000	**75.000**	*50.000*
5	40.000	**60.000**	**60.000**	**60.000**	5	20.000	**60.000**	*40.000*
6	50.000	**66.667**	66.667	**66.667**	6	16.667	50.000	*33.333*
7	**57.143**	**57.143**	71.429	71.429	7	28.571	42.857	*42.857*
8	**62.500**	**62.500**	75.000	**75.000**	8	25.000	50.000	*50.000*
9	**66.667**	**55.556**	77.778	**77.778**	9	33.333	44.444	**55.556**
10	**70.000**	50.000	**80.000**	**80.000**	10	30.000	40.000	50.000
11	**72.727**	45.455	**81.818**	**81.818**	11	27.273	45.455	45.455
12	**66.667**	50.000	**83.333**	**83.333**	12	25.000	41.667	41.667
13	**69.231**	**53.846**	**84.615**	**84.615**	13	23.077	38.462	46.154
14	**71.429**	50.000	**85.714**	**85.714**	14	21.429	35.714	*42.857*
15	**73.333**	**53.333**	**86.667**	**86.667**	15	20.000	40.000	40.000

Table 6.6: Dynamic behaviour of the index ARNP

#	$FS_{B;1}$	$FS_{B;2}$	$FS_{B;3}$	$FS_{B;II}$	#	$FS_{F;1}$	$FS_{F;2}$	$FS_{F;II}$
1	-100.000	**100.000**	-100.000	*-100.000*	1	-100.000	-100.000	-100.000
2	-100.000	**42.971**	-100.000	*-100.000*	2	**91.156**	**91.156**	**91.156**
3	-100.000	**34.155**	-87.668	-87.668	3	54.842	92.836	**92.836**
4	75.440	**91.914**	76.954	*76.954*	4	41.414	93.457	*76.113*
5	89.686	**96.604**	90.322	*90.322*	5	22.766	67.947	*52.890*
6	92.659	**97.583**	93.112	*93.112*	6	13.165	54.812	*40.933*
7	93.695	69.686	94.084	94.084	7	54.921	-19.632	69.336
8	94.087	71.568	94.451	94.451	8	41.046	-8.917	72.082
9	94.194	68.458	94.552	94.552	9	50.661	-23.772	76.636
10	94.235	67.263	94.591	94.591	10	32.243	-33.091	55.042
11	94.236	67.232	94.592	94.592	11	14.436	-15.170	34.165
12	54.988	73.853	95.685	95.685	12	-13.006	-35.512	1.992
13	65.954	80.223	96.736	96.736	13	-29.042	-47.400	20.058
14	70.440	56.477	97.166	97.166	14	-29.721	-47.903	18.909
15	72.407	59.373	97.355	97.355	15	-36.615	-33.395	7.245

6.2 2nd-Stage Results

In general, the 2nd ANN processing stage improves the results obtained by the 1st one for both the analyzed time series. Such an improvement is detectable by the 2nd-stage forecasting scenario IECs, in fact $IEC_{B;II} = 50,08691$ and $IEC_{F;II} = 3,18902$ (see, for the 1st-stage ones **Table 6.1**) and by the fifth and the last column values of **Table 6.2** to **Table 6.6**. In particular, in **Table 6.7** we report, for both the analyzed time series, the percentage in which the 2nd-stage index values are better than or, at least, equal to the corresponding best 1st-stage ones (↑), are better than or, at least, equal to the corresponding worst 1st-stage ones (↔) and are worse than the corresponding worst 1st-stage ones (↓).

With regard to the benchmark time series, such an improvement of the 2nd-stage index values is well evident (in particular, for the indexes R, T_r and CS). Moreover, such index values are comparable with the corresponding ones obtained, for the same time series, by using others sAI techniques (see, for example [Giove *et al.*, 1996]).

As far as the financial time series is concerned, the improvement of the 2nd-stage index values is quite satisfactory and is particularly evident, also from the "desirability" interval point of view, for the index ARNP, whose operative importance is well manifest. Anyway, only the 10.96% of the 2nd-stage index values are (slightly) worse than the corresponding 1st-stage ones.

Table 6.7: Improvement/worsening percentages

Index	$FS_{B;II}$ ↑	$FS_{B;II}$ ↔	$FS_{B;II}$ ↓	$FS_{F;II}$ ↑	$FS_{F;II}$ ↔	$FS_{F;II}$ ↓
MAPE	40.00%	60.00%	0.00%	33.33%	66.67%	0.00%
R	85.71%	14.29%	0.00%	35.71%	42.86%	21.43%
T	92.86%	7.14%	0.00%	14.29%	50.00%	35.71%
CS	86.67%	13.33%	0.00%	80.00%	20.00%	0.00%
ARNP	60.00%	40.00%	0.00%	80.00%	20.00%	0.00%
Global	**72.60%**	**27.40%**	**0.00%**	**49.31%**	**39.73%**	**10.96%**

7 Concluding Remarks

In this last section we give the following concluding remarks.

Looking at the results previously presented in section 6, the 2-stage ANN predictor we developed seems to be able, by suitably combining different 1st-stage forecasting scenario predictions, to generate a final output whose "quality" is higher than that of the corresponding 1st-stage outputs. Of course, in order to achieve a definitive judgement on this ANN forecasting methodology, other (both theoretical and empirical) analyses would be required.

Finally, because of the evidence of predictability we find in the financial time series, it seems indispensable to develop a new theoretical framework, within which the classical financial models, that, generally, are based on the assumption that the variations of stock prices are identically and indenpendently (log-normally) distributed, should be generalized.

8 References

[1] AZOFF, E. M. (1994) *Neural Network Time Series Forecasting of Financial Markets*. John Wiley & Sons, New York.
[2] BAESTAENS, D. E., VAN DEN BERGH, W. M. and WOOD, D. (1994) *Neural Network Solutions for Trading in Financial Markets*. Pitman Publishing, London.
[3] BAUM, E. B. and HAUSSLER, D. (1989) What Size Net Gives Valid Generalization?, in TOURETZKY, D. S. (ed.) (1989) *Advances in Neural Information Processing Systems 1*, 81-90, Morgan Kaufmann Publishers, 81-90.

[4] BELCARO, P. L., CANESTRELLI, E. and CORAZZA, M. (1996) Artificial Neural Network Forecasting Models: an Application to the Italian Stock Market, *Badania Operacyjne i Decyzje*, 3-4, 29-48.

[5] BLATTBERG, R. and GONEDES, N. (1974) A Comparison of Stable and Student Distributions as Statistical Models for Stock Prices, *J. of Business*, 47, 244-280.

[6] BOLLERSLEV, T. (1987) A Conditonal Heteroskedastic Time Series Model for Speculative Prices and Rates of Return, *Review of Economics and Statistics*, 69, 542-547.

[7] BOOTH, G. G., MARTIKAINEN, T., SARKAR, S. S., VIRTANEN, I. and YLI-OLI, P. (1992) Nonlinear Dependence in Finnish Stock Returns, lecture presented at *Euro Working Group on Financial Modelling*, 12th Meeting, Helsinki.

[8] BROCK, W., LAKONISHOK, J. and LeBARON, B. (1992) Simple Technical Trading Rules and the Stochastic Properties of Stock Returns, *The J. of Finance*, XLVII, 5, 1731-1764.

[9] CAMPBELL, J. Y., LO, A. W. and MacKINLAY, A. G. (1997) *The Econometrics of Financial Data*. Princeton University Press, Princeton.

[10] CORAZZA, M. (1993/94) *Caso e Caos Deterministico: un Approccio all'Analisi delle Leggi di Evoluzione dei Prezzi Speculativi*. Ph. D. Thesis, University of Brescia, Brescia.

[11] CORAZZA, M. (1996) Long-term Memory Stability in the Italian Stock Market, lecture presented at *Letters in Public Finance*, 1st Meeting, Acquafredda di Maratea (to be appear on *Economic & Financial Modelling*).

[12] CORAZZA, M., MALLIARIS, A. G. and NARDELLI, C. (1996) Searching for Fractal Structure in Agricultural Futures Market, lecture presented at *Euro Working Group on Financial Modelling*, 14th Meeting, Mantova (to be appear on *The J. of Futures Market*).

[13] CORAZZA, M. and NARDELLI, C. (1993) Fenomeno della Dipendenza a Lungo Termine nel Mercato Finanziario Italiano, *Atti del XVII Convegno A.M.A.S.E.S.*, Ischia, 359-372.

[14] DING, Z., GRANGER, C. and ENGLE, R. (1993) A Long Memory Property of Stock Returns and a New Model, *J. of Empirical Finance*, 1, 83-106.

[15] FARLOW, S. J. (1984) The GMDH Algorithm, in FARLOW, S. J. (ed.) (1984) *Self-Organizing Methods in Modeling*, 1-24, Marcel Dekker, Inc., New York.

[16] FELDMAN, K. and KINGDON, J. (1995) Neural Networks and some Applications to Finance, *Applied Mathematical Finance*, 2, 17-42.

[17] FIELITZ, B. D. and ROZELLE, J. P. (1972) Stable Distributions and the Mixtures of Distributions Hypotheses for Common Stock Returns, *J. of the American Statistical Association*, 78, 381, 28-36.

[18] FIELITZ, B. D. and SMITH, E. W. (1972) Asymmetric Stable Distributions of Stock Price Changes, *J. of the American Statistical Association*, 67, 340, 813-814.

[19] GATELY, E. (1996) *Neural Networks for Financial Forecasting*. John Wiley & Sons, New York.

[20] GIOVE, S., PELLIZZARI, P. and TEZZA, S (1996) RBF Networks for Financial Data Analysis and Forecasting: a Fuzzy-Cluster Approach, *Badania Operacyjne i Decyzye*, 3-4, 119-130.

[21] GREENE, M. T. and FIELITZ, B. D. (1977) Long-term Dependence in Common Stock Returns, *Journal of Financial Economics*, 4, 339-349.

[22] HECHT-NIELSEN, R. (1990) *Neurocomputing*. Addison-Wesley Publishing Co., Reading.

[23] HELMS, B. P., KAEN, F. R. and ROSENMAN, R. E. (1984) Memory in Commodity Futures Contracts, *The J. of Futures Markets*, 44, 559-567.

[24] HERTZ, J., KROGH, A. and PALMER, R. G. (1994) *Introduction to the Theory of Neural Computation*, Addison-Wesley Publishing Co., Reading.

[25] HINICH, M. J. and PATTERSON, D. M. (1989) Evidence of Nonlinearity in the Trade-by-trade Stock Market Return generating Process, in BARNETT, W.A., GEWEKE, J. and SHELL, K. (eds.) (1989) *Economic Complexity. Chaos, Sunspots, Bubbles and Nonlinearity*. Cambridge University Press, Cambridge.

[26] HSIEH, D. A. (1989) Testing for Nonlinear Dependence in Daily Foreign Exchange Rates, *J. of Business*, 62, 339-368.

[27] HSIEH, D. A. (1991) Chaos and Nonlinear Dynamics: Application to Financial Markets, *The Journal of Finance*, 46, 5, 1839-1877.

[28] HSU, D., MILLER, R. and WICHERN, D. (1974) On the Stable Paretian Behavior of Stock Market Prices, *J. of the American Statistical Association*, 69, 108-113.

[29] LO, A. W. (1991) Long-term Memory in Stock Market Prices, *Econometrica*, 59, 5, 1279-1313.

[30] MALLIARIS, A. G. and PHILIPPATOS, G. (1993) Random Walk vs. Chaotic Dynamics in Financial Economics, in GORI, F., GERONAZZO, L. and GALEOTTI, M. (eds.) (1993) *Nonlinear Dynamics in Economics and Social Sciences*, 99-122, Springer-Verlag, Berlin.

[31] MANDELBROT, B. B. (1963) The Variation of Certain Speculative Prices, *J. of Business*, in COOTNER, P. H. (ed.) (1964) *The Random Character of Stock Market Prices*, 307-332, The M.I.T. Press, Cambridge.

[32] McKEY, M. C. and GLASS, L. (1977) Oscillation and Chaos in Physiological Control Systems, *Science*, 197, 287-289.

[33] PETERS, E. E. (1991) *Chaos and Order in the Capital Market*. John Wiley & Sons, New York.

[34] PETERS, E. E. (1994) *Fractal Market Analysis*. John Wiley & Sons, New York.

[35] PRESS, W. H., FLANNERY, B. P., TEUKOLSKY, S. A. and VETTERLING (1986) *Numerical Recipies. The Art of Scientific Computing*. Cambridge University Press, Cambridge.

[36] REFENES, A.-P. (ed.) (1995) *Neural Networks in the Capital Martkets*. John Wiley & Sons, New York.

[37] SANDULESCU, G., LAZAR, S. and CARDINALI, S. (1995) Neural Network Applications in Finance. The Need of a Standardization of the Evaluation of the Performance related to Forecasting and Classification. Proposal and the Relation with Classical Methods, lecture presented at *Financial Applications of Neural Networks and Fuzzy Systems*, 1st Meeting, Venice.

[38] SCHEINKMAN, J. A. and LeBARON, B. (1989) Nonlinear Dynamics and Stock Returns, *The J. of Business*, 62, 3, 311-337.

[39] SIMKOWITZ, M. and BEEDLES, W. (1980) Asymmetric Stable Distributed

Security Returns, *J. of the American Statistical Association*, 75, 306-312.

[40] TURBAN, E. and TRIPPI, R. R. (eds) (1996) *Neural Networks in Finance and Investing*, Irwin Professional Publishing, Chicago.

Generic Neuro-Fuzzy-Chaos Methodology for Time-Series Analysis and Building Intelligent Adaptive Systems

Robert Kozma and Nikola K. Kasabov

Department of Information Science
University of Otago, P.O.Box 56, Dunedin, New Zealand
Phone: +64 3 479 8319, Fax: +64 3 479 8311
email: nkasabov@otago.ac.nz, rkozma@commerce.otago.ac.nz

Abstract. A general methodology for chaotic time series analysis is presented. The methodology begins with analysing the chaotic properties of the time series which is considered as a multi-level process evolving over time. In our approach, the prediction is implemented as a hierarchical process when the higher-level trends are predicted first, followed by the lower level values of the time-series. After the initial time series analysis, a corresponding hierarchical multi-modular structure is built to model the time series at different levels. A fuzzy neural network FuNN is used for the purpose of building each of the modules in the modular structure. FuNN has well-developed methods for adaptive learning, which include a method for structural learning with forgetting, methods for rules insertion and rules extraction. Fuzzy rules for explaining chaotic time series at different levels of its behaviour can be extracted. A case study of a stock index time series has been used through the paper to illustrate the proposed methodology and techniques.
Key words: fuzzy neural network, chaotic time series, prediction

1. Introduction

Analysis of chaotic time series data has been of interest to scientists for a long time [1]. In spite of the progress of research in this field, a comprehensive and effective methodology for chaos analysis is still lacking. A chaotic time-series is usually treated as a "flat", "multi-frequency" process which makes it predictable only in short term future, the length of which depends on the level of chaos characterised by the Lyapunov exponents [2-5]. This paper treats a chaotic process as a hierarchical, compound one consisting of components with different time scales. At the highest level it is the longest trend of the process and at the lowest level is the single time moment value. A long term analysis and prediction of a time series will include first predicting the highest-level trend, then within it - the next level trend, etc, until a prediction of a single time-moment value can be attempted.

A generic methodology of a chaotic time series analysis is presented in the paper which includes:

1. Building a model of the time series through a rigorous analysis of its chaotic behaviour
2. Building a connectionist-based modular hierarchical structure to model the time-series through adaptive training and to predict it
3. Extracting underlying rules to explain the chaotic process at its different levels of behaviour.

This approach, which is a generic one, is illustrated on a financial data set - the SE40 index data.

There have been many attempts to use neural networks for financial applications. These have included prediction for various markets, credit scoring, and bankruptcy prediction; for an overview, see [6]. Various types of networks can be used to this aim, e.g., recurrent, time-delay neural networks and multi-layer feed-forward architectures. In this paper, multi-layer feed-forward networks are used which are "forced" to learn the entire data and pick all the variations and trends in it. A disadvantage of standard feed-forward neural networks is that while they provide an effective means of discovering potentially non-linear mappings from an input space to the corresponding output space, this mapping is represented explicitly in the hidden layers. While various techniques have been proposed for examining a network's weight matrix which represents the model's behaviour, none have been entirely successful. This 'black box' effect severely limits the use of neural networks for knowledge discovery and hinders the verification of the model developed.

Another problem with such networks is that they are entirely data driven. While the ability to learn arbitrary models from data is perhaps the greatest strength of the neural network paradigm, the exclusion of knowledge from the model building process can be seen as wasteful. Techniques have been proposed for pre-weighting networks in such a manner as to start the network closer to a solution, but again have not been entirely successful.

An alternative approach is that of using fuzzy-neural networks [7-15]. These are generic tools that provide a semantically meaningful fuzzy structure within the neural network, allowing for rule insertion, model-free training on data, and most significantly the extraction of adapted rules. If no initial knowledge can be formulated, the network can still be trained on data after random initialisation, with rules extracted from the trained structure. Such a structure synergistically combines the strengths of fuzzy expert rules and neural network learning.

In this paper a special type of fuzzy neural network FuNN is used for modeling time series. It is illustrated how to use fuzzy neural networks (FuNN) and FuNN-based hybrid systems for both modeling and predicting time series. FuNN provides a powerful new approach for integrating knowledge and data into a single structure. Advanced new adaptation strategies have been developed to take full advantage of this technique. The nature of many problems in the financial domain, characterised by the employment alternative theories and the availability of large quantities of data, makes them well suited to this hybrid paradigm.

2. Multi-Scale Representation of Chaotic Time Series and Their Analysis

2.1 A General Method for Chaotic Time Series Analysis

The proposed time series analysis method consists of three major steps: (1) characterisation of the signal using various statistical and dynamical evaluation methods; (2) developing a model for the description of past and present behaviour and, within a certain time frame, for predicting future states; (3) iterative updating/refinement of the characterisation conducted in (1) using model calculations. In this section the following issues are discussed: estimation of fractal dimension and multi-fractal features, identification of major time scales of the process. Modeling the dynamic behaviour within the identified time frame is described in the consecutive sections of this paper.

The goal of the first step is to reveal some major features of the investigated process, e.g., stationarity/non-stationarity; presence/absence of periodic components; revealing whether the signal is random or it contains non-linear deterministic, chaotic components, etc. Results of the characterisation step have important implications on the choice of modeling methods in the further analysis. For example, if the signal is stationary with possible periodic components, conventional methods of correlation analysis in time- and frequency domains are usually sufficient. For non-stationary signals with non-linear dynamics, however, methods of chaos analysis can be more appropriate [1, 16-17].

Once the main properties of the signal have been identified, certain quantitative features are determined. These features include the dominant time scales in the signal; possible occurrence of self-similarity and fractal/multi-fractal features; dimensionality of the underlying phenomena. All these descriptors contain crucial information for the design of the system model.

In the present work we concentrate on signals with non-linear dynamics modelled by fuzzy neural networks FuNNs [10]. The level of chaos determines the reliability of the short- and long-term predictions. The chaosness is related to the dimensionality of the system which has to be taken into account when designing, training, and adaptively tuning the FuNN architecture. A time series with complex chaotic dynamic may require larger number of inputs and also a lot of rule nodes.

Finally, the properly trained and tuned FuNN is used for the extraction of knowledge on the dynamic system. The extracted knowledge can be used for updating the characterisation features of the signal. In this way a closed feedback loop is generated which can be used for iteratively refining the description and also for adapting the inferred model to the changing environment. In the following section, details of the applied dynamic characterisation are given.

2.2 Fractal Analysis

A significant part of the time series analysis methods is based on the assumption that the investigated signals can be described as stochastic processes with Gaussian probability density functions. Moreover, by calculating the power spectral density functions by the commonly used FFT algorithm, it is assumed that the data represent stationary processes. These assumptions are quite restrictive and they are rarely met in most of the examples in natural scenes. Methods of chaos analysis do not make such assumptions and they can provide a solution to the arising problems.

In the present work the dimensionality of the system is investigated (1) by calculating the fractal dimension of the temporal signals and also (2) by determining the effective memory of the system using the structure of the FuNN trained by a structural learning algorithm. The dimensionality of the system may change over time reflecting changes in the dynamics of the time series.

The fractal dimension of self-similar time series is estimated following the procedure elaborated and further refined in [16] and [18]. Starting from a time series $X(j)$, $(j = 1, 2, \ldots, N)$, the partial length of the graph of the time series, $L_m(k)$ is defined as follows:

$$L_m(k) = \left(\sum_{i=1}^{[(N-m)/k]} |X(m+ik) - X(m+(i-1)k)| \right) \frac{(N-1)/k}{[(N-m)/k]} \quad (2.1)$$

where k denotes the time interval, and m=1,2,...,k. Notation [a] stands for the integer part of a. N is the number of data points used for calculating a set of $L(k)$ values. A new set of $L(k)$ is calculated sequentially at each time instant when new data have been acquired. This is followed by the estimation of the fractal dimension based on the $L(k)$ values.

For each time interval k, the average value of the length, $\langle L(k) \rangle$ is given as:

$$\langle L(k) \rangle = \frac{1}{k} \sum_{m=1}^{k} L_m(k). \quad (2.2)$$

Here $\langle L(k) \rangle$ corresponds to the mean length of the curve when the wave number k is fixed. It is easy to see that Eq. (2.2) indeed gives a normalised length by summing up the absolute values of the step-by-step changes along the graph of the time series. If the relationship $L(k) \propto k^{-D}$ holds, the time series reveals fractal characteristics. In the case of a fractal time series, the log-log plot of k vs. $L(k)$ curve shows a linear behaviour and the negative slope of the curve gives the fractal dimension value D. In order to estimate the fractal dimension of a time series based on the slope, the least squares method has been used. If the signal is fractal, the following relationship holds between k and $L(k)$:

$$\log(L(k)) = x_1 + x_2 \log k, \tag{2.3}$$

where x_1 and x_2 are parameters estimated by the least squares method. Finally, the fractal dimension D is given simply as

$$D = -x_2. \tag{2.4}$$

In a lot of practically important cases, the power spectral density has a power-law behaviour, i.e., low frequencies have higher energies compared to high frequencies, following the unique relationship:

$$P(f) \propto f^{-\alpha}. \tag{2.5}$$

Here $P(f)$ is the power spectral density, f is the frequency, and α is a power law index. A curve with a single power law index for all frequencies is self-similar. The following approximate relationship has been obtained between power law index alpha and the fractal dimension D [16,17] over the range of $1 < D < 2$

$$D = (5 - \alpha)/2. \tag{2.6}$$

Note that the above relation is just an approximation. It strictly holds for a class of processes called fractional Brownian motion with $1 < \alpha < 3$, but it breaks down outside this region.

In many practical situations, the signal often reveals bi- or multi-fractal features; i.e., the slope of the k vs. $L(k)$ curve depends on the range of wave numbers k. In a multi-fractal signal, the estimation of a set of fractal dimension values is performed by dividing the whole k-range into several segments and applying linear fitting over each sub-region; see [16],[18]. Results obtained by using the above method of fractal analysis and statistical time series analysis can be used in the design of the FuNN architecture using an iterative procedure, as it has been described in the previous section.

2.3 The Case Study of NZSE40 Time Series

The NZSE40 data set contains the stock exchange index collected daily for a period of several years. Some major results are summarised in Fig. 2.1a-e. Figure 2.1a shows the SE40 time series. The power spectrum of the SE40 index is given in Fig. 2.1b. The behaviour of the power spectrum is close to a $1/f$ power law, although, large statistical fluctuations make it difficult to determine the exact shape of the spectrum, especially at high frequencies. Figure 2.1c illustrates the fractal properties of the time series. Two major ranges can be distinguished in the wave number space. Namely, the $L(k)$ versus k curve is less steep at low k values compared to the high k region. This is a typical bi-fractal behaviour with a breaking point at $k \approx 20$. The value of the fractal dimension D has been determined based on the least-square fit of the corresponding segments of the curve. The least-square fits to the fractal curve are shown shown as dashed lines in Fig. 2.1c. The obtained fractal dimension values are 1.35 ±0.02 and 1.70 ±0.03 over k-ranges [1 - 22] and [53 - 362], respectively, which suggests that at least two scales of modeling and prediction would be appropriate to apply.

Figures 2.1d-e contain additional information about the statistics of the data. The cross correlation function in Fig. 2.1d indicates a memory effect of up to about 15 days. The probability density function (histogram) in Fig.1e is far from having a Gaussian behaviour and its two distinct peaks represent an apparent bimodality of the SE40 values. The interpretation of these ob-

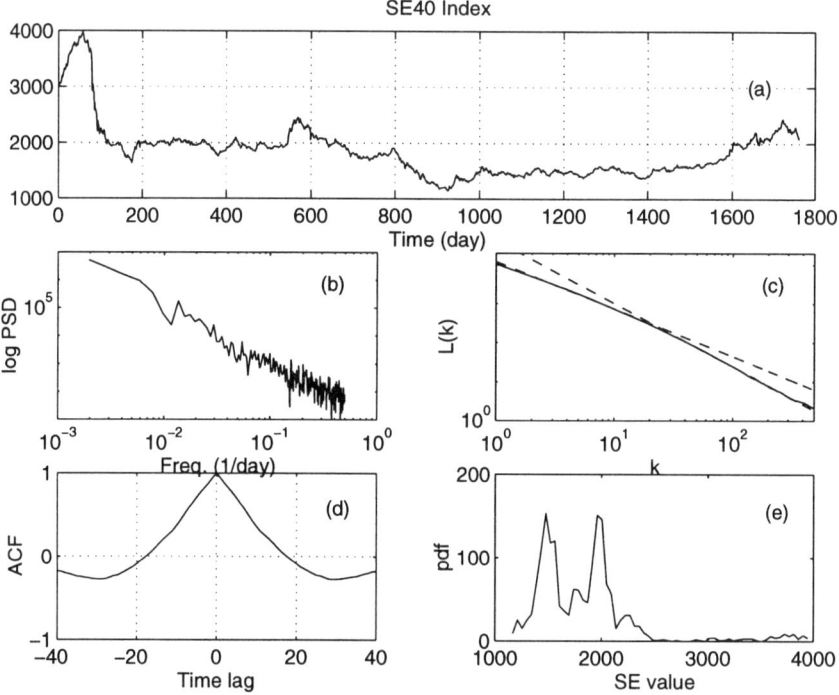

Fig. 2.1. Characterisation of the SE40 data; (a) time series; (b) power spectral density; (c) fractional length of the graph of the time series; (d) auto correlation function; (e) probability density (histogram).

servations will be given in the forthcoming discussions based on modeling the process by fuzzy-neural networks (FuNNs). Multi-scale model is experimented based on the chaos characteristics given above. The model has been implemented by making use of FuNN modules. The introduced modular structure, however, should be considered as a more general one which can be realised based on other modeling techniques as well.

3. Building Adaptive FuNN-based System Models

3.1 Fuzzy Neural Networks. The FuNN Architecture

The FuNN architecture facilitates learning from data and approximate reasoning, as well as fuzzy rules extraction and insertion. It allows for the combination of both data and rules into one system, thus producing the synergistic benefits associated with the two sources. In addition, it allows for several methods of adaptation in a dynamically changing environment. FuNN uses a multi-layer perceptron (MLP) network architecture and a modified backpropagation training algorithm. The general FuNN architecture consists of 5 layers of neurons with partial feedforward connections as shown in Fig. 3.1. A full mathematical presentation of the training algorithm developed for FuNN, which is a modified backpropagation algorithm, is given in [19-20]. The input layer of neurons represents the input variables as crisp values. These values are fed to the condition element layer which performs fuzzification with triangular membership functions. Using triangular membership functions makes the fuzzification and the defuzzification procedures in FuNN fast without compromising the accuracy of the solution. Initially the membership functions are spaced equally over the weight space, although expert knowledge can be used in its initialisation if such a knowledge is available.

In the rule layer, each node represents a single fuzzy rule. The layer is potentially expandable and shrinkable, i.e., nodes can be added or deleted, to represent increasing or decreasing number of rules as the network adapts. The activation function is the sigmoidal function. The semantic meaning of the activation of a node is the degree to which input data matches the antecedent component of an associated fuzzy rule. However, the synergistic nature of rules in a fuzzy-neural architecture must be remembered when interpreting such rules. The connection weights from the condition element layer to the rule layer represent semantically the degrees of importance of the corresponding condition elements for the activation of this node. The values of the connection weights to and from the rule layer can be limited during training to be within a certain interval, say [-1,1], thus introducing non-linearity into the synaptic weights.

In the action element layer a node represents a fuzzy label from the fuzzy quantisation space of an output variable. The activation of the node represents the degree to which this membership function is supported by the current data used for recall. The shape of the output membership functions is not restricted and may be changed during training and adaptation.

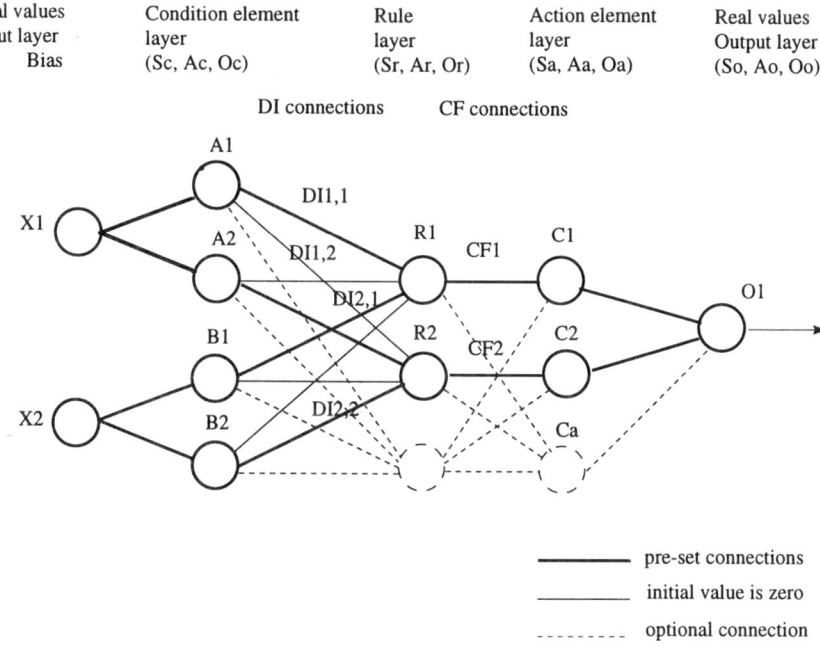

| Real values
input layer
Bias | Condition element
layer
(Sc, Ac, Oc) | Rule
layer
(Sr, Ar, Or) | Action element
layer
(Sa, Aa, Oa) | Real values
Output layer
(So, Ao, Oo) |

Fig. 3.1. A FuNN structure for two initial fuzzy rules: R1: IF x1 is A1 (DI1,1) and x2 is B1 (DI2,1) THEN y is C1 (CF1); R2: IF x1 is A2 (DI1,2) and x2 is B2 (DI2,2) THEN y is C2 (CF2), where DIs are degrees of importance attached to the condition elements and CFs are confidence factors attached to the consequent parts of the rules; adapted from [8].

One of the advantages of the FuNN architecture is that it manages to provide a fuzzy logic system without having to unnecessarily extend the traditional MLP. Since standard transfer functions, linear and sigmoidal, are used along with a slightly modified back-propagation algorithm, the main departure being the constraining rules, much of the large body of theory regarding such networks is still applicable.

3.2 Adaptation Strategies in FuNN

There are five versions of weight updating in the FuNN according to the mode of training and adaptation [10, 14-15]. These are not mutually exclusive versions but are all provided within the same environment and the versions can be switched between as needed. These methods of adaptation are:

– a partially adaptive training, where the membership functions (MF) of the input and the output variables do not change during training and a modified backpropagation algorithm is used for the purpose of rule adaptation. This adaptation mode can be suitable for systems where the membership functions to be used are known in advance or where the implementation is constrained by the problem in some way;

- a fully adaptive training with an extended backpropagation algorithm, as explained in [10]; this version allows changes to be made to both rules and membership functions, subject to constraints necessary for retaining semantic meaning;
- a partially adaptive version, where a forgetting factor is introduced;
- a partially adaptive version with the use of a genetic algorithm for adapting the membership functions; this mode does not alter the rules; the algorithm is described in [10];
- adaptive training with the use of the 'Method of Training and Zeroing' as described in [15]; this method employs a standard backpropagation algorithm but small connection weights (below a certain threshold) are "zeroed" regularly using a variable threshold; these connections can be left in the structure for further change or can be pruned.

These modes can either be used as alternatives or they can be used together in whatever combination is most appropriate for the given problem at a certain time. It may be useful to use several different modes in an alternative manner, with each version of the adaptation algorithm best suited to some part of the adaptation task.

3.3 Structural Learning Methods

A neural network can eventually be trained to approximate a chaotic function, but can a connectionist structure be trained with chaotic data in such a way that it captures structurally the main characteristics of the chaotic process? This problem is solved here by applying a method of structural learning with forgetting to a FuNN. After training with forgetting, the FuNN structurally represents the underlying rules of the chaotic process.

In the past few years, significant efforts have been devoted to elaborate algorithms which find optimal neural network architectures. Two major approaches can be distinguished: either growing an increasingly elaborate network starting from a simple architecture, or reducing the size and complexity of an initially very complex neural network; see [21-24]. The latter approach is called network pruning. In the present study, a special type of network pruning is applied, which is a modified backpropagation learning algorithm with forgetting the connection weights. Modified backpropagation with forgetting belongs to the class of structural learning algorithms. By applying learning with forgetting, the weights decrease continuously, unless they are reinforced by the backpropagation rule. At the end of the training, only the essential weights deviate significantly from zero. By pruning the weights which are close to zero, a skeleton network is obtained.

Based on the skeleton structure, knowledge can be obtained on the analysed data. A neural network which is able to create and process abstract knowledge is called an artificially intelligent network, compared to computational nets which simply process numerical data. The structural learning method applied in this work has the potential to generate artificially intelligent neural networks in the above sense. NNs trained by forgetting algorithm are expected to have better generalisation properties than the ones trained by standard BP, because the skeleton structure obtained after training with forgetting is usually more suitable for the given problem than a predefined architecture used in standard BP. Moreover, by decreasing the effective number of weights during training with forgetting, overtraining can be avoided. A disadvantage of BP with forgetting is the increased computational time. This problem, however, can be compensated for by removing the unnecessary connections.

Below, the main features of the backpropagation learning algorithm with forgetting are summarised. The basic idea is to update the connection weights as follows [19]:

$$\Delta w_{ij} = \Delta w'_{ij} - \gamma sgn(w_{ij}) \tag{3.1}$$

Here $\Delta w'_{ij}$ is the change of the ij-th weight using standard backpropagation algorithm, γ is the so-called forgetting rate, $sgn(x)$ denotes the sign function. The second term on the right hand side of Eq. (3.1) describes a decreasing tendency for the connection weights. Indeed, the weights decrease continuously, unless they are reinforced by the backpropagation rule. The corresponding cost function is given by:

$$J = \sum_i (y_i - y_i^*)^2 + \gamma' \sum_{i,j} |w_{i,j}| \tag{3.2}$$

Here y_i and y_i^* are the actual and the target values of the network outputs, respectively. $\gamma' = \lambda\gamma$, where λ is the learning rate and γ is the forgetting rate. The first term is the usual sum of squared errors (SSE) between the actual and target values of the output of the NN. The second term is the sum of the absolute values of weights (SW) with an appropriate proportionality constant.

3.4 Outline of the Multi-Modular System

A multi-modular architecture is proposed which consists of several FuNN modules, a rule extraction module and a module for adaptation, as given in Fig.3.2. Such systems can be efficiently used for example in classification tasks when one FuNN is trained to classify examples of one particular class. This structure allows for adaptive individual tuning of each of the class FuNN units according to the performance of this class unit during the operation of the whole system. Only the FuNN units which do not operate properly need to be tuned, while the remaining ones remain unchanged. This facilitates an efficient and adaptive tuning of the system in real time. The rules extracted may be used for a better adaptation in the adaptation module. FuNN-based

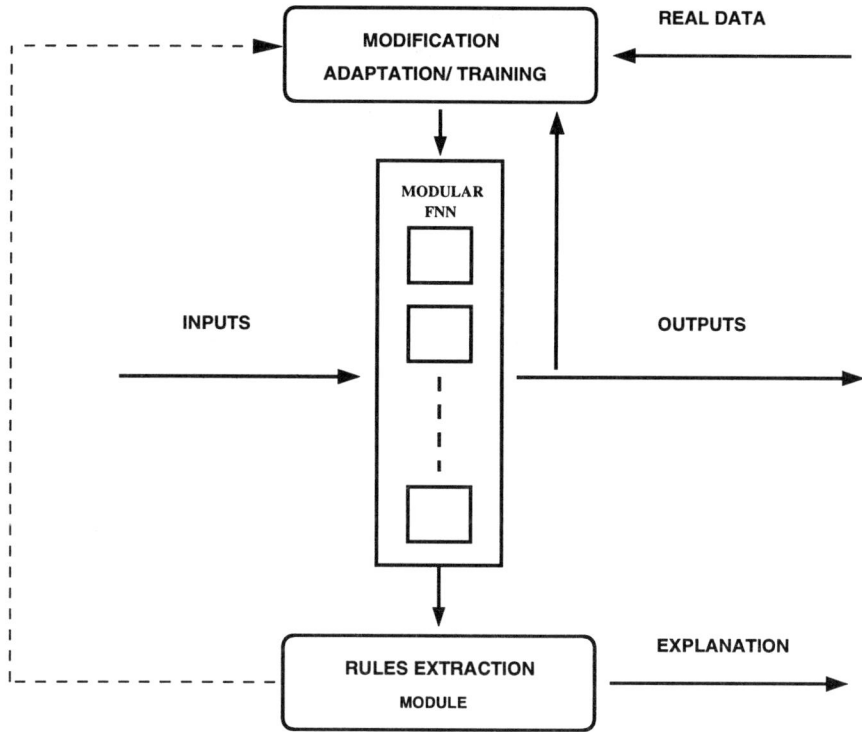

Fig. 3.2. Architecture of a multi-modular adaptive, intelligent FuNN-based system

hybrid systems, which consist of several modules for adaptive training, rules extraction and explanation, on-line data manipulation and analysis, are introduced here and illustrated in the next section as a powerful methodology for building on-line adaptive intelligent systems for chaotic time-series analysis.

4. Modeling, Predicting and Explaining the Underlying Rules of Chaotic Time Series

4.1 Implications of the Results of Chaos Analysis on FuNN Design

Usual statistical methods perform well if the analysed time series is a stationary process. In the presence of trends, seasonal patterns and cycles with not strictly periodic components, the effectiveness of traditional methods of signal analysis tends to diminish. In this section, a novel FuNN-based approach is proposed to complement or replace methods of correlation analysis.

Financial data represent very complex phenomena, therefore, even an advanced multivariate analysis technique can have only limited success in modeling these processes. We demonstrate our general methodology on a simple case study, which enables us to illustrate some major ideas in an easily understandable way. The results obtained by the very simple univariate model can be readily incorporated into a multi-modular system by using the FuNN modules described previously.

Consider the results obtained in the previous section when analysing the multi-fractalness of the SE40 index. It has been shown that there are two distinct time-scales in the data, i.e, the ones below about 20 time lags and another one above 20 to about 1 year. Time scales longer than 1 year has not been analysed because the limited amount of data. It has been found that the fractal dimension of the system is lower for small wave numbers k than for large k values, therefore different modeling methods are required to predict the time series for small and large k values.

It is an important question how the knowledge about the dominant time scales of the system can be utilised in the design of the FuNN architecture. The size and structure of the FuNN depends on the complexity of the modelled process. For a simple system, a few input nodes representing previous time steps are sufficient to describe the dynamics. It is important to note that an excessive use of input nodes makes the modeling not just more complicated but less accurate as well. Indeed, information supplied by the extra time lags is not used in generating the desired mapping, rather it acts as a noise component and makes the identification more difficult [4, 17]. Therefore, the optimum design of the structure of each FuNN module is a crucial issue.

In the following section it is outlined how structural learning methods can help to optimise the FuNN behaviour and how the FuNN structure can be used to obtain information about the chaotic properties of the system?

4.2 Prediction of SE40 index by FuNN and MLP

The operation of FuNN-based and MLP-based prediction modules are compared here for predicting the index value at the next time moment $t + 1$. In the initial FuNN model, 10 previous time steps have been used to model the SE40 value on the next day. Three triangular fuzzy membership functions have been used at each input node as well as at the output. Accordingly, there were 30 nodes in the condition layer and 3 nodes in the action layer. The number of rule nodes has been 20 and fully-connected weight matrices were used between the condition and rule, and the rule and action layers. Experiments have been performed with standard backpropagation and also with structural learning-with-forgetting. The choice of the forgetting rate γ is crucial, therefore, extensive parameter studies have been conducted to find an optimum value of γ. In the experiments shown in this paper, $\gamma = 5 \times 10^{-4}$ is used. This value allowed a proper convergence of the training on the one hand, and also an efficient pruning within several thousands iterations, on the other hand. In Figure 4.1a, results of training of the 10-30-20-3-1 FuNN

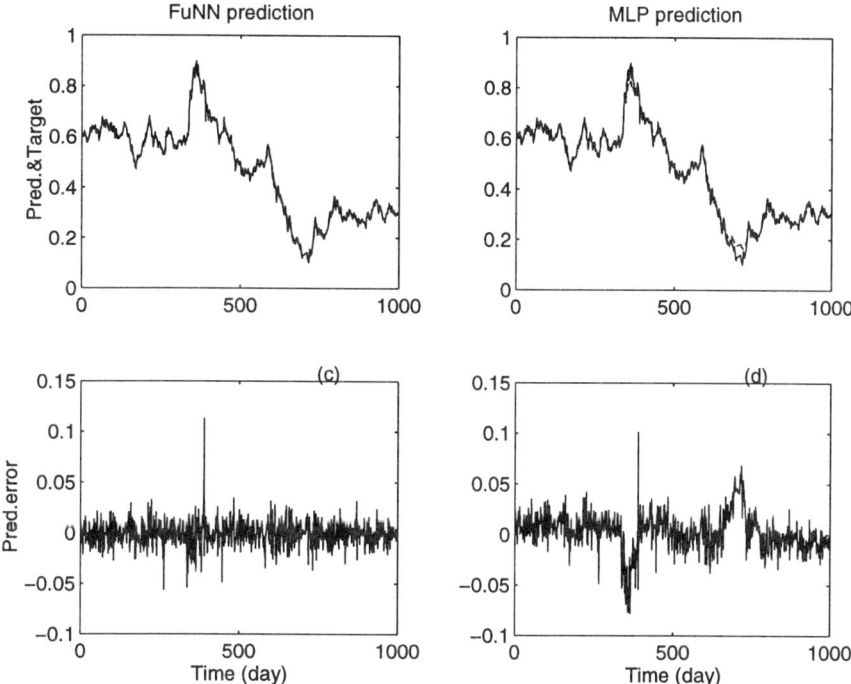

Fig. 4.1. Predicting the SE40 index by FuNN and standard MLP; (a) FuNN prediction, (b) MLP prediction, (c) prediction error by FuNN, (d) prediction error by MLP

are introduced, while Fig.4.1b corresponds to the case of standard three-layer perceptron (MLP). The one-step predicted and actual SE index values are in good agreement, therefore the two curves on Fig. 4.1a and Fig.4.1b significantly overlap. After careful inspection one can observe a noticeable discrepancy between the predicted and actual values in the MLP case, especially near the extrema; see Fig.4.1b. The differences are more clear on Figs. 4.1c-d, where the prediction error values are depicted for the FuNN and MLP, respectively. It is clear that the FuNN approximation is much better compared to the MLP. This advantage of the FuNN can be interpreted in the following way. There are relatively few training examples near the extrema of the training patterns, therefore, MLP learns slower over that part of the training set. FuNN, on the other hand, has dedicated membership functions distributed over the universe of discourse of the SE variable. The presence of membership functions helps to train better the model and to fine-tune the prediction.

It is interesting to calculate the absolute amount of gain or loss as the result of the prediction by FuNN when one tries to implement it in practice. Detailed calculation shows that the FuNN prediction yields an average daily success rate 54.01% compared to the 50% corresponding to the random choice. The performance of the forecasting system can be improved further by implementing the multi-modular scheme.

4.3 Extracting Rules via Structural Learning in FuNN

Finally, rule and knowledge extraction is performed based on the skeleton structure of the fuzzy neural network trained by structural learning with forgetting. Figures 4.2a and 4.2b illustrate the structure of the initial (fully-connected) and final (skeleton) structure of the hidden layers of FuNN. The input and output layers are not shown as they are not tuned during this set of experiments.

It is clear that only 6 rules remain active from the initial 20 rules after structural learning has been completed; see Fig. 4.2d. These rules are still quite complicated but a few interesting observations can be made. Nodes #14 and #16 represent rules which can be formulated as *"large stays large"* and *"small stays small"*, respectively. Rule node #10 supports an implication relation concerning the *medium (M)* future values and it writes:

IF [Y(t-7) is M (0.07)] and [Y(t-2) is M (0.06)] and [Y(t-1) is M (1.66)] and [Y(t-1) is not-L (0.22)] THEN [Y(t) is M (1.95)]

Interesting effects are seen in the condition layer as well. A clear memory effect takes place, i.e., the 3 membership functions belonging to the most recent time instant have far the highest contribution due to the large weight magnitudes at time $t - 1$, as it is shown in Fig.4.2c. In addition to the dominance of time $t - 1$, certain secondary effects are also obvious, which influence the nodes belonging to time points $t - 4$, $t - 7$, and $t - 10$. To emphasise this effect, the magnitudes of the weights W1 and W2 are depicted in Fig.4.2e-f in logarithmic coordinates. Figure 4.3 shows the importance of each time lag. The importance is calculated as the sum of the magnitudes of the weights linked with the given input node representing the given time lag. This result shows that the present skeleton structure describes a dynamical system with an effective memory of 4-5 time lags.

5. Conclusions

The paper presents, and illustrates on financial data, a neuro-fuzzy-chaos methodology for time series manipulation which includes: multi-scale analysis, modeling, prediction, knowledge acquisition and adaptation. In the first part, chaos and fractal analysis methods are introduced to analyse the chaosness of the data, to discover the time scales in which modeling and prediction would be possible, and to find out the dimensionality of the processes at the different time scales.

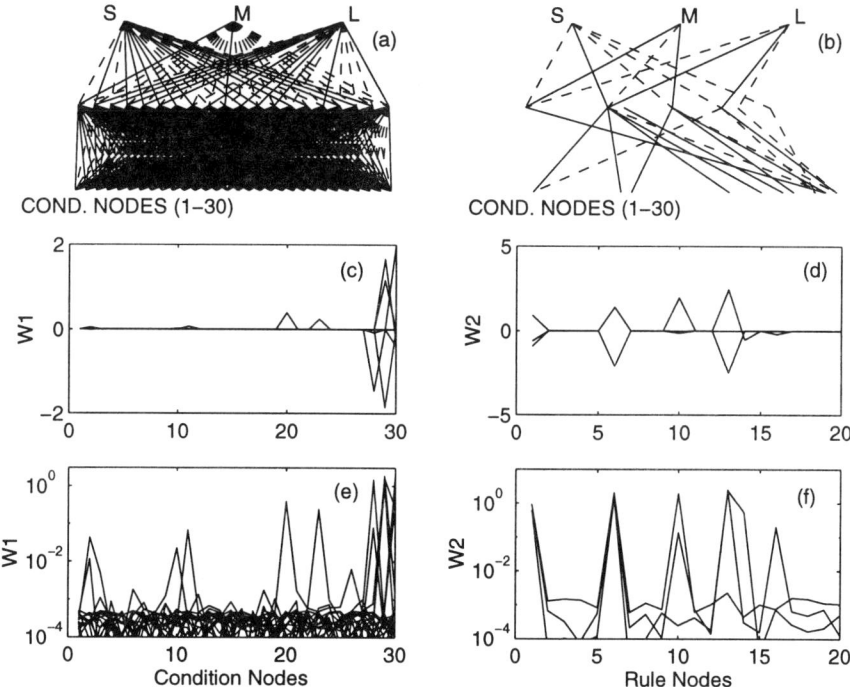

Fig. 4.2. Memory effect in the FuNN trained by learning with forgetting; (a) fully connected FuNN structure 10-30-20-3-1, (b) skeleton FuNN structure 4-12-6-3-1 (c) weights between condition and rule layers, (d) weights between rule and action layer, (e) log(abs(W1)), (f) log(abs(W2))

Based on the chaos and fractal analysis and on the multi-scale representation, a multi-modular system is built to model and predict the time series and to extract knowledge about its behaviour. In the modeling, fuzzy neural networks (FuNNs) were used which have been trained by a structural learning algorithm. In the paper the operation of a single module is analysed in detail. Rules have been extracted from the skeleton structure of the trained FuNN module.

In addition to time series prediction and rule extraction, the trained fuzzy neural network has been used also for estimating the effective memory of the process. This new, FuNN-based methodology of estimating the parameters of the chaotic process, in combination with evaluating the fractal dimension directly from the time series, can be used for iteratively refining our model and for improving the accuracy of the predictions made by the model.

There is a close connection between moving average prediction techniques and the time scales identified by multi-fractal analysis introduced in this paper. Future research should reveal the details of this relationship. Results

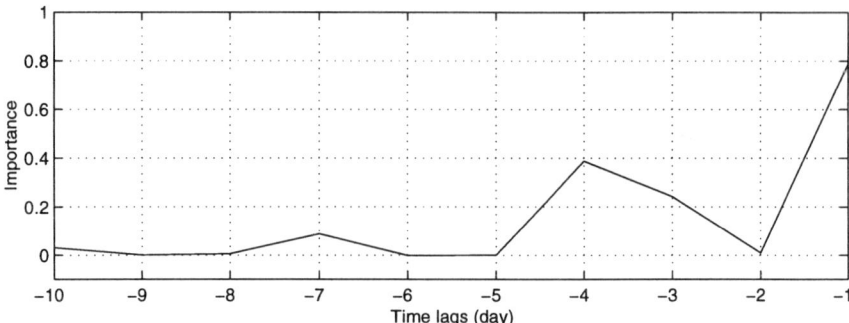

Fig. 4.3. Importance of input time lags calculated with structural learning in FuNN

of this study can be utilised in the implementation of the adaptive, multi-modular forecasting technique.

Our present study deals with a very simple one-variable model based on SE40 data. It is obvious that a reliable forecasting model should be a multi-variable one, which incorporates information on additional features of the NZ economy, and also financial data from major overseas countries.

References

1. Bai-Lin, H., Chaos II, World Scientific, 1990.
2. Farmer, J.D., Sidorowich, "Prediction Time Series," Phys. Rev. Lett., 59, 845-848 (1987)
3. Casdagli, M., "Nonlinear prediction of Chaotic Time Series," Physica D, 35, 335-356 (1989)
4. Sugihara, G., R.M. May, "Nonlinear Forecasting as a Way of Distinguishing Chaos from Measurement Error in Time Series," Nature, 344, 734-741 (1990)
5. Smith, L.A., "Local Optimal Prediction: Exploiting Strangeness and the Variation of Sensitivity to Initial Conditions," Phil. Trans. R. Soc. London A 446, 1-11 (1994)
6. Deboeck, G.J. (ed.) Trading on the Edge, Neural, Genetic, and Fuzzy Systems for Chaotic Financial Markets, John Wiley & Sons, N.Y. (1994)
7. Hashiyama, T., Furuhashi, T., Uchikawa, Y., "A Decision Making Model Using a Fuzzy Neural Network", in: Proceedings of the 2nd International Conference on Fuzzy Logic & Neural Networks, Iizuka, Japan, (1992) 1057-1060.
8. Kasabov, N. "Adaptable connectionist production systems". Neurocomputing 13 (2-4), 1996, 95-117
9. Kasabov, N., Foundations of Neural Networks, Fuzzy Systems and Knowledge Engineering, The MIT Press, CA, MA, 1996
10. Kasabov, N., Kim J S, Watts, M., Gray, A, "FuNN/2- A Fuzzy Neural Network Architecture for Adaptive Learning and Knowledge Acquisition", Information Sciences - Applications, 1997, in print

11. Hauptmann, W., Heesche, K., "A Neural Net Topology for Bidirectional Fuzzy-Neuro Transformation", in: Proceedings of the FUZZ-IEEE/IFES, Yokohama, Japan, (1995) 1511-1518.
12. Jang, R., "ANFIS: adaptive network-based fuzzy inference system", IEEE Trans. on Syst.,Man, Cybernetics, 23(3), May-June 1993, 665-685
13. Lin, C-T., Lin, C-J., Lee, C.T., "Fuzzy adaptive learning control network with on-line learning", Fuzzy Sets and Systems, 71 (1), 1995, 25-45
14. Kasabov, N. "Hybrid Connectionist Fuzzy Production Systems - Towards Building Comprehensive AI", Intelligent Automation and Soft Computing, 1:4 (1995) 351-360
15. Kasabov, N., "Investigating the adaptation and forgetting in fuzzy neural networks by using the method of training and zeroing", in: Proceedings of the International Conference on Neural Networks ICNN'96, Plenary, Panel and Special Sessions volume,1996, 118-123
16. Higuchi, T., "Approach to an Irregular Time Series on the Basis of the Fractal Theory," Physica D, Vol.31, pp. 277-283 (1988)
17. Tsonis, A.A., J.B. Elsner, "Nonlinear Prediction as a Way of Distinguishing Chaos from Random Fractal Sequences," Nature, 358, 217-220 (1992)
18. Sakuma, M., R. Kozma, M. Kitamura, "Characterisation of Anomalies by Applying Methods of Fractal Analysis," Nucl. Technol. 113, 86 99 (1996)
19. Ishikawa, M., "Learning of Modular Structured Networks", Artificial Intelligence (1995) 75, 51-62.
20. Kozma, R., M. Sakuma, Y. Yokoyama, M. Kitamura, "On the Accuracy of Mapping by Neural Networks Trained by Backpropagation with Forgetting", Neurocomputing, 13(2-4) (1996)
21. Reed, R., "Pruning algorithms - a survey", IEEE Trans. Neural Networks, 4(5) (1993) 740-747.
22. Sankar, A., R.J. Mammone, "Growing and Pruning Neural Tree Networks", IEEE Trans. Comput. 42(3) (1993) 291-299.
23. Le Cun, Y., J.S. Denker, S.A. Solla, "Optimal Brain Damage", in: D.S. Touretzky, ed., Advances in Neural Information Processing Systems, (Morgan Kaufmann, 1990) 2, 598-605.
24. Miller, D.A., J.M. Zurada, J.H. Lilly, "Pruning via Dynamic Adaptation of the Forgetting Rate in Structural Learning," Proc. IEEE ICNN'96, Vol.1, p.448 (1996)

Acknowledgement. This work has been completed as part of the Connectionist Based Information System (CBIS) project # UOO 606 funded by the Public Good Science Fund of the Foundation of Research Science & Technology (FRST) in New Zealand.

Dynamic Programming
and Fuzzy Reinforcement of Backpropagation
for Interest Rate Prediction

Maciej Krawczak
Systems Research Institute
Polish Academy of Sciences
ul. Newelska 6, 01-447 Warsaw, Poland
e-mail: krawczak@ibspan.waw.pl

1. INTRODUCTION

Our nature desires to know what is likely to happen in the future. The observation of the past can be used to anticipate the future behavior of the observed phenomenon *(prediction)*. The outcomes of the observed phenomenon over time form a *time series*. If a mathematical model of the phenomena is known then the prediction task is simple. Any mathematical model of interest rate is incomplete and the only way for prediction is to build a model that takes into account some previous outcomes and neglect any exterior influence. Formally a time series $\{x_t\}$ can be defined as a function x of an independent variable t. Sometimes the behavior of a time series can be anticipated by describing the series through probabilistic laws. Usually the considered interest rate as time series prediction problems are approached either by stochastic methods [1] or using artificial neural networks [12]. Both approaches have some advantages and some disadvantages. The stochastic methods are fast but commonly used linear models limit applicability. Neural networks methods from accuracy point of view are powerful but they are time consuming trial and error procedures.

The well-known dynamic programming can be applied to the dynamic process of multilayer neural networks learning. The learning error function as the return function is expanded into the Taylor series about some nominal network weights and corresponding states (neurons outputs). Using only the first term of the expansion of the return function the problem can be considered as differential dynamic programming of the first order [10].

Next it can be shown that obtained in this way these equations are exactly the same like those of the backpropagation algorithm [11]. The differential dynamic programming of the first order can elucidates the physical nature of the backpropagation algorithm.

In the last section it is proposed to improve the considered learning algorithm. The backpropagation algorithm is a descent gradient algorithm. All gradient based algorithms can be characterized by some very specific features, namely algorithms are very simple but the optimization is local and the converging rate is very low.

The neural networks models can be complemented with other successful approximation techniques based on fuzziness [3, 7]. Introducing linguistic descriptions of changing a learning rate and a gain parameter for each neuron we can speed up the learning process of the considered class of neural networks. Some numerical experiments were performed which showed the effectiveness of the neuro-fuzzy algorithm for practical applications.

2. STOCHASTIC MODELS

A general linear stochastic model of a stationary time series is the autoregressive moving average model of orders p and q (ARMA(p, q)). It describes the process value as a weighted sum of p previous process values and the current as well as q previous values of a random process. Formally, a stationary ARMA(p, q) process with zero mean $\{x_t\}$ is represented as:

$$x_t = \varphi_1 x_{t-1} + \varphi_2 x_{t-2} + \cdots + \varphi_p x_{t-p} + \alpha_t + \psi_1 \alpha_{t-1} \psi_2 \alpha_{t-2} + \cdots + \psi_q \alpha_{t-q}, \tag{1}$$

where $x_{t-1}, x_{t-2}, ..., x_{t-p}$ represent the process values at p previous time steps, $\alpha_t, \alpha_{t-1}, ..., \alpha_{t-q}$ are the current and the q previous values of a random process, usually emanating from a normal (Gaussian) distribution with mean zero and $\varphi_1 ... \varphi_p, \psi_1 ... \psi_q$ are the model parameters.

The ARMA(p, q) based predictor approximates the real process value x_t by a predicted value $\hat{x}_t$, computed as:

$$\hat{x}_t = \varphi_1 x_{t-1} + \varphi_2 x_{t-2} + \cdots + \varphi_p x_{t-p} + \alpha_t + \psi_1 \alpha_{t-1} \psi_2 \alpha_{t-2} + \cdots + \psi_q \alpha_{t-q}, \tag{2}$$

The AR(p) and MA(q) models are special cases of the ARMA(p, q) model, where AR(p) is described as:

$$x_t = \varphi_1 x_{t-1} + \varphi_2 x_{t-2} + \cdots + \varphi_p x_{t-p} + \alpha_t, \tag{3}$$

and MA(q) is described as:

$$x_t = \alpha_t + \psi_1 \alpha_{t-1} \psi_2 \alpha_{t-2} + \cdots + \psi_q \alpha_{t-q}. \tag{4}$$

A natural generalization of the linear ARMA and AR models to the nonlinear cases leads to the NARMA model

$$x_t = h(x_{t-1}, x_{t-2}, \cdots, x_{t-p}, \alpha_{t-1}, \alpha_{t-2}, \alpha_{t-q}) + \alpha_t, \tag{5}$$

and the NAR model

$$x_t = h(x_{t-1}, x_{t-2}, \cdots, x_{t-p}) + \alpha_t, \tag{6}$$

where *h* is an unknown smooth function.

The NARMA and NAR models are very complex, thus being unsuitable for real life applications. The neural networks models are closely related to NARMA ones and in the same time are more related to practical systems like systems of interest rate.

3. NEURAL NETWORKS

Feedforward neural networks work as universal approximators and can effectively construct approximations for unknown functions by learning from examples (known outcomes of the function). This ability to approximate unknown complex input-output mappings makes them attractive in practical applications.

The feedforward neural networks are considered as a number of simple processing units (*neurons*). The neurons are interconnected through synaptic links (*weights*) and are arranged in *layers*. There are three different types of layers, namely: *input, output* and one (or more) *hidden layers*. The considered architecture of neural networks is called *feedforward*, it means the signal flows from the input layer towards the output layer. Each neuron is characterized by an *activation function* (usually a nonlinear smooth and bounded function), the sum of its weighted inputs and a neuron specific parameter (called bias).

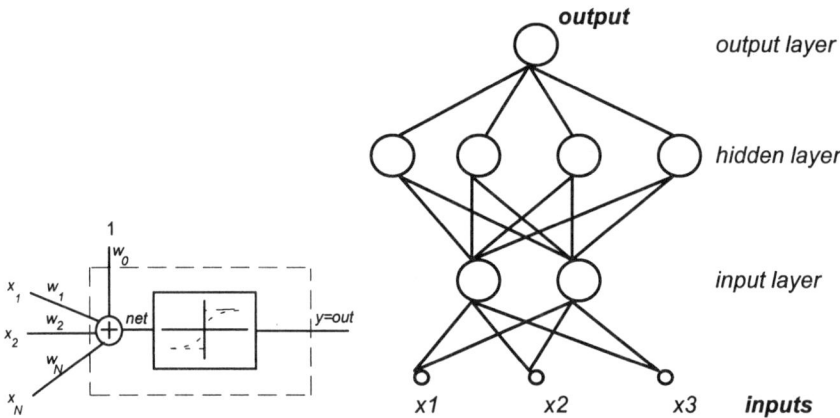

Fig.1. Processing unit - neuron   Fig.2. An example of a feedforward
                                          network with one hidden layer

Feedforward neural networks have been proposed [1] for simulating NARMA and NAR models. The NARMA predictor can be approximated as:

$$\hat{x}_t = h(x_{t-1}, \cdots, x_{t-p}, \alpha_{t-1}, \cdots, \alpha_{t-q}) \approx \sum_{i-1}^{m} W_i f(\sum_{j=1}^{p} w_{ij} x_{t-j} + \sum_{j=1}^{q} w'_{ij}(x_{t-j} - \hat{x}_{t-j}) + \theta_i) + \Gamma, \quad (7)$$

and the NAR predictor as:

$$\hat{x}_t = h(x_{t-1}, \cdots, x_{t-p}) \approx \sum_{i-1}^{m} W_i f(\sum_{j=1}^{p} w_{ij} x_{t-j} + \theta_i) + \Gamma, \quad (8)$$

where f represents a nonlinear, smooth and bounded function and $\alpha_k = x_k - \hat{x}_k$, , for all $k \in \{t - q, \cdots, t - 1\}$. This approximation of the NARMA model corresponds to neural networks in which W_i are the weights between hidden and output neurons, w_{ij} are the weights between external input neurons and hidden neurons, w'_{ij} are the weights between input neurons and hidden neurons, θ_i are the hidden neuron biases, Γ is the bias and f is the activation function of the hidden neurons.

3.1. Dynamic programming

The learning process can be treated as a dynamic system. In this case the required weights are treated as control to be optimal. The signals flow from the first layer to the last and next the value of the return function in the backwards way. Such structure of information flow is just the natural for the dynamic programming.

The supervised learning process of multilayer neural networks is based on somehow philosophical consideration of Pitts and McCulloch from 1947 [14], namely this process is of *iterative* nature. Considerations of Widrow and Hoff from 1960 [17] as well as the *backpropagation* algorithm of Rumelhart, Hinton and Williams from 1986 [15] have confirmed this idea of Pitts and McCulloch.

Let us denote each unit by the following expression

$$y_{pi}(k) = f_i \left(net_{pi}(k), \lambda_i(k), K \right) \quad (9)$$

$$net_{pi}(k) = \sum_{j=1}^{N_n} w_{ij}(k) x_{pj}(k) \quad (10)$$

where $y_{pi}(k)$ is a scalar output of the ith, $i=1,2,...,N$, unit within a layer k, $k=1,2,...,K$, the index $p=1,2,...,P$ indicates the number of a pattern, and next by $f_i(.)$ the activation function of an unit i in the network, while $\lambda_i(k)$ is a gain parameter (or temperature) of the unit.

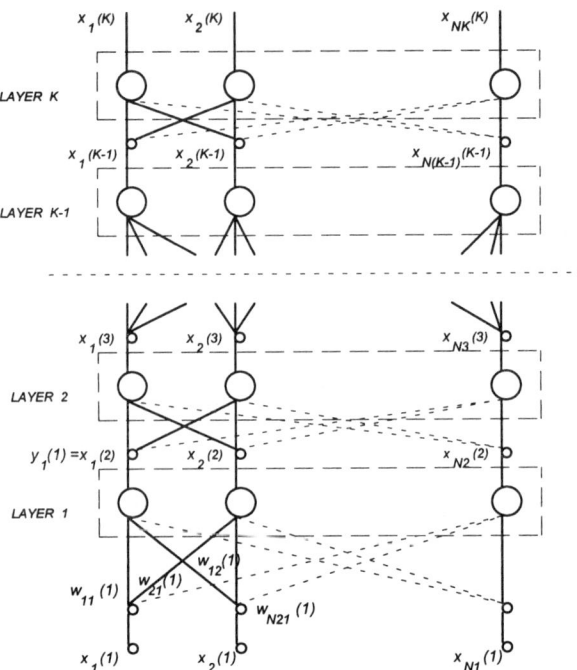

Fig. 3. Multilayer perceptron

Now let us aggregate units of any layer k, $k=1,2,...,K$, in the following way

$$Y_p(k) = \left[y_1(k), y_2(k),..., y_{N_{K+1}}(k) \right]^T$$

$$X_p(k) = \left[x_1(k), x_2(k),..., x_{N_K}(k) \right]^T$$

$$u_i(k) = \left[w_{i1}(k), w_{i2}(k),..., w_{N_K}(k) \right]^T$$

$$U(k) = \left[u_1(k), u_2(k),..., u_{N_{K+1}}(k) \right]^T$$

$$\Lambda(k) = \left[\lambda_1(k), \lambda_2(k),..., \lambda_{N_{K+1}}(k) \right]^T \tag{11}$$

the *K-stage* system is obtained, governed by the equation

$$X_p(k+1) = F\left[X_p(k), U_p(k), \Lambda_p(k) \right], \qquad k = 1,2,...,K \tag{12}$$

where F is a N_{k+1} dimensional vector of activation functions.

The supervised neural network learning is related to feeding the network with input patterns as the system input

$$X_p(1) = \left[x_{p1}(1), x_{p2}(1), ..., x_{pN_1}(1)\right]^T \qquad p = 1,2,...,P \qquad (13)$$

and at the same time the network output is compared to the corresponding pattern output

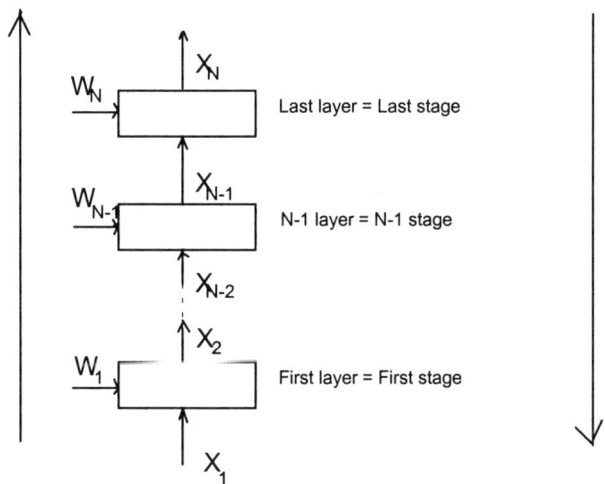

Fig. 4. Multilayer neural network as a multistage dynamic system

$$Y_p(K) = \left[y_{p1}(K), y_{p2}(K), ..., y_{pN_{K+1}}(K)\right]^T \qquad (14)$$

The error between the desired output and actual of the network, or square of such an error

$$E_p = \frac{1}{2}\left\|Y_p(K+1) - X_p(K+1)\right\|^2 \qquad p = 1,2,...,P \qquad (15)$$

can serve as a measure of weights adjustment. The error over all considered patterns

$$E = \sum_{p=1}^{P} E_p \qquad (16)$$

is a *performance index* for the considered multistage optimal control problem.

Equations (13-16) constitute just an optimal control problem. The application of the dynamic programming is strictly determined by the structure of the considered problem.

Let us consider a multilayer neural network as a multistage dynamic system shown in Fig. 2. Each stage of the multistage dynamic system is described by Eq.

(12) while the cost function, it means the learning error to be minimized w.r.t. controls (weighted) is defined by Eq. (16). For any $k = N - 1, n - 2, ..., 1$ the controls (weights) are chosen as

$$W(k) = \arg\min_{W(k)} V\big(\{W(k)\}, \{X(k)\}\big) \qquad (17)$$

where $V(\cdot)$ denotes the return function for the considered optimization problem and $\{\cdot\}$ is a sequence of the argument from k to $N - 1$. Now let us start from the first stage $k = 1$, it means let us consider the return function $V(1) = V\big(\{W(1)\}, \{X(1)\}\big)$ and the first-order Taylor expansion of this function about some nominal control $\{W^j(1)\}$, viz.

$$V^{j+1}(1) - V^j(1) = V_W^j(1)\big[\{W^{j+1}(1)\} - \{W^j(1)\}\big] \qquad (18)$$

for small enough control variations to ensure the expansion validity. If, for $\eta > 0$,

$$\{W^{j+1}(1)\} - \{W^j(1)\} = -\eta V_W^j(1)^T \qquad (19)$$

then we face a minimization problem.

For the arbitrarily chosen *nominal* weight (control) $\{W^j(1)\}$ the *nominal* states $\{X^j(1)\}$ can be computed *forward* from Eq. 12.

It can be shown [10] that the following *backward* equations are valid

$$V_X^j(k) = V_X^{j+}(k + 1) \cdot F_X^j(k) \qquad (20)$$
$$V_W^j(k) = V_X^{j+}(k + 1) \cdot F_W^j(k) \qquad (21)$$

and they can be applied to (19) in order to obtain the new nominal controls

$$\{W^{j+1}(k)\} \leftarrow \{W^j(k)\}.$$

For the new nominal controls $\{W^{j+1}(k)\}$ the new nominal states $\{X^{j+1}(k)\}$ are computed forward (see Fig. 4). This process is repeated until no improvement of the error (16) is obtained.

Equations (18) and (19) give a difference prescription how to change controls in order to minimize the performance index, these equations are similar to corresponding equations for the differential dynamic programming [9].

In sequence, the obtained formulae for control improvements are very similar to the backpropagation algorithm.

3.2. Backpropagation

The only known way to teach feedforward neural networks is to use backpropagation of the error of fitting the output of the network to the real data.

Here we consider a network built of neurons with sigmoidal activation function (Fig. 1)

$$y_i = f_i\left(net_i, \lambda_i\right) = \frac{1}{1 + e^{-\lambda_i net_i}} \tag{22}$$

where the input is denoted by

$$net_i = \sum_{j=1}^{N} w_{ij} x_j \tag{23}$$

where y_i is a scalar output of the ith unit within a layer l, the index $j=1,2,...,N$ indicates the input number and λ_i is a gain parameter (or temperature) of the unit.

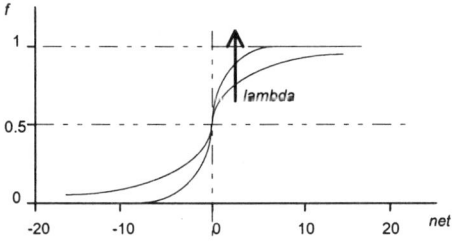

Fig. 5. Activation function

The backpropagation learning rule similar to Eq. (19) can be rewritten as

$$\Delta w_{ij}^l(k) = \eta \delta_j^i y_j^{(l-1)} \tag{24}$$

where η is the learning rate, δ_j is a generalized error of learning and $y_j^{(l-1)}$ denotes outputs of the previous layer. The new weights are generated by

$$w_{ij}^{(l)}(k+1) = w_{ij}^{(l)}(k) + \Delta w_{ij}^{(l)}(k) \,. \tag{25}$$

Here it should be emphasize that the Eq. (25) is very similar to the Eq. (19). This similarity allows to elucidate the background of the backpropagation algorithm, which was established as a heuristic procedure.

4. FUZZY REINFORCEMENT OF BACKPROPAGATION

The aim of the paper is to show how it is possible to implement the fuzzy logic for multilayer neural networks learning. We would like to use fuzzy logic to change the learning rate η in (24) as well as the gain parameter λ in (22) according to actual situation of the learning process. More precisely, during the learning process it can be noticed some regularities and some violation of this regularities. It is assumed that removing the violation the learning process can be speeded up. Changing the learning rate if necessary should make the learning process more fast while changing the gain parameter causes the change of the shape of the activation functions. It is easy to notice from Eq. (22) that

$$
\begin{aligned}
y &= f(-3,1) \approx 0.05 \\
y &= f(+3,1) \approx 0.95
\end{aligned}
\tag{26}
$$

and the sigmoidal curve in the neighborhood of (-3) and (3) is almost flat and even large change of the value of *net* does not change much the value of the neuron output.

It seems that proper choice of the learning rate η and the gain parameter λ should lead to possibility to avoid some local minima, to speed up computation by evasion from flat manifolds and to avoid oscillations.

We have tried to use some linguistic rules of the following form IF...THEN... which could cover these heuristics such as:

IF *The first derivative* **IS** *Negative Big* **AND**
  The second derivative **IS** *Negative Big*

THEN *Change of learning rate* **HAS TO BE** *Negative Small.* (27)

For such kind of linguistic notation of heuristic rules just the fuzzy logic methodology can be applied. It is known that:

- fuzzification transforms the crisp input values into linguistic ones,
- conclusion implements such linguistic rules,
- defuzzification gives again crisp results.

1. Quasioptimal change of the learning parameter η.

The approach for the learning rate η optimization is based on the following rules [3]:

IF *the I and II derivatives of the learning error are Small*
THEN *the learning rate η must be enlarged* (28)

IF *the I and II derivatives of the learning error are Large*
THEN *the learning rate η must be decreased.* (29)

For one cycle of learning (epoch) the learning error is similar to (15-16)

$$
E_e = \frac{1}{2} \sum_{p=1}^{P} \left\| Y_p(K+1) - X_p(K+1) \right\|^2
\tag{30}
$$

In the rules (28-29) there are first and second derivatives of the learning error with respect to the learning rate η which can be denoted by

$$\frac{\partial E_e}{\partial \eta} = E_{e\eta} \approx \alpha_1 \left(E_e - E_{e-1} \right) \qquad (31)$$

$$\frac{\partial^2 E_e}{\partial \eta^2} = E_{e\eta\eta} \approx \alpha_2 \left(E_{(e)\eta} - E_{(e-1)\eta} \right) \qquad (32)$$

where α_1, α_2 are scaling factors.

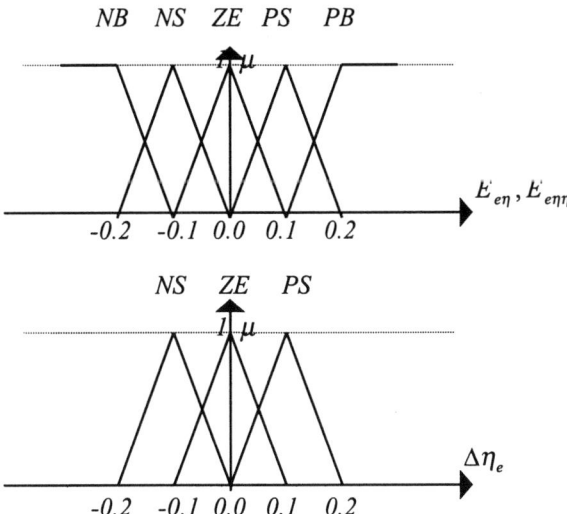

Fig. 6. Membership functions for changing of η

The membership functions for premises and conclusions for the chosen rules are of simple triangular shape, Fig. 6, where NB - means *Negative Big*, NS - *Negative Small*, ZE - *Zero*, PS - *Positive Small* and PB - *Positive Big*. The bases of rules development are shown in Table 1

Table 1. Rule bases for development of $\Delta\eta_e$

$E_{e\eta}, E_{e\eta\eta}$	NB	NS	ZE	PS	PB
NB	NS	NS	NS	NS	NS
NS	NS	ZE	ZE	NS	NS
ZE	ZE	ZE	PS	NS	NS
PS	NS	ZE	ZE	NS	NS
PB	NS	NS	NS	NS	NS

Using MIN-MAX conclusion for $\Delta\eta_e$ in the next epoch the learning rate will be changed in the following way:

$$\eta_{e+1} = \eta_e + \Delta\eta_e\alpha_1 \tag{33}$$

where α_1 is a scaling factor.

2. Quasioptimal change of the gain parameters λ .

For each neuron if the weighted input multiplied by its gain parameter has large either negative or positive value then it is proposed to reduce these weights for the next training epoch step. In this way the output of the neuron become smaller with the same input. It possible to obtain such results by modification of the gain parameter. First we need to assume some minimal and maximal points for the saturation of the activation function.

The difference between the actual output value with these points can describe the direction as well as the amplitude of the weights changes. The same we can get investigating the difference between the actual output and "middle" point, it means *output=1/2* for *net=0*.

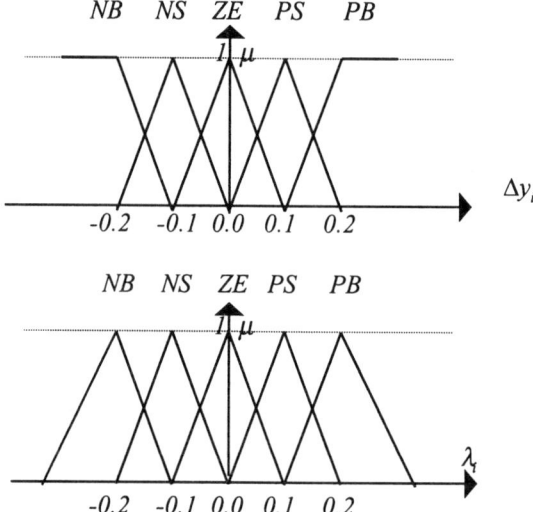

Fig. 7. Membership functions for changing of λ

It can be written as follows

$$\Delta y_i = y_i - \frac{1}{2} \tag{34}$$

Table 2. Rule bases for development of $\Delta\lambda$

$\Delta y, \Delta\lambda$	**NB**	**NS**	**ZE**	**PS**	**PB**
NB	PB	PS	ZE	NS	NB
NS	PS	PS	ZE	NS	NS
ZE	ZE	ZE	ZE	ZE	ZE
PS	NS	NS	ZE	PS	PS
PB	NB	NS	ZE	PS	PB

where y_i denotes the actual output of the neuron.

Fig. 8 illustrates the proposed procedure

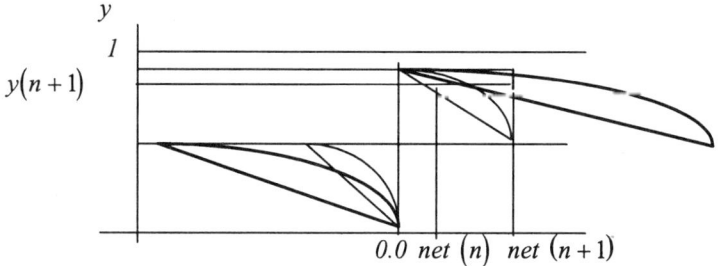

Fig. 8. Procedure illustration.

For any neuron, indicated by i, after each epoch n, the new gain parameter is calculated in a following way

$$\lambda_i(n+1) = \lambda_i(n) + \alpha_3 \Delta\lambda_i(n) \tag{35}$$

where $\Delta\lambda_i(n)$ is calculated with the help of Tab. 2, while α_3 is a scaling factor.

5. RESULTS

The proposed fuzzy reinforcement of backpropagation algorithm has been implemented on a PC computer. The new algorithm has been tested for some standard problems like 2- and 3- dimensional XOR problems. After that the computer program calculated several different tasks of prediction problem of real interet rates. It can be said that in average the number of epochs presented to the networks in order to teach the neural network was twice (sometimes less) smaller than using standard backpropagation algorithm.

6. CONCLUSIONS

We have studied neural networks as models for time series forecasting comparing the Box-Jenkins with the neural networks method.

First it was shown that the application of a method known in the optimal control theory, namely the differential dynamic programming (with the first order Taylor expansion of the return function) can elucidate the nature of the backpropagation algorithm applied to the supervised learning process of multilayer feedforward neural networks. The approach in a very elegant way can give a physical interpretation of the backpropagation algorithm. Then it was shown how to improve the backpropagation algorithm using some observation. As a result we proposed a heuristic algorithm which, with a help of fuzzy linguistic methodology, can speed up the convergence rate of the backpropagation algorithm. Considering the number of teaching epochs the improvement is twice in average.

REFERENCES

1. Abu-Mostafa, Y., 1995, "Financial Applications of Learning from Hints," in Advances in Neural Information Processing Systems (G. Tesauro et al, editors), Vol. 7, pp. 411-418.
2. Anderson J.A., Rosenfeld E.: Neurocomputing: Foundation of Research. Cambridge: MIT Press, 1988.
3. Arabashahi P. et el. (1995): Fuzzy Control of Backpropagation. Proc. Of 1st IEEE Int. Conference on Neural Networks.
4. Bellman, R.: Dynamic Programming. Univ. Press, Princeton, New Jersey, 1957 (6th ed. 1972).
5. Bowerman, B. L. and O'Connell, R. T. 1987. Time Series Forecasting: Unified Concepts and Computer Implementation, 2nd ed. Duxbury Press, Boston, TX.
6. Box G. and G. Jenkins, 1976, "Time Series Analysis. Forecasting and Control", Prentice-Hall.
7. Choi J.J. (1992): Fuzzy Parameter Adaptation in Neural Systems. Proc. Int. IEEE Joint Conference on Neural Networks.
8. Drossu R. and Z. Obradović, 1997, "Efficient Design of Neural Networks for Time Series Prediction", School of Electrical Engineering and Computer Science, Washington State University, Pullman, Working Paper, 99164-2752.
9. Jacobson D. H., Mayne D. Q.: Differential Dynamic Programming. Am. Elsevier Pub. Comp., N-Y, 1970.
10. Krawczak M. and Mizukami, K. (1994): The Control Theory Approach to Perceptron Learning Process. 44 Conference of IEE of Japan, Okayama, 1994.
11. Krawczak M. (1995): Perceptron Learning as an Optimal Control Problem. Proc. System Modelling Control, Zakopane 1995.
12. Lapedes A. and R. Farber, 1987, "Nonlinear Signal Processing Using Neural Networks: Prediction and System Modeling", Technical Report, LA-UR87-2662, Los Alamos National Laboratory, Los Alamos, New Mexico.

13. Lapedes, A. and Farber, R.1987. Nonlinear signal processing using neural networks: Prediction and System Modeling. Technical Report LA-UR-87-2662, Los Alamos National Laboratory.

14. Pitts, W. and McCulloch, W. S. (1947): How we know universals: the perception of auditory and visual forms. Bulletin of Mathematical Biophysics, 9, pp. 127-147. (Also in [1]).

15. Rumelhart, D., Hinton and Williams (1986): Parallel Distributed Processing., vol. 1, edited by D. Rumelhart, J. McClelland, and the PDP Research Group, MIT Press, Cambridge, MA, Chap. 8. (Also in [1]).

16. Werbos P., 1995, "Beyond Regression: New Tools for Predicting and Analysis in the Behavioral Sciences", Harvard University, Ph.D. Thesis, 1974. Reprint by J. Wiley and Sons.

17. Widrow, B. and Hoff, M. (1960): Adaptive Switching Circuits. 1960 IRE WESCON Convention Record, New York: IRE, pp. 96-104.

18. Yakowitz, S. and Rutherford, B. (1984): Computational Aspects of Discrete-Time Optimal Control. Applied Mathematics and Computation.

3

STOCK AND CURRENCY MARKETS

Portfolio Selection Based on Possibility Theory

Hideo Tanaka Peijun Guo

Department of Industrial Engineering, Osaka Prefecture University
Gakuencho 1-1, Sakai, Osaka 599-8531, Japan
tanaka@ie.osakafu-u.ac.jp guo@ie.osakafu-u.ac.jp

Abstract. An investor is faced with a choice from an enormous number of assets, such as stocks and bonds. It seems very difficult to decide which securities should be selected because of the inherent existence of uncertainty. Similar to other decision problems in an uncertainty environment, portfolio selection problems can also be modeled as stochastic programming problems and fuzzy programming problems, which supply a general frame to deal with the uncertainty in the real world from probabilistic and possibilistic viewpoints, respectively. The existing stochastic portfolio selection models and possibilistic portfolio selection models are introduced firstly. Then the emphasis will lie in the possibilistic models based on upper and lower exponential possibility distributions where experts' knowledge can be reflected.

1 Portfolio Selection Models Based on Probability Theory

Assume that there are n securities denoted by S_j ($j=1,...,n$). The return of the security S_j is denoted as x_j and the proportion of total investment fund devoted to this security is denoted as r_j. Thus, the following equation holds.

$$\sum_{j=1}^{n} r_j = 1 \tag{1}$$

Since the returns of the securities x_j ($j=1,...,n$) vary from time to time, those are assumed to be random variables which can be represented by the pair of the average vector and the covariance matrix. For instance, it is assumed that the observation data on returns of securities over m periods are given. At the discrete time i, the vector of n returns is denoted as $\mathbf{x}_i = [x_{i1}, \cdots, x_{in}]^t$. Thus, the total data over m periods are denoted as the following matrix.

$$\begin{pmatrix} x_{11} & x_{12} & \cdots & x_{1n} \\ x_{21} & x_{22} & \cdots & x_{2n} \\ \vdots & \vdots & \ddots & \vdots \\ x_{m1} & x_{m2} & \cdots & x_{mn} \end{pmatrix}, \tag{2}$$

where x_{ij} denoting the return of the jth security at the time i is defined as {(Closing price of the jth security at the time i)-(Its closing price at time i-1)+(Its dividends at the time i)}/(Its closing price at time i-1). The average vector of returns over m periods denoted as $\mathbf{x}^0 = [x_1^0, \cdots, x_n^0]^t$ is defined as

$$
\mathbf{x}^0 = \begin{bmatrix} \sum_{i=1}^{m} x_{i1}/m \\ \vdots \\ \sum_{i=1}^{m} x_{in}/m \end{bmatrix}.
\tag{3}
$$

The variance-covariance matrix $\mathbf{Q} = [q_{ij}]$ is defined as

$$
q_{ij} = \sum_{k=1}^{m}(x_{ki} - x_i^0)(x_{kj} - x_j^0)/m \quad (i=1,\ldots,n, j=1,\ldots,n).
\tag{4}
$$

Therefore, random variables x_j $(j=1,\ldots,n)$ can be represented by the average vector $\mathbf{x}^0$ and the covariance matrix $\mathbf{Q}$, denoted as $(\mathbf{x}^0, \mathbf{Q})$. Now, the return associated with a portfolio $\mathbf{r} = [r_1, \cdots, r_n]^t$ is given by

$$
z = \mathbf{r}'\mathbf{x}.
\tag{5}
$$

The average and variance of z are given as:

$$
E(z) = E(\mathbf{r}'\mathbf{x}) = \mathbf{r}'E\mathbf{x} = \mathbf{r}'\mathbf{x}^0,
\tag{6}
$$
$$
V(z) = V(\mathbf{r}'\mathbf{x}) = \mathbf{r}'\mathbf{Q}\mathbf{r}.
\tag{7}
$$

1.1 Markowitz's portfolio selection model

Since the variance of a portfolio return is regarded as the risk of investment, the best investment is one with the minimum variance (7) subject to a given average return c. This is the famous Markowitz's model [1]. It can be formalized as the following quadratic programming (QP) problem.

$$
\min_{\mathbf{r}} \quad \mathbf{r}'\mathbf{Q}\mathbf{r}
\tag{8}
$$
$$
\text{s.t.} \quad \mathbf{r}'\mathbf{x}^0 = c,
$$
$$
\sum_{i=1}^{n} r_i = 1,
$$
$$
r_i \geq 0.
$$

By changing the value of c in the QP problem (8), we can obtain the corresponding minimum variance of the portfolio return with the expected return given. The curve formed by the variance of the portfolio return and the corresponding expected return is called the efficient frontier (See Fig. 1). The points on the efficient frontier are the Pareto optimal solutions considering the bi-objectives, i.e., the expected return and the variance of the portfolio return. In Fig.1, the region under the efficient frontier is the feasible set for investment. Investors will choice the corresponding portfolio of the point P on the efficient frontier tangent to an indifferent curve of utility given by investors where A_1 is preferred to A_2 and A_2 is preferred to A_3.

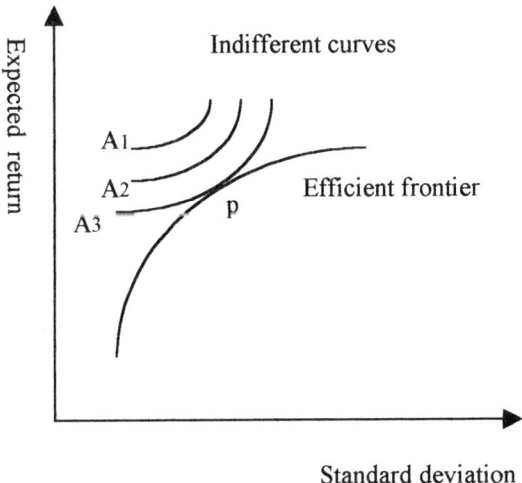

Fig. 1. The efficient frontier

1.2 Models based on probability measures

Let us consider the problem to maximize the probability of the event that the return of a portfolio is larger than a predetermined value c. Thus, the portfolio selection model for finding out such a portfolio **r** can be described as follows.

$$\max_{\mathbf{r}} \quad \Pr((\mathbf{r}'\mathbf{x}) \geq c) \tag{9}$$

$$\text{s.t.} \quad \sum_{i=1}^{n} r_i = 1,$$

$$r_i \geq 0.$$

For simplicity, we assume that the return vector $\mathbf{x}$ is from a normal probability distribution $N(\mathbf{x}^0, \mathbf{Q})$. Then the portfolio return z obeys the normal distribution $N(\mathbf{r}'\mathbf{x}^0, \mathbf{r}'\mathbf{Q}\mathbf{r})$. The objective function can be rewritten as follows:

$$\Pr(\mathbf{r}'\mathbf{x} \geq c) = \Pr(\frac{\mathbf{r}'\mathbf{x} - \mathbf{r}'\mathbf{x}^0}{\sqrt{\mathbf{r}'\mathbf{Q}\mathbf{r}}} \geq \frac{c - \mathbf{r}'\mathbf{x}^0}{\sqrt{\mathbf{r}'\mathbf{Q}\mathbf{r}}}) = 1 - \Phi(\frac{c - \mathbf{r}'\mathbf{x}^0}{\sqrt{\mathbf{r}'\mathbf{Q}\mathbf{r}}}), \tag{10}$$

where Φ is the probability distribution function of $N(0,1)$. It should be noted that $(\mathbf{r}'\mathbf{x} - \mathbf{r}'\mathbf{x}^0)/\sqrt{\mathbf{r}'\mathbf{Q}\mathbf{r}}$ obeys the standard normal distribution $N(0,1)$. As a result, maximizing the objective function (10) is equivalence to minimizing $(c - \mathbf{r}'\mathbf{x}^0)/\sqrt{\mathbf{r}'\mathbf{Q}\mathbf{r}}$, namely, maximizing $(\mathbf{r}'\mathbf{x}^0 - c)/\sqrt{\mathbf{r}'\mathbf{Q}\mathbf{r}}$. It leads to the following fractional programming problem, which can be solved by the methods proposed by Dinkelbach [2].

$$\max_{\mathbf{r}} \quad \frac{\mathbf{r}'\mathbf{x}^0 - c}{\sqrt{\mathbf{r}'\mathbf{Q}\mathbf{r}}} \tag{11}$$

$$\text{s.t.} \quad \sum_{i=1}^{n} r_i = 1,$$

$$r_i \geq 0.$$

Let us consider a dual model of (9), which maximize the expected portfolio return c under the condition that the probability of "the portfolio return being smaller than c" is at most α. The portfolio selection model for finding out such a portfolio $\mathbf{r}$ can be described as follows.

$$\max \quad c \tag{12}$$

$$\text{s.t.} \quad \Pr(\mathbf{r}'\mathbf{x} \leq c) \leq \alpha,$$

$$\sum_{i=1}^{n} r_i = 1,$$

$$r_i \geq 0,$$

where $0 < \alpha < 1/2$.

Similarly, we assume that the return vector $\mathbf{x}$ is from a normal probability distribution $N(\mathbf{x}^0, \mathbf{Q})$. The first constraint condition can be rewritten as follows:

$$\Pr(\mathbf{r}'\mathbf{x} \leq c) \leq \alpha \Leftrightarrow \Pr(\frac{\mathbf{r}'\mathbf{x} - \mathbf{r}'\mathbf{x}^0}{\sqrt{\mathbf{r}'\mathbf{Q}\mathbf{r}}} \leq \frac{c - \mathbf{r}'\mathbf{x}^0}{\sqrt{\mathbf{r}'\mathbf{Q}\mathbf{r}}}) \leq \alpha \Leftrightarrow \Phi(\frac{c - \mathbf{r}'\mathbf{x}^0}{\sqrt{\mathbf{r}'\mathbf{Q}\mathbf{r}}}) \leq \alpha. \tag{13}$$

From (13), we have

$$c \leq \mathbf{r}'\mathbf{x}^0 + K_\alpha \sqrt{\mathbf{r}'\mathbf{Q}\mathbf{r}}, \tag{14}$$

where K_α is the α-fractile of the standard normal distribution $N(0,1)$, i.e., $\Pr(x \le K_\alpha) = \alpha$. It follows from (14) that

$$\max c \iff \max \mathbf{r}'\mathbf{x}^0 + K_\alpha \sqrt{\mathbf{r}'\mathbf{Q}\mathbf{r}}. \tag{15}$$

Using (15), the optimization problem (12) becomes

$$\max \quad \mathbf{r}'\mathbf{x}^0 + K_\alpha \sqrt{\mathbf{r}'\mathbf{Q}\mathbf{r}} \tag{16}$$
$$\text{s.t.} \quad \sum_{i=1}^{n} r_i = 1,$$
$$r_i \ge 0.$$

It should be noted that $K_\alpha < 0$ because of $0 < \alpha < 1/2$. Thus, (16) is a convex programming problem. Using the method proposed by Kataoka [3], the model (16) can be solved.

2 Portfolio Selection Models Based on Possibility Theory

2.1 Portfolio selection models based on aspiration levels of decision-makers

From the relation between the expected returns and variances of portfolios in the efficient frontier of Markowitz's model, it is obvious that investors who pursue some portfolio with the higher expected return should take the larger risk. How to balance the expected return and the corresponding risk is a very important question for investors and contains some subjective factors. In what follows, a portfolio selection model, which employs fuzzy membership functions to reflect preferences with respect to return and risk, is introduced.

Generally speaking, investors always choose a portfolio from the feasible region according to the following two objectives

$$\max \quad E(\mathbf{r}'\mathbf{x}) = \mathbf{r}'\mathbf{x}^0,$$
$$\min \quad V(\mathbf{r}'\mathbf{x}) = \mathbf{r}'\mathbf{Q}\mathbf{r}. \tag{17}$$

The aspiration levels of the expected portfolio return and variance are represented by the membership function μ_E and μ_V, respectively [5]. The membership function μ_E shown in Fig. 2 is defined as

$$\mu_E(\mathbf{r}) = \begin{cases} 1 & : \quad E_u \le E(\mathbf{r}'\mathbf{x}) \\ 1 + \dfrac{E(\mathbf{r}'\mathbf{x}) - E_u}{E_u - E_l} & : E_l \le E(\mathbf{r}'\mathbf{x}) \le E_u \\ 0 & : \quad E(\mathbf{r}'\mathbf{x}) \le E_l \end{cases}, \tag{18}$$

where E_l and E_u are the given necessity and sufficiency levels for the expected return, respectively. The equation (18) means that the larger the expected return, the better the portfolio.

Similarly, the membership function μ_V shown in Fig.3 is defined as

$$\mu_V(\mathbf{r}) = \begin{cases} 1 & : \quad V(\mathbf{r}'\mathbf{x}) \le V_u \\ 1 - \dfrac{V(\mathbf{r}'\mathbf{x}) - V_u}{V_l - V_u} & : V_l \le V(\mathbf{r}'\mathbf{x}) \le V_u \\ 0 & : \quad V_l \le V(\mathbf{r}'\mathbf{x}) \end{cases}, \tag{19}$$

where V_l and V_u are the given necessity and sufficiency levels for risk, respectively. The equation (19) means that the smaller the variance is, the better the portfolio.

The total satisfaction level of the problem (17) for a portfolio $\mathbf{r}$, denoted as $\lambda(\mathbf{r})$, is defined as

$$\lambda(\mathbf{r}) = \min(\mu_E(\mathbf{r}), \mu_V(\mathbf{r})) . \tag{20}$$

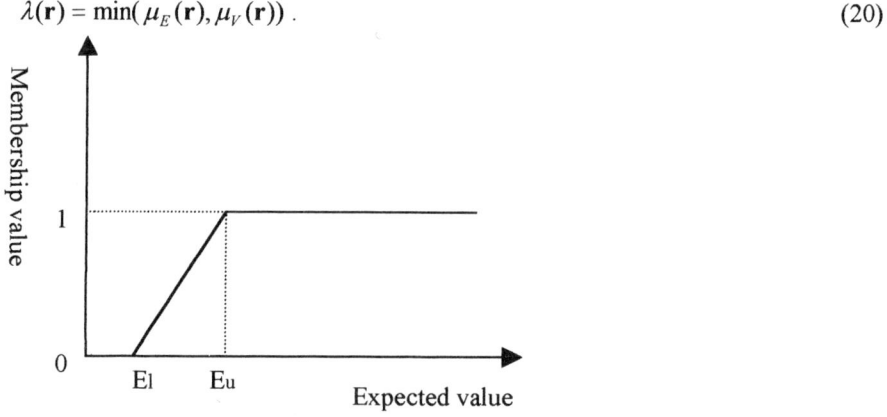

Fig. 2. The membership function for the expected portfolio return

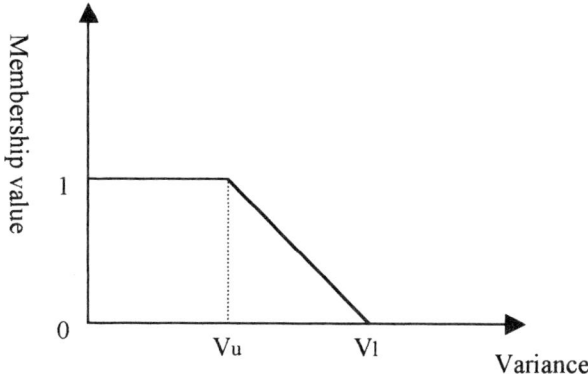

Fig. 3. Membership function for the variance of portfolio return

A compromise solution, which is regarded as the one maximizing the total satisfaction $\lambda(\mathbf{r})$, can be obtained by the following optimization problem.

$$\max \quad \lambda \tag{21}$$
$$\text{s.t.} \quad \lambda \leq \mu_E(\mathbf{r}),$$
$$\lambda \leq \mu_V(\mathbf{r}).$$

Substituting (18) and (19) into (21) and considering (17), the following optimization problem is obtained.

$$\max_{\mathbf{r}} \quad \lambda \tag{22}$$
$$\text{s.t.} \quad \mathbf{r}'\mathbf{x}^0 + (E_l - E_u)\lambda \geq E_l,$$
$$\mathbf{r}'\mathbf{Q}\mathbf{r} + (V_l - V_u)\lambda \leq V_l,$$
$$\mathbf{r}'\mathbf{I} = 1,$$
$$r_i \geq 0.$$

2.2 Portfolio selection models based on possibility and necessity measures

Let X be a possibilistic variable governed by a possibility distribution π_A. Given an inequality relation

$$X \leq z, \tag{23}$$

The possibility and necessity measures of (23), denoted as $Pos(X \leq z)$ and $Nes(X \leq z)$, respectively, are defined as follows:

$$\Pi_A(B) = \max_x (\min(\pi_A(x), \pi_B(x))),$$ (24)

$$N_A(B) = \min_x (\max(1 - \pi_A(x), \pi_B(x))),$$ (25)

where $\pi_B(x)$ is the membership function of fuzzy event B. In the cases of $Pos(X \le z)$ and $Nes(X \le z)$, B is the crisp set $(-\infty, z]$. From (24) and (25) we have

$$Pos(X \le z) = \max\{\pi_A(x) \,|\, x \le z\},$$ (26)

$$Nes(X \le z) = 1 - \max\{\pi_A(x) \,|\, x \ge z\},$$ (27)

whose explanations are shown in Fig. 4.

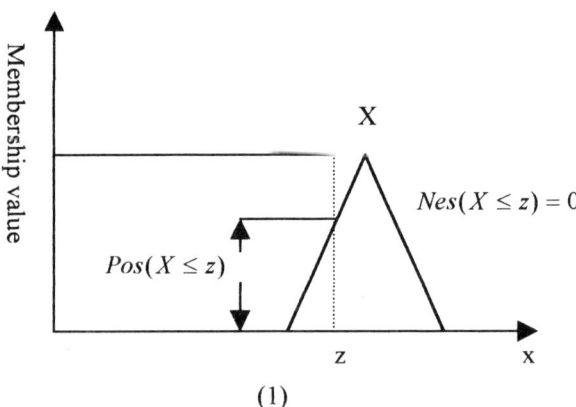

(1)

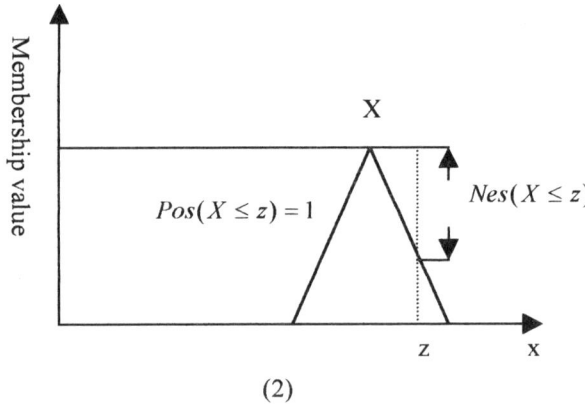

(2)

Fig. 4. The possibility and necessity measures of $X \le z$

Similarly, the following relations hold.

$$Pos(X \ge z) = \max\{\pi_A(x) \,|\, x \ge z\},$$ (28)

$$Nes(X \ge z) = 1 - \max\{\pi_A(x) \,|\, x \le z\}.$$ (29)

As in the portfolio selection models based on probability measures, the model based on necessity measures is given as follows:

$$\max_{\mathbf{r}} \quad Nes((\mathbf{r}'\mathbf{x}) \geq c) \tag{30}$$

$$\text{s.t.} \quad \sum_{i=1}^{n} r_i = 1,$$

$$r_i \geq 0,$$

where $\mathbf{x}$ is governed by a possibility distribution π_A rather than from a probability distribution. Its dual approach similar to the model (12) is given as follows.

$$\max \quad c \tag{31}$$

$$\text{s.t.} \quad Nes(\mathbf{r}'\mathbf{x} \leq c) \leq \alpha,$$

$$\sum_{i=1}^{n} r_i = 1,$$

$$r_i \geq 0.$$

Given a possibility distribution π_A, the models (30) and (31) can be solved with considering (27) and (29). Inuiguchi and Ramik [6] has given some detailed solutions of them by changing normal probability distributions to independent exponential possibility distributions.

2.3 Portfolio selection models based on fuzzy probabilities

The portfolio selection model based on fuzzy probabilities has been proposed by Tanaka et. al [7] where fuzzy probabilities are used to reflect experts' judgment in portfolio selection problems. In this method, the data are given as ($\mathbf{x}_i, h_i$) (i=1,...,m) where $\mathbf{x}_i = [x_{i1}, \cdots, x_{in}]'$ is a vector of returns of n securities S_j (j=1,...,n) at the ith period and h_i is a possibility grade reflecting a similarity degree between the future state of stock markets and the state of the ith sample offered by experts. These grades h_i ($i = 1,...,m$) are regarded as weights to determine the fuzzy average vector and covariance matrix in fuzzy probabilities.

2.3.1 Definition of fuzzy probabilities

Given the data ($\mathbf{x}_i, h_i$) ($i = 1,...,m$), the fuzzy weight average vector $\mathbf{a} = [a_1, \cdots, a_n]'$ can be defined as follows.

$$\mathbf{a} = \sum_{i=1}^{m} (h_i \mathbf{x}_i) / \sum_{i=1}^{m} h_i . \tag{32}$$

Similarly, the fuzzy weight covariance matrix $\Sigma = [\sigma_{ij}]$ can be defined by

$$\sigma_{ij} = \{ \sum_{k=1}^{m} (x_{ki} - a_i)(x_{kj} - a_j)h_k \} / \sum_{k=1}^{m} h_k \quad (i=1,\ldots,n, j=1,\ldots,n). \tag{33}$$

Thus, the given data (x_i, h_i) $(i = 1,\ldots,m)$ can be summarized as parametric representation (a, Σ), which is used to construct the fuzzy portfolio selection model.

2.3.2 Fuzzy probability portfolio selection model

Given the weight average vector and covariance matrix (a, Σ), the average and variance of the return z defined in (5) are given as follows:

$$E(z) = r'a, \tag{34}$$

$$V(z) = r'\Sigma r. \tag{35}$$

Thus, the fuzzy probability portfolio selection problem can be obtained as:

$$\begin{aligned}
\min_{r} \quad & r'\Sigma r \\
\text{s.t.} \quad & r'a = c, \\
& \sum_{i=1}^{n} r_i = 1, \\
& r_i \geq 0.
\end{aligned} \tag{36}$$

It should be noted that the average vector and the covariance matrix in Markowitz's model are replaced by the weight average vector and covariance, respectively, in which the expert judgment h_i is contained. The curve formed by the different given the values of c and the corresponding $r'\Sigma r$ obtained from the optimization problem (36) is called the fuzzy efficient frontier.

It is obvious that when the given data have the same important grades, the fuzzy probability portfolio selection model is just equivalent to Markowitz's model. It means that the fuzzy probability portfolio selection model (36) is an extension of the portfolio selection model (8).

2.4 Possibilistic portfolio selection model based on exponential distributions

The basic assumption for using probability models is that the situation of stock markets in future will be similar to the past one represented by the past security data. It is hard to ensure this kind of assumption for the real ever-changing stock markets. Possibility portfolio selection models has been proposed by Tanaka and Guo to reflect the experience of portfolio experts, which is characterized by the identified possibility distributions from the given possibility degrees to security data [8]. Because possibility portfolio models integrate security data in the past and experts' knowledge, it can catch variation of stock markets more feasibly.

2.4.1 Identification of possibility distributions

Let us begin with the given data ($\mathbf{x}_i, h_i$) ($i=1,...,m$) where $\mathbf{x}_i = [x_{i1}, \cdots, x_{in}]^t$ is an n-dimensional vector and h_i is an associated possibility grade given by experts to reflect the expert's judgement of how much the possibilistic grade of the ith sample is for some event. Assume that these grades h_i with $\mathbf{x}_i$ ($i=1,...,m$) are expressed by a possibility distribution $\mathbf{A}$ defined as

$$\Pi_A(\mathbf{x}) = \exp\{-(\mathbf{x}-\mathbf{a})^t \mathbf{D}_A^{-1}(\mathbf{x}-\mathbf{a})\} = (\mathbf{a}, \mathbf{D}_A)_e, \tag{37}$$

where $\mathbf{a} = [a_1, a_2, \cdots, a_n]^t$ is a center vector and $\mathbf{D}_A$ is a symmetric positive definite matrix, denoted as $\mathbf{D}_A > 0$.

Given the data, the problem is to determine an exponential possibility distribution (37), i.e., a center vector $\mathbf{a}$ and a symmetric positive definite matrix $\mathbf{D}_A$. According to two different viewpoints, two kinds of possibility distributions of $\mathbf{A}$, namely, the upper and the lower possibility distributions are introduced [9]. The upper and the lower possibility distributions denoted as Π_u and Π_l, respectively, should satisfy the inequality $\Pi_u(\mathbf{x}) \geq \Pi_l(\mathbf{x})$ with considering some similarities between our proposed methods and rough sets [10].

From (37), it is obvious that the vector $\mathbf{x}$ with the highest possibility grade should be closest to the center vector $\mathbf{a}$ among all $\mathbf{x}_i$ ($i=1,...,n$). Thus, the center vector $\mathbf{a}$ can be approximately estimated as

$$\mathbf{a} = \mathbf{x}_{i^*}, \tag{38}$$

where $\mathbf{x}_{i^*}$ denotes the vector with the grade such that $h_{i^*} = \underset{k=1,...,m}{\text{Max}} h_k$. The associated possibility grade of $\mathbf{x}_{i^*}$ is revised to be 1. Taking the transformation $\mathbf{y} = \mathbf{x} - \mathbf{a}$, the possibility distribution with a zero center vector is obtained as,

$$\Pi_A(\mathbf{y}) = \exp(-\mathbf{y}^t \mathbf{D}_A^{-1} \mathbf{y}) = (\mathbf{0}, \mathbf{D}_A)_e. \tag{39}$$

The upper and the lower distributions are used to reflect two kinds of distributions from the upper and the lower directions. In what follows, the matrices $\mathbf{D}_A$ in the upper and the lower possibility distributions are denoted as $\mathbf{D}_u$ and $\mathbf{D}_l$, respectively.

In order to determine the matrix $\mathbf{D}_u$ in the upper distribution, the following assumptions are given:

1) $\Pi_u(\mathbf{y}_i) \geq h_i$, $i=1,...,m$ (the constraint conditions),

2) minimize $\Pi_u(\mathbf{y}_1) \times \cdots \times \Pi_u(\mathbf{y}_m)$ (the objective function).

The problem can be described as determining $\mathbf{D}_u$ that minimizes the objective function 2) subject to the constraint conditions 1). It means to obtain the smallest distribution among $\Pi_u(\mathbf{y}_i) \geq h_i$ $(i=1,...,m)$ in the sense of minimizing $\Pi_u(\mathbf{y}_1) \times \cdots \times \Pi_u(\mathbf{y}_m)$. Fig. 5 illustrates the basic idea of the identification method. More detailed, the assumption 1) can be written as follows:

$$\Pi_u(\mathbf{y}_i) \geq h_i \Leftrightarrow \mathbf{y}_i' \mathbf{D}_u^{-1} \mathbf{y}_i \leq -\ln h_i, \ i=1,...,m. \tag{40}$$

The objective function can be rewritten as follows:

$$\max \sum_{i=1}^{m} \mathbf{y}_i' \mathbf{D}_u^{-1} \mathbf{y}_i. \tag{41}$$

Thus, the problem for obtaining $\mathbf{D}_u$ becomes the following optimization problem.

$$\max_{\mathbf{D}_u} \sum_{i=1}^{m} \mathbf{y}_i' \mathbf{D}_u^{-1} \mathbf{y}_i \tag{42}$$

$$\text{s.t.} \quad \mathbf{y}_i' \mathbf{D}_u^{-1} \mathbf{y}_i \leq -\ln h_i, \ i=1,...,m,$$
$$\mathbf{D}_u > 0.$$

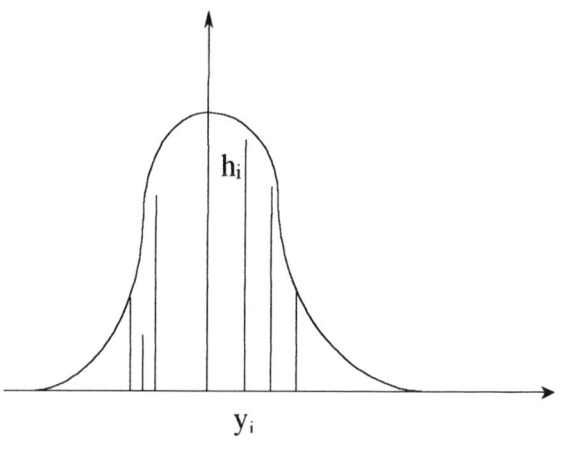

Fig. 5. Upper possibility distribution

Similarly, in order to determine the matrix $\mathbf{D}_l$ in the lower distribution, the following assumptions are given:

1) $\Pi_l(\mathbf{y}_i) \leq h_i$, $i=1,...,m$, (the constraint conditions),

2) maximize $\Pi_l(\mathbf{y}_1) \times \cdots \times \Pi_l(\mathbf{y}_m)$ (the objective function).

Likewise, the assumptions 1) and 2) can be converted into the following optimization problem to obtain the distribution matrix $\mathbf{D}_l$.

$$\min_{\mathbf{D}_l} \quad \sum_{i=1}^{m} \mathbf{y}_i' \mathbf{D}_l^{-1} \mathbf{y}_i \tag{43}$$

$$\text{s.t.} \quad \mathbf{y}_i' \mathbf{D}_l^{-1} \mathbf{y}_i \geq -\ln h_i, \qquad i=1,\dots,m,$$

$$\mathbf{D}_l > 0.$$

It means to obtain the largest distribution among $\Pi_l(\mathbf{y}_i) \leq h_i$, $i=1,\dots,m$ in the sense of maximizing $\Pi_l(\mathbf{y}_1) \times \cdots \times \Pi_l(\mathbf{y}_m)$. Fig. 6 shows the basic idea of the lower distribution.

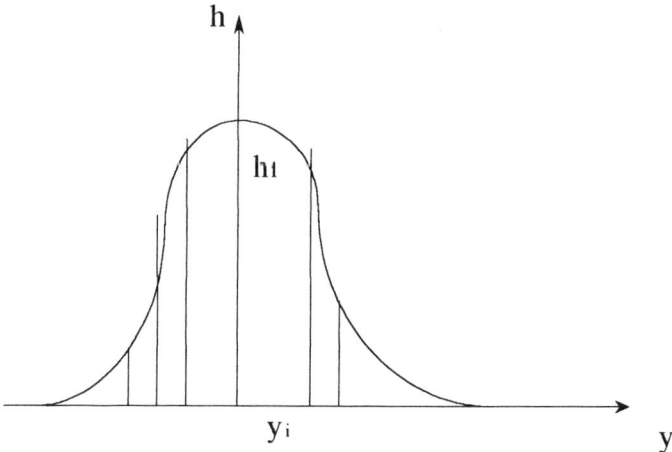

Fig. 6. Lower possibility distribution

From (42) the upper possibility distribution is obtained as the smallest possibility distribution subject to $\Pi_l(\mathbf{y}_i) \geq h_i$, namely, it is characterized as the least upper bound. And from (43) the lower possibility distribution is obtained as the largest possibility distribution subject to $\Pi_l(\mathbf{y}_i) \leq h_i$, namely, it is characterized as the great lower bound. If we solve these two optimization problems separately, it can not be ensured that $\Pi_u(\mathbf{y}) \geq \Pi_l(\mathbf{y})$ holds for an arbitrary $\mathbf{y}$. Let us consider the following model, which integrates (42) and (43) to find out $\mathbf{D}_l$ and $\mathbf{D}_u$, simultaneously with the condition that $\mathbf{D}_u - \mathbf{D}_l$ is a semi-positive definite matrix.

$$\min_{\mathbf{D}_u, \mathbf{D}_l} \quad \sum_{i=1}^{m} \mathbf{y}_i' \mathbf{D}_l^{-1} \mathbf{y}_i - \sum_{i=1}^{m} \mathbf{y}_i' \mathbf{D}_u^{-1} \mathbf{y}_i \tag{44}$$

$$\text{s.t.} \quad \mathbf{y}_i' \mathbf{D}_u^{-1} \mathbf{y}_i \leq -\ln h_i,$$

$$\mathbf{y}_i' \mathbf{D}_l^{-1} \mathbf{y}_i \geq -\ln h_i, \quad i=1,\dots,m,$$

$$\mathbf{D}_u - \mathbf{D}_l \geq 0,$$

$$\mathbf{D}_l > 0.$$

In this case, $\Pi_u(\mathbf{y})$ and $\Pi_l(\mathbf{y})$ are similar to rough sets concept shown in Fig. 7 because $\mathbf{D}_u - \mathbf{D}_l \geq 0$ ensures $\Pi_u(\mathbf{y}) \geq \Pi_l(\mathbf{y})$. It is obvious that (44) is a nonlinear optimization problem which is difficult to be solved.

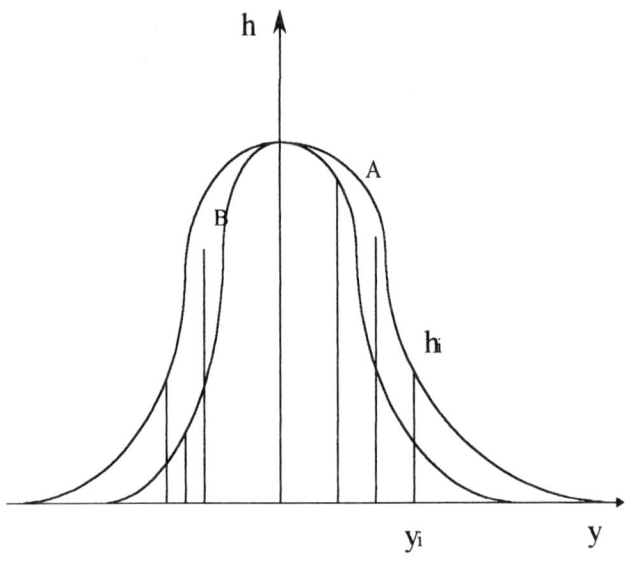

Fig. 7. Graphic explanation of upper and lower distributions(Curve A: $\Pi_u(\mathbf{y})$; Curve B: $\Pi_l(\mathbf{y})$)

In order to solve the problem (44) easily let us firstly consider a simple linear programming problem without the conditions $\mathbf{D}_u - \mathbf{D}_l \geq 0$ and $\mathbf{D}_l > 0$ in this problem. If the obtained matrix $\mathbf{D}_u$ and $\mathbf{D}_l$ can not satisfy the conditions $\mathbf{D}_u - \mathbf{D}_l \geq 0$ and $\mathbf{D}_l > 0$, we use principle component analysis (**PCA**) to rotate the given data $(\mathbf{y}_i, h_i)$ to obtain a positive definite matrix easily. Fig. 8 illustrates the rotation of orthogonal axes. The data can be transformed by linear transformation **T**. Columns of **T** are eigenvectors of the matrix $\Sigma = [\sigma_{ij}]$, where σ_{ij} is defined as

$$\sigma_{ij} = \{ \sum_{k=1}^{m} (x_{ki} - a_i)(x_{kj} - a_j) h_k \} / \sum_{k=1}^{m} h_k , \tag{45}$$

where the matrix Σ, called a correlation matrix, describes the scatter of the given data similar to the covariance matrix in statistic. Without loss of generality, we assume that $rank(\Sigma) = n$. It should be noted that $\mathbf{T}'\mathbf{T} = \mathbf{I}$. Using the linear transformation, the data $\mathbf{y}$ can be transformed into $\{\mathbf{z} = \mathbf{T}'\mathbf{y}\}$. Then we have

$$\Pi_A(\mathbf{z}) = \exp\{-\mathbf{z}'\mathbf{T}'\mathbf{D}_A^{-1}\mathbf{T}\mathbf{z}\}.$$ (46)

According to the feature of the PCA, $\mathbf{T}'\mathbf{D}_A^{-1}\mathbf{T}$ is assumed to be a diagonal matrix as follows:

$$\mathbf{T}'\mathbf{D}_A^{-1}\mathbf{T} = \mathbf{C}_A = \begin{pmatrix} c_1 & & 0 \\ & \ddots & \\ 0 & & c_n \end{pmatrix}.$$ (47)

Denote $\mathbf{C}_A$ as $\mathbf{C}_u$ and $\mathbf{C}_l$ for the upper and lower possibility distribution cases, respectively and denote c_{uj} and c_{lj} $(j=1,...,n)$ as the diagonal elements in $\mathbf{C}_u$ and $\mathbf{C}_l$, respectively. The integrated model can be rewritten as the following LP (linear programming problem):

$$\min_{\mathbf{C}_l,\mathbf{C}_u} \quad \sum_{i=1}^{m}\mathbf{z}_i'\mathbf{C}_l\mathbf{z}_i - \sum_{i=1}^{m}\mathbf{z}_i'\mathbf{C}_u\mathbf{z}_i$$ (48)

$$\text{s.t.} \quad \mathbf{z}_i'\mathbf{C}_l\mathbf{z}_i \geq -\ln h_i,$$

$$\mathbf{z}_i'\mathbf{C}_u\mathbf{z}_i \leq -\ln h_i, \quad i=1,...,m,$$

$$c_{uj} \geq \varepsilon$$

$$c_{lj} \geq c_{uj}, j=1,...,n,$$

where the condition $c_{lj} \geq c_{uj} \geq \varepsilon > 0$ makes the matrix $\mathbf{D}_u - \mathbf{D}_l$ semi-positive definite and matrices $\mathbf{D}_u$ and $\mathbf{D}_l$ positive. Thus, we have

$$\mathbf{D}_u = \mathbf{T}\mathbf{C}_u^{-1}\mathbf{T}',$$

$$\mathbf{D}_l = \mathbf{T}\mathbf{C}_l^{-1}\mathbf{T}'.$$ (49)

In what follows, let us show that in the LP problem (48), the matrices $\mathbf{C}_u$ and $\mathbf{C}_l$ always exist. Take $\mathbf{C}_u = q\mathbf{I}$ and $\mathbf{C}_l = p\mathbf{I}$ in (48). Thus the constraint conditions of (48) can be written as

$$p\mathbf{z}_i'\mathbf{z}_i \geq -\ln h_i, \quad i=1,...,m,$$

$$q\mathbf{z}_i'\mathbf{z}_i \leq -\ln h_i, \quad i=1,...,m,$$

$$q \geq \varepsilon,$$

$$p \geq q.$$ (50)

If we take $p = \max\limits_{i=1,\cdots,m-1, i \neq i'}(-\ln h_i / \mathbf{z}_i' \mathbf{z}_i)$, $q = \min\limits_{i=1,\cdots,m-1, i \neq i'}(-\ln h_i / \mathbf{z}_i' \mathbf{z}_i)$ and $\varepsilon \leq q$, inequalities (50) can hold. Therefore, there is an admissible set in the constraint conditions of the LP problem (50). It should be noted that the vector $\mathbf{z}_{i'} = \mathbf{0}$ is omitted, because $\mathbf{z}_{i'}' \mathbf{z}_{i'} = -\ln 1 = 0$ in (50). Thus, we consider $i=1,...,m-1$ without $\mathbf{z}_{i'} = \mathbf{0}$ in determining the values for p and q. This fact implies that we can always obtain the matrices $\mathbf{D}_u$ and $\mathbf{D}_l$ in the upper and lower possibility distributions.

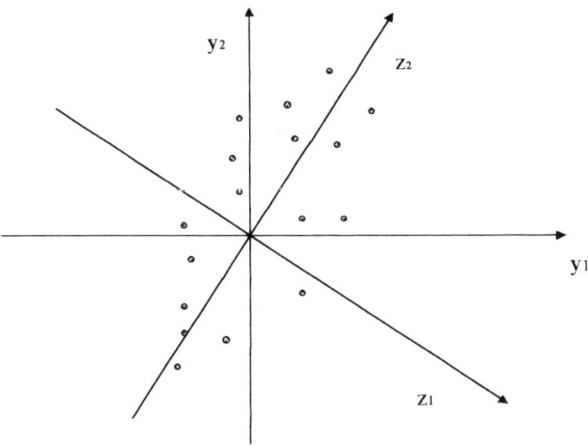

Fig. 8. Illustration of the linear transform by principle component analysis

Assume that the given data ($\mathbf{y}_i$, h_i), $i=1,...,m$, are obtained from an exponential possibility distribution $\mathbf{Y} = (\mathbf{0}, \mathbf{A}^\nabla)_e$ where the center vector is zero vector. In other words, the following equations hold.

$$\Pi_{\mathbf{Y}}(\mathbf{y}_i) = \exp\{-\mathbf{y}_i' \mathbf{A}^{\nabla^{-1}} \mathbf{y}_i\} = h_i, \text{ for } i=1,...,m. \tag{51}$$

Let us consider the following LP problem for finding out the upper distribution matrix $\mathbf{A}_u$ and the lower distribution matrix $\mathbf{A}_l$ from the above given data.

$$\min_{\mathbf{A}_l, \mathbf{A}_u} \quad J(\mathbf{A}_l, \mathbf{A}_u) = \sum_{i=1}^m \mathbf{y}_i' \mathbf{A}_l^{-1} \mathbf{y}_i - \sum_{i=1}^m \mathbf{y}_i' \mathbf{A}_u^{-1} \mathbf{y}_i \tag{52}$$

s.t.
$$\mathbf{y}_i' \mathbf{A}_l^{-1} \mathbf{y}_i \geq -\ln h_i,$$
$$\mathbf{y}_i' \mathbf{A}_u^{-1} \mathbf{y}_i \leq -\ln h_i,$$

where $i=1,...,m$.

It can be proved that the optimal solutions of $\mathbf{A}_u$ and $\mathbf{A}_l$ in the LP problem (52) are $\mathbf{A}^\nabla$ as follows. The LP problem (52) can be separated into the following two LP problems:

$$\max_{\mathbf{A}_u} \ J_1(\mathbf{A}_u) = \sum_{i=1}^m \mathbf{y}_i' \mathbf{A}_u^{-1} \mathbf{y}_i \tag{53}$$

s.t. $\quad \mathbf{y}_i' \mathbf{A}_u^{-1} \mathbf{y}_i \leq -\ln h_i, \ i=1,...,m.$

and

$$\min_{\mathbf{A}_l} \ J_2(\mathbf{A}_l) = \sum_{i=1}^m \mathbf{y}_i' \mathbf{A}_l^{-1} \mathbf{y}_i \tag{54}$$

s.t. $\quad \mathbf{y}_i' \mathbf{A}_l^{-1} \mathbf{y}_i \geq -\ln h_i, \ i=1,...,m.$

Since data $(\mathbf{y}_i, h_i)$ $(i=1,...,m)$ are obtained from the exponential possibility distribution $(\mathbf{0}, \mathbf{A}^\nabla)_e$, the data $(\mathbf{y}_i, h_i)$ $(i=1,...,m)$ satisfy (51). Therefore, $\mathbf{A}^\nabla$ is an admissible solution of (53) and (54). Assume that there is another matrix $\mathbf{A}'$ such as $J_1(\mathbf{A}') > J_1(\mathbf{A}^\nabla)$ in (53). Then, for some i,

$$\mathbf{y}_i' \mathbf{A}'^{-1} \mathbf{y}_i > \mathbf{y}_i' \mathbf{A}^{\nabla-1} \mathbf{y}_i = -\ln h_i, \tag{55}$$

which shows that $\mathbf{A}'$ is not admissible. Thus, $\mathbf{A}^\nabla$ is the optimal solution of (53). In the same way, we can prove that the optimal solution of (54) is also $\mathbf{A}^\nabla$. Therefore, both $\mathbf{A}_u$ and $\mathbf{A}_l$ are $\mathbf{A}^\nabla$, which means that our methods for determining an exponential possibility distribution can obtain the actual matrix $\mathbf{A}^\nabla$ if the given data are governed by an exponential possibility distribution with a distribution matrix $\mathbf{A}^\nabla$. Moreover, the upper and the lower possibility distributions are equal to $\mathbf{A}^\nabla$.

2.4.2 Portfolio selection model based on upper and lower possibility distributions
The portfolio return can be written as

$$z = \mathbf{r}' \mathbf{x}. \tag{56}$$

Because $\mathbf{x}$ is governed by a possibility distribution $(\mathbf{a}, \mathbf{D}_A)_e$, z becomes a possibility variable Z whose possibility distribution can be obtained as

$$\Pi_Z(z) = \exp\{-(z - \mathbf{r}' \mathbf{a})^2 (\mathbf{r}' \mathbf{D}_A \mathbf{r})^{-1}\} = (\mathbf{r}' \mathbf{a}, \mathbf{r}' \mathbf{D}_A \mathbf{r})_e, \tag{57}$$

where $\mathbf{r}' \mathbf{a}$ is the center value and $\mathbf{r}' \mathbf{D}_A \mathbf{r}$ is the spread of a portfolio return Z. After obtaining the lower and the upper possibility distributions, namely, $\mathbf{D}_u$ and $\mathbf{D}_l$, the corresponding portfolio selection models are given as:

Portfolio selection model based on upper possibility distributions

$$\min_{\mathbf{r}} \quad \mathbf{r}'\mathbf{D}_u\mathbf{r} \tag{58}$$

$$\text{s.t.} \quad \mathbf{r}'\mathbf{a} = c,$$

$$\sum_{i=1}^{n} r_i = 1,$$

$$r_i \geq 0, \ i{=}1,\ldots,n.$$

Portfolio selection model based on lower possibility distributions

$$\min_{\mathbf{r}} \quad \mathbf{r}'\mathbf{D}_l\mathbf{r} \tag{59}$$

$$\text{s. t.} \quad \mathbf{r}'\mathbf{a} = c,$$

$$\sum_{i=1}^{n} r_i = 1,$$

$$r_i \geq 0, \ i{=}1,\ldots,n,$$

where c is an expected center value of possibility portfolio return. It is straightforward that models (58) and (59) are quadratic programming problems minimizing the spread of a possibility portfolio return Z. If the constraint conditions $r_i \geq 0$ in (58) and (59) are eliminated, it means that a short sale is allowed. In this case, we can obtain the analytic solution of $\mathbf{r}$ as follows. Consider the following optimization problem

$$\min_{\mathbf{r}} \quad \mathbf{r}'\mathbf{D}\mathbf{r} \tag{60}$$

$$\text{s. t.} \quad \mathbf{r}'\mathbf{a} = c,$$

$$\sum_{i=1}^{n} r_i = 1,$$

where $\mathbf{D}$ is either $\mathbf{D}_u$ or $\mathbf{D}_l$. The optimal solution $\mathbf{r}^*$ can be obtained by minimizing the following Lagrangian function,

$$\min \quad L(\mathbf{r}, \lambda_1, \lambda_2) = \mathbf{r}'\mathbf{D}\mathbf{r} + \lambda_1(c - \mathbf{r}'\mathbf{a}) + \lambda_2(1 - \mathbf{r}'\mathbf{I}), \tag{61}$$

where $L(\mathbf{r}, \lambda_1, \lambda_2)$ is a convex function because of $\mathbf{D}{>}0$. The necessary and sufficient conditions for optimality of (61) are

$$\partial L / \partial \mathbf{r} = \mathbf{0},$$
$$\partial L / \partial \lambda_1 = 0,$$
$$\partial L / \partial \lambda_2 = 0, \tag{62}$$

which can be explicitly written as

$$2\mathbf{D}\mathbf{r} - \lambda_1\mathbf{a} - \lambda_2\mathbf{1} = \mathbf{0}, \tag{63}$$

$$c - \mathbf{r}'\mathbf{a} = 0, \tag{64}$$

$$1 - \mathbf{r}'\mathbf{1} = 0. \tag{65}$$

From (63), we have

$$\mathbf{r}' = 1/2(\lambda_1\mathbf{a}'\mathbf{D}^{-1} + \lambda_2\mathbf{1}'\mathbf{D}^{-1}) \tag{66}$$

Substituting (66) into (64) and (65) leads to the following equations.

$$c = 1/2(\lambda_1\mathbf{a}'\mathbf{D}^{-1}\mathbf{a} + \lambda_2\mathbf{1}'\mathbf{D}^{-1}\mathbf{a}), \tag{67}$$

$$1 = 1/2(\lambda_1\mathbf{a}'\mathbf{D}^{-1}\mathbf{1} + \lambda_2\mathbf{1}'\mathbf{D}^{-1}\mathbf{1}). \tag{68}$$

For simplicity, we let

$$\alpha = 1/2\mathbf{a}'\mathbf{D}^{-1}\mathbf{a}, \quad \beta = 1/2\mathbf{1}'\mathbf{D}^{-1}\mathbf{a}, \quad \gamma = 1/2\mathbf{1}'\mathbf{D}^{-1}\mathbf{1}. \tag{69}$$

It should be noted that α, β and γ are constant values. Thus, (67) and (68) can be rewritten as

$$\alpha\lambda_1 + \beta\lambda_2 = c, \tag{70}$$

$$\beta\lambda_1 + \gamma\lambda_2 = 1. \tag{71}$$

Assuming that $e = \alpha\gamma - \beta^2$ is not zero, we can solve the equations (70) and (71) to obtain λ_1 and λ_2 as follows:

$$\lambda_1 = (c\gamma - \beta)/e, \tag{72}$$

$$\lambda_2 = (\alpha - c\beta)/e. \tag{73}$$

Substituting (72) and (73) into (66) leads to

$$\mathbf{r}^{*\prime} = (c\gamma - \beta)/2e\mathbf{a}'\mathbf{D}^{-1} + (\alpha - c\beta)/2e\mathbf{1}'\mathbf{D}^{-1}. \tag{74}$$

Thus,

$$\mathbf{r}^* = ((\gamma/2e)\mathbf{D}^{-1}\mathbf{a} - (\beta/2e)\mathbf{D}^{-1}\mathbf{1})c + (\alpha/2e)\mathbf{D}^{-1}\mathbf{I} - (\beta/2e)\mathbf{D}^{-1}\mathbf{a}) = \mathbf{b}c + \mathbf{d}, \tag{75}$$

where $\mathbf{b} = (\gamma/2e)\mathbf{D}^{-1}\mathbf{a} - (\beta/2e)\mathbf{D}^{-1}\mathbf{1}, \tag{76}$

$$\mathbf{d} = (\alpha/2e)\mathbf{D}^{-1}\mathbf{I} - (\beta/2e)\mathbf{D}^{-1}\mathbf{a}. \tag{77}$$

Because **b** and **d** are constant vectors, it follows from (75) that the optimal solution $\mathbf{r}^*$ is a linear function of the given center c. Considering that $\mathbf{r}^{*t}\mathbf{D}\mathbf{r}^*$ is the smallest spread of the portfolio return denoted as τ, we have

$$\tau = \mathbf{r}^{*t}\mathbf{D}\mathbf{r}^* = (\mathbf{b}^t c + \mathbf{d}^t)\mathbf{D}(\mathbf{b}c + \mathbf{d}) = c^2 \mathbf{b}^t \mathbf{D}\mathbf{b} + 2c\mathbf{b}^t \mathbf{D}\mathbf{d} + \mathbf{d}^t \mathbf{D}\mathbf{d} . \tag{78}$$

Since $\mathbf{b}^t\mathbf{D}\mathbf{b}$, $\mathbf{b}^t\mathbf{D}\mathbf{d}$ and $\mathbf{d}^t\mathbf{D}\mathbf{d}$ are constants denoted as t_1, t_2 and t_3, respectively, (78) can be simply written as follows.

$$\tau = t_1 c^2 + t_2 c + t_3 , \tag{79}$$

which means that the spread τ is a quadratic function of the given center c.

It can be seen that the spread of the possibility portfolio return based on the lower possibility distribution is not larger than the one based on the upper possibility distribution as follows. Suppose that the optimal solutions obtained from (58) and (59) are denoted as $\mathbf{r}_u^*$ and $\mathbf{r}_l^*$, respectively, with considering the same center value. According to the relation between the upper and lower possibility distributions, i.e. $\mathbf{D}_u - \mathbf{D}_l \geq 0$, the following inequality hold.

$$\mathbf{r}_u^{*t}\mathbf{D}_u\mathbf{r}_u^* \geq \mathbf{r}_u^{*t}\mathbf{D}_l\mathbf{r}_u^* . \tag{80}$$

Because $\mathbf{r}_l^*$ is the optimal solution of (59), we have

$$\mathbf{r}_u^{*t}\mathbf{D}_l\mathbf{r}_u^* \geq \mathbf{r}_l^{*t}\mathbf{D}_l\mathbf{r}_l^* . \tag{81}$$

As a result,

$$\mathbf{r}_u^{*t}\mathbf{D}_u\mathbf{r}_u^* \geq \mathbf{r}_l^{*t}\mathbf{D}_l\mathbf{r}_l^* . \tag{82}$$

The nondominated solutions with considering two objective functions, i.e., the spread and the center of a possibility portfolio in the possibility portfolio selection models (58) and (59) can form efficient frontiers. Efficient frontiers from the upper and lower possibility portfolio selection models are called the possibility efficient frontiers **I** and **II**, respectively. Two spreads of possibility portfolio returns from the upper and lower possibility distributions with the same given center value form an interval. This interval is called a possibility risk interval, which is used to reflect the uncertainty in portfolio selection problems.

2.4.3 The model based on necessity measures

Referring to (31) with the obtained possibility distribution of **x**, i.e. $\Pi_A = (\mathbf{a}, \mathbf{D}_A)_e$, the following model can be considered.

$$\text{max} \quad c \tag{83}$$

$$\text{s.t.} \quad Nes(\mathbf{r}'\mathbf{x} \geq c) \geq \alpha,$$

$$\sum_{i=1}^{n} r_i = 1,$$

$$r_i \geq 0,$$

where α is a necessity level given by decision-makers. Using (29), we have

$$Nes(\mathbf{r}'\mathbf{x} \geq c) \geq \alpha \Leftrightarrow \mathbf{r}'\mathbf{x} - \sqrt{-\ln(1-\alpha)\mathbf{r}'\mathbf{D}_A\mathbf{r}} \geq c. \tag{84}$$

A graphic explanation is given in Fig. 9. Fig. 9 shows that the feasible region for c is $[0, q]$ where $q = \mathbf{r}'\mathbf{x} - \sqrt{-\ln(1-\alpha)\mathbf{r}'\mathbf{D}_A\mathbf{r}}$. It follows from (84) that maximizing the parameter c leads to

$$\max_{\mathbf{r}} \quad \mathbf{r}'\mathbf{x} - \sqrt{(-\ln\alpha)\mathbf{r}'\mathbf{D}_A\mathbf{r}}. \tag{85}$$

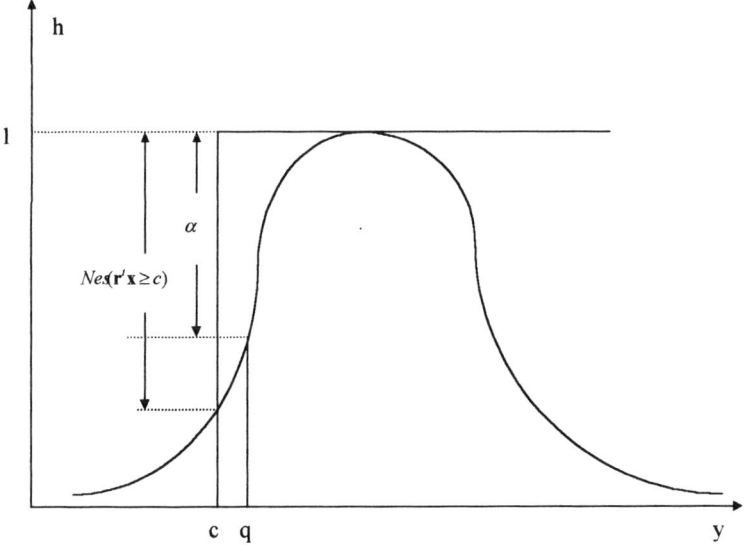

Fig. 9. Explanation of $Nes(\mathbf{r}'\mathbf{x} \geq c) \geq \alpha$

Thus, the problem (83) can be rewritten as

$$\max_{\mathbf{r}} \quad \mathbf{r}'\mathbf{x} - \sqrt{(-\ln\alpha)\mathbf{r}'\mathbf{D}_A\mathbf{r}} \tag{86}$$

$$\text{s.t.} \quad \sum_{i=1}^{n} r_i = 1,$$

$$r_i \geq 0.$$

It should be noted that the model (86) is a convex programming problem. It is obvious that the optimization problem (86) is similar to (16) in the forms. However, they analyze security data in very different way. The model (16) reflects the statistic viewpoint where $\mathbf{Q}$ is just from historical data while (86) reflects the experts' perspectives where $\mathbf{D}_A$ is from the historical data plus the experts' judgment.

3. Numerical Examples

In what follows, let us give a numerical example for illustration of the fuzzy probability portfolio selection model introduced in Section 2.3 and portfolio selection models based on upper and lower possibility distributions introduced in Section 2.4. The security data are listed in Table 1 introduced by Markowitz [2]. Since here we can consider that the recent sample is more similar to the future state, it is assumed that the possibility grade h_i can be obtained as

$$h_i = 0.2 + 0.7(t-1)/17 \quad (t=1,...,18). \tag{87}$$

In Table 6.1, No.1 to No.9 are American Tobacco, AT&T, United States Steel, General Motors, Atchison&Topeka&Santa Fe, Coca-Cola, Borden, Firestone and Sharon Steel, respectively. The return of the security S_j during a year is defined as

$$x_{t,j} = (p_{t+1,j} + d_{t,j} - p_{t,j})/p_{t,j}, \tag{88}$$

where $p_{t,j}$ is the closing price of the security S_j ($j=1,...,9$) in the year t and $d_{t,j}$ is the dividends of this security in the same year.

Table 1. Security data with possibility grades

hi	year	#1 Am.T	#2 A.T.&T.	#3 U.S.S.	#4 G.M.	#5 A.T.&S.	#6 C.C	#7 Bdn.	#8 Frstn.	#9 S.S.
0.2	1937(1)	-0.305	-0.173	-0.318	-0.477	-0.457	-0.065	-0.319	-0.4	-0.435
0.241	1938(2)	0.513	0.098	0.285	0.714	0.107	0.238	0.076	0.336	0.238
0.282	1939(3)	0.055	0.2	-0.047	0.165	-0.424	-0.078	0.381	-0.093	-0.295
0.324	1940(4)	-0.126	0.03	0.104	-0.043	-0.189	-0.077	-0.051	-0.09	-0.036
0.365	1941(5)	-0.28	-0.183	-0.171	-0.277	0.637	-0.187	0.087	-0.194	-0.24
0.406	1942(6)	-0.003	0.067	-0.039	0.476	0.865	0.156	0.262	1.113	0.126
0.447	1943(7)	0.428	0.3	0.149	0.225	0.313	0.351	0.341	0.58	0.639
0.488	1944(8)	0.192	0.103	0.26	0.29	0.637	0.233	0.227	0.473	0.282
0.529	1945(9)	0.446	0.216	0.419	0.216	0.373	0.349	0.352	0.229	0.578
0.571	1946(10)	-0.088	-0.046	-0.078	-0.272	-0.037	-0.209	0.153	-0.126	0.289
0.612	1947(11)	-0.127	-0.071	0.169	0.144	0.026	0.355	-0.099	0.009	0.184
0.653	1948(12)	-0.015	0.056	-0.035	0.107	0.153	-0.231	0.038	0	0.114
0.694	1949(13)	0.305	0.038	0.133	0.321	0.067	0.246	0.273	0.223	-0.222
0.735	1950(14)	-0.096	0.089	0.732	0.305	0.579	-0.248	0.091	0.65	0.327
0.776	1951(15)	0.016	0.09	0.021	0.195	0.04	-0.064	0.054	-0.131	0.333
0.818	1952(16)	0.128	0.083	0.131	0.39	0.434	0.079	0.109	0.175	0.062
0.859	1953(17)	-0.01	0.035	0.006	-0.072	-0.027	0.067	0.21	-0.084	-0.048
0.9	1954(18)	0.154	0.176	0.908	0.715	0.469	0.077	0.112	0.756	0.185

3.1 Portfolio selection model based on fuzzy probabilities

Using (32) we obtained the weight average vector as follows:

$\mathbf{a} = [0.07099, 0.07012, 0.19645, 0.20610, 0.23390, 0.05317, 0.13619, 0.21603, 0.14386]^t$

Using (33) we obtained the fuzzy covariance matrix Σ as follows.

$$
\begin{vmatrix}
0.04042 & 0.01593 & 0.01933 & 0.03277 & 0.01046 & 0.02665 & 0.0183 & 0.02816 & 0.02077 \\
0.01593 & 0.01119 & 0.01701 & 0.01875 & 0.00771 & 0.00705 & 0.00912 & 0.02106 & 0.01518 \\
0.01933 & 0.01701 & 0.09852 & 0.06287 & 0.04545 & 0.00694 & 0.0035 & 0.07752 & 0.03114 \\
0.03277 & 0.01875 & 0.06287 & 0.07954 & 0.04465 & 0.02072 & 0.00904 & 0.07894 & 0.01964 \\
0.01046 & 0.00771 & 0.04545 & 0.04465 & 0.09713 & 0.00585 & 0.01096 & 0.086 & 0.0285 \\
0.02665 & 0.00705 & 0.00694 & 0.02072 & 0.00585 & 0.0405 & 0.00953 & 0.01952 & 0.01095 \\
0.0183 & 0.00912 & 0.0035 & 0.00904 & 0.01096 & 0.00953 & 0.01986 & 0.01784 & 0.0079 \\
0.02816 & 0.02106 & 0.07752 & 0.07894 & 0.086 & 0.01952 & 0.01784 & 0.13343 & 0.03455 \\
0.02077 & 0.01518 & 0.03114 & 0.01964 & 0.0285 & 0.01095 & 0.0079 & 0.03455 & 0.06211
\end{vmatrix}
$$

Using the fuzzy probability portfolio selection model (36), we obtained the fuzzy efficient frontier shown in Fig.10. In Fig.10 the variance of a portfolio return is used to represent the risk of investment for fuzzy probability. Fig.11 shows the securities selected by the fuzzy probability model in the case of c=0.17

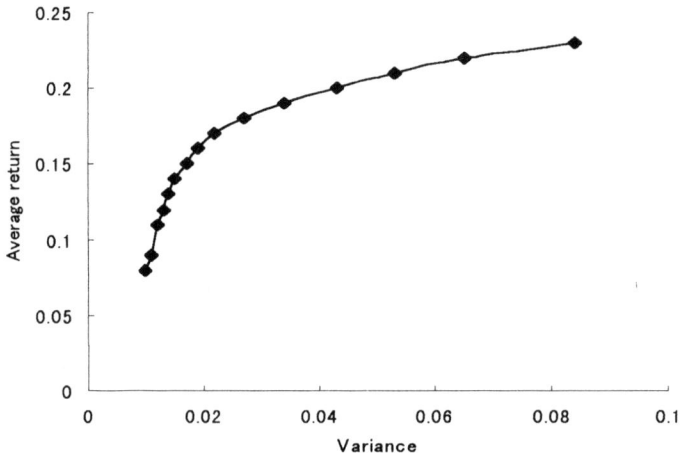

Fig. 10. Efficient frontier based on the fuzzy probability model

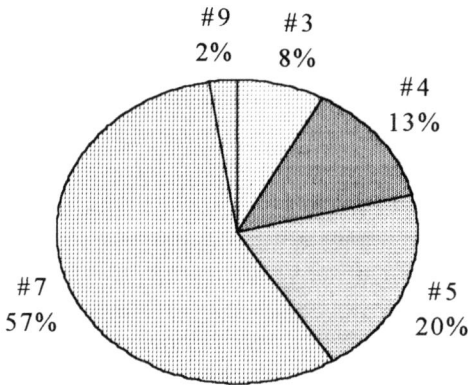

Fig. 11. Portfolio based on the fuzzy probability portfolio model(c=0.17)

3.2 Portfolio selection models based on upper and lower possibility distributions

The center vector, and upper and lower possibility distribution matrices were obtained by (38), (48) and (49) with ε =0.001 as follows.

a $=[0.154, 0.176, 0.908, 0.715, 0.469, 0.077, 0.112, 0.756, 0.185]$

52.242	39.936	-0.146	-52.592	-26.514	-61.637	149.506	67.634	-114.276
39.936	91.779	-21.404	-14.957	-93.979	-218.783	124.639	73.068	56.717
-0.146	-21.404	374.000	-381.493	89.657	102.189	112.117	-148.463	161.681
-52.592	-14.957	-381.493	476.694	-62.849	-47.444	-278.92	100.631	-43.709
-26.514	-93.979	89.657	-62.849	115.338	246.189	-70.492	-81.383	-78.534
-61.637	-218.783	102.189	-47.444	246.189	560.137	-193.902	-153.722	-244.533
149.506	124.639	112.117	-278.92	-70.492	-193.902	474.289	146.975	-238.171
67.634	73.068	-148.463	100.631	-81.383	-153.722	146.975	159.533	-183.809
-114.276	56.717	161.681	-43.709	-78.534	-244.533	-238.171	-183.809	720.757

51.951	39.730	-0.992	-53.331	-27.108	-61.831	149.395	66.677	-114.576
39.730	91.583	-22.443	-15.762	-94.476	-218.888	124.615	72.127	56.543
-0.992	-22.443	367.104	-386.498	87.167	101.954	112.314	-153.912	161.174
-53.331	-15.762	-386.498	472.979	-64.849	-47.724	-278.868	96.485	-44.235
-27.108	-94.476	87.167	-64.849	113.995	245.85	-70.628	-83.794	-79.083
-61.831	-218.888	101.954	-47.724	245.85	559.982	-194.014	-154.161	-244.76
149.395	124.615	112.314	-278.868	-70.628	-194.014	474.186	146.923	-238.328
66.677	72.127	-153.912	96.485	-83.794	-154.161	146.923	154.806	-184.575
-114.576	56.543	161.174	-44.235	-79.083	-244.76	-238.328	-184.575	720.418

Using models (58) and (59), we obtained two possibility efficient frontiers shown in Fig.12. It can be said from Fig.12 that the spread of the possibility portfolio return from (58) is always larger than that from (59). This fact stems from the concept of the lower and the upper possibility distributions. They can be regarded as two extreme opinions playing a reference role for an investor. The corresponding risk with $c=0.3$ is an interval value, i.e., [0.17978, 0.67318], which reflects the uncertainty in real investment problems. Fig. 13 and Fig. 14 show the securities selected by the possibility portfolio selection models (58) and (59) in the case of $c=0.3$, respectively. The result shows that the number of the obtained securities from (59) is more than the one from (58). It implies that the portfolio from (59) tends to take more distributive investment than the one from (58).

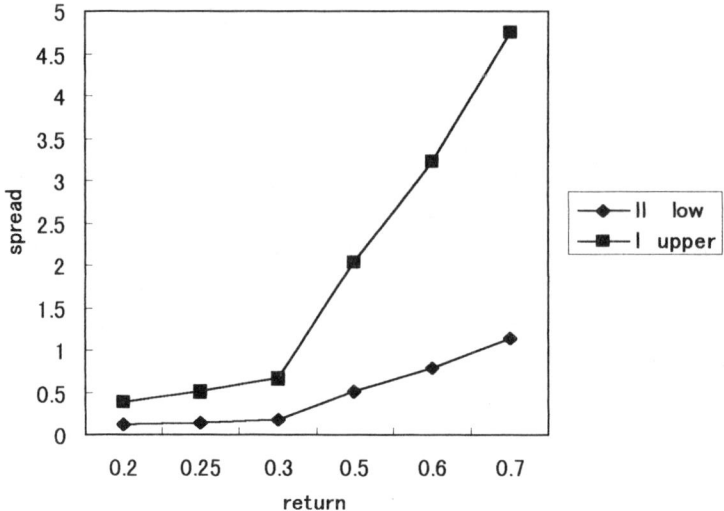

Fig. 12. Possibility efficient frontiers I and II

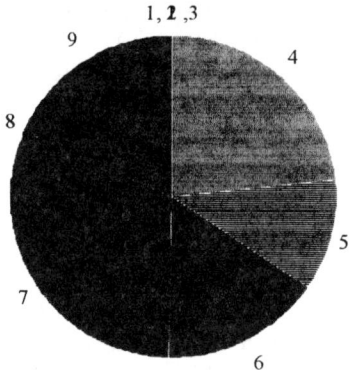

Fig. 13. Possibility portfolio based on the upper possibility distribution with c=0.3 (1,2,3,8: 0%, 4: 23.3%, 5: 11.1%, 6: 16.0%,7: 31.2%, 9: 18.4%)

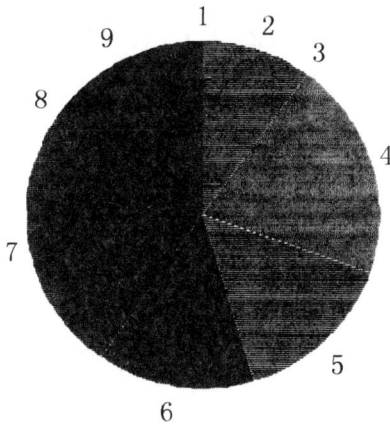

Fig. 14. Possibility portfolio based on the lower possibility distribution with c=0.3 (1,3,8: 0%, 2: 10.1%, 4: 20.1%, 5: 15.2%, 6: 14.3%, 7: 25.0%, 9: 15.3%)

References:
[1] W. Dinkelbach, On nonlinear fractiona programming, Management Since, 13 (1967) 492-498.
[2] H. Markowitz, Portfolio Selection: Efficient Diversification of Investments, John Wiley, New York, 1959.
[3] S. Kataoka, A stochastic programming model, Econometrica, 31(1963) 181-196.
[4] H. Konno and H. Yamazaki, Mean-absolute deviation portfolio optimization model and its applications to Tokyo stock market, Management Science 37(1991) 519-531.
[5] H. Mizunuma and J. Watada, Fuzzy portfolio selection: Realization of an aspiration level given by a decision maker, Transaction of the Institute of Systems, Control and Information Engineers 8 (1995) 677-684(In Japanese).
[6] M. Inuiguchi and J. Ramik, Fuzzy linear programming: A brief survey of techniques and application to portfolio selection, Fuzzy Sets and Systems (to appear)
[7] H. Tanaka, P. Guo and I. B. Turksen, Portfolio selection based on fuzzy probabilities and possibility distributions, Fuzzy Sets and Systems (to appear)
[8] H. Tanaka, P. Guo, Portfolio selection based on upper and lower exponential possibility distributions, European Journal of Operational Research (to appear)
[9] H. Tanaka and P. Guo, Identification methods for exponential possibility distributions, In: *Proceedings of Sixth IEEE International Conference on Fuzzy Systems* 2 (1997) 687-692.
[10] Z. Pawlak, Rough set, International Journal of Computer and Information Science, 11(1982) 341-356.

Neuro-Fuzzy Methods Applied to the German Stock Index DAX

Stefan Siekmann[1], Ralph Neuneier[1], Hans Georg Zimmermann[1], and Rudolf Kruse[2]

[1] Siemens AG, Corporate Technology
   D-81730 Munich, Germany
   Stefan.Siekmann@mchp.siemens.de
   E-mail: stefan.siekmann@mchp.siemens.de
[2] Otto-von-Guericke University Magdeburg
   Faculty of Computer Science
   D-39106 Magdeburg, Germany
   E-mail: Rudolf.Kruse@cs.uni-magdeburg.de

Abstract. Neural networks are able to learn from data but it is very difficult to extract useful information from an optimized neural network. Fuzzy-systems make use of expert knowledge but they can not learn from data. In this article, we present a neuro-fuzzy-system, combined with a semantic-preserving learning algorithm, which makes effective use of expert knowledge and of historical data.

The neuro-fuzzy-network can be initialized with a set of rules given by an expert or created with a rule generation algorithm and/or with some rules created at random. The particular architecture enables us not only to change the shape and the position of the membership functions and the rule weights but also to apply typical pruning algorithms to delete or insert single premises. The user can define some constraints on the premises, in order to avoid that the system create rules which are found in the data but semantically not correct. The learning algorithm optimize the rule base without destroying the semantic. Due to a sparse initial network structure the effective number of parameters is small which prevents the network from overfitting.

These methods are implemented in the *Simulation Environment for Neural Networks*, SENN, a product of Siemens AG. More information can be found at the web page `http://www.senn.sni.de`. We have tested the neuro-fuzzy-approach on different financial series. Here, we present encouraging results on the task to predict daily returns of the German Stock Index DAX using a simple technical model.

Keywords : neuro-fuzzy, daily prediction of DAX, semantic-preserving learning algorithm, pruning of rules and premises, rule generation

1 Financial Engineering and Neuro-Fuzzy-Methods

In the last few years neural networks have been applied to the problems of financial analysis. The advantages of neural networks in contrast to classical methods are established in the possibility to learn from data and the property of good approximation in high dimensional problems. It is very difficult to extract structural information from the optimized network. As a further disadvantage the expert knowledge is often ignored when applying classical statistical methods like linear regression as well as neural networks to time series prediction. An interesting approach is to combine fuzzy-methods with neural network learning algorithms [1] and to study so called neuro-fuzzy-architectures. The main problem with straight forward combination is that typical neuro-fuzzy-systems destroy their initial rule base during learning or have to use penalties which restrict the optimization [2]. The neuro-fuzzy-architecture is combined with a semantic-preserving learning algorithm which ensures that the rules always allow a meaningful interpretation after learning. Traders can relate their theories to the real data of the financial market by formulating a rule base and by observing the rule weights during learning. If some rules do not fit to the structure in the data, the learning algorithm will drive the rule weights to zero. Also integration of expert knowledge into a neural network can be useful to reduce the effect of overfitting. Bad generalization performance because of overfitting are typical in the field of financial analysis because the data is very noisy and often not available to the necessary extent [3]. Since rules given by an human expert are generally low dimensional and since each rule takes only a small number of input variables into account, the resulting architecture of our neuro-fuzzy-system is very sparse. The complexity of the network is further reduced by the mentioned semantic-preserving learning algorithm. The applicability of pruning techniques to delete non relevant or inconsistent premises and rules results in a even smaller number of parameters.

2 Transformation of Rules into a Neural Network

We describe, how a rule base given by an expert is transformed into the parameters of our neuro-fuzzy-architecture. First, an expert has to define a set fuzzy-rules $R_1,..,R_i,...,R_n$ of the following form:

Rule R_i:

IF	Δdax_t	$= increasing$
AND	Δusd_t	$= increasing$
THEN	Δdax_{t+1}	$= increasing$

where Δdax_t represents the daily difference of the DAX and Δusd_t the daily difference of the US-\$/DM-exchange rate at time step t. The linguistic expressions, e. g. *increasing* and *decreasing* are described by fuzzy sets, which are defined by one-dimensional membership functions, e. g. Gaussian or logistic functions. If describing particular economical relationships monotonous fuzzy-statements can be adequately expressed by a logistic membership function (figure 1, b).

$$m_j(x_i) = \exp\left(-0.5\frac{(x_i-\mu_{ij})^2}{\sigma_{ij}^2}\right) \quad \text{(Gaussian)}$$
$$m_j(x_i) = \left(1 + \exp(-4\frac{(x_i-\mu_{ij})}{\sigma_{ij}})\right)^{-1} \text{(logistic)} \tag{1}$$

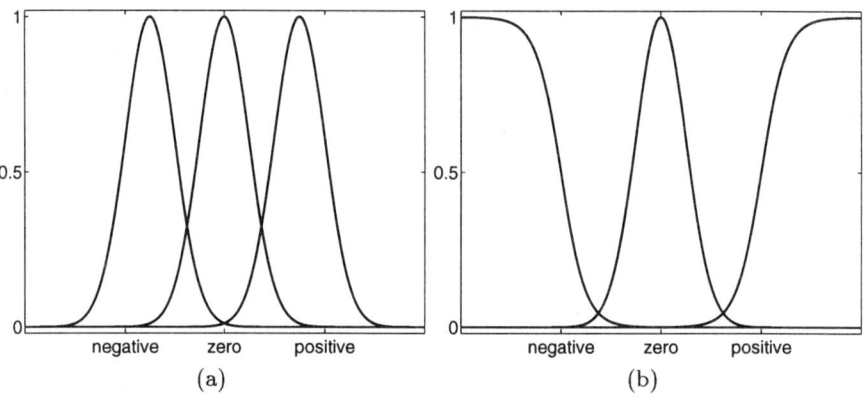

Fig. 1. Gaussian membership functions (a) and a combination of logistic and Gaussian membership functions (b).

The location of a membership function is determined by the parameter μ_{ij}, which represents the mean of the Gaussian resp. the turning point of the logistic function. The scope of a membership function depends on $\frac{1}{\sigma_{ij}}$, which is the inverse of the deviation of a Gaussian membership function, resp. is proportional to the slope at the turning point of the logistic function. Within this very general formulation we are free in specifying the form of a parameterized membership function. The product-operator is used to simulate the AND-Operation for rule evaluation. The "Center of Singleton" method is used for defuzzification (see also [2], [5], [6]). The output y for a given input vector $\underline{x} = (x_1, ..., x_j, ..., x_k)$ is computed by

$$y(\underline{x}) = \sum_{i=1}^{n} w_i \frac{b_i(\underline{x})}{\sum_{i=1}^{n} b_i(\underline{x})} \quad \text{with} \quad b_i(\underline{x}) = \kappa_i \Pi_{j=1}^{m}(m_j(x_{v(j)}))^{p_{ij}}. \tag{2}$$

where m represents the number of membership functions and $v(j)$ returns the index of the input variable corresponding to membership function j. The rules and membership functions are transformed into a neural network shown in figure 2. Each rule R_i corresponds to a neuron in the second hidden layer ("rule layer"). For each input variable x_k there is a set of membership functions m_j, corresponding to a neuron in the first hidden layer ("membership function layer"). The "membership function layer"(MF) is connected with the "rule layer", where the weights (p_{ij}) represents the premises. If rule R_i take the fuzzy-set m_j into account then the weight p_{ij} is set to 1, otherwise $p_{ij} = 0$. The singletons w_i are the weights of the connection between the "rule layer" and the output neuron.

The weight κ_i, which measures the "importance" of the rule R_i [7], are positive real numbers with their sum being equal to some a priori fixed constant. In this way unimportant or inconsistent rules are pruned automatically as the learning algorithm drives κ_i of such rules to zero [2], [8].

In figure 2 a neuro-fuzzy-model with two input variables (*dax*, *dollar*)and one output variable is shown. The system consists of three membership functions for each input and the output (*increase*, *stable*, *decrease*) and nine rules. This network acts like a normal feed forward network with one input

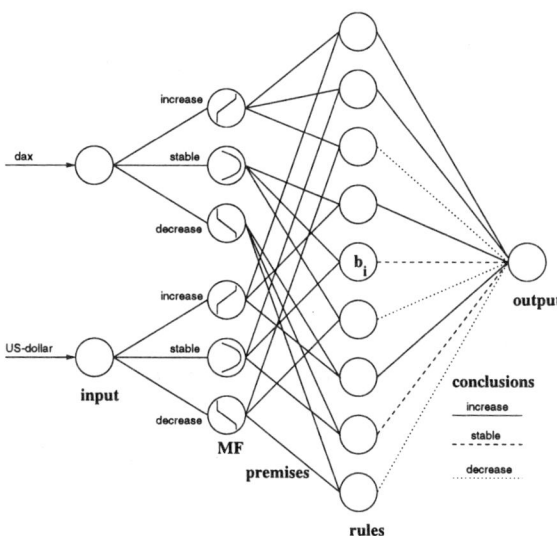

Fig. 2. The neuro-fuzzy-architecture

cluster, one output cluster and two hidden layers.

3   The Semantic-Preserving Learning Algorithm

After initializing the network with some rules, which was formulated by an expert or created with a rule generation algorithm, training on actual data can improve the network performance. Learning algorithms based on a gradient descent technique (e. g. back-propagation, conjugate gradient and others, see [4]) will destroy the initial rules. To avoid that the parameters of the membership functions move too far from their original values and destroy the initial semantic, the user can express two types of relations between the parameters of the membership functions. First, one may demand that the parameters of different membership functions to have the same value, e. g. belong to one equivalence class. For example, a rule describing a trend behavior looks like

$$
\begin{aligned}
\text{IF} \quad & \Delta dax_t \quad = increasing \\
\text{AND} \quad & \Delta dax_{t-1} = increasing \\
\text{THEN} \quad & \Delta dax_{t+1} = increase
\end{aligned}
$$

where Δdax_t measures the relative difference between the last two days of the DAX (time step $t-1$ to time step t). Since the fuzzy-set *increasing* is used by the same time series, the user may link all or some of the parameters of these membership function, e. g. the parameter μ:

$$
\mu^{increasing}_{\Delta dax_t} = \mu^{increasing}_{\Delta dax_{t-1}} \tag{3}
$$

Second, with order constraints we mean that the position parameters (μ_{ij}) shall be kept in their original semantic order or within some bounds, e. g. :

$$
-7 < \mu^{decrease}_{\Delta dax} < \mu^{zero}_{\Delta dax} < \mu^{increase}_{\Delta dax} < 7 \tag{4}
$$

After one training cycle the parameters are adapted in a direction computed by the learning algorithm. Before the new training cycle starts we have to insure that the user given constraints are fulfilled. Instead of using general constraint-optimization methods which would heavily enlarge the computing time, we solve that problem by ranking the constraints and applying a variation of a active set technique [9]. If two parameters have reversed the original order, they must be corrected. As the correction can lead to a situation where other constraints are not met, the process might have to be iterated. If all constraints can not be solved within a given number of iteration the user is given a warning that the rule base is not consistent with the data. Then one can change the rules or release some constraints. In our experiments the algorithm needs rarely more than one iteration and has always converged.

We want to stress that in contrast to the methods in [2], our technique preserves the initial semantic given by the relations among the fuzzy-expressions in the rule base. The semantic-preserving learning algorithm ensures that reinterpretation after training is always possible and can give useful insights for an improved system understanding. In addition, the constraints reduce the effective number of parameters which can avoid overfitting.

4 Pruning of Rules and Premises

4.1 Why Pruning ?

The main problem of time series prediction with neural networks is to avoid overfitting and pure memorizing the training data. Since the proposed neuro-fuzzy-approach is able to approximate any continuous function with arbitrary accuracy, one has to control the effective complexity of the model to avoid overfitting. One possibility to achieve models with high generalization performance is to eliminate neurons or parameters which are only approximating the noise in the data. How typical pruning algorithms can be applied to the neuro-fuzzy-network is described in the next section.

4.2 Pruning Rules

The positive rule weights κ_i are always unconstrained except that their sum has to be equal to a constant. If the learning algorithm increases a rule weight, others have to decrease their values. Ideally, this might lead to automatical elimination of unimportant or inconsistent rules. Alternatively, the user can delete rules with low κ_i.

4.3 Pruning Premises with Early Brain Damage

Due to the extended neuro-fuzzy-architecture it is possible to use typical (inexpensive) pruning algorithms [3, 4, 10] which compute a test value for each premise p_{ij}. Low values indicate that these premises are not relevant or inconsistent with the data. Based on these statistics the user can delete some premises, reducing the complexity of the neuro-fuzzy-system. In the following we describe the EBD, *Early-Brain-Damage*, pruning algorithm [10] because of our good experience using this algorithm for premise pruning [17]. This method is based on the often cited OBD, *Optimal-Brain-Damage*, pruning method of [15]. In contrast to OBD, EBD allows its application before the training has reached a local minimum. For every weight EBD computes as a test value an approximation of the difference between the error function for $w = 0$ versus the value of the error function for the best situation this weight can have ($w = w_{\min}$).

$$\text{test}_w = E(0) - E(w_{\min}) = -g'w + \frac{1}{2}w'Hw + \frac{1}{2}g'H^{-1}g, \qquad (5)$$

where $g = 1/T \sum_t g_t$, T represents the number of patterns and g_t is gradient for the weight w on pattern t. The Hessian H in this approach is computed in the same way as in the original OBD calculus [15]. The above approximation is motivated by a Taylor expansion of the error function. From

$$E(\tilde{w}) = E(w) + g(\tilde{w} - w) + \frac{1}{2}(\tilde{w} - w)'H(\tilde{w} - w) \qquad (6)$$

we get

$$E(0) = E(w) - g'w + \frac{1}{2}w'Hw \tag{7}$$

and as a solution to the minimum problem $E(\tilde{w}) \to \min$ we have

$$w_{\min} = w - g'H^{-1} \text{ together with } E(w_{\min}) = E(w) - \frac{1}{2}g'H^{-1}g. \tag{8}$$

The difference of these two error values is the proposed EBD test.

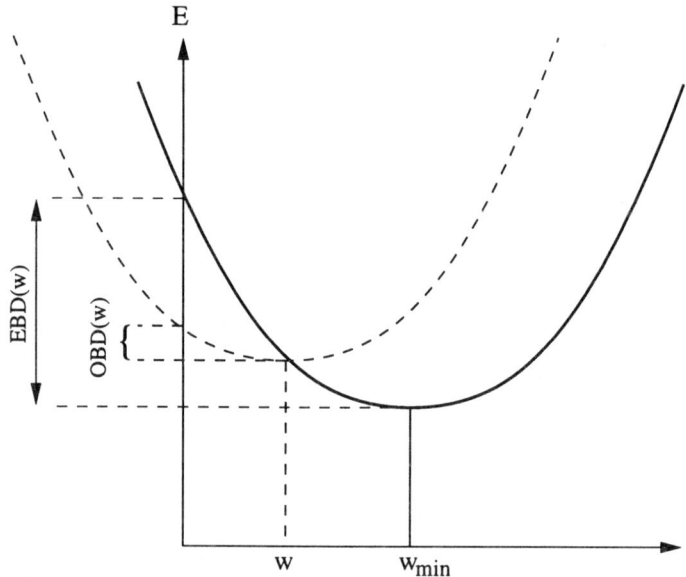

Fig. 3. EBD versus OBD weight pruning.

One of the advantages of EBD over OBD is the possibility to do the testing slidely away from a local minimum. EBD is also able to revive already pruned weights.

EBD favors weights with low rate of fluctuations. If a weight is pushed around by a high noise, the implicit curvature penalty would favor a flat minimum around this weight which leads to its elimination by EBD. For more information see [17].

After premise pruning, one trains the system again to convergence or until the error on a cross-validation set increases again [3]. These two steps might be iterated until one achieves a minimal network with good performance. Note, that the semantic-preserving learning algorithm still applies and keeps the optimized rule base interpretable.

It may happen that after pruning of premises rules have been derived which are identical. These rules are merged by adding their rule weights κ. It is also possible that the resulting rules differ only in their conclusions, they are inconsistent. The rule with lower κ could be deleted or the user can leave these rules unchanged because inconsistent knowledge can appear in financial analysis.

4.4 The "best per Rule" - Pruning Algorithm

Another (expensive) possibility to optimize the rule structure is to compute the exact influence of each premise p_{ij} on the error function and use this information for improvement. The algorithm works by iteration of two different steps: the "deletion"-step and the "insertion"-step.

The "deletion" - step: For the "deletion"- step the algorithm computes a test value for each active premise ($p_{ij} = 1$) of each rule based on the influence on the error function. The algorithm returns a lists of test values, with a negative value indicating an improvement of the error function.

The premise which leads to the most error reduction ("worst" premise) is deleted from the rule which is tested. If all test values are positive there is no improvement possible by deletion of a premise. Then, the rule will not be changed. The test value for deletion of the "worst" premise p_{ij} for each rule R_j is computed by :

$$t_j^{del} = \min_{i=1,..,m} \left(\sum_{t=1}^{P} \mathrm{E}(\mathrm{NN}(\underline{x_t})|p_{ij} = 0) - \sum_{t=1}^{P} \mathrm{E}(\mathrm{NN}(\underline{x_t})|p_{ij} = 1) \right), \qquad (9)$$

where $E()$ is the error function or another cost function, m is the number of membership functions, P represents the number of patterns. $\mathrm{NN}(\underline{x})$ is the output of the model on input vector $\underline{x}$.

If $t_j^{del} <= 0$ then $p_{ij} = 0$.

The "insertion"-step: The "insertion"-step works similar to the "deletion"-step. The algorithms returns a lists of test values for all dead premises ($p_{ij} = 0$) based on the change of the error function. A negative test value indicates an improvement of the error function if the premise is inserted into the rule. The premise with leads to the most error reduction ("best" premis) is inserted into the rule which is tested. If all test values are positive, no improvement is possible by insertion of a premise. Then the rule leaves unchanged. The test value for insertion of the "best" premise p_{ij} for each rule R_j is computed by:

$$t_j^{ins} = \min_{i=1,..,m} \left(\sum_{t=1}^{P} \mathrm{E}(\mathrm{NN}(\underline{x})|p_{ij} = 1) - \sum_{t=1}^{P} \mathrm{E}(\mathrm{NN}(\underline{x})|p_{ij} = 0) \right). \qquad (10)$$

If $t_j^{ins} <= 0$ then $p_{ij} = 1$.

Note, that there is no difference between deleted premises and premises which are not active because of the initial rule base structure. That means, that deleted premises could be reinserted by an "insertion" - step.

The user can iterate the two steps until the performance of the model is convenient. If the "deletion"-step and the "insertion"-step leave the rule base unchanged the algorithm is converged. The algorithm has to converge to a local minimum, because each change reduces the error of the system. The order of the two steps influences the local minimum to which the error of the model converges. The iteration should be begin with "deletion"-steps, especially if the rule base was created at random or by an expert, because some rules may be wrong. In this case all premises have to be deleted from a rule. That means, the number of "deletion"-steps at the beginning should be equal to the maximal number of single premises in a rule.

4.5 Insertion of Premises under Constraints

If premises are inserted into a rule, the system has to check if some constraints are not longer fulfilled. There are two types of constraints possible. The first one assures a consistent rules base and is called "Input Constraint". Two premises of the same input variable should **not** occur in the same rule, e. g. :

$$
\begin{aligned}
\text{IF} \quad & \Delta dax_t && = increasing \\
\text{AND} \quad & \Delta dax_t && = decreasing \\
\text{THEN} \quad & \Delta dax_{t+1} && = increase
\end{aligned}
$$

The user can define some constraints on the premises to assure economically "correct" rules ("User Constraints"), e.g. :

$$
\begin{aligned}
\text{IF} \quad & \Delta usd_t && = decreasing \\
\text{THEN NOT} \quad & \Delta dax_{t+1} && = increase
\end{aligned}
$$

That means, that it is not allowed to create a rule where a *decreasing* US-\$/DM-exchange rate leads to an *increasing* DAX at the next time step.

4.6 Rule Generation with Pruning

As we mentioned above, pruning algorithms can be used for rule generation. Assume that an expert has defined the fuzzy-sets for each input variable (e. g. 3) and the singletons for the output variable. Now the rules have to be to created. We indicate, how the algorithm works:

1. Randomize premises : $p_{ij} = \text{random}(0,1)$
2. Allow only a restricted number of premises per rule (e.g. 2)
3. Check "Input Constraints" (see section 4.5).
4. Check "User Constraints" (see section 4.5).

5. Iterate insertion of premises ("best per Rule") until no premise insertion leads to further improvement of the error or cost function.
6. Iterate deletion of premise ("worst per Rule") until no premise deletion leads to further improvement of the error or cost function.
7. Iterate step 5 and 6 until no premise could be inserted or deleted. Alternatively the procedure can stop if the system error or the system performance reached a defined value.

Note the the membership functions have their initial form. The system create the rule base in that way that the error is minimal using the initial membership functions. A further error reduction is possible while optimizing the parameters of the membership functions by the semantic-preserving learning algorithm.

5   Experiment: Daily Prediction of DAX

5.1   Introduction

We tested our neuro-fuzzy-approach intensively on different financial time series. Experiments with the daily returns of the US-\$/DM exchange rates are described in [11]. Here we present the results of the experiments to the German stock index (see also [12], [13], [14]). For the experiments, we used the neural network simulator SENN of Siemens Nixdorf , because it integrates all mentioned methods.

5.2   The German Stock Index DAX

The recently growing dynamics of the international stock markets has made portfolios consisting of such assets more attractive than bonds or other investments. In this article, we focus on the German stock index DAX because the 30 companies forming the index are responsible for about 70% of the turnover at the stock market in Frankfurt. Since the DAX is a weighted mixture of stocks it behaves like a real portfolio.

The task is to predict the daily returns (relative differences) of the DAX using only technical indicators computed from the DAX time series.

5.3   Technical Indicators

This section describes some technical indicators. Also some rules based on the indicators are presented. The rules are part of the initial fuzzy system. The **Moving Average** over the last u days is computed by

$$\text{MA}_t(x, u) = \frac{1}{u} \sum_{k=t-u+1}^{t} x_k, t = u, ..., T, \tag{11}$$

where T represents the number of all patterns. For instance, if $dax_t > MA_t(dax, u)$ then the conclusion is *increase*, $(target_{t+1} > 0)$, if $dax_t < MA_t(dax, u)$ then the conclusion is *decrease* $(target_{t+1} < 0)$, for given u and t.

The **Momentum** of a time series x is computed by

$$MOM_t(x, u) = x_t - x_{t-u}. \tag{12}$$

If $MOM_t(dax, u) > 0$ *(increasing)* then the conclusion is *increase*, otherwise the conclusion is *decrease*.

The **Relative Strength Index** of a time series x is calculated by

$$RSI_t(x, u) = \frac{\sum_{k=t-u+1}^{t} \text{profit}(x, k)}{\sum_{k=t-u+1}^{t} \text{loss}(x, k) + \sum_{k=t-u+1}^{t} \text{profit}(x, k)}, \tag{13}$$

with

$$\text{profit}(x, k) = \text{if } r_k(x) > 0 \text{ then } r_k(x) \text{ else } 0, \tag{14}$$

and

$$\text{loss}(x, k) = \text{if } r_k(x) < 0 \text{ then } -r_k(x) \text{ else } 0, \tag{15}$$

where

$$r_k(x) = (\frac{x_k}{x_{k-1}} - 1). \tag{16}$$

The values of $RSI_t(x, u)$ lie between 0 and 1.0. If $RSI_t(dax, u) > 0.7$ then the market is *overbought* and the prediction is *decrease*. If $RSI_t(dax, u) < 0.3$ then the market is *oversold* and the prediction is *increase*. Additionally one can compute the indicators **K-Stochastic** and **D-Stochastic** by

$$\text{K-Stochastic}_t(x, u) = \frac{x_t - max(x_t, u)}{max(x_t, u) - min(x_t, u)} * 100 \tag{17}$$

$$\text{D-Stochastic}_t(x, u) = \frac{1}{u} \sum_{k=t-u+1}^{t} \text{K-Stochastic}_k(x, u), \tag{18}$$

where the functions $max(x_t, u)$ resp. $min(x_t, u)$ returns the maximum resp. the minimum value over the last u days of a time series x beginning at time step t. if Stochastic < 0.7 then then market is *overbought* and the prediction is *decrease*. If Stochastic < 0.3 then the market is *oversold* and the prediction is *increase*.

5.4 Input Variables

In this section the 15 input variables of the technical model are explained.

Table 1. Inputs of the technical model at time step t.

input	description
Δdax_t	$(\frac{\text{dax}_t}{\text{dax}_{t-1}} - 1) * 100$
diffaver5_t	$(\ln(\text{dax}_t) - \text{MA}_t(\ln(dax), 5)) * 100$
diffaver10_t	$(\ln(\text{dax}_t) - \text{MA}_t(\ln(dax), 10)) * 100$
Δmomentum5_t	$(\text{MOM}_t(\ln(dax), 5) - \text{MOM}_{t-1}(\ln(dax), 5)) * 100$
Δmomentum10_t	$(\text{MOM}_t(\ln(dax), 10) - \text{MOM}_{t-1}(\ln(dax), 10)) * 100$
RSI5_t	$(\text{RSI}_t(\ln(dax), 5) - 0.7) * 10$
RSI10_t	$(\text{RSI}_t(\ln(dax), 10) - 0.7) * 10$
K-Stochastic5_t	$(\text{K-Stochastic}_t(\ln(dax), 5) - 0.7) * 10$
K-Stochastic10_t	$(\text{K-Stochastic}_t(\ln(dax), 10) - 0.7) * 10$
D-Stochastic5_t	$(\text{D-Stochastic}_t(\ln(dax), 5) - 0.7) * 10$
D-Stochastic10_t	$(\text{D-Stochastic}_t(\ln(dax), 10) - 0.7) * 10$
dayOfMonth	Day of month (positive integer between 1 and 31)
dayOfWeek	Day of Week (positive integer between 1 and 5)
monthOfYear	Month of Year (positive integer between 1 and 12)
daxcurve$_t$	$dax_t - 2 * dax_{t-2} + dax_{t-4}$

5.5 The Initial Rule Base

For each input variable of table 1 three fuzzy-sets are defined: *decreasing,*
stable and *increasing* resp. *oversold, normal* and *overbought.* Only the fuzzy-
set *stable* resp. *normal* is realized by a Gaussian membership function, the
others by logistic membership functions. The parameters of the membership
functions are defined by analyzing the distributions of the variables. The
center of the fuzzy-set *stable* is set to zero and can not be adapted. As
an example the membership functions of the input variable Δdax and the
distribution of input data are displayed in figure 4.

$$
\begin{aligned}
&decreasing : m_j(x_i) = (1 + \exp(-4(-0.25)(x_i + 2.0)))^{-1} \\
&stable \quad\; : m_j(x_i) = \exp(-0.5x_i^2) \\
&increasing : m_j(x_i) = (1 + \exp(-4(0.25)(x_i - 2.0)))^{-1}
\end{aligned} \tag{19}
$$

By relating the input Δdax_t to each of 10 technical indicators using all
combination of the fuzzy-sets we construct $90 = 9 * 10$ rules. Note, that only
pairwise correlations are used. The rules are constructed according assumed
structural relationships (for details, see [12]). Additionally we construct 4
rules concerning the time information and 16 rules concerning the information
taken from the curvature of the DAX (variable daxcurve$_t$).

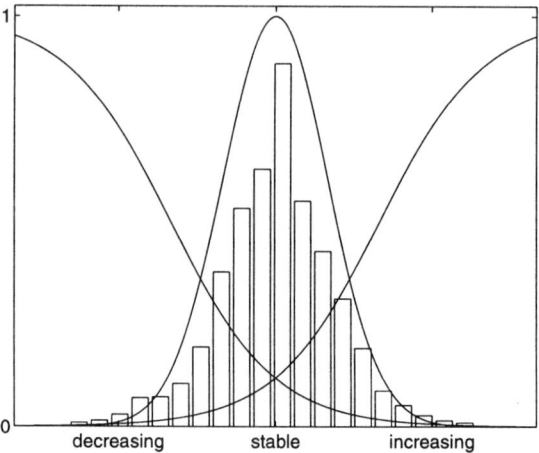

Fig. 4. membership function with histogram of the input variable DAX

5.6 Partitioning of Data

The partitioning of the data in training, cross-validation, and test set is shown in table 2. The cross-validation set is not used for training of the system, but gives a hint when to stop training [3]. If the error on this portion of the data starts to increase we usually stop training and try to reduce the complexity of the network by pruning. Afterwards we train again until the next increase of the error. To evaluate the resulting neuro-fuzzy-models we construct a

Table 2. Partitioning of the data.

Set	Start	End	Number of patterns
Training	1992/1/16	1995/2/9	800
Cross-Validation (CV)	1995/2/10	1995/6/29	100
Test	1995/6/30	1995/11/17	100

trading strategy going long if the network prediction is positive and selling short if the prediction is negative.

5.7 Benchmarks

The benchmarks which are used to compare the performance are the following trading systems respectively models:

1. **Buy&Hold:** buy the DAX at the beginning of the test set and sell it at the end. This strategy assumes an efficient capital market which does not allow excess return because the conditional expectation of the returns are zero. The Buy&Hold strategy gains only by exploiting the market trend.
2. **naive prediction:** buy or hold the DAX if the last difference is positive and sell otherwise. The naive prediction assumes that the market behaves like a random walk.

5.8   Measurements

The performance of the strategies are compared by computing the return on invest (*roi*) on the test set. This curve measures the return of a trading system by

$$roi = \sum_{t=1}^{T} (\frac{\text{dax}_{t+1}}{\text{dax}_t} - 1) * \text{sign}(\text{NN}(\underline{x_t})) \tag{20}$$

where $\text{NN}(\underline{x_t})$ is the output of the network for time step t and $\text{sign}(\text{NN}(\underline{x_t}))$ is the predicted direction of the DAX. *roi* increases if the predicted direction is correct, otherwise it decreases. The annualized return on invest ($aroi_{td}$ is computed by

$$aroi_{td} = \frac{td}{T} * roi. \tag{21}$$

where td represents the trading days per year (e. g. : $td = 260$). T represents the number of predicted patterns on test set.

5.9   Performance of Fuzzy-Systems

First, we measure the performance of the fuzzy-system defined by the expert. This result is not satisfying. Now we applicate the "best per Rule"-pruning algorithm described in section 4.2 on training set on the expert fuzzy-system until we achieved satisfying performance. Note, that the fuzzy-sets and rule weightings have their initial form. The performance of the expert fuzzy-system and the improved fuzzy-system on training and test set are displayed in figure 5.

5.10   Optimization

We use the following steps to optimize the fuzzy-system:

1. Optimizing of the initial fuzzy-system with "best per Rule"-pruning.
2. Training until the minimal mean squared error (MSE) on validation set is reached.
3. Pruning of rules with small rule weight (e. g. $\kappa_i < 0.1$).
4. Delete premises (e. g. EBD-Pruning).

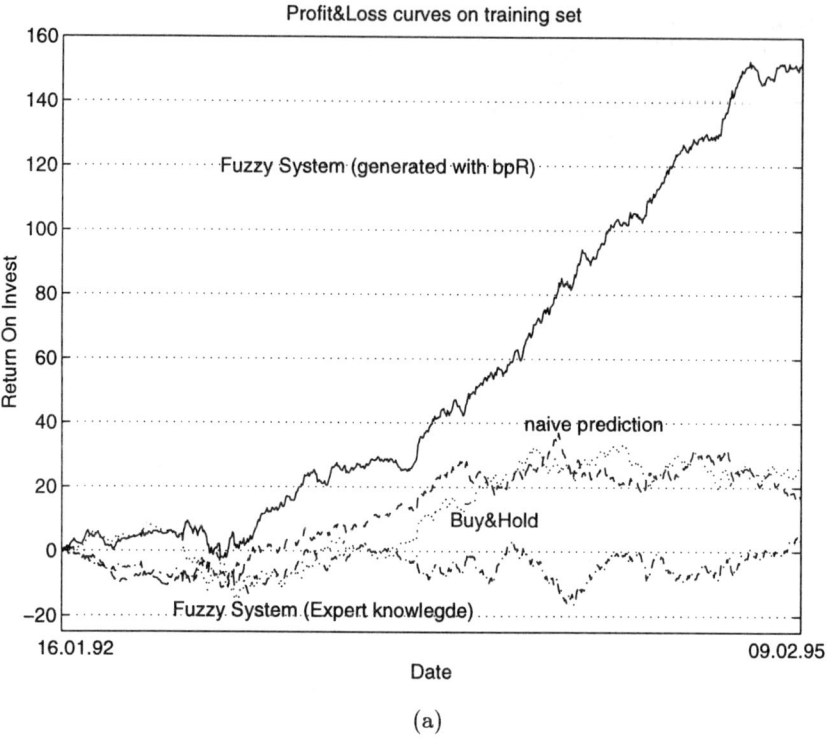

(a)

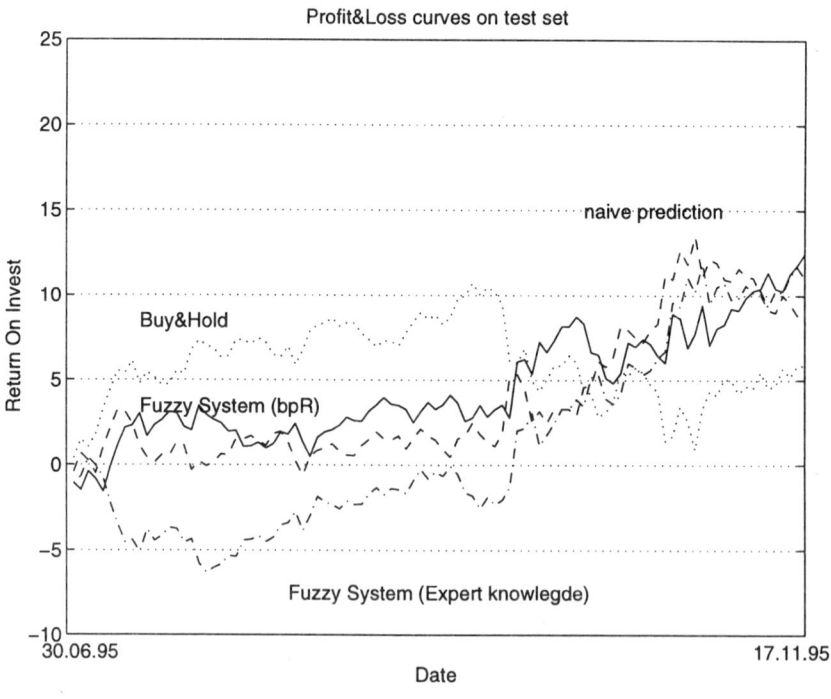

(b)

5. Iteration of training and pruning until the model can not be further improved.

The quality of the model during optimization is measured by the values described in section 5.8. Our experience is that the model with the best performance does not corresponds with the minimal error model.

6 Results

The optimization is stopped, when the model can not be further improved. This model is taken to predict the DAX on the test set. Note, that the optimized model is always interpretable due to the semantic preserving learning algorithm. The optimized neuro-fuzzy-system consists of only 55 Rules. In figure 6 the "Return on Invest" - curves of the neuro-fuzzy-model and the two trading benchmarks are displayed. At the begin of the test set the performance of the neuro-fuzzy-model is not very satisfying. Note, that this model takes only technical inputs into account and no fundamental influences are used. Additionally the performance of the initial fuzzy-model (expert), the fuzzy-model which was improved with the "best per Rule"-pruning algorithm (bpR), the neuro-fuzzy-model and the benchmarks are displayed in table 3.

Table 3. Results on test set.

Model	roi	$aroi_{260}$
naive prediction	+0.088	+0.230
Buy & Hold	+0.058	+0.152
Fuzzy(Expert knowledge)	+0.110	+0.286
Fuzzy(improved with bpR)	+0.124	+0.323
Neuro-fuzzy(55 rules)	+0.193	+0.500

7 Remarks

In [16] one can find the comparison of different approaches on the task to predict the daily returns of DAX using the partitioning defined above. Siegler uses 13 fundamental time series as input for different models. He uses a simple MLP with one hidden layer and a different number of hidden neurons, the machine learning algorithm M6.1 and linear regressions. He turns out, that neural network are able to build models of the DAX, which are better than the results of linear regression and M6.1 (see table 4). Note, that his models takes into account substantially more information as the presented neuro-fuzzy-system.

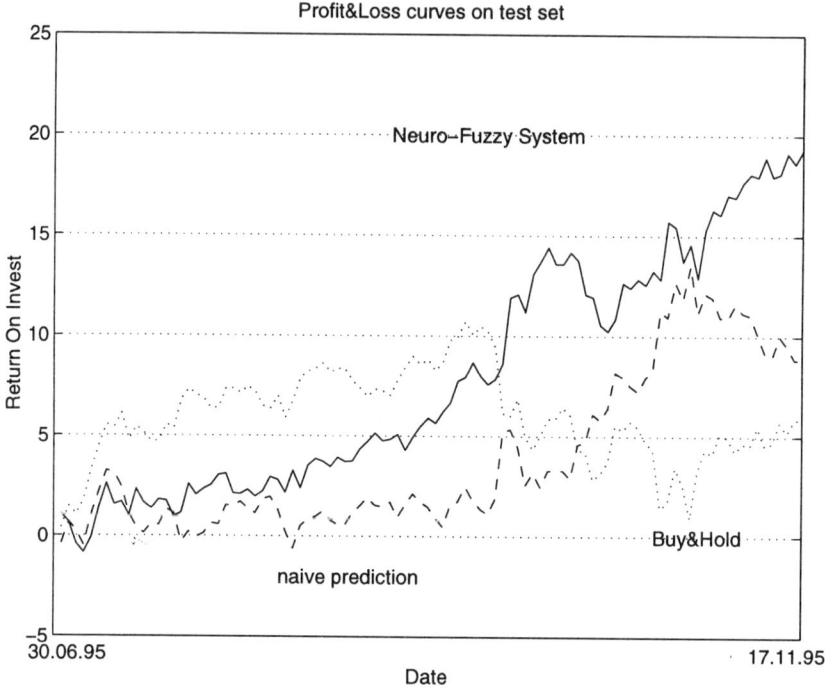

Fig. 6. Comparison of *roi*-curves of different models.

Table 4. Results of Siegler's models [16] on test set

Model	roi	$aroi_{260}$
linear regression	+0.083	+0.216
3-layer-MLP(average)	+0.130	+0.338
M6.1	+0.086	+0.224

8 Conclusions

Although the neuro-fuzzy-model takes only technical indicators into account the performance of the model especially on the last section on the test set is very encouraging. The "best per Rule"-Pruning algorithm generated a fuzzy system based on the initial structure of the fuzzy sets, which is superior to the fuzzy-system formulated by an expert. The optimization with the semantic preserving learning algorithm and the application of the EBD-Pruning algorithm leads to an further improvement of the model.

References

[1] D.Nauck, F.Klawonn, R.Kruse, Foundations of Neuro-Fuzzy-Systems, Wiley, 1997

[2] V. Tresp, J. Hollatz, S. Ahmad, Network Structuring and Training Using Rule-Based Knowledge. In S. J. Hanson, J. D. Cowan, C. L. Giles (editors), Advances in Neural Information Processing Systems 5, 1993.

[3] W. Finnoff, F. Hergert, H. G. Zimmermann, Improving Generalization by Nonconvergent Model Selection Methods. Neural Networks 6, 1992.

[4] H. G. Zimmermann, Neuronale Netze als Entscheidungskalkül. In H. Rehkugler, H. G. Zimmermann (editors), Neuronale Netze in der Ökonomie, Vahlen, 1994, München

[5] T. Takagi, M. Sugeno, Fuzzy identification of systems and its applications to modelling and control. IEEE Trans. on Syst., Man and Cybernetics, 1, Vol. 15, 1985.

[6] L. X. Wang, J. M. Mendel, Generating Fuzzy Rules from Numerical Data, with Applications. Univ. of Southern Cal., tech. report USC-SIPI REPORT 169, 1991.

[7] R.Kruse, E.Schwecke, J.Heinsohn, Uncertainty and vageness in knowlegde based systems, Springer, Heidelberg, 1991.

[8] R. Neuneier, V. Tresp, Radiale Basisfunktionen, Dichteschätzungen und Neuro-Fuzzy. In H. Rehkugler, H. G. Zimmermann (editors), Neuronale Netze in der Ökonomie, Vahlen Verlag, München, 1994.

[9] P. E. Gill, W. Murray, M. H. Wright, Practical Optimization. Academic Press, 1981.

[10] V. Tresp, H. G. Zimmermann, R. Neuneier, Early Brain Damage, Advances in Neural Information, Proc. NIPS, 1996.

[11] R. Neuneier, H. G. Zimmermann, A semantic-preserving learning algorithm for neuro-fuzzy systems with applications to time series prediction, ICANN-Workshop, 1995.

[12] H. Dichtl, Zur Prognose des Deutschen Aktienindex DAX mit Hilfe von Neuro-Fuzzy-Systemen, Institut für Kapitalmarktforschung, J. W. Goethe-Universität, Frankfurt, Germany, 1996.

[13] H. G. Zimmermann, R. Neuneier, S. Siekmann, H. Dichtl, Modeling the German stock index DAX with Neuro-Fuzzy, Proc. of EUFIT'96, 1996.

[14] S. Siekmann, R. Kruse, R. Neuneier, H. G. Zimmermann, Advanced Neuro-Fuzzy Techniques applied to the German Stock Index DAX, Proc. of EFDAN'97, Dortmund, 1997

[15] Y. le Cun, J. S. Denker, S. A. Solla, Optimal Brain Damage. In D. S. Touretzky, editor, Advances in Neural Information Processing Systems 2 (NIPS'89), pages 589-605, San Mateo, CA, 1990. Morgan Kaufmann.

[16] Siegler, Wolfgang, Kurzfristige Prognose des DAX, Abteilung Mathematik VII (Operations Research), Universität Ulm, Diplomarbeit, 1997

[17] Neuneier, R.; Zimmermann, H.G.: How To Train Neural Networks, to appear 1997

IBOVESPA Neuro-Fuzzy Forecasting:
A Case Study in Brazilian Capital Markets

Maria Augusta Soares Machado[*], Luiz Alfredo Rodrigues Gaspar[**],
Antonio Araújo de Freitas Jr.[**] and Reinaldo Castro Souza[*]

[*] Dept. Eng. Elétrica
Pontificia Universidade Católica
Rio de Janeiro, Brazil
E-mails: augusta@omega.lncc.br, reinaldo@puc.br

[**] Information Systems Research Dept.
IBMEC - Brazilian Institute of Capital Markets
Rio de Janeiro, Brazil
E-mail: {lalfredo,afreitas}@ibmec.br

Abstract. This paper focuses on a presentation and a comparison of two fuzzy inference adaptive systems and Box and Jenkins' time series forecasting model, used to make out-of-sample crisp predictions for the very liquid IBOVESPA nominal spot index traded in BOVESPA's STOCK EXCHANGE. The central theme of this study is to establish how empirical knowledge (numerical data) could be used to improve the effectiveness of fuzzy inference systems. We conclude, on the basis of the obtained forecasting results, that we could say this type of models are very powerful to solve data-driven non-linear ill-posed financial problems.

Keywords: fuzzy neural networks; forecasting; neuro-fuzzy models; fuzzy inference adaptive systems; soft computing.

1. Introduction

Today's researchers and practitioners have plenty of scientific artifacts (analytical and statistical mathematical models, economic/econometric models, chaotic/fractal models, and artificial intelligence models) offering the flexibility to focus (model) and solve given financial problems from different points of view. Perhaps one of these financial problems that have been dealt with by using almost all of this kind of models are the nominal value or the trend's prediction (or trading) of stock prices and indexes. Actually, there are many kinds of fuzzy knowledge base reasoning approaches to solve this kind of problems [1], [2].

Recently some combinations of the neural networks and fuzzy logic technologies have being used to deal with financial problems [3], [4], [5], [6]. In this work we choose the ANFIS (Adaptive Neuro-Fuzzy Inference System) [7], [8] and the numerical-fuzzy inference system [9] to solve our problem.

In Section 2 we give a motivation for the incorporation of empirical knowledge in the process of developing more practical and maintainable fuzzy inference systems.

In Sections 3 and 4 we present some features of the ANFIS model and the results obtained by using this model with the time series chosen to be predicted.

Sections 5 and 6 present the counterpart for the numerical-fuzzy inference system.

In Sections 7 and 8 we present some considerations about the Box and Jenkins time series forecasting model, and the results obtained using this approach with the same time series.

In Section 9 we do the comparison of results obtained by the three models.

Conclusions are presented in Section 10.

2. Motivation for the use of neuro-fuzzy models

As is well known, in early examples of fuzzy modeling attempts were made to extract the fuzzy model directly from the experts' knowledge. To use this direct approach to construct fuzzy (or linguistic) inference systems we can follow the following steps [9], [10], [11], [12], [13]:

1. definition of input and output numerical (crisp or ordinary) relevant variables based on human experience;
2. specification of the universe of discourse (domain) of each variable identified;
3. determination of the linguistic labels (reference fuzzy sets) into which these variables are partitioned;
4. formation of a fuzzy rule base (a set of linguistic if-then production rules) that represents relationships between the system variables;
5. determination of a mapping from the input space to the output space based on the combined fuzzy rule base using a defuzzifying procedure;
6. validation of the results and evaluation of model adequacy.

Though this kind of approach has been successfully applied in many areas where conventional model-based approaches are difficult or not cost-effective to implement (as, for example, control theory applications in the industrial setting [9],[14]), this direct approach fails if expert knowledge is faulty or if the system's complexity (number of membership functions and fuzzy rules) increases.

Furthermore, due to the dynamic nature of financial applications, membership functions and fuzzy rules must be adaptive to the changing environment in order to be useful [3], [10].

Therefore, seeking more objectivity in constructing fuzzy inference systems, we could try to use an available empirical knowledge (input-output data using the statistical terminology or examples from the neural networks community) of the system being studied to adapt it to the dynamic nature of the financial problem considered.

In this work we focus on the two adaptive fuzzy inference systems mentioned above.

3. The ANFIS model

We could illustrate the ANFIS architecture considering a fuzzy system with only two inputs and one output for a first order Sugeno model, defining the linguistic if-then rules as:

rule 1: if x is A1 and y is B1, then f1 = p1 * x + q1 * y + r1
rule 2: if x is A2 and y is B2, then f2 = p2 * x + q2 * y + r2

The ANFIS architecture for this system is showed in Figure 1 (adapted from [7],[8]).

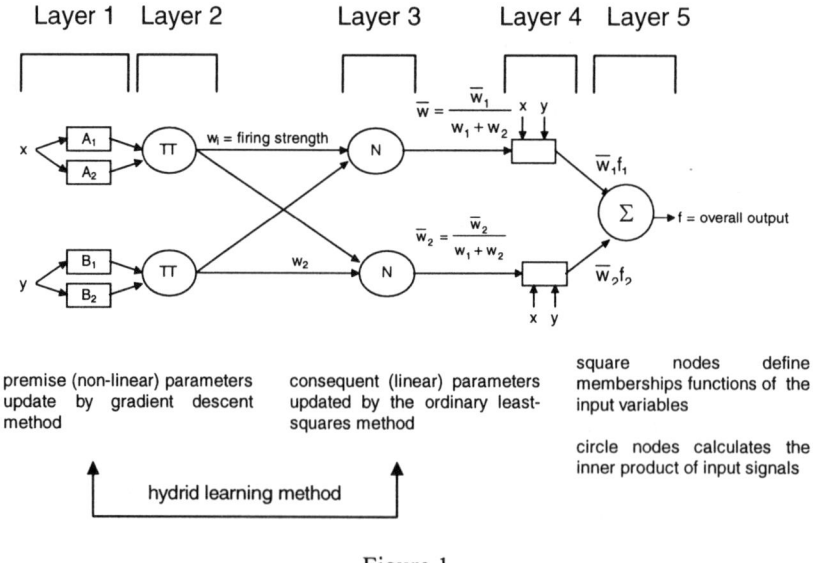

Figure 1

The meaning of each of the five layers for the ANFIS model can be described as follows, assuming that the output of each layer is the input for the next layer:

input: each crisp variable value for the whole set of linguistic labels which is related to

layer 1:

type of node: adaptive for the non-linear parameters
process: fuzzification of each numeric input variable
output: value of each membership function

• **antecedent part of the ANFIS (layer 2 and layer 3)**

layer 2:

type of node: non-adaptive
process: T-norm (triangular norm) operation of each combination of the defined fuzzy sets
output: value (firing strength) of each T-norm operation

layer 3:

type of node: non-adaptive
process: normalization of all firing strengths
output: normalized firing strengths

• **consequent part of the ANFIS (layer 4 and layer 5)**

layer 4:

type of node: adaptive for the linear parameters
process: product of each normalized firing strength by each of the Sugeno first-
              order crisp function value
output: products defined above

layer 5:

type of node: non-adaptive
process: summation of all products
output: our desired prediction.

The adaptivity is introduced in this model by the utilization of the topological ordering representations of the Werbos backpropagation training algorithm version

that works as follows:
1. Initial data are presented and the corresponding output is calculated.
2. The error between the calculated output and the expected value is computed.
3. Membership functions are adjusted through the estimation of new parameters.
4. At a desired number of epochs and training rate some useless fuzzy rules are deleted and the useful ones are added.
5. If the error goal is achieved, a good solution is obtained; otherwise, new data has to be presented.

4. Results of ANFIS experiments

The rationale used in the selection of the numeric (crisp) input variables using the ANFIS model was like the one adopted in any data-driven model used in the financial market literature. Therefore, we based our selection of variables on the compromise that we have to establish between the scarcity of data points and the input fuzzy space partitioning's methods most frequently used. Since we have chosen the grid method of partitioning, we have selected three of the fundamental and technical variables most commonly used in data-driven financial market models.

They are:

- CDI/Over (the daily certificate of interbanks deposits, a proxy of interest rate),
- IBOVESPA's daily volume, and
- IBOVESPA's time series values one-step backward returns specified as:
  $(p_{t+1} - p_{tt}) / p_t$.

This simple type of data preprocessing provides a reasonable performance of the ANFIS algorithm.

The data collecting period was from January 3 to March 12, 1997, that provides 295 usable data points. First of all, we have done a data validation process before using the data in the model.

We define 252 as the number of training data (observations) set points and 43 as the number of the checking data set points, to be compatible with the selected structure of 27 ($= 3^3$) fuzzy rules, induced by our choice of the numbers of input variables (3), memberships functions (3) and parameters (2) of the Gaussian membership function. This definition was based on the fact that the selected structure of the ANFIS model has 108 ($= 27 \times 4$) linear parameters and 18 ($= 3 \times 3 \times 2$) non-linear parameters.

What we have done, in summary, was the utilization of the following two heuristics:
- that simpler structures have a better chance to avoid the problem of overfitting

the data utilized in the training phase, and

- selection of the best (minimum root mean squared error) ANFIS model by using a validation data set to determine when training should be terminated to prevent overfitting the data utilized in the training phase by overtraining.

After defining the objective of the neuro-fuzzy model as one to predict the behavior of IBOVESPA's one step ahead time series values (tomorrow's day) and the input variables defined above, we collected the pertinent data to our experiment.

The specific values related to each of the five layers for the ANFIS model developed are defined as follows:

input: three crisp variable values for each set of three linguistic labels named LOW, MEDIUM and LARGE

crisp variable 1: CDI / Over
crisp variable 2: IBOVESPA=s Daily Volume
crisp variable 3: IBOVESPA=s Time Series values one step backward.

layer 1:

For each of the numeric variables x_i , $i = 1,2,3$, we set:

A1 = fuzzy set LOW;   A2 = fuzzy set MEDIUM;   A3 = fuzzy set LARGE,

and obtain:

$A_j(x_i)$ = degree of membership of each specific value of x_i relative to fuzzy set A_j, $j = 1,2,3$

We have selected the Gaussian membership function defined in the MATLAB's fuzzy toolbox to represent all of these fuzzy sets [15].

- **antecedent part of the ANFIS model**

layer 2:

We have defined the following antecedent parts of the fuzzy rule base:

```
rule 1 :   if x1 is  A1 ( x1 )  and  x2 is  A1 ( x2 )  and  x3 is  A1 ( x3 )
rule 2 :   if x1 is  A1 ( x1 )  and  x2 is  A1 ( x2 )  and  x3 is  A2 ( x3 )
rule 3 :   if x1 is  A1 ( x1 )  and  x2 is  A1 ( x2 )  and  x3 is  A3 ( x3 )
rule 4 :   if x1 is  A1 ( x1 )  and  x2 is  A2 ( x2 )  and  x3 is  A1 ( x3 )
rule 5 :   if x1 is  A1 ( x1 )  and  x2 is  A2 ( x2 )  and  x3 is  A2 ( x3 )
rule 6 :   if x1 is  A1 ( x1 )  and  x2 is  A2 ( x2 )  and  x3 is  A3 ( x3 )
rule 7 :   if x1 is  A1 ( x1 )  and  x2 is  A3 ( x2 )  and  x3 is  A1 ( x3 )
```

rule 8 : if x1 is A1 (x1) and x2 is A3 (x2) and x3 is A2 (x3)
rule 9 : if x1 is A1 (x1) and x2 is A3 (x2) and x3 is A3 (x3)
rule 10 : if x 1 is A2 (x1) and x2 is A1 (x2) and x3 is A1 (x3)
rule 11: if x1 is A2 (x1) and x2 is A1 (x2) and x3 is A2 (x3)
rule 12: if x1 is A2 (x1) and x2 is A1 (x2) and x3 is A3 (x3)
rule 13: if x1 is A2 (x1) and x2 is A2 (x2) and x3 is A1 (x3)
rule 14: if x1 is A2 (x1) and x2 is A2 (x2) and x3 is A2 (x3)
rule 15: if x1 is A2 (x1) and x2 is A2 (x2) and x3 is A3 (x3)
rule 16: if x1 is A2 (x1) and x2 is A3 (x2) and x3 is A1 (x3)
rule 17: if x1 is A2 (x1) and x2 is A3 (x2) and x3 is A2 (x3)
rule 18: if x1 is A2 (x1) and x2 is A3 (x2) and x3 is A3 (x3)
rule 19: if x1 is A3 (x1) and x2 is A1 (x2) and x3 is A1 (x3)
rule 20: if x1 is A3 (x1) and x2 is A1 (x2) and x3 is A2 (x3)
rule 21: if x1 is A3 (x1) and x2 is A1 (x2) and x3 is A3 (x3)
rule 22: if x1 is A3 (x1) and x2 is A2 (x2) and x3 is A1 (x3)
rule 23: if x1 is A3 (x1) and x2 is A2 (x2) and x3 is A2 (x3)
rule 24: if x1 is A3 (x1) and x2 is A2 (x2) and x3 is A3 (x3)
rule 25: if x1 is A3 (x1) and x2 is A3 (x2) and x3 is A1 (x3)
rule 26: if x1 is A3 (x1) and x2 is A3 (x2) and x3 is A2 (x3)
rule 27: if x1 is A3 (x1) and x2 is A3 (x2) and x3 is A3 (x3)

and obtain 27 firing strengths w_i

layer 3:

normalization of all firing strengths (w_i), i = 1, ..., 27)

- **consequent part of the ANFIS**

layer 4:

$f 1 = p1 * x1 + q1 * x2 + r1 * x3 + s1$ for rule 1
$f 2 = p2 * x1 + q2 * x2 + r2 * x3 + s2$ for rule 2
$f 3 = p3 * x1 + q3 * x2 + r3 * x3 + s3$ for rule 3
...
and so on till rule 27;

$f_i * w_i$, i = 1, ..., 27

layer 5:

$f_i * w_i$ = the desired output

The results that we have chosen to present from our experiments with this model, using the MATLAB's fuzzy toolbox, are shown and explained in the following figures.

Figure 2 shows the IBOVESPA's time series values for the time window selected. The three memberships functions for the linguistic variables LOW, MEDIUM and HIGH for each of the three crisp variables used before training are given in Figure 3.

Figure 4 shows the three memberships functions for the linguistic variables LOW, MEDIUM and HIGH for each the three crisp variables used after training.

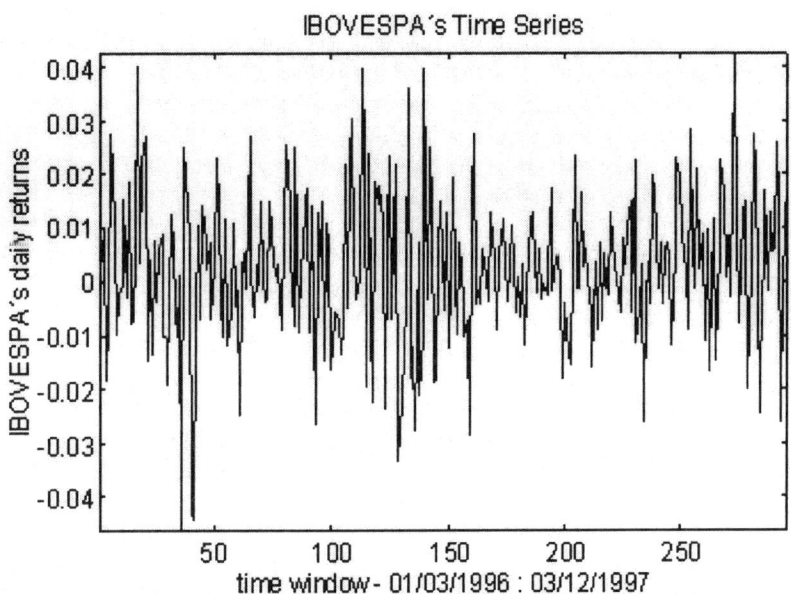

Figure 2

As we can see, comparing Figure 3 (Membership Functions before Training) and Figure 4 (Membership Functions after Training), the spreads for the linguistic sets of variable 1 (CDI / Over), for the linguistic sets of variable 2 (IBOVESPA's Daily Volume), and for the linguistic sets of variable 3 (IBOVESPA's time series values one step backward) are very reduced after training, showing that *learning+ decreases "vagueness".

Figure 5 shows the behavior of the root mean squared error for both training and checking phases versus the number of epochs used for training. It is important to see that the performance after the first epoch is usually a good index of how well the ANFIS model will perform after further training [9].

Finally, Figure 6 shows the errors (actual values minus predicted values)

212

generated by the ANFIS model. It is important to see that the differences are reasonably short.

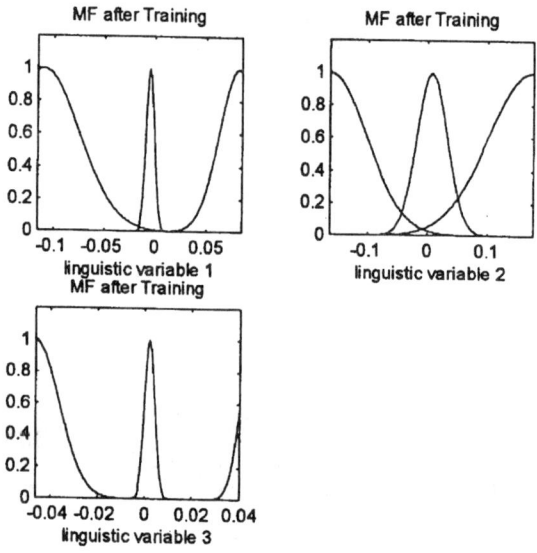

Figure 3

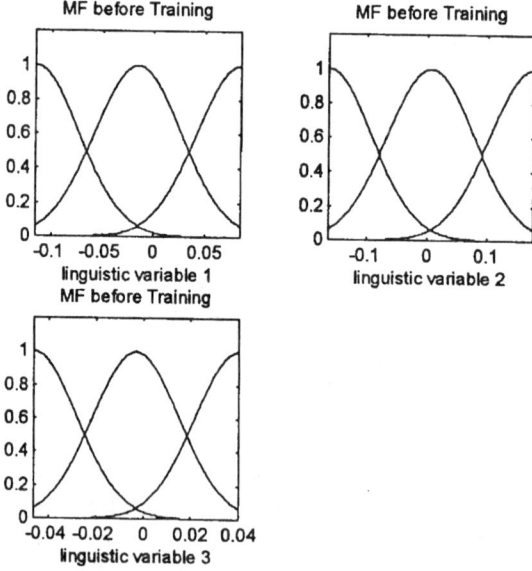

Figure 4

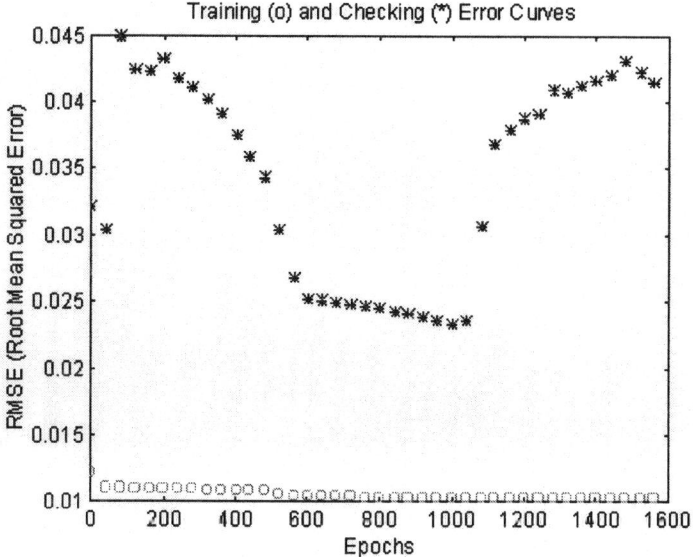

Figure 5

5. Numerical-fuzzy model

The numerical-fuzzy model consists of the following five steps [9]:

1. division of the input and output variables spaces of a given numerical data pairs into fuzzy regions; this step is similar to the process developed in layer 1 in the ANFIS model.
2. generation of fuzzy rules from the given numerical data pairs doing the substeps:

   a) determination of the degrees of the variables in different fuzzy regions
   b) assignment of a given value of each variable to the region of maximum degree
   c) obtaining of one rule from one pair of desired input-output numerical data;

3. assignment of a degree of each of the generated fuzzy rules for the purpose of resolving conflicts among this rules;
4. creation of a combined fuzzy rule based on both the generated fuzzy rules and linguistic rules of human experts;
5. determination of a mapping from input space to output space based on the combined fuzzy rule base using a defuzzifying procedure.

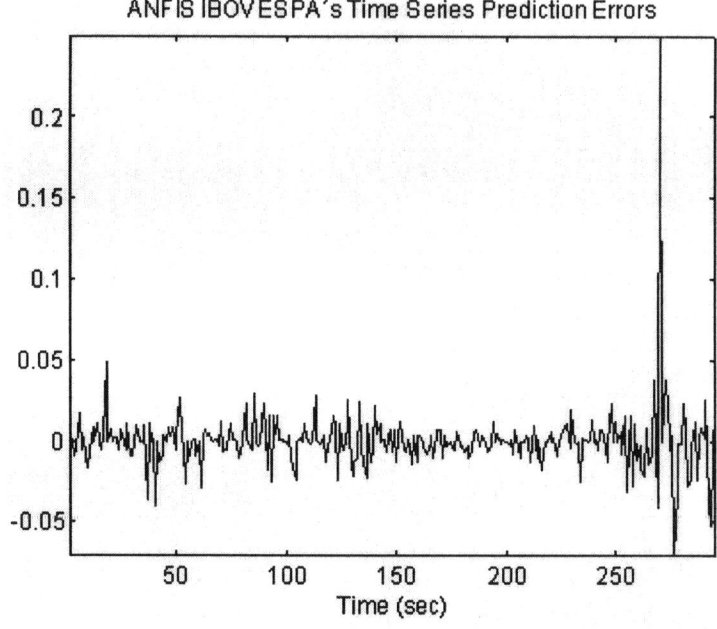

Figure 6

6. Results of experiments with the numerical-fuzzy model

In order to make a comparison of the ANFIS model with the numerical-fuzzy inference model, we use the data that was used before for the ANFIS model, but instead of using three regressor variables we use only the past values of IBOVESPA's series to explain the foregoing values of this series.

We have implemented the five model's steps as follows:

1. we define six inputs variables named as: Monday, Tuesday, Wednesday, Thursday, Friday and Monday;
2. an example of the rules that was generated follows bellow:

if

IBOVESPA	was	0.0005400	in	06/01/97	and
IBOVESPA	was	0.0000670	in	07/01/97	and
IBOVESPA	was	0.0000540	in	08/01/97	and
IBOVESPA	was	0.0000078	in	09/01/97	and
IBOVESPA	was	0.0000032	in	10/01/97	and

IBOVESPA was 0.0000030 in 13/01/97

then

IBOVESPA was 0.0000053 in 14/01/97.

This type of fuzzy rule is represented by each line in the following tables:

- thirty six fuzzy rules to forecast 03/10/97 (Monday seven days after):

Fuzzy Rule	Antecedent Part	Consequent Part
1	01/06/97 to 01/13/97	01/14/97
2	01/07 to 01/14	01/15
.	.	.
.	.	.
.	.	.
36	02/27 to 03/06	03/07

- thirty five fuzzy rules to forecast 03/07/7 (Friday seven days after):

Fuzzy Rule	Antecedent Part	Consequent Part
1	01/06/97 to 01/13/97	01/14/97
... 2	01/07 to 01/14	01/15/97
.	.	.
.	.	.
.	.	.
35	02/26 to 03/05	03/06/97

- thirty four fuzzy rules to forecast 03/06/97 (Thursday seven days after):

Fuzzy Rule	Antecedent Part	Consequent Part
1	01/06/97 to 01/13/97	01/14/97
2	01/07 to 01/14	01/15
.	.	.
.	.	.
.	.	.
34	02/25 to 03/04	03/05/97

- thirty three fuzzy rules to forecast 03/05/97 (Wednesday seven days after):

Fuzzy Rule	Antecedent Part	Consequent Part
1	01/06/97 to 01/13/97	01/14/97
2	01/07 to 01/14	01/15
.	.	.
.	.	.
.	.	.
33	02/24 to 03/03	03/04/97

- thirty two fuzzy rules to forecast 03/04/97 (Tuesday seven days after):

Fuzzy Rule	Antecedent Part	Consequent Part
1	01/06/97 to 01/13/97	01/14/97

2	01/07 to 01/14	01/15
. . .	. . .	. . .
32	02/21 to 02/28	03/03/97

- thirty one fuzzy rules to forecast 03/03/97 (Monday seven days after):

Fuzzy Rule	**Antecedent Part**	**Consequent Part**
1	01/06/97 to 01/13/97	01/14/97
2	01/07 to 01/14	01/15
. . .	. . .	. . .
31	02/20 to 02/27	02/28/97

3. we have assumed, for the sake of simplicity, that all degrees of the data pairs are equal to unity;
4. the combined fuzzy rule base consists of a fuzzy associative memory (hypercube) with six dimensions, where we use «max» as the aggregation method;
5. the defuzzification method used was the "centroid".

The graphical results of this method are shown in Figure 7.

7. The Box and Jenkins time series forecasting model

One of the deficiencies in the analysis of time series in the past has been the confusion between fitting a series and forecasting it. It was common to decompose the series arbitrarily into three components: a trend, a seasonal component and a random component.

The trend might be fitted by a polynomial and the seasonal component by the Fourier series. A forecast was then made by projecting these fitted functions.

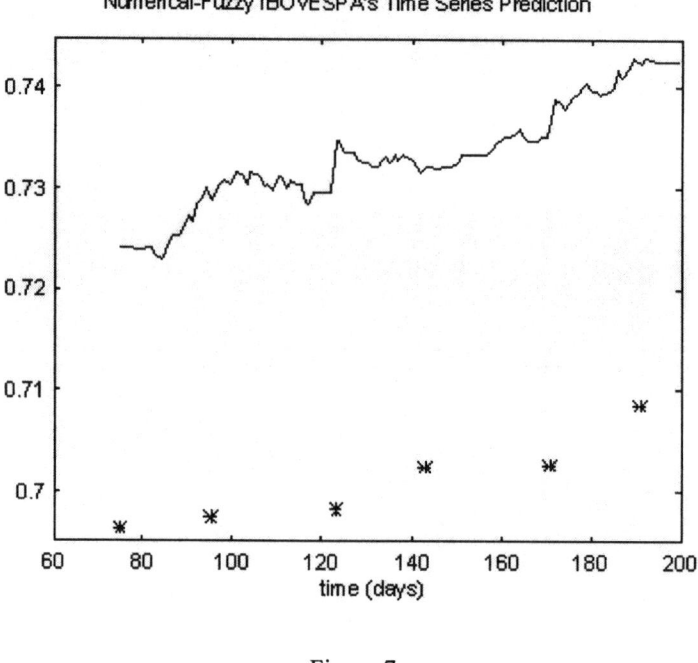

Figure 7

The numerical non-fuzzy model consists on the following steps:

1. model identification through the use of estimated autocorrelation functions and their standard errors, to select some possible models;
2. model diagnostic checking of overfitting using statistical tests applied to residuals (for example, the autocorrelation check, Portmanteau lack-of-fit test, model inadequacy, cumulative periodogram test, etc.) with the aim to select a parsimonious model (since, in practice, parsimonious models generally produce better out-of-sample forecasts than models with too many parameters because they don't overfill the available data).

8. Results of the Box and Jenkins model experiments

In order to make comparison with the ANFIS and the numerical-fuzzy inference results, we present this section using only past values of IBOVESPA's series. We have implemented the following steps [16],[17]:

1. fit, as the simplest approach, an AR model to a transformation on the series that is nearly stationary;
2. examine the time series estimated autocorrelation and partial autocorrelation functions that exhibit significant peaks on lag two;
3. fit, as a consequence, two AR models:

   - an AR(2) model where we it autocorrelation had a significant on lag two,
   - an AR(3) (overfitted) model that had no significant estimated parameters;

4. introduce, based on these facts, short MA terms to capture the stochastic structure of the time series being analysed;
5. fit, using the parsimonious principle, an ARIMA (2, 0, 2) model.

STATISTICA RELEASE 4.3 was used to estimate parameters of the model and for forecasting [18].

In Figure 8 the real series and its forecasting are shown for the selected ARIMA (2, 0, 2) model.

The adequacy of fit of this model was done by examining the residuals from the following fitted ARMA (2,2):

$$\hat{z}_t = -0.3442\hat{z}_{t-1} + 0.29141\hat{z}_{t-2} - 0.418\hat{a}_{t-1} + 0.52984\hat{a}_{t-2}$$

The estimated autocorrelations of the residuals are shown in Figure 9. The partial autocorrelations of the residuals are presented in Figure 10.

The overall check is provided by the quantity

$$Q = \sum_{k=1}^{n-2} r_k^2(\hat{a}_k)$$

which is approximately χ_{n-2}^2. The observed values of «Q», and on hypothesis of adequacy of the model, the check does not provide any evidence of inadequacy in the model identified.

The Kolmogorov-Smirnoff test which provides a very rough guide to the significance for the residuals, fails in this instance to indicate any significant departure from the assumed model.

9. Comparison of experiments results for the models

Comparing the results obtained by using the numerical-fuzzy inference system and

ANFIS for the same days, we obtain the results presented in Table 1.

Comparing the forecasting error results obtained using the three models, we can see the best performance of ANFIS.

Table 1

Forecasting	Forecasting Error		
	Learning from Fuzzy Rules	ANFIS	Box-Jenkins
Monday eight weeks after (03/10/97)	0.3788	0.00032	0.14212
Friday seven weeks after (03/07/97)	0.3605	0.00006	0.14249
Thursday seven weeks after (03/06/97)	0.4069	0.00012	0.14240
Wednesday seven weeks after (03/05/97)	0.4148	0.00007	0.15432
Tuesday seven weeks after (03/04/97)	0.3262	0.00016	0.14310
Monday seven weeks after (03/03/97)	0.3654	- 0.00047	0.14586

10. Conclusions

The results obtained using the three forecasting models that we have selected in this work, suggest the use of the ANFIS model to predict the BOVESPA index based in its better out-of-sample performance.

On the other hand, what we suppose that the most important contribution of this work is to show to the finance community, that neuro-fuzzy inference systems are excelent tools to model and solve problems involving situations where exist uncertainties expressed as ambiguity and imprecision and not only uncertainties expressed as randomness.

So based on these facts   we   can recommend the use of this powerful technology to make, for example, financial forecasting.

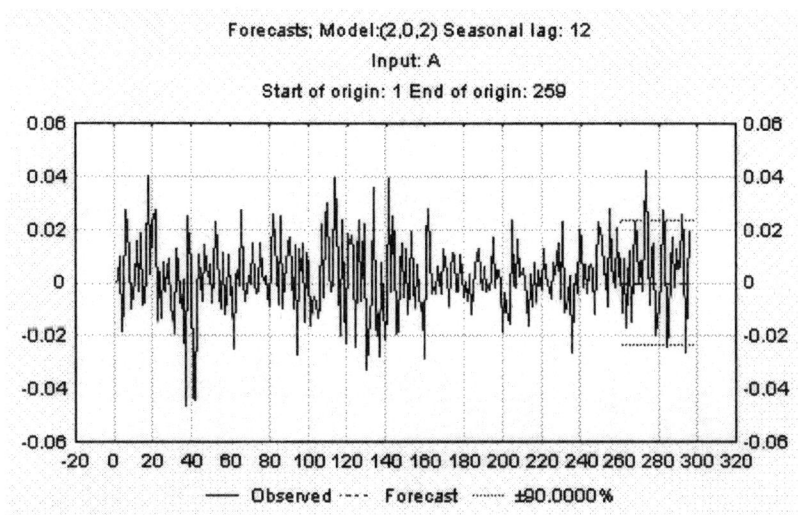

Figure 8

11. Acknowledgments

This research was supported by the Brazilian Institute of Capital Markets - IBMEC (Rio de Janeiro Unit and Faculty of Economics and Business). We thank Berta Maria Rodrigues Silveira for her help in the financial analyses and data validation process developed.

References

1. LAM, K. P, CHUI, K.C., CHAN, W. K. (1995) An Embedded Fuzzy Knowledge Base for Technical Analysis of Stocks, in *Neural Networks in Financial Engineering, Proceedings of the Third International Conference on Neural Networks in the Capital Markets*, REFENES, A-P N., ABU-MOSTAFA, Y., MOODY, J, & WEIGEND, A., World Scientific.

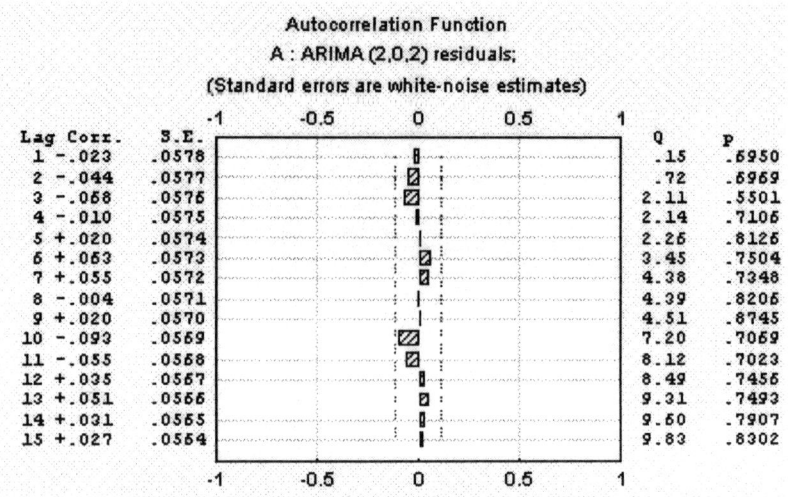

Figure 9

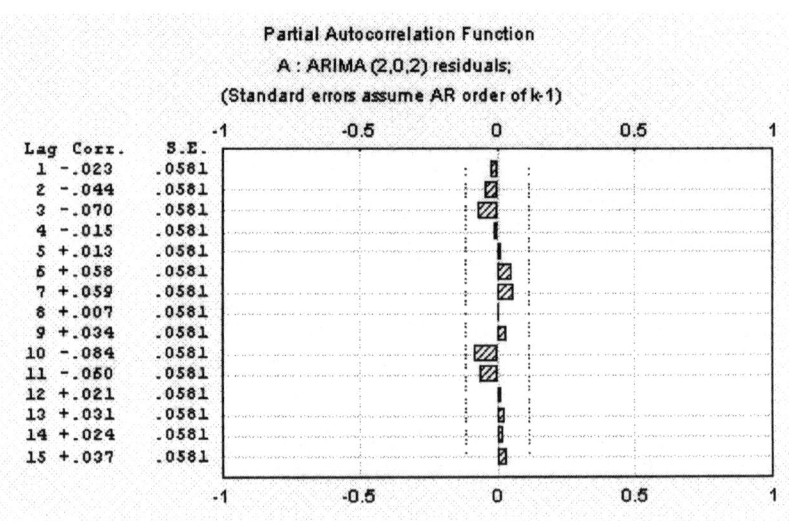

Figure 10

2. ZHONGSING, Y. & LITING, G. (1994) A Fuzzy System for Trading the Shanghai Stock Market in Trading on the Edge - Neural, Genetic and Fuzzy

Systems for Chaotic Financial Markets. Deboeck G.J., Editor, John Wiley & Sons.

3. WONG, F. (1994) Neurofuzzy Computing Technology, NeuroVet Journal Guest Editorial, May/June.

4. DERRY J. (1994) Neurofuzzy Hybrid Systems, NeuroVet Journal, May/June.

5. PAN Z., X. LIU & O. MEJABI (1997) A Neural-Fuzzy System for Financial Forecasting, NeuroVet Journal, January/February.

6. ALTROCK, CONSTANTIN VON (1997) Fuzzy Logic & Neurofuzzy Applications In Business & Finance, Prentice Hall, New Jersey.

7. JANG, J.-S. R. (1993) Adaptive-Network-Based Fuzzy Inference System, IEEE TRANSACTIONS ON SYSTEMS, MAN, AND CYBERNETICS, VOL. 23, NO. 3, MAY/JUNE.

8. JANG, J.-S. R., C-T. SUN, E. MIZUTANI (1997) Neuro-Fuzzy and Soft Computing: A computational Approach to Learning and Machine Intelligence, Prentice Hall, New Jersey.

9. WANG, L-X. and MENDEL J. M. (1992) Generating Fuzzy Rules by Learning from Examples, IEEE Transactions on Systems, Man and Cybernetics, Vol. 22, Number 6. Nov/Dec.

10. YAGER, R. R. and FILEV, D. P. (1994) Essentials of Fuzzy Modeling and Control, John Wiley & Sons.

11. BENACHENCOU, D. (1994) A Smart Trading with FRET in Trading on the Edge, in *Neural, Genetic and Fuzzy Systems for Chaotic Financial Markets.* Deboeck G.J., Editor, John Wiley & Sons.

12. BOJADZIEV, G. & BOJADZIEV, M. (1997) Fuzzy Logic for Business, Finance, and Management, Advances in Fuzzy Systems - Applications and Theory, Vol. 12, World Scientific, London.

13. BRAGA, M.J., BARRETO, J.M.& MACHADO, M.A.S. (1995) Conceitos de Matematica Nebulosa na Analise de Risco, Artes & Rabiskus.

14. ROSS, T. (1995) Fuzzy Logic with Engineering Applications, McGraw-Hill.

15. FUZZY LOGIC TOOLBOX - The Math Works Inc., Jan/1995.

16. HAMILTON, D.J (1994) *Time Series Analysis*, Princeton Press, New Jersey.

17. SOUZA, C.R., CAMARGO, M.E. (1996) Analise E Previs|o de Series Temporais: Os modelos ARIMA, Sedigraf.

18. STATISTICA for Windows, Release 4.3, 1993.

Application of Fuzzy Regression Models to Predict Exchange Rates for Composite Currencies

K. K. Yen and S. Ghoshray
Department of Electrical Engineering
Florida International University
Miami, Fl 33199, USA
E-mail : ghoshray@fiu.edu

Abstract

Predicting the exchange rates for composite currencies have been one of the most interesting and critical aspects in international finance owing to the inherent volatile nature and uncertainty involved in the phenomenon. With the increase in number of variables that interact in a complex economic environment, the accumulation of perfect knowledge for the purpose of prediction has become increasingly unrealistic. Thus, predicting future exchange rates for a composite currency has become increasingly difficult. This work is an effort in that direction in which we try to predict certain key parameters based on the imperfect and uncertain information obtained from the related economic variables. This in turn helps generate significant accuracy in the prediction process. Here we utilize the fact that the relationship between the dependent variable and the independent variables is not sharply defined as in the non-fuzzy linear regression analysis. The most important assumption for this work is that the deviations between the estimated values and the corresponding real values of the output variables lie in the imprecision or the ambiguity in the system parameters. The significant contribution of this research lies in its efficient modeling of a fuzzy prediction analysis system which can be implemented in an uncertain economic environment such as fluctuations of composite currency. In this paper, we have used the results of fuzzy regression analysis using fuzzy number coefficients from our earlier work.

Keywords*:* measurement of uncertainty, fuzzy regression analysis, non-symmetric fuzzy number coefficients, exchange rate prediction, composite currencies, European currency unit

1. INTRODUCTION

This paper is intended to deal with problems resulting from uncertainty that is inherent in complex economic environment. Uncertainty in data comes from both randomness and vagueness. Randomness involves only uncertainties in the outcomes of an experiment; vagueness, on the other hand, involves uncertainties in the description of the data. Fuzzy axiomatic structure usually increases both the mathematical tractability and physical realism of the problems dealing with uncertainty. In this research, we have taken the case of European Currency Unit(ECU) currency as a test example. At a time when the prospect of creating a European Economic and Monetary Union (EMU) has highlighted the benefits of currency integration, another extraordinary development has been taking place in the European financial sectors. Rapid growth of the private ECU has caused concerns due to its volatile nature [1,2]. In this paper, we are going to take a detail look at the private ECU; how to determine the value of it, and its future implications. The official ECU is defined as a basket of fixed amounts of 12 ECU currencies used to denominate some types of official transactions [3,4]. The official ECU is defined dually: a) by its composition and b) by its functions. At the day of entry on 13 May 1979, it was defined as the sum of fixed amounts of 9 European Community currencies [5]. On 17 September 1984, the Greek drachma and on 21 September 1989, the Spanish peseta and the Portuguese escudo were included [6]. The fixed amounts and weights of currencies of the ECU basket were changed as the ECU evolved [7].

The private ECU, on the other hand, is a basket of several European Union (EU) currencies whose individual amounts are driven by the market demand. The main difference between the official and the private ECUs is in the fact that, the official ECU is created by mutual agreement between the authorities representing the different European countries, whereas, no official agreement among the respective authorities govern the existence of private ECU. Secondly, the official ECU is exchangeable into the fixed basket of currencies into an equivalent value of a single currency, while, there does not exist a guaranteed one-for-one exchange rate of private ECUs into units of the ECU Basket. The holder of private ECU-denominated bank deposits cannot convert them into the Basket at par at all times. The same is true for the conversion of a private ECU-denominated treasury bill or bond into an equal value in units of the Basket. The private use of the ECU (or private ECU) is a contract between private agents that agree to accept payment obligations in ECU. These contracts are usually based on the "open-side ECU" definition [8]. It is called so because it is based on the official composition of the ECU though it changes composition when the official composition changes. Thus, if a ten-year ECU bond was concluded in 1983, it was based on the initial composition of the ECU basket. But when the bond matures in 1993, it will be repaid with ECU containing the drachma, peseta, and escudo. The private ECU has made a breakthrough in ECU bond issues, ECU money market and even in ECU derivatives. The private ECU has assumed many attributes such as, a financing currency, hedging and trading instrument, and an investment currency. It is thus important to explore the implications for and the meaning of the divergence between the actual ECU exchange rate from its theoretical value (i.e., the rates that can be obtained by unbundling the currencies that constitute the ECU) as well as the divergence between the actual rate of interest from its theoretical value. The private ECU embarked into the financial environment at a time when the European Community was embracing the benefits of currency integration, without analyzing the pitfalls of it. It is well known among the international community that, the more currencies there are, the higher the costs of doing business and the currency risks. These factors impair the function of money as a medium of exchange and as a store of value. As the existence of more currencies being perceived as a barrier to international trade and investment, the idea of currency integration gained its popularity [9]. Against this backdrop, the official ECU was created and the need to develop a reliable prediction model for the exchange rate was perceived.

Having established the volatility and uncertainty of the ECU, we embark on the urgency to establish the technical innovation required to build an efficient prediction model that can handle volatility and uncertainty. Modeling of fuzzy linear systems has been addressed in the literature [11,12]. The following model of a fuzzy linear system shows the dependence of an output variable on inputs variables,

$$\tilde{Y} = f(\mathbf{x}, \tilde{A}) = \tilde{A}_0 + \tilde{A}_1 x_1 + \cdots + \tilde{A}_n x_n \tag{1}$$

where $\tilde{Y}$ is the fuzzy output, $\mathbf{x} = [x_1, x_2, \ldots, x_n]^{\mathrm{T}}$ is the input vector, and $\tilde{A} = \{\tilde{A}_0, \tilde{A}_1, \cdots, \tilde{A}_n\}$ is a set of fuzzy numbers. The regression analysis problem is defined as: Given a set of crisp data points $<\mathbf{x}_1, y_1>$, $<\mathbf{x}_2, y_2>$, ..., $<\mathbf{x}_m, y_m>$, the aim of regression problem is to find a set of fuzzy parameters $\tilde{A}_0, \tilde{A}_1, \cdots, \tilde{A}_n$ for which the equation expresses the best fit to these data points, according to some criterion of goodness. The purpose of this research is to propose a fuzzy regression method that uses non-symmetric triangular fuzzy number coefficients. Before describing the fuzzy regression analysis based on fuzzy coefficients, we describe how the regression problem in (1) can be solved by using symmetric triangular fuzzy number coefficients. The theoretical foundation for this work has been laid in fuzzy arithmetic on fuzzy numbers [13]. Finally, the theoretical development described in this research has been applied in the financial environment for composite currency exchange rate prediction purposes.

2. FUZZY LINEAR MODEL

Earlier, we have introduced $\tilde{A}_i$ as the coefficient of the variable x_i in the regression model of the additive form. In this section we describe the fuzzy linear model where symmetric triangular membership functions are used as in Figure 1. The symmetric triangular fuzzy number coefficient $\tilde{A}_i$ can then be defined by the pair (a_i^C, a_i^W), where a_i^C is the center and a_i^W the width. In the following discussion, we write $\tilde{A}_i = \{a_i^C, a_i^W\}$. This can be further expressed as $\tilde{A}_i = \{a_i^L, a_i^C, a_i^U\}$, where a_i^L is the lower limit and a_i^U the upper limit. The property of symmetry for the fuzzy coefficient $\tilde{A}_i$ helps us establish the following relations:

$$a_i^C = (a_i^L + a_i^U)/2; \tag{2}$$

$$a_i^W = a_i^C - a_i^L$$

$$= a_i^U - a_i^C \tag{3}$$

Having established the relationships pertaining to the fuzzy coefficients, the fuzzy linear model $f(\mathbf{x})$ can be calculated according to fuzzy arithmetic on fuzzy numbers [14,15],

$$\tilde{Y} = f(\mathbf{x}, \tilde{A}) = (f^C(\mathbf{x}, \tilde{A}), f^W(\mathbf{x}, \tilde{A})) \tag{4}$$

where $f^C(\mathbf{x})$ is the center of the fuzzy linear model $f(\mathbf{x})$, and defined as

$$f^C(\mathbf{x}, \tilde{A}) = a_0^C + a_1^C x_1 + \ldots + a_n^C x_n \tag{5}$$

$f^W(\mathbf{x})$ is the width of the fuzzy linear model $f(\mathbf{x})$, and defined as

$$f^W(\mathbf{x}, \tilde{A}) = a_0^W + a_1^W |x_1| + \dots + a_n^W |x_n| \tag{6}$$

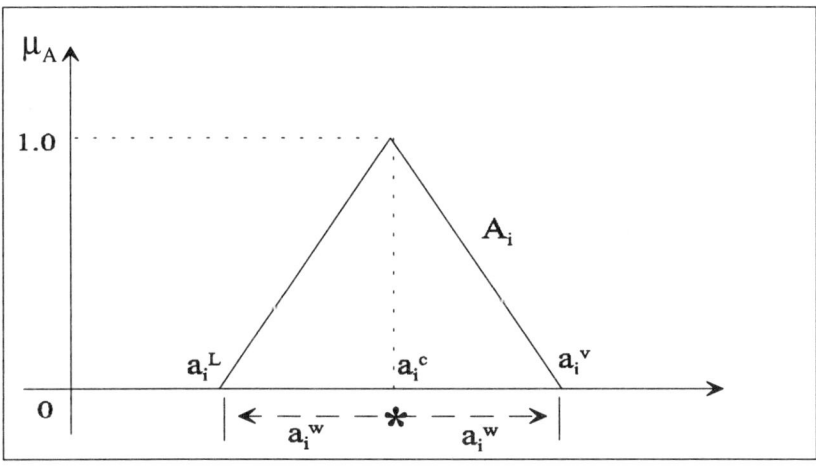

Figure 1. Membership Function for the Symmetric Triangular Fuzzy Number
Coefficient $\tilde{A}_i$

In this context, the grade membership equation of Section 2 can be rewritten as follows:

$$\mu_{\tilde{Y}}(y_j) = \begin{cases} 1 - \dfrac{|y_j - \sum_{i=1}^n a_i^C x_{ij}|}{\sum_{i=1}^n a_i^W |x_{ij}|}, & x_i \neq 0 \\[3mm] 1, & x_i = 0, y = 0 \\[3mm] 0, & x_i = 0, y \neq 0 \end{cases} \tag{7}$$

3. REGRESSION WITH NON-FUZZY DATA

The objective of the regression model with nonfuzzy data is to determine the optimum parameters $\tilde{A}^*$ such that the fuzzy output set, which contains y_j, is associated with a membership value greater than h, that is,

$$\mu_{\underset{Y}{\sim}}(y_j) \geq h, \quad j = 1, \dots, m \tag{8}$$

In this context, the degree h is specified by the user, such that by changing h a subsequent change in the fuzziness of the output is observed. The above equation states value is such that it is centered at $\sum_{i=1}^{n} a_i^c x_{ij}$, with a spread of $\sum_{i=1}^{n} a_i^w \mid x_{ij} \mid$.

In regression, our objective is to find the fuzzy coefficients that minimize the above mentioned spread of fuzzy output for all the data sets. The cost function, J, to be minimized can be written as $J = \sum_{j=1}^{m} \sum_{i=1}^{n} a_i^w x_{ij}$ (9) which can also be written as:

$$\text{Minimize } z = f^W(\mathbf{x}_1) + f^W(\mathbf{x}_2) + \dots + f^W(\mathbf{x}_m) \tag{10}$$

Tanaka et al [16] formulated a linear programming problem (LPP) to determine the fuzzy number coefficients $\tilde{A}_i$ of the fuzzy linear model, where $i = 0, \dots n$, and data available is non-fuzzy. If the data is a two dimensional data $(\mathbf{x}_j, y_j)$, where, $j = 1, \dots, m$, then the problem to be solved becomes as follows:

$$\text{Minimize } z = f^W(\mathbf{x}_1) + f^W(\mathbf{x}_2) + \dots + f^W(\mathbf{x}_m) \tag{11}$$

subject to the set of constraints

$$y_j \in [f(\mathbf{x}_j)]_h$$

where $[f(\mathbf{x}_j)]_h = [\tilde{A}_0]_h + [\tilde{A}_1]_h \mathbf{x}_{j1} + \ldots + [\tilde{A}_n]_h \mathbf{x}_{jn}$ such that $[\bullet]_h$ represents the h-level set of a fuzzy number. In this context, the h-level set of a fuzzy number $\tilde{A}$ is defined by its membership function $\mu_{[\tilde{A}]_h}(a) = \{a \mid \mu_{\tilde{A}}(a) \geq h\}$, where the following conditions have to be satisfied:

(i) $0 < h \leq 1$

(ii) R is the set of all real numbers

(iii) $a_i^w \geq 0$, $i = 0,1, \ldots, n$

It can be seen that, the minimization of the objective function in the LPP, $z = f^W(\mathbf{x}_1) + f^W(\mathbf{x}_2) + \ldots + f^W(\mathbf{x}_m)$ is equivalent to the minimization of the total fuzziness of the linear model $f(\mathbf{x})$. Henceforth, the linear programming problem expressed above evaluates the fuzzy linear model having the minimum fuzziness such that the model includes all the given data in its h-level set.

The objective of the regression model with non-fuzzy data is to determine the optimum parameters $\tilde{A}^*$ such that the fuzzy output set, which contains y_j, is associated with a membership value greater than h, that is,

$$\mu_{\tilde{y}}(y_j) \geq h, \quad j = 1, \ldots, m \tag{12}$$

where the value of h is chosen for the purpose of generating the best fitting model. In this context, vagueness is a very important aspect to be considered in any fuzzy mathematical modeling.

In regression, our goal is to find the fuzzy coefficients that minimize the above-mentioned spread of fuzzy output for all the data sets. The cost function, J, to be minimized can be written as

$$J = \sum_{j=1}^{m} \sum_{i=1}^{n} a_i^S \mid x_{ji} \mid \tag{13}$$

which can also be written as:

$$\text{Minimize } Z = f^S(\mathbf{x}_1) + f^S(\mathbf{x}_2) + \cdots + f^S(\mathbf{x}_m) \tag{14}$$

subject to the set of constraints

$$y_j \in [f(\mathbf{x}_j)]_h, \tag{15}$$

where $\quad [f(\mathbf{x}_j)]_h = [\tilde{A}_0]_h + [\tilde{A}_1]_h x_{j1} + \cdots + [\tilde{A}_n]_h x_{jn} \quad$ such that $[\bullet]_h$ represents the h-level set of a fuzzy number. Therefore, the minimization of the objective function in the LPP is equivalent to the minimization of the total fuzziness of the linear model $f(\mathbf{x})$. Henceforth, the linear programming problem expressed above evaluates the fuzzy linear model having the minimum fuzziness such that the model includes all the given data in its h-level set.

4. UNSYMMETRIC COEFFICIENTS

In the previous section, we have shown that each symmetric triangular fuzzy coefficient $\tilde{A}_i$ can be uniquely described by two parameters, either $\{ a_i^L, a_i^U \}$ or $\{ a_i^S, a_i^C \}$. However, if these triangular numbers are not symmetric, we need a minimum of three parameters to uniquely describe each. For example, $\tilde{A}_i$ can be described by the triplets $\{ a_i^L, a_i^P, a_i^U \}$ or by $\{ s_i^L, a_i^P, s_i^R \}$, where a_i^P is the point at which $\mu_{\tilde{A}_i}(a_i^P) = 1$, s_i^L is the left-side spread from the peak point a_i^P, and s_i^R represents the right-side spread as shown in Fig.2.

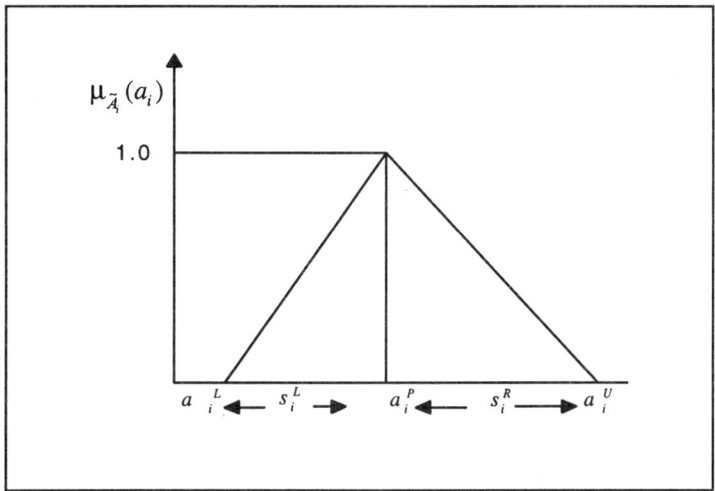

Figure 2. Showing Unsymmetric spreads for fuzzy coefficients

Another representation is also possible, if we normalize the spreads. Since $s_i^L = a_i^c - a_i^L$ and $s_i^R = a_i^R - a_i^P$, we can use either spread as the base to normalize the other one. Let us choose s_i^L as the base, then s_i^R can be expressed as

$$s_i^u = k_i s_i^L \tag{16}$$

where k_i are the skew factors and are positive real numbers. Based on the a priori knowledge, we decide the values of k_i. Then $\tilde{A}_i$ can be described by the triplets $\{s_i^L, a_i^P, k_i\}$. The membership function for each $\tilde{A}_i$ has the form either

$$\mu_{\tilde{A}_i}(a_i) = \begin{cases} 1 - \dfrac{a_i - a_i^P}{s_i^L}, & a_i^P \le a_i \le a_i^P + s_i^L \\[2mm] 1 - \dfrac{a_i^P - a_i}{s_i^R}, & a_i^P - s_i^R \le a_i \le a_i^P \\[2mm] 0, & \text{otherwise} \end{cases}$$

$$\tag{17}$$

or

$$
\mu_{\tilde{A}_i}(a_i) = \begin{cases}
1 - \dfrac{a_i - a_i^P}{s_i^L}, & a_i^P \le a_i \le a_i^P + s_i^L \\[2mm]
1 - \dfrac{a_i^P - a_i}{k_i s_i^L}, & a_i^P - k_i s_i^L \le a_i \le a_i^P \\[2mm]
0, & \text{otherwise}
\end{cases}
$$

(18)

or

$$
\mu_{\tilde{Y}}(y) = \begin{cases}
1 - \dfrac{y - \sum_i a_i^P x_i - a_0^P}{s_0^L + \sum_i s_i^L |x_i|}, & a_0^P + \sum_i a_i^P x_i \le y \\[1mm]
& \quad \le a_0^P + \sum_i a_i^P x_i + (s_0^L + \sum_i s_i^L |x_i|) \\[3mm]
1 - \dfrac{a_0^P + \sum_i a_i^P x_i - y}{k_0 s_0^L + \sum_i k_i s_i^L |x_i|}, & a_0^P + \sum_i a_i^P x_i - (k_0 s_0^L + \sum_i k_i s_i^L |x_i|) \le y \\[1mm]
& \quad \le a_0^P + \sum_i a_i^P x_i \\[3mm]
0, & \text{otherwise}
\end{cases}
$$

(19)

Following the Principle of Extension, the fuzzy membership function for the output can be obtained by either

$$
\mu_{\tilde{Y}}(y) = \begin{cases}
1 - \dfrac{y - \sum_i a_i^P x_i - a_0^P}{s_0^L + \sum_i s_i^L |x_i|}, & a_0^P + \sum_i a_i^P x_i \le y \le a_0^P + \sum_i a_i^P x_i + (s_0^L + \sum_i s_i^L |x_i|) \\[3mm]
1 - \dfrac{a_0^P + \sum_i a_i^P x_i - y}{s_0^R + \sum_i s_i^R |x_i|}, & a_0^P + \sum_i a_i^P x_i - (s_0^R + \sum_i s_i^R |x_i|) \le y \le a_0^P + \sum_i a_i^P x_i \\[3mm]
0, & \text{otherwise}
\end{cases}
$$

(20)

From the above expression, we get

$$1 - \frac{y - \sum_i a_i^P x_i - a_0^P}{s_0^L + \sum_i s_i^L |x_i|} \geq h \tag{21}$$

and

$$1 - \frac{a_0^P + \sum_i a_i^P x_i - y}{s_0^R + \sum_i s_i^R |x_i|} \geq h \tag{22}$$

if we have taken membership function values at h-cut.

Let us look at the Figure 4. Here, $a_i^P - a_i^L \neq a_i^R - a_i^P$, such that $k_i \neq 1$. Rearranging equations (22) and (23), we get

$$s_0^L + \sum_i s_i^L |x_i| - y + \sum_i a_i^P x_i + a_0^P \geq h(s_0^L + \sum_i s_i^L |x_i|) \tag{23}$$

and

$$s_0^R + \sum_i s_i^R |x_i| + y - \sum_i a_i^P x_i - a_0^P \geq h(s_0^R + \sum_i s_i^R |x_i|) \tag{24}$$

After simplification, equations (24) and (25) have the form

$$(1-h)s_0^L + (1-h)\sum_i s_i^L |x_i| + \sum_i a_i^P x_i + a_0^P \geq y \tag{25} \tag{25}$$

and

$$(1-h)s_0^R + (1-h)\sum_i s_i^R |x_i| - \sum_i a_i^P x_i - a_0^P \geq -y \tag{26} \tag{26}$$

or

$$(1-h)k_0 s_0^L + (1-h)\sum_i k_i s_i^L |x_i| - \sum_i a_i^P x_i - a_0^P \geq -y \tag{27} \tag{27}$$

Now the problem at hand is to minimize the fuzziness of the output. Since, the value of the membership function of the fuzzy output is a function of the spread, minimizing the spread corresponds to the minimization of the fuzziness of the output. Therefore, we develop the expression for the sum of the spreads in a multi-input fuzzy output function. The sum of the spread is given by

$$\Delta S = (s_0^L + s_0^R) + \Sigma_i (s_i^L + s_i^R) |x_i| \tag{28}$$

or

$$\Delta S = (1 + k_0) s_0^L + \Sigma_i (1 + k_i) s_i^L |x_i| \tag{29}$$

5. APPLICATION TO EXCHANGE RATE PROBLEM

If all the k_i are made equal to 1, then the non-symmetric case above is reduced to the symmetric triangular case, and the expression of ΔS becomes $2[s_0^L + \Sigma_i s_i^L |x_i|]$. The problem therefore, becomes a linear programming problem (LPP) in which we have to estimate the variables, a_i^S and a_i^C under two sets of constraints, equations (26) and (27) or (26) and (28), where a_i^S is the spread of the fuzzy number and a_i^C is the center of the fuzzy number. Therefore, we can apply our fuzzy regression model to predict the exchange rate of composite currency by using only two variables. Let us clarify this concept with the following example.

Example : For the given data in the Table, find the values
for a_i^S and a_i^C.

j	y_j	x_{j1}	x_{j2}
1	1.1	1.823	0.33
2	1.08	1.75	0.40
3	1.09	1.79	0.30
4	1.12	1.81	0.32
5	1.1	1.83	0.2

In this case the dependent variable is the exchange rate of ECU per dollar, the two independent variables are, x_{j1} and x_{j2}, which respectively represent the exchange rates of DM/\$ and FF/\$.

Solution:

If the value for h is selected to be 0.5, we can set up the LPP for minimization as follows:

$$\text{Minimize } Z = a_0^S + \sum_j (a_1^S |x_{j1}| + a_2^S |x_{j2}|) \tag{30}$$

subject to the constraints:

$$.5a_0^S + .5x_{j1}a_1^S + .5x_{j2}a_2^S + a_0^C + x_{j1}a_1^C + x_{j2}a_2^C \geq y_j \tag{31}$$

$$.5a_0^S + .5x_{j1}a_1^S + .5x_{j2}a_2^S - a_0^C - x_{j1}a_1^C - x_{j2}a_2^C \geq -y_j \tag{32}$$

where x_{ji} denotes the i-th component of x in the j-th data set. The actual number of functional constraints depends on the number of data set available; in this example a data set containing 5 different sets of values of $\{y, x_1, x_2\}$ will generate 10 functional constraints.

Substituting the known data values, the LPP for the given problem has the form

$$\text{Minimize } Z = a_0^S + 9.00a_1^S + 1.59a_2^S \tag{33}$$

subject to:

$$0.5 a_0^S + 0.9115 a_1^S + 0.165 a_2^S + a_0^C + 1.823 a_1^C + 0.33 a_2^C \geq 1.1 \tag{34}$$

$$0.5 a_0^S + 0.9115 a_1^S + 0.165 a_2^S - a_0^C - 1.823 a_1^C - 0.33 a_2^C \geq -1.1 \tag{35}$$

$$0.5 a_0^S + 0.875 a_1^S + 0.2 a_2^S + a_0^C + 1.75 a_1^C + 0.4 a_2^C \geq 1.08 \tag{36}$$

$$0.5 a_0^S + 0.875 a_1^S + 0.2 a_2^S - a_0^C - 1.75 a_1^C - 0.4 a_2^C \geq -1.08 \tag{37}$$

$$0.5 a_0^S + 0.895 a_1^S + 0.15 a_2^S + a_0^C + 1.79 a_1^C + 0.3 a_2^C \geq 1.09 \tag{38}$$

$$0.5 a_0^S + 0.895 a_1^S + 0.15 a_2^S - a_0^C - 1.79 a_1^C - 0.3 a_2^C \geq -1.09 \tag{39}$$

$$0.5\,a_0^S + 0.905\,a_1^S + 0.175\,a_2^S + a_0^C + 1.81\,a_1^C + 0.35\,a_2^C \geq 1.12 \quad (40)$$

$$0.5\,a_0^S + 0.905\,a_1^S + 0.175\,a_2^S - a_0^C - 1.81\,a_1^C - 0.35\,a_2^C \geq -1.12 \quad (41)$$

$$0.5\,a_0^S + 0.915\,a_1^S + 0.16\,a_2^S + a_0^C + 1.83\,a_1^C + 0.32\,a_2^C \geq 1.1 \quad (42)$$

$$0.5\,a_0^S + 0.915\,a_1^S + 0.16\,a_2^S - a_0^C - 1.83\,a_1^C - 0.32\,a_2^C \geq -1.1 \quad (43)$$

and

$$a_0^S \geq 0, \quad a_1^S \geq 0, \quad a_2^S \geq 0, \quad a_0^C \geq 0, \quad a_1^C \geq 0, \quad a_2^C \geq 0$$

Using the software Mathprog [17], the solution set is given by $a_0^S = 0.02417$, $a_1^S = 0$, $a_2^S = 0$, $a_0^C = 0.59542$, $a_1^C = 0$, $a_2^C = 0.0833$, and the minimized value of the objective function on the spread is 0.238. This gives us the number coefficients as follows: $\tilde{A}_0 = (0.02417, 0.59542)$, $\tilde{A}_1 = (0.0, 0.0)$, $\tilde{A}_2 = (0.0, 0.0833)$. The above result can be explained as follows:

When ECU exchange rate is determined using FF/\$ rate and DM/\$ rate, respectively, we see that DM/\$ rate does not influence the ECU. Since the coefficient for the DM/\$ rate is 0, the regression equation can be written as

Predicted ECU/\$ = $\tilde{A}_0 + \tilde{A}_2$ (FF/\$ rate), or

Predicted ECU/\$ = $(0.02417, 0.59542) + (0, 0.0833)$ (FF/\$ rate) . \quad (44)

For a given rate of FF/\$ = 6.00, we get

$$\text{Predicted ECU/\$} = (0.02417, 0.59542) + (0, 0.0833)\,(6.0)$$
$$= (0.02417 + 0, 0.59542 + 0.4998)$$
$$= (0.02417, 1.09522) \quad (45)$$

This means that for the exchange rate of FF/\$ = 6.0. we get the ECU/\$ rate varies between 1.07105 to 1.11937, which is accurate within 2.2%. Incidentally, this 2.2% is lower than an average transaction cost.

Let us now try another example.

$$\text{Minimize } Z = a_0^S + 9.00 a_1^S + 191.2 a_2^S \tag{46}$$

subject to:

$$0.5\,a_0^S + 0.9115\,a_1^S + 18.8\,a_2^S + a_0^C + 1.823\,a_1^C + 37.6\,a_2^C \geq 1.1 \tag{47}$$

$$0.5\,a_0^S + 0.9115\,a_1^S + 18.8\,a_2^S - a_0^C - 1.823\,a_1^C - 37.6\,a_2^C \geq -1.1 \tag{48}$$

$$0.5\,a_0^S + 0.875\,a_1^S + 19.05\,a_2^S + a_0^C + 1.75\,a_1^C + 38.1\,a_2^C \geq 1.08 \tag{49}$$

$$0.5\,a_0^S + 0.875\,a_1^S + 19.05\,a_2^S - a_0^C - 1.75\,a_1^C - 38.1\,a_2^C \geq -1.08 \tag{50}$$

$$0.5\,a_0^S + 0.895\,a_1^S + 19.0\,a_2^S + a_0^C + 1.79\,a_1^C + 38.0\,a_2^C \geq 1.09 \tag{51}$$

$$0.5\,a_0^S + 0.895\,a_1^S + 19.0\,a_2^S - a_0^C - 1.79\,a_1^C - 38.0\,a_2^C \geq -1.09 \tag{52}$$

$$0.5\,a_0^S + 0.905\,a_1^S + 19.5\,a_2^S + a_0^C + 1.81\,a_1^C + 39.0\,a_2^C \geq 1.12 \tag{53}$$

$$0.5\,a_0^S + 0.905\,a_1^S + 19.5\,a_2^S - a_0^C - 1.81\,a_1^C - 39.0\,a_2^C \geq -1.12 \tag{54}$$

$$0.5\,a_0^S + 0.915\,a_1^S + 19.25\,a_2^S + a_0^C + 1.83\,a_1^C + 38.5\,a_2^C \geq 1.1 \tag{55}$$

$$0.5\,a_0^S + 0.915\,a_1^S + 19.25\,a_2^S - a_0^C - 1.83\,a_1^C - 38.5\,a_2^C \geq -1.1 \tag{56}$$

and

$$a_0^S \geq 0, \quad a_1^S \geq 0, \quad a_2^S \geq 0, \quad a_0^C \geq 0, \quad a_1^C \geq 0, \quad a_2^C \geq 0$$

In this case the dependent variable is the exchange rate of ECU per dollar, the two independent variables are, x_{j1} and x_{j2}, which respectively represent the exchange rates of DM/\$ and BelgianFF/\$

After running the software, we obtain $a_0^S = 0.01548$, $a_1^S = 0$, $a_2^S = 0$, $a_0^C = 0.18445$, $a_1^C = 0.17065$, $a_2^C = 0.01587$, and the objective function gives us the minimal value 0.01547 on the spread. The fuzzy number coefficients are: $\tilde{A}_0 = (0.01548, 0.18445)$, $\tilde{A}_1 = (0.0, 0.17065)$, $\tilde{A}_2 = (0.0, 0.01547)$.

The result shows that where ECU exchange rate is determined using Belgian FF/$ rate and DM/$ rate respectively, we get the following fuzzy regression equation :

$$\text{Predicted ECU/\$} = \tilde{A}_0 + \tilde{A}_1 (\text{DM/\$ rate}) + \tilde{A}_2 (\text{Belgian FF/\$ rate}), \text{ or} \quad (57)$$

$$\text{Predicted ECU/\$} = (0.01548, 0.18445) + (0.0, 0.17065)(\text{DM/\$ rate})$$
$$+ (0.0, 0.01547)(\text{Belgian FF/ \$ rate}). \quad (58)$$

With a given rate of BelgianFF/$ = 39.0, and DM/$ = 1.8, we obtain

$$\text{Predicted ECU/\$} = (0.01548, 0.18445) + (0.0, 0.17065)(1.8) + (0.0, 0.01547)$$
$$(39.0).$$
$$= (0.01548 + 0 + 0, \ 0.18445 + 0.30717 + 0.60333)$$
$$= (0.01548, 1.09495) \quad (59)$$

This means that for the exchange rates of the two different currencies, Belgian FF/$ and DM/$, we get for every dollar, an amount of ECU which varies between 1.07947 and 1.11043. This predicted value is accurate within 1.4%, lower than an average transaction cost again.

Thus, we can see that fuzzy linear regression analysis can be efficiently used to predict the exchange rates for composite currencies. We can also see that the proposed method works well for ECU, where uncertainty and volatility has been a factor since its inception. The following diagrams depict how the model works.

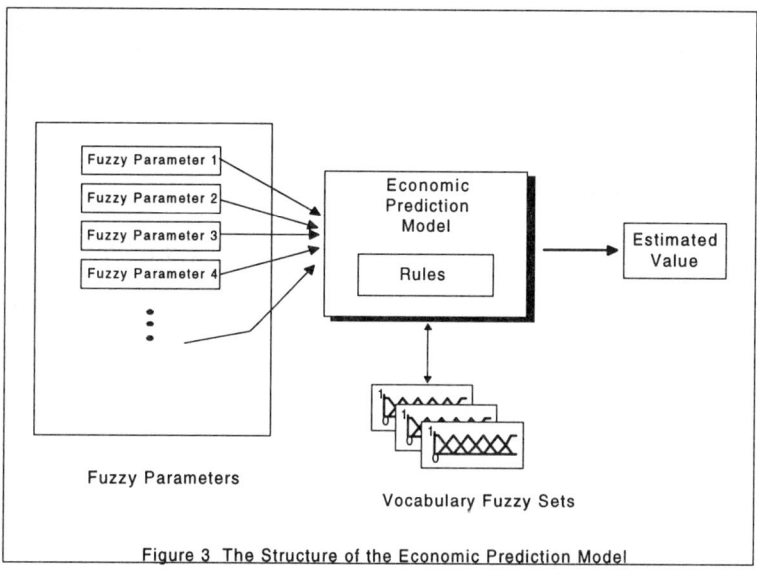

Figure 3 The Structure of the Economic Prediction Model

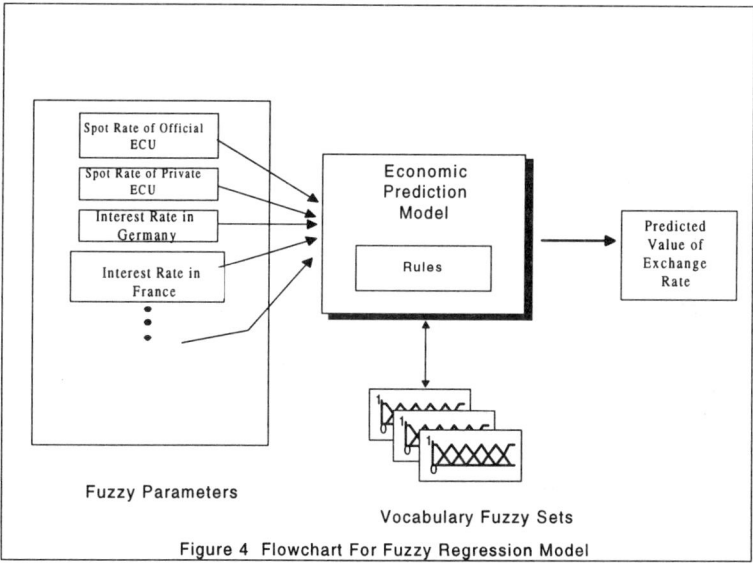

Figure 4 Flowchart For Fuzzy Regression Model

6. CONCLUSION

Our primary objective in this paper is to develop a fuzzy regression model that can efficiently predict the exchange rate for a composite currency as described. We further want to understand the nature of a composite currency from a truly finance perspective. The volatile nature of the private ECU as well as its interaction with other economic determinants has been examined and an efficient prediction model has been proposed. It has been established that the private ECU's unpredictability and its deviation from the par value relative to the official ECU is mainly due to the lack of a real monetary mechanism and a controlling strategy for the composite currency. This modeling methodology can be extended to any other set of composite currencies that we wish to examine. Finally, it is prudent to say that the analysis of unpredictability and uncertainty as well as fluctuation in bilateral exchange rates of a composite currency is a relatively new field and not much literature is available yet. Therefore, this study is an endeavor to pave the way for a better prediction of exchange rates based on fuzzy statistical methods.

REFERENCES

1. Bayoumi, T. & Eichengree, B., "Shocking Aspects of European Monetary Union," in *Adjustment and Growth in the European Monetary Union*, Cambridge University Press, 1993, pp. 193-229.
2. Bean, C., "Economic and Monetary Union in Europe", *Journal of Economic Perspectives*,Vol. 6, 1992, pp. 31-52.
3. Committee of Governors of the Central Banks of the Member States of the European Economic Community, *Statistical Review*, February 1991.
4. ECU Banking Association, "The ECU--To BE or Not to Be a Basket - That is the Question", *EBA Newsletter*, June 1991.
5. Commission of the EC. *The European Monetary System: Commentary*, Documents, Brussels:Kredietbank.1979.
6. Commission of the EC. "On Developing the European Monetary System",

Brussels: Com(84) 678 Final, November 29. 1984.
7. De Cecco, M., and Giovannini, A." A European Central Bank?" *Perspectives on Monetary Unification after Ten Years of the EMS*, Cambridge: University Press. 1989
8. Abraham, F., Abraham, J.P., and Lacroix,Destree, Y. "EMS, ECU and Commercial Banking", *Revue de la Banque*, No.2, pp.5-35, 1984.
9. Chaphekar, P., Keating, G. & Mason, R., "ECU Recomposition and the True Synthetic Yield", *Credit Suisee First Boston*, September 1998.
10. Colligon, S."The Economic Consequences of a Single European Currency on Centre- Periphery Relations within the Community in Association for the Monetary Union of Europe", *A Strategy for the ECU*, London. 1990.
11. Tanaka, H., Vejima, S., Asai., K. "Linear Regression Analysis with Fuzzy Model", *IEEE Trans.on Systems, Man, and Cybernetics*, Vol. 12, No. 6, pp. 903-907, 1982.
12. Yen, K.K., Ghoshray, S., "Fuzzy Regression Analysis for Prediction in Complex Economic Environment," *Proc. of the 3rd Int'l Conf. on Fuzzy Logic*. Zurich, Switzerland, 1995.
13. Kaufmann, A., Gupta, M.M.,"Introduction to Fuzzy Arithmetic", Van Nostrand Reinhold, New York, 1985.
14. A. Kandel and W. Byatt, "Fuzzy Sets, Fuzzy Algebra, and Fuzzy Statistics", *Proceedings of the IEEE*, vol. 66, no. 12, December 1978, pp 1619-1639.
15. Ross, Timothy, "Fuzzy Logic with Engineering Applications", McGrawHill, Inc., New York, 1995.
16 . H. Tanaka et al, "Fuzzy Linear Regression Model", *IEEE Transaction on Systems, Man, and Cybernetics*, vol. 10, no. 4, 1980, pp 2933- 2938.
17. Hillier, Mark. MathProg and ProbMod Software. McGraw-Hill, Inc., 1995.

A Fuzzy Inferencing Approach Towards the Chaotic Nature of Foreign Currency Interactions

S. Ghoshray and K.K. Yen
Department of Electrical Engineering
Florida International University
Miami, Fl 33199, USA
E-mail : ghoshray@fiu.edu

Abstract

Foreign currency exchange rate prediction has been a well-researched topic in international finance. However, most prediction techniques suffer from drawbacks due to the inherent uncertainty in the data acquisition method, which we seek to alleviate by using fuzzy reconstruction. This study, we have analyzes the time series data from a pure dynamic system point of view and explores the deterministic chaos inherent in it. A method of predicting time series data based on deterministic dynamically system has been proposed in this work. The study revolves around the concepts of chaotic time series, its embedding based on Takens' Thereom, and fuzzy reconstruction. Here we propose a new prediction methodology based on efficient unification of chaos theory and fuzzy reconstruction method.

Keywords: deterministic chaos, nonlinear prediction, fuzzy reconstruction, embedding, strange attractor, fuzzy inferencing

1. INTRODUCTION

An estimation problem of particular importance in the field of financial engineering is the problem of forecasting, or predicting trends in the foreign exchange market or in the stock market. All the various methods that have been applied in predicting the future movements of various financial instruments can be categorized by two broad class; the fundamental analysis and the technical analysis [1]. Fundamental analysis is based on the relationships between the various factors that influence the economy and eventually develop some empirical models, such as, the balance of payments flow model, monetary models of exchange rate determination, currency substitution model, the hybrid monetary/fiscal policy model etc [2]. On the other hand, in the technical analysis, the prediction is done by analyzing a set of past data by various methods such as time series analysis, regression analysis, expert systems, etc [3].

Because exchange rate movements affect so many businesses, investment and policy decisions, the proper determination of the currency exchange rate has become the primary objective of all market participants. However, the correct determination of exchange rate on a consistent basis has become very difficult. In their continuous efforts to develop the best model, the economists and the financial analysts have come up with a wide range of prediction methodologies. Research has indicated that fundamental analysis based models can be used in explaining long-range trend in currency movements, whereas it is inadequate in explaining the short-range and medium-range fluctuations in exchange rate data [4]. Against this backdrop, many technical-analysis based models have been developed to be somewhat successful in predicting currency exchange rates over short-run periods. This relative success of the technical models in currency exchange rate prediction, compared to the lack of success of the fundamental-based models, has made the technical analysis become extremely popular among market participants. However all these methods suffer from drawbacks in their inability to predict the future values with consistent accuracy [5,6,7]. This occurs due to the lack of reliable knowledge base as the data available is not well organized or not coherent enough. Secondly, the movements of both the foreign exchange and the stock market follow a chaotic path based on dynamic deterministic systems which we will explain in detail in the subsequent sections. Therefore, present methods are not adequate enough to model the dynamic systems that represent the fluctuations in stock market or foreign exchange market. In this research, we have examined several uncertainty modeling techniques, analyzed the behavior of time series data and developed a fuzzy inferencing technique to predict the future values of time series.

2. PREDICTION METHODOLOGIES BASED ON LINEAR ANALYSIS

Where the fundamental-based predictions rely on independent projections of the related economic variables and then determine exchange rates, technical models predict analyze and subsequently extrapolate the set of past data by various methods as mentioned in the previous section and then predict exchange rates. There exists a wide variety of foreign currency exchange rate prediction methods which is based on trend, but, in all fairness, they share a common thread which is the property of extrapolation. Herein comes the inherent drawback. Since these models generate forecasts by extrapolating the recent past trend of exchange rates into the future, the buying or selling decisions can be made only after the currency has already started rising or falling. Therefore, these prediction models cannot catch the very top or bottom of market moves. Instead, they rely on the assumptions that the exchange rates must always move in large swings such that the model can capture enough of a market move in order to be able to earn a sizable profit. Let us now analyze the trends in the market in more detail.

2.1 Identifying Market Trends by Linear Analysis of Patterns

In any existing prediction methodology, the pattern in market prices is defined as a series of primary and secondary waves. In a pattern diagram depicting the market trend, the primary waves can be seen as the large, broad moves in the prices. In this case, the underlying market trend can be seen as either upward or downward as depicted in Figure 1.

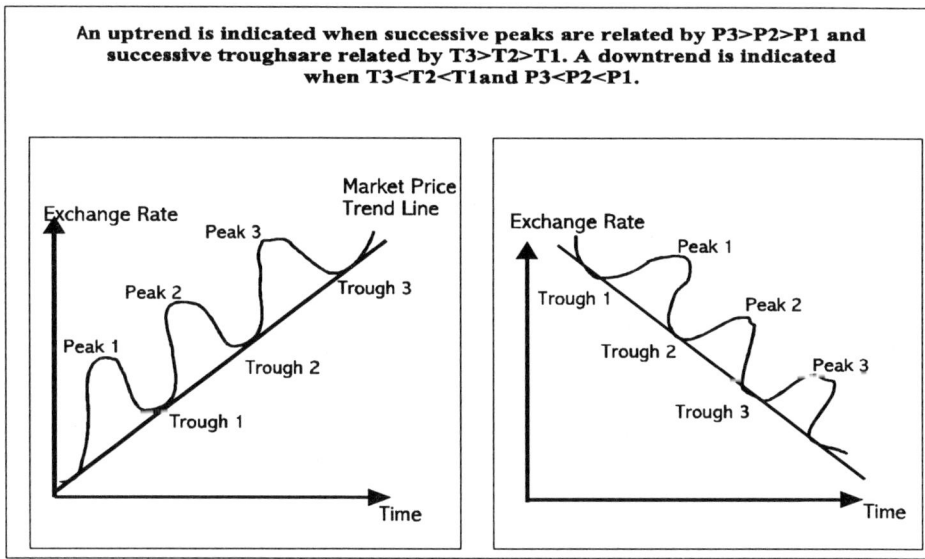

An uptrend is indicated when successive peaks are related by P3>P2>P1 and successive troughsare related by T3>T2>T1. A downtrend is indicated when T3<T2<T1and P3<P2<P1.

Figure 1. Identification of Trend in Exchange Rates Based on the Wave Pattern

The secondary waves can be seen as retracements over the primary trend, which indicates a temporary correction from the original trend. By analyzing the directions of the successive peaks in the wave, a prediction as to the future behavior of the market is generated. If exchange rates achieve successive higher peaks and the intermediate troughs do not fall below the preceding troughs, an upward trend is indicated. On the other hand, if the falling rates establish a succession of lower troughs and the intermediate advances fall below the preceding peaks, a downward trend is declared. A reversal in the market is indicated when the wavelike series of rising peaks and troughs is as depicted in Figure 2.

248

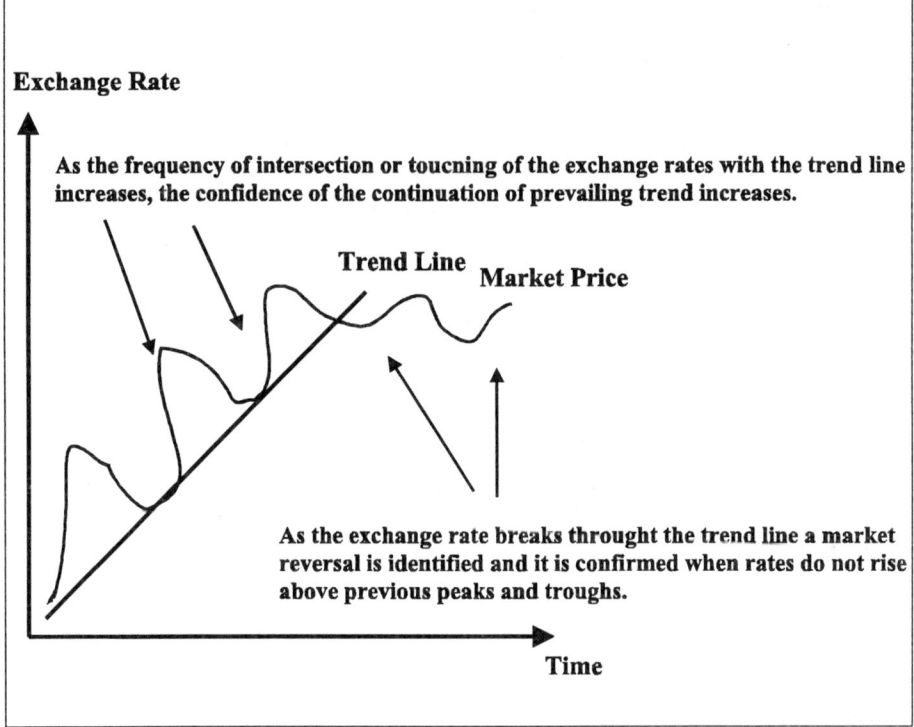

Figure 2. Identification of Market Reversal

There are several patterns that can be identified as the characteristics for market reversal. However, the common characteristic of the reversal pattern is that all reversals must be preceded by the failure of market prices to achieve successively higher peaks and troughs. Figure 3 exhibits another type of reversal of market pattern, in which three consecutive rallies show market reversal after gradual weakening of demand.

A major drawback in the current models of exchange rate prediction lies in the fact that the buy and sell signals are late in drawing attention to a shift in market direction. This is because the prediction generated by extrapolating the past sequence of exchange rate movements into the future. Henceforth, the buy and sell signals may be issued only after a currency has already started rising or falling. This is defined as the "recognition lag" in the existing prediction methodologies [6].

2.2 Efficiency Analysis of Prediction Based on Past Data

Various studies have been performed to ascertain whether changes in exchange rates can be forecasted solely on the basis of their past behavior [7,8]. One trend among the researchers is to seek the existence of stable linear relationships between the current change in the exchange rate (saturated at time t) ΔE_t with the exchange rate in the preceding period ΔE_{t-1}. If there exists a stable positive linear relationship that would confirm the existence of a trend in the currency exchange rates. This subsequently would ascribe validity to the numerous prediction methodologies of today. However, most studies have concluded that there exists no stable positive linear relationship between ΔE_t and ΔE_{t-1}. Series correlation test would determine if there exists a stable linear relationship between ΔE_t and ΔE_{t-1}. Evidence of positive serial correlation will indicate that a positive change in a currency's value at time t will be followed by another positive change tomorrow [9]. The estimated serial-correlation coefficient could vary between +1, 0, and -1, based on whether there exists a strong positive, zero, or negative relationship between successive exchange rate changes.

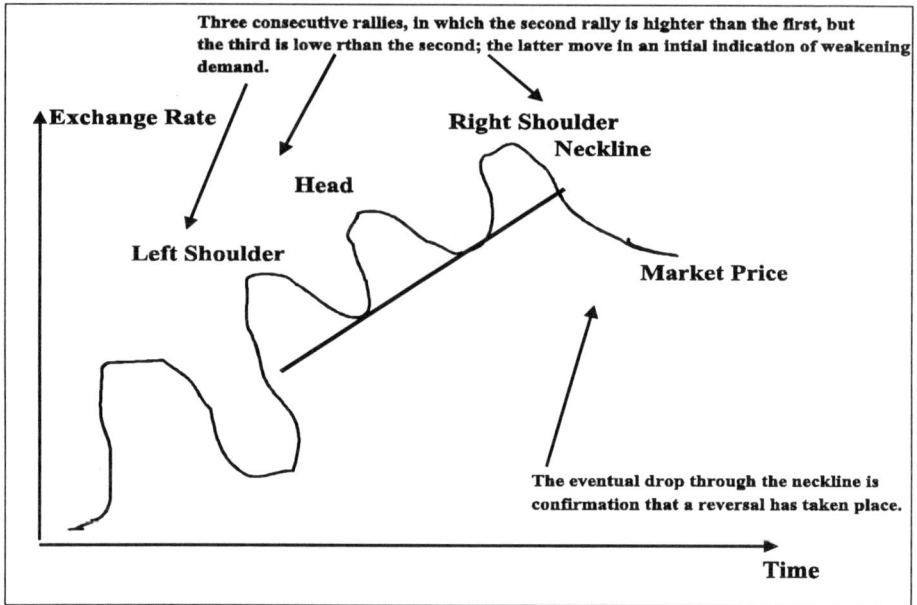

Figure 3. Identification of Some Reversal Patterns

3. THE FAILURE OF LINEAR PARADIGM

In its current form, the financial market theory, which is also known as capital market theory is based on a few key concepts, (a) Rational investors, (b) Efficient markets and, (c) Random walks. Rational investor concept tells us that the investors assess potential returns by a probabilistic weighting method that generates expected returns, such that, the risk is measured as the standard deviation of returns. According to Efficient Market Hypothesis (EMH), changes in prices are not related, except possibly for some very short-term dependence, which dissipates quickly. These two concepts bring us the third concept, according to which, return follows a random walk. Therefore, the probability distribution is approximately normal or log-normal, indicating thereby that the distribution of returns has a finite mean and variance. Empirical studies have attempted to prove this Gaussian assumption of the capital market theory, but have often encountered contradictory results. While developing the above mentioned concepts two possibilities have been ignored, which are (i) markets and securities are interdependent and, (ii) the rational investor model is not realistic. It has been observed that, people do not behave in the manner described by rational expectations theory. In previous studies, the view that market participants may not know how to interpret all known information and may react to trends, thereby incorporating past information into their current actions, was treated as unnecessary complexities with insignificant change in outcome [10,11]. It has been however, acknowledged recently, that this previously neglected information is more crucial than thought before, hence needed further analysis, even if the mathematics get messy. That is why the linear paradigm, despite its simplicity and conceptual elegance, is seriously flawed.

Several complete studies have been done to discount the normality assumption of market returns, the very fundamental building block of the linear paradigm. The first complete study on daily returns was done by Fama in 1965, who found that returns were negatively skewed: more observations were in the left-handed (negative) tail than in the right-hand tail. In additions, the tails were fatter, and the peak around the mean was higher than predicted by the normal distribution, a condition called "leptokurtosis" [12] Sharpe also noted this in his 1970 textbook, *Portfolio Theory and Capital Markets* [13]. When Sharpe compared annual returns to the normal distribution, he noted that "normal distribution assign little likelihood to the occurrence of really extreme values. But such values occur quite often." More recently, Turner and Weigel in 1990 performed an extensive study of volatility, using daily S&P index returns from 1928 to 1990, with similar results [14]. They found that "daily return distributions for the Dow Jones and S&P 500 are negatively skewed and contain a larger frequency of returns around the mean interspersed with infrequent very large or very small returns as compared to a normal distribution. In another recent study of quarterly S&P 500 returns, from 1946 to 1988, Friedman and Laibson pointed out that "the 22.6 percent *one-day* decline in stock prices on October 19, 1987 was unique, but from the perspective of a quarterly time frame, the 1987 episode was one of several unusually large rallies or crashes" [15]. These authors note that, in addition to being leptokurtotic, "large movements have been often crashes than rallies" and significant leptokurtosis "appears regardless of the period chosen."

These studies prove in unmistakable terms that the market returns are not normally distributed. If the market returns are not normally distributed, then much of the statistical analysis, particularly diagnostics such as correlation coefficients and t-statistics, is seriously weakened and may give misleading answers. Therefore, the case for a random walk in market prices is also seriously weakened. Therefore, we can see that the three simplifying assumptions, rational investors, efficient markets, and random walks, have led to an entire analytic framework that may be a castle built on sand. These concepts were constructed to justify the use of probability calculus by giving an economic framework to the crucial assumption of independence of observations of returns. The assumption that the market participants react to information in a linear way, as the information arrives, can profoundly change the nature of the markets if, instead, market participants react in a nonlinear delayed fashion.

4. EXISTENCE OF CHAOS IN FINANCIAL SYSTEMS

Behind the new tools available for non-traditional research are developments in physical sciences that have a direct impact on financial trading and portfolio management. The new methods have originated from the theories of the physical sciences. The most fundamental characteristic that gives them an edge over the traditional methods is the fact that all forms of organizations simultaneously map themselves into two states that apparently are at odds with each other, *change and order*. *Change* is characterized by the freedom to move away from the status quo by altering things in a manner reflecting new developments and by taking full account of the forces behind the process of innovation [16]. The representation of this change is complex, and the transition between change and order involves a great number of uncertainties. By a sharp contrast, *order* is represented by simpler and more settled paths to regulation and is often expressed in a structured, hierarchical manner [17]. Both change and order are essential, though they are contradictory to each other. The theory of complexity interfaces the chaos and order and addresses the problems of transition. Therefore, in a complex system chaos and order go through transitions. Furthermore, chaotic systems are essentially periodic. What makes them appear random is a continual transition from one periodic orbit to another. To delve deeper into chaos and its applicability in financial markets, it is essential to understand the relationships among chaos, non-equilibrium and instability. A chaotic system could be stable if its particular irregularity persisted in the event of small disturbances. Thus, in spite of having a pattern of irregularity and being locally predictable, chaos may be globally stable. These patterns of disturbances in chaos can be defined as orderly disorder. Therefore, by analyzing the way in which patterns change with respect of time, it is possible to make more sense out of chaotic behavior of complex systems, such as financial markets. In this context, the failure of existing models of economy in efficiently predicting future events lies in the fact that these models fail to establish the relationships among chaos, instability and equilibrium. It is to be noted that, there can be no equilibrium condition in the transitions in a dynamic environment that is steadily characterizing the alterations of change and order. The existing models of economy such as the equilibrium theory and the efficient marker hypothesis fail to recognize this aspect. It is therefore, of paramount importance to understand that no dynamic system can be correctly modeled if the analysis either ignores time or treats time as a controllable variable.

In financial analysis, most of the modeling processes aim at the study of time series of values resulting from measurements attributed to specific events. Traditionally, the changes in values of a specific variable have been represented as a function of time. In this regard, mostly linear algorithms are being used to exploit and visualize the relationship that exists between time series values. Our research has found that both linearity and randomness have been used for predictive reasons. This explains why determinism and randomness have been seen as opposites for a long time. Based on this, it is therefore assumed that complex phenomena originates from systems with many degrees of freedom and are analyzed as random processes. On the other hand, simple phenomena are modeled deterministically. As a result, this procedure ends by producing unpredictable behavior in the longer run. However, under the influence of nonlinearity, only a few degrees of freedom are necessary to generate chaotic motion. That is why, researchers have been working on methods and tools for nonlinear modeling motivated by the observation that nonlinear approaches underlining chaotic dynamics produces superior prediction capabilities as compared to existing linear or quasi-linear models.

Nonlinear approaches to short-term forecasting employ chaotic attractors, making it possible to predict impending crisis. This is done by dynamically examining time series taken near the catastrophic bifurcation threshold. Chaos theory can be helpful in this context because it represents the possibility that random systems might actually be modeled by simple procedures and rules, thereby making them predictable. The objective in chaos theory in the context of financial markets is to develop models that can predict with unprecedented accuracy. Therefore, the aim of this research is to apply prediction capabilities to financial markets and financial instruments so that a high degree of significance in term of predictability is attained.

The implementation of chaos theory in currency exchange rate prediction essentially revolves around the dynamics of nonlinear solution spaces. The results obtained from chaotic system apparently can look random, which however, is not truly random. In this case, each chunk of values are limited within a given region. This chaotic behavior allows us to predict short range time series data more accurately.

5. DYNAMIC BEHAVIOR OF THE TIME SERIES DATA

In this section, we explain in somewhat detail as to what is meant by the term "chaos" as applied to deterministic dynamic systems. We investigate the mechanisms that give rise to chaotic dynamics and also review the analytical techniques for prediction (in terms of system parameters). There has been a great deal of interest in recent years in the application of chaos theory to a variety of real world time dependant systems. There has also been much attention given to the ability of computational intelligence tools such as Neural Networks, Genetic Algorithms, and Fuzzy Logic to model fuzzy or ill defined real world problems. There are many times series, notably in the natural sciences and finance, that had proved difficult to analyze with conventional linear methods and, are now beginning to be modeled using non-linear and non-parametric methods [18].

Most of these series suffer from a major limitation of non-stationary time series, such as, noisy and inadequate. The numbers of points available are probably small by any of the data point measurements that have been previously suggested. Most of these studies check the reliability of their results given the small amount of data available by comparing estimate with distribution from simulated stochastic processes [19]. Thus, we can see that there is interesting evidence of potential predictability in many of these series. However, the problem is related to how much forecastibility can be left around in a time series. In this context, by using Chaos we can estimate a Lyapunov exponent, of a time series which can provide some idea of forecast degradation over a short horizon. This obviously implies that over the shortest horizon, good forecast were available to analyze how their performance drops after several periods have gone by.

Thus, the continuity properties of a dynamical system, whether flow or map imply unique solutions and predictable behavior. This determinism imply chaotic characteristics, in which case the faithful reconstruction from a single observed time series of the attractor for the underlying dynamics is possible via embedding methods [20].

5.1 Fundamentals of Chaos Theory

Chaos is the mathematical term for the behavior of a system which is inherently unpredictable. A dictionary definition of chaos is "a disordered state of collection; a confused mixture," which is an accurate description of dynamic systems theory today. A dynamic system is one which changes with time. To understand a dynamic system means to know how the states vary through time. One of the ingredients of a chaotic system is feedback. Let us explain this with the logistic equation that is introduced to explain the basics of chaos theory:

$X_t = K * X_{t-1} * (1 - X_{t-1})$, where K is a constant [21].

In this logistic equation, the results from the previous iteration is fed back repeatedly into the next one. In this context, we can see how trivial the above equation is. It is a simple quadratic formula in the variable X_{t-1}. Given X_{t-1} and K, we can compute X_t, accordingly. Our experiments have shown, when K is small the value X_t can be quite predictable. For K=0.5, the value of X_t tends to 0; whereas for K=1, 2, and 3, it tends to stabilize or reach a definite limiting value. At above 3, different values of K yield significantly different results. This example illustrates in unmistakable terms the consequences of chaos in deterministic systems because of the following observations: First and foremost, it is not possible to accurately predict the result and secondly, the search for a specific solution in a chaotic system is *inefficient*. Therefore, in dealing with chaotic systems, we focus on a more global viewpoint and instead of trying to predict the particular behavior of a solution, we seek to identify the totality of all these solutions.

In the search for solutions in a chaotic dynamic system, an important object is the *strange attractors*. From a dynamic system point of view, an *attractor* can be defined as an object toward which all nearby solutions adhere to as time moves on. If we consider a dynamic system, in which the state space W can be fined as an open set in some real *Banach space B*, such that K is a nonempty compact set having a neighborhood N in W with the following properties: every trajectory starting in N has compact closure in W and has all its limit points in K; K is defined as an attractor. Chaotic dynamic systems are sometimes said to have "strange attractors" or even "*strange strange attractors*"[22]. In spite of some vagueness associated in this concept, it means, *K* is neither a single stationary point or a single periodic orbit.

6. PREDICTION METHODOLOGY

In order to analyze and predict time series we must first reconstruct a state space. In this context, a state s(t) is an information set that fully describes the system at a fixed instant in time *t*. If it is known with complete accuracy and if the system is strictly deterministic, then the state contains sufficient information to determine the future of the system. This means that the past behavior of the time series contains information about the present state. Therefore, in order to construct a dynamical model for the time series or the current state of the system, we are going to use the immediate past behavior of the time series. In this context, the measurements making up a time series are of lower dimension than the dynamics that generate them. The past behavior of the time series can be represented as $x(t) = (x(t), ..., x(t-(n-1)()))$, where $x(t)$ is a delay vector of embedding dimension n. The use of past information to construct a state has been a standardized convention in time series analysis and literature is replete with such work. In this context, Takens' theory of embedding has been the guiding light in the reconstruction of state space [17]. According to this theory, if the original state s(t) has a separation dimension d, then the mapping of s(t) to $x(t)$ is possible if $n \geq 2d + 1$, provided there is no noise. Here, the appropriate values of d and n are important to ensure accurate results. In the absence of theory to guide us, empirical methods seem very attractive so long as the search space is not too large. One can define practical bounds for embedding parameters, and thus define a search space. Reasonable bounds for these parameters can be determined based on the empirical rules: (i)The embedding and the separation dimensions are integer-valued, (ii) Prediction is unlikely to be possible for anything requiring an embedding dimension greater than 8, because in that case we are going to have separation dimension greater than 16, which is too large [23]. As we can see that there is no formula or equation governing the choice of embedding parameters. This, therefore, prompts us to use the value of some derived metric such as prediction performance to determine the optimum. Let us explain embedding with some known values of the parameter. Literature has shown that fractal dimension of the Lorenz attractor is 2.06. Therefore, according to Takens, the upper bound for a successful embedding in this case is 5], whereas it is known that the practical embedding dimension of the series in reference is 3 [24].

As for the Lyapunov exponent is concerned, it has been ascertained in the literature, that when dealing with large amounts of noiseless data, a choice of a larger dimension may not matter when calculating Lyapunov exponents. However, a choice of a larger dimension can be fatal where modeling is concerned. This has been shown by Martin Casadagli in which he used a brute force search through various embedding dimensions and constructed models of various types of each dimension value, which he subsequently tested on fresh data [18]. The reasons for this effect are most likely to be parsimony, or the lack of it. Any model generated with more than the required number of inputs and thus more than the required parameters or model complexity is less likely to perform well on out of sample data. With this in mind we embark on a description of the time series predictor.

6.1 Description of Time Series Predictor

Due to the complexity of the data, its availability in vast quantities, and the growing interest in the prediction methodologies, financial time series has been the focus of attention for quite sometime. In this section, we are going to describe the development of a time series predictor dealing with the financial time series. Figure 4 shows a crude diagram of the proposed time series predictor. In this system, we have arranged the input data ordered in time, rather than sampled at equal intervals of time. This was designed for the system to be able to handle multivariate data. At the present time we are still testing our technique and fine tuning it. More information about the time series data will be provided in our future communication, once we finalize the construction of the predictor. However, based on the work done so far, the following steps have been implemented:

1. Storing and Reformatting Input Data

   As has been established so far that the data updates are used as the fundamental time-bases for prediction and analysis in the proposed method, whereas the frequency of the data updates assume significant role as they vary enormously over time, especially for financial time. Therefore, in order to get better results we must order the data points efficiently in the data base which is used for input. Each data point is therefore stored with multiple fields containing the time stamp and the data value. This allows us to sample the series at discrete intervals in time.

2. Re-arranging Input Data

   After the input data is placed in a multiple field database, we reorganize the data so that the system is be able to handle multivariate data. Here each data point is contained in a multiple field record and time stamped. We then place the data structure in a multiple record linked structure, so that any data point can be accessed in accordance with its time of creation.

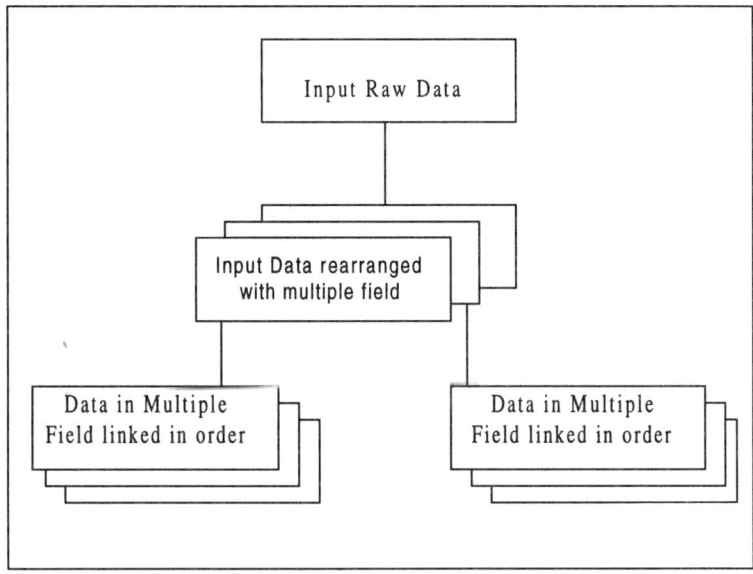

Figure 4. Organization of the Database

Once our database is constructed as described, all sorts of input, such as, the training sets, validation sets, input sets for chaos analyzer, are all extracted from the database. In this regard, the data used is sampled with regular time intervals between samples. Because of the flexibility incorporated in the our structure, the sampling intervals can be changed during the data manipulation as well as the prediction generation process.

3. Data Normalization

The input data goes through training process before producing output values. From simulation runs, we have observed that sometimes if data is not normalized, the training algorithms become severely slowed down and their performance suffers. This is because, non-normalized data is sometimes out of scale and therefore generate predictions outside the range of given input values. We have seen that the training as well as the generation of prediction proceeds more efficiently and if input data is normalized. In this regard, normalization consists of finding the highest and lowest level in the data supplied, and calculating a scaling value based on the application and initial simulation results. In this work, we used the following formulas:

$$\text{Scale} = \frac{1 + 2\lambda}{(\text{max} - \text{min})}$$

Where λ is a safety margin to be tested and determined later. At this point, we tested values that range from 0.05 to 0.5. The safety margin is added to ensure that we can safely represent a prediction outside of the prices historical range.

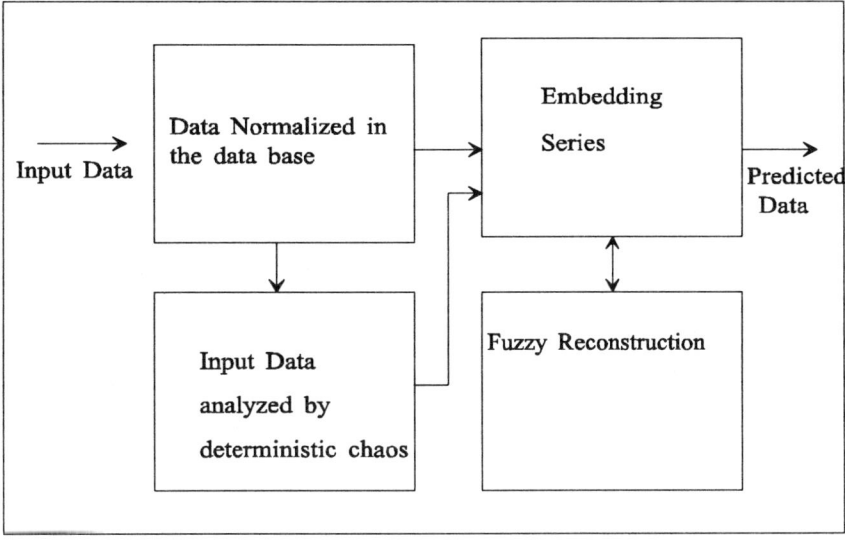

Figure 5. Block Diagram of Proposed Predictor

6.2 Lyapunov Exponent Implementation

This measure describes how adjacent trajectories on the attractor under study diverge as they are evaluated in time. As a chaotic system evolves, no trajectory will ever be the same as a preceding one. This is fundamental to the definition of a chaotic system; by looking at pairs of trajectories and how they diverge, we can estimate how rapidly we will cease to know the exact location of a projected trajectory, and thus the maximum achievable predication accuracy. The measure calculated in practice is the average of this accuracy over the whole of the attractor, or at least our knowledge of it. Calculation of the Lyapunov spectrum can be derived analytically where the equations of the processes are known [25].

6.3 Embedding Analysis

The two most prominent tasks involved in generating a time series prediction are: finding a suitable model for the data, and finding a suitable method for presenting the data to the modeling algorithm. With the growth of non-parametric modeling techniques the latter problem has been much simplified, however, the earlier problem presents the greater difficulty.

Using the financial time series analysis presented in this work there are effectively three unknowns. They are (i) the correct embedding dimension to use for a series, (ii) the correct sample separation to use for a series, and (iii) the number and type of helper series to use. Literature is not clear at all in the derivation of these parameters. Therefore, it is up to the individual researcher to come up with the burden of estimating the time of search that is required to find the appropriate parameters. In this context, it is possible to automate the process using either brute force search or a more efficient method such as Genetic Algorithms [26]. These methods are of incredibly time consuming but definitely effective. However, we do not have much confidence in their robustness. That is why we have used fuzzy reconstruction for prediction in this work.

However, in attempting time series prediction no real assumptions can be made about the underlying function driving the time series. If we find a choice of parameters that give good predictions, we might only found some chance alignment of data values. Since the model and parameters are to be effectively trained together it is not certain that the best solution to be found cannot be a combination of say a good model and mediocre embedding parameters or vice versa. An analytical method for determining the correct parameters without reference to a model would give the most confidence in the results.

6.4 Training Pattern Generation

Takens' theorem [17] states that a chaotic process can be predicted by a smooth function if properly embedded. Supervised algorithms are used in this work to generate these smooth functions from the time series. These learnt functions are mappings form input data provided as tuples to one or more predictions of the future value of the time series. The process of embedding a single time series is as follows:

The scalar series is converted to a series of vectors:

$$X_t = X_t, X_{d+t}, X_{2d+t}, \ldots\ldots, X_{nd+t}$$

where d is the *separation*, and n the *embedding dimension*.

In practice, in order to perform predictions for a given time series, first the separation is calculated, then the embedding dimension (this is to that the separation calculated can be used in the optimal dimension calculations). Finally, the embedded vectors are used as training set to some example of a supervised learning algorithm, along with some future value of the time series representing the point to be predicted.

In our case, multivariate prediction are to be obtained by maintaining separate database for each input series, selecting embedding parameters for that series, embedding them appropriately and concatenating the input vectors and output scalars. Great care is taken to ensure that the sampling intervals are the same for each series and that the input vectors are completely synchronized.

6.5 Local Approximation Algorithm

Here the time series is embedded using the methods discussed earlier. A binary tree is to be formed form the embedded data, and the tree is stored. Thus, by completing the learning phase in this way, we would move forward towards prediction. To make a prediction from a similarly embedded predictee vector the $n+1$ nearest neighbors are to be sought in the binary tree, where n is the selected embedding dimension. The idea behind this is that the simplest figure that can be created in n dimensions must have $n+1$ vertices. We implemented an exponential schemes to weigh the nearest neighbors according to Euclidean distance from the predictee. We can pictorially describe this interpolation scheme as follows:

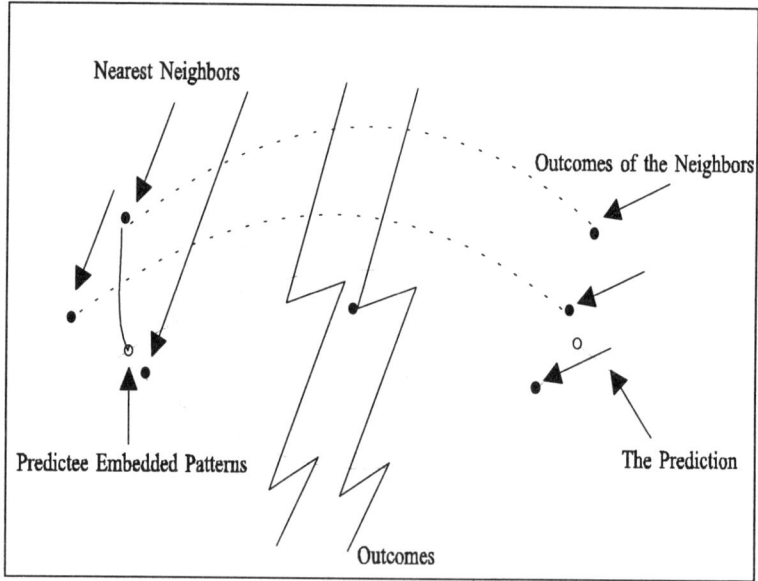

Figure 6. Local Approximation Interpolation

6.6. Prediction Methodology

Now we embark on explaining the distinction between the nonlinear short-term prediction and the long term prediction from the view point of deterministic dynamic systems. How the attractor and the state space are reconstructed by using a given time series data from the original dynamic system is the focus of this section. In this regard, the necessary and sufficient condition for the reconstruction of state space of the dynamic system into a one-dimensional Euclidean space R has been substantiated in accordance to Taken's Theory [17]. The first step involves the construction of the n-dimensional time series. The n-dimensional time series are to be constructed from n consecutive quotes of an one-dimensional series. The chaotic dynamic system generates the one-dimensional time series as this state evolves in phase space. In practice, it is not known a priori the dimension of the phase space, henceforth, it is not possible to determine the number n for the reconstruction. In our experiment, we have tested with all the numbers in the set $1 \leq n \leq 10$ and computed the largest Lyapunov exponent as well as the correlation dimension corresponding to each of the reconstruction. According to Takens, the method of determining the correlation dimension of an attractor or W-limit set in a physical experiment consists of two parts. First, the "reconstruction of the phase space" in R^n and second the determination of the correlation dimension of a bounded subset in R^n. In the first part, a sequence $\{a_0, a_1, a_2, \ldots\}$, obtained as a time sequence of experimental data $(a_i \in R)$, is used to produce a sequence $\{A_0, A_1, A_2 \ldots\}$ in R^n ; this sequence is defined by $A_i = (a_i, a_{i+1}, \ldots, a_{i+n-1})$. The experiment involves a finite dimensional deterministic model with phase space X, if the sequence $\{a_i\}$ is obtained by composing the orbit $x(i) \in X$, describing the evolution during the experiment with the mapping, $y: x \rightarrow R$, such that $a_i = y(x(i))$. Then the sequence $\{A_i\}$ and the set A in R^n are the image of $\{x(i)\}$. It has been proven that if n is sufficiently big, and if y together with the dynamics in x satisfy certain generic condition, then this transformation form x to R^n is termed as embedding [24].

In the present experiment, the vector represents a single point of an n-dimensional reconstructed state space R^n . Figures 8 and 9 show how the embedding of the original trajectory takes place for a sufficiently large value of the embedding dimension n. If we have a time series $\quad \varphi(t), \varphi(t + \tau), \varphi(t - 2\tau)$, ... $\varphi(t - (n -1) \tau))$, where τ represents the time delay, the method of reconstruction generates a data vector $\psi(T)$ in the state space. In this reconstruction process, $\Phi(i)$ is the past data and the state $\Phi(i + s)$ is the state which is "s" steps ahead. Analysis of the time series subsequently results in the predicted value $\hat{\Psi}(T + S)$ of $\Psi(T + S)$.

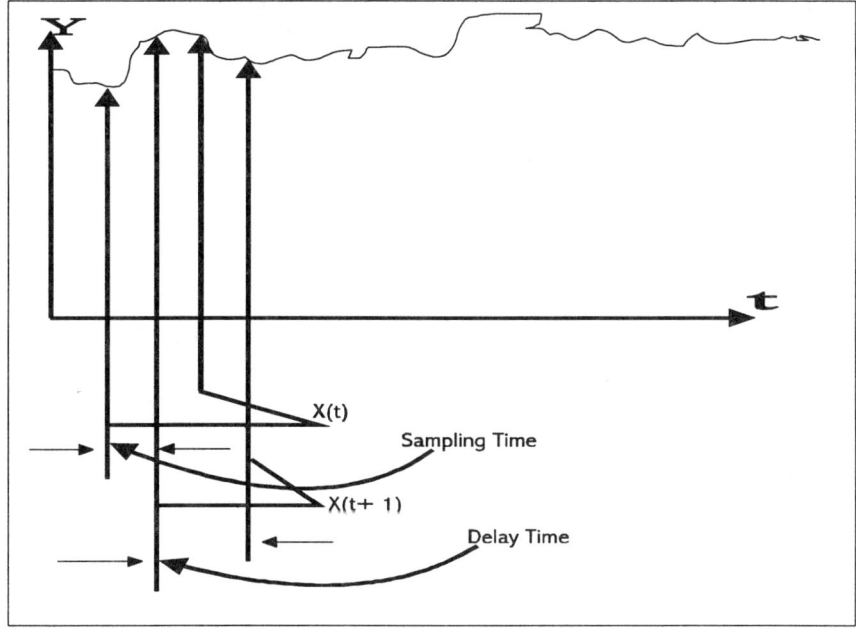

Figure 7. Reference Time Series

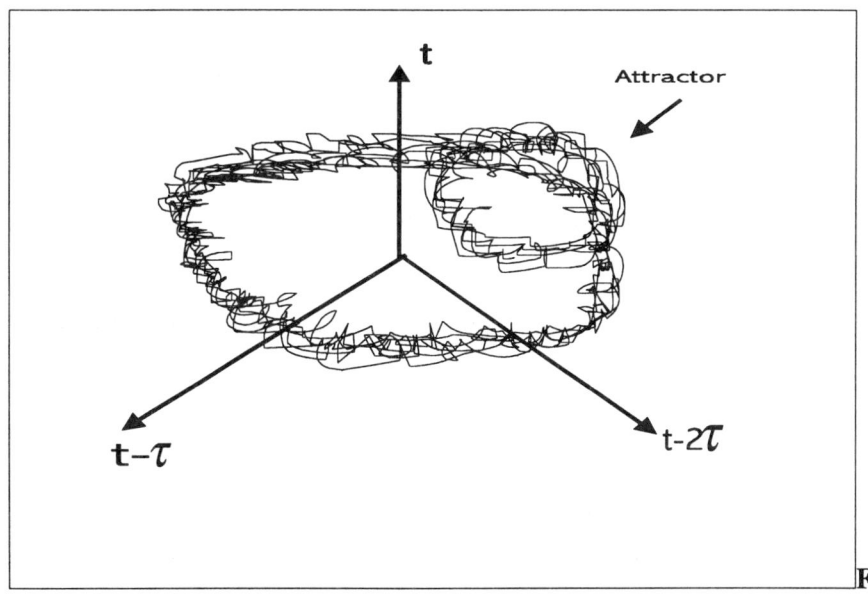

Fi

Figure 8. Reconstructed State Space

7. LOCAL FUZZY RECONSTRUCTION METHOD

Once the behavior of the time series has been ascertained to have corresponded to deterministic chaos, as shown in the earlier figures, the transition form state ϕ (i) to ϕ (i + s), "s" steps ahead in the future can be assumed to be dependent on the dynamics related to determinism. In this case, the dynamics can be represented by fuzzy function according to figure 10 as follows:

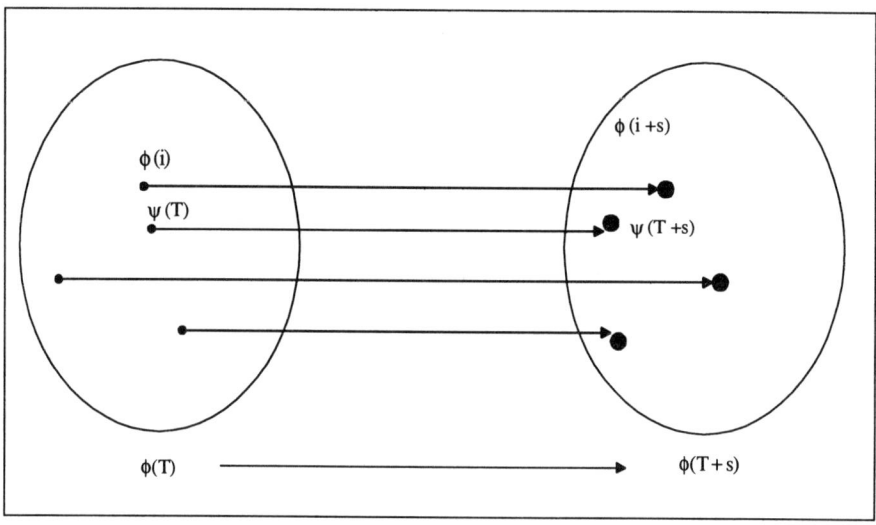

Figure 9. Fuzzy Reconstruction Method: Linguistic Expression of Dynamics

Thus, if ϕ (T) is the set of data vector neighboring to ψ (T) in n-dimensional reconstruction state space, ϕ (T + s) is the set expressing a data vector at s th step after ϕ (T), and ϕ (i) is the data vector neighboring to ψ (T), the fuzzy rule is:

If ϕ (T) is ϕ (i) THEN ϕ (T + s) is ϕ (i + s).

Let us explain the mechanism, with respect to the following example.

Example 1:

Here we develop the fuzzy inference rules that express the dynamics Involved in the problem. We take,

> Embedding dimension: $n = 3$
>
> Delay time: $\tau = 3$
>
> Number of data vectors neighboring $\psi(T)$: $N = 3$
>
> Number of predicting steps: $p = s$

Therefore, we have the resulting data vectors. Neighborhood of $\psi(T)$:

$$\psi(T) = (y_1(T),\ y_2(T-3),\ y_3(T-6))$$
$$\phi(t_0) = (y_1(T),\ y_2(T-3),\ y_3(T-6))$$
$$\phi(t_0) = (y_1(t_0),\ y_2(t_0-3),\ y_3(t_0-6))$$
$$\phi(t_2) = (y_1(t_2),\ y_2(t_2-3),\ y_3(t_2-6))$$

Similarly, data vectors in the neighborhood of $\psi(T+s)$ can be written as:

$$\psi(T+s) = (y_1(T+s),\ y_2(T+s-3),\ y_3(T+s-6))$$
$$\phi(t_0+s) = (y_1(t_0+s),\ y_2(t_0+s-3),\ y_3(t_0+s-6))$$
$$\phi(t_1+s) = (y_1(t_1+s),\ y_2(t_1+s-3),\ y_3(t_1+s-6))$$
$$\phi(t_2+s) = (y_1(t_2+s),\ y_2(t_2+s-3),\ y_3(t_2+s-6))$$

The above data vectors were evaluated according to the relations:

$$X(i) = (y(i), y(i-\tau), \ldots, y(i-(n-1)\tau))$$

$$X(i+s) = (y(i+s), y(i+s-\tau), \ldots, y(i+s-(n-1)\tau))$$

In this context, the trajectory from $\psi(T)$ to $\psi(T+s)$ is determined based on the Euclidean distance from $\psi(T)$ to $\phi(i)$ according to the local approximation algorithm as explained in the earlier section. Since, the embedding dimension, n =3 there are three axes of reconstruction states space, the fuzzy inference rules are as follows:

1st dimension of reconstruction states space:

IF axis 1(T) is $\hat{y}_1(t_o)$ THEN axis 1(T+s) is $\hat{y}_1(t_o+s)$

IF axis 1(T) is $\hat{y}_1(t_1)$ THEN axis 1(T+s) is $\hat{y}_1(t_1+s)$

IF axis 1(T) is $\hat{y}_1(t_2)$ THEN axis 1(T+s) is $\hat{y}_1(t_2+s)$

2nd dimension of reconstruction states space:

IF axis 2(T) is $\hat{y}_2(t_o)$ THEN axis 2(T+s) is $\hat{y}_2(t_o+s-3)$

IF axis 2(T) is $\hat{y}_2(t_1)$ THEN axis 2(T+s) is $\hat{y}_2(t_1+s-3)$

IF axis 2(T) is $\hat{y}_2(t_2)$ THEN axis 2(T+s) is $\hat{y}_2(t_2+s-3)$

3rd dimension of reconstruction states space:

IF axis 3(T) is $\hat{y}_3(t_o)$ THEN axis 3(T+s) is $\hat{y}_3(t_o+s-6)$

IF axis 3(T) is $\hat{y}_3(t_1)$ THEN axis 3(T+s) is $\hat{y}_3(t_1+s-6)$

IF axis 3(T) is $\hat{y}_3$ (t₂) THEN axis 3(T+s) is $\hat{y}_3$ (t₂+s-6)

We can see that the *j*-axis component of ψ (T) in the *n*-dimensional fuzzy reconstructed state space is equal to y_j(T). Thus, the *j*-axis is component of predicted value $\hat{ψ}$ (T+s) of data vector ψ (T+s), *s* steps in the future is obtainable by fuzzy inference.

Tables 1(a), 1(b), and 1(c) present some results as to the short-term prediction of foreign exchange rates by this fuzzy reconstruction method. Time series data of the exchange rates of several European Currencies versus US $ have been tested. It has been observed that as the dimension of embedding (*n*) and delay time (τ) decreases and the number of neighboring data vector (N) increases, the correlation coefficient between the currencies increases, which verifies the effectiveness of the proposed method.

Table 1: (a) Experimental Values For Exchange Rates Between FF/US $

Embedding Dimension (n)	Delay Time (τ)	Numbering of Neighboring Data Vector (N)	Correlation Coefficient (λ)
6	3	6	0.982
5	2	7	0.984
7	3	5	0.979

Table 1: (b) Experimental Values For Exchange Rates Between SFr/US $

Embedding Dimension (n)	Delay Time (τ)	Numbering of Neighboring Data Vector (N)	Correlation Coefficient (λ)
8	4	5	0.979
6	3	8	0.982
10	2	4	0.978

Table 1: (c) Experimental Values For Exchange Rates Between DM/US $

Embedding Dimension (n)	Delay Time (τ)	Numbering of Neighboring Data Vector (N)	Correlation Coefficient (λ)
7	2	7	.985
9	3	5	.983
11	4	4	.978

We have tested the time series with several embedding dimensions and data vectors. We find that the accuracy of prediction increases initially with the increase of embedding dimension, but it starts degrading after certain embedding dimension. In this regard, correlation coefficient is obtained between the original exchange rate and the predicted exchange rate. Thus, closer the value of correlation coefficient goes to 1.0, better is the prediction. Based on the results, we suspect that there is a specific range of embedding dimensions available, within which the currency exchange rate provides the best prediction. However, we are still working on this aspect and in our upcoming communication, we intend to provide more information. The following figure shows how the prediction changes with respect to the embedding dimension.

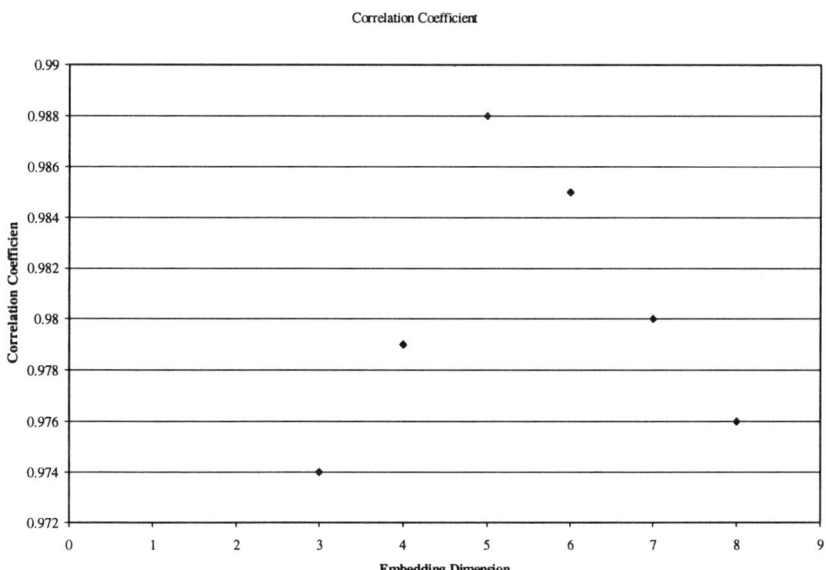

Figure 10. Effect of Embedding Dimension on Accuracy of Prediction

8. CONCLUSION

This research embarked on proposing a prediction methodology for one of the most sought after topics in international finance. Here we have integrated Chaos theory and Fuzzy Logic to predict future values of exchange rates of currencies based on their past values. Determination of chaos in the frequency fluctuations of Foreign Exchange Prices and Stock Market quotes have been the topic of much investigation for the last several years. The departure from Gaussianity of the high and medium frequency fluctuations in foreign exchange rate prices have been ascribed to the low-dimensional deterministic chaos. The type of deterministic chaotic structure observed in the data may be a reflection of very high frequency oscillatory changes of prices from one local equilibrium to another. Our work on the development of a robot long-term prediction model for currency exchange rate is still being continued. The analysis about the relationships among embedding dimension, delay time and the correlation coefficient between the actual value and the predicted value serve as guiding light towards developing better and more accurate prediction model.

REFERENCES

1. Rosenberg, M., "Currency Forecasting: A Guide To Fundamental and Technical Models of Exchange Rate Determination", Irwin Publishing, (1996), pp. 345-373.

2. Rosenberg, M., "Is Technical Analysis Right For Currency Forecasting?", *Euromoney*, (1981), pp. 125-131.

3. Koteh, Y., Yuize, H., Yoneda, K., Takahashi & Tano, S., "Gradual Rules in Decision Support System for Foreign Exchange Trading", *International Conference on Fuzzy Logic and Neural Networks*, (1992), pp. 625-0628.

4. Yansunobu, C., Kosaka, M. & Yokomura, K., "A fuzzy Dealing Support System", Denshi Tokyo, No. 32, *IEEE*, Tokyo Section, (1993), pp.85-88.

5. Rogler, H., "Analyzing the Stock Market: Statistical Evidence and Methodology", (1978), Columbus, OH. Grid.

6. Silber, W., "Technical Trading: When It Works and When It Doesn't", *The Journal of Derivatives*. Spring- Verlag, (1994).

7. Takagi, S., "On the Statistical Properties of Floating Exchange Rates: A Reassessment of Recent Experience and Literature Bank of Japan Monetary and Economic Studies", G, No.1, (1988), pp. 61-91.

8. Hsieh, P., "Testing for Nonlinear Dependence in Daily Foreign Exchange Rates", *Journal of Business*. 62, No. 3, (1989), pp. 339-368.

9. Boothe, P., Glassman, D., "The statistical distribution of exchange rates". *Journal of International Economics*. No. 22, (1987), pp. 297-319.

10. Bachelier, L. "Theory of Speculation, " in P.Cootner, ed., *The Random Character of Stock Market Prices*, Cambridge, MA:M.I.T. Press, 1964.

11. Black, F., Jensen, M.C., and Scholes, M. "The Capital Asset Pricing Model: Some Empirical Tests," in M.C. Jensen, ed., *Studies in the Theory of Capital Markets*. New York: Praeger, 1972.

12. Fama, E.F. "The Behavior of Stock Market Prices," *Journal of Business* 38, 1965.

13. Sharp. W. F. "Capital Asset Prices: A Theory of Market Equilibrium Under Conditions of Risk. " Journal of Finance, September 1964, pp 425-422.

14. Turner, A.L., and Weigel, E.J. "An Analysis of Stock Market Volatility,"*Russell Research Commentaries*, Frank Russell Co. Tacoma, WA, 1990.

15. Friedman, B.M., and Laibson, D.I. "Economic Implications of Extraordinary Movements in Sock Prices," *Brookings Papers on Economic Activity 2*, 1989.

16. Hirch, M., "The Chaos In Dynamical Systems", *Chaos, Fractals, and Dynamics*. New York, (1986), pp. 189-196.

17. Takens, F., "In Dynamical Systems and Turbulence", *Springer - Verlag,Berlin*, 1981, (1981), pp. 366 -381.

18. Casdagli, M. "Non-Linear Prediction o f Chaotic Time Series". Physica Vol. D.35 pp. 335.

19. Tong, H. "Non-Linear Time Series". A Dynamical System Approach". Oxford University Press, 1990.

20. Ellner, S., Gallant, A., McCaffrey, D., & Nychka, D. "Convergence Rates and data requirements for Jacobian based estimates of Lyapunov exponents from data, Physics Letters A Vol. 153, pp.357-363, 1992.

21. Lorenz, E. "Deterministic Non-Periodic Flow". Journal of Atmospheric Science, Vol. 20. pp.130-146.

22. Abarbanel, H, Brown R., & Kennel, M. " Local Lyapunov Exponents from observed Data". Journal Nonlinear Science, Vol.2, pp.343-365. 1992.

23. Benettin, G. Galgani, L. & Strelcyn, J. "Lyapunov Characteristic Exponents for Smooth Dynamical Systems and for Hamiltonian Systems; A Method for Computing All of them". Mechanica Vol.15, pp 9.

24. Kennel, M. Brown, R. Abarbanel H.D.I., "Determining Embedding dimension for phase space reconstruction using a geometrical construction". Physical Review A, Vol. 45 Number 6 3403-3411. 1993.

25. Wolf, A., Swift, J., Swinney, H., & Vastano, J. "Determining Lyapunov Exponents from a Time Series". Physica vol D16. 1985. pp. 285.

Application of Fuzzy Methodologies to Financial Fields: FOREX, Case Studies and Generalizations

Shun'ichi Tano

Graduate School of Information Systems
University of Electro-Communication
1-5-1 Chufugaoka, Chofu-shi
Tokyo 182, Japan
E-mail: tano@is.uec.ac.jp

Abstract. In this chapter, a fuzzy expert system called FOREX (Foreign Exchange Trade Support Expert System) and a fuzzy system development tool called FINEST (Fuzzy Inference Environment Software with Tuning) are described. FOREX is one of the biggest fuzzy expert systems, implemented with approximately 300 fuzzy frames and 5000 fuzzy rules. FOREX was developed at LIFE (Laboratory for International Fuzzy Engineering Research, in Japan) as a case study to check the applicability of fuzzy theory to intelligent information systems. FINEST, on the other hand, is a knowledge-based system shell, developed at the same laboratory, based on the experience of the development of FOREX.

Keywords. fuzzy inference, foreign exchange, fuzzy expert system

1 Introduction

Fuzzy theory is being applied in many other fields besides control engineering. Here we show a challenge of applying fuzzy theory to intelligent information systems. The application domain we chose is foreign exchange trade, as it implies various kinds of fuzziness.

The main goal of this chapter is to describe a fuzzy expert system called FOREX (Foreign Exchange Trade Support Expert System) and a fuzzy system development tool called FINEST (Fuzzy Inference Environment Software with Tuning). Actually, FOREX [1,2] is one of the biggest fuzzy expert systems, implemented with approximately 300 fuzzy frames and 5000 fuzzy rules. FOREX was developed at LIFE (Laboratory for International Fuzzy Engineering Research, in Japan) as a case study to check the applicability of fuzzy theory to intelligent information systems. FINEST [3,4], on the other hand, is a knowledge-based system shell (not an expert system but an expert system shell), developed at the same laboratory, based on the experience of the development of FOREX.

In the following sections, we first describe the characteristics of the application domain, i.e. foreign exchange trade. Next, we show the system architecture of FOREX and evaluate its performance with actual data. Finally, we analyze the drawbacks of fuzzy theory applied to this domain and describe FINEST, which was designed based on the results of the analysis.

2 The Application Domain

Foreign exchange rates strongly depend not only on numerical data such as economic indices, stock prices and interest rates, but also on information conveyed verbally (text data), such as comments from governments' high officials, monetary agencies or news broadcast about international politics. Thus, to forecast foreign exchange rates with a computer, it is necessary (1) to devise a method to unify the information obtained from numerical data and text data as people involved in the foreign exchange market (dealers...) do, (2) to develop a prediction method on the basis of such information.

Recently, several expert systems for the prediction of trends in foreign exchange and stock markets have been developed [5]. Input are limited to numerical data and the systems provide with nothing more than predictions based on expert knowledge concerned with technical analysis. However, other factors such as news regarding national policies or statements from trade officials also have a great effect on foreign exchange rates.

Moreover, as explained in the next section, numerical data as well as text data have inherent fuzziness, and the fuzziness plays an essential role in trends' prediction.

3 Fuzziness in Foreign Exchange Trade

The features of foreign exchange trade with respect to fuzziness can be classified as follows.

3.1 Fuzziness of Information (Data)

The information obtained on political issues may be ambiguous. Besides, economic data have varying degrees of freshness. The latest data better represent the current status. Some data, such as stock prices and foreign exchange rates, are released every day whereas some other ones (commodity price indices, trade balance, etc.) are released semi-annually or quarterly only.

For statistical data, moreover, it is very often the case that preliminary figures are released first and that final figures are released later. In many cases, however, there is large difference between preliminary and final figures. Moreover, statistics are released in an indefinite period. Therefore, it is necessary to assess the reliability and importance for each figure.

It is important to interpret the meaning of each numerical value in the context of the market. For example, different people in the market will feel that the prices of commodity is high or low, depending on the situation of the market, even if the price increasing rate is equal to 4.5%. This illustrates the difficulty of predicting market trends if, for example, a usual commodity price is taken into consideration. There will always be a dispersion of around 3.3% in the various perceptions.

3.2 Fuzziness in Knowledge (Rule)

Fuzziness is inherent in the economic knowledge (rules) used in the foreign exchange market. For instance, statements like " If the business activity is vigorous, the prices of commodity will increase" contain fuzziness.

- Fuzziness related to the reliability of rule
In an economic issue, it is sometimes difficult to completely grasp and describe the conditions behind an event. For instance, the causes of the increase of a commodity price can not be perfectly described in the condition part of a rule. The result is that the conclusion of the rule can not always be true, even if the condition of the rule is satisfied. In such cases, the reliability of the rule must be taken into consideration.

- Fuzziness in the condition part of the rule
The fact that the economic activity is vigorous can not be expressed with crisp data only. Though many indices can be used to describe the economic activity, it is more appropriate to express it with a membership function, rather than simply say that it is vigorous.

- Fuzziness related to the strength of the relation between the condition and the conclusion of the rules
In general, the more the conditions of a rule are satisfied, the stronger the conclusion of the rule is believed in. For example, the more vigorous the economic activators are, the faster the prices of commodity will increase.

3.3 Fuzziness on a Evaluation Structure

Suppose that the current economy is booming. One possible scenario is that the prices of commodity increase, so that the interest rates may be increased to suppress the prices of commodity. In this case, the foreign exchange rate will rise. It is also possible to imagine a quite different scenario: the booming economic activity results in inflation, which reduces the value of the currency. In this case, the foreign exchange rate will go down.

So it is very important to evaluate the current status subjectively as well as objectively. The relative importance of indices such as the prices of commodity and the unemployment rate reflects the subjective evaluation of each dealer. This subjective evaluation leads to the quite different predictions exemplified above.

4 Case Study : FOREX
- Foreign Exchange Trade Support Expert System -

4.1 Basic Structure and Special Features

Fig. 1 shows the basic structure of FOREX and its special features. FOREX consists of two parts, a state recognition part and a scenario evaluation part. First, numerical data and news data are input into the state recognition part and each data is transformed into one or a collection of qualitative linguistic values. Several important indices with a great influence on the foreign exchange market are deduced and used as inputs to the scenario evaluation part. The indices are used to select the most suitable scenario, indicating the possible future changes of the exchange rate.

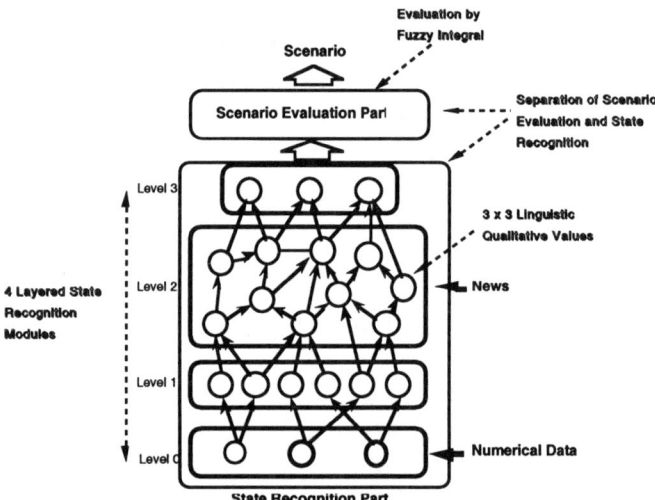

Fig. 1 Basic structure of FOREX and its special features

The four special features of FOREX are summarized as follows :

- Separation of the State Recognition Part and the Scenario Evaluation Part
In the state recognition part, numerical data and news information are analyzed and transformed into abstract indicators of the foreign exchange market. These indicators are used in the scenario evaluation part to choose the most possible scenario, stored

in FOREX as a Knowledge.

- 4-layered State Recognition
The state recognition part is divided into 4 levels (0 to 3), the highest of which presents the highest degree of abstraction. The raw numerical data in level 0 are evaluated and translated into qualitative data, such as 'the FF rate of the US is very high', then stored in level 1. Level 2 represents the state transition network, where each state stands for an aspect of economic fundamentals. News data are directly input in level 2. The status of the network is summarized into a few dozens of indicators in level 3, for the use of the scenario evaluation part.

- State Representation by 3x3 Linguistic Qualitative Values
Each state in levels 1, 2 and 3 is represented by 3x3 variables, expressing the combination of past / current / future and level / differential / quadratic differential values. The values of all the variables are linguistic qualitative data, not numerical data.

- Scenario Evaluation by Fuzzy Integral
The condition of each scenario is given as a fuzzy measure on the state values used in the level 3 of the state recognition part. Each scenario is evaluated by Fuzzy Integral and the results are sorted using Fuzzy Ranking.

4.2 State Recognition by Fuzzy State Description and Fuzzy Rules

The state recognition part is divided into four levels, the highest of which represents the highest degree of abstraction. These levels correspond to the following three standpoints : "Numerical data are converted into linguistic variables", "Information is synthesized based on economic mechanisms" and "States are integrated for evaluation as a whole."

Level 0
This level is used for time-dependent numerical data. Items handled here include stock prices, interest rates and various economic indicators from countries such as Japan, the U.S. and Germany.

Level 1
This level is for maintaining the results of interpreted (standardized) numerical data. Items on level 1 generally correspond to those on level 0. However, there are more items in this level than in level 0, because some numerical data can be interpreted in different ways (e.g., price index in terms of either the annual or monthly rate of change).

284

Level 2

This level is used for state recognition. This includes the identification of possible future trends for all items, based on the state values in levels 1 and 2 and on information extracted from news data.

Level 3

In general, this level is used to represent abstract, macro items obtained from integrating two or more items from level 2. The scenario evaluation function evaluates scenarios by referring to items from this level. Items in level 3 are prices, international expenditures, employment trends, productivity trends, personal consumption, stock market trends, long-term interest rates, short-term interest rates and official positions of trade ministries from countries such as Japan, the U.S. and Germany.

Fig. 2 shows a small part of the state recognition network. The network consists of blocks, representing state values, and arcs, representing causal relations between these states. In FOREX, each state is represented by 3x3 qualitative fuzzy variables and each causal relation is described by a fuzzy production rule as explained below.

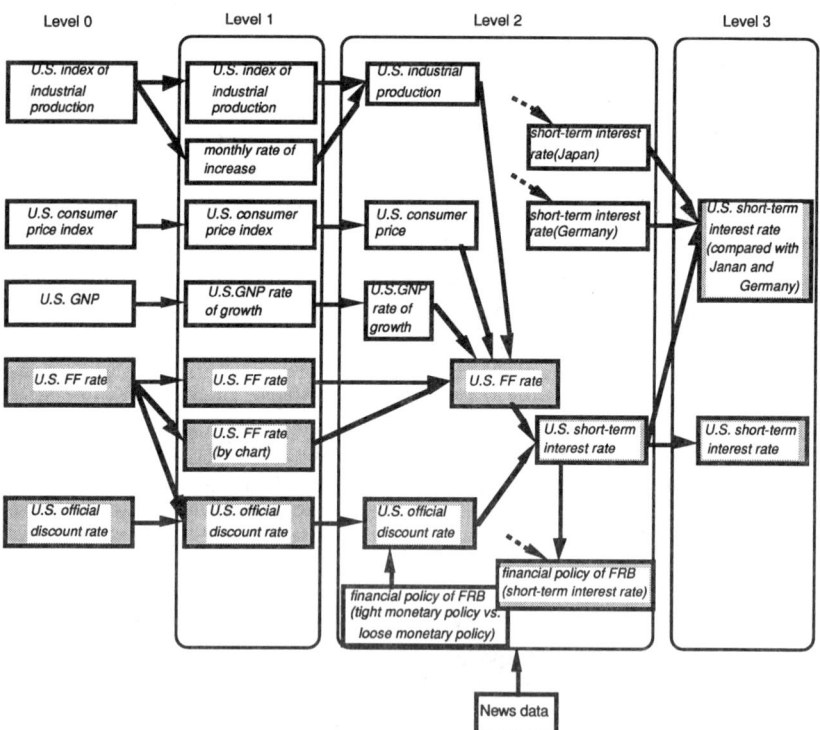

Fig. 2 Example of State Recognition Network

- 3x3 qualitative fuzzy variable

A state (corresponding to a block in Fig. 2) is not a physical value but a psychological value and is represented by 3x3 fuzzy variables as shown in Fig. 3. "3x3" comes from the combination of past / current / future and present / movement / pressure (or level / differential / quadratic differential). This representation was suggested by the expert psychological view of the market.

The numerical data in level 0 must be transformed into qualitative fuzzy values. A qualitative fuzzy value is a fuzzy set on an ordered set of seven distinct natural language words. This also corresponds to the psychological view of experts. For example, concerning the state "the financial policy of the FRB", y is defined as a fuzzy set on the ordered set {very tight, tight, more or less tight, normal, somewhat loose, loose, very loose}. Similarly, y' is defined as a fuzzy set on {very strong pressure toward tight policy, strong pressure toward tight policy, some pressure toward tight policy, no pressure, some pressure toward loose policy, strong pressure toward loose policy, very strong pressure toward loose policy}.

Namely, all the state values, except the ones in level 0, are represented using a 3x3 relative representation. Reference values are therefore needed to transform numerical values into relative values (qualitative fuzzy values). However, it is also difficult to represent a reference value as a numerical number. In FOREX, reference values are represented using fuzzy numbers, that is, fuzzy sets on real numbers. In the example of Fig. 3, the fuzzy numbers y and y' are used as reference values for the evaluation of the actual state values, y and y'.

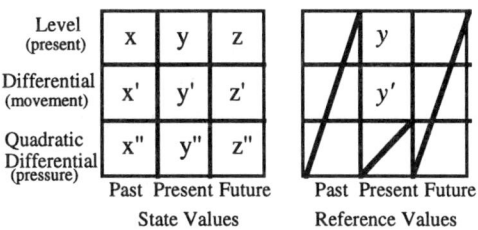

Fig.3 3x3 fuzzy qualitative values

Fig. 4 shows how to transform a raw numerical value X, e.g. short-term interest rate 5.9%, into a fuzzy qualitative value Z. Note that the raw numerical value X is a crisp value (5.9%), whereas the reference value Y is a fuzzy number (about 6.5%). First, "X - Y" is calculated and the result is expressed as a distribution on the real number "around zero". Then, the interpretation function, defining the meaning of natural language words, is used to define the qualitative value Z, in this case {0.1/low, 1/kind of low, 0.5/normal}.

286

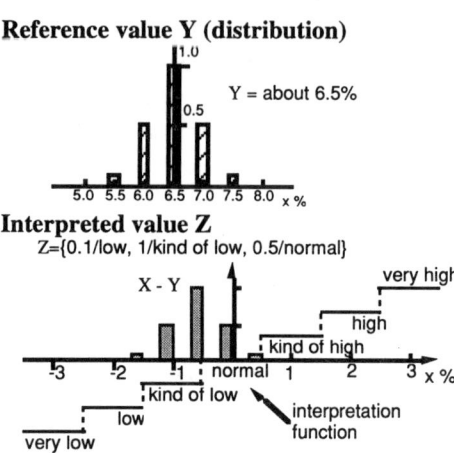

Numerical data X to be interpreted
X : 5.9% (short-term interest rate)

Reference value Y (distribution)

Y = about 6.5%

Interpreted value Z
Z={0.1/low, 1/kind of low, 0.5/normal}

Fig. 4 Interpretation of Numerical Data

- Handling News Data

At the present time, news information is processed manually. All the news are first converted into the following format :

      (date of news, type of news, person who makes the statement, ...,

        state variable name = value, state variable name = value, ...)

The value of each state is represented using 3x3 qualitative fuzzy variables. State values and news are processed by conjunctive combination. The actual example given below shows how a news about the U.S. short-term interest rates is converted. The date of the news as well as the person making the statement are omitted.

News Example: "U.S. Secretary of State, James Baker, announced in the afternoon of the 5th that economic growth, fueled by low inflation, is expected to continue and that there is a conservative attitude towards any increase in official interest rates."

The above news is transformed as follows:

      y' for official discount rate = {0.6/no pressure, 1.0/some pressure to rise}

      y' for U.S. price trend = {0.3/kind of low, 1.0/reasonable level}

      y" for U.S. price trend = {0.3/no pressure, 1.0/some pressure to rise}

The policy for inflation is usually to increase the official discount rate. In this case, the degree of inflation is low, so that the pressure for a rise of the official discount rate is 'a little'.

- Production Rule

Causal relations between the states in Fig. 2 are represented by fuzzy production rules. An example of rule is shown below :

Rule 1

IF   y" for U.S. official discount rate (level 1) is high pressure to rise, and
      y for financial policy of FRB (level 2) is tight,
THEN y" for U.S. official discount rate (level 2) is high pressure to rise.

Fuzzy propositions in the condition part and the consequent part of the rules are described using the 3x3 fuzzy qualitative variables (x, x', x", y, y', y", z, z' and z") and fuzzy predicates (such as "high pressure to rise" and "tight").

Rules are usually interpreted using gradual equivalence [6,7], where the value of conclusion is determined by the antecedent input data. Another interpretation of the rules is the one based on the Generalized Modus Ponens.

4.3 Scenario Evaluation by Fuzzy Measure and Integral

The value of the macro states is obtained in the state recognition part. In the scenario evaluation part, these values are used to generate the actual predictions. In FOREX, it is necessary to provide the system with scenarios and to store several of them together with the conditions under which they are likely to occur. The most likely scenario is chosen by matching the conditions with the state values.

One feature of the scenario evaluation part is that the likelihood of each scenario is evaluated using the fuzzy integral with respect to a fuzzy measure[8]) defined on the set of conditions of the scenario. The integrated values are the results of the matching of each (usually fuzzy) condition with the value of the corresponding state.

The main reason for using fuzzy integral in the evaluation part is to obtain appropriate values for the overall condition part of each scenario[9,10]. This can not be accomplished by merely connecting the conditions using t-norm (logical "and") and t-conorm (logical "or") operations.

Data are collected on a 24 hour basis, from 9 AM one day to 9 AM the next day. They are processed and scenarios are evaluated using fuzzy integral. Finally, the results of the evaluation are ordered using fuzzy ranking. The processing steps are described below and an example is shown in Fig. 5.

Step 1: Calculate the matching degree of each condition. For instance, it calculates the matching degree between the value of the state (x for U.S. business condition) and the fuzzy predicate (high).

Step 2: Perform the Fuzzy Integral, using the matching degrees of all the conditions and a fuzzy measure.

Step 3: Perform Step 1 and Step 2 for all the scenarios prepared in FOREX.

Step 4: Order the scenarios according to the results of fuzzy integral, by the fuzzy ranking method [11,12] .

Scenario

A change in uptrend of the U.S. output, reduced feeling of over-heating in the U.S. business, smaller concern over the U.S. inflation, all of these lead to the decrease in upward pressure on U.S. interest rates and the dollar depreciation.

Conditions of Scenario

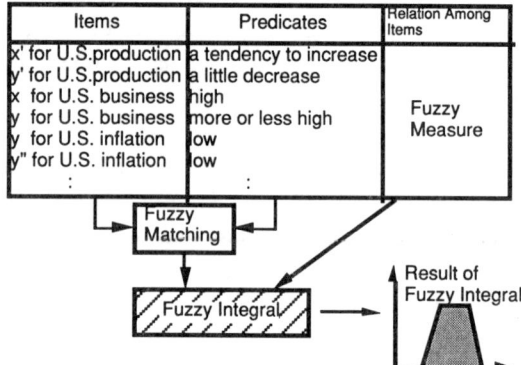

Fig. 5 Example of Scenario and Processing Flow

4.4 Evaluation

To evaluate the performance of FOREX, we carried out a simulation for the period of June 1988. This period was chosen due to the three events which occurred at this time, as shown in Fig. 6. These events were interpreted by experts (articles in newspaper) as follows :

Point 1 (6th)
The increase of the unemployment rate in the US indicates the cooling of the expansion of the economic activity. It means that the government will not increase the official discount rate in the near future. Therefore, the dollar will be sold and the exchange rate will go down.

Point 2 (15th)
The amount of the trade deficit is less than expected. It should lead to the rising dollar. However, the foreign exchange rate is stable because Japanese fundamental indices are still very good.

Point 3 (22nd)
The yen is constantly going down due to the following facts: (1) improvement of the

trade balance of the US, (2) US monetary agencies seem to consider that a strong dollar is preferable, (3) high interest rates in Germany and (4) Japanese monetary agencies cannot manipulate the interest rate at this time.

FOREX succeeded in selecting the most suitable scenario which meets the analysis mentioned above. Not only were the predictions correct but the values of 3x3 qualitative fuzzy variables in the state recognition part were also adequate to compare with those of experts'.

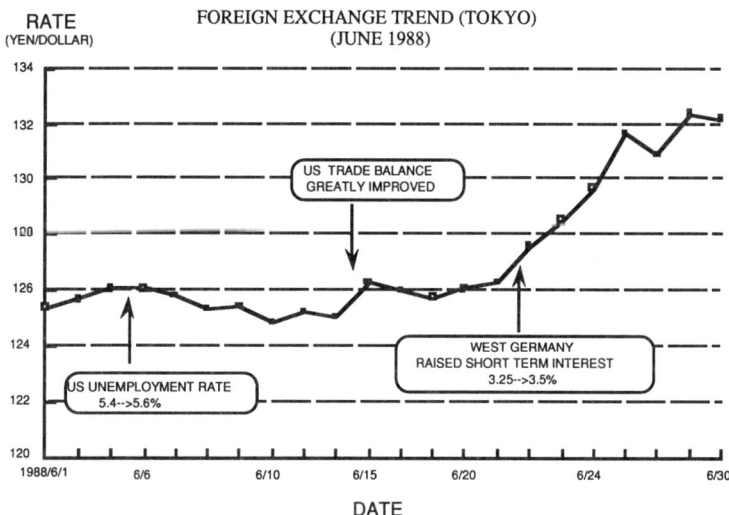

Fig.6 Real Data of Foreign Exchange Trend in Tokyo in June 1988

5 Fuzzy Expert System Shell: FINEST

5.1 Problems Found through the Experience of FOREX

We implemented FOREX using various methods based on fuzzy theory such as fuzzy sets, fuzzy logic, fuzzy measure and fuzzy integral, in order to verify the applicability of fuzzy theory not only to control systems but also to intelligent information systems. The experience proved that fuzzy methodology is feasible and quite effective. However, at the same time, we found several serious problems in fuzzy inference. We classified the problems and made up research themes to study at LIFE and we have developed FINEST, which is short for Fuzzy Inference Environment Software with Tuning[3,4].

The main problems we found through the FOREX experience are (1) the insufficiencies of usual fuzzy inference methods and (2) the difficulty in selecting a suitable inference method from a huge numbers of candidates.

5.2 Extended Fuzzy Inference and Tuning Function in FINEST

Concerning the first problem mentioned in Section 5.1, we improved the conventional inference methods on the following four points.

- Aggregation with synergy and cancellation[13]

Even though, in many cases, a rule is simply expressed in the form " If X and Y Then Z", the "and" operator has a vague meaning. It may have a strict "and" nature, or a weak one. When we developed FOREX, we found that many "and" operators have a synergistic nature.

We defined a new aggregation operator '*and*' by adding a synergistic effect to an ordinary t-norm operator.

This operator has four parameters expressing the strength of the synergistic effect and the area where this effect is required. When the user sets the value of the parameter controlling the strength of the synergistic effect to 0, our operator behaves like a standard t-norm. Otherwise, the operator has a synergistic effect controlled by the value of the parameters.

Furthermore, the cancellation property, which is of the same nature as the synergistic effect, can be expressed as a special kind of synergistic effect.

- Parameterized implication method[14]

Although there are various implication functions in the field of fuzzy theory, it is difficult to select a suitable one for actual applications. However, if we can define the implication function as a parameterized function, we can easily select a suitable inference method by changing the value of the parameters. For example, a parameterized implication function could be defined as a combination of some parameterized t-norm and t-conorm operators.

- Fuzziness Reducing Combination method[15]

A combination method indicates how to combine the results derived from different inference processes. Many systems use the max operator as a combination method, but this causes a constant increase of the fuzziness. Then, the more the inference process proceeds, the more the fuzziness of the result increases. Based on the concept of positive/negative belief and using stochastic rules representing the dependency, we defined a parameterized combination function which can reduce the fuzziness.

- Fuzzy Backward reasoning[16]

Although backward reasoning is an indispensable inference method for knowledge processing, its formulation has not yet been achieved. First of all, we regarded fuzzy backward reasoning as a problem of solving fuzzy relational equations. Two cases occurred : when a solution exists, it is not unique and on the other hand, there are many cases where no solution exists. As a result, only a few rules can be used for fuzzy backward reasoning. Therefore, we extended the goal representation to interval-valued fuzzy sets instead of ordinary fuzzy sets.

Concerning the second problem mentioned in Section 5.1, i.e. the difficulty of selecting a suitable inference method, we reached the conclusion that the automatic tuning of the inference method is indispensable. There have been many studies on the tuning of fuzzy predicates in the field of fuzzy inference. But as mentioned before, the inference method has many tuning factors. Up to now however, only fuzzy predicates were tuned, and the tuning of the inference method has never been considered. We adopted a method similar to back-propagation, which tunes a network representing the calculation flow of the inference process[17].

5.3 Knowledge Representation of FINEST

FINEST can be seen as a tool for building fuzzy knowledge-based systems. Since all the knowledge is represented by units and the final system is built as a collection of units, units play a very important role in FINEST. A unit is defined as an object that simply gets inputs through its input interface, processes them in a specified way, and sends the results through its output interface. Each unit consists of three parts: the input interface, the data processing body, and the output interface (Fig. 7).

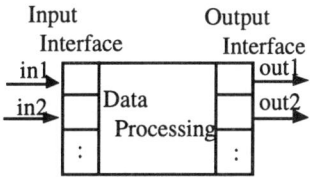

Fig.7 Abstract view of Unit

Notice that units are independent from the way data is processed in the unit. Even data storage areas are defined as units (i.e., as memory units).

A unit is regarded as a basic constituent of the target system. Usually, the target system is built as a combination of several blocks. FINEST can deal with the hierarchical structure of units.

FINEST now has five types of units: rule units, function units, external units, memory unit and composite units (Fig. 8).

Knowledge Source		Role	Item to be defined	Tuning
Unit	Memory Unit	Memory unit stores the status of inference and system.	Input & output variable Attribute name, value Fuzzy predicate	
	Rule Unit	A rule unit consists of several fuzzy rules.	Input & output variable Rule Attribute name Fuzzy Predicate ◄——————— OK Parameters of Inference ◄——————— OK	
	Function Unit	An algorithmic procedure can be defined by LISP.	Input & output variable LISP function Parameter ◄——————— OK Derivation function	
	External Unit	A UNIX process	Input & output variable Unix process ID	
	Composite Unit	A set of connected units can be treated as a unit.	Input & output variable Connection among units	
Tuning Data Set		Teaching data for tuning	Attribute name, value Fuzzy predicate	

Fig. 8 Knowledge Source

- Rule unit

A rule unit is composed of one or more rules. The rules inside a rule unit use input data for inference and the result is output through the rule unit's output interface. Rule-type knowledge is expressed in the form " If x is F and/or G is B then z is H," where x, y, and z are attribute names and F, G, and H are attribute values. These attribute names and attribute values (linguistic labels, etc.) are also defined in the rule unit, as is the inference method for each rule of the rule unit. Normally, the parameters of the aggregation operators, the implication function, and the combination function can also be defined inside the unit.

- Function unit

A function unit differs from a rule unit insofar as calculations are done using LISP functions instead of rules. A function unit evaluates its input data from the input interface as arguments, and it outputs the evaluated value through the output interface. A function unit can have some parameters inside, and the parameters can be tuned if the derivative functions are given. A function unit can be used to represent a defuzzification process or a process whose behavior is known algorithmically. That is, if the defuzzification function is represented using some parameters and the derivative functions with respect to the parameters are given, that function can be tuned.

- *External unit*

An external unit corresponds to an executable UNIX file, and the calculation process of the external unit is executed as a UNIX process. The external unit provides its input data to this process, receives the result from the process, and then outputs the result through its output interface. An external unit to be used can be combined with an existing system, but it cannot be tuned.

- *Memory Unit*

A memory unit is an area to store information relative to the status of the system and to store the intermediate results of the inference. For example, rules in one rule unit refer to and update data in memory units. Similarly, functions in a function unit sometimes read from and write to a memory unit. Data in a memory unit are expressed in the form "x is A," where "x" represents an attribute name and "A" is its attribute value. The attribute value is a numeric value, character, fuzzy set, or linguistic label. For example in the case of "the temperature is 22.5" and "the height is tall," "temperature" and "height" are the attribute names and "22.5" and "tall" are the attribute values. Furthermore, "tall" is a linguistic label characterized by a fuzzy predicate.

- *Composite unit*

Units can be combined with each other, and a combination of units is called a composite unit. Using a composite unit, the user can build a system step by step and hierarchically.

In addition to these five units, FINEST has a tuning data set as a knowledge source.

5.4 User Interface

Units and tuning data sets are the basic knowledge sources in developing an application, and most operations with FINEST are regarded as operations on these knowledge sources. Therefore, the user must generate these knowledge sources on the root window and must operate on these knowledge sources. Fig. 9. shows an example of a composite unit window.

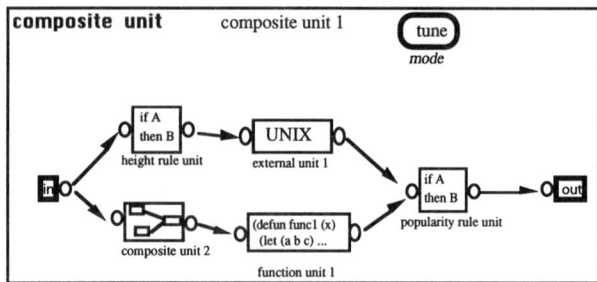

Fig. 9 Example of a composite unit

This composite unit (composite unit 1) consists of two rule units (height rule unit, popularity rule unit), an external unit (external unit 1), a function unit (function unit 1), and a composite unit (composite unit 2). The composite unit 2 has a structure similar to that of composite unit 1.

Detailed information about a unit will be shown if a user clicks with a mouse on a unit making up composite unit 1. For example a network window expressing the calculation flow of the inference will appear as shown in Fig. 10 if the user clicks on the height rule unit. If the user clicks on the external unit, a window expressing a LISP function and its input and output variables will appear.

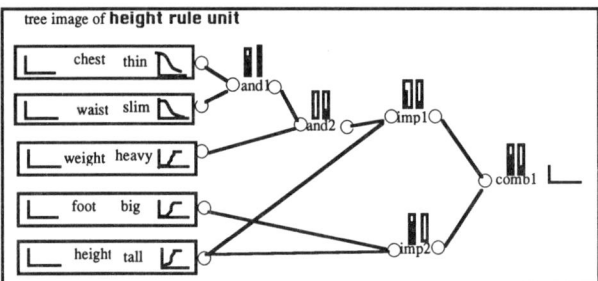

Fig. 10 Example of a rule unit

The user can tune a unit on the window of the unit if the user provides the tuning data set for the unit. If the user tunes a composite unit, all the members of the composite unit except external units will be tuned. For example, in the case of the composite unit 1 (Fig. 9), the height rule unit, the popularity rule unit, the function unit 1, and the composite unit 2 are tuned, but the external unit 1 is not. The user can also designate particular parameters to be tuned. In that case, only the designated parameters are tuned. Fig. 11 shows a window when the tuning mechanism is working. In this case, only the fuzzy predicate "slim" and the implication function "imp1" of the height rule unit are assigned to be tuned.

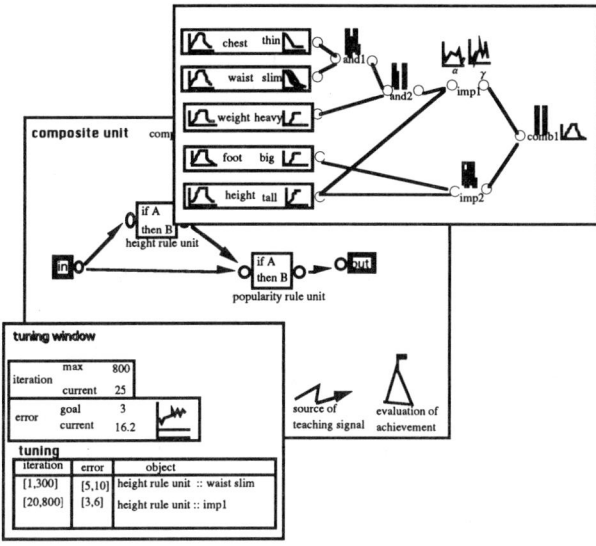

Fig. 11   Example of a window when tuning

5.5 Examples of Building a System

We illustrate the typical system construction flow by using the example of a simple fuzzy controller for a one input and one output plant (Fig. 12). The fuzzy controller keeps the system's state y close to a fixed value x. The problem here is to construct the fuzzy controller under the assumption that the modeling of the plant is completed. In other words, the model of the plant is given by a certain method, such as a procedural algorithm, a neural network, and so on.

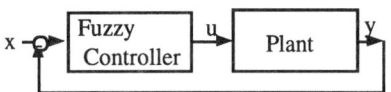

Fig. 12 Example of a process controller

We have first to divide the system shown in Fig. 12 into several units. Here we assume that the plant is represented by one function unit. The fuzzy controller is represented as a rule unit containing several rules. A unit is needed for defuzzification, since the output of the rule unit is a fuzzy set. So a function unit for defuzzification is located between the controller and the plant. Because rules in the rule unit require e and de, it is necessary to store the system state and calculate e and de. So a memory unit and a function unit are also necessary. Finally, we get a static structure of units like that shown in Fig. 13.

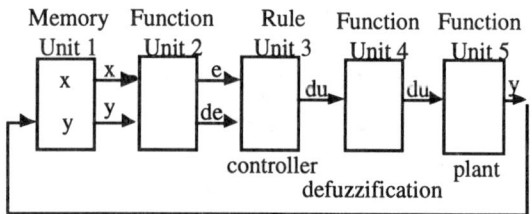

Fig. 13 Unit structure

Next we have to describe the data processing method of each unit. For example, the defuzzification algorithm defined in the function unit 4 is written in LISP source code. It is possible to define a defuzzification algorithm whose nature is modified by parameters. If the derivative function is given, the parameters can be tuned. Of course, several rules should be stored in the rule unit 3 for the fuzzy controller. The inference process consists of "and" operations, implication functions, and combination functions. If there are parameterized functions, the parameters can be automatically tuned as explained in the following section.

5.6 Tuning Function

FINEST supports the following two tuning methods.

- Tuning based on input/output data set
In this method the user specifies the input variables and output variables of the target system to be tuned and provides the tuning data set; that is, a set of desired input and output data pairs.

For example, if we want to tune the units 3, 4, and 5 in Fig. 13 simultaneously, we inform the tuning mechanism that e and de are the input variables and y is the output variable, and we give a tuning data set consisting of a lot of desired input/output data set such as (e, de, y). This tuning method can be seen as a neural network-like tuning.

- Tuning to minimize the summation of an observed variable.
The system described in Fig. 13 can also be used by another tuning method. If the user indicates some initial values, the time (or number of iterations) the system should be observed, and a variable to be observed, the parameters of the system can be tuned to keep the summation of the value of the observed value as close to zero as possible.

6 Summary

FOREX is one of the biggest fuzzy expert systems, implemented with approximately 300 fuzzy frames and 5000 fuzzy rules, making full use of fuzzy theory. The experience of the development of FOREX convinced us that fuzzy theory can provide with a lot of methodologies to deal with the fuzziness found in foreign exchange trade.

Furthermore we found several serious problems in fuzzy inference. To solve the problems, we are developing FINEST which has an improved fuzzy inference and a powerful tuning mechanism. FINEST can be seen as a tool for quantifying the fuzzy meaning of natural language expressed in the form of rules. For example, aggregation operators, implication methods, combination methods as well as fuzzy predicates can be tuned with FINEST, and as a result the nature of the sentences is made clear. The interpretation is, for example, "the 'and' in this rule has a strong synergistic nature", "the 'or' has a weak cancellation property", "this rule expresses knowledge of the form 'The more ..., the more...' " , etc.

We are convinced that the treatment of fuzziness is indispensable in building a intelligent system connected to human activities and believe that fuzzy theory is one of the most important technologies for the treatment of fuzziness.

References

[1] Tano, Yuize, Yagyu, Yoneda, Katoh, Grabish and Fukami, FOREX: Foreign Exchange Trade Support Expert System, International Fuzzy Engineering Symposium - IFES '91, pp.1114-1115 (1991).

[2] Yuize, H., Yagyu, T., Yoneda, M., Katoh, Y., Tano, S., Grabisch, M. and Fukami, S., Decision Support System for Foreign Exchange Trading - Practical Implementation -, Proceedings of IFES'91, pp. 971-982 (1991).

[3] Tano, S., Oyama, T., Kato, Y., Miyoshi, T., Arnould, T. and Bastian, A., Overview and Special Features of FINEST: Fuzzy Inference Environment Software with Tuning, First Asian Fuzzy Systems Symposium, pp. 294-302 (1993).

[4] Tano, Miyoshi, Kato, Oyama, Arnould and Bastian, Fuzzy Inference Software - FINEST: Overview and Application Examples, IEEE International Conference on Fuzzy Systems - FUZZ-IEEE'95 , pp. 1051-1056 (1995).

[5] Akiyama, T., New Technologies related to AI that have started to be used for establishing a new financial DSS, NIKKEI computer Feb. 26 (1990).

[6] Dubois, D. and Prade, H., Gradual Inference Rules in Approximate Reasoning, Information Sciences, Vol. 61, pp. 103-122 (1992).

[7] Kato, Y., Yuize, H., Yoneda, M., Takahashi, K., Tano, S., Yagyu, T., Grabisch, M. and Fukami, S., Gradual Rules in a Decision Support System for Foreign Exchange Trading, Proceedings of IIZUKA'92, pp. 625-628 (1992).

[8] Sugeno, M., Fuzzy Measures and Fuzzy Integrals - a survey, Fuzzy Automata and Decision Process (Gupta, Saridis and Gains eds.), North Holland (1987).

[9] Grabisch, M., Yoneda, M. and Fukami, S., Subjective Evaluation by Fuzzy Integral: Crisp and Possibility Case, Proceedings of IFES'91 (1991).

[10] Yoneda, M., Fukami, S. and Grabisch, M., Fuzzy Evaluation and Decision Making in the Decision Making Support System, Collection of Monographs of Society of Measure Automatic Control, Vol. 28, No. 9, pp. 1125-1134 (1992).

[11] Borotolan, G. and Degani, R., A Review of Some Methods for Ranking Fuzzy Subsets, Fuzzy Sets and Systems, Vol.15, pp. 1-19 (1985).

[12] Tseng, T.Y. and Klein, C.M., New Algorithm for the Ranking Procedure in Fuzzy Decision Making, IEEE Trans. on SMC, Vol. 19, pp. 1289-1296 (1989).

[13] Kato, Y., Arnould, T., Miyoshi, T. and Tano, S., Conjunction and disjunction with synergistic effect, FUZZ-IEEE'93, pp. 225-230 (1993).

[14] Oyama, Tano and Arnould, A Parameterized Implication Function Derived from the Relations to be Satisfied between a Premise and the Conclusion, IEEE International Conference on Fuzzy Systems - FUZZ-IEEE'95, pp. 359-366 (1995).

[15] Tano, Oyama and Arnould, Deep Combination of Fuzzy Inference and Neural Network in Fuzzy Inference Software - FINEST, Fuzzy Set and Systems (1996).

[16] Arnould and Tano, Interval-valued Fuzzy Backward Reasoning, IEEE Transactions on Fuzzy Systems, Vol.3, No.4, pp.425-437(1995).

[17] Oyama, Tano and Arnould, A Tuning Method for Fuzzy Inference with Fuzzy Input and Fuzzy Output, IEEE International Conference on Fuzzy Systems - FUZZ-IEEE'94, pp. 876-881 (1994).

4

CORPORATE FINANCIAL ANALYSES

Possibilistic Rule-Based Inference:
A Case Study in Financial Analysis[†]

Salem Benferhat, Henri Farreny and Henri Prade

Institut de Recherche en Informatique de Toulouse (IRIT) – CNRS,
Université Paul Sabatier, 118 route de Narbonne,
31062 Toulouse Cedex 4, France

Abstract. The paper presents an inference machinery, based on a possibilistic
Assumption-based Truth Maintenance System (ATMS), which is able to deal with
uncertain propositions and imprecisely-known numerical variables, and to handle
exceptions properly. A knowledge base in financial analysis provides an illustration
of the problems to handle (rules pervaded with uncertainty, fuzzy thresholds, ill-
known facts), and a test case. Possibility theory is used for the representation of
uncertain or imprecise pieces of information. The basic approximate reasoning
machinery, which relies on possibilistic logic is explained in detail.

Keywords. Possibilistic logic; uncertainty; ATMS; fuzzy rule; fuzzy pattern
matching; expert system.

1   Introduction

Financial analysis is one of the fields of applications where the expert system
methodology has raised much interest for a long time (e.g., Abel, Menu and Probst,
1984; Kerschberg and Dickinson, 1985). Besides, the idea of using fuzzy set
aggregation operations for modelling complex notions involving multiple criteria,
such as credit worthiness, dates back to Zimmermann and Zysno (1983); see also
Zimmermann (1997). This research trend has led to recent developments of fuzzy
logic-based decision support systems in credit analysis (e.g., Barczewski et al., 1996;
Güllich, 1996). This paper reports on a case study concerning a computer-assisted
device for facilitating the analysis of the financial situation of companies. In this case,
the expert system approach seems particularly natural due to the granularity of the
knowledge to be encoded and since the ability to modify or to complete this
information is often needed. A rule-based approach has also the advantage to be
easier to exploit than a multiple criteria aggregation-based approach, if explanations
have to be provided for the obtained conclusions. Moreover, as we shall see, we can

---

[†] This article borrows its case study to a ten year old conference paper (Farreny, Prade and
Wyss, 1986). However, the inference machinery which is presented here has been
completely renewed, although uncertainty is still represented in the framework of possibility
theory.

also deal with fuzzy thresholds and graded uncertainty in the rule-based framework.

In order to design a system able to exploit a given set of rules and facts, and to derive plausible conclusions from this information, three problems must be considered in the traditional expert system view: i) the representation language issue: how to formalize the pieces of information expressed by the rules and facts in a correct and consistent way; ii) the inference issue: how to model and mechanize the inference which can be applied to the knowledge base; iii) the control and strategy issues: how to design an inference engine in order to control and to organize the inference process. In (Farreny, Prade and Wyss, 1986), these three problems were discussed in the framework of our test case, with a special emphasis on the two first questions, and an inference engine named TAIGER[1] was presented. One of the most interesting features of TAIGER was its ability to deal both with uncertain and with imprecise information using an approach based on possibility theory (Zadeh, 1978; Dubois and Prade, 1988). Its inference mechanism (with the three usual steps: estimation of the certainty with which the condition part of a rule is satisfied, propagation of the uncertainty along the rule, combination of an obtained result with other available pieces of information, see, e.g., Buchanan and Shortliffe (1984)) was taking advantage of a possibilistic handling of uncertainty under the form of a simple matrix calculus (Farreny and Prade, 1986).

Since this time, the blind combination step of partial conclusions pervaded with uncertainty has been widely recognized as being ad hoc, especially when rules with various levels of specificity were used in the knowledge base; see, e.g., (Dubois and Prade, 1989). A new inference machinery is presented in the following, which is now completely embedded in the framework of possibilistic logic (Dubois, Lang and Prade, 1994a, b), and which, as such, has a strong theoretical basis. Nonmonotonic reasoning can be encoded in possibilistic logic (Benferhat et al., 1992), and thus rules with various levels of specificity can be properly handled. Moreover, the inference machinery is implemented as a possibilistic Assumption-based Truth Maintenance Systems (Π–ATMS for short), which provides explanation capabilities to the system (Dubois et al., 1991; Benferhat et al., 1994).

Section 2 of this paper analyzes the main characteristics of the knowledge we have to deal with in our test case and lists the encountered problems. Section 3 presents the possibility theory-based representation which is used for the rules and facts, including the treatment of uncertain rules with exceptions. Section 4 is devoted to the presentation of a short background on possibilistic logic. Section 5 introduces the Π-ATMS machinery, while Section 6 illustrates the approach with the financial test case.

2 The Main Characteristics of the Test Case

Table 1 gives some examples of the rules to deal with. A real number belonging to the interval [0,1] is attached to each rule. According to the expert, it estimates the certainty of the conclusion when the conditions expressed in the "if part" of the rule are certainly satisfied. Total certainty corresponds to 1, and total uncertainty to 0. It should be emphasized that this numerical encoding of uncertainty is a matter of convenience. What matters is the ordering which is thus induced between the rules

---

[1] An acronym for "Treatment of Approximate Inference by Graded Expert Rules".

according to their uncertainty. A linearly ordered scale with a finite number of levels can be used in practice as well. For instance, the second rule in Table 1 states that if we are completely sure that long-dated lending is not feasible, then we are moderately certain (the degree 0.4) that long-dated investment is not feasible either. Most of the rules in the test case have a certainty below 1 (i.e., they are somewhat uncertain), and about 15 percent of their certainty levels is below 0.5 (i.e., they are far from providing almost certain conclusions).

• If "financial expense ratio" ≤ 0.03 and "financial structure ratio" > 0.5 then (0.7) "long-dated lending is not feasible"
• If "long-dated lending is not feasible" then (0.4) "long-dated investment is not feasible"
• If "profit ratio" > 0.15 and "capitalization ratio" > 0.8 then (0.4) "long-dated investment is feasible"
• If "treasury is negative" and "financial expense ratio" > 0.03 then (0.8) "short-dated lending is not feasible"
• If "working capital" > "needs in working capital" and "profit ratio" > 0.1 then (0.7) "supplier credit ratio" := "supplier credit ratio" * 1.30

Table 1.

Several other observations can be made on the rules of Table 1.

• Logical propositions and their negations appear in the expression of rules (e.g., "long-dated investment is feasible"). These propositions can be either true or false; however there may be some uncertainty pervading their truth status.

• A proposition which appears in the conclusion part of a rule may also appear in the condition part of another rule. Consequently, we have to be able to estimate the certainty of the conclusion of a rule, when the satisfying of its condition(s) remains somewhat uncertain, in order to be able to chain the rules.

• Expressions like "financial expense ratio" or "profit ratio" underlie numerical variables. These variables are involved in propositions stating that they belong to some subinterval of the real line (e.g., "financial expense ratio" ≤ 0.03), or in comparative statements, as in the last rule of Table 1. Such propositions will be referred to as "numerical variable propositions" (NVP); their truth may be uncertain as for any propositions. Besides, the thresholds should be understood with some flexibility rather than drastically, in most cases.

• Rules may have compound conditions: conjunctions of propositions may appear in the condition parts of rules.

• A proposition or its negation may be found in the conclusion parts of several rules. We may also have different NVP's relative to the same numerical variable but involving different subintervals in the conclusion parts. Then a combination procedure is needed in order to synthesize the partial conclusions pervaded with uncertainty, which are obtained from the different rules. However, there are situations where the combination is undesirable. In particular, when a conclusion obtained by a rule which is fairly specific of the current situation competes with a conclusion obtained with more general rules. In such a case, priority should be given to the conclusion obtained with the most specific rule (see Section 3.4).

- We need to determine the certainty with which a condition involving a numerical variable (e.g., "profit ratio" > 0.15) in a given rule is satisfied, from the available knowledge concerning this variable (e.g., the certainty that the "profit ratio" is smaller than 0.20, is equal to 0.8). Here we have a pattern matching problem between a condition (which may become fuzzy if the threshold, or the inequality relation is interpreted in a flexible way), and a piece of information pervaded with imprecision and uncertainty. A similar problem is encountered when comparing quantities which might be ill-known, as in the last rule of Table 1. Indeed, a strict inequality relation may have to be interpreted in some cases in a fuzzy way, if it really means, e.g., "much stronger", or on the contrary, "greater or approximately equal".

- The conclusion part of the last rule in Table 1 exhibits an example of a value of a numerical variable (which may be ill-known) which has to be modified; in this case we have to determine in which subinterval the new value lies and with which uncertainty. Such a rule should clearly be used only one time.

The test case is quite representative of the different problems raised by the management of imprecise and uncertain knowledge. Note that here we have not only to deal with uncertain rules, but also to evaluate to what extent conditions, which involve one or several numerical variables and possibly a comparator, are satisfied knowing some imprecise and uncertain information on the values of the involved variables.

3 Modeling the Uncertainty of Rules and Facts

Possibility theory (Zadeh, 1978; Dubois and Prade, 1988) is used here as a general framework for the modeling of uncertainty and imprecision. The main characteristics of possibility theory for the representation of the available information, are now recalled.

3.1 Uncertain Propositions

Let p be a proposition (e.g., "long-dated investment is feasible"). Our certainty that p is true will be expressed by means of a number belonging to the interval [0,1]; this degree will be denoted by $N(p)$ and will express to what extent p can be considered as necessarily true. A proposition p is all the more certain as the contrary proposition $\neg p$ is impossible; we shall write $N(p) = Imp(\neg p)$. On the scale [0,1] it is natural to set that the impossibility of p, $Imp(p)$, corresponds to the complement to 1 of the possibility $\Pi(p)$ of p. Then we have:

$$N(p) = 1 - \Pi(\neg p) \text{ and } \Pi(p) = 1 - N(\neg p). \tag{1}$$

In case we are using a discrete totally ordered scale, $1 - (\cdot)$ would be replaced by the order-reversing map of the scale. Using the scale [0,1], $N(p) = 1$ means that there is no uncertainty on the truth of p; p is surely true. Indeed $N(p) = 1 \Leftrightarrow \Pi(\neg p) = 0$. Since p and $\neg p$ are either true or false, and satisfy the excluded-middle and contradiction laws, we must have:

$$N(p \vee \neg p) = 1 \text{ and } N(p \wedge \neg p) = 0 \tag{2}$$

and consequently

$$\Pi(p \wedge \neg p) = 0 \text{ and } \Pi(p \vee \neg p) = 1. \tag{3}$$

The characteristic axioms of necessity and possibility degrees are:

$$N(p \wedge q) = \min(N(p), N(q)) \tag{4}$$

or equivalently

$$\Pi(p \vee q) = \max(\Pi(p), \Pi(q)) \tag{5}$$

which yields

$$\min(N(p), N(\neg p)) = 0 \quad \text{and} \quad \max(\Pi(p), \Pi(\neg p)) = 1. \tag{6}$$

Note that the equalities (6) completely depart from the situation in probability theory where Prob(p) + Prob(¬p) = 1; here we remain free to consider that two contrary propositions are both possible, since as soon as one is completely possible (at least one must be such due to the excluded-middle law), the possibility of the other remains unconstrained. Conversely, only one of two contrary propositions may be somewhat certain. For differences between probability and possibility, and discussions of representational issues, the reader may consult (Dubois and Prade, 1988; Dubois et al., 1996). Note also that we only have the inequalities $\Pi(p \wedge q) \leq \min(\Pi(p), \Pi(q))$ and $N(p \vee q) \geq \max(N(p), N(q))$ (indeed we may have q = ¬p).

$\Pi(p)$ and $\Pi(\neg p)$ define a so-called possibility distribution (Zadeh, 1978) on the set of two mutually exclusive alternatives {p, ¬p}. This may be represented as in Figure 1 where the horizontal axis has been arbitrarily partitioned in two parts corresponding to p and ¬p respectively.

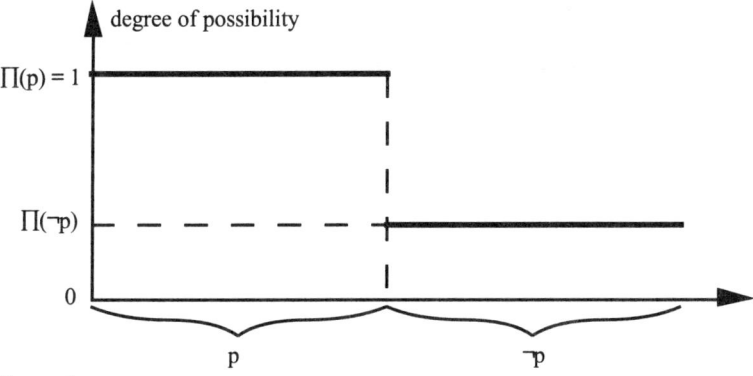

Figure 1.

3.2 Numerical Variables

Similarly, a NVP is represented by means of a possibility distribution on the domain of the variable. The possibility distribution restricts the more or less possible values of the variable; these values are mutually exclusive. For instance, the two possibility distributions attached to the NVP's p_1 = "the certainty that the profit ratio is greater than 0.25 is equal to 0.8" and p_2 = "the certainty that the profit ratio is smaller than 0.40 is equal to 0.7" are pictured in Figure 2.

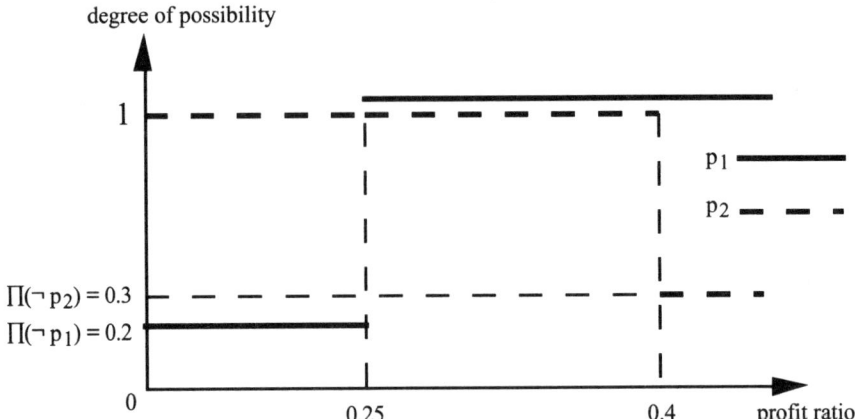

Figure 2.

We have $\Pi(p_1) = 1$ and $\Pi(\neg p_1) = 1 - 0.8 = 0.2$. In case the information concerning a NVP comes from several sources, we would have to combine several possibility distributions relative to the same variable, using the min operation pointwisely on the domain of the variable. If the pieces of information remain consistent, the resulting possibility distribution should remain normalized (i.e., at least one value has a possibility degree equal to 1).

The possibility distributions which are used here are step functions; more general possibility distributions can be manipulated in approximate reasoning as well (see Dubois and Prade, 1988). Any kind of possibility distribution associated with a factual information can be handled, as we are going to see now.

3.3 Evaluation of a Proposition

The evaluation of the condition part p of a rule w.r.t. the available (fuzzy) information also leads to a possibility distribution $(\Pi(p), \Pi(\neg p))$ on $\{p, \neg p\}$. For computing it, we have to compare a piece of information with the requirement expressed by p. This can be done in the following way, using a fuzzy pattern matching procedure (Cayrol et al., 1982).

Let D be the domain of the variable, say x, associated with the NVP p. Let π_x be the possibility distribution representing the available information about x (i.e., the quantity x is certainly between $\underline{r}_0$ and $\overline{r}_0$, and more plausibly between $\underline{r}_1$ and $\overline{r}_1$, which can be represented by a trapezoidal distribution, as in Figure 3). Then, letting [p] denote the set of models of a proposition p, in D, we can compute $\Pi(p)$ (and similarly $\Pi(\neg p)$), as

$$\Pi(p) = \sup_{d \in [p]} \pi_x(d). \tag{7}$$

When we use a discrete, totally ordered, scale rather than [0,1], π_x should be first approximated on this scale before computing $\Pi(p)$ and $\Pi(\neg p)$.

degree of possibility

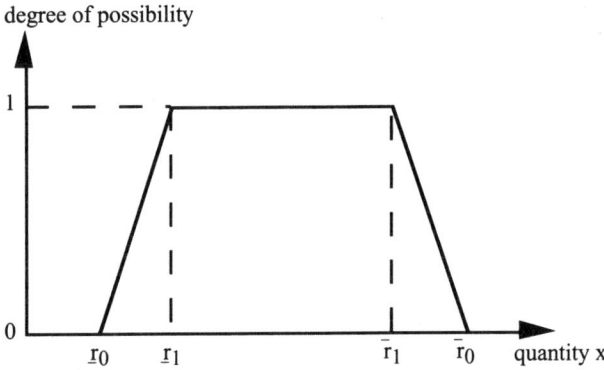

Figure 3

When p is a non-fuzzy proposition, we have $\max(\Pi(p), \Pi(\neg p)) = 1$ (and thus, $\min(N(p), N(\neg p)) = 0$). Then the factual information pertaining to numerical variables and represented by possibility distributions gives birth to uncertain, non-fuzzy, propositions p with $N(p) > 0$. This is no longer true when p is a fuzzy proposition (e.g., 'ratio x is strongly greater than a') and [p] is a fuzzy set (represented by the membership function $\mu_{[p]}$) if we use the usual definition of the possibility of a fuzzy event which extends (7), namely

$$\Pi(p) = \sup_{d \in D} \min(\mu_{[p]}(d), \pi_x(d)). \tag{8}$$

This is useful, as we shall see, for evaluating the condition part of rules of the form "the more x is A, the more certain the proposition q" (with $\mu_{[p]} = \mu_A$). When the information is precise (i.e., $x = d_0$, which corresponds to $\pi_x(d_0) = 1$, and $\pi_x(d) = 0$ if $d \neq d_0$), we have $\Pi(p) = \mu_{[p]}(d_0) = N(p)$, even when [p] is fuzzy (with $N(p) = 1 - \Pi(\neg p)$). This enables us to deal with fuzzy thresholds and fuzzy comparators in presence of a precise piece of information $x = d_0$. Indeed, for a condition of the form $p = 'x > a'$, we compute $\Pi(p)$ as

$$\Pi(p) = N(p) = \mu_{>a}(d_0)$$

where $\mu_{>a}$ represents the (fuzzy) set of values greater (or e.g., strongly greater, in the fuzzy case) than a. If 'a' is itself a fuzzy threshold represented by μ_a, $\mu_{>a}$ will be computed as the set of values certainly greater than the fuzzy quantity a (see Dubois and Prade, 1988), namely

$$\mu_{>a}(d_0) = \inf_d \max(\mu_>(d_0, d), 1 - \mu_a(d))$$

where > may be a fuzzy relation (otherwise $\mu_>(d, d') = 1$ if $d > d'$ and is 0 otherwise). Similarly, when comparing two precisely known quantities $x = d_0$ and $y = d'_0$, $\Pi(p)$ for $p \equiv 'x > y'$ is computed as $\Pi(p) = N(p) = \mu_>(d_0, d'_0)$.

In the more general case, where both the information is not precise and the proposition to evaluate is fuzzy, we directly compute N(p) as

$$N(p) = \inf_{d \in D} \max(\mu_{[p]}(d), 1 - \pi_x(d))$$

(e.g., $\mu_{[p]} = \mu_{>a}$), or in case of a comparative statement,

$$N(p) = \inf_{d \in D, d' \in D} \max(\mu_>(d,d'), 1 - \pi_x(d), 1 - \pi_y(d')).$$

Thus, in practice, from the factual information corresponding to the value of variables, represented by possibility distributions, the certainty of any proposition of interest can be computed.

In case of rules with a compound condition made of a conjunction of elementary conditions p_1 and... p_n, the elementary matching degrees $N(p_i)$ are aggregated by means of min operation, in agreement with the fact that the $N(p_i)$'s are necessity degrees.

3.4 Rules and Nonmonotonicity

A rule of the form 'if p then q' (where p and q are non-fuzzy propositions) is understood in the possibilistic framework as the constraint (Benferhat et al., 1992)

$$\Pi(p \wedge q) > \Pi(p \wedge \neg q) \tag{9}$$

if the rule may have exceptions. In case the rule has no exception (i.e., as soon as, if p is true for sure, then q is certainly true) a more drastic constraint holds, namely $\Pi(p \wedge \neg q) = 0$, which is equivalent to $N(\neg p \vee q) = 1$. Note that (9) is equivalent to $\Pi(p) > \Pi(p \wedge \neg q)$ since $\Pi(p) = \max(\Pi(p \wedge q), \Pi(p \wedge \neg q))$. It is still equivalent to $N(q \mid p) > 0$ where $N(q \mid p) = 1 - \Pi(\neg q \mid p)$ and

$$\begin{aligned} \Pi(q \mid p) &= 1 \text{ if } \Pi(p) = \Pi(p \wedge q) \\ &= \Pi(p \wedge q) \text{ if } \Pi(p) > \Pi(p \wedge q). \end{aligned} \tag{10}$$

Note also that (9) entails (but is not equivalent to) $N(\neg p \vee q) > 0$. Thus a knowledge base made of n rules of the form "if p_i then q_i" is represented by the set of constraints $\Pi(p_i \wedge q_i) > \Pi(p_i \wedge \neg q_i)$ for i = 1,n. In (Benferhat et al., 1992), it is shown that choosing the greatest possibility measure (the one allocating the greatest possibility degrees to the interpretations) satisfying these constraints, when this possibility measure exists, completely agrees with the postulates proposed by (Kraus et al., 1990) for nonmonotonic reasoning and more particularly the so-called, rational consequence relation. If this possibility distribution does not exist, it means that the knowledge base is inconsistent. Moreover, it is shown in (Benferhat et al., 1992) that each constraint can be translated into a constraint of the form

$$N(\neg p_i \vee q_i) \geq N^*(\neg p_i \vee q_i) \tag{11}$$

where N^* is the necessity measure associated by duality with the greatest solution Π^* of the set of constraints. An algorithm is given in (Benferhat et al., 1992) which enables us to stratify the set of rules into a set of layers of formulas of the form $\neg p_i \vee q_i$, where all the formulas in a layer have the same "certainty" level

N*(¬p$_i$ ∨ q$_i$). This approach makes sure that a rule ¬p$_i$ ∨ q$_i$ which is more specific than another rule ¬p$_j$ ∨ q$_j$ (taking into account the knowledge provided by the other rules) will be in a layer with a higher level such that N*(¬p$_i$ ∨ q$_i$) > N*(¬p$_j$ ∨ q$_j$). For instance, in the famous example, which is prototypical of nonmonotonic reasoning, namely: "birds fly", "penguins are birds", "penguins do not fly", the last rule is more specific than the rule "birds fly". Then, applying the possibilistic logic machinery presented in the next section, priority will be automatically given to the more specific rules (which can be applied to the current set of facts which constitutes the available knowledge).

This procedure goes well with the assessment by the expert of levels of confidence to the rules, provided that the ordering induced by these levels of confidence is compatible with the one induced by N*.

Thus, the rules we consider, which are of the form "if p then (α) q" (see Table 1), are understood as "N(¬p ∨ q) ≥ α" (after checking that this does not violate the ordering between the rules induced by the constraints of the form (9), as just explained). The constraint N(¬p ∨ q) = 1 will be associated with the completely certain rule "if p then (1) q".

When a rule 'if p then q' has a fuzzy condition part (rules with fuzzy conclusion parts are not considered here), we shall model it by a constraint of the form

$$N(q) \geq N(p) \tag{12}$$

where N(p) is computed from the available factual knowledge, as explained in Section 3.3. This is in complete agreement with the semantics of certainty rules (Dubois and Prade, 1996a), which are of the form "the more X is A, the more certain q", with p ≡ 'x is A' here. When x becomes ill-known, the semantics becomes "the more certain we are that x is A with a high degree, the more certain q".

4 Possibilistic Logic

The reader is referred to Dubois, Lang and Prade (1994a and b) for introductory and detailed presentations on possibilistic logic respectively. In the following, we only recall some basic points.

A possibilistic logic formula is made of a pair constituted by a classical logic formula φ and a weight α belonging to a totally ordered scale, e.g., [0,1], or a finite scale. Here φ is a proposition p. (p, α) is semantically interpreted as a constraint of the form N(p) ≥ α where N is a necessity measure. Then the following resolution rule is in agreement with this semantics:

$$\frac{(\neg p \vee q, \alpha)}{(q \vee r, \min(\alpha, \beta))}$$

This resolution rule extends classical resolution for α = β = 1. Refutation can be extended to this framework. Let Σ be a possibilistic knowledge base made of a set of possibilistic logic formulas put under clausal form (this can be always done, since if p = ∧$_i$ p$_i$ then N(p) ≥ α ⇔ ∀i, N(p$_i$) ≥ α). Then proving (p,α) from Σ, which can be written symbolically Σ ⊢ (p, α), amounts to prove (⊥,α), where ⊥ denotes the empty clause, by applying the resolution rule to $\Sigma \cup \{(\neg p, 1)\}$ repeatedly. Moreover we have, $(p, \alpha') \vdash (p, \alpha)$ iff $\alpha \leq \alpha'$; besides, if $\Sigma \vdash (p, \alpha)$ and $\Sigma \vdash (p, \alpha')$, then $\Sigma \vdash (p, \max(\alpha, \alpha'))$. So we are looking for the refutation which provides the greatest lower bound. This syntactic machinery is sound and complete with respect to a semantics in terms of a possibility distribution encoding an ordering on the interpretations, in agreement with the semantic understanding of (p, α) as $N(p) \geq \alpha$.

Let us for instance consider the possibilistic knowledge base which contains the two formulas $(\neg p \vee q, \alpha)$, $(\neg p \vee \neg p' \vee q, \alpha')$ with $\alpha' > \alpha$. Then if we add the information $(p, 1)$, we can infer that (q, α), while if we have both $(p, 1)$ and $(p', 1)$, we can infer a more certain conclusion, namely (q, α') using the more "specific" clause $(\neg p \vee \neg p' \vee q, \alpha')$, since $\alpha' > \alpha$.

Possibilistic logic can cope with partial inconsistency. The inconsistency degree $\text{Inc}(\Sigma)$ of a possibilistic knowledge base Σ is the greatest α such that $\Sigma \vdash (\bot, \alpha)$ can be proved by repeated application of the resolution rule. Then any conclusion (p, β) such that $\Sigma \vdash (p, \beta)$ with $\beta > \alpha = \text{Inc}(\Sigma)$ remains valid since (p, β) is obtained by applying the resolution rule to a *consistent* subpart of the base (made of formulas whose certainty level is greater or equal to β; inconsistency can only be created by formulas whose certainty level is at most α). Note also that if we have the two clauses $(\neg p \vee r, \beta)$ and $(\neg p \vee \neg p' \vee \neg r, \beta')$ with $\beta' > \beta$, the more specific clause when we have both $(p, 1)$ and $(p', 1)$ leads to the valid conclusion $(\neg r, \beta')$ since β' is greater than the inconsistency degree β of the set of the four above clauses. When we only have $(p, 1)$ and the two first clauses, the inconsistency degree is 0 and the valid conclusion (r, β) is obtained (while $(\neg r, \beta')$ cannot be produced). This example illustrates how nonmonotonic reasoning is handled in possibilistic logic, and why more specific clauses should be associated with a greater certainty level in order to give priority to their conclusion when we have enough information to be sure of being in the corresponding specific situation. See (Dubois, Lang and Prade, 1994b).

As explained in the preceding section, all the information (facts and/or rules) can be turned into a set of possibilistic logic constraints of the form $N(c) \geq \alpha$, where c is a clause. Note that, the certainty rule "the more x is A, the more certain q" corresponds to the possibilistic framework $(q, \mu_A(x))$ with a "variable" weight depending on the degree to which the value of x satisfies the fuzzy property A (see Dubois, Lang and Prade, 1994a).

Besides, in possibilistic logic it is always possible to move literals from the formula slot to the weight slot. Indeed, it can be shown that there is a semantic equivalence between $(\neg p \vee q, \alpha)$ and $(q, \min(\alpha, \mu_{[p]}(\omega)))$ for instance, where $\mu_{[p]}(\omega)$ denotes the truth-value (1 for 'true', 0 for 'false') of p for an interpretation ω. It means that saying that $\neg p \vee q$ is at least α-certain is semantically equivalent to say that q is α-certain provided that p is true. This remark can be exploited when some literal cannot be eliminated in the resolution process, and more generally in hypothetical reasoning.

5   Hypothetical Reasoning with Possibilistic ATMS

In this section, we recall how possibilistic logic can deal with hypothetical reasoning, by means of an extended Assumption-based Truth Maintenance System (ATMS), called "possibilistic ATMS" (or Π-ATMS for short), where the management of uncertainty is integrated inside the basic capabilities of the ATMS.

Assumption-based Truth Maintenance Systems (ATMS) (De Kleer, 1986) are automated reasoning systems oriented towards hypothetical reasoning since they are able to determine under which set of assumption(s) a given proposition is true. ATMSs use two kinds of propositional symbols (or data): those which correspond to the choice of the users (called assumption data) and the others (called non-assumption data) which often correspond to the conclusions obtained from a knowledge base and facts. For instance, in fault diagnosis, assumptions data are associated with each component which may be faulty (e.g., there is no oil, the engine belt is broken,…) and the non-assumption data describe observable facts whose truth value may be known by the user (e.g., the temperature indicator is red, the charge ammeter is positive,…).

Classical ATMSs require that the clauses contained inside the knowledge base (justifications and disjunctions of assumptions) are certain; we may wish to handle more or less uncertain information without losing the capacities of the ATMS. The basic principle of the Π-ATMS (Dubois et al., 1991, Benferhat et al. 1994) is to associate to each clause a weight α which is a lower bound of its necessity degree. Assumptions may also be weighted, i.e. the user or the inference engine may decide at any time to believe in an assumption with a given certainty degree. A Π-ATMS is able to answer the two following questions:

i) Under what configuration of the assumptions is a fact d certain to some degree? Namely, what assumptions shall we consider as true, and with what certainty degrees in order to have d certain to a degree α? For example, in fault diagnosis problem, we can ask for sets of configuration of the assumptions which explain a given observation.

ii) What is the inconsistency degree of a given configuration of assumptions? For example, in fault diagnosis problem, we can ask if it is consistent or not (and to what degree) that a given breakdown is issued from a set of configuration of the assumptions (e.g., we can ask if it is coherent to assume that the faulty comes simultaneously from the facts that there is no oil and that the engine belt is broken).

The basic notions attached to the classical ATMS can be generalized to the possibilistic setting. Let Σ be a set of possibilistic logic clauses of the form (p,α) (understood as $N(p) \geq \alpha$). Let E be a set of assumptions; we only consider non-weighted assumptions (i.e., they will have the implicit weight 1). The following definitions are useful:

- $[E\ \alpha]$ is an environment of the fact d if $N(d) \geq \alpha$ is a logical consequence of $E \cup \Sigma$;
- $[E\ \alpha]$ is an α-environment of d if $[E\ \alpha]$ is an environment of d and if $\forall\ \alpha' > \alpha$, $[E\ \alpha']$ is not an environment of d (α is maximal);
- $[E\ \alpha]$ is an α-contradictory environment, or α-nogood, if $E \cup \Sigma$ is α-inconsistent with α maximal. The α-nogood $[E\ \alpha]$ is said to be minimal if there is no β-nogood $[E'\ \beta]$ such that $E \supset E'$ and $\alpha \leq \beta$.

The label of the fact d, $L(d) = \{[E_i\ \alpha_i], i \in I\}$ is the unique fuzzy subset of the set of environments for which the four following properties hold:

- soundness: $\forall\ [E_i\ \alpha_i] \in L(d)$ we have $E_i \cup \Sigma \vdash (d\ \alpha_i)$; i.e., $L(d)$ contains only environments of d.

- minimality: there do not exist two environments $(E_1\ \alpha_1)$ and $(E_2\ \alpha_2)$ of L(d) such that $E_1 \subset E_2$ and $\alpha_1 \geq \alpha_2$. It means that L(d) only contains the most specific α-environments of d.

- completeness: for every environment E' such that $E' \cup \Sigma \vdash (d\ \alpha')$, there exists $[E_i\ \alpha_i] \in L(d)$ such that $E_i \subseteq E'$ and $\alpha_i \geq \alpha'$, i.e., all minimal α-environments of d are present in L(d).

- (weak) consistency: $\forall\ [E_i\ \alpha_i] \in L(d)$, $E_i \cup \Sigma$ is either consistent, or the inconsistency degree of $E_i \cup \Sigma$ is strictly less than the certainty with which d can be deduced from $E_i \cup \Sigma$ (i.e., $Inc(E_i \cup \Sigma) < \alpha_i$).

These notions of nogoods and of labels allow respectively to answer to the questions (i) and (ii). The set of nogoods can be seen as a way to restricting the set of inputs in order to preserve the consistency while the label of a given datum d exhibits the necessary conditions to deduce this datum. An algorithm for computing labels and nogoods is developed in (Benferhat et al., 1994). This algorithms, based on a restricted form of resolution, offers:

- a uniform representation for all pieces of knowledge (no differentiated storage and treatment between justifications, i.e. Horn clauses (i.e., clauses with one negative literal), and disjunctions of assumptions, i.e., non-Horn clauses),

- a capability of handling negated assumptions i.e., environments and nogoods may contain negations of assumptions; this approach differs from De Kleer "NATMS" (De Kleer, 1988) where negated assumptions do not appear inside the environments.

Ranking environments according to their weight in the label of each fact provides a way for limiting the consequences of combinatorial explosion: indeed when a label contains too many environments, the Π-ATMS can help the user by giving the environments with the greatest weight(s) only. This same advantage appears for rank-ordering "*interpretations*" (maximal consistent sets of assumptions) which are practically used in revising inconsistent knowledge bases. These interests can be seen in (Benferhat et al., 1996) where an application of Π-ATMS to a data fusion problem is given. See also (Bos-Plachez, 1997) for another application.

6 Application to the Financial Analysis Test Case

The complete knowledge base which is used in our financial analysis test case can be found in (Wyss, 1988). It contains about forty rules, and about twenty propositional symbols are necessary for the complete description of a situation. This section applies a Π-ATMS to a fragment of this financial knowledge base (this fragment refers to a subpart of the factual knowledge only). We distinguish two kinds of propositional symbols:

— Propositional symbols which encode "numerical variable propositions". These variables are involved in clauses stating that they belong to some sub-interval of the real line (e.g., "financial expense ratio" > 0.03). Since Π-ATMSs are based on propositional logic, we encode numerical variables by Boolean propositional symbols. For instance, the expression "FE" > 0.03 is encoded by a proposition "FE > 3" which is true if the numerical variable "financial expense ratio" is strictly greater than 0.03, and false otherwise. These numerical variables are considered as the assumptions data of the Π-ATMS since they represent characteristic (financial) data of the enterprise. In the fragment of the knowledge base used here, we only have six assumption data denoted by:

FE > 3 (financial-expense-ratio is strictly greater than 0.03),
FI > 3 (financial-independence-ratio is strictly greater than 0.03),
FS <= 5 (financial-structure-ratio is less or equal than 0.05),
PR > 15 (profit-ratio is strictly greater than 0.15),
CA > 8 (capitalization-ratio is strictly greater than 0.08),
WC > 0 (working-capital is positive).

— Non-numerical propositions which correspond to the non-assumption data of the Π-ATMS. In our knowledge base we consider three non-assumption data:

lenfea (long-dated lending is feasible),
invfea (long-dated investment is feasible),
invrec (long-dated investment is recommended).

The fragment of knowledge base used here is described by the following rules:

R1. if financial-expense-ratio is strictly greater than 0.03
    then long-dated lending is not feasible (0.7)

R2. if financial-expense-ratio is less or equal than 0.03
    and financial-independence-ratio is less or equal than 0.03
    then long-dated lending is not feasible (0.5)

R3. if financial-expense-ratio is less or equal than 0.03
    and financial-structure-ratio is strictly greater than 0.05
    then long-dated lending is not feasible (0.7).

R4. if financial-expense-ratio is less or equal than 0.03
    and financial-independence-ratio is strictly greater than 0.03
    then long-dated lending is feasible (0.9)

R5. if financial-independence-ratio is less or equal than 0.03
    and financial-structure-ratio is less or equal than 0.05
    then long-dated lending is feasible (1).

R6. if long-dated lending is feasible
    then long-dated investment is feasible (1)
    otherwise long-dated investment is not feasible (0.7)

R7. if profit-ratio is strictly greater than 0.15
    and capitalization-ratio is strictly greater than 0.08
    then long-dated investment is feasible (0.5).

R8. if long-dated investment is feasible and WC>0
    then long-dated investment is recommended (0.7)
    otherwise long-dated investment is not recommended (0.7).

Using the previous notations and putting the above rules in a clausal form we get a set of 11 clauses:

C_1:	$\neg FE > 3 \vee \neg lenfea$	0.7
C_2:	$\neg lenfea \vee FE > 3 \vee FI > 3$	0.5
C_3:	$\neg lenfea \vee FE > 3 \vee FS <= 5$	0.7
C_4:	$\neg FI > 3 \vee lenfea \vee FE > 3$	0.9
C_5:	$\neg FS <= 5 \vee lenfea \vee FE > 3$	1.
C_6:	$\neg lenfea \vee invfea$	1.
C_7:	$\neg invfea \vee lenfea$	0.7
C_8:	$\neg PR > 15 \vee \neg CA > 8 \vee invfea$	0.5
C_9:	$\neg invfea \vee \neg WC>0 \vee invrec$	0.7
C_{10}:	$\neg invrec \vee invfea$	0.7
C_{11}:	$\neg invrec \vee WC>0$	0.7

The clauses C_1-C_5 encode R_1-R_5 respectivley. C_6 and C_7 encode rule R_6; C_8 corresponds to R_7, while R_8 is captured by C_9-C_{11}. The notation $\neg FE > 3$ means FE<=3, i.e., the negation $\neg$ applies to the proposition 'FE > 3'. Note that from the clauses C_4 and C_5 alone we can remark that the set A = {[{FI > 3 ¬FE > 3} 0:9], [{FS<=5 ¬FE > 3} 1.]} contains two environments of the datum lenfea and that using only the clause C_8, the set B = {[{PR > 15 CA > 8} 0.5]} contains an environment of the datum invfea. The last environment expresses that "long-dated investment is feasible" to a certainty degree equal to 0.5 provided that we are completely certain that the profit ratio is strictly greater than 0.15 and that the capitalization ratio is strictly greater than 0.08. These two sets A and B cannot be considered as the respective labels of lenfea and invfea since they do not contain all the environments of these data.

To get the label of different non-assumption data, ∏-ATMS applies a restricted form of possibilistic resolution between clauses of the knowledge base in order to get new clauses which are interesting for the ∏-ATMS (see Benferhat et al. (1994) for more details). We list below all the clauses (some of them are deduced) which permit to immediatly recover the different labels and nogoods:

C_{12}:	$\neg CA > 8 \vee \neg PR > 15 \vee lenfea$	0.5
C_{13}:	$\neg FS <= 5 \vee invfea \vee FE > 3$	1.
C_{14}:	$\neg FI > 3 \vee invfea \vee FE > 3$ 0.9	
C_{15}:	$\neg WC > 0 \vee \neg CA > 8 \vee \neg PR > 15 \vee invrec$	0.5
C_{16}:	$\neg WC > 0 \vee \neg FS <= 5 \vee invrec \vee FE > 3$	0.7
C_{17}:	$\neg WC > 0 \vee \neg FI > 3 \vee invrec \vee FE > 3$	0.7
C_{18}:	$\neg FI > 3 \vee \neg FS<= 5 \vee FE > 3$	0.7
C_{19}:	$\neg FS <= 5 \vee \neg FI > 3 \vee FE > 3$	0.5
C_{20}:	$\neg FE > 3 \vee \neg CA > 8 \vee \neg PR > 1$	0.5
C_{21}:	$\neg CA > 8 \vee \neg PR > 15 \vee \neg FI > 3$	0.5
C_{22}:	$\neg CA > 8 \vee \neg PR > 15 \vee \neg FS <= 5$	0.5

The label of the different non-assumption data are hence:

$$
\begin{aligned}
\text{label (lenfea)} = \{ \ & [\{CA > 8 \ PR > 15\} \ 0.5], \\
& [\{FS <= 5 \ \neg FE > 3\} \ 1.], \\
& [\{FI > 3 \ \neg FE > 3\} \ 0.9]\} \\
\text{label (invfea)} = \{ \ & [\{CA > 8 \ PR > 15\} \ 0.5], \\
& [\{FS <= 5 \ \neg FE > 3\} \ 1.], \\
& [\{FI > 3 \ \neg FE > 3\} \ 0.9]\} \\
\\
\text{label (invrec)} = \{ \ & [\{WC > 0 \ CA > 8 \ PR > 15\} \ 0.5], \\
& [\{WC > 0 \ FS <= 5 \ \neg FE > 3\} \ 0.7], \\
& [\{WC > 0 \ FI > 3 \ \neg FE > 3\} \ 0.7]\}.
\end{aligned}
$$

The two last environments in the label of the non-assumption datum "lenfea" can be obtained immediatly from the clauses C_4 and C_5 as already said, while the first environment [$\{CA > 8 \ PR > 15\}$ 0.5] can be obtained using the clauses C_7 and C_8. Note that the labels of the datum "invfea" and the datum "lenfea" are the same. This is due to the clause C_6 which implies that each environment of the datum "lenfea" is also an environment of the datum "invfea". However, the converse is weakly true using the clause C_7. Indeed, if [E α] is an environment of the datum "invfea", then only [E min(α, 0.7)] is also an environment of the datum "lenfea".

The set of clauses $\{C_{18}, C_{19}, C_{20}, C_{21}, C_{22}\}$ represents the nogood base:

$$
\begin{aligned}
\text{nogood} = \{ \ & [\{FI > 3 \ \neg FS <= 5 \ \neg FE > 3\} \ 0.7], \\
& [\{FS <= 5 \ \neg FI > 3 \ \neg FE > 3\} \ 0.5], \\
& [\{FE > 3 \ CA > 8 \ PR > 15\} \ 0.5], \\
& [\{CA > 8 \ PR > 15 \ \neg FI > 3\} \ 0.5], \\
& [\{CA > 8 \ PR > 15 \ \neg FS <= 5\} \ 0.5]\}
\end{aligned}
$$

Each environment [E α] in the set of nogoods means that if all the assumptions in E are observed to be true then there will be an inconsistency to a level α in the knowledge base. For instance let us consider the environment [$\{FI > 3 \ \neg FS <= 5 \ \neg FE > 3\}$ 0.7] which belongs to the set of nogoods. Clearly the following set of completely certain formulas $\{(FI > 3 \ 1), (\neg FS <= 5 \ 1), (\neg FE > 3 \ 1)\}$ together with the clauses C_3 and c_4 is inconsistent to a level 0.7. Thus, nogoods are useful for determining the sets of factual data which are inconsistent with the expert knowledge. The computation of labels enables us to determine under what factual conditions a conclusion of interest can be reached with a given certainty level.

Assume now that we have received (or obtained through fuzzy pattern matching as explained in Section 3.3) a new fact:

- It is certain to a degree 0.9 that financial-expense-ratio is less or equal than 0.03.

This is added to the knowledge base in the following clausal form:

C_{25}: $\neg FE > 3$ 0.9

Then, the different labels of the data become:

label (lenfea) = LABEL (invfea) = { [{CA > 8 PR > 15} 0.5]
                                      [{FI > 3} 0.9]
                                      [{FS <= 5} 0.9]
                                      [{FS <= 5 ¬FE > 3} 1]
                                      }
label (invrec) = {[{WC > 0 CA > 8 PR > 15} 0.5]
      [{WC > 0 FI > 3} 0.7]
      [{WC > 0 FS <= 5} 0.7]}

nogood = {[{FS <= 5 ¬FI > 3} 0.5]
      [{CA > 8 PR > 15 ¬FI > 3} 0.5]
      [{CA > 8 PR > 15 ¬FS <= 5} 0.5]
      [{FI > 3 ¬FS <= 5} 0.7]
      [{FE > 3} 0.9]}

Note that in the labels of the datum "lenfea" we get four environments rather than three as it would be the case if the classical ATMS (namely when all the clauses in the knowledge base are completly certain). The reason is that the two environments [{FS <= 5} 0.9] and [{FS <= 5 ¬FE > 3} 1] are not redundant, the first environment means that if financial-structure-ratio is less or equal than 0.05 then the datum "lenfea" will be certain to a degre 0.9, but the second environment specifies that if moreover we learn that financial-expense-ratio is less or equal than 0.03 then the datum "lenfea" will be completely certain.

The new set of nogoods also contains a new environment [{FE > 3} 0.9] which is obtained from the new information C_{25}. Besides, the environment [{FE > 3 CA > 8 PR > 15} 0.5] is no longer in the new set of nogoods. It is subsumed by the new added environment [{FE > 3} 0.9]. Indeed, [{FE > 3 CA > 8 PR > 15} 0.5] means that the addition of the three possibilistic formulas {(FE > 3, 1), (CA > 8, 1), (PR > 15, 1)} leads to a partial inconsistency with a level 0.5; however a stronger result is obtained using the nogood [{FE > 3} 0.9], since adding {(FE > 3, 1)} alone leads to an inconsistency with a higher degree of inconsistency (i.e., 0.9).

Now, let us assume that moreover we have two certain pieces of information:

• It is completely certain that the working capital is positive.
• It is completely certain that the financial-structure-ratio is less or equal than 0.05.

These rules are added to the knowledge base in the following clausal form:

C_{26}:   WC > 0   1
C_{27}:   FS <= 5   1.

The new sets of labels and nogoods are:

label (lenfea) = label (invfea) = { [{} 0.9]
                                     [{¬FE > 3} 1]
                                     }

label (invrec) = {[{} 0.7]}

nogood = { [{¬FI > 3} 0.5]
            [{FE > 3} 0.9]
            [{¬FS <= 5} 1]
            [{¬WC > 0} 1]
            }.

These results mean that "long-dated lending is feasible" is certain 0.9, namely we do not need to assume any further assumption data to get "lenfea" at degre 0.9. If we want to get "lenfea" completely then it is enough to have FE >= 3. The label of "invrec" means that "long-dated investment is recommended" is certain to a degree .7 with no further conditions, and we cannot have "long-dated investment is recommended" with a higher certainty degree.

7 Conclusion

This paper has illustrated the potentials of fuzzy set-based inference techniques for handling expert knowledge pervaded with uncertainty and qualitative numerical information (here pertaining to financial ratio and fuzzy thresholds) in a financial analysis advising problem. The approach has mainly taken advantage of the fuzzy pattern matching technique for evaluating the condition part of rules, and of the possibilistic logic inference machinery for handling uncertain rules (which may have various levels of specificity). A possibilistic ATMS then enables us to compute under what possible sets of factual conditions a conclusion can be reached (with a given certainty level). The financial analysis test case is only representative of the kind of expert rules which can be encountered in this type of application, and should not be necessarily regarded as uptodate pieces of expert knowledge in their final form. Clearly, financial analysis is only one of many fields where fuzzy logic can be successfully applied to fuzzy information engineering problems. See (Dubois, Prade and Yager, 1997) for other applications of this type (which may use other types of approximate reasoning machineries, see (Dubois and Prade, 1996b) for an overview of these other techniques.

References

Abel J., Menu J., Probst A.R. (1984) Un prototype de système expert pour la finance. Proc. of the 4th Inter. Conf. on Expert Systems & Their Applications, Avignon, France.

Barczewski T., Rust H.J., Weber R., Zygan H. (1996) A fuzzy system for credit analysis in a German credit insurance company. Proc. of the 4th Europ. Congress on Intelligent Techniques and Soft Computing (EUFIT'96), Aachen, Germany, Sept. 2-5, 2215-2218.

Benferhat S., Chehire. T, Monai F. F. (1996) Possibilistic ATMS in a data fusion problem. In: Fuzzy Information Engineering: A Guided Tour of Applications (D. Dubois, H. Prade, R.R. Yager, eds.), Wiley, New York, 417-435.

Benferhat S., Dubois D., Lang J., Prade H. (1994) Hypothetical reasoning in possibilistic logic: Basic notions and implementation issues. In: Advances in Fuzzy Systems: Applications and Theory, Vol. 1 (P.Z. Wang, K.F. Loe, eds.), World Scientific Publ., Singapore, 1-29.

Benferhat S., Dubois D., Prade H. (1992) Representing default rules in possibilistic logic. Proc. of the 3rd Inter. Conf. on Principles of Knowledge Representation and Reasoning (KR'92), Cambridge, MA, Oct. 26-29, 673-684.

Bos-Plachez C. (1997) A possibilistic ATMS contribution to diagnose analog electronic circuits. Int. J. of Intelligent Systems, Vol. 12, pp. 849-864.

Buchanan B.G., Shortliffe E.H. (Eds.) (1984) Rule-Based Expert Systems — The MYCIN Experiments of the Stanford Heuristic Programming Project. Addison-Wesley, Reading.

Cayrol M., Farreny H., Prade H. (1982) Fuzzy pattern matching. Kybernetes, 11, 103-116.

De Kleer J. (1986) An assumption-based TMS. Artificial Intelligence, 28, 127-162.

De Kleer J. (1988) A general labeling algorithm for assumption-based truth maintenance. Proc. of the National Conf. on Artificial Intelligence (AAAI'88), Saint Paul, Minnesota, Aug. 21-26, 188-192.

Dubois D., Lang J., Prade H. (1991) A possibilistic assumption-based truth maintenance system with uncertain justifications, and its application to belief revision. In: Truth Maintenance Systems (J.P. Martins, M. Reinfrank, eds.), Springer Verlag, Berlin, 87-106.

Dubois D., Lang J., Prade H. (1994a) Automated reasoning using possibilistic logic: semantics, belief revision and variable certainty weights. IEEE Trans. on Data and Knowledge Engineering, 6(1), 64-71.

Dubois D., Lang J., Prade H. (1994b) Possibilistic logic. In: Handbook of Logic in Artificial Intelligence and Logic Programming, Vol. 3 (D.M. Gabbay, C.J. Hogger, J.A. Robinson, D. Nute, eds.), Oxford University Press, 439-513.

Dubois D., Prade H. (with the collaboration of Farreny H., Martin-Clouaire R., Testemale C.) (1988) Possibility Theory — An Approach to Computerized Processing of Uncertainty. Plenum Press, New York.

Dubois D., Prade H. (1989) Handling uncertainty in expert systems: pitfalls, difficulties, remedies. In: The Reliability of Expert Systems (E. Hollnagel, eds.), Ellis Horwood, Chichester, UK, 64-118.

Dubois D., Prade H. (1996a) What are fuzzy rules and how to use them. Fuzzy Sets and Systems, 84, 169-185.

Dubois D., Prade H. (1996b) Fuzzy sets in approximate reasoning: A personal view. In: Fuzzy Logic — Implementations and Applications (M.J. Patyra, D.M. Mlynek, eds.), Wiley, New York and B.G. Teubner, Stuttgart, 3-35.

Dubois D., Prade H., Smets P. (1996) Representing partial ignorance. IEEE Trans. on Systems, Man and Cybernetics, 26(3), 361-377.

Dubois D., Prade H., Yager R.R. (Eds.) (1997) Fuzzy Information Engineering: A Guided Tour of Applications. Wiley, New York.

Farreny H., Prade H. (1986) Default and inexact reasoning with possibility degrees. IEEE Trans. Systems, Man & Cybernetics, 16(2), 270-276.

Farreny H., Prade H., Wyss E. (1986) Approximate reasoning in a rule-based expert system using possibility theory: a case study. In: Information Processing'86 (Proc. of the 10th World FIIP Cong., Dublin, 1-5 Sept. 1986) (H.J. Kugler, ed.), North-Holland, Amsterdam, 407-413.

Güllich H.P. (1996) Fuzzy-logic decision support system for credit risk evaluation. Proc. of the 4th Europ. Congress on Intelligent Techniques and Soft Computing (EUFIT'96), Aachen, Germany, Sept. 2-5, 2219-2223.

Kerschberg L., Dickinson J. (1985) FINEX: An expert support system for financial analysis. Proc. of the 5th Inter. Conf. on Expert Systems & Their Applications, Avignon, France, May 13-15, 919-942.

Kraus S., Lehmann D., Magidor M. (1990) Nonmonotonic reasoning, preferential models and cumulative logics. Artificial Intelligence, 44, 167-207.

Wyss E. (1988) TAIGER, un générateur de systèmes experts adaptés au traitement de données incertaines et imprécises. Thèse de Doctorat de l'Université Paul Sabatier, Toulouse, France.

Zadeh L.A. (1978) Fuzzy sets as a basis for a theory of possibility. Fuzzy Sets and Systems, 1, 3-28.

Zimmermann H.J. (1997) Operators in models of decision making. In: Fuzzy Information Engineering: A Guided Tour of Applications (D. Dubois, H. Prade, R.R. Yager, eds.), Wiley, New York, 471-496.

Zimmermann H.J., Zysno P. (1983) Decisions and evaluations by hierarchical aggregation of information. Fuzzy Sets and Systems, 10, 243-260.

Financial Analysis of Non-Financial Companies with Neural Networks

Rita Almeida Ribeiro and Fernando Moura-Pires

Departamento Informática, Faculdade Ciências Tecnologia, Universidade Nova de Lisboa, 2825 Monte Caparica, Portugal.

E-mail: {rr, fmp}@di.fct.unl.pt

Abstract

This paper presents a neural network approach to classify the 500 biggest Portuguese companies. The objective is to find relations and correlations between their relevant financial and economic attributes. Further, we want to elicit information according to the most important market players, such as banks, stockholders, managers and government. Thus, our proposal is a neural network analysis of financial and economic attributes using the most important market players perspectives.

Keywords: market player perspective, financial and economic analyses, neural networks

1 Introduction

There are various perspectives on defining what a good company is. The government focuses on their contributions to the national economy; managers are concerned with efficiency, profits and productivity; bankers focus on financial aspects; and stockholders are primarily interested in profits.

For an individual investor the availability of all the above information can represent a complementary source of knowledge about the stock market. Further, it also provides the investor with measures for risk assessment, allowing an in-depth analysis of the companies performance.

Every year, the biggest non-financial 500 companies are ranked in the Portuguese magazine Exame [Exame, 1996]. In this paper we used 1995 data, where the companies are ordered by their net sales volume and the 500 selected are those with net sales above 4,522 million escudos (about 27.4 million dollars), i.e. they are the 500 bigger Portuguese companies. The magazine also presents a financial and economic ordering, per sector of activity, of those biggest firms. This latter ordering uses a weighted average aggregation to select the best 10 companies per activity sector, with eight criteria: sales growth; net profits growth; net assets profitability; owners equity profitability; sales profitability; gross added value; solvency and general liquidity. Summarising, the classification used in the magazine [Exame, 96] for selecting the bigger and best NON-financial Portuguese companies is:

 _ Bigger: net sales greater than 4,522 million escudos
 _ Better: weighted average aggregation of grades for sales growth, net profits growth, net assets profitability, owners equity profitability, sales profitability, gross added value, solvency and general liquidity.

In this paper we used a neural network analysis approach because we want to automate the process of finding relations and correlation's between attributes, which a grade aggregation method cannot provide. Further, we also want to include information about financial and economic ratios [Aubert-Krier, 77], [Whalen, 86], according to the most important market players, such as banks, stockholders, managers and government. The most appropriate technique to meet our objectives is neural newtorks because it automates the classification by similar attributes (see examples in (Trippi and Turban 1992)). Thus, we develop a neural network analysis of financial and economic attributes with four main market player perspectives, as follows:

A) Government, that is concerned with the contribution to the national economy. The indicators used are: a.1.) Gross added value (GAV) - sum of the net sales, production fluctuations, subsidies and net extraordinary profits; a.2.) Gross added value (GAV)/Net sales. This measures how much a company contributes to the national economy per escudo sold.

B) Management, that is concerned with the firms profitability, dynamism and efficiency. The attributes used are: b.1) Sales growth; it is given by the ratio Sales 95/Sales 94 ; b.2) Net profits growth; it is given by the ratio Net profits 95/Net profits 94, that measures the dynamism and the capacity to maintain or increase the market quota; b.3) Assets turnover; given by Net Sales/Assets, that represents the degree of efficiency of available resources; b.4) Productivity; it is the ratio gross added value (GAV)/Number of workers which measures the degree of efficiency of human resources.

C) Stockholders, that are mainly concerned with profitability. The indicators are: c.1) ROI (return on investment); it is the profit per unit of capital invested in the company; c.2) ROE (return on equity); ratio of Net profits/Owners equity. This ratio measures the profitability of the owners capital; c.3) Profit margin on sales; it is the ratio of profits after taxes/ sales; c.4) Sales profitability; measured with Current profits/ Sales.

D) <u>Banks,</u> that are concerned with the financial health of companies. The attributes used are: d.1) Indebtedness; given by the ratio Liabilities/Net Assets. It measures the capacity of the firm to contract loans (the bigger the worse); d.2) Solvency; given by the ratio Owners equity/Liabilities. It measures the long-term capacity to fulfil commitments; d.3) Financial autonomy; given by the ratio Owners equity/Net assets. It measures the participation of the owners equity in financing of the company activities (complement of Indebtedness); d.4) General liquidity; given by the ratio Assets/Current liabilities. It measures the capacity to fulfil the short-term commitments; d.5) Cash flow. It measures the auto-financing capacity of the company.

The reason for this grouping is linked, as mentioned, with the different interests of managers, bankers, stockholders and government, as well as, with the idea of offering a general view, to new stock market investors, of the best Portuguese firms.

2 Classification Techniques

In order to reason one needs to classify one´s knowledge. This process of classification can be defined as an ideal arrangement of the alike and unlike. According to Mirkin [Mirkin, 96] the purpose of the arrangement is:

"1) to shape and record knowledge;

2) to analyze the structure of phenomena; and

3) to relate different aspects of a phenomena in question to each other."

Classification has been used in many fields of knowledge, as for instance: mathematics, artificial intelligence, chemistry, physics, geology, and social sciences. In mathematics it comprises two kinds of activities: computation (find the exact or approximate solutions to various equations and optimization problems) and deductions about properties of mathematical concepts (the art to construct, analyze and connect classifications of mathematical objects by means of logical tools). In artificial intelligence the process is similar, but sometimes the knowledge representation is different and it uses heuristics for optimization problems. Addressing other fields is beyond the scope of this paper.

Here our focus is on neural network techniques within the artificial intelligence field. Three of the most important techniques for classification are, conceptual clustering [Genari, 89], clustering [Mirkin, 96] and neural networks [Haykin, 94]. The first technique is usually used for problems where the attributes are nominal while the others are used when the attributes are numeric. In our case, the attributes are numeric, hence, either clustering or neural networks can be used. These two techniques are equivalent, since they use a measure of similarity based in the

Euclidean distance. We opted for a neural network approach for the classification because of software availability and prior experience of one of the authors [Nascimento, 1997 #837].

In classification problems one of the best well-known neural network technique is denoted Self-Organizing Maps or Kohonen neural network [Kohonen, 85]. We selected this neural network for our classification approach. Since our objective is the classification of non-financial companies, only a brief overview of classification with Kohonen neural networks is presented.

Kohonen neural network uses competitive learning [Kohonen, 95]. The neurons are placed at the nodes of a lattice, usually a two-dimensional one. The neurons become selectively tuned to various inputs patterns in the course of a competitive learning process. The location of the winner neuron tends to become ordered, with respect to each other, in such a way that a meaningful coordinate system for different input spaces is created over the lattice. A Kohonen neural network attribute map is, therefore, characterized by a formation of a topographic map of input patterns, in which the spatial locations of the neurons in the lattice, correspond to the attributes of the input patterns.

The essential aspects of a Kohonen neural network, which are the same we used for the classification, are [Haykin, 94]:

1) the neurons compute a discriminate function (usually based on Euclidean distance);
2) there is a mechanism that compares these discriminate values and selects a winner;
3) there is another mechanism to activate the selected winner and its neighbours (function of a radius);
4) it contains an adaptive process that enables activated neurons to increase their discriminate function values, in relation to the input signal (it is dependent of a neighbourhood function and a learning rate).

The whole process is iterative, i.e. each example is classified one at a time, and then the algorithm is repeated until the error stabilizes. The size of the error defines the stopping criterion for the iterative procedure.

3 Neural Network Analysis

In this section we describe the assumptions used for handling the data and the parameters of the Kohonen neural network. After we discuss the results obtained with this classification approach.

3.1 Data Normalization

As mentioned in the introduction, only a subset of all available attributes is used in this paper. Following to the four perspectives defined, each attribute, its range, its average and its standard deviation is shown in Table 1. As can be observed, the attribute scales are very different. This fact represents a problem for classification techniques which are based in dissimilarity measures using Euclidean distances [Kaufman, 90].

Persp	Parameters	Raw data values			
		Min	Max	Mean	Std Dev.
A	Gross added value (GAV)	-1,683.0	424,732.0	6,606.2	31,400.6
	GAV / Net Sales	-35.5	196.5	24.5	21.2
B	Sales growth	-43.6	397.0	23.7	177.7
	Net profits growth	-30,025.7	167,360.4	434.6	8,438.5
	Assets turnover	0.1	53.9	2.2	3.2
	Productivity	-36.6	2,092.3	14.1	94.7
C	Return on investment (ROI)	-37.4	44.3	2.7	7.1
	Return on equity (ROE)	-585.7	290.9	6.0	45.8
	Profit margin on sales	-176.7	30.6	1.5	10.2
	Sales profitability	-52,534.0	131,395.0	877.5	8,003.5
D	Indebtedness	0	266.9	65.5	23.5
	Solvency	-0.6	11.7	0.8	1.1
	Financial autonomy	-1.7	1	0.3	0.2
	General liquidity	1.0	16	1.7	1.4
	Cash flow	-49,346.0	197,334.0	1,869.0	11,102.4

Table 1. Attributes characterization

In order to compare the different attributes, it is usual to normalize the raw data. The most frequent methods of normalization are:

Normalization [0, 1], *i.e.*

$$y_j = \frac{x_j - a}{D}$$

where x_j is the value of the attribute of the example *j*, *a* is its minimum and *D* is the range of the attribute raw data (D= Max-Min).

Gaussian normalization, *i.e.*

$$y_j = \frac{x_j - m}{\sigma}$$

m is the average of the attribute and is its standard deviation.

S normalization, *i.e.*,

$$y_j = \frac{1}{n} \times \frac{x_j - m}{\sum_{i=1}^{n} |x_i - m|}$$

where *n* is the number of samples in the raw data.

The choice of the normalization method is a challenging problem and it is problem dependent. The Gaussian normalization is good if the raw data follows a normal distribution, i.e., if the values are not very different. In our case, since the values are very different, a Gaussian normalization yields a distribution where the values near the average are not very discriminating. The S normalization seems more appropriate in our case because it provides a wider discrimination. In order to illustrate this point, Table 2 depicts the range of values for two attributes, without normalization, with Gaussian normalization and with S-normalization. For the first attribute the Gaussian normalization could have been used. For the second attribute the Gaussian normalization should not be used because the range is to small (not discriminative).

Attributes	Normalization	Min	Max
Financial Autonomy	without	-1.7	1
	Gaussian	-8.6	2.8
	S-Normal	-11.5	3.7
Sales profitability	without	-52,534.0	131,395.0
	Gaussian	-6.7	16.3
	S-Normal	-30.9	75.5

Table 2. Example of normalization's.

Based on the data in Table 1 we have chosen, for our classification tests, the following two kind of analyses: no normalization (raw data) and the S-normalization.

3.2 Kohonen Neural Network Parameters

For each market player perspective - government, managers, banks and stockholders/investors - we performed tests with different neural network sizes. To chose the best dimension for the neural network to be analyzed, we performed tests for the following neural network dimensions: 5 x 15, 10 x 20, 30 x 40 and 40 x 60. We believe the dimension 30 x 40 is rich enough to discriminate our data. Other neural network sizes proved either too sparse (almost no companies were similar) or too concentrated (too many very different companies were grouped in the same group).

After some tests, the other parameters selected for the learning process of the neural network are : number of iterations greater than 1,000,000; learning rate varying in the interval [0.01, 0.1] and radius (neighbourhood function) varying in the interval [0, 40]. When the number of iteration increases, the learning rate and the radius decrease. Both the learning rate and the neighbourhood function belong to the adaptative process of the Kohonen neural network, as mentioned in section 2.

There are two tools to analyze the Kohonen neural network: U-mat maps and Sammon maps.

The U-mat maps are described in Ultsch [Ultsch, 93]. These maps are similar to the Kohonen neural network where the neurons are represented by a hexagon with a number (identity of the company, following the ordering of the magazine for big companies) or with a point ("•"). Each neuron is surrounded by other hexagons, with different grey levels representing the distance (in input space) between the neurons. The grey levels codification is the following: black - extremely distant; almost black - very distant; dark grey - quite distant; grey - distant; light grey - close; almost white - very close.

The Sammon maps [Sammon Jr, 69] represent the projection of the input space to a 2-dimensional space where the distances between the image points tend to approximate the Euclidean distances of the input vectors.

3.3 Analysis of Results

In this section an additional explanation about the figures to be discussed is needed. We discuss the U-mat maps and their respective Sammon maps. The latter is a graphic representation of the former and it was used to improve readability. Both maps are generated by a program package [Kohonen, 96] which allows for the visualization of distances, the U-mat using neighbouring distances with grey levels and the Sammon using Euclidean distances.

Two neural networks are generated for each of the four perspectives, one using raw data and other S-normalized data. Thus, we obtained a total of eight neural networks. For reasons of space only the normalized maps are shown. Further, for each neural network it was computed two outputs, a U-mat map and a Sammon map. These maps are used in the result analysis.

In order to improve the visualization of distinct groups, only partial regions of the entire U-mat maps are show. They correspond to the most distinctive groups here analyzed. The distinctive groups are also manually underlined, both in the U-mat and Sammon maps, to further improve the visualization. A reduced example of a complete U-mat is depicted in Fig. 1 to show the complete size of a 30x40 Kohonen neural network.

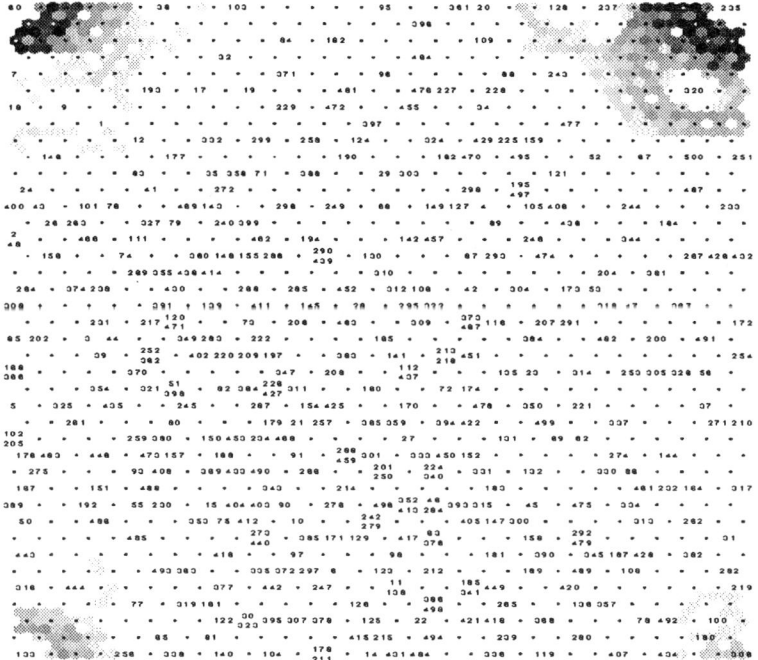

Fig. 1 - U-mat map example (perspective B)

The focus here is to unveil how the classification process provides an important tool for a financial and economic analysis of similarities and dissimilarities between companies.

The groups allow for a detailed analysis (neuron by neuron) of which companies are included and the respective raw values show why they are similar. However, here we only analyze the groups extremely distant/distinct (surrounded by black neurons), very distant (surrounded by almost black) and distant (surrounded by dark grey and grey). Thus, we only analyze the groups including companies that are very distinguishable from the average. In addition, the discussion is not an in-depth financial and economic analysis of the results obtained for the indicators, but solely a discussion of the reasons why these groups are far away from others.

After introducing our assumptions, it is now possible to discuss the results obtained. In order to do so, we follow the four perspectives of the market players, as described in the introduction.

A) Government Perspective - Contribution to the National Economy

The most interesting attributes which provide a measure of the contribution of companies to the national economy are the GAV and the GAV/Sales. Fig. 2 depicts the distinct groups in the U-mat map and the complete Sammon map.

The results in the U-mat show three very distinct groups (surrounded by black, almost black and dark grey neurons) containing companies 1, 2, 3. After, there are three quite distinct groups (surrounded by dark grey and grey neurons) containing companies 16, 9, 7. Then there are two other distinct groups (surrounded by grey neurons), one containing company 5 and another with companies 18, 24, 43, 55, 44, 48, 151, 444. The remaining companies in the figure are all considered very similar since they are surrounded by almost white neurons (very close). Finally, there is a far away group, in the down right corner, containing company 475 (not shown to save space). This last company has negative values both for the GAV and the GAV/Sales, with values: -1,683 and -35.5, respectively. Hence, it is obvious why it was classified in an opposite group (extremely distant).

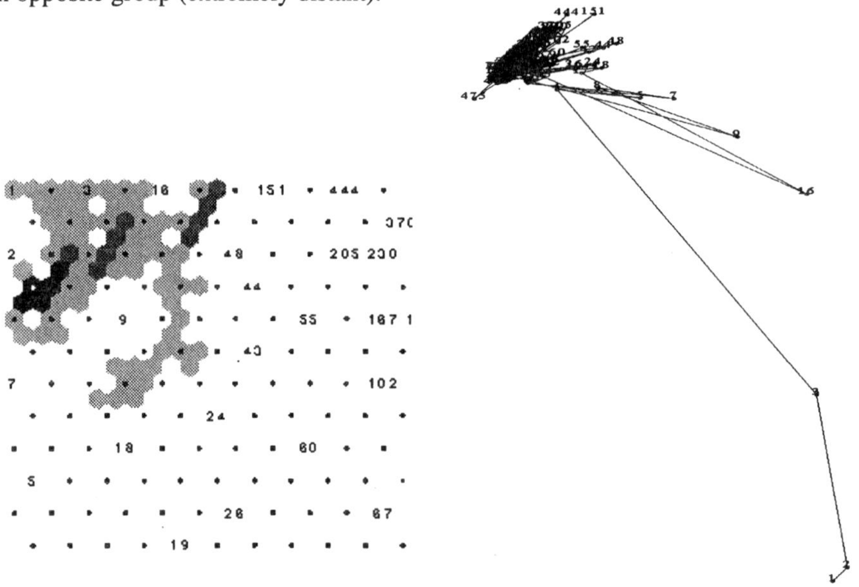

Fig. 2. Partial Umat and complete Sammon maps of contribution to National Economy

The results in the U-mat show two very distinct groups (surrounded by black, almost black and dark grey neurons) each containing respectively companies #1, #2 and #3. After, there are three quite distinct groups (surrounded by dark grey and grey neurons) containing companies #16, #9, #7. Then there are two other distinct groups (surrounded by grey neurons), one containing company #5 and another with companies #18, #24, #43, #55, #44, #48, #151, #444. The remaining companies in the figure are all considered very similar since they are surrounded by almost white neurons (very close). Finally, there is a far away group, in the lower right corner, containing company #475 (not shown to save space). This last company has negative values both for the GAV and the GAV/Sales, with values: -1,683 and -35.5, respectively. Hence, it is obvious why it was classified in an opposite group (extremely distant).

The reason for the first very distant (distinct) groups is due to big differences in their GAV values. Their GAV values are: #1 = 424,731 (thousand escudos); #2 = 416,080; #3 = 292,591. The GAV values for the next closest groups are: #16 = 153,712; #9 = 123,746; #7 = 75,721. The other distinct groups (surrounded by grey neurons) have values in the order of 30.000-50.000. Since all other companies have GAV values ranging from -134 to around 20.000 they are considered rather similar and grouped in big group, all within almost white neurons (not shown in the Fig. 2 for reasons of clarity).

Observing the Sammon map, we can now see how distant (Euclidean distance) the companies really are. We see that company #1 and #2 are more or less similar, company #3 is more distant and than the closest ones are company #16 and #9. Further up, we can still distinguish companies #7, #5, #48, #44, #8, #151, #444, #42 and #4. After these ones, all the other companies are almost identical (overlapping black area). Finally, we observe that company #475 lies in the opposite side of companies #1 and #2 and it is also distinct from the big group.

The results obtained using raw data have similarities with the ones in Fig. 2 but with less distinctive groups. For example, company #1 and #2 are considered identical, when in reality the GAV values are similar but the other attribute values, GAV/Sales, are quite different: #1 = 56.1 and #2 = 77.2. For the other groups the same problem arises. It should be pointed out that using normalized values generates much better comparative results because we are using distances as a similarity measure. When the scales are very different the values are not easily comparable.

In summary, the U-mat unveils that after the small subset of companies located in the upper left hand corner, almost all the others are very similar in what concerns the GAV and GAV/ Sales attributes (all included in almost white neurons). In financial terms they contribute much less to the national economy. The higher contribution to the Portuguese national economy is due to the companies #1, #2, #3, #16, #7 and #5. One interesting point about these companies is that they are all state-owned companies, except number #7 (a petrol company, SHELL). Hence, in reality, the only private company with a significant national contribution is number #7 (SHELL).

B) Management Perspective - Dynamism, Efficiency and Profitability

Although profitability is an issue of relevance to managers, we postpone its discussion till latter because it is the major concern of stockholders and investors. Also in this test we eliminated 90 companies from the set of examples, since there were no data available for more than one attribute. It should be stressed that when one attribute has no numerical value, the aggregated distance obtained will, necessarily, be smaller than the one of other companies with similar values in the other attributes. Non available data distorts groups because of the disparity of the aggregated values.

The most relevant attributes for evaluating the efficiency and dynamism of companies are sales growth, net sales growth, assets turnover and productivity. Fig. 3. depicts the more distinctive groups in the U-mat maps and the complete Sammon map with the 500 companies analyzed.

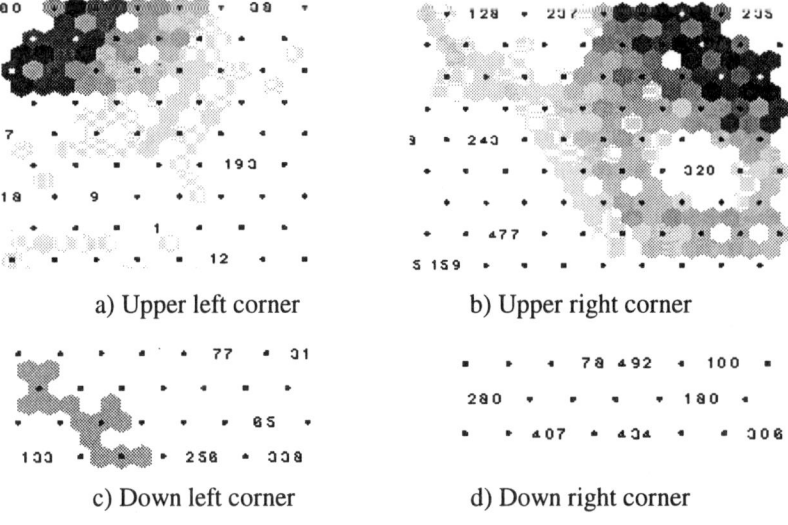

a) Upper left corner

b) Upper right corner

c) Down left corner

d) Down right corner

Fig. 3. A) b) c) d) U-mat map for Dynamism Efficiency and Profitability
In Fig. 3 there are four distinct sets of groups, located in the upper left corner, upper right corner, lower left corner and lower right corner. The upper left corner group includes company #60. The upper right corner includes three groups, the farthest with company #235 (surrounded by black and almost black neurons), then another surrounded by dark grey neurons with company #320 and the last (surrounded by grey neurons) includes companies #128 and #237. In the lower left corner (surrounded by dark grey and grey neurons) there is a group with company #133 and in the lower right corner (surrounded by grey and almost grey neurons) has a group with company #306. The group with company #60 has the greatest value for productivity of the whole set, and this is the reason for being extremely distant (black

surroundings). The value for productivity is #60 = 2,092.3 (see table 1) while the next greatest value is only #7 = 244.2 (in a light grey neuron).

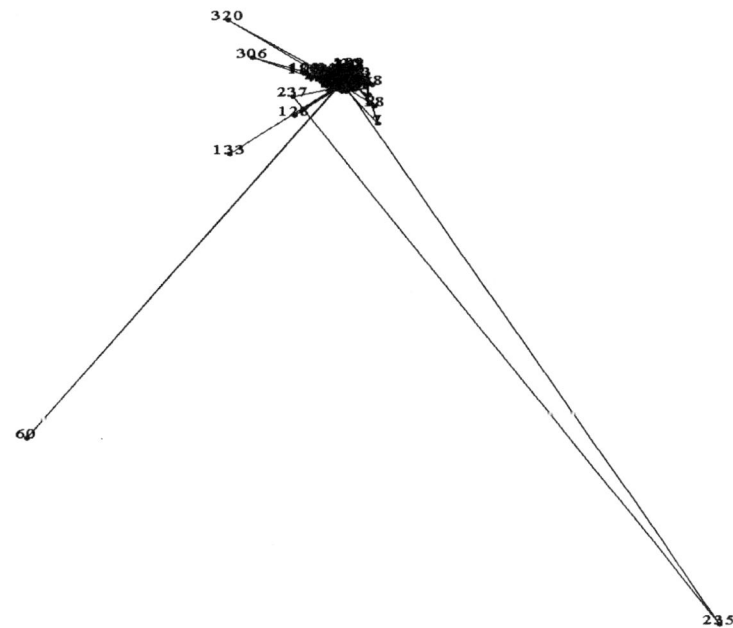

Fig. 3 – e) Complete Sammon maps for Dynamism and Efficiency

The reasons for the distinct groups in the upper right corner are quite different. The farthest group has the biggest value for Net sales growth, #235 = 167,360.4, but a low value for productivity #235 = 1.9. The next closer group, with company #320 has a lower value for Net sales growth, #320 = 29,218, but it compensates with a larger value for productivity, #320 = 10.6. The next closest group, with companies #128 and #237 have a much smaller values for Net sales growth, #128 = -75.6 and #237 = 2,839.8, but a good productivity level (#128 = 12.1 and #237 = 8.9). Further, these two companies share the best values for sales growth, #128 = 397 and #237 = 315.8. The distances between the groups just described are clearly visualized in the respective Sammon map (Fig. 3e).

Observing again Fig. 3,. the opposite group in the lower side of the U-mat includes company #133, which has the worst bad result for Net sales growth, #133 = -30,025.7 (see table 1). Looking at the opposite group, which includes company #306, the value for Net sales growth is not bad #306 = 219.5, but it belongs to a distinct group because it has small values for all other attributes, sales growth #306 = -26, assets turnover #306 = 53.9 and productivity #306 = 2.1.

The situation in terms of efficiency and dynamism for all the companies located in the upper side of the U-mat is very good while the lower side of the U-mat contains the worst companies. It should also be noted that the attribute, Assets turnover, has small value variations for all companies and, hence, it is not important in the differentiation of the groups. The Sammon map (Fig. 3e) shows that companies #60 and #235 are really very distinct form the others and that companies #320, #306, #237, #128 and #138 are distinct, but closer to all the more average ones (black area).

C) Stock Holder Perspective - Profitability

In this perspective the most important indicators to discuss are return on investment (ROI), return on equity (ROE), profit margin on sales and sales profitability. Fig. 4 depicts the partial U-mat maps with the most distinctive groups and the complete Sammon map.

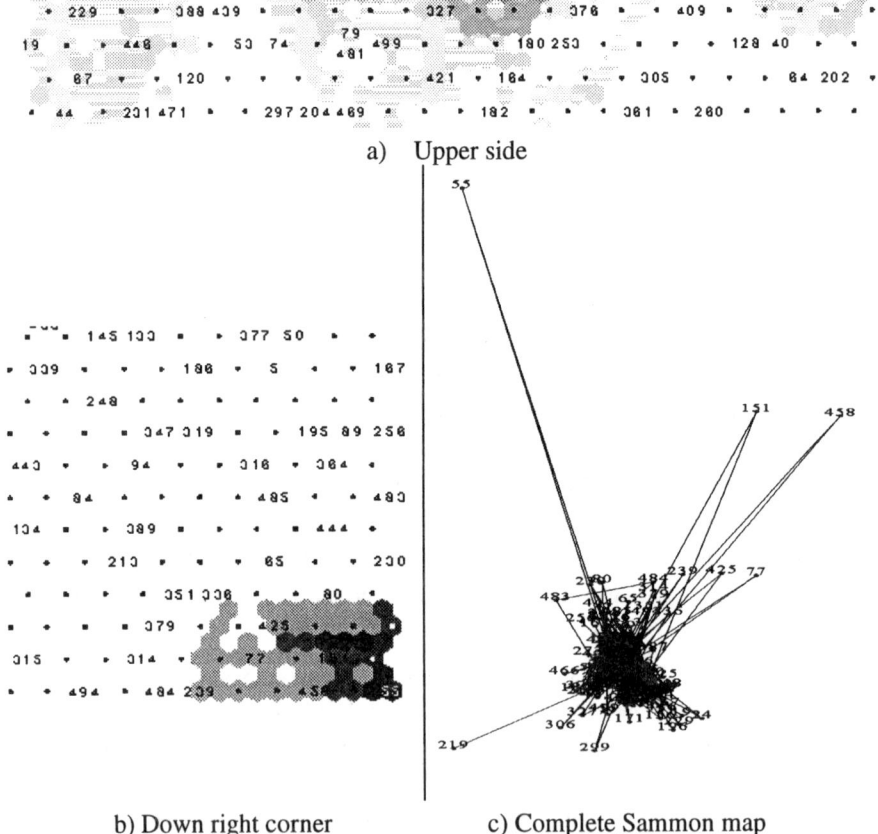

a) Upper side

b) Down right corner   c) Complete Sammon map

Fig. 4. a)b) c) Partial U-mat and Complete Sammon maps for Profitability

In Fig 4.a) the left upper corner has a group including companies: #24, #43, #196, #156, #229, #446, #67, #19, #44 (also light grey). In the upper middle section there are three groups, one with company #219, another with company #299, another with company #306 and another with company #466. In the U-mat lower right corner (Fig. 4 b) there are four distinct groups, one with company #55, another with companies #151 and #458, another with company #77, another with companies #239, #425 and quite a huge one including companies: #494, #484, #314, #379, #351, #336, #65, #80, #230, #444, #485, #483, #316, #364, #256, #89, #195, #167 (light grey - close).

Looking at the Sammon map, Fig.4. c), we verify that the left upper corner group is not very significant since it is quite close to the other companies (in the U-mat they were light grey) and that the same problem applies to the big group in the lower right hand corner. These two groups are not discussed in detail here because, as previously mentioned, we focus in distinctive groups (from black to grey).

Observing the groups located in the upper middle U-mat map (Fig. 4 a), we have the group with company #299 (dark grey) and then three others surrounded by grey. The raw values for these are depicted in table 3. The values are almost all positive for all the profitability attributes (except in company #466). In summary, these companies are quite profitable in financial terms.

Company	ROI	ROE	Profit margin on sales	Sales profitability
#219	16.2	290.9	1.3	123
#306	38.9	NA	0.7	37
#299	44.3	108.9	17.4	1,740
#466	14.3	23.1	10.1	-811

Table 3– Raw results comparison - stock holder perspectives

An interest point to highlight is given by analyzing the raw data of the upper left corner group (even though it is light grey). This is the furthest group in relation to the almost black one and, hence, it is the group with the most profitable companies in the whole set tested. It includes the companies with the maximum (table 1) values for all the attributes. The values are not detailed because it is a light grey group.

Observing now the attribute values for company #55 (Fig 4. b), located in the black and almost black group (lower right hand corner) we see that it has the worst values (see its values in table 1) for all attributes except for the ROI. It is clear that it is disastrous in profitability terms. It should also be noted that company #55 is the Portuguese public railroad and usually public railroad companies are not profitable. Companies #458 and #151, located in the closest group, also have quite bad values for ROI, ROE, the profit margin on sales and sales profitability (table 4). The next closest group (company #77) also shows bad values for all attributes as can be observed in table 4. The last group also has bad values for all attributes (except for ROE which has no available data).

Another interesting conclusion to elicit from table 4 data, is the effect of using an aggregated normalized distance for generating the groups. Companies #458 and #151 are in the same group, though they have very different values for Sales profitability because the overall value is similar. These distortions can only be studied by looking at the raw data.

Company	ROI	ROE	Profit margin on sales	Sales profitability
#458	-26.3	-568.2	-15.2	-671
#151	-20.5	NA	-41.4	-5,664
#77	-3.9	-233.2	-2.2	-562
#425	-13.1	NA	-10.3	-565
#239	-34.1	NA	-8.1	-388

Table 4 – Raw results comparison - stockholder perspectives

In addition, the results obtained in the Kohonen neural network for the raw data (not shown in the paper) were slightly different from the ones obtained with the normalized values because they are less discriminating. I.e. some companies are included in a group that has rather different values in the comparable attributes. For reasons of space these differences are not discussed further in this paper.

D) Banks Perspective - Financial Health

In this section we will discuss the most import indicators to assess the financial health of the 500 biggest Portuguese companies.

The relevant attributes of financial health are, indebtedness, solvency, financial autonomy, general liquidity and cash flow.. Fig. 5 depicts the U-mat map with the most dissimilar groups and Fig. 6 depicts the Sammon map

In the upper left corner of the U-mat (Fig. 5 a) and Sammon map (Fig.6) we observe that there are two very distinct groups containing companies #2 and #3. Then there are four other distinct groups (surrounded by grey neurons), one including companies #1, #8, #48, another including company #17, another including company #24 and finally another with company #19. In the upper right corner (Fig 5 b) there are two other groups, one with company #55 and another with companies #128 and #306. Finally, there are other groups in the lower left corner (Fig. 5 c), but since they are surrounded by light grey neurons (close) we will not discuss them here. However, these light grey groups are quite distinct in the Sammon map (companies #365, #422,

#67, #159 and #24) as can be observed. It should be highlighted that company #24 is included in a different group in the U-mat due to the different distances algorithm used (it is the only case in all tests performed).

a) Upper left corner   b) Upper right corner

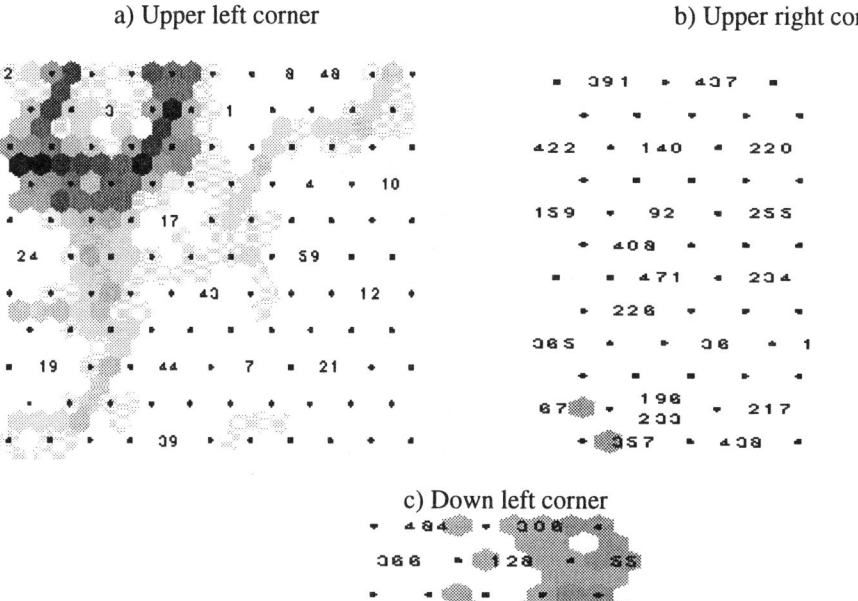

c) Down left corner

Fig. 5.a) b) c) Partial Umat map for Financial Equilibrium

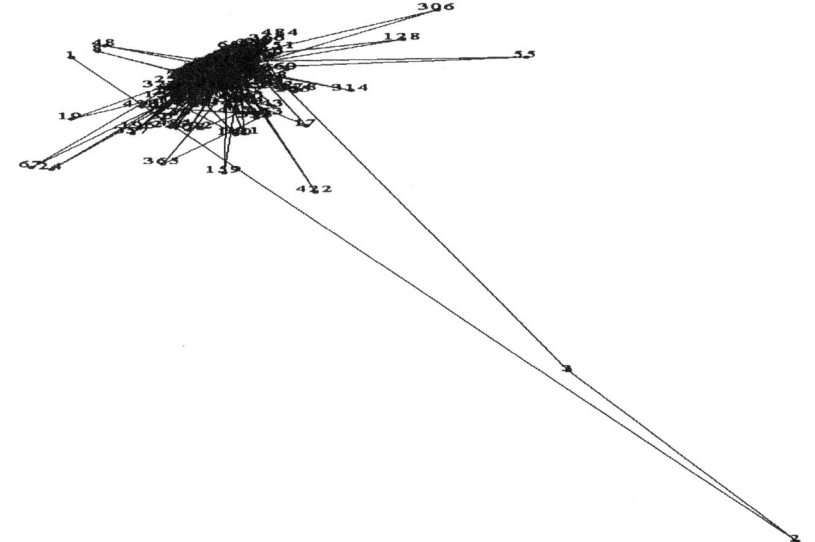

Fig.6. Complete Sammon map for Financial Equilibrium

Looking at the companies raw values we observe that company #2 is extremely different from the others. The main reason is that, comparatively, it has a very high cash-flow: #2 = 197,334. The next closest group in Fig 5 a) (surrounded by black and dark grey neurons) includes company #3, which has a smaller cash flow, #3 = 124,550. Then, the closest four groups (surrounded by grey neurons) include companies #8, #48, #1; #17; #19; #24. The values of the cash flow for the first group are #8 = 22,912, #48 = 22,406, #1 = 26,924; for the second group the value is #17 = 25,840; for the third group the value is #19 = 24,993 and for the fourth group the value is #24 = 26,670. The distinct four groups are due to the values of the other attributes. In the first group the Indebtedness and Solvency ratios are similar (respectively #8 = 80.9; #48 = 85.2; #1 = 72 and #8 = 0.24; #48 = 0.17; #1 = 0.39). In the second group the values for Indebtedness and Solvency are #17 = 44.6 and #17 = 1.24. In the third group the values for Indebtedness and Solvency are #19 = 17.7 and #19 = 4.6. In the fourth group the values for Indebtedness and Solvency are, #24 = 9.4 and #24 = 9.68. After looking at the values it is quite obvious why these companies belong to different groups and why they are very distinct from companies #2 and #3.

We will now discuss the two groups located in the upper right corner (Fig 5 b) one including company #55 and another including companies #306 and #128. The raw data for their financial health are shown in table 5.

Company	Indebtedness	Solvency	Financial autonomy	General liquidity	Cash flow
#55	97.7	0.02	0.02	1	-49,346
#128	192.6	-0.48	-0.92	6	1,414
#306	266.9	-0.63	-1.60	NA	57

Table 5 - Results comparison - banks perspectives

It is very clear that company #55 is considered at the opposite extreme of companies #2 and #3 since its cash flow is rather negative (the minimum found for this attribute). Regarding the next closest group to company #55, we observe that the indebtedness, solvency and financial autonomy are similar and quite different from company #55. However, they are also quite different from the values of the companies in the groups in the opposite direction. An interesting aspect in this last set, is that the classification process grouped together almost bankrupt companies (when the indebtedness ratio is bigger than 100, firms are technically bankrupt). Further, it should be noted that all the companies near this area have bad indebtedness and solvency indicators.

Much more information can be extract from the analysis of the groups and individual neurons, but here we just focused in the most distinctive aspects. In addition, this classification process can facilitate the risk assessment done by banks, since it immediately separates the bad companies from good ones. Further, in this point we do not address the results obtained with raw data because those were more or less similar, though less discriminated. As previously mentioned this is due to using distances as a similarity measure.

Conclusion

We introduced a neural network method for classification of the most important financial and economic attributes of the 500 biggest non-financial Portuguese companies. Our objective was to detect which are the best and worst companies in financial and economic terms according to the most important market players.

The four market perspectives used are: government, stockholders, managers and banks. Market players have different interests when evaluating companies, hence, they look at different indicators. Our group analysis detected, for each market perspective, which are the distinctive companies both in good and bad terms. The information obtained can also be of use for individual investors, which can assess companies following their preferred criteria. An interesting conclusion that the group analysis also unveiled, is that the majority of the companies are quite similar, within each perspective, and only a handful present some outstanding feature(s). This fact is due to the relatively few distinctive groups detected.

In summary, we used a neural network analysis for performing a financial and economic analysis of non-financial companies. With this approach, relevant financial information about similar and dissimilar companies can be extracted. Another advantage of this approach is that the automated isolation of groups could also have been used for a further in-depth financial and economic analysis.

References

Aubert,-Krier, J., (1977), Os Meios de Informação e Decisão, Editorial Presença.

Genari, J. H. et al, (1990), Models of Incremental Concept Formation, in Machine Learning - Paradigms and Methods, Jaime Carbonell (ed). MIT Press/Elvesier

Exame, Edição especial No. 1, As melhores e maiores (1996), Out/Nov

Haykin, S. (1994), Neural Networks - A comprehensive Foundation. Macmillan College Publishing Company.

Kaufman, L. and P. J. Rousseeum, (1990), Finding Groups in Data, A Wiley-Interscience Publucation, New York

Kohonen, T. (1989), Self-Organization and Associative Memory. Springer-Verlag, Berlin, 3rd edition.

Kohonen, T. (1995), Self-Organizing Maps. Springer-Verlag, Heidelberg.

Kohonen, T. et al. (1996), SOM_PAK: The Self-Organizing Map Program Package, Report A31, January 1996, Helsinki University of Technology, Faculty of Information Technology, Laboratory of Computer and Information Science, Finland.

Mirkin, B. (1996), Mathematical Classification and Clustering. Kluwer Academic Publishers.

Nascimento, S. and F. Moura-Pires (1997). A genetic approach to fuzzy clustering with a validity measure fitness function. 2nd International Symposium on Intelligent data Analysis, IDA-97, London, UK, Springer-Verlag.

Sammon Jr., J.W. (1969), A nonlinear mapping for data structure analysis. IEEE Transactions on Computers, C-18(5):401-409, May 1969

Ultsch, A. (1993), Self organized feature maps for monitoring and knowledge acquisition of a chemical process. S. Gielen, B. Kappen (editors), Proceedings of the International Conference on Artificial Neural Networks (ICANN93), 846-867, London. Springer-Verlag.

Whalen, T. and B. Schott, (1986), Financial Ratio Analysis, in: Fuzzy Logic in Knowledge Engineering, (ed) H. Prade and C.V. Negoita, Verlag TUV Rheinland.

Trippi, R. R. and E. Turban, Eds. (1992). Neural networks in Finance and Investing, Irwin. Publishers.

Customer Segmentation with Fuzzy Clustering

Peter Hofmeister

Department of Operations Research, RWTH Aachen

52056 Aachen, Templergraben 64, Germany

peter@or.rwth-aachen.de

Abstract. Due to the increasing competition in the financial market banks have to manage the shift from a seller's to a buyer's market. Consumer's requirements which are at the heart of the strategy have to be identified early by analyzing customers' files. Intelligent data analysis techniques like the fuzzy c-means algorithm use a non-dichotomous assignment to represent the fuzzy customers in homogenous segments. Mathematical hints and the experience of banking experts guarantee are a sufficient validity.

Keywords. Consumer segmentation, financial sector, cluster analysis, fuzzy sets, fuzzy c-means algorithm, validity measure

1   Introduction

Due to the liberalization of the common market in the European Community competition in the financial sector has been increasing for years. The two prevailing reasons for this increase are the reduction of entry barriers, originally raised by government policy and the admission of former prohibited financial products to the market. New competitors from foreign countries and other sectors of the financial market like, for example insurance companies, confront the established commercial banks and intensify the trend to expand the product range. Simultaneously demand shifts from standard to more sophisticated products based on a higher education and information level of the customers. As a result, the exodus of capital and customers compels the banks to adjust their business strategies from an inside to an outside orientation and to manage the shift from a seller's to a buyer's market.

Therefore, the consumer's requirements are at the heart of the strategy. The early identification of demand and the development of appropriate and reasonably prized products become the major challenge of product managers in the financial services sector. Since patents cannot successfully prohibit imitation of service products, supreme effort is placed on the identification. To identify which products should be developed or imitated, respectively, the established banks have the advantage of keeping files on the transactions carried out for their customers. The customers' records cover not only past transactions (e.g. savings, loans, net margin) but also personal data like income, real property, age and so on. Based on these files it is possible to detect latent desires and needs, which can be used to select or to develop products to satisfy them. Moreover, it is possible to estimate the sales potential more accurately in avoidance of wasting resources in marginal, i.e. less valuable segments of the market. When the segments and their assigned products have been identified, one has to select qualified media to promote each product to the focused segment without leakage due to non-selective advertising. In summary, one has to work out what kinds of (potential) customers are in the market and to cover their needs by well-promoted products.

2 Data Analysis Techniques

Since the penetration of a market in its entirety is less effective than to target single customers - the latter being less efficient in most situations - a compromise has to be made. The aim of such a method is to divide the heterogeneous total market in homogeneous sub-markets. Due to the homogeneity each sub-market can be served efficiently partly preserving the efficiency by targeting each group of customers in its entirety.

The underlying rationale for dividing the market requests the segmentation of customers by distinguishing features like, for example, age or income. Therefore, a promising method has to identify meaningful features and to segment the market relative to them. The features must permit to infer the customers' future market behavior and to classify the customers into different groups with respect to their behavior. It is noteworthy that the market behavior includes not only the action undertaken by customers but also the possibilities of a company to influence it by marketing activities. The objects, i.e. the customers belonging to a group must have an almost identical feature profile and are assumed to act (and react) at the market in the same way.

Both, the identification of relevant features and the grouping of objects are issues of data analysis. Data analysis methods provide powerful techniques to reduce complexity and to uncover the structure in the data. Traditional methods like factor analysis, discriminant analysis, AID or regression analysis give hints for selecting the most expressive attributes. Apart from techniques like multidimensional scaling and Q-factor analysis, cluster analysis plays a primary role in grouping objects [Aaker and Day, 1986].

Cluster techniques are categorized in graph-theoretic, hierarchical, and objective-functional methods [Zimmermann, 1996, p. 245-249]. Graph-theoretic methods regard the objects as nodes, and the weights of the edges represent the similarity between the objects. Typically, one breaks edges in a minimal spanning tree to form sub-graphs which are interpreted as clusters (see Figure 1).

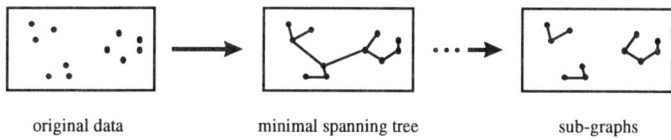

original data   minimal spanning tree   sub-graphs

Figure 1. Graph-theoretic clustering methods

Hierarchical techniques assign each object to a class irrevocably and a partially grouping cannot be undone. The starting point of agglomerative (or bottom up) hierarchical methods is a total segmentation, i.e. each object represents one cluster, and the method proceeds by merging successively the two most similar clusters. The divisive (or top down) method heads in the opposite direction starting with one cluster containing all objects and successively splits the groups of objects (see Figure 2).

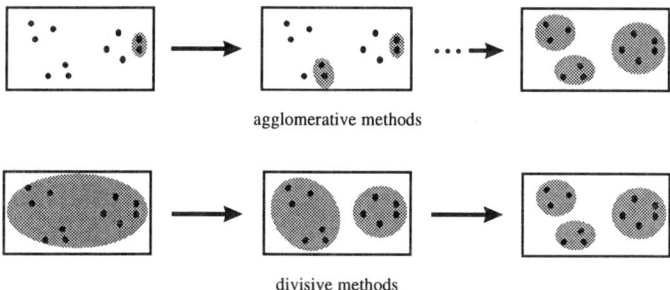

agglomerative methods

divisive methods

Figure 2. Agglomerative and divisive clustering methods

One disadvantage of these methods are the contradicting similarity criteria (for example single, average, and complete linkage) indicating at different clusters to merge or to split, respectively. Another disadvantage is the irrevocable assignment, which does not take into account subsequent steps and therefore can cause a sub-optimal segmentation.

Objective-functional methods avoid this way of short-sighted segmentation because they allow to change the assignment according to a segmentation criterion and to rearrange the clusters in the iterations (see Figure 3). The criterion measures the fit of the overall segmentation by minimizing the distance between the objects and center of the nearest cluster.

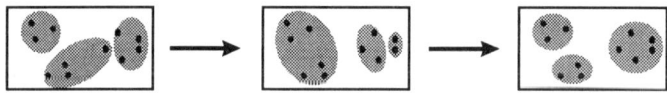

Figure 3. Objective-functional clustering methods: Rearrangement of clusters

But this method has two limitations: First, optima of the objective function are not identified as local extrema and pretend an unwarranted global optimality. Second, this method requires the number of the clusters as an input. Since for most problems this is not available from the outset, one has to carry out the procedure for several numbers of clusters and to identify the appropriate number of clusters according to some criteria, e.g. the elbow criterion at the end.

The most important limitation of these clustering techniques is up to a more general issue: Each object is assigned to exactly one cluster indicating at a distinct separation of the groups. They use crisp methods to partition objects even if these objects are not defined in a crisp way, and if they are crisply defined, there can still be a fuzzy separation.

A classical example, the butterfly, is shown below to explicate the difficulties of clustering crisp objects in a dichotomous way (see Figure 4). The original data in the middle is represented by fifteen objects that have to be clustered in (obviously) two classes. Any traditional cluster technique bears one drawback: the object in the middle has to be classified either to the left (result A) or to the right (result B) segment. Since it not possible to settle this problem by a compromise and no further information is available, one has to assign it randomly.

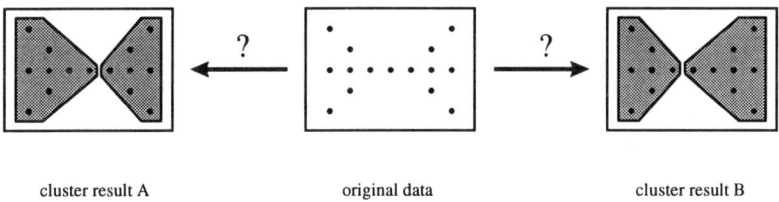

cluster result A   original data   cluster result B

Figure 4. The butterfly [Ruspini, 1970]

The dichotomous methods are called crisp (or traditional) because they are non-fuzzy approaches. Since their validity of representing fuzzy phenomena (as most objects are) in a proper way can be questioned, fuzzified versions of several fuzzy data analysis techniques were developed to overcome this limitation [Zimmermann, 1996]. Fuzzy linear regression analysis and fuzzy clustering techniques like the fuzzy c-means algorithm are two of these well-known non-dichotomous methods. In recent years other intelligent data analysis techniques matured: Knowledge-based clustering approaches emerged from the area of artificial intelligence using (linguistic) rules for the segmentation of objects. Another promising technique descended from the field of neural networks and can closely be connected with the knowledge-based approaches by the hidden learning of clustering rules. But up to now, the fuzzy c-means algorithm remains one of the best-known and explored techniques with an impressive number of successful applications.

3 Fuzzy C-Means Algorithm

The fuzzy c-means algorithm [Bezdek, 1981, pp. 65-70] descends from the ISO-DATA algorithm, a dichotomous objective-functional clustering technique, by expanding the binary assignment to fuzzy membership values.

Let $X = \{x_1, x_2, ..., x_n\}$ be a set of given objects, so that each x_i denotes a vector representing the values of the attributes $j = 1, ..., m$ of the object. Each object is related to a cluster $k = 1, ..., c$ by assigning a value μ_{ik}. The center of each cluster is depicted by an m-dimensional vector v_k that stands for the objects belonging to the cluster in their entirety.

The ISODATA algorithm [Ball and Hall, 1967] minimizes the sum of distances between the objects and the center of the cluster to which they are assigned to unequivocally, i.e. the μ_{ik} are restricted to be binary:

$$\mu_{ik} \in \{0, 1\}$$

An object i belongs to the cluster k (1) or not (0) and it has to be assigned to exactly one cluster:

$$\sum_{k=1}^{c} \mu_{ik} = 1 \quad \forall \; i = 1, ..., n$$

The widely accepted criterion to minimize is the sum of the variances of all attributes j and objects i in each cluster k:

$$\min \quad \frac{1}{n} \sum_{k=1}^{c} \sum_{i=1}^{n} \sum_{j=1}^{m} \left(x_{ij} - v_{kj} \right)^2 \cdot \mu_{ik}$$

Fuzzy clustering techniques expand the restrictive range of the assignment to the unit interval, so that they are the well-known degrees of membership of the fuzzy set theory:

$$\mu_{ik} \in [0, 1]$$

The variance in each cluster is influenced by every object whose membership is not zero. Since it is not plausible to let objects, which belong strongly to cluster A, contribute to the variance of a cluster B, an exponent m is given to the membership values in the objective function.

$$\min \quad \frac{1}{n} \sum_{k=1}^{c} \sum_{i=1}^{n} \sum_{j=1}^{m} \left(x_{ij} - v_{kj} \right)^2 \cdot \mu_{ik}^m$$

The range of m is restricted to $[1, \infty)$, taking the lower value the fuzzy c-means algorithm converges "in theory" to a generalized hard c-means, i.e. a crisp, binary assignment similar to that obtained by the ISODATA algorithm [Bezdek, 1981, p. 70]. As m increases, the fuzzification is amplified. For $m \to \infty$, all centers of the clusters coincide with the arithmetic mean of the values of all objects and, therefore, each object is uniformly assigned to the clusters, i.e. $\mu_{ik} \to 1/c$. As a result, any existing structure in the data is concealed [Zimmermann, 1996, p. 259]. Up to now, no theoretically justified rule for choosing m exists, but as pointed out by Bezdek, it seems plausible to choose $m = 2$ to minimize the equivalent total squared error [Bezdek, 1981, p. 72].

Since the minimization of the objective function is hard to solve, even for a small number of clusters and objects, one approximates the minimum by an iterative algorithm including the following four steps [Zimmermann, 1996, p. 258].

1) Initialization.

The algorithm starts with a selection of the parameters for the number of the clusters c and the weighting exponent m. In addition, a first assignment of objects to clusters expressed by membership values μ_{ik} in a membership matrix has to be given (see Table 1). To terminate the iterative process, a termination criterion ε has to be chosen. By reducing this criterion the degree of precision is increased, i.e. the approximation deviates less from the (local) optimal solution.

Table 1. Membership matrix

		cluster k				
		1	2	...	c-1	c
	1	0.3	0.01	...	0.08	0.23
object i	...			μ_{ik}		
	n	0.17	0.05		0.09	0.45

2) Update of the centers.

Based on this assignment all values of the single attributes of the centers can be computed by

$$v_{kj} = \frac{\sum\limits_{k=1}^{n}(\mu_{ik})^m x_{ij}}{\sum\limits_{k=1}^{n}(\mu_{ik})^m} \qquad \forall\, j=1,...,m \quad \forall\, k=1,...,c$$

3) Update of the membership values.

Since the centers moved, one has to calculate new membership degrees by

$$\mu_{ik} = \frac{1}{\sum\limits_{s=1}^{c}\left(d_{ik}/d_{is}\right)^{\frac{2}{m-1}}} \qquad \forall\, k=1,...,c \;\; \forall\, i=1,...,n$$

where $$d_{ik} = \sum_{j=1}^{m} \left(x_{ij} - v_{kj} \right)^2 \quad \forall\, k, i$$

4) Termination.

The algorithm terminates if the change of the membership values is smaller than ε.

$$\left| \mu_{ik}^{old} - \mu_{ik}^{new} \right| \leq \varepsilon \quad \forall\, k = 1,...,c \quad \forall\, i = 1,...,n$$

Otherwise, a new iteration starts at step 2.

Since there are five parameters to choose, the fuzzy c-means algorithm represents a class of clustering techniques. As already pointed out, the value of ε influences the exactness of the approximation and the exponent m weights each object to control fuzziness of the final segmentation. The choice of the membership matrix has an effect on the optimality, because different starting points can lead to different local optima. In addition, one can use other distance measures instead of the Euclidean distance, especially if the scale level of the data does not justify this distance measure.

Another problem arises by the choice of the proper number of clusters. Since the number of segments is not obvious at the outset in most situations, different heuristics can be suggested. At first, it is possible to use hierarchical clustering techniques to find the appropriate value by detecting qualitative leaps. Secondly, there are several criteria introduced in the literature to compare fuzzy partitions with respect to their number of clusters [Ismael, 1988, p. 455]. The prevalent criteria are the partition coefficient F and the partition entropy H whose definitions and properties are given below [Bezdek, 1981, p. 100-112].

$$F(c) = \sum_{k=1}^{n} \sum_{i=1}^{c} \frac{\left(\mu_{ik} \right)^2}{n} \qquad \frac{1}{c} \leq F(c) \leq 1$$

$$H(c) = -\frac{1}{n} \sum_{k=1}^{n} \sum_{i=1}^{c} \mu_{ik} \cdot \log_e \left(\mu_{ik} \right) \qquad 0 \leq H(c) \leq \log_e(c)$$

The crisper a partition becomes, the higher is the value of the partition coefficient and the partition entropy decreases. The limitations of these criteria are due to their lack of any suitable benchmark. Following the elbow criterion, a heuristic rule to choose the "best" number of clusters is to take the value of c* so that the increase of F from c*-1 to c* lies below the trend and the same holds for the decrease of the partition entropy that should be above the trend [Zimmermann, 1996, p. 263]. All criteria should be used carefully since they are only mathematical hints that needs to be augmented by experience and knowledge of the analyzed objects.

4 Data

The study is based on a random sample taken from the data base of a German commercial bank. Companies and customers of the public sector were excluded, because there already exists a customer oriented policy to serve them individually. The random sample contains 300 customers who are described by one demographic and four socio-economic features, namely age, income, money property, credit and contributed profit margin. Since the identification of all relevant attributes is of high significance, personal bankers were integrated in the process of the feature selection. All identified features have a sufficient discriminatory potential with only a small correlation indicating their independence (see Figure 5). In addition, all attributes can be measured on a ratio scale, therefore, allowing to use the Euclidean norm to calculate the distance between the objects.

Correlation Matrix - Bankdat dat		Age [Ages]	Income [DM/Month]	Money_Property [DM]	Credit [DM]	Contr._Margin [DM/Year]
1	Age	1,000	0,274	0,330	-0,024	0,282
2	Income	0,274	1,000	0,437	-0,305	0,194
3	Money_Propert	0,330	0,437	1,000	0,025	0,336
4	Credit	-0,024	-0,305	0,025	1,000	-0,213
5	Contr._Margin	0,282	0,194	0,336	-0,213	1,000

Figure 5. Correlation matrix

Since the dimensions of the attributes vary to a considerable amount (see Figure 6), the data is normalized to the unit interval in order to avoid an unjustified weighting. Without normalization, for example, the age would not influence the segmentation compared to the credit.

DataEngine$^©$, a software tool of MIT GmbH, is used for the calculation. It contains several easy-to-use modules for data analysis based on intelligent techniques like neural nets, knowledge-based reasoning, and the fuzzy c-means algorithm. It supports the preprocessing of data by putting several statistical tools at the user's disposal and provides tools for graphical representation of data and results.

		Age [Ages]	Income [DM/Month]	Money_Property [DM]	Credit [DM]	Contr._Margin [DM/Year]
1	Minimum	1,000	0,000	0,000	210.000.000	-1.000,000
2	Maximum	94,000	12.500,000	175.000,000	0,000	1.620,000
3	Mean Value	41,670	3.085,950	19.465,747	-10.576,193	126,863
4	Variance	541,707	569.093,011	808.953.688,183	7222E+009	117.663,978
5	Std. Deviation	23,275	2.563,024	28.442,111	33.274,944	343,022
6	Range	93,000	12.500,000	175.000,000	210.000,000	2.620,000
7	Skewness	0,157	0,971	2,908	-4,046	1,339
8	Kurtosis	-0,901	0,914	10,666	16,792	4,635
9	Sum	12.501,000	925.785,000	5.839.724,000	172.858,000	38.059,000
10	Sum of Squares	682.887,000	1085E+009	3,555517E+011	6161E+011	40.009.821,000
11	Number of Values	300,000	300,000	300,000	300,000	300,000
12	Number of missing Values	0,000	0,000	0,000	0,000	0,000

Figure 6. General statistics of the data

The fuzzy c-means algorithm is initialized with $m = 2$, a random membership matrix, and $\varepsilon = 0.001$. Since for this problem an upper bound of 10 clusters seems to be reasonable, the calculation is carried out for $c = 2,...,10$. To select the "best" number of clusters, one refers to the mathematical hints. The shapes of both the partition coefficient and the partition entropy indicate 7 clusters, because the partition entropy is below the trend when c moves from 6 to 7, and the opposite holds for the partition coefficient (see Figure 7).

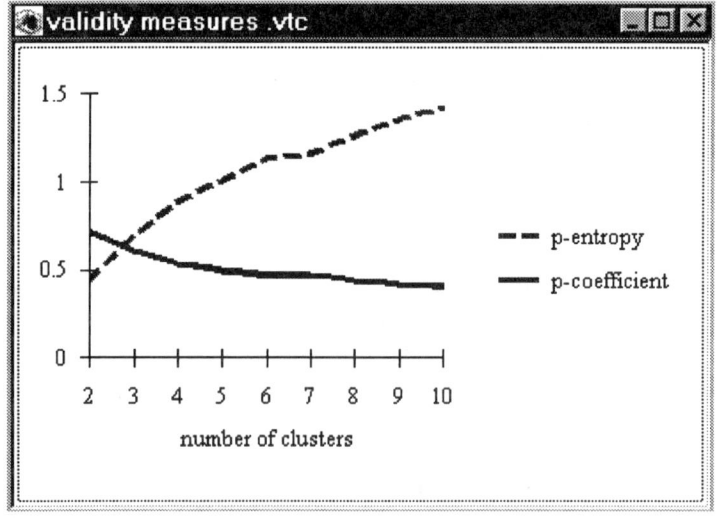

Figure 7. Validity measures

After the selection of the appropriate number of clusters, their centers can be investigated. To obtain the real values of the centers v_k of the seven clusters the normalization is offset (see Figure 8).

		Age [Ages]	Income [DM/Month]	Money_Property [DM]	Credit [DM]	Contr._Margin [DM/Year]
1	Cluster_A	59,883	2.859,464	13.045,347	-4.028,722	85,545
2	Cluster_B	52,086	5.302,008	47.157,455	-11.332,604	254,160
3	Cluster_C	77,398	2.166,579	30.687,449	-1.810,677	287,553
4	Cluster_D	30,699	2.650,055	8.731,271	-4.659,572	26,567
5	Cluster_E	9,640	143,882	3.640,496	456,568	7,932
6	Cluster_F	44,822	5.276,313	25.973,416	-44.396,258	266,545
7	Cluster_G	38,343	5.704,428	16.645,518	-8.783,750	68,954

Figure 8. Centers of the segments

5 Discussion

Since the "best" number of clusters is selected only by mathematical measures of validity the results of the analysis were presented to banking experts to reconsider the validity by their experience. Subsequent interviews revealed, that the segmentation obtained by the cluster analysis is a good reflection of the existing customer pool. Each segment is easily recognized as a real customer, for example, cluster E represents young children with only small "income", money property, and credit. Their margin can be neglected in comparison to clients of cluster B, C, and F. The latter contribute considerably to the (actual) profit of the bank, are middle-aged, have a high income, and a small amount of money property compared to their credit.

To address marketing activities one has to know, which customers belong to a segment. Traditional clustering techniques offer this dichotomous partition, but they have a drawback. Since all customers are assigned equally to the segment one can not select the most typical objects to concentrate the resources. Attention has to be paid to each customer of a segment, because all kinds of selection are an arbitrary act. Quite the reverse, the fuzzy partition enables to rank the customers by referring to their membership values. In addition, depending on an α-level a customer i can be assigned to a segment k if and only if his membership μ_{ik} value is not less than the threshold α. By varying the α-level, marketing activities can be directed to customers in a very flexible way. Figure 9 presents the membership values of five selected customers, whose ranking for cluster A is 61, 63, 65, 62, 64.

Bank 7 clusters.dat	Cluster_A	Cluster_B	Cluster_C	Cluster_D	Cluster_E	Cluster_F	Cluster_G
61	0,756	0,041	0,074	0,041	0,013	0,036	0,039
62	0,051	0,160	0,026	0,069	0,023	0,144	0,527
63	0,334	0,086	0,381	0,051	0,022	0,065	0,061
64	0,006	0,004	0,003	0,024	0,950	0,005	0,007
65	0,138	0,058	0,687	0,028	0,013	0,040	0,034

Figure 9. Membership values of selected customers

For $\alpha = 0.3$, Figure 10 contains the crisp assignment of the clients. Since, for example, cluster C comprises client 63 and client 65, both are targets of a marketing activity prepared for cluster C. Client 63 is also a member of cluster A, so that he is involved in marketing programs for cluster A, too.

Bank 7 clusters 0.3-level.dat	Cluster_A	Cluster_B	Cluster_C	Cluster_D	Cluster_E	Cluster_F	Cluster_G
61	1,000	0,000	0,000	0,000	0,000	0,000	0,000
62	0,000	0,000	0,000	0,000	0,000	0,000	1,000
63	1,000	0,000	1,000	0,000	0,000	0,000	0,000
64	0,000	0,000	0,000	0,000	1,000	0,000	0,000
65	0,000	0,000	1,000	0,000	0,000	0,000	0,000

Figure 10. Assignment at a 0.3-level

The advantage of the fuzzy clustering is the possibility to select a threshold appropriate for each problem. It is, therefore, possible, to assign a customer to one or more segments, depending on the α-cut. There is a also chance not to assign an object to any cluster. This anomaly is caused by an economical view: Since the budget to serve clients is limited, one selects only clients, who fit to the cluster very well. Clients with a small membership indicate small sensibility to cluster-specific marketing actions, thus wasting resources to unpromising customers. These customers are removed from the cluster or expelled from the marketing activity, respectively.

DataEngine supports the representation of the membership degrees by a tool which allows to display the membership graphically (see Figure 11).

Graphically, client 61 can be regarded as a member of segment A, since his membership function takes the highest value for cluster A. The other clients can be assigned in the same way. This goes along with a hard c-means algorithm which assigns each object to one class.

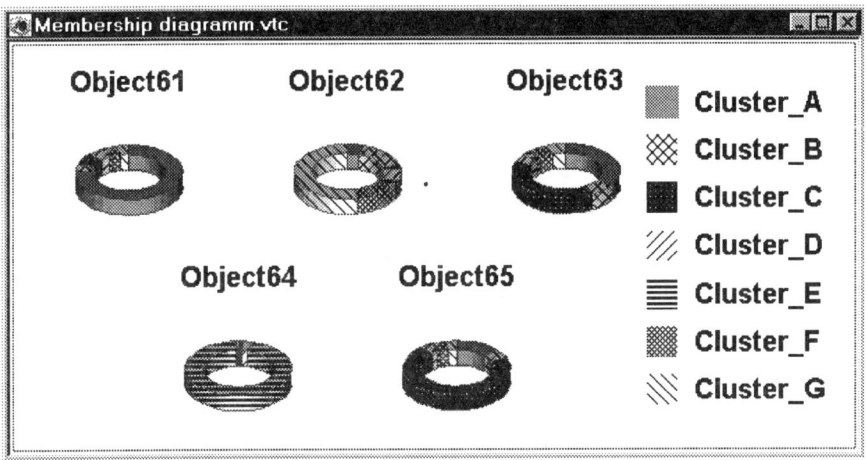

Figure 11. Membership degrees of selected customers

Thereby, one gets a good understanding of the quality of the segmentation. Customers without an unequivocal membership like client 63, who can be assigned to cluster A or C, have to be reviewed in detail. The reason for the ambiguous assignment can be twofold: at first, the client can be closely related to both clusters, i.e. he can be regarded as a member of both segments. Secondly, he lies between both segments, but is not close to them, i.e. he is an outlier. Since his membership degrees have to sum up to unit, and the closest clusters are A and C, he is assigned to them to a large extent. If the number of those outliers is large, one has to examine, whether the segmentation is too coarse, and gets another hint for a more appropriate, i.e. larger, number of clusters that can be included in the validation process as well as the mathematical hints.

To decide which number of clusters is appropriate one has to consider not only the data but also the purpose of the clustering. Even if the data are better reflected by a larger number of clusters there can still be a reason to reduce c. As more clusters are taken into account the size of each cluster decreases. From an economic point of view it can be too expensive to serve these small segments.

The means to influence clients by marketing activities have to be considered as well. The granulation level determines the effectiveness of the marketing program because fine-grained segmentation allows to address to very homogenous classes. The more custom-made the activities are the more increases the chance to succeed. To obtain homogenous clusters, one has to raise the α-level. As a result, the size of each segment decreases. Therefore, by choosing an α-level - appropriate for a marketing program - one can estimate the size of a segment. Since the α-level is positively related to the homogeneity of the buyer's behavior and has an unfavorable effect on the size of the segment the calibration of α and the focus of the marketing program depend closely on each other.

6 Conclusions

Crisp clustering algorithms have the drawback that an assignment of a customer to a cluster excludes him or her from another segment. Although this seems reasonable at first sight, problems will arise if two almost similar customers are members of two different classes. A product or a marketing activity is not focused on crisp target markets but on segments with fuzzy boundaries. Therefore it is more convenient to assign membership degrees to each customer in each market segment. Besides, the reliability of the underlying crisp values must be taken into account. Sometimes the values are well-estimated but have to be interpreted as representations of a narrow interval, which prohibits one from separating values with small differences too strictly. Another advantage is the possibility to rank the customers with reference to their membership to a selected class. The ranking enables marketing specialists to select a set of customers either by specification of a threshold value for the membership degree or by restricting the number of elements in the set and selecting only customers with a high membership degree. For example, the resulting crisp subset enables a product manager to determine which customers should receive a mailing.

The quality of the input data is of importance, too. The coarser and more unreliable the information is the less it is justified to use crisp algorithms. Fuzzy clustering techniques are less sensitive to incorrect data because the membership values do not change significantly because of a small deviation. A crisp clustering is likely to assign the object another segment if the deviation exceeds a specific - even small - threshold.

On the other hand, the fuzzy clustering approach is more sensitive to dynamic processes. The needs of customers vary in time by a slow process indicated by small changes in the attributes. In general, crisp clustering techniques change the assignment less frequently, because a threshold has to be exceeded, and they do it more abruptly compared to fuzzy methods. Therefore, fuzzy approaches follow the advance more immediately and exactly, and offer more hints for forecasting techniques.

The limitations of the presented method study are twofold. At first, there arise problems with respect to the validity of the data. The study is oriented toward the past, because it relies on - perhaps obsolete - data of the past. In addition, only existing customer relations are analyzed which can obstruct the view toward the total market including its potential. Secondly, the problem of the appropriate choice for the parameters of the fuzzy c-means algorithm can be a process of trial and error.

Despite the limitations one gains a valuable insight into the problem. This became plain by the favorable reception given to the results by the commercial bank. Since the banking experts were involved in the study, they were confident that the method can support their market research and use them for their marketing activities. In summary, the fuzzy c-means algorithm is a means to an end with which one can achieve impressive results if it is augmented by theory, experience, and common sense.

7 References

Aaker, D.A. and Day, G.S. [1986]. *Marketing Research*. 3ed. New York.

Ball, G.H. and Hall, D.J. [1967]. A Clustering Technique for Summarizing Multivariate Data. *Behavior Science*, Vol. 12, pp. 153-155.

Bezdek, J.C. [1981]. *Pattern Recognition with Fuzzy Objective Function Algorithms*. New York.

Gupta, M.M. and Yamakawa, T. (eds.) [1988]. *Fuzzy Computing: Theory, Hardware, and Applications*. New York.

Ismail, M.A. [1988]. Soft Clustering: Algorithms and Validity of Solutions. In *Gupta and Yamakawa*, pp. 445-471.

Ruspini, E. [1970]. Numerical Methods for Fuzzy Clustering. *Information Science*, Vol. 2, pp. 239-253.

Zimmermann, H.-J. [1996]. *Fuzzy Set Theory - and its Applications*. 3ed. Boston.

A Rejects Management Information System by Means of Fuzzy Logic

Nina Vojdani[1] and Michael Bellmann[2]

[1] University of Dortmund, Department of Computer Science I,
Otto-Hahn-Str. 16, 44227 Dortmund, Germany.
E-Mail: vojdani@ls1.informatik.uni-dortmund.de
[2] KPMG Unternehmensberatung GmbH, Am Bonneshof 35,
40474 Düsseldorf, Germany. E-Mail: mbellmann@kpmg.com

Abstract. A dynamic changing business environment demands management information systems to sustain and improve the competitive capabilities of manufacturing enterprises. To consider practical and specialized issues of the use of fuzzy logic in those systems, a Rejects Management Information System (R-MIS) to detect problems and irregularities in the manufacturing of goods has been developed. The multi-dimensional database system pcExpress and the graphical tool Express/EIS from ORACLE have been used to implement R-MIS. This project has been a cooperation between the University of Dortmund and a subsidiary company of a well known German automotive enterprise.

Keywords. Rejects Management Information System, Fuzzy Logic, Fuzzy Set, Linguistic Variable, Linguistic Term, Fuzzy Query, Selector, Manufacturing, Production Process, Partial Information System, pcExpress, Express/EIS, OLAP, Multidimensional Database System

1
Differentiation of Information Systems for Management

The terminus management information system was born in the middle of the 60s. It was intended to model enterprises with their complex embedding in environment in a single information system and to store *all* relevant data. This integrated system was supposed to deliver information for every relevant state of affairs for management. The so called "total systems approach" has revealed itself to be too complex and not practical [1,2,3]. As a result of its failure, management information systems are realized today as partial information systems, which differentiate with respect to the following issues [4]:

- Hierarchical adjustment / Addressees of information systems
- Functional adjustment
- Computer-technical support
- Structuredness of the task

Hierarchical adjustment / Addressees of information systems

A management information system can support management at different hierarchical levels. The management concept of Anthony for example distinguishes three tasks with respect to the functional dimension of management [4]:

1. Strategic Planning
2. Management Control
3. Operational Control

The characteristics of decisions and needed data differs on every management level. To reduce the complexity of the design of information systems and to improve their usefulness, it makes sense to focus on a limited number of addressees on the same management level.

Functional adjustment

In a similar manner, it is useful to limit the thematic focus of a management information system to a coherent, manageable complex of problems. Currently, business information systems are usually focused on a special functional area of an enterprise, for example procurement, manufacturing, sales, finance & accountancy as well as personnel. In future, process-oriented approaches will increasingly gain importance.

Computer-technical support

Computer-technical support means the selective application of software concepts and hardware technologies in information systems. The employment of appropriate software simplifies the process of constructing such a system. Examples are: Decision Support System generators, specific planning languages, database systems and model/method base systems. Methods for the modularization of software are subsumed as well. On the other hand it has to be determined, which is the best fit for the hardware of the information system. This deals with the choice of computers (PC, workstation, host) and appropriate equipment (screen, mouse, touch-screen, colour printer, etc.).

Structuredness of the task

Computers can solve only well structured problems, but integrated man-machine-systems can solve semistructured problems in an interactive decision process. Research in artificial intelligence deals with the problem to approximate badly structured problems through expert systems. The structuredness of the task determines the involved methods and techniques as well as the handling of the management information system.

The practical necessity of the differentiation of management information systems with respect to these issues has led to a variety of terms in this area, e.g. executive information systems, decision support systems and expert systems [1,2,3,4].

2
Fuzzy Logic and Management Information Systems

The success of using Fuzzy Logic in management information systems has to be measured by the benefit for the addressee. Fuzzy Logic seems to be especially appropriate for the use in information systems because of the following considerations [5,6,7,8]:

- The man-machine communication can be handled more human,
- the information processing capacity of the human being can be better used and
- it allows the implementation of human reasoning and heuristics.

3
The Concept of the Rejects Management Information System (R-MIS)

3.1
Main Features of R-MIS

In recent research, no special interest has been paid to the transformation of data to *information* concerning the topic of rejects [9]. Within the scope of this prerequisite it is indispensable to prevent "data overload" by devoting extensive attention to the structure of the user-interface of the information system [8].

The Rejects Management Information System (R-MIS) is realized as partial information system. R-MIS can be described as information reporting system with capabilities for fuzzy-analysis. The aim is to give the production manager the possibility to detect problems and irregularities in the manufacturing of goods [9,10].

The Rejects Management Information System

- gives the production manager the possibility to shorten reaction times for taking countermeasures to eliminate reasons for undesired production states or reduce their effects;
- assists the production manager in optimizing the production process by providing high quality information.

In the end, this means cost saving for companies. R-MIS has the following main features:

- An analysis of rejects data is on different aggregation levels easily possible.
- Contextsensitive graphics visualize time series and the composition of rejects cost with respect to different base dimensions.
- The selector is the tool to identify hot spots in the quantity of data. Natural language queries are supported. Corresponding linguistic variables and terms could be interactively defined and used in a query.

For example, trends like an increase of *rejects share* should be recognizable to the user to allow the early taking of countermeasures. Therefore, the system has to offer a variety of aggregate information, but it also has to place detailed information at the user's disposal to enable the identification of the concrete weak spot. Fuzzy Logic is used to build up query-like selections to crystallize out the most promising spots.

R-MIS operates on PC-basis with the operating system MS-DOS and the software pcExpress and Express/EIS from ORACLE[1] [11,12,13,14]. PcExpress and Express/EIS are OLAP(On-Line Analytical Processing)- tools. PcExpress is characterized by the manufacturer as an integrated Decision Support System for a wide area of business planning and analysis applications. Its core consists of a database system and a 4'th generation language. The database system is based on a multidimensional data model. Express/EIS is an front-end, which allows the easy construction of an userfriendly interface. Rejects data is imported from an IBM AS/400 host via network and is automatically stored in the database by the use of update procedures.

3.2
Data Acquisition

Problems in data acquisition are frequently neglected, but nevertheless it is a very important area in the construction of management information systems. In any case, the cost-benefit-ratio with respect to the effort for data acquisition and the validity as well as the expressiveness of data has to be evaluated. This issue has to be considered separately for every enterprise and production structure.

---

[1] In 1995, the field of OLAP-technology of IRI Software was sold to ORACLE Corporation.

3.3
Organization of Rejects Data in R-MIS

Rejects data like *rejects cost* and *rejects share* can be organized along base dimensions[2]

- month
- part number
- burden center
- operation[3]
- flaw cause

One can imagine the data to be stored in a five-dimensional cube, where each axis is built out of the values of a dimension. Each field in the cube is determined by a combination of values for each of the five dimensions and stores the corresponding rejects data. Because not every combination of these base dimensions values is of practical relevance, R-MIS uses the special pcExpress-structure of a conjoint dimension to avoid most of the redundancy in the system.

The rejects data can be easily aggregated by the user over one or more base dimensions to get a top-level view. For example, one may want to see the *rejects cost* per month, part number, burden center and operation aggregated over all flaw causes, or one may want to see the *rejects cost* differentiated only per month and part number.

Actual and recent data of *rejects cost* or *rejects share* as well as related indexes of time series are an important analysis-tool:

- maximum of time series
- minimum of time series
- average value of time series
- standard deviation of time series

In addition, data on the quantity of rejects and good (intermediate) products are available.

Additional information like for example the share of the *rejects cost* caused by a specific flaw in relation to the total *rejects cost* is also at one's disposal[4].

R-MIS also uses a parts list. This parts list contains information about the parts, which are assembled to the final product. The grouping of final products with respect to the criterion *product type*, which is another very practical information, is also stored. On the other hand, parts can be grouped by the criterion *part type*. R-MIS

---

[2] This data organization is appropriate for many, but not all companies. However, an adaption is easily possible.

[3] It is possible, that the same operation is carried out at different burden centers.

[4] i.e. the composition of *rejects cost* of a part in a specific month, concerning a specific operation and a specific burden center.

stores the part type for every part. These data serve for the purpose of improving the ease of the selection of information by the user of R-MIS.

3.4
Fuzzy Sets and Rejects Data

Fuzzy sets are an appropriate tool to model rejects data. Figure 1 shows an exemplary definition of a linguistic variable *rejects cost*[5].

A feature of R-MIS is, that the user can interactively define linguistic variables and terms, assign them to the data and use them in a query. For example, the user can freely change the definition of the variable *rejects cost* according to his needs.

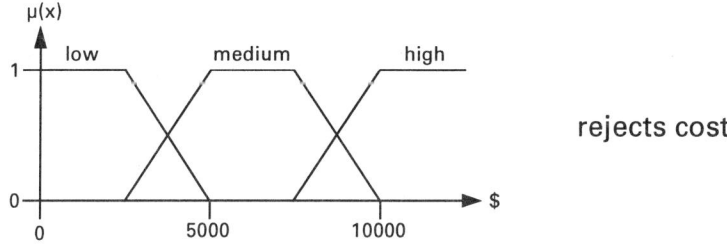

Figure 1: Example of a linguistic variable *rejects cost*

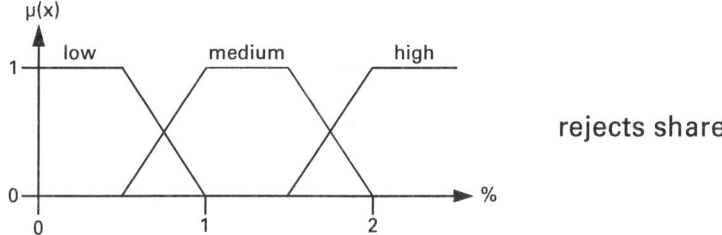

Figure 2: Example of a linguistic variable *rejects share*

Figure 2 shows an exemplary definition of a linguistic variable *rejects share*. The sense of the use of a linguistic variable *rejects share* in R-MIS can be illustrated by a simple scenario: When you tell someone that *rejects share* is 1% for the manufacturing of a special part during a special operation, only production specialists can tell you whether it is high or not. Tell someone that *rejects share* is high, an assessment is implicit and the less important detail of the concrete value is left out. In this sense, the

---

[5] Without any restriction of universal applicability we consider only normalized fuzzy sets.

fuzzyfication prevents data overload. Another effect is, that the comparison of values between different parts is easily feasible. Usually, the definition of linguistic variables *rejects share* is fixed in advance for every part and operation by the corresponding production specialists and needs to be changed only in case of production process modifications.

3.5
The Selector of R-MIS

3.5.1
Selection Types

The selector is to formulate and execute queries. It is a constituent part of R-MIS and the tool to identify the most promising spots in the production process. These spots hint at weak points.

R-MIS allows the following selection types:

- Selection of database entities[6] based on direct criteria with respect to the base dimensions
- Selection of database entities based on indirect criteria with respect to the part number
- Selection of database entities based on sharp criteria with respect to the data
- Selection of database entities based on linguistic variables and corresponding terms associated with the data

The user can combine these selection types in a single query. In the same way, he can freely construct his query from fuzzy and sharp components by connecting them with AND or OR. To support the manager, who is the determined addressee, R-MIS deliberately avoids the use of an editor to enter a specific query and uses instead a pre-structured grid of fields, which pull down on a mouseclick and offer the possible choices to the user.

---

[6] Database entities are rejects data, which are determined by specific values of the base dimensions month, part number, burden center, operation and flaw cause. The combination of specific base dimension values can be integrated into a conjoint dimension value.

3.5.2
Query Elements

Selection of database entities based on direct criteria with respect to the base dimensions

The base dimensions values are laid down by referencing to concrete values in the query. Base dimensions are month, part number, burden center, operation and flaw cause.

Examples: Select all database entities, where part number is in the list [7]
               ´A1000000000, A1000000002, A1000000008´[7]

              Select all database entities, where month is one of the last 5

Selection of database entities based on indirect criteria with respect to the part number

These selections use the parts list and the grouping of parts and final products by the criterion *type*.

Examples: Select all database entities, where part number is a piston

              Select all database entities, where part number is a part of
                                steering system No. 1

              Select all database entities, where part number is a component of
                                a gear pole steering system

Selection of database entities based on sharp criteria with respect to the data

These selections relate to the data and not - as the previous selections - to the base dimensions.

Examples: Select all database entities, where rejects cost are
                                greater than 20000 $

              Select the database entities,   where rejects share shows
                                the 5 highest values

---

[7] A1000000002 etc. are company specific codings of parts.

Selection of database entities based on linguistic variables and corresponding terms associated with the data

This selection method is very useful to managers. They can use linguistic terms like for example *low*, *medium* and *high* to reference to the data.

Example: Select all database entities, where rejects cost is high

3.5.3
Construction and Evaluation of Fuzzy Queries

Sharp queries[8] are a special case of fuzzy queries[9]. Therefore, sharp queries are also subsumed under the terminus fuzzy query. As already mentioned, elementary queries are put together to a compound query by connecting them with AND or OR. The setting of brackets determines the evaluation order. R-MIS uses the following operators for the interpretation of the linguistic AND and OR[10]:

$$\mu \cup \lambda: \quad G \to [0,1] \quad \text{mit} \quad (\mu \cup \lambda)(x) := \max\{\mu(x), \lambda(x)\}, x \in G$$

$$\mu \cap \lambda: \quad G \to [0,1] \quad \text{mit} \quad (\mu \cap \lambda)(x) := \min\{\mu(x), \lambda(x)\}, x \in G$$

These operators include the special case of union and intersection in classical set theory. Fuzzy queries allow users to express selections on database entities in a natural way.

Figure 3 shows the evaluation of the query

Select all database entities, where rejects cost is high OR rejects share is high

for a database entity with *rejects cost* equal to 7000 $ and *rejects share* equal to 1.9 %. The acceptance threshold is set to 0.5. Like shown in Figure 3, the corresponding database entity belongs with a membership value of 0.75 to the resulting set of database entities. An analogous evaluation has to be done for every entity in the database.

---

[8] A sharp query evaluates to 0 or 1.
[9] A fuzzy query evaluates to a value in the interval [0;1].
[10] Other operator definitions are discussed in literature. The selection of operators is determined in practice amongst other criteria by field of application, mathematical characteristics of the operator and computing efficiency [15,16].

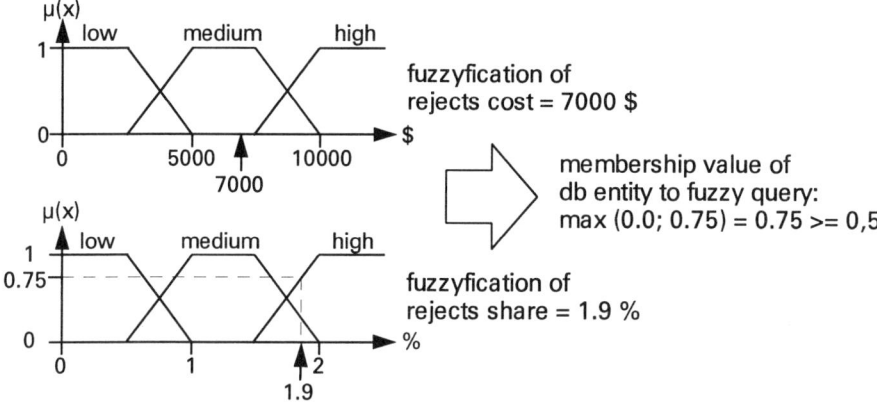

Figure 3: Evaluation of a fuzzy query for a database entity with *rejects cost* = 7000 $ and *rejects share* = 1.9 %

In a similar manner, more complicated fuzzy queries can be constructed. A possible compound query from a production manager for gear pole steering systems might be formulated like following:

Select all database entities, where

```
(           rejects share is very high
OR  (       rejects cost is high
    AND     rejects share is high
    AND     standard deviation of rejects share of the last six month is high ) )
AND part number is a component of a gear pole steering system
```

R-MIS automatically uses the to a special part and a special operation affiliated linguistic variable *rejects share*. If no special linguistic variable is defined, a default variable is used. Generally, R-MIS allows a great degree of freedom by the interactive definition and assignment of linguistic variables.

4
The Realization of the Rejects Management Information System

The Rejects Management Information System is realized on base of the multidimensional database system pcExpress from ORACLE Corporation. The interface to the user is designed with the front-end Express/EIS (ORACLE). Data is imported into the multidimensional database from an IBM AS/400 host via network. The foundation stone of R-MIS is a screen structure for Dataviews, which consists of four areas, like shown in Figure 4.

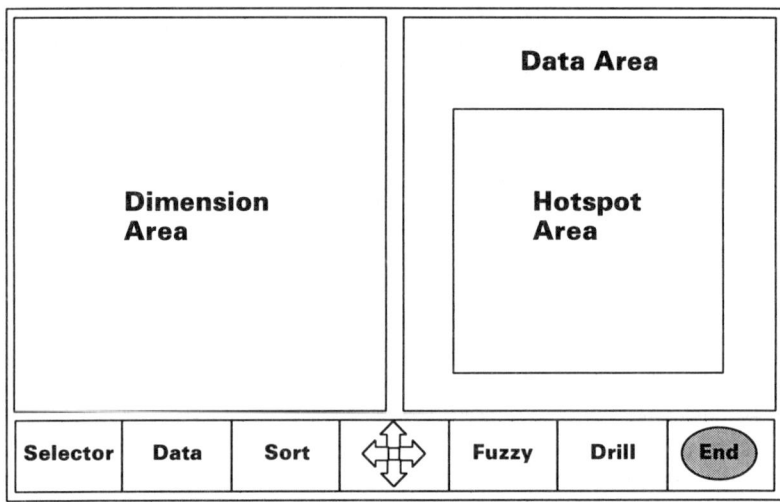

Figure 4: Screen Structure of Dataviews

The Dimension Area is a pure display area where the values of the conjoint dimension - which consists of the dimensions month, part number, burden center, operation and flaw cause - of the data is shown. The actual data is displayed in the data area. A mouseclick on sensitive fields leads to the display of specific graphic screens. These fields are called hot spots. A mouseclick on different hot spots leads to different graphics. These graphics are also influenced by the status[11] of the dataview. The menu area has several buttons which allow the execution of different tasks.

Figure 5 exemplarily shows a dataview screen of R-MIS. It is a base dataview at the most detailed level with chosen data *rejects cost* and *rejects share*. With the Drill-Button, you can aggregate the data in any possible direction, although not all theoretically possible options are of practical relevance. For example, you may want to see the *rejects cost* per month, part number, burden center and operation aggregated over all flaw causes, or you may want to see the *rejects cost* differentiated only per month and part number.

---

[11] The status of the dataview comprises all currently selected database entities. These entities are visible on the screen or could be made visible by scrolling the screen.

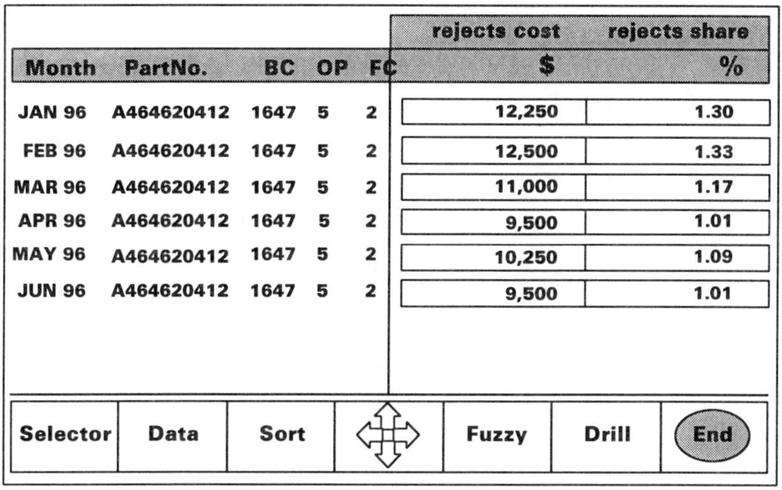

Month	PartNo.	BC	OP	FC	rejects cost $	rejects share %
JAN 96	A464620412	1647	5	2	12,250	1.30
FEB 96	A464620412	1647	5	2	12,500	1.33
MAR 96	A464620412	1647	5	2	11,000	1.17
APR 96	A464620412	1647	5	2	9,500	1.01
MAY 96	A464620412	1647	5	2	10,250	1.09
JUN 96	A464620412	1647	5	2	9,500	1.01

Selector	Data	Sort		Fuzzy	Drill	End

Figure 5: A base Dataview of R-MIS[12]

With the Data-Button, you can choose different data to see, like for example average values of *rejects cost* for the last months and the corresponding standard deviation, maximum and minimum values as well as the share of the special flaw cause with respect to all flaw causes belonging to this month, part, burden center and operation. The Data-Button also allows to display the query results, i.e. the membership values concerning a query which has been evaluated by the selector.

As already explained in 3.5, the selector is the tool to formulate and execute queries. Supplemental to the selection of entities from the entirety of the database, you can reference the current status which is displayed in the dataview and keep or remove entities to this status which satisfy the query. Another possibility is to add all database entities satisfying the query to those in the current status of the dataview.

The Sort-Button allows the sorting of the database entities in the current status, i.e. the rows of the dataview. The rows can be sorted according to values of data or the numerical respectively alphabetical order of the base dimensions.

The user accesses the fuzzy tools with the Fuzzy-Button. Here one can interactively define linguistic variables and terms as well as assign them to the data.

Through a mouseclick on hot spots one activates the procedures for the graphical representations of data. Usually this is done after the user has selected special database entities. He has focused on a smaller number of elements and makes further investigations. Figure 6 and 7 show examples for those graphical representations which visualize the current state concerning rejects. Figure 6 shows the course of time for the *rejects cost* of a special part. Figure 7 illustrates the composition of flaw causes in a special month, for a special part, burden center and operation.

---

[12] BC: burden center; OP: operation; FC: flaw cause

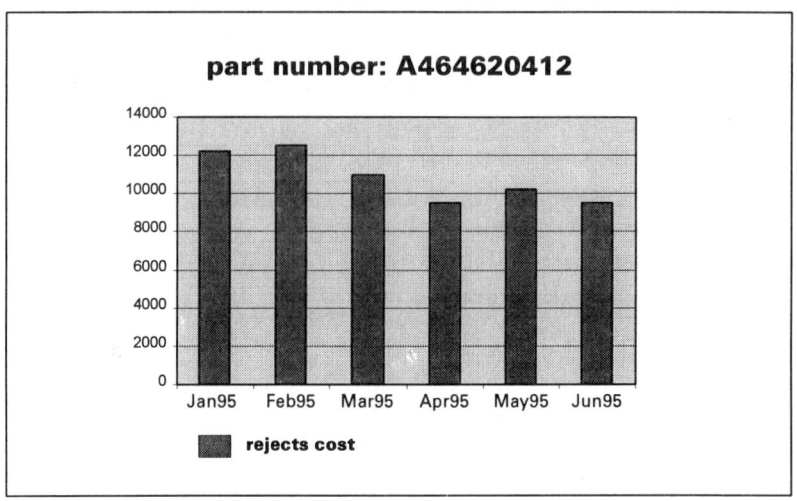

Figure 6: The course of time for *rejects cost* of a specific part

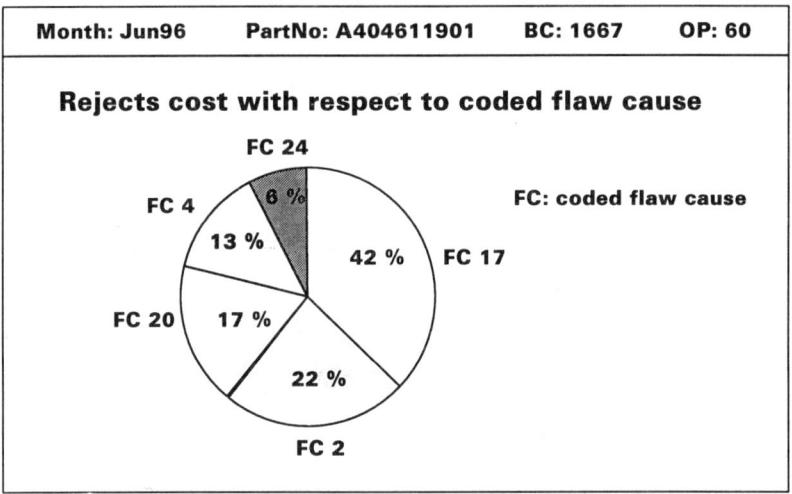

Figure 7: The composition of *rejects cost* with respect to coded flaw cause[13].

---

[13] BC: burden center; OP: operation.

5
Conclusion

The developed Rejects Management Information System R-MIS gives the production manager the possibility to detect problems and irregularities in the manufacturing of goods. It is implemented on base of the multidimensional database system pcExpress from ORACLE Corporation. The interface to the user is designed with the front-end Express/EIS.

Rejects data like for example *rejects cost* and *rejects share* are organized along the base dimensions month, part number, burden center and flaw cause. An analysis of rejects data is on different aggregation levels easily possible. Contextsensitive graphics visualize time series analysis and the composition of *rejects cost* with respect to different base dimensions.

The selector is the tool to identify hot spots in the quantity of data. Natural language queries are supported. To interpret those queries, Fuzzy Logic is used. Corresponding linguistic variables and terms could be interactively defined and used.

References

[1]   P. G. Keen, M. S. Scott Morton (1987). *Decision Support Systems: An Organizational Perspective.* Mass.: Reading.

[2]   D. W. Kroeber, H. J. Watson (1987). *Computer-Based Information Systems: A Management Approach.* New York: Macmillan Publishing Company.

[3]   J. A. O'Brien (1990). *Management Information Systems: A Managerial End User Perspective.* Homewood: Irwin.

[4]   U. Guthunz (1994). *Informationssysteme für das strategische Management.* Wiesbaden: Dt. Univ.-Vlg.

[5]   H.-H. Over, S. Roppel, C. Womser-Hacker (1994). *A Fuzzy Query Formulation Mode in a Knowledged Based Materials Information System.* Proceedings, EUFIT 94 - Second European Congress on Intelligent Techniques and Soft Computing, Vol. I, Aachen, Page 205-211.

[6]   H. Tashiro, N. Ohki, R. Kamekura, T. Nomura, T. Yokoyama, Y. Matsushita (1992). *A Fuzzy Database System Considering Each User's Subjectivity.* A. M. Tjoa, I. Ramos (eds). *Database and Expert Systems applications.* Proceedings of the International Conference in Valencia, Spain, Page 231-236.

[7]   N. Vojdani (1996). *An Intelligent Fuzzy Decision Support System for Production Management.* Proceedings, ENERGY WEEK '96, Energy Information Management Conference, Symposium Computers in Engineering, Houston, Texas, January 29- February 2.

[8]   M. Zemankova (1989). *FILIP: A Fuzzy Intelligent Information System with Learning Capabilities.* Information Systems, Vol. 14, No. 6, Page 473-486.

[9] M. Bellmann (1995): *Entwicklung und Modellierung eines Management-Informations-Systems mit Hilfe der Fuzzy-Logik am Beispiel der Lenkungsproduktion in der Automobilindustrie.* Diplomarbeit, University of Dortmund.

[10] N. Vojdani, M. Bellmann (1996). *A Rejects Management Information System by Means of Fuzzy Logic.* Proceedings, IPMU 96 - Sixth International Conference on Information Processing and Management of Uncertainty in Knowledge-Based Systems, Vol. I, Granada, Page 193-196.

[11] Manual pcExpress (1993). *pcExpress. Introduction. Version 4.0.* Waltham: Information Resources.

[12] Manual pcEcpress (1993). *pcExpress. User's Guide. Version 4.0.* Waltham: Information Resources.

[13] Manual pcExpress (1993). *pcExpress. Reference Manual. Version 4.0.* Waltham: Information Resources.

[14] Manual Express/EIS (1993). *Express/EIS. Developer's Guide. Version 4.0.* Waltham: Information Resources.

[15] H.-J. Zimmermann (1987): *Fuzzy sets, decision making and expert systems.* Boston: Kluwer.

[16] H.-J. Zimmermann (1993): *Fuzzy set theory and its applications.* Boston: Kluwer.

5

ANALYSES AND CALCULATION OF RISK AND VALUE

Fuzzy Logic Based Systems for Checking the Credit Solvency of Small Business Firms

Heinrich J. Rommelfanger

J. W. Goethe-University Frankfurt am Main
Institute of Statistics and Mathematics
Mertonstr. 17-23, D-60054 Frankfurt am Main
Rommelfanger@wiwi.uni-frankfurt.de

Abstract: In this paper it is analyzed, how the proceeding commonly used in fuzzy control can be applied to non-technical expert systems. The new ideas are explained by means of a system for checking the credit solvency of small business firms. Additionally we present some results received from working on expert systems which support analytic procedures of auditors.

Keywords: fuzzy logic, membership functions, checking credit solvency, annual audit, fuzzy inference, vague input data

1. Introduction

Decisions and evaluations in economic and business problems are usually complex. A lot of variables and relations have to be specified. The expectations of the fifties and sixties of this century - that it would be possible to model all problems in form of adequate mathematical systems - could not be satisfied. Today we know this can only be achieved for relatively simple problems.

However, it has always been necessary to make decisions in complex situations. A circumstance which is still valid no matter whether it concerns economic, business respectively jurisprudential problems or everyday situations like, for example, driving a car during rush hour. Based on qualifications and practical knowledge, individuals attempt to come to a satisfying solution. A person who obtains extraordinarily good results is called an „expert" in this field.

The motivation within the last decade was to model the decision process of experts instead of the decision situation. Expert knowledge does normally not consist of confirmed theories, it is rather composed of heuristic rules the expert obeys during his own decision making. Expert rules are usually formulated by linguistic terms which is why it is difficult to transform them into classical mathematical terms or to apply them to computer-aided processing.

In my contribution I want to demonstrate that the fuzzy set theory offers adequate instruments for modeling and dealing with expert rules. By modeling linguistic variables in form of fuzzy sets, it is possible to transform expert rules into mathematical terms. Moreover the fuzzy set theory offers a great variety of operators which are able to aggregate and combine these rules.

The advantages of fuzzy logic for controlling technical processes have become well-known, not only in Japan but by the last four years in America and Europe, too. Now the question arises, whether the procedures, used very successfully in fuzzy control, can also be applied to non-technical expert systems.

I am convinced that a transfer of the basic ideas of fuzzy control to non-technical decision support systems is possible. At the Institute of Statistics and Mathematics of the University Frankfurt am Main we are working at the following research projects using expert rules and fuzzy logic processing:
- Checking the creditability of small business firms, see [1, 6, 7, 8]
- Checking the credit solvency of persons buying a car on the installment plan
- Evaluating capital structure, financial assets and revenue of firms in order to support the business of auditors, see [9]
- Analytical procedures in the course of audits, see [4]
- Portfolio management
- Evaluating suppliers

In this paper I want to mainly explain the new ideas by means of a system for checking the creditability of small business firms. With regard to the construction of linguistic variables, I will present results of an empirical study where membership functions are designed using data of different branches of business.

2. Hierarchical Systems for Determinants of the Material Business Creditability

Complex and not directly measurable criteria, as for example the credit solvency of a business firm, may often be explained more transparent and more intelligible by a hierarchical system of subaspects. In Figure 1 a hierarchical system for determinants of the material creditworthiness is presented which was developed in 1991 by Bagus [1], based on empirical studies of Rommelfanger/Unterharnscheidt [7, 8]. For evaluating the creditworthiness of a specific firm, at first the aspects on the bottom level have to be evaluated. Then those evaluations of the subattributes need to be aggregated step by step until the top level of the hierarchical concept is reached.

Usually this aggregation process is accomplished by means of aggregation operators depending on parameters or weights which ask for further specification by the decision maker, see e.g. [8], [13].

An disadvantage of these operators is that they portray the complex conjunction mechanism of the human mind only incompletely. In literature and practice there exist a lot of examples, that the weights within an objective system depend not only on the objectives but often change with the obtained values. The hierarchical system in Figure 2 combined with the rule set in Table 1 is a good example for this fact; it seems impossible or at least very difficult to describe this aggregation pattern by means of operators. Therefore it is necessary to look for other ways of modeling the decision process of credit managers.

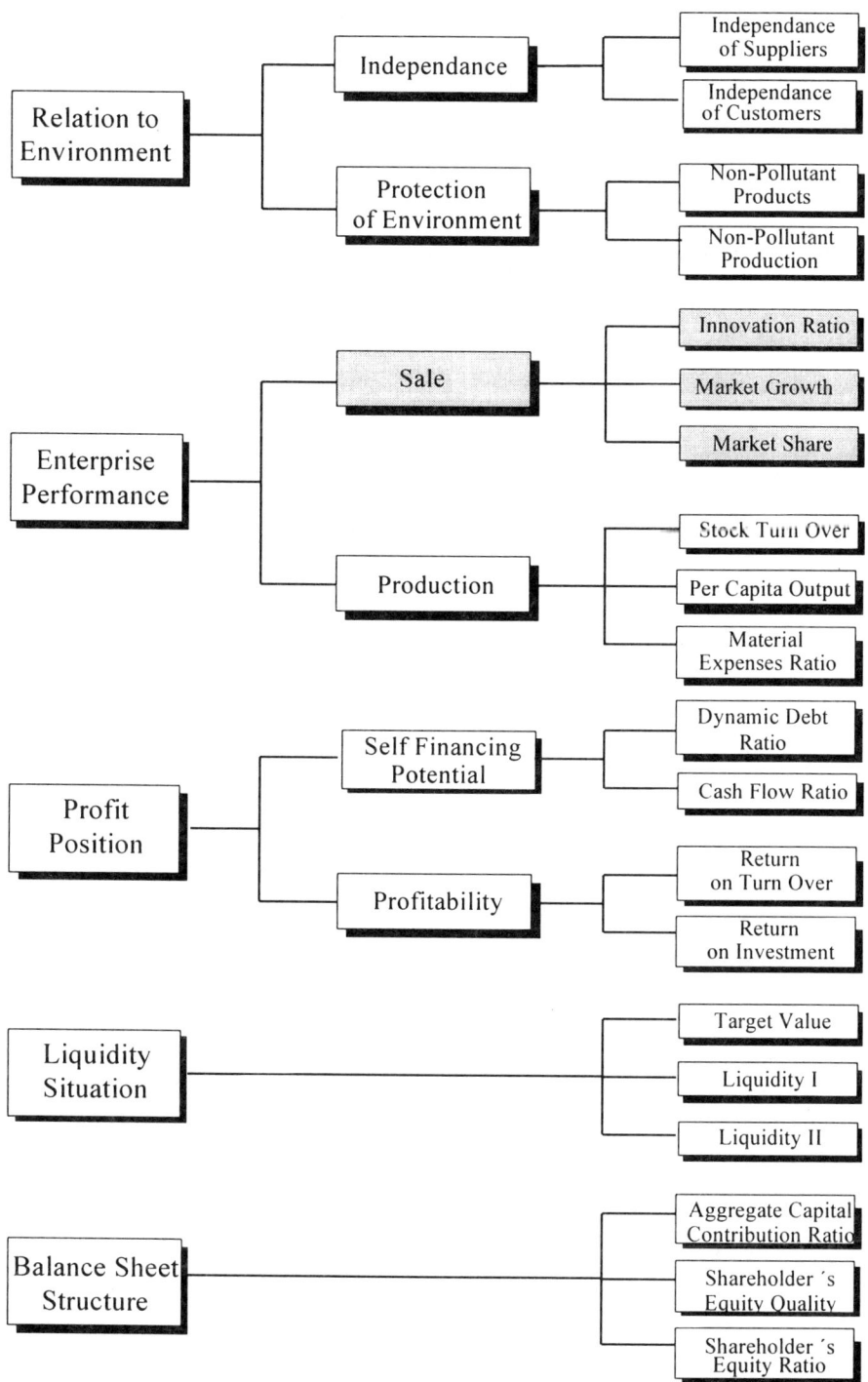

Figure 1: Hierarchical System for Evaluating Material Business Creditability

374

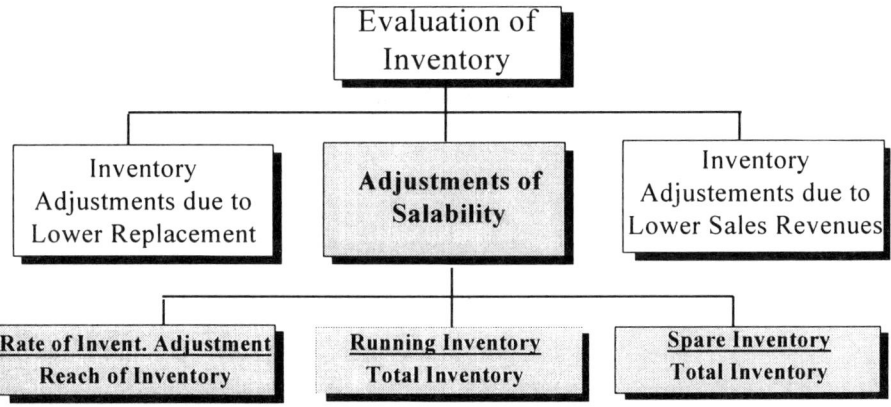

Figure 2: Analysis of Adjustments of Salability

Rate of inv. Adjust. Reach of Inventory	Running Invent. Total Inventory	Spare Inventory Total Inventory	Adjustments of Salability
low	low	low	low
low	low	medium	low
low	low	high	low
low	medium	low	low
low	medium	medium	low
low	medium	high	medium
low	high	low	medium
low	high	medium	medium
low	high	high	high
medium	low	low	low
medium	low	medium	medium
medium	low	high	medium
medium	medium	low	medium
medium	medium	medium	high
medium	medium	high	medium
medium	high	low	high
medium	high	medium	medium
medium	high	high	low
high	low	low	medium
high	low	medium	high
high	low	high	medium
high	medium	low	high
high	medium	medium	medium
high	medium	high	low
high	high	low	medium
high	high	medium	low
high	high	high	low

Table 1: Evaluation of Adjustments of Salability

3. Aggregation of Determinants by Expert Rules

In the artificial intelligence literature we can find many models in which the human decision process is described by means of rules formulated by experts. The following table presents a rule map established by an expert team of the Commerzbank AG Frankfurt am Main, see [5].

Market Share	Market Growth	Rate of Innovation	Sales
p	p	p	p-
p	p	m	p-
p	p	g	p
p	m	p	p
p	m	m	p
p	m	g	p+
p	g	p	p+
p	g	m	m-
p	g	g	m
m	p	p	p
m	p	m	m-
m	p	g	m-
m	m	p	p+
m	m	m	m
m	m	g	m
m	g	p	p+
m	g	m	m
m	g	g	g-
g	p	p	p
g	p	m	p+
g	p	g	m-
g	m	p	m-
g	m	m	m
g	m	g	m+
g	g	p	g-
g	g	m	g
g	g	g	g+

Table 2: Evaluation of Sales

In this rule-based model the evaluation of determinants is described by the linguistic terms „poor", „medium" and „good". For every possible situation on the lower hierarchy level an aggregation rule was defined. In this study only three values per criterion were distinguished, yet additional ratings (- and/or +) were allowed for the aggregation results.

In the study of the Commerzbank AG the ratios are defined as

$$\text{Market Share} = \frac{\text{Sales volume of the firm}}{\text{Sales volume of all firms}},$$

$$\text{Market Growth} = \frac{\text{Predicted Market Volume in the year t+1}}{\text{Market Volume in the year t}},$$

$$\text{Rate of Innovation} = \frac{\text{Number of Innovative Products}}{\text{Total Number of Products}},$$

and the linguistic evaluations are described by means of intervals represented in the Tables 3, 4 and 5.

Market Share (MS)		Rate of Innovation (RoI)
MS < 5 %	poor (p) (big risk)	RoI < 10 %
5 % ≤ MS < 20 %	medium (m) (medium risk)	10 % ≤ RoI < 30 %
20 % ≤MS	good (g) (small risk)	30 % ≤ RoI

Table 3: Evaluation of
Market Share

Table 4: Evaluation of
Rate of Innovation

Market Growth (MG)	Grade	
MG < -5 %	6	poor (p) (big risk)
-5 % ≤ MG < 0 %	5	
0 % ≤ MG < 5 %	4	medium (m) (medium risk)
5 % ≤ MG < 7 %	3	
7 % ≤ MG < 10 %	2	good (g) (small risk)
10 % ≤ MG	1	

Table 5: Evaluation of Market Growth

Objections against those rules can be raised due to the fact that the rules are very inaccurate; the terms „good", „medium", „poor" allow a comparably large interpretation spectrum, see Tables 3, 4, 5.

To demonstrate this disadvantage we consider the following three firms:
Firm A : Market Share 5 %,   Market Growth 0 %, Rate of Innovation 10 %
Firm B : Market Share 15 %, Market Growth 5 %,   Rate of Innovation 25 %
Firm C : Market Share 4,9 %, Market Growth 6,9 %, Rate of Innovation 19,9 %

According to the rule 14 in Table 2 the firms A and B get the same valuation „medium" for the determinant „Sales", though firm B is much better in all three basic criteria. On the other side, firm C gets the worse valuation „poor" according to the rule 5, though it has a better valuations for the criterion „Market Growth" and „Rate of Innovation" than the other firms and the valuation of „Market Share" is only insignificant worse compared with firm A. Moreover the strong distinctions between the three classes give the impression of an arbitrary classification.

To improve this situation we could try to enlarge the number of valuations for each criterion. This, however would result in an explosive increase of the number of rules as for m aspects with r possible valuations there exist r^m rules. In the case of the valuation of „Sales" in Table 2, we have now $3^3 = 27$ rules. An increase in the number of valuations to 5 would result in $5^3 = 125$ rules.

Therefore it is necessary to restrain the number of valuations for each aspect. Moreover if the rule map gets too large the expert team will not be able to guarantee a conscious distinction of each situation.

4. Description of Expert Rules by Fuzzy Sets

As demonstrated in the example above different values of the same interval portray a linguistic term not correspondingly. This is a result of the fact that intervals only allow Yes/No-statements. Therefore we propose to model the linguistic terms by fuzzy sets; this theory makes it possible to describe the different membership degrees according to the categories of „poor", „medium" or „good" credit solvency as precise as the credit expert can express it. These membership functions must be specified as carefully as possible, because they will decisively influence the valuation process. Nevertheless we will never obtain membership functions which are accurate in every detail, because a lot of data about similar firms and knowledge of the trade must be collected by the expert team. Therefore the form of membership functions in expert systems will be very simple and the same design will be used repeatedly. In practice it is sufficient to work with fuzzy numbers or fuzzy intervals of the LR-type, see [10], [12].

Whereas fuzzy control applications usually employ very simple triangular or trapezoid fuzzy sets, we propose to use reference functions of the s-type, which take pattern to normal probability distributions in non-technical applications. In the following figures the reference function $\exp(-u^2)$ is used. To specify the form of a membership function for small membership degrees is particularly difficult. To avoid errors we propose to neglect all membership degrees smaller than a minimum level ε, in this paper the minimum membership level is fixed at $\varepsilon = 0.05$.

The membership functions in the Figures 3, 4 and 5 are modeled by experts using the Tables 3, 5 and 4. In contrast with these membership functions the membership functions $\mu = \mu(x)$ in the Figures 6, 10 and 11 are based on a fictive scale.

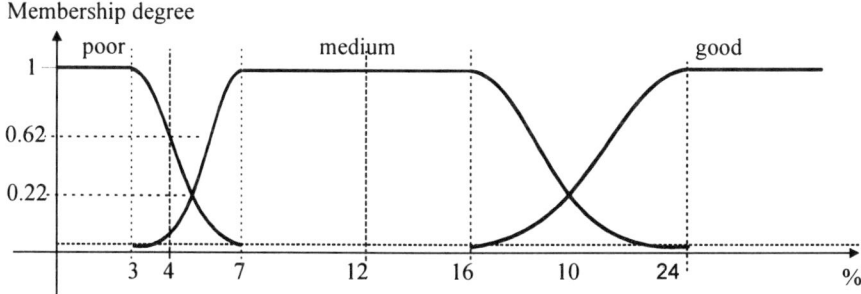

Figure 3: Valuation of Market Share

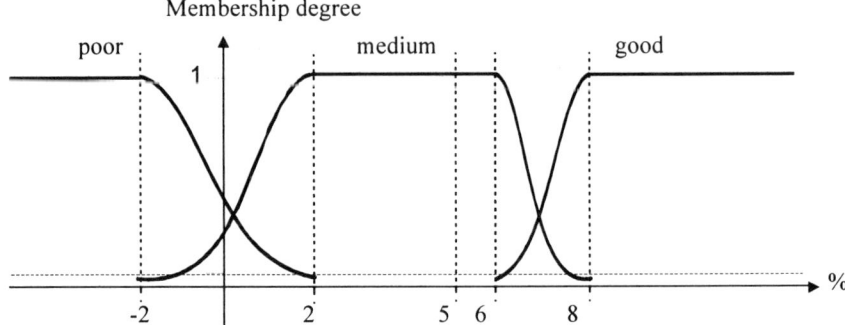

Figure 4: Valuation of Market Growth

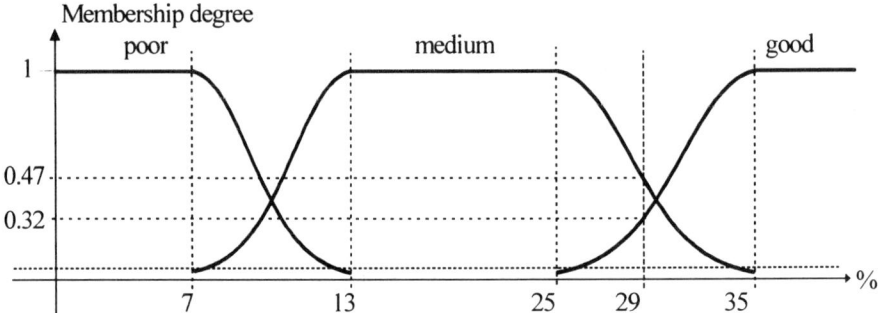

Figure 5: Valuation of Rate of Innovation

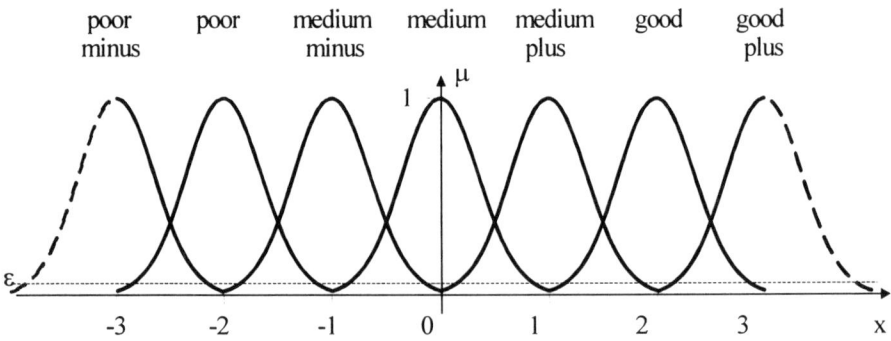

Figure 6: Valuation of Sales

Presenting fuzzy sets as categories of valuation provides the opportunity to precisely inform users of expert systems about their valuation basis. Moreover by comparing data of different branches of business this proceeding allows to resort to knowledge already stored in data bases.

A way for a practical transformation has been analyzed in a pilot study at the Institute of Statistics and Mathematics of the University of Frankfurt am Main, see

[2]. The intention was to design membership functions in the course of an expert system for supporting the evaluation of the financial and operating position of business firms as part of the annual audit, see [9].

At first on the base of a suitable data bank the median, the 25%-quantil and the 50%-quantil of the characteristic number were calculated for the branch the observed firm belongs to. Then, according to the „standard operating procedure" the 1-level set (1-cut) of the membership function of „average" is the central 25%-quantil. The 1-cut of the membership function of „low" is below the 50%-quantil whereas the 1-cut of the membership function of „high" is situated above the 50%-quantil, see Figure 7.

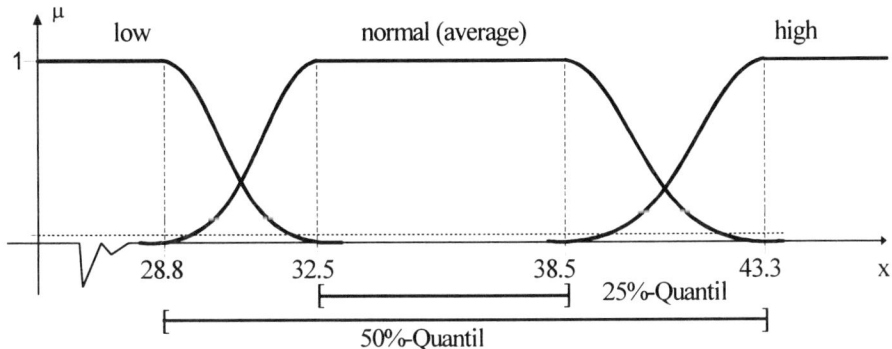

Fig. 7: Membership function of „Personnel Cost/Total Output"

This procedure was then modified for „risk indicators" and „alteration reference numbers". For „risk indicators" the 1-cut of the „risk area" is extended to the border of the 25%-quantil and the 1-cut of the evaluation „average" is shorten to the 12,5%-quantil in this part, see Figure 8. The 1-cut of the membership function of „average" is the 25%-quantil.

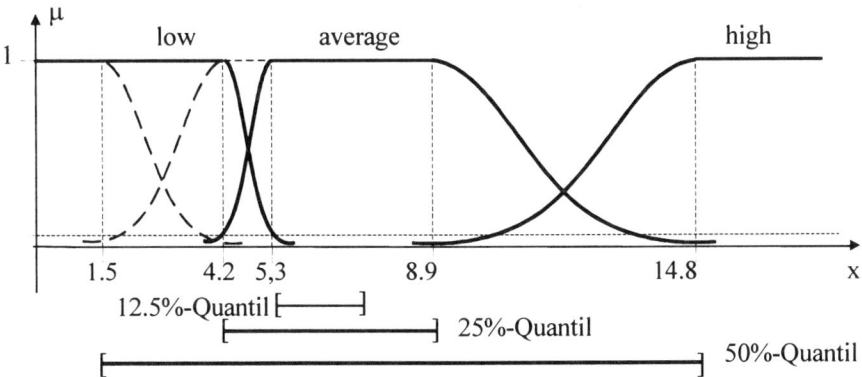

Fig. 8: Membership function of „ Cash Flow/Borrowed Capital"

For „alteration reference numbers" the 1-cut of the membership function of „average" is shortened to the 12,5%-quantil and the 1-cuts of the membership function of the other valuations are now situated below or above the 25%-quantil, see Figure 9.

The limitation to a standardized procedure with three types implies the advantage that the data of a firm's data bank can be extensively used. By that fuzzy membership functions can be defined for any reference number and any branch of business with little effort - as long as the necessary information is available. As a consequence a data bank supplier gets the chance to implement an instrument of analysis, for example the described expert system, into his data bank for annual financial statements. The user then obtains the opportunity to carry out an evaluation of a company based on comparing data of different branches of business.

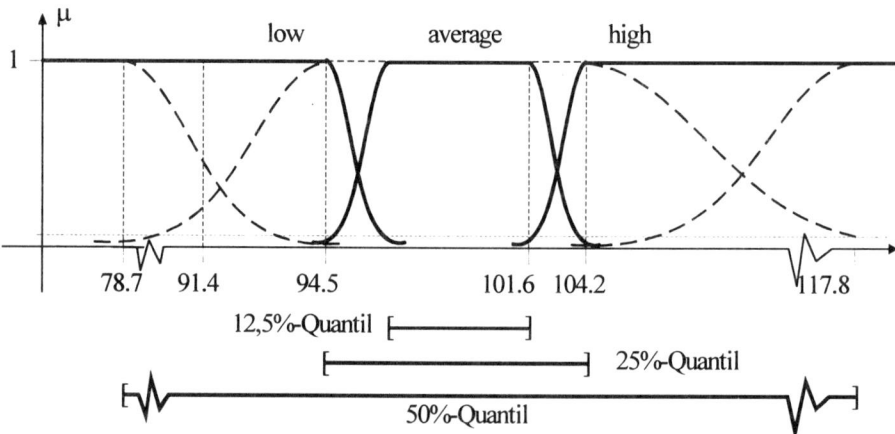

Fig. 9: Membership function of „Difference Stocks/ Difference sales"

Discussions with qualified auditors confirmed that the membership functions defined according to the described procedures are able to simulate the evaluation behavior of experts quite accurately. The pilot study however, can only provide a first approximation. Before starting the practical application of the expert system on a large scale a fundamental empirical check has to be carried out: The established fuzzy membership functions as well as the expert rules which are necessary for processing the evaluations of the reference numbers need to be confirmed. In this context the influence of the economic situation on the position and shape of the particular membership function has necessarily to be examined. Especially due to the fact that all the data at disposal refers to the past, the classification of reference numbers may be distorted.

It also makes sense to check the valuation intervals of different branches of business against one another. In the course of this study it was discovered that within the sectors *mechanical engineering and computers, building construction and civil engineering* as well as *department stores* a company can only be rated adequately if it is analyzed on the basis of data of its own branch. Still it remains to be checked whether there are other branches of that kind that their companies show resembling financial and operating positions as well as a corresponding economic situation. In that case those branches could be considered alike for the determination of fuzzy membership functions without cutting down the quality of the received valuations.

5. Fuzzy Controller and Rule-Based Aggregation

When modeling the linguistic evaluation terms by fuzzy sets, the aggregation rules are only applied to those cases, in which the evaluations produce a membership degree 1 for all subaspects. Then the corresponding rule of the rule map is applied and leads to a distinct evaluation of the upper-aspect with the membership degree 1, too. Therefore the use of fuzzy sets helps users to understand the basic principles of the expert knowledge more easily. This „understanding" is an essential factor for the acceptance of an expert system and related to that for its successful realization.

As an example, we contemplate a firm with the characteristics

(Market Share , Market Growth , Rate of Innovation) = (28 % , 3 % , 5 %).

Then according to the 22nd rule In Table 2 the Sales gets the valuation „medium minus" with the membership degree 1.

For all the other cases, where at least one evaluation has a membership degree smaller than 1, no special rules have been stated by the experts. We assume that the given rules can be extended to situations in the vicinity. The rules are softened with the consequence that now many rules can be used simultaneously in a weakened manner.

For a real situation we denote the degree of fulfillment with the descriptions of state in the rule maps by DOF. According to the proceeding in fuzzy control, DOF is defined as the minimum of the membership degrees attached to the „inputs" of this rule. Having examined various operators regarding their ability to describe the human conjunction behavior in specific cases, we came to the conclusion that the minimum operator should be used. Besides others the minimum operator has the advantage that only few rules with positive DOFs exist, whereas by using compensatory operators almost all rules will show positive DOFs and we therefore have to expect intermediate evaluation.

For example, a firm D with the characteristics

(Market Share , Market Growth , Rate of Innovation) = (4 % , 5 % , 29 %)

can be described by means of vectors containing membership degrees:

$$(\mu_{poor}^{MS}(4\%), \mu_{medium}^{MS}(4\%), \mu_{good}^{MS}(4\%)) = (0.62, 0.22, 0) \quad \text{and}$$

$$(\mu_{poor}^{RoI}(29\%), \mu_{medium}^{RoI}(29\%), \mu_{good}^{RoI}(29\%)) = (0, 0.47, 0.32).$$

This „fuzzification" of the crisp input values produces a connection between the observed values and the linguistic valuations in the rule base.

In accordance with Table 2, we get for firm D the following 4 positive DOFs $\geq \varepsilon$:

$\text{DOF}_{\text{Rule 5}} = \text{Min} \left(\mu_{\text{poor}}^{\text{MS}}(4\%), \mu_{\text{medium}}^{\text{MG}}(5\%), \mu_{\text{medium}}^{\text{RoI}}(29\%) \right)$

$= \text{Min} (0.62, 1, 0.47) = 0.47$ *poor*

$\text{DOF}_{\text{Rule 6}} = \text{Min} \left(\mu_{\text{poor}}^{\text{MS}}(4\%), \mu_{\text{medium}}^{\text{MG}}(5\%), \mu_{\text{good}}^{\text{RoI}}(29\%) \right)$

$= \text{Min} (0.62, 1, 0.32) = 0.32$ *medium minus*

$\text{DOF}_{\text{Rule 12}} = \text{Min} \left(\mu_{\text{medium}}^{\text{MS}}(4\%), \mu_{\text{medium}}^{\text{MG}}(5\%), \mu_{\text{medium}}^{\text{RoI}}(29\%) \right)$

$= \text{Min} (0.22, 1, 0.47) = 0.22$ *medium*

$\text{DOF}_{\text{Rule 13}} = \text{Min} \left(\mu_{\text{medium}}^{\text{MS}}(4\%), \mu_{\text{medium}}^{\text{MG}}(5\%), \mu_{\text{good}}^{\text{RoI}}(29\%) \right)$

$= \text{Min} (0.22, 1, 0.32) = 0.22$ *medium*

Now all rules with positive DOF contribute to the valuation of Sales Potential in proportion to their DOFs.

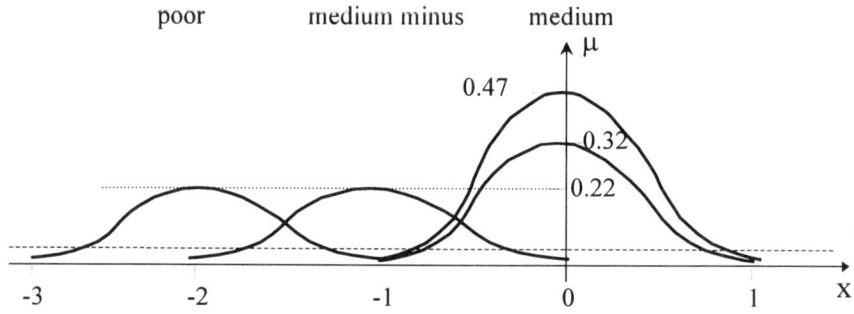

Fig. 10. Valuation of Sales using Max-Prod-Inference

When „turning down" the evaluations corresponding to the individual rules we recommend the use of the Max-Prod-inference which means that the membership values are fixed in proportion to the corresponding DOF, see Figure 10. We are convinced that the Max-Prod-inference is more adequate than the Max-Min-inference which is often used in Fuzzy Control applications, because the elimination of membership values which go above the DOFs implies that rules with medium DOF get more influence.

In this context we want to remark that there is an essential difference between fuzzy control applications and non-technical evaluation and decision problems. Usually technical control processes are rapidly repeated, see [6, 10]. Therefore it is sufficient when an approximately correct action is carried out, because the correction will follow immediately. On the contrary decision support systems require a definite decision for every section which evidently has to be correct. As a consequence the procedure in decision support systems has to be handled more carefully than in fuzzy control. Not only the linguistic evaluation terms have to be defined more carefully but also the calculation of the DOFs and the influence of the DOFs on the final result require an exact empirical examination.

In fuzzy control the total result is calculated by applying the Maximum-operator for aggregating the evaluations of the rules with positive DOF. But in decision support systems corrections should be considered. In our example the valuation „medium" for the Sales can be found twice. On the one hand we do not consider it to be right that the rating „medium" only counts with a DOF Max(0.47, 0.32) = 0.47 which means that the rule with the second best positive DOF is completely neglected. On the other hand it seems absurd to add the DOFs if two or more rules turn up with the same „output", because it would then be possible to get DOF-values greater then 1. We propose to adopt a middle course and suggest the use of the algebraic sum. By doing so we get - in the example above - for the valuation „medium" the total DOF 0.47 + 0.32 - 0.47 × 0.32 = 0.64 which presents a more balanced valuation.

Then the self financing potential is vaguely evaluated by means of the member-ship function shown in Figure 11.

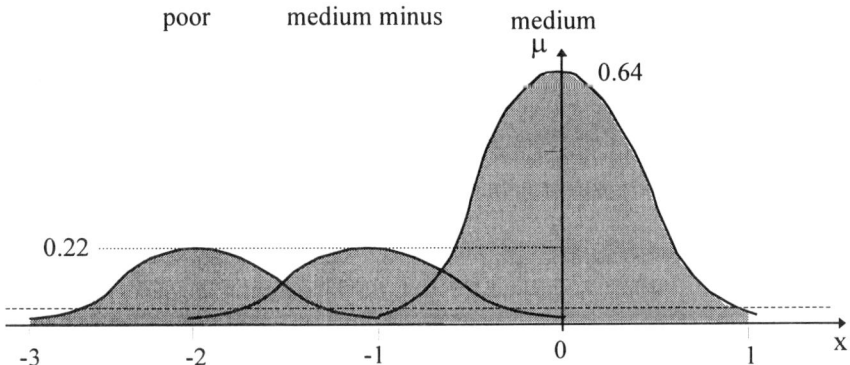

Figure 11: Valuation of Sales for the firm D

If it is intended to „compress" the data to a unique valuation, the well known defuzzification procedures can be used. The best-known are the center of gravity method and the center of area method. But in hierarchical systems defuzzifying is not necessary, because it is better to use directly the fuzzy valuations as inputs for the next aggregation step, where the corresponding DOFs are interpreted as membership values. For evaluating the „Enterprise Performance" on the higher level of the hierar-chy the firm D gets the „fuzzified" valuation of Sales (S):

$$(\mu^S_{poor}(D), \mu^S_{poor \atop min\,us}(D)\mu^S_{medium \atop min\,us}(D), \mu^S_{medium}(D), \mu^S_{medium \atop plus}(D), \mu^S_{good}(D), \mu^S_{good \atop plus}(D))$$

$$= (0, 0.22, 0.22, 0.64, 0, 0, 0)$$

see Figure 11.

Here, we recognize the problem, mentioned in sector 3, connected with using too many valuation grades. Only on the top level of the hierarchy there is no trouble if we use more than three evaluation classes. As the sum of the membership values can differ from 1, it is recommended to normalize the membership degrees.

7. Fuzzy Inference in the Case of Vague Input Data

In economic applications we sometimes have the problem that some of the input data are not known precisely but can be usually modeled by fuzzy numbers or fuzzy intervals. Obviously, this case is only uncomplicated in the case that the specific input value corresponds to a linguistic input data of the rule base. The problem with vague input data is only marginally mentioned in literature, because in the technical applications of fuzzy control and in most of the economic applications crisp input data are assumed.

The easiest way to deal with vague input data is to replace them by a "mean" value. In case of the vague data are modeled in form of fuzzy numbers or fuzzy intervals, all defuzzification methods can be used to reduce a vague input value to a crisp representative.

We want to discuss this problem by means of the ratio"Staff Costs Rate" which is defined as $\text{Staff Costs Rate} = \dfrac{\text{Staff Costs}}{\text{Total Costs}}$. In the Figures 12 and 13 experts explain their valuation of Staff Costs Rates by means of the linguistic variables "poor", "average" and "high". Moreover, we assume that the Staff Costs Rate of a firm is not exactly known but it can be described by a triangular fuzzy number $\tilde{X}_T$ or a trapezoid fuzzy interval $\tilde{X}$, compare Figures 12 and 13.

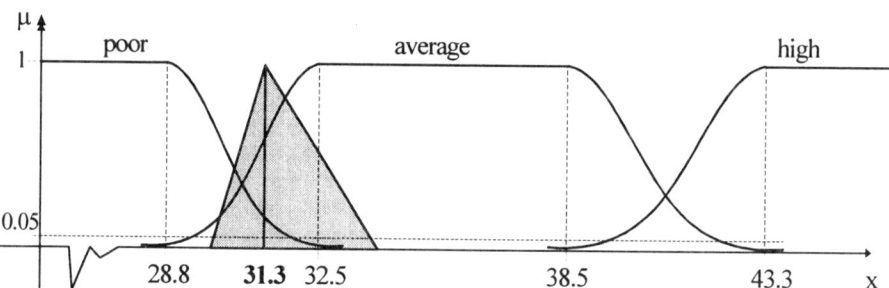

Figure 12: Valuations of Staff Costs Rate and triangular input data $\tilde{X}_T$

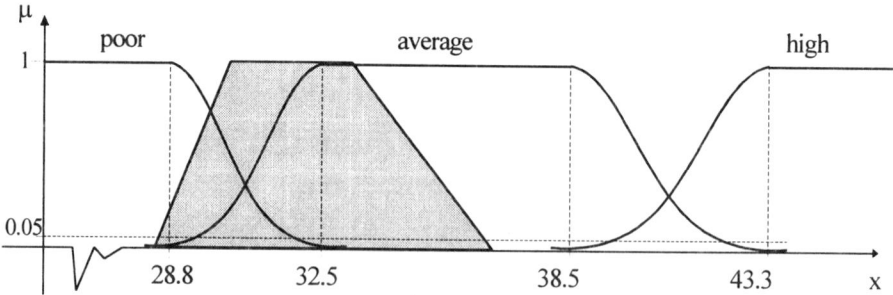

Figure 13: Valuations of Staff Costs Rate and trapezoid input data $\tilde{X}$

In the case of trapezoid input data $\widetilde{X}$, we get the following mean values and corresponding fuzzified input values, using different defuzzification methods:

Maximum-Mean-Method $\qquad \overline{x}_M = 31.78$

$$(\mu_{poor}(\overline{x}_M); \mu_{medium}(\overline{x}_M); \mu_{high}(\overline{x}_M)) = (0.1\,;0.76\,;0)$$

Center of Gravity-Method $\qquad \overline{x}_S = 32.236$

$$(\mu_{poor}(\overline{x}_S); \mu_{medium}(\overline{x}_S); \mu_{high}(\overline{x}_S)) = (0.05\,;0.89\,;0)$$

Center of Area Method $\qquad \overline{x}_F = 32.18$

$$(\mu_{poor}(\overline{x}_F); \mu_{medium}(\overline{x}_F); \mu_{high}(\overline{x}_F)) = (\approx 0\,;0.92\,;0)\,.$$

All these crisp input data state the valuation "medium" with a light tendency to low.

For getting more expressive results we propose to use the intersection between the fuzzy input data and the linguistic input valuations of the rule base. For the examples in the figures 12 and 13 we get the intersections presented in figure 14.

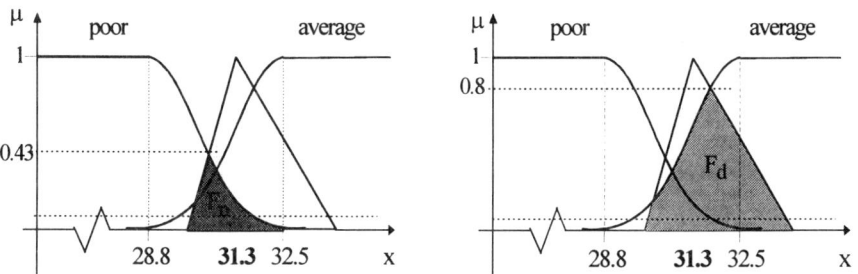

Figure 14: Fuzzy intersections in the case of triangular input data $\widetilde{X}_T$

Tilli [11] and Kahlert; Frank [3] propose to fuzzify the triangular input data in figure 13 in the form

$$(\mu_{poor}(\widetilde{X}_T); \mu_{medium}(\widetilde{X}_T); \mu_{high}(\widetilde{X}_T))$$

$$= (\underset{x}{Max}\,Min(\mu_{poor}(x); \mu_{X_T}(x))\,;\underset{x}{Max}\,Min(\mu_{medium}(x); \mu_{X_T}(x))\,;$$

$$\underset{x}{Max}\,Min(\mu_{high}(x); \mu_{X_T}(x)))$$ (1)

$$= (0.43\,;0.8\,;0)\,.$$

This procedure corresponds to the fuzzification of crisp data, see section 5.

An important disadvantage of this procedure is visible in the case of trapezoid input data, see figure 15. Using formula (1), the trapezoid input data $\widetilde{X}$ is fuzzified in

$$(\mu_{poor}(\widetilde{X}); \mu_{medium}(\widetilde{X}); \mu_{high}(\widetilde{X})) = (0.7\,;1\,;0)\,.$$

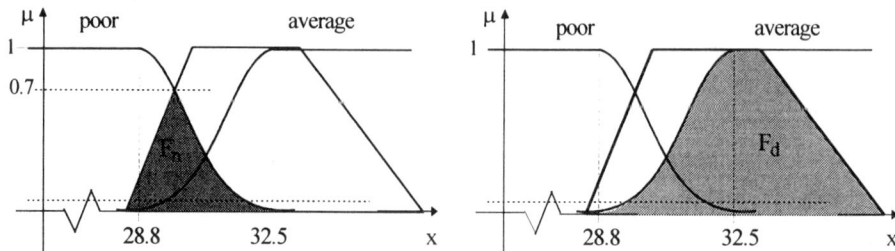

Figure 15: Fuzzy intersections in the case of trapezoid input data $\widetilde{X}$

This result is not a appropriate representation of the real situation; both member-ship degrees are too high. Moreover, the value $\mu_{poor}(\widetilde{X})$ is too large compared with $\mu_{medium}(\widetilde{X})$, as the normalization $(\frac{0.7}{1.7};\frac{1}{1.7};0) = (0.41;0.59;0)$ reveals. Further-more, the fuzzified input value does not react on alternations of $\widetilde{X}$, as long as the right border of the 1-cut is greater or equal 3.25.

Obviously, we will get no better results, if we use the center of gravity method or the center of area method for calculating mean values of the planes F_n and $F_{d\cdot..}$

In order to get a more appropriate description of the fuzzy input data, we propose to take into account the areas $S(F_n)$ and $S(F_d)$ of the planes F_n and F_d. Choosing the sum $S(F_n) + S(F_d)$ as base for the normalization, we have

$$(\mu_{poor}(\widetilde{X});\mu_{medium}(\widetilde{X});\mu_{high}(\widetilde{X})) = (\frac{S(F_d)}{S(F_d) + S(F_d)};\frac{S(F_d)}{S(F_n) + S(F_d)};0)$$

$$= (\frac{1.33}{4.69};\frac{3.36}{4.69};0) = (0.28;0.72;0).$$

Another base value can be the area $S(\widetilde{X})$ below the membership function $\mu_X(x)$ of $\widetilde{X}$. Then we get

$$(\mu_{niedrig}(\widetilde{X});\mu_{durch}(\widetilde{X});\mu_{hoch}(\widetilde{X})) = (\frac{S(F_d)}{S(\widetilde{X})};\frac{S(F_d)}{S(\widetilde{X})};0)$$

$$= (\frac{1.33}{5.65};\frac{3.36}{5.65};0) = (0.24;0.59;0).$$

In this case the sum of the membership degrees of a fuzzified input value does not generally equal 1. Carrying out a normalization, we get in the example the result $(0.29;0.71;0)$. It seems a likely supposition that the two proposed methods hardly differ.

8. Final Remarks

The application of linguistic variables and the employment of fuzzy conjunction methods offer an appropriate method to model the human reflection process. By doing so expert systems are constructed which actually deserve this name. There are still a lot of questions left to be answered, but I am convinced that this concept aims at the right direction. In the meantime, the first applications are used in practice.

References

1. Bagus, T.: Wissensbasierte Bonitätsanalyse für das Firmenkundengeschäft der Kreditinstitute. Peter Lang-Verlag Frankfurt a. M. 1992

2. Flach, J.: Ermittlung typisierter Fuzzy-Zugehörigkeitsfunktionen auf der Grundlage von Branchendaten als Komponente eines wissensbasierten Systems zur Unternehmensbeurteilung. Diplomarbeit am Institut für Statistik und Mathematik der J.W. Goethe Universität Frankfurt am Main 1995

3. Kahlert, J.; Frank, H.: Fuzzy-Logik und Fuzzy-Control. Vieweg Verlag, Braunschweig/Wiesbaden 1993

4. Müller, C.: Entwicklung eines wissensbasietren Systems zur Unterstützung der Analytischen Prüfungshandlungen im Rahmen der Jahresabschlußprüfung. Peter Lang Verlag, Frankfurt am Main 1996

5. Nolte-Hellwig, K.U.; Leins, H.; Krakl, J.: Die Steuerung von Bonitätsrisiken im Firmenkundengeschäft. In: Lüthje, B (Ed.): Risikomanagement in Banken - Konzeptionen und Steuerungssysteme. Verband öffentlicher Banken, Bonn (Berichte und Analysen Bd. 13) 1991

6. Rommelfanger, H.: Entscheiden bei Unschärfe.- Fuzzy Decision Support-Systeme. Springer-Verlag Berlin Heidelberg 1988, second edition 1994

7. Rommelfanger, H.; Unterharnscheidt, D.: Entwicklung einer Hierarchie gewichteter Bonitätskriterien für mittelständische Unternehmen. *Österreichisches Bank-Archiv* **33** , 419-437, 1986

8. Rommelfanger, H.; Unterharnscheidt, D.: Modelle zur Aggregation von Bonitätskriterien. *Zeitschrift für betriebswirtschaftliche Forschung* **40**, 471-503, 1988

9. Scheffels, R.: Fuzzy Logik in der Jahresabschlußprüfung. - Entwicklung eines wissensbasierten Systems zur Analyse der Vermögens-, Finanz- und Ertragslage. Deutscher Universitätsverlag, Wiesbaden 1996

10. Sugeno, M. (Ed.): Industrial Applications of Fuzzy Control. North Holland Amsterdam 1985

11. Tilly, T.: Fuzzy-Logik. Franzis-Verlag, München 1991

12. Yager, R.R.; Zadeh, L.A.: An Introduction to Fuzzy Logic Applications in Intelligent Systems. Kluwer Dordrecht 1992

13. Zimmermann, H.J.: Fuzzy Sets, Decision Making and Expert Systems. Kluwer Academic Publishers, Boston 1987

Applications of Fuzzy Logic for Creditworthiness Evaluation

Richard Weber
Management Intelligenter Technologien GmbH
Promenade 9
52076 Aachen, Germany
E-mail: rw@mitgmbh.de

Abstract. One of the first applications of fuzzy logic to financial engineering has been performed to evaluate creditworthiness of private bank customers. Here, a hierarchical aggregation of different criteria with subjective evaluations has been used. In the meantime, different methodological approaches for similar tasks have been suggested. Amongst others, there are rule-based techniques and fuzzy connectionist models which also belong to the area of soft computing.

This contribution explains the methods mentioned above and presents an application for creditworthiness evaluation which has been implemented for a credit insurance company.

Keywords. creditworthiness evaluation, rule-based fuzzy system

1 Introduction

Creditworthiness evaluation is one area of financial engineering where many soft computing techniques have been used in the past. Starting with approaches where a hierarchy of criteria has been aggregated using appropriate aggregation operators, connectionist models, rule-based systems and other techniques using genetic algorithms and neural networks have been suggested.

Chapter 2 of this contribution gives an overview on different soft computing approaches for creditworthiness evaluation. In chapter 3 a fuzzy system is presented which has been developed for a credit insurance company. The software tools used in this project are described in chapter 4. Chapter 5 gives concluding remarks and points to some future applications of systems similar to the one proposed in this contribution.

2 Overview on Different Soft Computing Approaches for Credit-worthiness Evaluation

In the literature many approaches for automatic creditworthiness evaluation have been presented. This chapter gives an overview on such methods using techniques from soft computing. The focus, however, lies on fuzzy methods which are described in the following three sub-chapters where hierarchical aggregation, fuzzy connectionist models, and rule-based techniques are presented. Further applications of soft computing techniques for credit evaluation are given in e.g. [Walker et al. 1995] and [Geyer-Schulz 1995] where genetic algorithms have been suggested or in [Leigh 1995] where neural networks are proposed for credit scoring. Of course, this overview does by far not claim to be exhaustive.

2.1 Hierarchical Aggregation of Information to Evaluate Creditworthiness

The approach presented in this chapter has been proposed in order to model the judgment of credit managers when evaluating creditworthiness of customers [Zimmermann, Zysno 1983]. In an empirical research project a hierarchy of criteria was developed which could be used to assess the top-level criterion creditworthiness based on a set of criteria describing each customer. Since the concept of a creditworthy customer could be described only by a large number of criteria (descriptors), it turned out to be impossible for the experts to handle all these descriptors simultaneously. In this sense, the term creditworthiness contains informational uncertainty which is due to an information overload. To treat this kind of uncertainty it has been proposed to split the top-criterion (here: creditworthiness) into two or more sub-criteria which are easier to describe. In the above mentioned empirical research project a concept hierarchy of creditworthiness has been developed which is shown in figure 2.1.

When evaluating the creditworthiness of applicants experts distinguish between their financial basis and their personality. In further steps these two criteria are split further as shown.

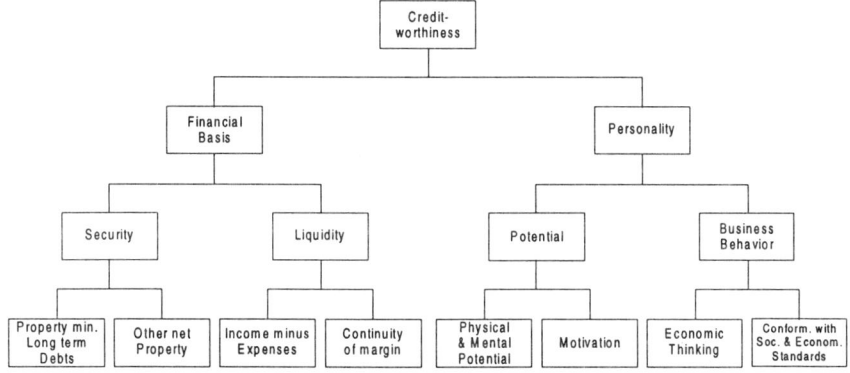

Fig. 2.1. Concept hierarchy of creditworthiness

After this hierarchical structure has been defined, the procedure how to compute the degree of creditworthiness for applicants has to be fixed. In particular, the degree to which each criterion at the bottom is fulfilled and their aggregation to arrive at the top-level is needed. Several aggregation operators including min-, max-, geometric mean, and the γ-operator have been tested [Zimmermann, Zysno 1980]. Based on previous publications where min- and product-operators have been investigated [Thole et al. 1979], it turned out that the γ-operator provided best results. The general formula to aggregate m membership values μi to an overall value using the γ-operator is:

$$(\prod_{i=1}^{m} \mu_i)^{1-\gamma} * (1- \prod_{i=1}^{m}(1-\mu_i))^{\gamma}$$

If necessary, each membership value could be weighted by an exponent δi which is not shown here explicitly; for further details see e.g. [Zimmermann, Zysno 1983].

Based on data from several credit seeking applicants the presented model based on the γ-operator has been applied and compared to other operators [Zimmermann, Zysno 1983]. Comparing observed creditworthiness evaluations with computed ones has shown a very good performance of the proposed model. This research has initiated many other publications where fuzzy logic has been used in the area of decision making, especially for evaluation of creditworthiness . Some of them are referred to below.

An empirical investigation similar to the one mentioned in this chapter so far has been performed in a project that aimed at the explanation how credit managers of banks arrive at creditworthiness evaluations of small firms [Rommelfanger 1993]. Since the techniques used there are already described above, no further details on the respective investigations are given here.

2.2 Fuzzy Connectionist Models for Decision Making on Creditworthiness

Based on the application presented in chapter 2.1 of this contribution a fuzzy connectionist model for decision making on creditworthiness has been developed. This fuzzy connectionist expert system "uses fuzzy logic for the implementation and reasoning under uncertainty and takes advantage of a connectionist architecture" [Romaniuk, Hall 1992].

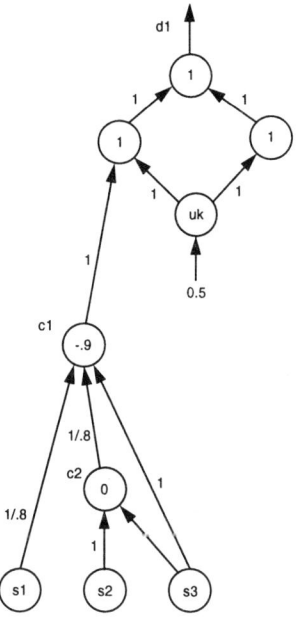

Fig. 2.2. Learning example with input vector [Romaniuk, Hall 1992, p. 17]

The connectionist model consists of three types of cells (input, output, and hidden cells) and has in its simplest format no feedback loops. Such cells are connected with each other via weighted links. Operators which are used e.g. in the above mentioned hierarchical system for creditworthiness evaluation are represented by cells in this connectionist model. The following figure shows such a structure for a given input vector.

Based on the same input data as specified in [Zimmermann, Zysno 1983] the proposed connectionist model could learn fuzzy rules for creditworthiness evaluation [Romaniuk, Hall 1992].

This system has been applied in subsequent studies to different domains and methodological improvements are presented e.g. in [Romaniuk 1993].

2.3 Processing of Rules for Evaluating the Creditability of Firms

In literature, it has been proposed to use the rule-based approach known from many fuzzy control applications in order to model expert knowledge in the non-technical domain. One example for this approach is described e.g. in

[Rommelfanger 1993] where a rule-based fuzzy system for evaluating material business creditability is presented. The techniques to apply such a rule-based fuzzy systems are similar to most of the fuzzy control applications and explained in detail in e.g. [Zimmermann 1996].

In a project with a major German bank an expert team of this bank has formulated fuzzy if-then rules which reflect their knowledge concerning the evaluation of business creditability. These rules are based on the respective linguistic variables and membership functions which have been defined in meetings of knowledge engineers and bank experts. The rules are given by tables as shown below.

Table 2.1. Rules for the Evaluation of "State of Liquidity"

Liquidity I	Liquidity II	Target Value		State of Liquidity
p	p	p		p-
p	p	m		p-
p	p	g		p
...	...	...		...
g	g	p		g-
g	g	m		g+
g	g	g		g+

The expressions used in this table have the following meaning: p: poor, m: medium, g: good; +/- denote a very good / bad fulfillment

Each row represents one rule, e.g. the rule given by the first row says: If (Liquidity I is poor) and (Liquidity II is poor) and (Target Value is poor) Then (State of Liquidity is very poor)

The proposed rule-based system gave promising results and is considered in many other similar applications [Rommelfanger 1993].

3 An Application at a Credit Insurance Company

This chapter describes a fuzzy system developed for the German credit insurance company Allgemeine Kreditversicherung AG and presents its implementation and results.

3.1 Problem Formulation

In daily business, companies offer and deliver their products and / or services to their customers. If, however, some of the customers are not solvent, problems for the supplier may occur if open bills are not or not fully paid. To avoid such cases, credit insurance companies offer two kinds of products:

Firstly, if an insurance contract for such businesses has been signed between supplier and a credit insurance company, the insured sum will be paid to the supplier in case of a claim. Secondly, by analyzing the economic situation of the supplier's customer, the credit insurance company will examine his financial standing. In case of poor solvency, bad debts could possibly be avoided before the transaction takes place. Therefore, a credit insurance company offers indemnification as well as loss prevention to suppliers.

The supplier has to name his customers to the credit insurance company which will then analyze the risks caused by these customers. If a company is analyzed for the first time, it will be stored in the insurer's data base and the corresponding information will be regularly updated in order to have a basis for future investigations. Other information sources are newspapers, inquiry offices, and domestic and foreign information agencies. Additionally, the policy holder is obliged to inform the credit insurance company about all circumstances relevant to credit analysis. Figure 3.1 displays the relations described.

There are many different forms of credit insurance contracts. In this investigation we have considered the credit insurance which includes domestic credit insurance and export credit insurance. The first deals with businesses between German suppliers and German customers. The latter covers the same kind of business between German suppliers and foreign customers. To gather information is, however, much more difficult in the case of export credit insurance. Therefore, some credit insurance companies are organized in the International Credit Insurance Association (ICIA) where member companies exchange information. The information-giving company shares also in the risk insured so that each member in this organization has an advantage of keeping the information most up-to-date.

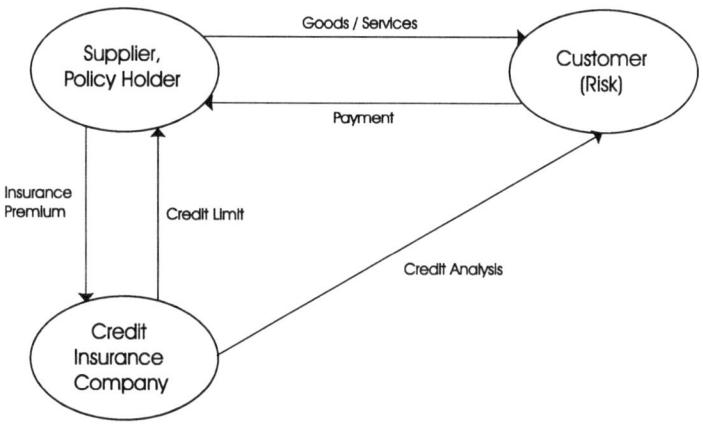

Fig. 3.1. Relationships between supplier, customer, and insurance company

3.2 Current Solution

At Allgemeine Kreditversicherung, 50,000 credit analyses are performed each month [Barczewski et al. 1996]. Obviously, these cannot be solely done by human operators. This high volume of potential risks has led to the first On-line Service for credit analysis offered by a German credit insurance company. This system was installed in 1990 and provides direct access to a data base where a customer has to state the name of his customer and credit limit requested. Based on this information an EDP-based system puts this inquiry into one of three cases. A request may be accepted or rejected automatically or, in case of doubts, be transferred to the credit department where experts analyze the financial standing. This process is shown graphically in figure 3.2. The already installed system is based on rules which are checked sequentially and model certain criteria, respectively.

If all rules are satisfied, the risk will be accepted and insured up to the limit specified by the policy holder. If one of the rules is violated, the risk will be rejected. Some of these rules contain thresholds for the individual decision. One rule, for example, considers the age of the company under investigation. There is a crisp threshold of two years which is used to decide on acceptance or rejection.

The installed system has worked fairly well since 1990. There are, however, at least two directions for further improvement. Firstly, for several decisions, crisp thresholds are used. This does not always reflect experience and knowledge of credit analysts and therefore leads to automatically derived decisions which deviate from expert decisions. Secondly, sequential evaluation of such rules does not allow for compensation between criteria which are modeled by different rules. If, for example, the first rule decides rejection, no other rule is considered, even if their criteria could be fulfilled quite well. The fuzzy system for credit analysis proposed in this contribution mitigates these two shortcomings.

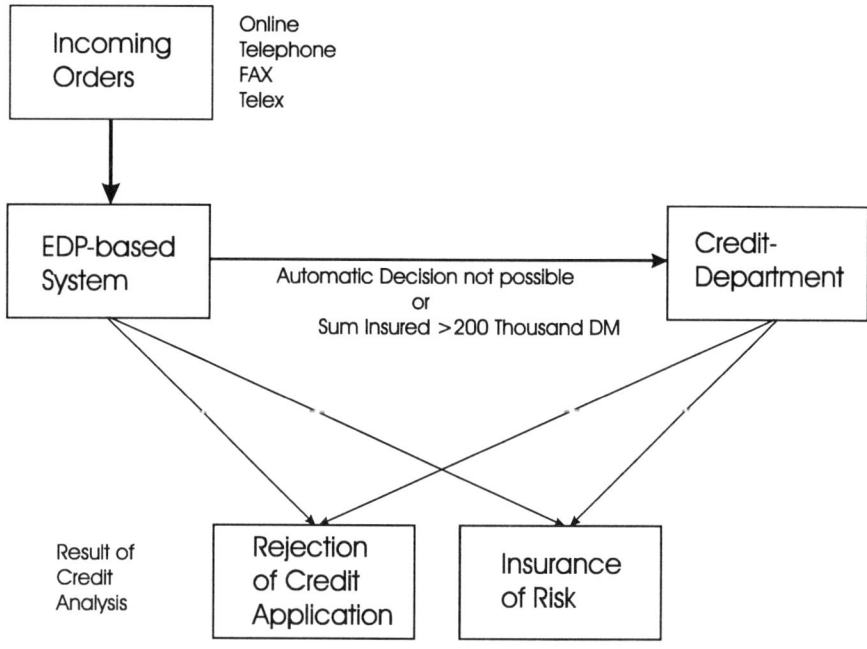

Fig. 3.2. Process of Credit Analysis

3.3 Development of the Fuzzy System for Credit Analysis

In this paper we describe the system for credit analysis in the area of domestic credit insurance as it has been implemented for a German credit insurance company [Barczewski et al. 1996]. A similar system has been developed for export credit insurance.

In this project a system for credit analysis was developed which models the way human experts analyze companies and judge about their creditworthiness. The input variables for this system were determined by the information stored in the existing data base. One of these variables is the age of a company for which a crisp threshold is defined in the conventional system. During the project it became apparent that experts do not work with such thresholds nor do they examine sequentially by considering one criterion after the other. Therefore, it has been decided to build a rule-based fuzzy system to model the way how experts analyze the financial standing of companies. In such a system both shortcomings mentioned above can be treated adequately. Vague judgment instead of crisp thresholds is described by linguistic variables for the respective input variables, as shown in figure 3.3 for the linguistic variable age with its terms young, medium, and old.

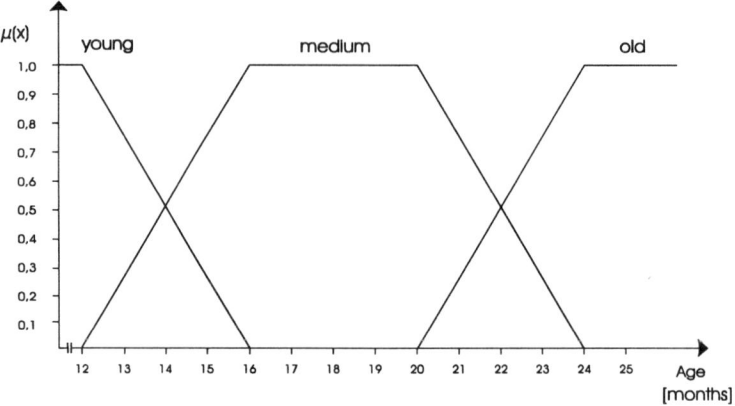

Fig. 3.3. Linguistic variable age

Second, the problem of sequential consideration of criteria can be handled by considering all relevant criteria simultaneously, as shown in figure 3.4 where the structure of the respective fuzzy system is sketched.

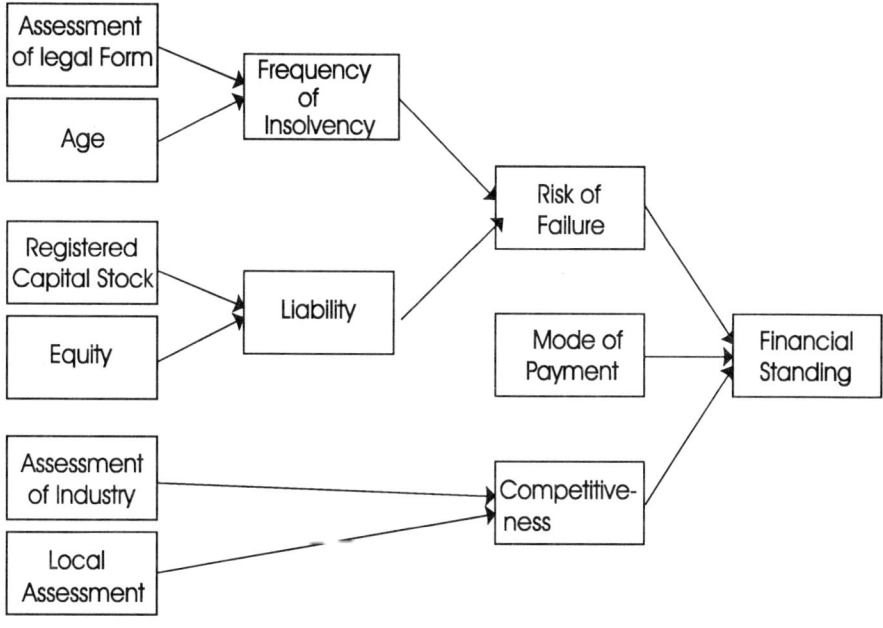

Fig. 3.4. Structure of the fuzzy system for credit analysis

For each branch in this tree, fuzzy rules have been formulated based on their terms. The entire system consists of 48 rules which are processed by standard fuzzy inference procedures as described e.g. in [Zimmermann 1996]. An example for such a rule is:

If „Age is young" and „Assessment of Legal Form is bad" Then „Frequency of Insolvency is very high"

3.4 Implementation and Results of the Credit Analysis System

The proposed system has been implemented and tested using DataEngine [MIT 1997a]. This software tool for intelligent data analysis uses different soft computing techniques and is described in more detail in the following chapter. To apply the proposed system for automatic credit analysis, the rule base had to be transferred to the insurance company's mainframe. For this purpose, a special interface was developed in order to ensure an on-line application of the fuzzy rule base.

The developed system was tested based on 46 real cases from the data base. The respective results were compared to the results given by the already installed conventional system as well as to decisions made by a group of seven experts.

Group of 7 experts	Fuzzy System	Conventional System
32 risks accepted by group of experts	31 risks accepted (96.875 %) 1 risk rejected (3,125 %)	23 risks accepted (71,875 %) 8 risks rejected (25 %) 1 risk could not be decided (3,125 %)
14 risks rejected by group of experts	12 risks rejected (85.7 %) 2 risks accepted with in-surance sum between minimum and maximum given by the experts (14,3 %)	13 risks rejected (92.9 %) 1 risk could not be decided (7,1 %)

Table 3.1. Results of the developed fuzzy system for credit analysis

Based on the input variables the conventional system accepts a proposal if all criteria are satisfied. In such cases the required credit limit is given. The fuzzy system, however, computes a degree of solvency for the respective company. Based on this degree, which is a number between 0 and 1, a credit limit is specified.

Both automatic systems are said to give correct decisions, if the suggested amount of the system lies between the minimal and maximal credit limit given by the experts. Table 3.1 shows the results of this comparison. The percentage given for the two automatic systems is based on the decision by the group of experts in the respective row. It can be seen that the fuzzy system accepts more risks than the conventional system. This is due to the fact, that a compensation between criteria takes place instead of a sequential evaluation of rules with sharp threshold. The insured sum, however, is lower for the fuzzy system than for the conventional system, since the conventional system insures the amount requested in case of acceptance whereas the fuzzy system computes a degree of solvency as a basis for the insurance.

The presented fuzzy system will be used in daily operation in order to decide automatically about incoming proposals. This application will lead to a further improvement of the fuzzy system. These experiences from domestic credit insurance will also influence the system for export credit insurance which will be implemented in a second step.

4 Software Tools for Creditworthiness Evaluation

In this chapter we present DataEngine, the software tool for data analysis we have used for creditworthiness evaluation.

DataEngine contains different methods for data analysis, like fuzzy clustering, fuzzy rule based systems and neural networks as well as statistics [MIT 1997a]. In addition to these modules, DataEngine supplies standard signal processing capabilities such as fast fourier transformation, smoothing, digital filtering and more.

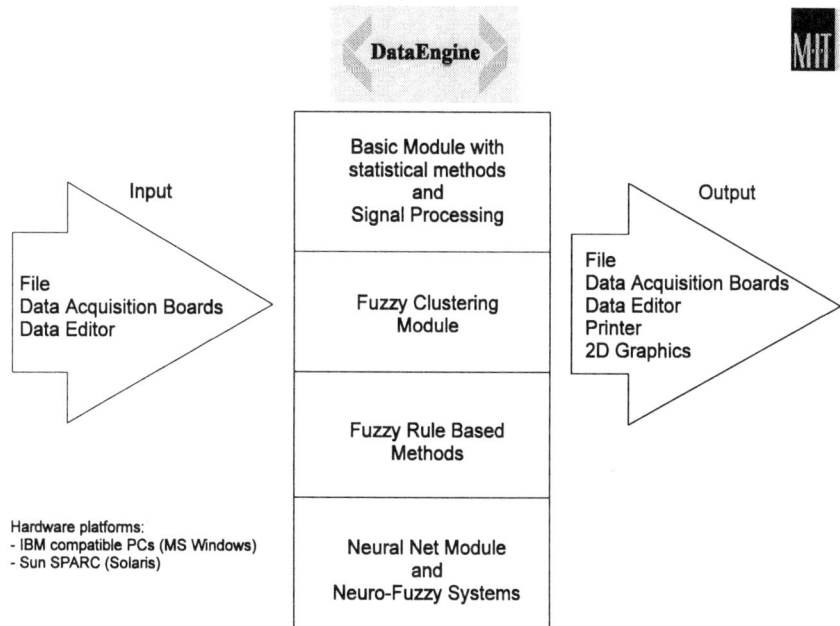

Fig. 4.1. Structure of DataEngine

The integration of a system developed in DataEngine into an already existing application program at an insurance company could be performed by DataEngine ADL - Application Development Library. This is a software component which is available as a C++ class library for various compilers and platforms [MIT 1997b]. DataEngine ADL has been used in the above described project to integrate the fuzzy system for creditworthiness evaluation developed in DataEngine into the application program that can be used for the overall decision process of credit insurance.

5 Conclusions

The fuzzy system for credit analysis presented in this paper has shown good results on the test cases. The advantage of fuzzy techniques to model human knowledge and experience enables the generation of the proposed system. The used approach where various criteria are aggregated to a top-criterion could be transferred to a high variety of tasks not only in the area of insurance companies. There are similar problems from other financial institutions, but also from totally different fields which could be modeled using the same structure. Just to mention a few of them, one could think of risk assessment in e.g. power plants [Jovanovic et al. 1993], evaluation of patient conditions in medicine, and environmental assessments.

References

Barczewski, T., Rust, H. J., Weber, R., Zygan, H. (1996): A Fuzzy System for Credit Analysis in a German Credit Insurance Company. Proceedings EUFIT '96 - Fourth European Congress on Intelligent Techniques and Soft Computing, Aachen, Germany, September, 2-5, 1996, 2215-2218

Geyer-Schulz, A. (1995): Fuzzy Rule-Based Expert Systems and Genetic Machine Learning. Physica-Verlag, Heidelberg

Jovanovic, A., Psomas, S., De Witte, M., Bath, U.: Development of an Integrated System for Decision Optimization in Power Plants Maintenance. Proceedings EUFIT '93 - First European Congress on Fuzzy and Intelligent Technologies, Aachen, September 1993, S. 83-86

Leigh, D. (1995): Neural Networks for Credit Scoring. In: Intelligent Systems for Finance and Business, S. Goonatilake, P. Treleaven (eds.), John Wiley & Sons, Chichester, 61-69

MIT (1997a): DataEngine 2.1. Manual, Aachen

MIT (1997b): DataEngine ADL - Application Development Library 2.1. Manual, Aachen

Romaniuk, S.G. (1993): Fuzzy Rule Extraction for Determining Creditworthiness of Credit Applicants. In: Proceedings of the First European Congress on Fuzzy and Intelligent Technologies, Aachen, Germany, 1356-1361

Romaniuk, S.G., Hall, L.O. (1992): Decision Making on Creditworthiness, using a Fuzzy Connectionist Model. Fuzzy Sets and Systems 48, p. 15-22

Rommelfanger, H. J. (1993): Fuzzy Logic-Based Processing of Expert Rules Used for Checking the Creditability of Small Business Firms. In: Klement, E.P., Slany, W. (Eds.): Fuzzy Logic in Artificial Intelligence. Springer-Verlag, p. 103-113

Thole,U., Zimmermann, H.-J., Zysno,P. (1979): On the Suitability of Minimum and Product Operators for the Intersection of Fuzzy Sets. Fuzzy Sets and Systems 2, 167-180

Walker, R.F., Haasdijk, E.W., Gerrets, M.C. (1995): Credit Evaluation Using a Genetic Algorithm. In: Intelligent Systems for Finance and Business, S. Goonatilake, P. Treleaven (eds.), John Wiley & Sons, Chichester, 39-59

Zimmermann, H.-J. (1996): Fuzzy Set Theory - And Its Applications. 3rd rev. ed., Kluwer, Boston

Zimmermann, H.-J., Zysno, P. (1980): Latent Connectives in Human Decision Making. Fuzzy Sets and Systems 4, 37-51

Zimmermann, H.-J., Zysno, P. (1983): Decisions and Evaluations by Hierarchical Aggregation of Information. Fuzzy Sets and Systems 10, 243-260

Rough Set Predictor of Business Failure

R. Slowinski[*], C. Zopounidis[**],
S. A.I. Dimitras[***] and R. Susmaga[****]

[*,****]Institute of Computing Science
Poznań University of Technology
Piotrowo 3a

60–965 Poznań, Poland

E-mail: [*]slowinsk@sol.put.poznan.pl,
[****]roberts@sirius.cs.put.poznan.pl

[**,***]Decision Support Systems Laboratory
Technical University of Crete
University Campus

73100 Chania, Greece

E-mail: [***]kostas@ergasya.tuc.gr

Abstract

We are addressing the problem of business failure prediction using the rough set methodology. A learning sample of 80 Greek firms, divided into healthy and bankrupt ones and described by 12 financial attributes, is analysed with the aim to evaluate the relevance of particular attributes for bankruptcy prediction, and to find satisfactory approximations of the two classes of firms using minimal sets of attributes. Then, a generalised description of these approximations is induced in form of decision rules. In order to evaluate the predictive capabilities of the decision rules, the rules are applied on the firms from the learning sample, but described by data from 4 consecutive years prior to the reference year, and on the firms from a testing sample, in 3 consecutive years prior to the reference year. The results of the rough set analysis are compared to those of a well-known inductive learning method, called C4.5. It appears that the rough set approach provides a good tool for the prediction of business failure.

Keywords. Business failure prediction, rough set theory, inductive learning, decision rules, decision trees, classification

1 Introduction

Business failure prediction is a research direction in which many academic and professional people have been working for, at least, three last decades. Also, financial organisations, such as banks, credit institutions, clients, etc., need these predictions for firms in which they have an interest.

This interest gave rise to many methods for business failure prediction. They are based on discriminant analysis, logit and probit analysis, recursive partitioning, mathematical programming, survival analysis, expert systems, neural networks and multicriteria decision aid methodology. Most of these methods mentioned above have already been investigated in the course of comparative studies related in several review articles (see Altman (1984), Jones (1987), Keasey and Watson (1991), Scott (1981), Zavgren (1983), among others). Dimitras *et al.* (1995) and Zopounidis (1995) gave a complete review of methods used for the prediction of business failure and of new trends in this area.

Recently, new methods of predicting business failure have been developed. Due to the advancement of computer and information science, they offer the financial institution's managers significant aid in the evaluation and selection of viable firms for financing. One of these new methods is based on the rough set theory introduced by Pawlak (1982). In the course of our previous studies, the rough set approach proved to be an effective tool for the analysis of information tables (financial information tables) describing a set of objects (firms) by a set of multi-valued attributes (financial ratios) (see Slowinski and Zopounidis, 1995). In Slowinski *et al.* (1997) and Dimitras *et al.* (1997) the rough set approach has been compared with the classic method of discriminant analysis on financial applications. The aim of this paper is to compare the rough set approach with one of well-known inductive learning methods, namely C4.5 (see Quinlan (1993)), on a real case of business failure prediction.

Section 2 recalls the basic concepts of the rough set theory. The application of the rough set approach on a sample of Greek firms is presented in section 3. Three sets of decision rules obtained using the rough set-based induction algorithms were put to a reclassification test summarised in section 4. In section 5, a comparison of results obtained using the rough set approach and the inductive learning method C4.5 is presented. In the concluding remarks, the merits of the rough set approach for the business failure prediction are discussed.

2 Basic concepts of the rough set theory

2.1 Introductory remarks

Rough set theory was introduced by Z. Pawlak (1982). It is an excellent tool to handle granularity of data. It has attracted attention of many researchers and practitioners all over the world, who contributed to its development and applications during the last decade (see e.g. Pawlak (1991), Slowinski (1992), Ziarko (1994), Lin and Wildberger (1995), Pawlak *et al.* (1995), Slowinski (1995)). Rough set theory may be used to describe dependencies between attributes, to evaluate relevance of attributes, and to deal with inconsistent data, to name just a few possible uses. As an approach to handling imperfect data (uncertainty and vagueness), it complements other theories that deal with data uncertainty, such as probability theory, evidence theory, fuzzy set theory, etc.

The rough set philosophy is founded on the assumption that with every object of the universe of discourse we associate some information (data, knowledge). Objects characterized by the same information are indiscernible in view of the available information about them. The indiscernibility relation generated in this way is the mathematical basis for the rough set theory.

Any set of all indiscernible objects is called an elementary set, and forms a basic granule of knowledge about the universe. Any set of objects being a union of some elementary sets is referred to as crisp (precise) — otherwise the set is rough (imprecise, vague). Consequently, each rough set has boundary-line cases, i.e. objects which cannot be classified with certainty as members of the set or of its complement.

Therefore, a rough set can be represented by a pair of crisp sets, called the lower and the upper approximation. The lower approximation consists of all objects which certainly belong to the set and the upper approximation contains objects which possibly belong to the set.

2.2 Information table and indiscernibility relation

For algorithmic reasons, knowledge about objects will be represented in the form of an information table. The rows of the table are labelled by *objects*, whereas columns are labelled by *attributes*. Entries of the table are *attribute values*. In general, we will use the notion of attribute instead of criterion because the former is more general than the latter; the domain (scale) of a criterion has to be ordered according to decreasing or increasing preference while the domain of the attribute does not have to be ordered. We will use the notion of criterion only when the preferential ordering of the attribute domain will be important in a given context.

Formally, by an *information table* we understand the 4-tuple S=<U,Q,V,f>, where U is a finite set of objects, Q is a finite set of *attributes*, $V = \bigcup_{q \in Q} V_q$, where V_q is a domain of the attribute q, and $f : U \times Q \rightarrow V$ is a total function such that $f(x,q) \in V_q$ for every $q \in Q$, $x \in U$, called an *information function* (Pawlak, 1991).

Let S=<U,Q,V,f> be an information table and let $P \subseteq Q$ and $x,y \in U$. We say that x and y are indiscernible by the set of attributes P in S iff $f(x,q)=f(y,q)$ for every $q \in P$. Thus every $P \subseteq Q$ generates a binary relation on U, called *P-indiscernibility relation*, denoted by I_P. Obviously, I_P is an equivalence relation for any P. Equivalence classes of the relation I_P are called *P-elementary sets* in S and $I_P(x)$ denotes the P-elementary set containing the object $x \in U$.

2.3 Approximation of sets

Let $P \subseteq Q$ and $Y \subseteq U$. The *P-lower approximation* of Y, denoted by $\underline{P}Y$, and the *P-upper approximation* of Y, denoted by $\overline{P}Y$, are defined as:

$$\underline{P}Y = \{x \in Y : I_P(x) \subseteq Y\}, \tag{1}$$

$$\overline{P}Y = \bigcup_{x \in Y} I_P(x). \tag{2}$$

The *P-boundary* (doubtful region) of set Y, denoted by $BN_P(Y)$, is defined as:

$$BN_P(Y) = \overline{P}Y - \underline{P}Y. \tag{3}$$

Set $\underline{P}Y$ is the set of all elements of U which can be certainly classified as elements of Y using the set of attributes P. Set $\overline{P}Y$ is the set of elements of U which can be possibly classified as elements of Y, using the set of attributes P. The set $BN_P(Y)$ is the set of elements which cannot be certainly classified to Y using the set of attributes P.

With every set $Y \subseteq U$, we can associate an *accuracy of approximation* of the set Y by P, or in short, accuracy of Y, defined as:

$$\alpha_P(Y) = \frac{card(\underline{P}Y)}{card(\overline{P}Y)} \tag{4}$$

where card() means cardinality of a set.

Let S be an information table, $P \subseteq Q$, and let $Y = \{Y_1, Y_2, ..., Y_n\}$ be a classification, or partition, of U. The origin of this classification is independent from attributes contained in P. Subsets Y_i, i=1,...,n, are classes of the classification Y. By P-lower (P-upper) approximation of Y in S we mean sets $\underline{P}Y = \{\underline{P}Y_1, \underline{P}Y_2 ,..., \underline{P}Y_n\}$ and $\overline{P}Y = \{\overline{P}Y_1, \overline{P}Y_2 ,..., \overline{P}Y_n\}$, respectively. The coefficient

$$\gamma_P(Y) = \frac{\sum_{i=1}^{n} card(\underline{P}Y_i)}{card(U)} \tag{5}$$

is called the *quality of approximation of classification* Y by the set of attributes P, or in short, *quality of classification*. It expresses the ratio of all P-correctly classified objects to all objects in the system.

2.4 Reduction and dependency of attributes

We say that the set of attributes $R \subseteq Q$ depends on the set of attributes $P \subseteq Q$ in S (denotation $P \rightarrow R$) iff $I_P \subseteq I_R$. Discovering dependencies between attributes is of primary importance in the rough set approach to information table analysis.

Another important issue is that of attribute reduction, which is performed in such a way that a reduced set of attributes P, $P \subseteq Q$, is to ensure the same quality of classification $\gamma_P(Y)$ (see formula (5)) as the original set of attributes Q. The minimal subset $R \subseteq P \subseteq Q$ such that $\gamma_P(Y) = \gamma_R(Y)$ is called *Y-reduct* of P (or, simply, *reduct* if there is no ambiguity in the understanding of Y) and denoted by $RED_Y(P)$. Let us notice that an information table may have more than one Y-reduct. Intersection of all Y-reducts is called the Y-core of P, i.e. $CORE_Y(P) = \cap \, RED_Y(P)$. The core is a collection of the most relevant attributes in the table.

2.5 Decision rules

An information table can be seen as *decision table* assuming that $Q = C \cup D$ and $C \cap D = \emptyset$, where set C contains so called *condition attributes*, and D contains *decision attributes*.

From the decision table $S = <U, C \cup D, V, f>$, defined as in section 2.2, a set of *decision rules* can be derived. Let us assume that D is a singleton, i.e. $D = \{d\}$, which does not decrease the generality of further considerations. The d-elementary sets in S are denoted by Y_t (t=1,...,n) and called *decision classes*. Describing decision classes in terms of condition attributes from C, one gets lower and upper approximations, $\underline{C}Y_t$ and $\overline{C}Y_t$, respectively, as well as the boundaries $BN_C(Y_t) = \overline{C}Y_t - \underline{C}Y_t$, t=1,...,n, according to formulae (1), (2) and (3).

A *decision rule* can be expressed as a logical statement:

IF *conjunction of elementary conditions*
THEN *disjunction of elementary decisions*

The elementary condition formulae over subset $A \subseteq C$ and domain V_{a_i} of attribute $a_i \in A$ are defined as: $f(x, a_i) = v_i$, where $x \in U$, $v_{a_i} \in V_{a_i}$. By $cond_A$ we denote a conjunction of elementary condition formulae, i.e.

$$f(x, a_1) = v_{a_1} \wedge ... \wedge f(x, a_r) = v_{a_r}, \text{ for all } a_i \in A,$$

and by $[cond_A]$ we understand the set of all objects satisfying conjunction $cond_A$. Obviously, if object $x \in [cond_A]$ then $[cond_A] = I_A(x)$.

Similarly, we define elementary decision formula $f(x, d) = v_t$, where $v_t \in V_d$. By dec_D we denote a disjunction of elementary decision formulae, i.e.

$$f(x, d) = v_1 \vee ... \vee f(x, d) = v_s, \text{ where } 1 \leq s \leq n,$$

and by $[dec_D]$ we understand a set of objects belonging either to the lower approximation of one of the decision classes (if $s = 1$) or to the common boundary of s decision classes (if $s > 1$). Precisely:

$$[dec_D] = \begin{cases} \underline{C}Y_t, & \text{if } s = 1 \text{ and } (f(x, d) = v_t) \equiv dec_D \\ \bigcap\limits_{t:\, (f(x,d)=v_t) \in dec_D} BN_C(Y_t), & \text{if } s > 1. \end{cases} \qquad (6)$$

The decision rule 'IF $cond_A$ THEN dec_D' is *consistent* iff $[cond_A] \subseteq [dec_D]$. If $s = 1$, i.e. dec_D consists of one elementary decision only, the decision rule is *exact*, otherwise it is *approximate*. Approximate rules are consequences of an approximate description of decision classes in terms of blocks of objects (granules) indiscernible by condition attributes. It means that using the available knowledge, one is unable to decide whether some objects (from the boundary region) belong to a given decision class or not.

Each decision rule r is characterised by the *strength* of its suggestion, which is defined as the number of objects satisfying the condition part of the rule (we say, *covered* by the rule) and belonging to the suggested decision class. In the case of approximate rules, the strength is calculated for each possible decision class separately. Stronger rules are usually more general, i.e. their condition parts are shorter and less specialised.

Procedures for generation of decision rules from a decision table operate on inductive learning principles. The objects are considered as examples of decisions. In order to induce decision rules describing a set of objects [dec_D], the examples belonging to [dec_D] are called *positive* and all the others are called *negative*. A decision rule is *discriminant* if it is consistent, i.e. distinguishes positive examples from negative ones, and minimal, i.e. removing any elementary condition from $cond_A$, producing $cond_{A'}$, would result in [$cond_{A'}$]⊆[dec_D] (consistency violation).

It may be also interesting to look for *partly discriminant* rules (see Mienko *et al.* 1996b). These are rules which besides positive examples cover a relatively small number of negative ones. They are characterised by a coefficient called *level of discrimination* specifying to what extent the rule is consistent, i.e. what is the ratio of positive examples to all examples covered by the rule.

Procedures for induction of decision rules from decision tables were presented by Grzymala-Busse (1992), Skowron (1993), Stefanowski and Vanderpooten (1994), Mienko *et al.* (1996b), and by Ziarko *et al.* (1993).

The existing induction algorithms use one of the following strategies:

(a) generation of a minimal set of rules covering all objects from a decision table,
(b) generation of an exhaustive set of rules consisting of all possible rules for a decision table,
(c) generation of a set of 'strong' decision rules, fully or partly discriminant, covering relatively many objects each, but not necessarily all objects from the decision table.

2.6 Decision support using decision rules

Decision rules derived from a decision table can be used for recommendations concerning new objects. Specifically, the classification of a new object can be supported by matching its description to that of the decision rules. The matching may lead to one of four situations (Slowinski and Stefanowski 1994):

(a) the new object matches one exact rule,
(b) the new object matches more than one exact rule indicating, however, the same decision class,
(c) the new object matches one approximate rule or several rules indicating different decision classes,
(d) the new object does not match any of the rules.

In case (a) and (b), the recommendation is univocal. In the case of ambiguous matching (c), the user is informed about the total strength of all matching rules with respect to suggested decision classes.

In the case of no rules matching the new object (d), one can help the user by presenting him/her a set of the rules 'nearest' to the description of the new object. In (Slowinski, 1993), a distance measure has been proposed based on a *valued closeness relation* (VCR), having some good properties. It involves indifference (q_i), strict difference (p_i) and veto (v_i) thresholds on each attribute a_i, provided by the area expert together with relative weights k_i of the attributes. This additional information is used in concordance and discordance tests whose goals are to:

(i) characterise a group of attributes considered to be in concordance with the affirmation 'object x is close to rule y', and assess the relative importance of this group,
(ii) characterise among the attributes which are not in concordance with the above affirmation the ones whose opposition is strong enough to reduce the credibility of the closeness which would result from taking into account just the concordance, and to calculate the possible reduction that would thereby result.

The same tests have been used for construction of the outranking relation by Roy (1985).

3 Application of the rough set approach

3.1 The data

A large number of firms which failed in Greece in the years 1986–1990 were collected. From this large set, 40 firms from 13 industries having been in business for more than five years were selected. The financial statements of these firms were collected for a period of five years, starting from year −5 (five years before bankruptcy) and ending with the year −1 (one year prior to the year of bankruptcy, the last year that the firm has been in business). Obviously, the actual year of bankruptcy (year 0) is not the same for all the firms, as they did not failed all in the same year.

The 40 failed firms were matched one by one to 40 'healthy' firms, i.e. firms that did not failed for bankruptcy. The healthy firms were chosen among those of the same industry and having also similar total assets and number of employees for the year −1 to the corresponding failed firm. For healthy firms there were also collected the financial statements for five years, similarly to the failed ones. This way of composing the sample of firms was also used by several researchers in the past, e.g. Beaver (1966), Altman (1968), Zavgren (1985). Its aim is to minimise the effect of such factors as industry or size that in some cases can be very important.

Except from the above learning sample a second testing sample was collected, consisting of 19 firms bankrupt in the period from 1991 to the middle of 1993, as well as 19 healthy firms, using a similar approach.

Using the financial statements of the firms (i.e. balance sheets and net income statements), 28 financial ratios were calculated. The small number of ratios is due to missing data and no availability of the sales volume reported by Greek firms, mainly for taxation reasons. Unfortunately, qualitative characteristics of the firms providing satisfactory reliability were not available either, as it is the case in many countries.

More details about the design of the samples and their characteristics are given in (Dimitras, 1995).

For the application of the rough set approach, the credit manager of a large Greek bank was employed to act as a decision maker (DM). The DM played an important role in:

(i)   the choice of the attributes (financial ratios) entering the information table,
(ii) the discretisation of the continuous attributes, by setting norms dividing the original domains of the attributes into sub-intervals,
(iii) the selection of a satisfactory reduct of attributes from among all reducts calculated for the learning sample, and
(iv) the test of decision rules on the testing sample.

Firstly, from the set of the 28 available financial ratios, 12 were selected by the DM to enter the information table (see Table 1). This choice was justified by:

(i)   the fact that the selected ratios represent well all three categories proposed by Courtis (1978), i.e. (a) profitability, (b) managerial performance and (c) solvency ratios,
(ii) a primary analysis of the characteristics of the two groups of firms (bankrupt versus healthy firms) presented to the DM, and
(iii) the preferences of the DM, his knowledge and experience about the Greek economy and Greek industrial firms.

Then, the DM was asked to discretise the continuous financial ratios providing norms according to his knowledge and the primary analysis of the groups. The discretisation is performed because the precision of financial ratios is rather doubtful and, moreover, it prevents drawing general conclusions from data in term of dependencies, reducts and decision rules.

The sub-intervals proposed for discretisation are presented in Table 2. Firms for which the values of these financial ratios are in the same sub-intervals are supposed to have very similar characteristics and behaviour. Using these sub-intervals and the principle: 'the higher the code, the better the sub-interval', a coded information table was obtained. According to this principle, decreasing attributes a7 and a11, for which the lower the value of the ratio the better for the firm, were given codes in the inverse order of the sub-intervals. It was also an opportunity to make some corrections of the preference scale in the case where the preference of the DM was not concordant with the increasing or decreasing sequence of sub-intervals. For example, this happened for attribute a1, where the fourth sub-interval $(1, +\infty)$ has the lowest preference because values higher than 1 mean a loss in Net Income as well as in Gross Profit, so it was given the code number 1 while the first, second and third sub-intervals were given the code numbers 2, 3, and 4, respectively.

The coded information table prepared for further analysis consisted of 80 firms (objects) belonging to the learning sample; they were described by 12 coded attributes (financial ratios), using data from one year before bankruptcy (year -1), and by the binary assignment to a decision class (healthy or bankrupt, coded by 1 and 0, respectively).

3.2 Presentation of the results

The rough set analysis of the coded information table has been performed using the systems RoughDAS and ProFIT (Mienko *et al.*, 1996a). It produced the following results.

The whole set of attributes C provided perfect approximation of the decision classes as well as the quality of classification. It means that $\alpha_C(Y^1) = 1$ and $\alpha_C(Y^0) = 1$, where Y^1 and Y^0 are the decision classes corresponding to the healthy and to the bankrupt firms, respectively. In consequence, $\gamma_C(\{Y^1, Y^0\}) = 1$ (quality of approximation of the classification is equal to one). See formulae (4) and (5).

Table 1: Attributes (financial ratios) considered in the information table

Attribute	
a1	Net Income / Gross Profit
a2	Gross Profit / Total Assets
a3	Net Income / Total Assets
a4	Net Income / Net Worth
a5	Current Assets / Current Liabilities
a6	Quick Assets / Current Liabilities
a7	(Long Term Debt + Current Liabilities) / Total Assets
a8	Net Worth / (Net Worth + Long Term Debt)
a9	Net Worth / Net Fixed Assets
a10	Inventories / Working Capital
a11	Current Liabilities / Total Assets
a12	Working Capital / Net Worth

Table 2: Sub-intervals (norms) and their codes defined for the 12 attributes

Attri-bute	1st	2nd	Interval / Code 3rd	4th	5th
a1	(-∞, 0.00]/ 2	(0.00, 0.25]/ 3	(0.25, 1.00]/ 4	(1.00, +∞)/ 1	
a2	(-∞, 0.00]/ 1	(0.00, 0.25]/ 2	(0.25, 0.50]/ 3	(0.50, +∞]/ 4	
a3	(-∞, -0.05]/ 1	(-0.05, 0.05]/ 2	(0.05, 0.20]/ 3	(0.20, +∞)/ 4	
a4	(-∞, 0.00]/ 1	(0.00, 0.25]/ 2	(0.25, +∞)/ 3		
a5	[0.00, 0.70]/ 1	(0.70, 1.00]/ 2	(1.00, 1.50]/ 3	(1.50, 2.00]/ 4	(2.00, +∞)/ 5
a6	[0.00, 0.50]/ 1	(0.50, 0.80]/ 2	(0.80, 1.00]/ 3	(1.00, 1.20]/ 4	(1.20, +∞)/ 5
a7	[0.0, 0.67]/ 4	(0.67, 0.80]/ 3	(0.80, 1.00]/ 2	(1.00, +∞)/ 1	
a8	(-∞, 0.00]/ 1	(0.00, 0.50]/ 2	(0.50, 1.00]/ 3		
a9	(-∞, 0.00]/ 1	(0.00, 0.30]/ 2	(0.30, +∞)/ 3		
a10	(-∞, 0.00]/ 1	(0.00, 0.50]/ 5	(0.50, 0.75]/ 4	(0.75, 1.00]/ 3	(1.00, +∞)/ 2
a11	[0.0, 0.25]/ 5	(0.25, 0.50]/ 4	(0.50, 0.75]/ 3	(0.75, 1.00]/ 2	(1.00, +∞)/ 1
a12	(-∞, 0.00]/ 1	(0.00, 0.50]/ 2	(0.50, +∞)/ 3		

The core of attributes was empty (see section 2.4). This indicates that no single attribute is absolutely necessary for perfect approximation of the decision classes. Non-empty core would indicate that there are attributes in the system which are indispensable from the discriminating point of view because removal of any of the attributes contained in the core leads immediately to the decrease of the quality of approximation. Additionally, non-empty core helps in determining the most important attributes as far as the approximation of classes is concerned.

54 reducts were obtained for the coded information table (see section 2.4). They contain from 5 to 7 attributes, which is considerably less than 12 – the total number of attributes. This result gives the idea of reduction a strong support because each of the reducts contains fewer attributes which, however, ensure the same quality of approximation as the whole set of attributes Q (the value is equal to 1.0). The attribute with the highest frequency of occurrence in reducts is a11 (47 reducts) and the one with the lowest frequency is a3 (15 reducts). The reducts are presented in Table 3.

The reducts were presented to the DM who was asked to select the one that best fits his/her preferences. This selection was made taking into account two criteria:

(i) the reduct should contain as small number of attributes as possible,
(ii) the reduct should not miss the attributes judged by the DM as the most significant for evaluation of the firms.

The reduct selected was the #16, which includes: a4 (profitability ratio), a5, a7, a9 (solvency ratios) and a11 (managerial performance ratio).

The remaining attributes were then eliminated from the coded information table and a set of decision rules has been derived from the reduced table. Since the quality of classification was equal to 1.0, the boundaries of decision classes were empty and thus all decision rules were exact (one elementary decision per rule).

Three decision rules have been derived from the reduced coded information table according to different possible strategies listed at the end of section 2.5:

(i)   the minimal set of rules is presented in Table 4,
(ii) the exhaustive set of rules, composed of 45 rules, was discarded because of low readability and relatively poor classification accuracy in the reclassification test,
(iii) the set of 'strong' (support: at least 8 objects) and fully discriminant (level of discrimination: 100%) rules is presented in Table 5,
(iv) the set of 'strong' (support: at least 8 objects) and partly discriminant (level of discrimination: 90%) rules is presented in Table 6.

In all three sets of decision rules the number of rules describing the bankrupt (d=0) firms is greater than the number of rules describing the healthy (d=1) firms: 9 or 6 vs. 5 or 4. This means that it is harder to generalize the description of the bankrupt firms than that of the healthy ones.

Before testing the decision rules, the DM was asked to provide information necessary for the definition of the Valued Closeness Relation (VCR). The thresholds and the weights corresponding to the five attributes from the selected reduct are presented in Table 7. According to the DM's preferences, the most important attributes are a5 and a11, followed by a7, a9 and a4.

The sets of decision rules together with the VCR will be considered as predictors of business failure for new firms.

Table 3: Reducts of the coded information table

#	Reduct	#	Reduct
1	{a4, a8, a10, a11, a12}	28	{a1, a5, a7, a8, a11, a12}
2	{a1, a7, a9, a10, a11, a12}	29	{a1, a2, a6, a7, a12}
3	{a1, a3, a8, a10, a11, a12}	30	{a1, a2, a5, a7, a11}
4	{a1, a7, a8, a10, a11, a12}	31	{a1, a4, a5, a9, a11, a12}
5	{a4, a7, a9, a10, a11}	32	{a1, a4, a5, a8, a11, a12}
6	{a4, a5, a9, a10, a11, a12}	33	{a1, a3, a5, a7, a11}
7	{a1, a3, a6, a11, a12}	34	{a2, a4, a6, a7, a9, a12}
8	{a1, a3, a5, a11, a12}	35	{a2, a4, a5, a6, a9, a12}
9	{a3, a4, a6, a9, a11, a12}	36	{a1, a2, a3, a5, a6, a12}
10	{a2, a4, a6, a9, a11}	37	{a2, a3, a4, a6, a9, a10, a12}
11	{a1, a4, a6, a9, a11, a12}	38	{a1, a2, a4, a6, a10, a12}
12	{a1, a2, a7, a10, a11}	39	{a1, a2, a4, a5, a6, a12}

13	{a1, a2, a4, a6, a11, a12}	40	{a1, a6, a7, a9, a10, a11}
14	{a1, a2, a4, a5, a11}	41	{a1, a6, a7, a8, a10, a11}
15	{a1, a3, a7, a10, a11}	42	{a1, a5, a6, a7, a9, a11}
16	{a4, a5, a7, a9, a11}	43	{a1, a5, a6, a7, a8, a11}
17	{a3, a4, a5, a9, a11, a12}	44	{a1, a2, a3, a8, a10, a11}
18	{a2, a4, a5, a9, a11}	45	{a1, a2, a3, a6, a10, a11}
19	{a4, a6, a8, a11, a12}	46	{a1, a2, a3, a5, a11}
20	{a4, a5, a7, a8, a11}	47	{a1, a2, a6, a7, a9, a11}
21	{a3, a4, a5, a8, a11, a12}	48	{a1, a2, a3, a6, a9, a11}
22	{a2, a4, a5, a8, a11}	49	{a2, a4, a8, a10, a11}
23	{a4, a6, a7, a9, a11, a12}	50	{a4, a7, a8, a10, a11}
24	{a4, a5, a6, a9, a11, a12}	51	{a1, a2, a4, a6, a10, a11}
25	{a1, a6, a7, a9, a11, a12}	52	{a2, a4, a6, a8, a11}
26	{a1, a5, a7, a9, a11, a12}	53	{a1, a2, a6, a7, a8, a11}
27	{a1, a6, a7, a8, a11, a12}	54	{a1, a2, a3, a6, a8, a11}

Table 4: The minimal set of decision rules

Rule #	Elementary conditions					Decision	
	a4	a5	a7	a9	a11	d	Strength
#1	1		2			0	15
#2		1				0	12
#3			1			0	12
#4			3		2	0	4
#5	1	3				0	10
#6	2		2			0	3
#7		2	3			0	3
#8				2		0	9
#9		2	4			0	1
#10	2		4			1	18
#11	3			3		1	18
#12	2	3			3	1	5
#13		4	3			1	1

Table 5: The set of 'strong' decision rules (strength≥8)

Rule #	Elementary conditions					Decision	
	a4	a5	a7	a9	a11	d	Strength
#1		1				0	12
#2			1			0	12
#3				1		0	12
#4					1	0	9
#5				2		0	9
#6	1		2			0	15
#7	1	2				0	11
#8	1	3				0	10
#9	1				2	0	12

#10		5				1	12
#11	2		4			1	18
#12			4		4	1	13
#13	3	3				1	9
#14	3			3		1	18

Table 6: The set of 'strong' and partly discriminant decision rules (strength≥8, level of discrimination≥90%)

		Elementary conditions				Decision		Decision	
Rule #	a4	a5	a7	a9	a11	d	Strength	d	Strength
#1		1						0	12
#2			1					0	12
#3				1				0	12
#4					1			0	9
#5				2				0	9
#6	1					1	1	0	33
#7	2				2	1	11	0	1
#8	3					1	18	0	1
#9			4			1	24	0	1
#10		5				1	12		

Table 7: Parameters of the Valued Closeness Relation

Parameter	Attribute				
	a4	a5	a7	a9	a11
q	0	0	0	0	0
p	1	3	1	1	3
v	2	4	3	2	4
k	1.3	1.5	1.4	1.3	1.5

4 Reclassification test using three sets of decision rules and VCR

The three sets of decision rules, shown in Tables 4, 5 and 6, were tested first on the firms from the learning sample characterised, however, by data from the years −2, −3, −4 and −5, i.e. 2, 3, 4 and 5 years before the state described in the information table.

Next, the three sets of decision rules were used for the classification of the firms from the testing sample in years −1, −2 and −3. All reclassification tests were run twice: with and without the VCR technique. This gave a clear insight into the efficiency of the VCR technique, which is designed to classify unclassified objects. On the average, 60% of objects not classified by rules were classified correctly by the VCR, while 40% were classified incorrectly. This is a better result than random classification of these objects.

Another general conclusion is that weak rules #9 and #13 (supported by one object each) were almost never used in the reclassification test. This means that the supporting objects no. 25 and 73, respectively, played a marginal role in this process.

The classification accuracy in percent of correctly classified objects by the three sets of rules for the learning sample in 5 years prior to the reference year and for the testing sample in 3 years prior to the reference year are summarised in Tables 8 to 10.

Going back from year −1, the classification accuracy is generally decreasing faster for bankrupt firms (class 0) than for healthy ones (class 1). This was expected because several years prior to the bankruptcy characteristic problems for bankrupt firms could have not been present yet, while the healthy firms should have had relatively stable performance during all five years.

Table 8: Classification accuracy for the minimal set of rules

Classif. Accuracy	Learning sample					Testing sample		
	Year −1	Year −2	Year −3	Year −4	Year −5	Year −1	Year −2	Year −3
Class 0	100%	85.0%	82.1%	82.5%	71.1%	84.2%	57.9%	42.1%
Class 1	100%	87.5%	71.8%	75.0%	78.9%	57.9%	52.6%	68.4%
Total	100%	86.3%	76.9%	78.8%	75.0%	71.1%	55.3%	55.3%

Table 9: Classification accuracy for the set of 'strong' rules

Classif. Accuracy	Learning sample					Testing sample		
	Year −1	Year −2	Year −3	Year −4	Year −5	Year −1	Year −2	Year −3
Class 0	97.5%	85.0%	79.5%	72.5%	65.8%	73.7%	47.4%	36.8%
Class 1	97.5%	85.0%	87.2%	80.0%	81.6%	57.9%	68.4%	68.4%
Total	97.5%	85.0%	83.3%	76.3%	73.7%	65.8%	57.9%	52.6%

Table 10: Classification accuracy for the set of 'strong', partly discriminant rules

Classif. Accuracy	Learning sample					Testing sample		
	Year −1	Year −2	Year −3	Year −4	Year −5	Year −1	Year −2	Year −3
Class 0	95.0%	85.0%	82.1%	75.0%	71.1%	94.7%	78.9%	42.1%
Class 1	90.0%	85.0%	79.5%	72.5%	78.9%	57.9%	42.1%	57.9%
Total	92.5%	85.0%	80.8%	73.8%	75.0%	76.3%	60.5%	50.0%

The classification accuracy for the testing sample is not so good as for the learning sample due to differences between the two samples, which were collected in distinct time periods (see Dimitras 1995).

In general, however, the results obtained are quite satisfactory. It can be observed that while the set of 'strong' and partly discriminant rules performs slightly better on the testing sample, the minimal set of rules performs slightly better on the learning sample. Indeed, the differences are rather small.

5 Comparison of the rough set approach with the C4.5 inductive learning technique

The algorithm known as C4.5 is one of the most popular classifiers. It was introduced by J.R. Quinlan as an extension of the ID3 tree classifier (Quinlan, 1986; Quinlan, 1993). Due to the widely acknowledged efficiency of ID3 and C4.5, the results generated by these algorithms have been used in comparative tests in numerous papers and have become characteristic benchmarks for efficiency in the field of machine learning.

C4.5 is an inductive algorithm for learning decision trees from preclassified examples. The input to this algorithm is a set of examples (objects) described by vectors of values of condition attributes. Each example is additionally labelled with a value of the decision attribute that determines the decision class to which the example belongs.

Given the set of examples, C4.5 builds a decision tree in which:

- the nodes are defined by tests on the attribute values,
- the leaves are decision classes to be assigned to the classified objects.

C4.5 may process both qualitative and quantitative data. In case of a continuous attribute (all the condition attributes appearing in all the analysed data sets are of this type), the attribute is internally discretised by finding a threshold T, which is subsequently used in a corresponding test of the following form: (attribute_value $\leq$ T ?).

The basic procedure used to generate the decision tree is as follows:

For a given set of preclassified examples:
(i) If all examples in the set belong to one class:
- create a tree leaf labelled with the class of the examples,
- place the examples in the created leaf.
(ii) Otherwise, for all examples in the set:

- find the attribute test which partitions the examples in the best possible way according to the assumed consistency measure,
- create a tree node using this test,
- divide the set of examples into disjoint subsets according to the results of the test,
- perform the procedure recursively in all of the resulting subsets.

Because for non-trivial data this simple scheme tends to build a very large decision tree with relatively few examples in each leaf (the phenomenon known as overfitting), the technique of tree pruning has been introduced. Its main objective is weakening the condition in (i) by a more general stopping condition. It results in creation of trees in which a single leaf may contain examples belonging to different classes. Trees modified in this way (pruned) have been proved to be much simpler and generally better classifiers for new examples than the original trees (Gelfand *et al.*, 1991).

One of the strongest aspects of the C4.5 algorithm is the *information gain* – an information-based consistency measure used by the method to evaluate partitioning of the examples into disjoint subsets (point (ii) of the algorithm above). The measure is defined as follows. Let U denote a set of examples, n – the number of different classes of examples in U and $p(U,j)$ — the proportion of those examples in U which belong to the j-th class. Informativeness of the set U is expressed as:

$$\text{Info}(U) = -\sum_{j=1}^{n} p(U, j) \log(p(U, j)) . \qquad (7)$$

If the set U is partitioned into k disjoint subsets X_i, the corresponding information gained by this partition is computed as:

$$\text{Gain}(U, k) = \text{Info}(U) - \sum_{i=1}^{k} \frac{|X_i|}{|U|} \text{Info}(X_i) . \qquad (8)$$

Application of the C4.5 algorithm to our original, non-reduced learning sample resulted in the pruned tree presented in Fig. 1.

Each node of the tree contains an attribute test. As it can be seen, only two attributes from among twelve have been used. The leaves contain prescribed classes and some additional information in form of two numbers in parentheses: (N / E). The numbers represent respectively: N – the number of training examples covered by the leaf, and E – the estimated numbers of misclassifications if N testing examples were classified.

According to this estimate, the considered decision tree would misclassify $(1.4+2.1+3.8) / (37+3+40) \times 100\% = 7.3 / 80 \times 100\% = 9.125\%$ of testing examples, which proves strongly over-optimistic (see the tree leaves for the original values from which the formula has been constructed). Actual results of applying the tree to the older versions of the learning sample and to the testing samples are presented in Table 11.

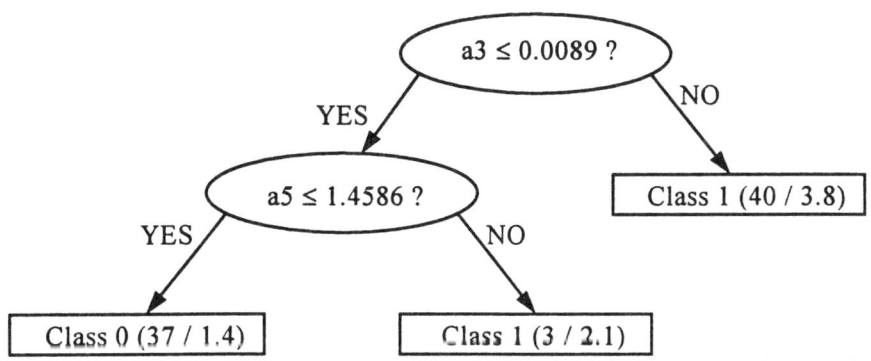

Fig. 1. The pruned decision tree generated by C4.5 from the learning sample

Table 11: Classification accuracy of the C4.5 decision tree

Classif. Accuracy	Learning sample					Testing sample		
	Year −1	Year −2	Year −3	Year −4	Year −5	Year −1	Year −2	Year −3
Class 0	92.5%	67.5%	65.0%	57.5%	57.5%	68.4%	52.6%	36.8%
Class 1	100.0%	95.0%	90.0%	87.5%	82.5%	63.2%	78.9%	68.4%
Total	96.3%	81.2%	79.5%	72.5%	73.7%	65.8%	65.8%	52.6%

A detailed comparison of the classification results obtained by C4.5 and by the sets of rules is presented in Table 12. Particular comparisons include, among others: averaging all of the total results, averaging totals of the learning and the testing samples separately, and comparison of the results for the testing sample in Year −1 and the learning sample in Year −2.

The contents of Table 12 shows superiority of the rule set results over those obtained with C4.5.

Table 12: Comparison of classification results by the sets of rules and by
C4.5. Columns RS-1, RS-2 and RS-3 contain averaged totals of Tables 8, 9
and 10. LS/TS stands for the learning/testing sample, respectively.

Summarised results	RS-1	RS-2	RS-3	C4.5
Average of all totals	74.8%	74.0%	74.2%	73.4%
Average of all totals but the LS Year −1	71.2%	70.7%	71.6%	70.2%
Av. of the totals of LS (Years −2, −3, −4, −5)	79.3%	79.6%	78.7%	76.7%
Av. of the totals of TS (Years −1, −2, −3)	60.6%	58.8%	62.3%	61.4%
Results for LS Year −2	86.3%	85.0%	85.0%	81.2%
Results for TS Year −1	71.1%	65.8%	76.3%	65.8%

The above comparison gives final evidence of the ability of the rough set
approach to respond efficiently to the business failure prediction problem.

6 Concluding remarks

In this study, the rough set method has been examined as an operational
decision tool for the prediction of business failure in Greece. This method,
especially conceived for multi-attribute classification problems, suits well the
problem of business failure prediction. The prediction model has the form of
decision rules. The decision rules take into account preferences of the DM
(in our case, the credit manager of a Greek commercial bank) who takes part
in the construction process. Moreover, the derived decision rules reveal the
most relevant attributes which should be considered by the credit manager in
order to evaluate the risk of failure of a firm. In the present study, the rough
set analysis has underlined the relevance of the financial profitability,
liquidity, debt capacity and working capital ratios. It is important to mention
that the rules were derived from a particular data set and as such they
represent a generalised description of the experience of a particular bank.
Following this, the rules cannot be applied uncritically to other banks. If
such a need arises, however, a new data set may be created and the rough set
method can be used to analyse this data set and generate appropriate rules
that will represent the experience of any bank supplying the data.

Concerning the classification of firms considered by the credit manager of
the Greek commercial bank, the rough set method had very satisfactory
results and better than those obtained with another well-known inductive
learning technique – the C4.5 classifier. In particular, the rough set approach
outperformed the C4.5 technique as far as the explicative character of the
results is concerned. In consequence, the rough set approach becomes, for
the future, a strong alternative tool for the analysis of financial management
problems.

Summarising, the main advantageous characteristics of the rough set approach are as follows:

- It discovers important facts hidden in data, expressed in a natural language of decision rules.
- It accepts both quantitative and qualitative attributes and specifies their relevance for approximation of the classification.
- It can contribute to the minimisation of the time and cost of the decision making process.
- It offers transparency of classification decisions, allowing for their argumentation.
- It takes into account background knowledge (preferences) of the decision maker.
- It can be incorporated into an integrated DSS for the evaluation of corporate performance and viability (see Siskos *et al.*, 1994; Zopounidis *et al.*, 1992, 1995).

Acknowledgements

R. Slowinski and R. Susmaga wish to acknowledge financial support of the grant no. 8 T11C 013 13 from the State Committee of Scientific Research (KBN) and of the CRIT2 – Esprit Project no. 20288.

References

Altman, E.I. (1968) Financial ratios, discriminant analysis and the prediction of corporate bankruptcy, *The Journal of Finance* 23, 589–609.

Altman, E.I., Avery, R., Eisenbeis, R. and Stinkey, J. (1981) *Application of classification techniques in business, banking and finance*, Contemporary Studies in Economic and Financial Analysis, Vol. 3, JAI Press, Greenwich.

Altman, E.I. (1984) The success of business failure prediction models : An international survey, *Journal of Banking and Finance* 8, 2, 171–198.

Beaver, W.H. (1966) Financial ratios as predictors of failure, *Empirical Research in Accounting: Selected Studies, supplement to vol. 4, Journal of Accounting Research*, 71–111.

Courtis, J.K. (1978) Modelling a financial ratios categoric framework, *Journal of Business Finance and Accounting* 5, 4, 371–386.

Dimitras, A.I. (1995) Multicriteria Methods for Business Failure Prediction, Ph.D. dissertation, *Technical University of Crete*, Chania, Greece (in Greek).

Dimitras, A.I., Zanakis, S.H. and Zopounidis, C. (1996) A survey of business failures with an emphasis on prediction methods and industrial applications, *European Journal of Operational Research* 90, 487–513.

Dimitras, A.I., Zopounidis, C. and Hurson, Ch. (1995) A multicriteria decision aid method for the assessment of business failure risk, *Foundations of Computing and Decision Sciences* 20, 2, 99–112.

Gelfand, S., Ravishankar, C., Delp, E., (1991) An iterative growing and pruning algorithm for classification tree design, *IEEE Transactions on Pattern Analysis and Machine Intelligence* 13, 2, 163–174.

Gloubos, G. and Grammatikos, T. (1988) The success of bankruptcy prediction models in Greece, *Studies in Banking and Finance* 7, 37–46.

Grzymala-Busse, J.W. (1992) LERS — a system for learning from examples based on rough sets, in: R. Slowinski (ed.), *Intelligent Decision Support. Handbook of Applications and Advances of the Rough Sets Theory*, Kluwer Academic Publishers, Dordrecht, 3–18.

Jones, F.L. (1987) Current techniques in bankruptcy prediction, *Journal of Accounting Literature* 6, 131–164.

Keasey, K. and Watson, R. (1991) Financial distress prediction models: A review of their usefulness, *British Journal of Management* 2, 89–102.

Lin, T.Y., Wildberger, A., eds. (1995) *Soft Computing: Rough Sets, Fuzzy Logic, Neural Networks, Uncertainty Management, Knowledge Discovery*, Simulation Councils, Inc., San Diego, CA.

Mienko R., Slowinski R., Stefanowski J., Susmaga R., (1996a) Rough family — software implementation of rough set based data analysis and rule discovery techniques, in: S. Tsumoto., S. Kobayashi., T. Yokomori., H. Tanaka., A. Nakamura., (eds), *Proceedings of the 4th International Workshop on Rough Sets, Fuzzy Sets and Machine Discovery*, Tokyo, 437–440.

Mienko, R., Stefanowski, J., Toumi, K., Vanderpooten, D., (1996b) Discovery-oriented induction of decision rules, *Cahier du LAMSADE* no. 141, Université de Paris Dauphine, Paris, 1996.

Pawlak, Z. (1982) Rough sets, *International Journal of Information and Computer Sciences* 11, 341–356.

Pawlak, Z. (1991) *Rough Sets. Theoretical Aspects of Reasoning about Data*, Kluwer Academic Publishers, Dordrecht.

Pawlak, Z., Grzymala-Busse, J.W., Slowinski, R., Ziarko, W. (1995) Rough sets, *Communications of the ACM* 38, 11, 89–95.

Pawlak, Z., Slowinski, R., (1994), Rough set approach to multi-attribute decision analysis, *European Journal of Operational Research* 72, 443–459.

Quinlan J.R., (1986) Induction of decision trees, *Machine Learning* 1, 81–106.

Quinlan J.R., (1993) *C4.5: Programs for Machine Learning*, Morgan Kaufmann Publishers, Los Altos, California.

Roy, B. (1985) *Méthodologie multicritère d'aide r la décision*, Economica, Paris.

Scott, J. (1981) The probability of bankruptcy: A comparison of empirical predictions and theoretical models, *Journal of Banking and Finance* 5, 317–344.

Siskos, Y., Zopounidis, C. and Pouliezos, A. (1994) An integrated DSS for financing firms by an industrial development bank in Greece, *Decision Support Systems* 12, 151–168.

Skowron, A. (1993) Boolean reasoning for decision rules generation, in: J. Komorowski and Z. W. Ras (eds.), *Methodologies for Intelligent Systems*, Lecture Notes in Artificial Intelligence vol. 689, Springer-Verlag, Berlin, 295–305.

Slowinski, R., ed. (1992) *Intelligent Decision Support. Handbook of Applications and Advances of the Rough Sets Theory*, Kluwer Academic Publishers, Dordrecht.

Slowinski, R. (1993) Rough set learning of preferential attitude in multi-criteria decision making, in: J. Komorowski and Z. W. Ras (eds.), *Methodologies for Intelligent Systems*. Lecture Notes in Artificial Intelligence vol. 689, Springer-Verlag, Berlin, 642–651.

Slowinski, R. (1995) Rough set approach to decision analysis, *AI Expert Magazine* 10, 3, 18–25.

Slowinski, R., Stefanowski, J. (1994) Rough classification with valued closeness relation, in: E. Diday *et al.* (eds.), *New Approaches in Classification and Data Analysis*, Springer-Verlag, Berlin, 482–488.

Slowinski, R. and Zopounidis, C. (1995) Application of the rough set approach to evaluation of bankruptcy risk, *International Journal of Intelligent Systems in Accounting, Finance and Management* 4, 27–41.

Stefanowski, J., Vanderpooten, D. (1994) A general two-stage approach to inducing rules from examples, in W. Ziarko (ed.) *Rough Sets, Fuzzy Sets and Knowledge Discovery*, Springer-Verlag, London, 317–325.

Vranas, A.S. (1992) The significance of financial characteristics in predicting business failure: An analysis in the Greek context, *Foundations of Computing and Decision Sciences* 17, 4, 257–275.

Zavgren, C.V. (1983) The prediction of corporate failure: The state of the art, *Journal of Financial Literature* 2, 1–37.

Zavgren, C.V. (1985) Assessing the vulnerability to failure of American industrial firms. A logistic analysis, *Journal of Business Finance and Accounting* 12, 1, 19–45.

Ziarko, W., ed. (1994) *Rough Sets, Fuzzy Sets and Knowledge Discovery*, Springer-Verlag, London.

Ziarko, W., Golan, D., Edwards, D. (1993) An application of DATALOGIC/R knowledge discovery tool to identify strong predictive rules in stock market data, in *Proceedings of the AAAI Workshop on Knowledge Discovery in Databases*. Washington D.C., 89–101.

Zopounidis, C. (1987) A multicriteria decision making methodology for the evaluation of the risk of failure and an application, *Foundations of Control Engineering* 12, 1, 45–67.

Zopounidis, C., Pouliezos, A. and Yannacopoulos, D. (1992) Designing a DSS for the assessment of company performance and viability, *Computer Science in Economics and Management* 5, 41–56.

Zopounidis, C. (1995) *Evaluation du risque de défaillance de l'enterprise : Méthodes et cas d'application,* Economica, Paris.

Zopounidis, C., Dimitras, A.I., and Le Rudulier, L. (1995) A multicriteria approach for the analysis and prediction of business failure in Greece, *Cahier du LAMSADE*, no. 132, Université de Paris Dauphine.

Zopounidis, C., Matsatsinis, N.F., and Doumpos, M. (1996) Developing a multicriteria knowledge-based decision support system for the assessment of corporate performance and viability: The FINEVA system, *Fuzzy Economic Review* 1, 2, 35–53.

Zopounidis, C., Doumpos, M. and Matsatsinis, N.F., (1996) Application of the FINEVA multicriteria knowledge-based decision support systems to the assessment of corporate failure risk, *Foundations of Computing and Decision Sciences* 21, 4, 233–251.

Fuzzy Insurance Premium Principles

Maria Rosaria Simonelli

Faculty of Economics, I. U. N., Via Acton, 38, 80133 - Naples, Italy
e-mail: Simonelli@naval.uninav.it

Abstract. If we consider a premium principle for insurance contracts as a problem of decision theory we see that a relevant part is the fuzzy integration. This theory is more adaptable to represent the real problems of the pricing insurance because we do not know the probability distribution of the risk insured but only its frequency. With Choquet's and Sugeno's integrals we build premium functionals enjoying properties which assure conditions of no arbitrage and we define index of fuzziness of the claims. As a particular case we build up a "variance-fuzziness premium principle" which is a generalization of the variance principle.

Keywords. Premium principles of an insurance, fuzzy integrals, measure of fuzziness.

1. Introduction

A *premium principle* or *premium functional* is a functional, H, that allows us to pricing the premium of an insurance. H is a function from a set of risks to the positive real number $\mathbb{R}^+$. It assigns at every risk, X, a real positive number, $H(X)$, which represents the price of an insurance policy on a future random damage. We have two kinds of principles of insurance premium:

i)   *classical principles;*

ii)   *fuzzy principles.*

In case *i)* we use probability measure and Lebesgue integral; in case *ii)* we use fuzzy measures and integrals of Choquet and Sugeno.

We find that using fuzzy integral with fuzzy measure we have premium functionals with elementary and plausible requirements that the classical principles does not satisfy. Moreover, we see the necessity of H having some of the following properties (cf.[4]):

— $H(X) > E_P[X]$; where $E_P[X]$ is the expected value of X with respect to the probability P and is called net premium;

— $H(X) < \max_{\omega \in \Omega} X(\omega)$ (the price of the insurance policy has to be less than the maximum possible risk);
— if X, Y are independent then H is additive: $H(X+Y) = H(X)+H(Y)$;
— in general H is sub-additive, i.e. $H(X + Y) \leq H(X) + H(Y)$;
— if X and Y vary in the same way, then H is additive;
— H is always additive.

With Choquet's and Sugeno's integrals we define index of fuzziness of the claims and we build premium functionals enjoying some or all these properties which assure conditions of no arbitrage. As a particular case we build up a "variance-fuzziness premium principle" which is a generalization of the variance premium principle.

2. Preliminaries

Let $(\Omega, \mathcal{A}, P)$ be a probability space where Ω is a set representing the eventualities linked to the damage insured, $\mathcal{A}$ is a σ-field representing all the random events linked to the damage and P is a probability defined on $\mathcal{A}$. In this paper we take Ω equal to an interval $[a, b]$ of real numbers and $\mathcal{A}$ equal to the σ-field of Borel $\mathcal{A} = \mathcal{B}([a, b])$ on Ω. The set of the fuzzy events corresponding to $(\Omega, \mathcal{A})$ is the set, $\mathcal{F}$, of all $\mathcal{A}$-measurable functions $f : \Omega \longrightarrow [0, 1]$. We refer to [12] and [13] for the theory of the fuzzy sets. The choices of Ω and P depend on the knowledge of the damage insured. In general, P is linked to the observed frequencies, for example, it may be a probability which interpolates the frequencies of the claim observed from the Insurance Companies in the past. So, instead of P we may also consider a *fuzzy measure*, μ, i.e. a non decreasing set function $\mu : \mathcal{A} \longrightarrow [0, 1]$, continuous from below, with $\mu(\emptyset) = 0$, $\mu(\Omega) = 1$. This fuzzy measure μ may be sub-modular, i.e.

$$\forall A, B \in \mathcal{A}, \quad A \cap B = \emptyset, \quad \mu(A \cup B) < \mu(A) + \mu(B).$$

In this case if we take $B = A^c$, then we have:

$$1 = \mu(\Omega) = \mu(A \cup A^c) < \mu(A) + \mu(A^c)$$

this say that we do not have enough information on the event A. This is the reality: in the insurance problem we have not enough information: we do not have the distribution of the risk but only its fuzzy frequencies.

The *risk*, i.e. the present value of the fuzzy and random claim which will be payed from the Insurance Company to compensation for the damage insured, may be represented in two different ways:

(i) by a positive random variable X: $\forall \omega \in [a, b] \longrightarrow X(\omega) > 0$ defined on $(\Omega, \mathcal{A}, P)$. We will denote with $\mathcal{X}$ the appropriate set of random variables, e.g., the space L^1 or L^2, or the set of bounded and A-measurable functions;

(ii) by a convex, normal and upper semi continuous fuzzy number $V : \Omega \longrightarrow [0,1]$ with support closed, limited and inclosed in the set of the positive real number.

We denote with $\mathcal{N}$ these fuzzy number. If $A, B \in \mathcal{N}$, then, $V = A \otimes (1 \oplus R)^{-n}$, where A and R represent the future fuzzy claim and the rate of interest respectively and $\otimes$, $\oplus$ are defined with Zadeh's extension principle. With our assumptions on $\mathcal{N}$ the fuzzy number V has an interval support which represents an interval of present values of future claims. We refer to [1] and [2] for the theory of the fuzzy mathematics of finance which can be also used for the insurance operations.

In this paper we will use *fuzziness* to build up an additive pricing functional, so, for easy reading, let us set out this notion. We should remember that given two fuzzy numbers f and g, we say that f has more fuzziness than g if the values that f assumes are nearer to $1/2$, while the values of g are nearer to 1 and 0. The fuzzy number denoted by $\Omega/2$ and defined by the function $f(\omega) = 1/2$, $\forall \omega \in \Omega$, is the fuzziest fuzzy set that one can imagine because every element ω has the same value of membership function both in $\Omega/2$ and in its complementary $1 - \Omega/2$. The classical events $E \in \mathcal{A}$ have fuzziness equal to zero.

The fuzziness measures $d(f)$ of a fuzzy set f is defined as an integral of a function composed by two functions, ψ and f, i.e. $d(f) = \int_\Omega \psi(f(\omega))d\mu(\omega)$, where μ may be a fuzzy measure or a probability measure and where ψ is a fuzziness norm function, i.e. ψ is a measurable function, $\psi : [0,1] \longrightarrow [0,1]$, enjoying the following properties:
(a) $\psi(0) = \psi(1) = 0$;
(b) $\psi(1/2) = 1$;
(c) $\psi(t)$ is non decreasing in $[0, 1/2]$, non increasing in $[1/2, 1]$;
(d) $\psi(t) = \psi(1 - t)$, $\forall t \in [0, 1]$.
An example of fuzziness norm function is Shannon's function (cf.[9], [11])

$$\psi(t) := -t\log_2(t) - (1 - t)\log_2(1 - t).$$

The function ψ is a scale function such that $d(f)$ belongs to the real interval [0,1] where zero represents the smallest measure of fuzziness and 1 the greatest. We have $d(f) = 0$ if f is equal to a characteristic function of a crisp subset of Ω, while $d(f) = 1$ if $f = \Omega/2$ i.e. the fuzziest fuzzy set. The fuzziness measure of a fuzzy set f is equal to the fuzziness of its complement. The measures of fuzziness $d(f)$, $f \in \mathcal{F}$ are useful to compare the fuzziness of risks. In the next paragraph we use the fuzziness norm function to build additive pricing functionals. Fuzziness measures are different from the variance and the standard deviation that are indexes of dispersion from the expectation and are not indexes of the fuzziness of the knowledge of a risk.

3. Classical Principles

We refer to [5], [6], [7] for the insurance theory. A premium calculus principle is a functional, H, defined in $\mathcal{X}$ and with positive values, $H : X \to H(X) > 0$. The more used classical principles may assume the following forms

(i) The expected value principle: $H : X \longrightarrow H(X) = E_P[X](1 + \gamma)$, the number $\gamma > 0$ is the rate of loading;

(ii) The variance principle: $H : X \longrightarrow H(X) = E_P[X] + aVar_P[X]$, where $Var_P[X]$ is the variance with respect to P of the risk $X \in L^2$, and $a > 0$;

(iii) The standard deviation principle:

$$H : X \longrightarrow H(X) = E_P[X] + b\sqrt{Var_P[X]},$$

with $b > 0$;

(iv) The expected utility principle: the insured individual has a certain capital c and may have a risk loss X. With the insurance he pays a premium p and he passes from the random capital $Y = c - X$ to the sure capital $c - p$. Instead, the insurer, that is the Insurance Company, passes from the sure capital c' to the random situation $Z = c' + p - X$, with $c' >> c$. Let u(x) be an utility function. Then, the insurance is advantageous for the insured individual if the premium p is such that $E[u(c - X)] < u(c - p)$ obviously. The advantageous condition of insurer is: $u(c') < E[u(c' + p - X)]$. The insurance is made if p is a number which satisfies both the inequalities.

4. Fuzzy Principles

Alternative models for the premium calculus are obtained using Choquet's and Sugeno's integrals. Choquet's integral is the functional $C : \mathcal{X} \longrightarrow \mathbb{R}^+$ defined in this way:

$$C(\mu, X) = \int_{[0,+\infty[} \mu(\omega \in \Omega : X(\omega) > z)dz.$$

it may be interpreted as an expectation of X with respect to μ. The measure μ may be:

(i) a fuzzy measure which may originate from frequencies of the damages indemnified in the past by Insurance Companies;

(ii) a measure which may be build with the probability P and another measure Q, i.e.

$$\mu(E) = P(E) + cQ(E), c > 0 \tag{1}$$

where Q is defined by a density g with respect to P, i.e.

$$\forall E \in \mathcal{A}, \quad Q(E) := \int_\Omega \chi_E(\omega)g(\omega)dP(\omega),$$

The function g is useful to represent a global index of both fuzziness and dispersion as we see in the sequel.

Using (1) we may obtain a premium functional $C(\mu, X)$ less than the greatest claim $\max X$ and greater than the expected value $E_P[X]$ if we take the constant c such that:

$$c < \frac{\max_{\omega \in \Omega} X(\omega) - E_P[X]}{E_Q[X]} \tag{2}$$

that is, we have the following theorem:

Theorem 1 *Let $(\Omega, \mathcal{A}, \mathcal{P})$ be the probability space, Q a measure, μ defined as in (1) where c is a positive constant satisfying the relation (2). Then, the Choquet integral $C(\mu, X)$ is equal to $E_\mu[X]$ and it is an additive, homogeneous, and monotonic premium functional with the following properties:*
(a) $C(\mu, X) > E_P[X]$;
(b) $C(\mu, X) < \max_{\omega \in \Omega} X(\omega)$.

Proof. From (1) we have

$$E_\mu[X] = E_P[X] + cE_Q[X]. \tag{3}$$

and for (2) $E_\mu[X]$ satisfies the conditions (a) and (b). By Fubini's theorem we have that $E_\mu[X]$ is equal to the Choquet's integral:

$$C(\mu, X) = \int_{[0,+\infty[} \mu(\omega \in \Omega : X(\omega) > t)dt = E_\mu[X].$$

The additivity, homogeneity and monotonicity are properties of the expected value with respect to the measure μ. $\qquad\square$

As a particular case, if we take

$$g(\omega) := (X(\omega) - E_P[X]) + \psi(f(\omega)), \tag{4}$$

where $\psi(f(\omega))$ is a fuzziness norm function defined in the preliminaries, then we have

$$E_Q[X] = \int_\Omega X(\omega)dQ(\omega) = Var_P[X] + E_P[X\psi \circ f].$$

$E_P[X\psi \circ f] = \int_\Omega X(\omega)\psi(f(\omega))dP(\omega)$ represents a fuzziness index on the knowledge of the risk X. So, for the assumption (4), the relation (3) becomes

$$C(\mu, X) = E_P[X] + c\{Var_P[X] + E_P[X\psi \circ f]\} \tag{5}$$

which we call *mean-variance-fuzziness pricing functional*. Obviously, homogeneity, additivity and monotonicity are importante properties of no arbitrage of our pricing functional. The homogeneity, i.e. $C(\mu, bX) = bC(\mu, X)$,

$0 < b < 1$, say that if there is a proportional insurance of the risk X then also the premium is proportional. The monotonicity, i.e.

$$\forall \omega \in \Omega, \qquad X(\omega) \geq Y(\omega) \implies C(\mu, X) \geq C(\mu, Y),$$

it says that if the claims X is always greater than Y, then the premium for the insurance of X has to be greater than the premium of Y.

If μ is not a measure but a fuzzy measure, then Choquet's integral is not additive but comonotonic additive. Let us give the definition of comonotonic functions:

Definition 2 Two functions $X, Y \in \mathcal{X}$ are comonotonic if

$$\forall s, t \in [a, b], \qquad (X(s) - X(t)) \cdot (Y(s) - Y(t)) \geq 0.$$

This means that X and Y represent two claims that vary in the same way, so X and Y cannot compensate. Dellacherie and Schmeidler show that if $X, Y \in \mathcal{X}$ are comonotonic functions, as a consequence, Choquet's integral is additive:$C(\mu, X + Y) = C(\mu, X) + C(\mu, Y)$. So, if we interprete Choquet's integral as an expectation for pricing claims X and Y, then we have that the price of two comonotonic claims $C(\mu, X + Y)$ is equal to the addition of the prices $C(\mu, X), C(\mu, Y)$.

We note a important difference from Choquet's premium functional and, for example, the classical variance principle which is independent-additive: if X and Y are independent we have that $H(X + Y) = H(X) + H(X)$. The comonotonic additivity of $C(\mu, \cdot)$ is completely different from the indipendence-additivity of H. Comonotonicity is an alternative property to independence. Two random variables X and Y cannot be comonotonic and independent simultaneously. Thus, for independent claims we may use premium functionals indipendent-additive, while for comonotonic claims, premium functional comonotonic-additive. Let us give an example of this second case:

Example 3 The comonotonic additivity of Choquet's integral may be used for pricing claims that are comonotonic, for example in the reinsurance. Let $Z = X + Y$ be a random total claim and $a > 0$. Define $v(z) := (z - a)^+$, $u(z) := z - v(z)$ and $X := u(Z)$, $Y := v(Z)$. Then X is the part of the total claim Z to be covered by the primary insurer (he will indemnify the damage for an amount less than a) and Y the part to be covered by the reinsurer (he will indemnify the damage for an amount greater than a). X and Y are comonotonic. The Choquet's integral is compatible with this type of reinsurance: $C(\mu, X + Y) = C(\mu, X) + C(\mu, Y)$.

In general, if μ is a fuzzy measure, then Choquet's premium functional is sub-additive, i.e.

$$C(\mu, X + Y) \leq C(\mu, X) + C(\mu, Y)$$

and this represent the discount in case of an insurance of $X + Y$, additivity is obtained where comonotonicity is present.

We may define a measure of the fuzziness of a fuzzy claim also with the Sugeno's integral. Let us give the definition.

Definition 4 Let a fuzzy measure space $(\Omega, \mathcal{A}, \mu)$ be given, and, let $\mathcal{F}$ the set of all $\mathcal{A}$-measurable functions, $f : \Omega \longrightarrow [0,1]$. Sugeno's integral is the functional $S(\mu, f) : \mathcal{F} \longrightarrow [0,1]$ defined in the following way:

$$(\forall f \in \mathcal{F}) \quad S(\mu, f) := \vee_{z \in [0,1]} [z \wedge (\mu\{\omega \in \Omega : f(\omega) > z\})].$$

Analogously as made with Choquet's integral we may define a premium functional with Sugeno's integral $S(\mu, f)$. Sugeno's integral enjoys some properties similar as Choquet's.
(i) $S(\mu, \chi_E) = \mu(E)$;
(ii) monotonicity: $(\forall v, h \in \mathcal{F})\big((\forall \omega \in \Omega)v(\omega) \geq h(\omega) \Longrightarrow S(\mu, v) \geq S(\mu, h)\big)$;
(iii) $\wedge$-homogeneity $(\forall v \in \mathcal{F})$ $S(\mu, kv) = k \wedge S(\mu, v)$, $k \in \mathbb{R}^+$.

If $v, h \in \mathcal{F}$ are comonotonic, Sugeno's integral is $\vee$-additive, that is $S(\mu, v \vee h) = S(\mu, v) \vee S(\mu, v)$, but we may have that μ is a $\vee$-additive fuzzy measure also if v, h are not comonotonic.

We may use Choquet's or Sugeno's integral for define a fuzziness measure of a fuzzy set f linked to a claim:

$$(\forall f \in \mathcal{F}) \quad d_1(f) := C(\mu, \psi(f(\omega))), \qquad d_2(f) := S(\mu, \psi(f(\omega))).$$

where ψ is a fuzziness norm function defined in the preliminaries and μ is measure or a fuzzy measure. Then, we may generalize (5) and build up a fuzzy premium functionals of the type

$$E_P[X] + c\{Var_P[X] + d_i(Xf)\}, \quad i \in \{1, 2\}.$$

References

1. L. Biacino, M.R. Simonelli: The internal rate of return of fuzzy cash flow, Rivista di matematica per le scienze ecenomiche e sociali, **14**, 3–13, 1991.
2. J.J. Buckley: The fuzzy mathematics of finance, Fuzzy Sets and Systems **21**, 257–273. North Holland, 1987.
3. C. Dellacherie: Quelques commentaires sur les prolongements de capacités, Séminaire Probabilités, V, Lecture Notes in Math., vol.**191**, Springer, 1970.
4. D. Denneberg: Premium Calculation: why standard deviation should be replaced by absolute deviation, Astin Bullettin, Vol. **20**, 181–190, 1990.
5. H.U. Gerber: Life insurance mathematics, Springer, Zurich, 1990.
6. M.J. Goovaerts, F. De Vylder, J. Haezendonck: Insurance Premium: Theory and Applications, North Holland, 1984.

7. J. Lemaire: Fuzzy insurance, Astin Bulletin, **20**, 33–55, 1990.

8. D. Schmeidler: Integral representation without additivity, Proc. Americ. Math. Soc., **97**, 1986.

9. D. Vivona: Mathematical aspects of the theory of measures of fuzziness, Mathware and Soft Computing **3**, 211–224, 1996.

10. Wang Shaun: Premium calculation by trasforming the layer premium density, Astin Bullettin, Vol. **26**, 71–92, 1996.

11. R.R. Yager: Entropy and specificity in a mathematical theory of evidence, International Journal of General Systems **8**, 139–146, 1982.

12. L.A. Zadeh: Probability measure of fuzzy events, J. Math. Anal. Appl. **23**, 421–427, 1968.

13. H.J. Zimmermann: Fuzzy set theory and its applications, third ed., Kluwer, 1997.

Second Order Data Mining:
Fire Risk Classification in a Newly-Developed Country

Gwangyong Gim   **Thomas Whalen**

Soong Sil University,   The Georgia State University,
Seoul, Korea   Atlanta, GA, USA
gygim@SAINT.soongsil.ac.kr   whalen@gsu.edu

I. Introduction

1. Deregulation of Korean Insurance Market

The Korean insurance market is changing rapidly in both the life insurance sector and the non-life insurance sector. Liberalization and deregulation are two key words symbolizing Korean insurance markets; most rates will be liberalized by 1998. Deregulation and liberalization bring price competition. With price competition, rate-making becomes one of the most important functions in insurance companies. [1]

2. Objectives of the Paper

The objectives of this paper are; (1) to examine the fire risk classification system in Korea and (2) to attempt to develop fire risk assessment models for individual property in the "general building" category. Specifically, for the first objective, we compare the current manual-based fire insurance rate classification system with statistical loss-based rates.

For the second objective, we divided samples into four groups (no fire and three categories of fire severity) and used two models, linear additive discriminant analysis and supervised back-propagation neural networks, to predict which category a case belongs to. We also develop second-order logical linguistic models of these numerical models using rule induction and compare the rule bases that result from this.

II. Korean Fire Insurance Risk Classification System

The practice of fire insurance rating in Korea follows a manual-based rating plan. [2] All companies use the same manual provided by the Korean Insurance Development Institute. The rating system uses four main categories of exposure units: houses, warehouses, factories, and general buildings. Each category has 16 subclasses based on crossing four location codes and four construction codes. The manual gives a rate for each subclass, which is adjusted by applying 8 merit factors and 6 demerit factors to the base rates. Merit-demerit factors include the usage of exposure units and the existence of fire protection facilities in the units, among others (see Table 1). Although the current fire insurance rating system employs a conventional property actuarial rating method, several potential problems have been noted. The first problem is whether the current classification system reflects fairly the policyholders' risks; this has not been empirically examined. Further, the merit-demerit factors selected appear to be based on convenience rather than statistical evidence. A search of the literature reveals no studies which test the validity of the Korean risk classification system

Table 1: Korean Fire Insurance Merit, Demerit Factors

Merit Factors		Demerit Factors	
Factors	Categories	Factors	Categories
Free Space	houses, general	Design	houses, general
Fire Extinguisher	houses, general	High building	houses, general
Special Building	houses, general	Risky products	general
High Insurance Amount	houses, general	Occupation	general
Fire Protection Facility	general	Operation	general
Design of fire protection	general	Usage	general
Public building	general		
Defense industry	general		

Experience-based relative rates are compared to the class rates of the manual. In order to calculate experience-based relative rates, loss ratios of each Location and Construction level are obtained from all of the policy cases from the year of 1990 to 1994 . Premiums and loss amounts are adjusted by CPI index in order to remove inflation factors before dividing to find the Loss Ratios. Raw Construction Relative Price is the Loss Ratio for one construction type divided by the overall loss ratio. Finally, Construction Relative price (CRP) is calculated by employing a credibility factor. CRP of each construction type is calculated by setting overall mean at one. Table 2 shows CRP calculation for Houses.

Location Relative Price (LRP) is also calculated by the same principle used in CRP calculation. The sixteen Relative Price (RP) factors for (Location, Construction) pairs are found by multiplying the LRP times the CRP. Tables 3 and 4 show the RP (Relative Price) of each pair for House properties and General Building properties respectively.

Table 2: Construction Relative Prices For Houses

Construction Type	Const 1	Const. 2	Const. 3	Const. 4	Total
# of Policies	401,964	395,774	69,331	5,152	872,221
Earned Premiums	13,086	15,959	2,566	195	31,806
Adj. Earned Prem.	14,623	17,542	2,876	222	35,263
Loss Cases	1,139	1,381	204	27	2,751
Loss Amounts	10,613	9,246	1,802	283	21,966
Adj. Loss Amts.	12,556	10,736	2,128	330	25,750
Loss Ratios	85.9	61.2	74	148.7	73
Raw Construction Relative Prices	1.18	0.48	1.01	2.04	1
Credibility Factors	1	1	0.45	0.1	1
Construction Relative Prices	1.15	0.71	0.93	1.19	1

Table 3: Relative Prices for (Location, Construction) Pairs

Houses	Constr. 1	Constr. 2	Constr. 3	Constr. 4	LRP
Location 1	1.36	0.84	1.10	1.40	1.18
Location 2	0.97	0.60	0.78	1.00	0.84
Location 3	1.15	0.71	0.93	1.19	1.00
Location 4	1.35	0.83	1.09	1.39	1.17
CRP	1.15	0.71	0.93	1.19	1.00

Table 4: Relative Prices for (Location, Construction) Pairs

General Bldg.	Constr. 1	Constr. 2	Constr. 3	Constr. 4	LRP
Location 1	0.70	1.16	2.00	2.49	1.03
Location 2	0.73	1.22	2.10	2.61	1.08
Location 3	0.54	0.90	1.55	1.94	0.80
Location 4	0.66	1.10	1.88	2.35	0.97
CRP	0.68	1.13	1.94	2.42	1.00

Tables 5 and 6, respectively, compare the RP (relative price) of each subclass in Table 3 and 4 with corresponding class rates in the Korean Fire Insurance Rate Manual. In order to make the comparison meaningful, both manual rates and RP are expressed as a percentage of the respective values for subclass 11 (Location 1 and Construction 1).

Table 5: Manual Rates (M.R.) *vs.* Calculated Relative Price (R.P.)

Houses	Constr. 1		Constr. 2		Constr. 3		Constr. 4	
	M.R.	R.P.	M.R.	R.P.	M.R.	R.P.	M.R.	R.P.
Loc. 1	100	100	163	62	263	81	400	103
Loc. 2	126	71	200	44	316	57	489	74
Loc. 3	142	85	232	52	379	68	579	88
Loc. 4	168	99	268	61	437	80	674	102

Table 6: Manual Rates (M.R.) *vs.* Calculated Relative Price (R.P.)

General Buildings	Constr. 1		Constr. 2		Constr. 3		Constr. 4	
	M.R.	R.P.	M.R.	R.P..	M.R.	R.P..	M.R.	R.P.
Loc. 1	100	100	158	166	257	285	396	356
Loc. 2	128	105	204	174	332	299	510	373
Loc. 3	156	78	249	129	404	222	622	276
Loc. 4	185	94	294	156	478	269	736	335

As shown in Tables 5 and 6, there are big differences between manual rates and experienced relative price rates, for both houses and general buildings. In other words, the manual overestimates the risk of the low-risk subclasses such as subclass 11 but underestimates the risk of the higher risk subclasses such as subclass 22 or 33. Therefore, we may say the existing manual rate does not express the real risk of fire losses, or each subclass does not hold a homogeneous group due to adverse selection.

III. Linear Discriminant Model and Neural Model

As discussed before, the merit-demerit fire insurance risk classification system based on the location-construction base rate was proved to be an inefficient risk classification system. In other words, adverse selection may be happening due to unfair risk classification. Furthermore, after OECD participation, Korea fire insurance companies may lose their market if foreign fire insurance companies which have relatively fair risk classification start to do business in Korea. Therefore, in this section, data-based rating models for the fire insurance risk classification will be developed using linear additive methods or connectionist methods, and the models' prediction accuracy for fire risk will be compared. In the next section, second-order logical linguistic models will be constructed on top of the numerical models to allow comparison of the rule bases that can be induced from them.

1. Data Preparation

A random sample of 131 General Buildings was drawn from a database of 55,858 no-loss cases from 1990 - 1994, and a random sample of 370 General buildings was drawn from a database of 4,257 loss cases. The criterion variable for this study was an index of relative severity (RS) which is the quotient of loss (indemnity) amount divided by insurance amount for each observation, considering both loss frequency and loss severity. To simplify the process of implementing and evaluating predictive models, the cases were divided into a non-loss category and three loss categories with roughly equal frequencies. The discretized RS index is "0" if there is no fire and "1" if the fire is so severe that the total coverage amount is paid as indemnity. Intermediate values between "0" and "1" show the relative fire severity. The Criterion values of relative severity grouping the samples into several risks are summarized in Table 7.

Table 7: Relative Severity Criteria for General Buildings

	Cases in Sample	Relative Severity (RS)	
No Fire	131		RS = 0
Small Fire	131	0	< RS ≤ 0.008525
Medium Fire	113	0.008525	< RS ≤ 0.1011
Severe Fire	126	0.1011	< RS ≤ 1

Table 8: Samples (General Buildings)

	Training Sample	Test Sample	Total
No Fire	68	63	131
Small Fire	61	70	131
Medium Fire	50	63	113
Severe Fire	70	56	126
Total	249	252	501

Finally, these samples are randomly divided into two sub-samples, a training sample and a test sample. The linear model using discriminant analysis and nonlinear model using neural networks are generated from the training sample and each model's prediction accuracy is tested in the test sample. The detail description of each sample by risk group is shown in Table 8.

2. Linear Additive Model

Linear additive models start by regressing the decision variable (fire or non-fire category) against the attributes (loss predictors) in the training sample to determine a weight for each attribute. Then, the products of the attributes and their weights are summed to produce final scores in a test sample and the scores are compared with some threshold in making the decision. The simplest and most widely used form of linear additive model is ordinary linear regression. In the present study, an ordinary linear regression model was produced by fitting coefficients to the nine predictor variables shown in Table 9 to minimize the sum of squared deviations of the model equation from the relative severity code (1, 2, 3, or 4).

Table 9: Predictor Variables

Location Codes:
dunji: building's Location; 4 groups gujo: building's materials used in construction; 4 groups
Merit Factors:
kongji: free space around building: 　　　　　　　　　　　2 groups: (space discount: 1, no discount: 0) sowha: building's fire extinguisher equipment; 　　　　　　　　　　　2 groups (fire discount: 1, no discount: 0) tuksu: building's specialty like fire wall protection; 　　　　　　　　　　　2 groups (special discount: 1, no discount: 0)
Demerit Factors:
jikup: building's operation used; 　　　　　　　　　　2 groups: (operation's penalty: 1, no penalty: 0) jakup: building's purpose used; 　　　　　　　　　　2 groups: (purpose penalty: 1, no penalty: 0) kochung: building's height: 　　　　　　　　　　2 groups: (height penalty :1, no penalty: 0) kunchuk: building's design style for fire protection: 　　　　　　　　　　2 groups; (design penalty: 1, no penalty: 0)

Since the current study has four qualitative categories (no fire and three fire severity levels), a more appropriate form of linear additive model is multiple discriminant analysis (MDA) [3]. In MDA, the dependent variables are three special discriminant functions that divide the sample space into four categories. The predictor variables represent the observed information about the object.

Which category an observation falls into determines which of the four risk classifications the system assigns it to.

The MDA system can generate model values that are roughly analogous to estimates of the probability that an object with particular values of the predictor variables will belong to the several risk categories, implicitly taking into consideration both the probability and severity of fire.

3 Connectionist Models

Neural networks (NN) [4], a representative example of connectionist models, emulate a simplified view of a living brain. A NN consists of a collection of nodes grouped in layers. The layers of a standard neural net application can be structured hierarchically as the input layer, the hidden layer, and the output layer. Each connection between nodes has a numerical weight associated with it, which models the influence of an input node on an output node. Positive weights indicate activation and negative weights correspond to inhibition. In other words, weights express the relative importance of each input to a processing element. These weights adjust continuously in a machine analogue of animal or human "learning." The result is a highly nonlinear, configural system that is roughly similar to aspects of the learning and deciding processes of living organisms.

An important consideration in NN work is the appropriate use of algorithms for learning. Back Propagation is the most widely used among several different learning algorithm. It requires training data for conditioning the network. A network is considered "feed forward" when there are no interconnections between the output of a processing element and the input of a node on the same layer or on a preceding layer. Supervised back-propagation NN is used as a representative example of the connectionist approach because it guarantees minimum squared error and is available in current software.

The other important consideration of NN is to decide the number of hidden nodes. Too many hidden nodes usually fit the training data well but lose generalizability. Too few hidden nodes may have difficulty in getting the pattern of training data. Therefore, the proper using of hidden nodes is very important in NN modeling. Based on a pilot study and experience with similar databases in the insurance industry, we used a neural network with three hidden nodes for the main analysis.

IV. Second Order Linguistic Models

We derived three second order linguistic models [5] to classify general buildings into the four risk categories according to the nine predictor variables in Table 9. The three second order linguistic models corresponded, respectively, to the regression, discriminant analysis, and neural network models discussed above.

A second order linguistic model is a collection of if-then rules derived by rule induction from the training sample by means of a generalized ID3 algorithm [6].

The algorithm recursively creates rules by adding clauses to split existing rules in such a way as to minimize the conditional entropy of the criterion variable at each step. The process continues until all training cases satisfying any given rule have the same value of the criterion variable (conditional entropy =0).

In a standard ("first order") rule induction application, the criterion variable is a nominal or ordinal measure of a training case, paired with that case's values on all the predictor variables. Such systems require very clean training data since they produce rules that account exactly for every training case. Thus, they are very sensitive to outliers or exceptional cases, and they require special 'fixes" to handle cases with identical predictor values but different criterion values.

In the training of a second order linguistic model, the actual criterion category for each case in the training sample is replaced by the calculated category found by applying that case's predictor values to a "first order" numerical system; in this study, either the regression equation, the discriminant model, or the neural network. The numeric model serves as a pre-processor to clean the data, giving the resulting system the robustness for which linear and neural models are well known. [7] On the other hand, the rule induction process gives the system a much greater perspicuity. The if-then rules, expressed in a near-natural language, are easy for a human expert to understand, critique, and improve. They also allow a decision support system based on the system to explain its recommendations to a user. Explanation is important because it helps the user to place an appropriate degree of reliance on the system on a case by case basis. In contrast, the regression model has much lower perspicuity, while the discriminant functions and the neural network have virtually none at all.

Table 10 shows the statistical results of the three first order models and the three corresponding second order models. The first column shows the percentage of cases whose computed classification was identical to the actual classification. The second column shows the "kappa" statistic which adjusts the percentage correct to account for the fact that a null model would average 24% correct by pure chance. Kappa=0 means chance level, negative kappa means worse than chance, and kappa=100% means a perfect match. The third column contains Spearman's nonparametric correlation coefficient (corrected for ties). This is a more flexible measure that takes the ordinal nature of the criterion into account, punishing large deviations (scoring a 1 as a 4) more severely than small deviations like scoring a 1 as a 2.

Probably the most striking thing to be observed from this table is the very great improvement in the Spearman correlation when the neural net is converted into a second order linguistic model. If this phenomenon is stable across other studies, it would seem to imply that the highly complex and nonlinear neural model can reap a benefit in generalizability from being converted into a simpler, but still configural, linguistic model.

Table 10: Accuracy of the Six Models on the Test Sample

Numerical Method	First Order Model	Second Order Model
Regression	% Correct = 39% Kappa = 19% Spearman's r = 29%	% Correct = 38% Kappa = 18% Spearman's r = 29%
Discriminant Analysis	% Correct = 45% Kappa = 26% Spearman's r = 18%	% Correct = 45% Kappa = 27% Spearman's r = 18%
Neural Network	% Correct = 38% Kappa = 17% Spearman's r = 12%	% Correct = 37% Kappa = 16% Spearman's r = 36%

Tables 11, 12, and 13 contain the linguistic if-then rules created, respectively, from the regression, discriminant, and neural systems. They are most meaningful to someone who is familiar with the Korean fire insurance industry. A follow-on study will ask such people to review and critique these rule sets. In a very real sense, it is precisely because these rules are more meaningful to Korean insurance practitioners than to the general reader interested in computer models or financial engineering that the three sets of rules are the real fruit of this data mining exercise.

V. Conclusion

1. Summary of Analysis Results

The comparison of manual rates used in the Korean fire insurance industry to experience rates derived from past five years experience indicates that great discrepancies exist between the two rates. Current Korean fire insurance rate classification is not consistent with loss experiences. Properties in Location 1 which are supposedly superior to properties in Locations 2 and 3 have actually poorer loss experience than properties in Location 2 and 3. The reason why loss experience of Location 1 is worse than that of Location 2 and 3 deserves some speculation.

The discrepancies found in the current rating system are best understood in the light of the fact that loss ratios of all Location and Construction levels are very low. Loss ratios of Houses and General buildings are 73% and 48%, respectively. Fire insurance lines are so profitable that an insurance company does not really care about risk classification. It is speculated that insurance companies locate their customers in better risk cells in order to attract customers. Underwriting standards are so loose companies may purposely put risky properties into the low risk categories such as cell 1 (Location 1, Construction 1) to win business. Since pricing competition is very weak due to tariff rate, insurance companies fight vigorously to increase market share. In the marketing war, underwriting does not function but the marketing competition might be the wrong direction in doing business with the participation of OECD.

2. Implication to Policy Making

All sectors of the Korean insurance market have been transforming dramatically. Liberalization and deregulation are the key words: almost all of Korean insurance markets will be liberalized by 1998. With the price liberalization of Property/Casualty insurance in 1997, could Korean P/C insurance companies afford these marketing practices? The industry should realize underwriting and rate-making, at last, have become a serious business function in order to win competition.

This paper may contribute to the field of risk estimation of individual property, particularly risk classification in the Korean fire insurance system. First, the research may shed some light on the validity of current risk classification systems in many newly developed countries and improve those risk classification systems. Second, methodologically, comparing NN approaches with linear approaches enable researchers to asses potential benefits and costs of each technique. A hybrid system combing NN and traditional approaches could be an alternative for future risk classification problems without losing the advantage of the law of large numbers. In particular, it is hoped that the rule bases displayed in Tables 13, 14, and 15 may be a useful springboard for the thinking of those who will be guiding the Korean insurance industry in the next century.

References

[1] Korean Insurance Development Institute, *Insurance Annual Statistics*, 1990-1994

[2] Gim, G., Kim, K., Kim, H., "Korean Fire Risk Classification Systems", The Proceeding of American Risk and Insurance Association, 1996 .

[3] Altman, E.I., Financial Ratios, Discriminant Analysis and the Prediction of Corporate Bankruptcy, The Journal of Finance, September, 589-609, 1968

[4] Rumelhart, D., Hinton, G. and Williams, R., "Learning internal representations by error propagation." in Rumelhart, D. and McClelland, J, Eds.: Parallel Distributed Processing: Explorations in the Microstructure of Cognition p.318-362, MIT Press, 1986

[5] Whalen, T., Gim, G., "Second Order Logical System for Risk Classification in a Newly Developed Country" Int. Journal of Uncertainty, Fuzziness and Knowledge-Based Systems 4:5 (1996), p. 421-430

[6] Quinlan, J., "Discovering rules by induction from large collections of examples," in D. Michie, Ed.: Expert Systems in the Microelectronic Age, pages 165-201, Edinburgh University Press, 1979.

[7] Daws, R.M. and Corrigan, B., Linear Models, Psych. Bulletin, 81:2,95-106, 1974

Table 11: Rules of Second Order Regression System
If gujo=1, jakup=0, kongji=0, dunji=1, jikup=0 then model=2;
If gujo=1, jakup=0, kongji=0, dunji=1, jikup=1, sowha=0, kunchuk=0, tuksu=0 then model=4;
If gujo=1, jakup=0, kongji=0, dunji=1, jikup=1, sowha=0, kunchuk=0, tuksu=1 then model=3;
If gujo=1, jakup=0, kongji=0, dunji=1, jikup=1, sowha=0, kunchuk=1, tuksu=0 then model=3;
If gujo=1, jakup=0, kongji=0, dunji=1, jikup=1, sowha=0, kunchuk=1, tuksu=1 then model=2;
If gujo=1, jakup=0, kongji=0, dunji=2, jikup=0 then model=2;
If gujo=1, jakup=0, kongji=0, dunji=2, jikup=1, kunchuk=0, tuksu=0 then model=3;
If gujo=1, jakup=0, kongji=0, dunji=2, jikup=1, kunchuk=0, tuksu=1 then model=2;
If gujo=1, jakup=0, kongji=0, dunji=2, jikup=1, kunchuk=1 then model=3;
If gujo=1, jakup=0, kongji=0, dunji=3 then model=2;
If gujo=1, jakup=0, kongji=0, dunji=4 then model=2;
If gujo=1, jakup=0, kongji=1 then model=1;
If gujo=1, jakup=1, tuksu=0, dunji=1 then model=4;
If gujo=1, jakup=1, tuksu=0, dunji=2 then model=4;
If gujo=1, jakup=1, tuksu=0, dunji=3, jikup=0 then model=3;
If gujo=1, jakup=1, tuksu=0, dunji=3, jikup=1 then model=4;
If gujo=1, jakup=1, tuksu=1 then model=2;
If gujo=2, dunji=1 then model=4;
If gujo=2, dunji=2, jikup=0, jakup=0 then model=3;
If gujo=2, dunji=2, jikup=0, jakup=1 then model=4;
If gujo=2, dunji=2, jikup=1 then model=4;
If gujo=2, dunji=3, jakup=0, jikup=0 then model=2;
If gujo=2, dunji=3, jakup=0, jikup=1, tuksu=0 then model=4;
If gujo=2, dunji=3, jakup=0, jikup=1, tuksu=1 then model=2;
If gujo=2, dunji=3, jakup=1 then model=4;
If gujo=2, dunji=4 then model=4;
If gujo=3, dunji=1 then model=4;
If gujo=3, dunji=2 then model=4;
If gujo=3, dunji=3, jakup=0 then model=3;
If gujo=3, dunji=3, jakup=1 then model=4;
If gujo=3, dunji=4, jikup=0 then model=2;
If gujo=3, dunji=4, jikup=1 then model=4;
If gujo=4, kongji=0 then model=4;
If gujo=4, kongji=1 then model=1;

Table 12: Rules of Second Order Discriminant Analysis System
If tuksu=1 and kochung=1 then model = 1;
If tuksu=1 and kochung=0 then model = 2;
If tuksu=0 and gujo=1 and dunji=1 and sowha=1 then model =2;
If tuksu=0 and gujo=1 and dunji=1 and sowha=0 then model =3;
If tuksu=0 and gujo=1 and dunji=2 and jikup=1 then model =3;
If tuksu=0 and gujo=1 and dunji=2 and jikup=0 and jakup=1 then model=3;
If tuksu=0 and gujo=1 and dunji=2 and jikup=0 and jakup=0 then model=1;
If tuksu=0 and gujo=1 and dunji=3 and jakup=1 then model=3;
If tuksu=0 and gujo=1 and dunji=3 and jakup=0 then model=1;
If tuksu=0 and gujo=1 and dunji=4 then model=1;
If tuksu=0 and gujo=2 and jakup=1 then model=4;
If tuksu=0 and gujo=2 and jakup=0 and jikup=1 and dunji=1 then model=4;
If tuksu=0 and gujo=2 and jakup=0 and jikup=1 and dunji=2 then model=4;
If tuksu=0 and gujo=2 and jakup=0 and jikup=1 and dunji=3 then model=4;
If tuksu=0 and gujo=2 and jakup=0 and jikup=1 and dunji=4 then model=1;
If tuksu=0 and gujo=2 and jakup=0 and jikup=0 then model=1;
If tuksu=0 and gujo=3 and dunji=1 then model=4;
If tuksu=0 and gujo=3 and dunji=2 then model=4;
If tuksu=0 and gujo=3 and dunji=3 and jakup=1 then model=4;
If tuksu=0 and gujo=3 and dunji=3 and jakup=0 then model=1;
If tuksu=0 and gujo=3 and dunji=4 and jikup=1 then model=4;
If tuksu=0 and gujo=3 and dunji=4 and jikup=0 then model=1;
If tuksu=0 and gujo=4 then model=4;

Table 13: Rules of Second Order neural System

If tuksu= 0 and dunji=I then model= 4

If tuksu= 0 and dunji=2 then model= 4

If tuksu= 0 and dunji=3 and gujo= I and jikup=0 and jakup= 0 then model= 3
If tuksu= 0 and dunji=3 and gujo= I and jikup=0 and jakup= I then model= 4
If tuksu= 0 and dunji=3 and gujo= I and jikup=I then model= 4
If tuksu= 0 and dunji=3 and gujo= 2 and jikup=0 and jakup= 0 then model= I
If tuksu= 0 and dunji=3 and gujo= 2 and jikup=0 and jakup= I then model= 4
If tuksu= 0 and dunji=3 and gujo= 2 and jikup=I then model= 4
Iftuksu= 0 and dunji=3 and gujo= 3 then model= 4
Iftuksu= 0 and dunji=3 and gujo= 4 then model= 3

If tuksu= 0 and dunji=4 and jikup 0 and gujo= I then model= I
If tuksu= 0 and dunji=4 and jikup 0 and gujo= 2 then model= No
If tuksu= 0 and dunji=4 and jikup 0 and gujo= 3 then model= I
If tuksu= 0 and dunji=4 and jikup 0 and gujo= 4 then model= 3
If tuksu= 0 and dunji=4 and jikup I then model= 4

If tuksu= I and jikup=0 then model= 2

If tuksu= I and jikup=I and gujo= I and dunji=I then model= 4
If tuksu= I and jikup=I and gujo= I and dunji=2 then model= 4
If tuksu= I and jikup=I and gujo= I and dunji=3 then model= 2
If tuksu= I and jikup=I and gujo= I and dunji=4 then model= 2

If tuksu= I and jikup=I and gujo= 2 then model= 2

If tuksu= I and jikup=I and gujo= 3 then model= 2

If tuksu= I and jikup=I and gujo= 4 then model= 4

Automated Residential Property Valuation:
An Accurate and Reliable Approach
Based on Soft Computing

Piero P. Bonissone, William Cheetham, David C. Golibersuch
and Pratap Khedkar

General Electric Company
Corporate Research and Development
One Research Circle
Niskayuna, NY 12309
USA

Emails: :Bonissone@crd.ge.com, Cheetham@crd.ge.com,
Golibers@crd.ge.com,Khedkar@crd.ge.com

Abstract

We present a soft computing system which uses multiple fuzzy logic algorithms to determine an estimate of residential property values. The system combines multiple estimates into a single value for the real estate value and an estimate of the reliability of that value. The system was built using enhanced neural networks and case-based reasoning techniques with aspects of fuzzy logic. Fuzzy techniques are also used to generate a reliability value for the estimates. The system has been successfully tested on thousands of real estate transactions. Both of the techniques were found to have typical errors of 5% - 7% relative to the actual sales price. This is close to the best possible[1], given the limited efficiency and liquidity of this market. The process of combining the individual estimates enhances the reliability and robustness of the resulting final estimate and provides guidance to the user regarding the applicability of each estimate to a particular business application.

1 Introduction

Residential property valuation [1] is the process of determining a dollar estimate of the property value for given market conditions. For this paper residential property is restricted to a single family residence designed or intended for owner-occupancy. The value of a property changes with market conditions, so any estimate of its value must be periodically updated to reflect those market changes. Any valuation must also be

---

[1] Time series analysis of repeat sales by Case and Shiller indicates that the time independent standard deviation of the variability in the sale process is 5.5-7.0% - see [6].

supported by current evidence of market conditions, e.g. recent real estate transactions.

1.1 Problem Description and Motivation

Many financial institutions grant mortgages and purchase mortgage packages on the secondary market as investments. These packages can contain up to 1000 mortgages. Valuations are needed to grant most new mortgages and to evaluate the current value of mortgage packages that may be purchased. In addition, valuations are sought as guidance by buyers and sellers and are needed for a variety of insurance purposes.

The current manual process for valuing properties usually requires an on-site visit by a human appraiser, takes several days, and costs about $500 per subject property. This process is too slow and expensive for batch applications such as those used by banks for updating their loan and insurance portfolios, verifying risk profiles of servicing rights, or evaluating default risks for securitized packages of mortgages. The appraisal process for these batch applications is currently estimated, to a lesser degree of accuracy, by sampling techniques. Verification of property value on individual transactions may also be required by secondary buyers. Thus, this work is motivated by a broad spectrum of application areas.

In most cases, the most credible method used by appraisers is the *sales comparison* approach. This method consists of finding comparables, i.e. recent sales that are comparable to the subject property (using sales records); contrasting the subject property with the comparables; adjusting the comparables' sales price to reflect their differences from the subject property (using heuristics and personal experience); and reconciling the comparables adjusted sales prices to derive an estimate for the subject property (using any reasonable averaging method). This process assumes[2] that the item's market value can be derived by the prices demanded by similar items in the same market.

To automate the valuation process we have developed the Automated Residential Property Valuation (ARPV) system, which uses fuzzy logic [13,19] to enhance neural networks and case-based reasoning techniques [14].

1.2 Chapter Structure

In Section 2, we will discuss the data used to develop and test our algorithms. This is followed in Section 3 by a brief overview of the methods employed to build the individual estimators. In Sections 4 and 5 respectively, a Neuro-Fuzzy-based estimator and a Case-Based Reasoning (CBR) estimator, will be described in detail. We will describe the theory behind each approach, then illustrate each with test results. Both approaches provide an estimated value for the subject property and compute a reliability value for that estimate. Finally, in Section 6, we will present a method for combining the two approaches into a single estimate and reliability value.

---

[2] It is also assumed that sales comparable are instances of arm-length transactions of willing buyers and sellers in a reasonably efficient market.

2 Data Description

The database used consists of a sales record of every property that has been sold in certain counties in Northern and Southern California during the five years preceding the development work. These records were stored in a Sybase database. The records were purchased from the California Market Data Corporation (CMDC) and TRW. These data vendors provided a description of each property which, in some cases, contained up to 166 property attributes. In addition, sales information (such as price and date) were also provided. A subset of the attributes which describe a property is given in Table 1.

Table 1: Subset of Property and Sale Attributes

Attribute	Value
Sale Price	$ 175,500
Sale Date	7/23/93
Address1	12 Bronco Lane
City	Contra Costa
State	CA
Zip Code	94063
Living Area	2,200 sq. ft.
Lot Size	10,000 sq. ft.
Bedrooms	3
Bathrooms	2
Total Rooms	6
Age	10 years

Using the address, each sold property was then geocoded using commercial software to provide a latitude and longitude for each record.

3 Overview of Approaches

In a team effort with other researchers at GE, we developed multiple methods for estimating the value of a property. The first approach was based on the location and living area of properties, see Figure 1. All properties within the county were combined to produce two output values, the locational_value and deviation_from_prevailing. Locational_Value (also referred to as LOCVAL) is an approximate estimator of property value. It uses all known, filtered historical sales in a county to construct a smooth surface spanning the county that represents a $/sq. ft. value at every point of longitude and latitude. This is derived by smoothing using radial basis functions that drop off exponentially with distance. The smoothing function used here has a "space" constant of about 0.15-0.2 miles. It can be described as the weighted sum of radial basis functions (all of the same width), each situated at the site of a sale within the past 1 year and having an amplitude equal to the sales price. Deviation from Prevailing value is the standard deviation for houses within the area covered and is derived using a similar approach.

Done before use

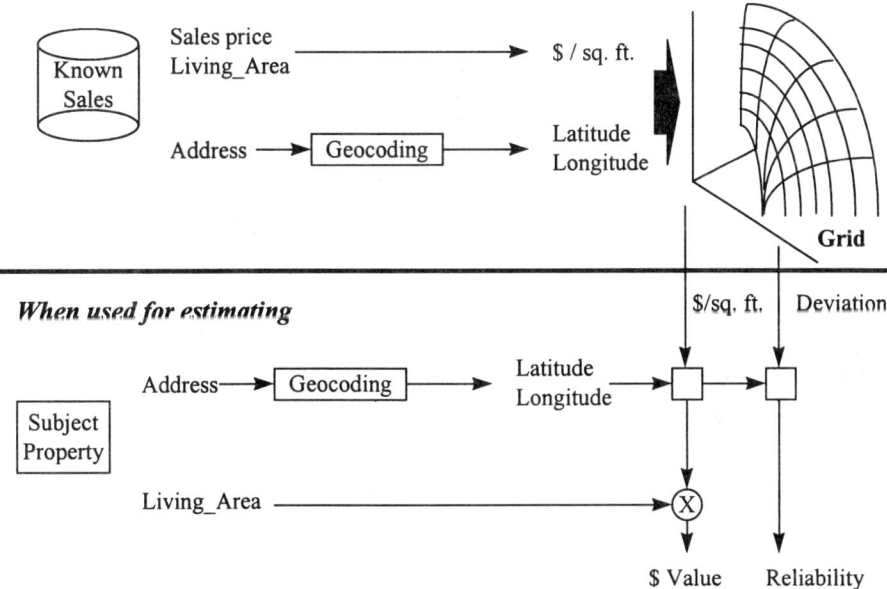

Figure 1: Locational Value method (LOCVAL)

The input values (namely, a valid, geocoded address and a living area in sq. ft.) must be present and accurate for the locational estimator to work correctly. If either is missing, or clearly out-of-range, the estimator will refuse to make a prediction.

The second method, called AIGEN, is a generative AI method which trained a fuzzy-neural net using a subset of cases from the case-base, and produced a run-time system to provide an estimate of the subject's value. This method will be described in greater detail in Section 4.

The third method, called AICOMP, used a Case Based Reasoning (CBR) process similar to the sales comparison approach to determine an estimate of the subject's value. This method will be described in Section 5.

The computation times, required inputs, errors and reliabilities for these three methods are shown in figure 2. The locational_value method takes the least time and information, but produces the largest error. The CBR approach takes the largest time and number of inputs, but produces the lowest error.

4 AIGEN Estimator

The AIGEN estimator is a generative system based on the combination of fuzzy logic systems and neural networks, which we explain in this section. First, some background on fuzzy-neural networks will be given, then the AIGEN estimator will be described, and finally, results will be given for multiple data sets.

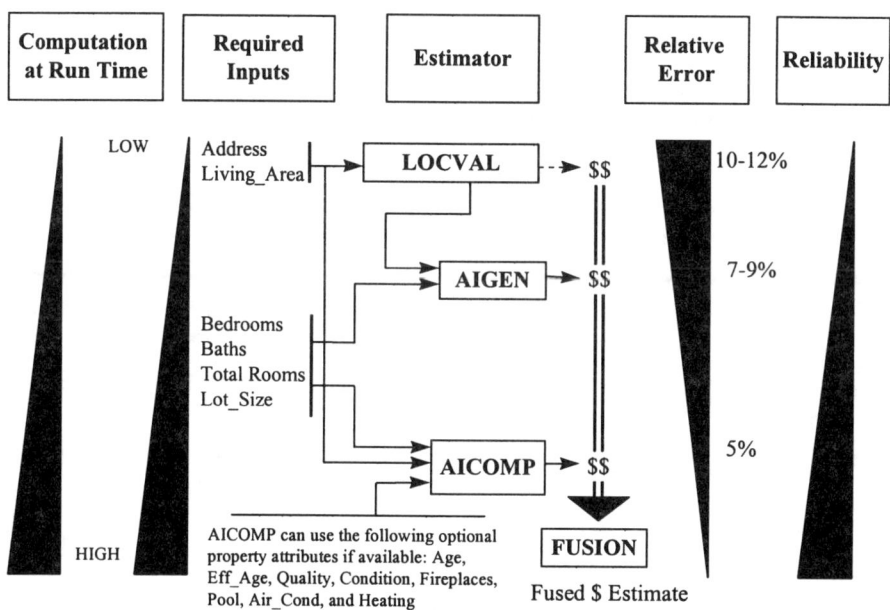

Figure 2: Data comparison of multiple approaches

4.1 Neuro-Fuzzy Systems

Neural Networks and Fuzzy Logic are two separate approaches to modeling knowledge and identifying complex, unknown systems. Each has some advantages over the other, depending on the context in which it is put to use. Table 2 summarizes the relative merits and demerits of each in isolation. The table shows that neural-nets need to use large amounts of input data, are adaptive, can have many inputs are difficult to interpret and understand, may or may not produce smooth models, and can not incorporate domain knowledge. On the other hand, fuzzy systems do not require large amounts of data, are not adaptive, are best with few inputs, can be evaluated for meaning, provide smooth results, and can contain domain knowledge.

System identification using neuro-fuzzy systems has become very popular in recent years. Some combination of neural nets and fuzzy systems can be found in a large number of consumer products, industrial applications, image processing equipment, financial applications, etc. Many of these applications use the two as distinct black boxes, working in tandem within the product or as tools in product development. On the other hand, neuro-fuzzy systems fuse the two approaches together such that the properties of each complement those of the other.

Table 2: Neural Nets vs. Fuzzy Systems

Property	Neural Nets	Fuzzy Systems
# data	large	small
Adaptive	yes	no
# inputs	many	few
Interpretable	no	yes
Smooth	unknown	yes
Knowledge	unusable	usable

Figure 3 brings out the reasons why such a fusion is desirable and how, in principle, it can be achieved. The best of both worlds is achieved by fusing the two into the hybrid neuro-fuzzy approach. Figure 3 shows one such approach, where knowledge from the domain is used to build the fuzzy rules, whose parameters can then be refined or made adaptive with the use of data and neural network tuning techniques.

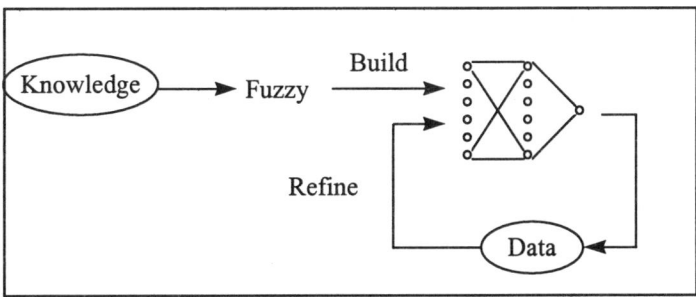

NN + Fuzzy = Adaptive Knowledge Bases

Figure 3: Fuzzy Neural Net

The specific model that we chose for the AIGEN estimator is a network-based implementation of fuzzy inference. Part of it is based on ANFIS [11], which implements a fuzzy system as a 5-layer neural network so that the structure of the net can be interpreted in terms of high-level rules. This net is then trained automatically from data. We have developed an extension of this methodology (referred to as E-ANFIS) which we use in AIGEN. ANFIS and E-ANFIS use a slightly different philosophy of fusion than that shown in Figure 3 --- they implement the fuzzy reasoning process as a neural net, and need to rely less on expert knowledge. In essence, the fuzzy logic helps to specify the structural component of the model only.

4.2 E-ANFIS

Figure 4 shows the architecture that we have used for the automated property valuation problem. The central difference between ANFIS and E-ANFIS is that E-ANFIS allows the output to be linear functions of variables that do not necessarily occur in the input. Another way of stating that is to allow the segmentation of the input space on a proper subset of the total variable set only (and then using a cylindrical projection of that segmentation for the whole space).

Figure 5 shows a schematic for the fuzzy inference process, where the rules have the following form:

Rule 1: IF x is A_1 and x is B_1 THEN z is $f_1(x,y)$

Rule 2: IF x is A_2 and y is B_2 THEN z is $f_2(x,y)$

Here, there are two variables x and y, which take on real values. However, the predicate A_1 against which x is matched, is a fuzzy set rather than a crisp value or an interval. All the sets A_i and B_i above are fuzzy sets. The IF part is referred to as the antecedent or precondition of the rule, and the THEN part is the consequent or postcondition. These rules are used to map inputs to outputs by a fuzzy logic inference system which works in several steps:

1. Match the inputs against the fuzzy sets A_i and B_i.
2. Determine the degree w_i of each rule by multiplying together the degrees to which its antecedent clauses match.
3. Determine the outputs recommended by each rule by evaluating $f_i(x,y)$ on the input.
4. Defuzzify the output by combining the outputs of all rules, by a normalized, weighted sum, where the weight of a rule is its degree w_i.

The specific form which we will use for f(x,y) is a crisp, linear function of the inputs, such that the general rule is of the form

Rule i: IF x is A_i and y is B_i THEN z is $c_{i0} + c_{i1} x + c_{i2} y$

Such a rule will be referred to as a TSK-type rule (after Sugeno, and Kang [18], who suggested this form). A special case of this is when all c_{ij} except c_{i0} are 0, in which case each rule recommends a fixed, crisp number. The inference procedure with TSK-type rules yields

$$z = \sum_i w_i (c_{i0} + c_{i1}x + c_{i2}y) / \sum_i w_i$$

where w_i is the weight of Rule i, computed as a weighted sum.

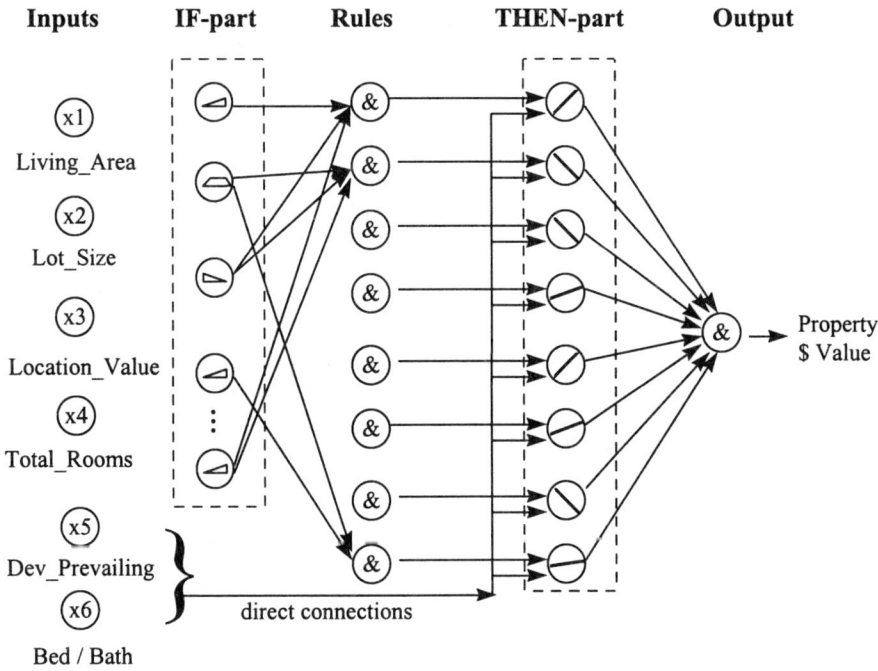

Figure 4: An E-ANFIS network

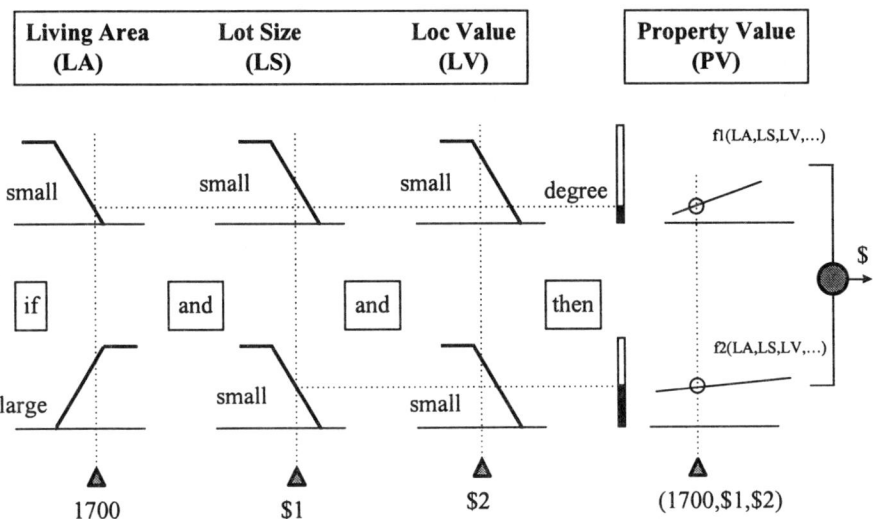

Figure 5: The Fuzzy Inference Process

For the antecedent fuzzy membership functions, we use softened trapezoids given by

$$\mu_A(x) = 1 / (1 + ((x-c) / a)^{2b})$$

Such a membership function is centered symmetrically around c, has a width controlled by a, and has a curvature controlled by b. For b=∞, we get a crisp interval [c-a, c + a]. For b → ∞, the set A tends to the non-fuzzy interval [c-a, c + a]. For b=0, its membership curve does not bend at all. An initial value of b=2 is used for our purposes. This choice is not critical as the algorithm will change it if required by the data. In subsequent experiments, we found that tuning the value of b is not critical.

The weight w_i of each rule is obtained by multiplying the $\mu(x)$ of the two clauses in that rule's IF part. The choice of granularity (how many fuzzy functions per axis?) is governed by the tradeoff between simplicity and accuracy. A high number of rules leads to a more "folded" surface and is to be avoided unless absolutely necessary for fitting the data. We propose using up to two membership functions per input dimension for our problem.

The E-ANFIS network architecture is determined by the number of membership functions assigned to each input dimension. For instance, if there are six inputs in all, and two membership functions are assigned to each of four of the inputs, the net has 6 input units, 8 units in the first layer (which come from the two fuzzy functions for each of the four variables), 16 in the next two layers (since 2x2x2x2 = 16 rules), and finally one summation unit to produce the output in the output layer. Each of the 16 rules has a TSK-type consequent which depends on all 6 inputs. Since each antecedent membership function has 3 degrees of freedom (a, b, and c), and each consequent has 7 coefficients here, there are 8x3+16x7 = 136 degrees of freedom for this E-ANFIS model.

Once the architecture is constructed in this fashion, the parameters can be initialized in a reasonable manner instead of randomly as in neural networks. For instance, the membership functions can be spaced at uniform distances over the axis so as to cover the range of the data points. The consequent linear functions are initialized to zero.

4.2.1 Training E-ANFIS

A variant of the gradient descent technique is used to train the network based on the training data. In brief, this algorithm tries to minimize the mean squared error between the network outputs and the desired answers, when presented with the data points in the training set. It proceeds as follows:

- Present a sample point in the training data set to the network and compute its output.
- Compute the error between the network output and the desired answer.
- Holding the IF-part parameters fixed, solve for the optimal values of the THEN-part parameters using a least-mean-squares optimization method. A recursive Kalman filter method is used here.
- Compute the effect of the IF-part parameters on the error, using derivatives of the functions implemented by intermediate layers.

- Using the above, change the IF-part parameters by small amounts so that the error at the output is reduced.
- Repeat the above steps several times using the entire training set, until the error is sufficiently small.

This procedure is as discussed in [11], with the extension of the Kalman filter to input variables that are not part of the antecedents of the fuzzy rules.

This procedure converges to a locally-optimal configuration where the error becomes fixed or decreases very slowly. Training is stopped at this point. The resulting network can be interpreted as a fuzzy rulebase, with each parameter in the net having a definite meaning in terms of the fuzzy sets or consequent functions. Learning speed is very fast compared to the conventional neural net paradigm. Additional data, if available, can always be used to further train the model using the same backpropagation-type algorithm. The resulting surface is very well-behaved and provably smooth. The rule base is extremely compact, so a large number of models can be stored easily.

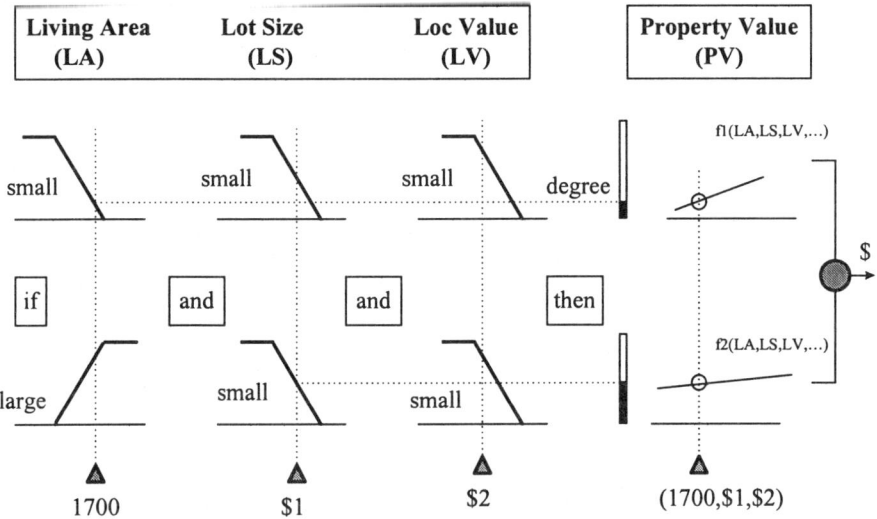

Figure 6: AIGEN method for appraisals

4.3 AIGEN Estimator

The AIGEN estimator uses an E-ANFIS network to do inference. By changing the inputs to the neuro-fuzzy network, or by varying its architecture, we can obtain different AIGEN models for the same problem. For instance, one could make the dollars/sq. ft. value for the property as the dependent variable, use E-ANFIS to compute this, and then multiply by living area to generate the predicted price. As another example, one could make the logarithm of the sale price the dependent variable (the output of E-ANFIS), or one could use different combination of property attributes as the inputs to E-ANFIS. We have explored some of these combinations. The following remarks apply to all of the models discussed in the subsequent section:

Each model uses an E-ANFIS net with 6 inputs and 1 output. Four of the inputs are used to partition the input space into 16 overlapping sets, and give rise to 16 rules. The remaining two inputs are used only by the consequents of the rules. The attributes used for these 6 inputs were changed as we tried different models.

Each of the 16 fuzzy rules make a prediction based on the 6 variables listed. Their outputs are then combined using interpolative reasoning to produce the estimate. The overall map is from 6 inputs to 1 output, and is a nonlinear, differentiable map that is constructed by melding together 16 hyperplanes in 7-dimensional space. However, the semantics of the 16 rules are easy to understand, and are of the form : if *lot_size is small* and *living_area is small* and *locational_value is high* .. then price is f(.), where f(.) is a linear function of the 6 input variables.

The properties used for training the AIGEN model were restricted to be in a certain price range. This is to eliminate obvious outliers. For this reason, it should not be used to make a prediction on a property outside this range. It will make a prediction if given such a property, but will bound its output to the said range. It will also issue a warning to the user in this case. There is one model for the entire price range, instead of a separate model for each range of price. We found that one uniform model worked better, and also made matters much simpler.

The question of which model is better depends on what error metric is used to judge it. A choice of several metrics is available. Here, we focus on one of the obvious measures of estimation accuracy --- E = (actual_price - estimated_price) / actual_price. This magnitude of relative discrepancy can be measured for each point in the test set, and its mean, median, RMS value, or distribution computed. Alternatively, one can look at the coefficient of correlation between the actual and estimated price, with or without outlier pruning. These issues are discussed in greater detail in the section on results.

4.4 Extracting AIGEN Models

We have tried a variety of AIGEN models, using different inputs and input combinations, including joint considerations such as dollars per square foot, or dollars per total room. We also tried different models for two price ranges (below and above 250K). In addition, we started with simpler models (three to four inputs only) and increased the complexity progressively till we reached the 6-input stage. This accuracy vs complexity tradeoff reduces error as the complexity goes up, but may cause overfitting as well as higher computational cost. The training algorithm used was the backpropagation-like method described earlier. We reduced the computational cost associated with training AIGEN by using a heuristic to reduce the dimensionality of the parameter space during training.

The 16 rules have 112 degrees of freedom in the consequent. This is a large share of the dimensionality of the parameter space, which uses a variant of the Kalman filtering algorithm to train the parameters in the consequent. It was found easier to train the consequent partially (4 inputs = 80 parameters) in the interleaved backpropagation process described earlier, followed by a final batch phase where all

112 consequent parameters were retrained again while holding the antecedent parameters constant. This reduces the computational cost somewhat.

Recall that the model extraction process minimizes the Mean Squared Error over a training set at the present time. All the training, models, and results discussed here are with respect to this optimization metric. The choice of optimization criteria is pivotal to the model that is extracted by the process.

Training set size: We have used about 5% of the total available data for training purposes. For Contra Costa County (in CA), this means that out of the 37712 potential test records that were available from CMDC, 1768 records were extracted and used for training the AIGEN model. For another data source, less than half of this (14-15 thousand records) was available, so that 10% of the total data was used for training the models. This corresponds to approximately 1400-1500 records for training.

These had to be error-free and more or less randomly distributed so as not to bias the estimator. The specific size of the training set is not significant. Since there are 136 degrees of freedom in all, a good rule of thumb is to use ten times as many examples for training. Moreover, it is important to use a small part of the total data, so that overfitting to the data can be avoided. The results discussed below apply to this training scheme.

We now discuss some of the models that we explored. As we shall see, the performance does not vary greatly, and no one model unambiguously dominates over another. The choice of which model to deploy must depend on the evaluation or error metric. The models preferred are the ones which estimate Sales Price directly, and the one based on estimating Sale price per unit of building area.

4.4.1 Estimating Sale Price Directly

Inputs to the E-ANFIS net are based on 7 attributes of the property:

- *total_rooms,*
- *num_bedrooms,*
- *num_baths,*
- *living_area,*
- *lot_size,*
- *locational_value,*
- *deviation_from_prevailing_value.*

The number of bedrooms and bathrooms is combined to produce a *bedrooms/bathrooms ratio* which is fed along with the other five values to the E-ANFIS net. Of these 6 inputs, *total_rooms, living_area, lot_size, locational_value* are used for partitioning the space into 16 fuzzy regions. The output variable is simply the dollar value of the house. The median error E is 8.6% (Data source A) 9.34% (Data source B), 6.9--7.2% (Data Source C). Overall, reducing the price range of interest, filtering and cleaning up the data has considerably helped our accuracy to the point where the median error is about 7%. Since data cleanliness and filtering play a significant role in the final accuracy of the models, we have chosen not to publicly associate the datasets A, B, and C with the companies that produce it.

4.4.2 Estimating Log of Sale Price

The output of E-ANFIS is $\log_{10}$(sale_price). Its inputs are:

- $\log_{10}$(total_rooms),
- $\log_{10}$(lot_size),
- $\log_{10}$(living_area),
- $\log_{10}$(locational_value),
- bedrooms/bathrooms, and
- deviation_from_prevailing_value.

The first four inputs are used for input space partitioning. In such a model, the median E is 8.50% (Source A) and 9.7%(Source B). This is a slight improvement over the previous model, but the outliers may suffer more in this model, since a small error on the log scale translates into a very large error in terms of dollars.

4.4.3 Estimating Sale Price per Unit Area

The output of E-ANFIS is sale_price per square foot of living area. Inputs to the E-ANFIS net are:

- *total_rooms,*
- *living_area,*
- *lot_size,*
- *locational_value/living_area,*
- *bedrooms/bathrooms, and*
- *deviation_from_prevailing_value.*

The final dollar value is computed by multiplying the output of E-ANFIS by the living area of the house. The median E here is 8.62% (for Data source A) and 9.17% (Data source B).

4.5 Results and Validation

Validation is done by testing the model on the entire dataset available from a data source, after it has been filtered to remove atypical properties. The filters used for testing are the same as the ones used for screening the training set. Recall that the training metric was mean squared dollar difference between the actual and estimated price. We have used the median of relative error as the principal test metric.

For the purposes of this evaluation, we define the error E on a given test property as the difference in the predicted sale price and the actual sale price, normalized by the actual price (all in $).

$$E = (\text{actual\_price} - \text{estimate}) / \text{actual\_price}$$

This is the absolute-value relative error in sale price per property. One can then analyze various statistics related to E, e.g. its mean (with or without the absolute value), median, percentiles, standard deviation, probability mass function, cumulative distribution function etc. We have elected to focus on the median (because it is robust to outliers), and the probability distributions (since they encapsulate the entire set of errors in one diagram).

4.5.1 Data Source A

The test dataset used for validation consists of 35370 property records. The training data size is 1768 points -- only 5% of the total data. The quantity E has been measured over a set of 35370 data points. This means that the model has never before seen the remaining 95% of the data set, when it is tested on these.

The median value of E is in the range of 8.5% --- 8.64%. This implies that half of the test properties have an estimation error of this or less. Let us consider the straightforward model which estimates sale price directly, as discussed in the previous section. The average bias of the estimator is about $557, which implies that the estimator is very slightly biased towards the conservative side, which is not undesirable in this context. The bias shown by the unsigned relative error is higher, but this is purely because the same dollar value error translates into different relative errors, depending on the value of the property. The average E value is around 12%, since it counts extreme outliers. The median is a better metric than the mean or RMS value, since both of these tend to give weight to outliers. The types of outliers causing this discrepancy between the mean and median error are discussed later.

Note that some limited amount of outlier elimination is taking place in the model itself, since it bounds its own estimate to lie in the range used for training. Without the truncation, median and mean of E are not significantly affected, and the RMSE increases slightly, but this is to be expected since it attaches very high weights to the few far outliers.

If we focus on the [5,95] percentile range of signed relative error, for the model which estimates sale price directly, (i.e. the middle 90% of the % errors in sale price), then the coefficient of correlation between the actual and the estimated AIGEN price is 0.97.

The cumulative probability distributions for error E over the test set (35370 points for A, 15733 for B, 14277 for C) were also compared. There are 3 sets of curves, corresponding to each of the three types of experiments done, and the models discussed earlier (3 for A, 5 for B, 3 for C). We found that models based on dataset B are worse that the ones based on dataset A , but that the spread between model performances within each of the two sets is not very large (with A again doing better than B). Changing filters and price ranges improves the performance with respect to data B.

4.5.2 Data Source B

The test data used for validation is the entire data set of 15733 records. Training was done using 10% of these.

For the model based on estimating price per unit area, recall that the median E was 9.17%. The mean value of the error is slightly negative as was the case in A, though the median value for signed E is 0.947%. The mean value of the absolute-valued error E is higher and heavily influenced by outliers.

If we consider the [5,95] percentile range of signed E values, then the mean is -0.56%, the standard deviation is 9.9%, and these errors range from -26.7% to +15.5%. Also, the coefficient of correlation between the actual and the estimated AIGEN price is 0.924.

We also did cross-checking experiments where a model trained on data source A was tested on data source B and vice versa. As expected, test performance deteriorated, partly due to data quality and partly due to inconsistent semantics used by the collectors of the two data source companies. This demonstrates the intuitive fact that when the model is used, the inputs to it should not only be accurate and complete, but consistent with the semantics of the training data.

4.6 AIGEN Reliability and Outliers

No model working on real-world data will ever achieve perfect accuracy. We have used filters for training and testing with both data sources to eliminate and clean up the data as far as possible. Despite this, there are properties on which the models do not perform well. These outliers are due to several reasons, and it is possible to treat this problem.

Roughly speaking, a very bad estimate of sale price is due to two reasons. The first is that the sale price itself is fraudulent or due to a non-arms-length transaction. An instance would be a large property with high TotalValue and TaxAmount and selling for $56000 in Contra Costa County. On such properties, the model will rightly predict a high sale price, but since the actual price happened to be low, a very large relative error will be recorded. Clearly, such sales need to be weeded out, and it is not a fault of the model if it makes a mistake when predicting an incorrect sale price. We can use filters based on TaxAmount, TotalValue and LocationalValue to filter out obviously bad sales during the training set selection process.

The second type of high-error case is a genuine mistake. This is caused by having an incorrect locational value prediction. The locational value estimator (LOCVAL) is very well correlated to actual price, so that AIGEN uses it as an input and gives it a significant weight in their determination. So when locational value is predicted wrongly, this error propagates through to AIGEN's output. These types of errors do not cause large magnitude errors often. A related problem is that of unusual properties where the physical characteristics are too extreme to conform to the typical cases on which AIGEN was trained.

An ideal solution to the problem of outliers and high errors would be to have an automated module which could detect them. Then AIGEN would be able to supplement its estimate with an indication of the appropriateness of the model for that data point. Such an accompanying reliability measure has been constructed for AIGEN. It is based on the reliability of the locational value and overall "averageness" of the subject based on its physical attributes. These concepts are converted to a numerical measure by using fuzzy sets.

The resulting reliability measure varies continuously from 0 (minimum) to 1 (maximum). The value depends on the following factors, of which the first three are relevant because they influence Location Value, and that is one of the inputs to AIGEN:

- *The number of sales that were used by the modeling step to construct the Locational Value surface at the location of the subject.* This is represented by the variable NumIn1mile, which is approximately the number of properties with sales records within a mile of the subject in the time period used. A value of 50 or more is preferred (reliability = 1). If the value is < 25, the reliability is 0. Intermediate values lead to a reliability between 0 and 1. A fuzzy set (S-shaped) can now be defined on the variable NumIn1mile.
- *The local variation in the Locational Value $/sq. ft. surface.* If the surface is flat where the subject is, then there is little variation in the immediate neighborhood, and the reliability should be high. This variation is specified by LocalVar, and is the standard deviation of $/sq. ft. values at the four corners of the grid cell in which the subject is located. A variation of < $4/sq. ft. is preferred (reliability=1), whereas a variation exceeding $13/sq. ft. will yield 0 reliability. Intermediate values lead to a reliability between 0 and 1.
- *The living area of the subject.* If the property is extremely small or extremely large, then the estimator has less reliability in its estimate. A value between 1000 and 3800 sq. ft. is preferred (reliability = 1). If the living area is less than 900 sq. ft. or more than 4200 sq. ft., the reliability is 0. Intermediate values lead to a reliability between 0 and 1.
- *Atypicality of the subject.* Sales in the subject's 5-digit ZIP have a mean and standard deviation associated with their physical features. The subject is assigned a score based on how "far away" it is from these mean values. An average house gets a score of 0 whereas a high score is associated with an unusual property. An Atypicality score of 0 to 1 is preferred (reliability = 1). If this exceeds 1.5, AIGEN reliability will be 0. Intermediate values lead to a reliability between 0 and 1.
- *Lot Size.* AIGEN prefers that the lot size be at most 0.8 acres. A value >= 1 acre leads to a 0 reliability. Intermediate values yield a reliability between 0 and 1.
- *Total Rooms.* This should ideally be 6 through 12. Less than 5 or more than 12 total rooms result in a 0 reliability value. Intermediate values lead to a reliability between 0 and 1.

The net AIGEN reliability value is the conjunction of these factors taken as the minimum of the individual reliabilities. This follows from the fuzzy conjunction (minimum) operator which ANDs all the above considerations together. All the specific thresholds were chosen by residual analysis and can be easily changed.

4.7 Discussion

Considering that AIGEN looks only at 5 structural variables, no style, no condition, no quality of construction, and no economic trend metrics, these are encouraging results. The other physical variables were not used since they tended to be missing a significant fraction of the time, and a model's usefulness is reduced if a crucial variable used by it is not available.

Further improvement in E will largely be metric-driven, and is unlikely to be drastic since the market is both imperfect and inefficient, meaning that the ideally maximal information model will also have a residual.

4.8 Other Approaches

We have used E-ANFIS, which is an extended version of ANFIS, as explained before. Other AI-based generative approaches could be tried to solve problems where an I-O relationship has to be identified from data. We briefly mention some of these and discuss why they may be inappropriate for the application at hand.

Fuzzy systems and neural networks could be used in isolation for solving this problem. Each of them is capable of implementing a multi-input, single-output numeric map. We have used a combination of these two approaches in E-ANFIS above, so that we get the advantages of both.

Non-AI approaches such as statistical linear regression use a similar philosophy of training and testing the models. The AI-based approach provides a transparent explanation of the model in terms of a small number of rules which are comprehensible to a human. In addition, it implements a nonlinear regression model.

As compared to the statistical tool CART [4], AIGEN uses a fuzzy generalization of the CART concept of a decision tree. CART may have a discontinuity problem, since the antecedent regions as determined by the decision tree are crisp sets. AIGEN gets the advantage of smoothness in behavior owing to its use of fuzzy sets.

An AI-based approach could be non-generative, in the sense that it may use more than just the subject property to make an estimation of its value. It could use data on other similar properties, as is done by a human appraiser. This process is captured by the AI-comparable based estimator, which is discussed elsewhere in this chapter.

4.9 Scalability and Computational Cost

The results and discussion of data issues presented above corresponded to data from Contra Costa County in California. The next important question is : how well will this approach generalize to other counties and other sources?

Since our AIGEN model has at most 100-150 degrees of freedom, it should not require more than 1500-2000 well-chosen training examples for extracting the model. This implies that the size requirements on training data are very modest, but their quality is required to be very good. None of the 3 data sources should have a problem meeting this requirement. The computational cost can be easily handled by a typical workstation. This argument continues to be valid even if each county is updated with new data every three months (for example). This decision is driven principally by the volatility of the economy, the needs of the business application, and the ease of maintenance required.

Testing an estimator on a subject property is computationally very fast and very simple. No database access is required. Only one property needs to be geocoded and its locational value estimated. This function is performed by the Locational Value estimator, after which the AIGEN model is equivalent to computing a single formula.

4.10 Conclusions

We have seen that a hybrid neuro-fuzzy approach is suitable for attacking the property valuation problem. We have discussed the architecture and algorithms of AIGEN, one of our proposed solutions. We have also shown that encouraging results have been obtained on the Contra Costa properties, based on multiple data sources. This is despite the limited number of attributes used in the computation. The next section will show an alternative approach which uses CBR.

5 Fuzzy Case Based Reasoning (CBR) Process

The CBR process consists of selecting relevant cases, adapting them, and aggregating those adapted cases into a single estimate of the property value

The possibility of using CBR to automating the valuation process was first shown by Gonzalez [9]. However, his CBR approach never captured the intrinsic imprecision of the basic steps in the sale comparison approach: finding the *most similar* houses, located *close* to the subject property, sold *not too long* ago; and selecting a *balanced* subset of the *most promising* comparables to derive the final estimate. Therefore we developed AICOMP, a fuzzy CBR system that uses fuzzy predicates and fuzzy-logic based similarity measures [2] to estimate the value of residential property. Our approach, described in [3], consists of:

1. Retrieving recent sales from a case-base using a small number of features to select potential comparables.
2. Comparing the subject property with the retrieved cases and deriving a partial ordering (similarity measure) from the aggregation of fuzzy preference values.
3. Adjusting the sales price of the retrieved cases to reflect their differences from the subject using a rule set.
4. Aggregating the adjusted sales prices of the retrieved cases, selecting the best comparables, deriving a single value estimate for the subject, and qualifying the estimate with a reliability value.

The property valuation process is shown in Figure 7.

Upon entering the subject property attributes, AICOMP retrieves potentially similar comparables from the case-base. This initial selection uses six attributes: address, date of sale, living area, lot area, number of bathrooms, and bedrooms. The comparables are rated and ranked on a similarity scale to identify the most similar ones to the subject property. This rating is obtained from a weighted aggregation of the decision making preferences, expressed as fuzzy membership distributions and relations. Each property's sales price is adjusted to better reflect the subject's value. These adjustments are performed by a rule set that uses additional property attributes, such as construction quality, conditions, pools, fireplaces, etc. The best 4 to 8 comparables are then selected. Finally, the adjusted sales price and similarity of the selected properties are combined to produce an estimate of the value of the subject, a reliability in that estimate, and a justification for the estimate.

5.1 Example

We will now provide an example of the property valuation process, consisting of the following steps:

- Retrieval of comparables from a database

- Evaluation of each comparable's attribute on a
- preference scale from 0 to 1
- Computation of each comparable's similarity with the subject, (weighted sum of preference values)
- Adjustment of comparables sale prices to reflect
- differences from the subject property
- Removal of poor quality comparables
- Weighted aggregation of best comparables

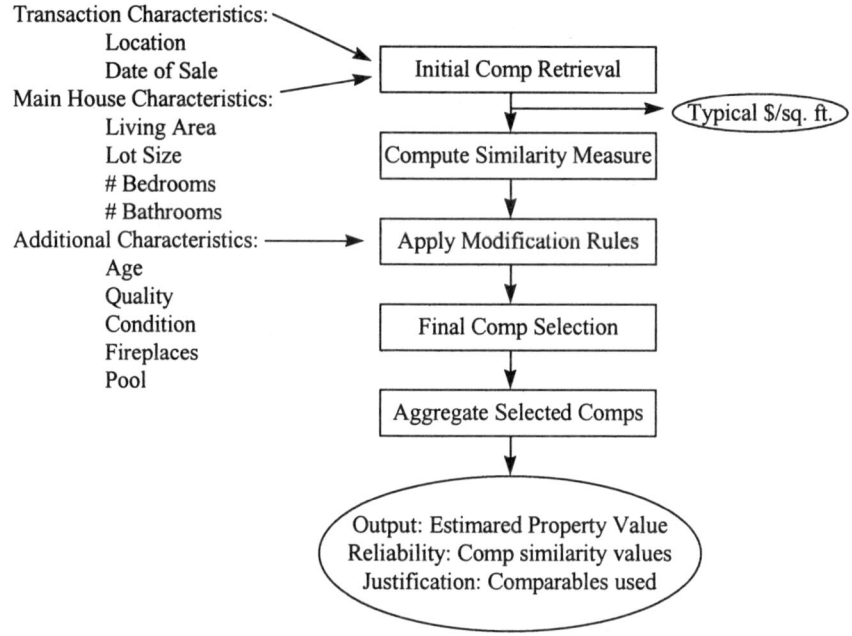

Figure 7: CBR Process

5.1.1 Case Retrieval

The initial retrieval extracts a set of potential comparables using standard SQL queries for efficiency purpose. The selection is performed by comparing specific attributes of the subject with the corresponding attribute of each comparable. All the comparables in the retrieved set have values within the allowable deviations. If the size of the retrieved set is too small, e.g., less than 10, the allowable deviations could be relaxed to increase its at the expense of retrieval quality.

This initial retrieval stage uses the following attributes and their corresponding maximum allowable deviations (written after each attribute):

- Date of sale (within 12 months)
- Distance (within 1 mile)
- living area (+ / - 25%)
- lot size (+ 100% / - 50%)
- Number of bedrooms (+/- 3)
- Number of bathrooms (+/- 3)

These ranges correspond to the support of the fuzzy sets shown in Figure 8 and the fuzzy relations of Figures 9-10.

Rationale for attribute selection. After performing a completeness analysis on CMDC and TRW data bases, we decided to use the above six key attributes because their fields contained a value in over 95% of the records in the data bases. The first two attributes (number of months since the date of sale, and distance from subject) are market and region dependent. Their range of allowed values could be manually modified or automatically indexed to reflect slow or fast markets, as well as urban, suburban, and rural regions. The remaining four variables (living area, lot area, number of bedrooms, number of bathrooms) reflect some of the subject's main characteristics. The range of values used in the initial retrieval stage have been obtained from several knowledge engineering sessions with practicing appraisers.

5.1.2 Preference Criteria Definition and Evaluation

Figure 8 describes our preference criteria for the first four features. The trapezoidal membership distributions representing these criteria have a natural preference interpretation. For each feature, the *support* of the distribution represents the range of *tolerable* values and corresponds to the interval-value used in the initial retrieval query. The *core* represents the most *desirable* range of values and establishes our top preference. By definition, a feature value falling inside the core will receive a preference value of 1. As the feature value moves away from the most desirable range, its associated preference value will decrease from 1 to 0. At the end of this evaluation, each comparable will have a *preference vector*, with each element taking values in the (0,1] interval. These values represent the partial degree of membership of each feature value in the fuzzy sets and fuzzy relations representing our preference criteria.

For example, by using the preference distributions shown in Figure 8 we can see that the preference value for the attribute *date-of-sale* of a comparable that was sold within 3 months of today's date is 1. If the date was 6 months ago, its preference value would be 2/3. Any comparable with a date of sale of more than 12 months would be given a preference value of zero.

The remaining two features, *Number of Bedrooms* and *Number of Bathrooms,* are evaluated in a similar fashion. Their preference functions are represented by two reflexive asymmetric fuzzy relations, illustrated in Figure 9 and 10, respectively.

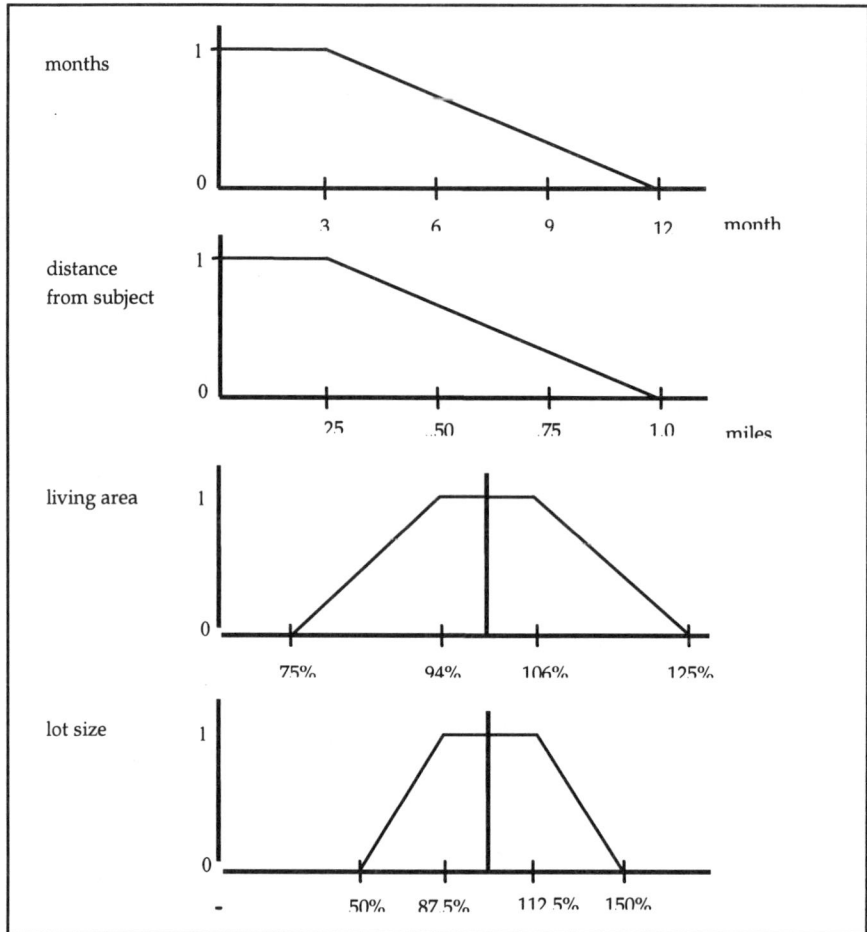

Figure 8: Attribute Preference Functions

Comparable's		1	2	3	4	5	6+
# Bedrooms							
	1	1.00	0.50	0.05	0.00	0.00	0.00
Subject's	2	0.20	1.00	0.50	0.05	0.00	0.00
# Bedrooms	3	0.05	0.30	1.00	0.60	0.05	0.00
	4	0.00	0.05	0.50	1.00	0.60	0.20
	5	0.00	0.00	0.05	0.60	1.00	0.80
	6+	0.00	0.00	0.00	0.20	0.80	1.00

Figure 9: Preference Function for Number of Bedrooms

For instance, using Figure 9, we can observe that for a subject with 5 bedrooms the preferred comparable would also have 5 bedroom (preference =1), while a 6 bedroom comparable would meet that preference criterion to a degree of 0.8. Similarly, using Figure 10, we can observe that, for a subject with 2 bathrooms, the preferred comparable would also have 2 bathrooms (preference value =1), while a 2.5 bathroom comparable would meet that preference criterion to a degree of 0.7.

Subject	Comparable								
	1	1.5	2	2.5	3	3.5	4	4.5	5+
1	1.00	0.75	0.20	0.05	0.01	0.00	0.00	0.00	0.00
1.5	0.60	1.00	0.60	0.25	0.10	0.05	0.00	0.00	0.00
2	0.10	0.70	1.00	0.70	0.25	0.05	0.00	0.00	0.00
2.5	0.05	0.20	0.75	1.00	0.75	0.20	0.05	0.00	0.00
3	0.01	0.10	0.40	0.80	1.00	0.80	0.40	0.10	0.05
3.5	0.00	0.05	0.15	0.45	0.85	1.00	0.85	0.45	0.30
4	0.00	0.00	0.05	0.20	0.50	0.90	1.00	0.90	0.70
4.5	0.00	0.00	0.00	0.10	0.30	0.70	0.95	1.00	0.95
5+	0.00	0.00	0.00	0.05	0.15	0.35	0.75	0.95	1.00

Figure 10: Preference Function for Number of Bathrooms

5.1.3 Similarity Measure Computation

The next step consists in computing a similarity measure between each potential comparable and the subject. The similarity measure is a function of the preference vector computed above and of the decision maker's priorities. These priorities are reflected by the weights used before the aggregation. Figure 11 (sixth column) illustrates a set of values obtained by interviewing expert appraisers, using Saaty's pairwise comparison method [17], and validated in our tests.

Figure 11 shows an example of the similarity measure computation between the subject and a comparable. Attributes (living area, lot area, bedrooms, bathrooms) and derived values (date, distance) used for the calculation are listed in the column labeled *Attribute*. The values of those attributes for the subject and comparable are listed in the columns labeled *Subject* and *Comparable*. The evaluation representing the attributes' degree of matching, obtained by using Figure 8, 94, and 10 are listed in the *Preference* column. The weights reflecting an attribute's relative importance in the specific market area are listed in the *Weight* column. The sum of the score and weights for an attribute is given in the *Weighted Preference* column. Finally, the total score of the weighted preferences represents the similarity measure.

5.1.4 Comparables Adjustments

All of the properties found by the initial retrieval will undergo a series of adjustment in their sales price to better reflect the subject property value. Any difference between the subject and comparable property that would cause the comparable to be more (or less valuable) than the subject produces an adjustment. If the comparable is superior to the subject that adjustment will decrease the comparable price, and vice versa for comparable that are inferior to the subject. After all the adjustments are applied to the comparable sales price the resulting value is called the comparable *Adjusted price*.

The adjustment rules, illustrated in Table 3, were obtained from numerous knowledge engineering sessions with expert appraiser and from the analysis of hundreds of existing appraisals. These rules will be triggered by differences between subject's and comparable's attributes.

Table 3: Adjustment Rule Set

> *Living Area (subject - comp) * (22 + (Sales_Price_of_comp * .00003))*
> *Lot Area (subject - comp) * 1*
> *Bathrooms   see figure 10*
> *Fireplaces   (subject - comp) * 2000*
> *Effective Year Built*
> *w * (Age_comp-Age_subject) * (Sale_Price_comp/1000)*
>   *if (Age_subject + Age_comp) / 2 < 4 then w = 4 else*
>   *if (Age_subject + Age_comp) / 2 < 6 then w = 3 else*
>   *if (Age_subject + Age_comp) / 2 < 8 then w = 2 else*
>   *if (Age_subject + Age_comp) / 2 < 15 then w = 1 else*
>   *w = .5*
> *max of 10% of salePrice*
> *Quality   (.02 * sale price) for each level of difference:*
> *(Luxury >Excellent > Good> Average > Fair > Poor)*
> *Pool $10000 for a pool*

Figure 12 shows the adjustments (in thousands of dollars) to be made to the comparable's price, as a function of the different number of bathrooms between the subject and the comparable property. The last column and row indicate the required adjustments for each additional bathroom when either the subject or the comparable have more than five bathrooms.

Figure 13 shows the computation of the comparable's adjusted price. The adjustments shown in the figure are:

- The Living Area is adjusted by (22 + (175000 * .00003)) = $27.25 per square foot which is 200 * $27.25 = $5450.
- The Lot Area is adjusted by $1/sq ft for a total of -$5000 since the comparable has a larger lot size.
- The Bathrooms are adjusted using Figure 10 (adjustment figures in 1,000 of dollars).
- There are the same number of Bedrooms so there is no adjustment.
- The subject has one more Fireplace than the comparable so the adjustment is $2000.
- The Effective Year Built formula produces an adjustment of $2800.
- The subjects Quality is one step better than the comparable so the adjustment is 2% of the sale price of the comparable.
- The subject has a Pool and the comparable does not so the adjustment is $10000.

Attribute	Subject	Comparable	Comparison	Preference	Weight
Months since date of	X	6 months	6 months	0,67	0,222
Distance	X	0.2 miles	0.2 miles	1,00	0,222
Living Area	2000	1800	90%	0,79	0,333
Lot Size	20000	35000	175%	0,33	0,111
# Bedroom	3	3	0%	1,00	0,056
# Bathrooms	2,5	2	2.5 -> 2	0,75	0,056

Figure 11: Similarity Measure Computation

Subject	Comp								
	1	1.5	2	2.5	3	3.5	4	4.5	5+
1	0.00	-1.50	-3.00	-5.00	-8.00	N/A	N/A	N/A	N/A
1.5	1.00	0.00	-1.00	-3.50	-6.00	-9.00	N/A	N/A	N/A
2	4.00	1.50	0.00	-2.25	-4.00	-6.50	N/A	N/A	N/A
2.5	7.00	4.50	2.00	0.00	-2.00	-4.50	-7.00	N/A	N/A
3	9.00	6.50	3.00	2.00	0.00	-2.50	-5.00	-7.50	'@*-5
3.5	N/A	8.50	6.50	4.50	2.50	0.00	-3.00	-5.50	'@*-5
4	N/A	N/A	8.50	7.00	5.50	3.00	0.00	-3.00	'@*-5
4.5	N/A	N/A	N/A	10.00	8.00	6.00	3.00	0.00	'@*-5
5+	N/A	N/A	N/A	'@*5	'@*5	'@*5	'@*5	'@*5	0.00

Figure 12: Adjustment Function for Number of Bathrooms

Attribute	Subject	Comparable	Adjustment
SalePrice	?	175000	175000
LivingArea	2000	1800	5450
LotArea	20000	25000	-5000
SFRTotalBaths	2.5	2	2000
SFRBedrooms	3	3	
SFRFireplaces	1	0	2000
EffYearBuilt	93	89	2800
Quality	Good	Average	3500
Condition	Average	Average	
Pool	Yes	No	10000
Adjusted Price =			195750

Figure 13: Example of Adjustments

5.1.5 Comparables Filtering

A good comparable selection is key to the property valuation process. We have found that the range of four to eight comparables is optimal for this process. By using less than four comparables, we are not correctly reflecting the current market. By using more than eight, we risk to include some comparables which are not similar enough to the subject property. If it is not possible to find four comparables similar to the subject property then no value estimate may be calculated for the subject. Typically, the initial retrieval yields an average of 22 comparables (up to a maximum of 100). Therefore, finding the best 4 - 8 comparables will usually require removing the less desirable comparables. We would like the selected comparables to have the following properties:

- No single adjustment should be larger (in absolute value) than 10% of sales price
- Net adjustment should not exceed 15% of sales price
- Gross adjustment should not exceed 25% of sales price
- The unit price for living area of the comparables should not vary more than 15% from each other and should bracket that of the subject
- Comparables should be as close as possible to the subject
- The value estimated for the subject should be bracketed by the sales price of the comparables

After adjusting all the comparables found in the initial retrieval, any comparable violating any of the first three constraints is removed from the process.

The best comparables are selected from the remaining ones by the method show in Figure 14. First, we determine the comparables with the highest similarity score, lowest net adjustments, and lowest gross adjustments. Figure 15 shows how these three values are combined into a single ranking of the comparables. Each comparable has its similarity score ranked with the other comparables such that the comparable with the best similarity score receives the lowest rank. Net adjustment and gross adjustment are similarly ranked. The sum of the three ranks is computed for each comparable, determining its *Total Rank*. The comparables with the lowest total rank are considered the best.

This method induces a cardinal ordering on the set of comparables, but does not tell us how many comparables to use. The sales prices of the comparables should bound the estimated sales price of the subject. Therefore, we would like to select comparables with both negative and positive net adjustments. Typically, a comparable with a negative net adjustment is likely to have an unadjusted price greater than the final estimate, and viceversa for a comparable with a positive net adjustment. To achieve this bracketing effect, we create a temporary set of candidates by repeatedly adding the comparable with the best similarity score to the set until:

1. there are at least four comparables in the set, and
2. at least one comparable has a net adjustment sign different from the others.

For the example in Figure 15, the comparables with the top six similarity scores would be included in the set. All other comparables are discarded. Of the comparables in the set we retain only four of each sign net adjust. The selected ones are the four with the lowest total rank. In the example from Figure 16, comparable number 305-006 would be discarded since there are four comparables with a positive net adjust and lower total rank. The five comparables selected form the final set of comparables.

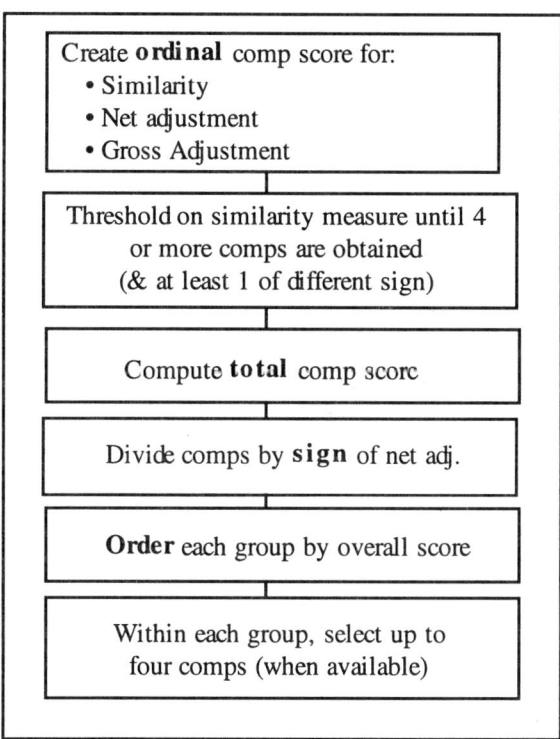

Figure 14: Comparable Final Selection

Comparable	Score Value	Score Rank	Net Adjust Value	N. A. Rank	Gross Adjust Value	G. A. Rank	Total Rank
113-012	0.95	1	1344	2	5924	4	7
306-018	0.88	2	3586	5	4186	1	8
093-011	0.78	3	5686	7	8191	7	17
305-006	0.67	4	6150	8	6160	6	18
685-046	0.64	5	3139	3	6099	5	13
847-984	0.58	6	-948	1	5670	3	10
873-005	0.53	7	-5261	6	9261	8	21
431-023	0.48	8	3546	4	4410	2	14
331-018	0.44	9	9310	9	11300	9	27

Figure 15: Comparable Selection Example

5.1.6 Weighted Aggregation of Comparables Sales Price

After the best 4-8 comparables are found, their prices must be combined to produce the final estimate. Each comparable's contribution to this result is weighted by its similarity score. Figure 16 shows the calculation of a final estimate from adjusted values of the selected comparables and their similarity scores.

In addition to producing the final estimate of the value of the subject, the CBR estimator provides a reliability in the estimate and the comparables that justify the estimate.

Comparable	Adjusted Price	Score	Weighted Price
113-012	197000	0.95	187150
306-008	202000	0.88	177760
093-011	196500	0.78	153270
685-046	192000	0.64	122880
847-984	201000	0.58	116580
Total		3.83	757640
Final estimate = 757640/ 3.83 =			199900

Figure 16: Comparable Aggregation

5.2 Reliability Value Assessment

The users will make critical decisions based on the estimates generated. Therefore, we need to tell them when the system produces an accurate, reliable solution. We achieve this goal by attaching a reliability measure to each estimate. Ideally we would like to have subjects with the highest reliability exhibiting the lowest errors. At the same time we would like to assign high reliability values to as many subjects as possible.

The reliability value is calculated from the following five quantitative characteristics of the case-based reasoning process:

• Number of cases found in the initial retrieval
• Average of the similarity values for the best four cases
• Typicality of problem with respect to the case-base (i.e. if the attributes of the subject fall within typical ranges for the subjects five digit zip code region)
• Span of adjusted sales prices of highest reliability solutions (i.e. the highest adjusted sale price minus the lowest adjusted sale price among the selected comparables)
• Distribution of adjusted sales prices of highest reliability solutions (i.e. average percentage deviation of the adjusted sales price of the comparables from the estimated value of the subject)

These characteristics are evaluated using the fuzzy membership functions illustrated in Figure 17. These functions map the numerical value of each parameter into a standard numerical reliability, which ranges from 0 to 1. These standardized reliability values are then aggregated into a final reliability value. Given the conjunctive nature of this aggregation, we decided to use the *minimum* of the standardized reliability values.

Figure 17a) shows that if two or less comparables are found then the standardized reliability for comparables found is 0. If between two and seven comparables are found, the reliability is $((n-2)*0.15))$, i.e. the reliability increases 0.15 for each comparable over two to reach 0.75 when there are seven comparables. Between seven and twelve comparables, the reliability is $((n-7)*0.05)+0.75)$, i.e. the reliability increases 0.05 for each comparable over seven and reaches 1.0 with twelve comparables. Since the aggregation method is minimum operator, a low reliability in any of the characteristics will cause a low reliability in the result regardless of other excellent reliability values for the other characteristics. The other figures show similar membership functions for the other reliability measures.

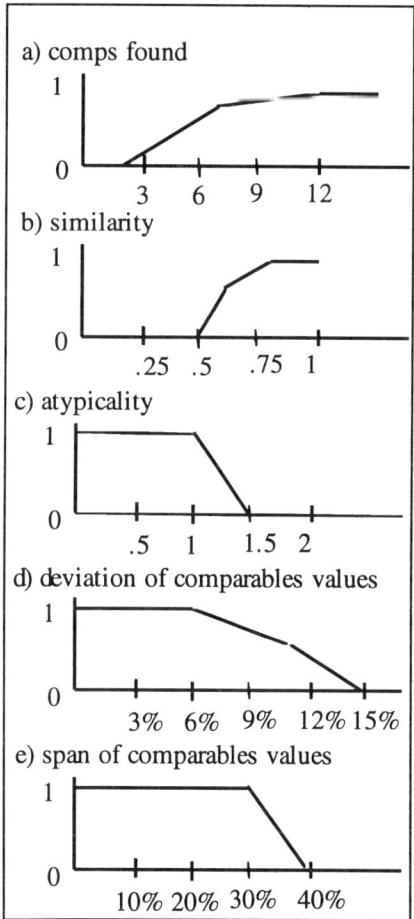

Figure 17: Membership functions for reliability

Figure 17b) shows that we have no reliability in an estimate whose similarity is lower than 0.5. Otherwise the reliability rises to 1 at a similarity of 0.8, and is 1 for anything over 0.8. Figure 17c) is used to determine our reliability based on the subject's atypicality. Atypicality is computed as a normalized deviation in the region's average lot size, living area, number of bedroom, bathrooms, etc. We have no reliability in subjects with atypicality greater than 1.5. Our reliability rises linearly as the atypicality decreases from 1.5 to 1.0 and is one when atypicality is less than 1.0. Figure 17d) shows our reliability for the average deviations in the values of the comparables. We have zero reliability in an estimate if the average comparable deviates from the estimated price by more than 15%. Finally, Figure 17 e) is used to determine our reliability based on the size of the span of the adjusted values of the comparables. If the span is greater than 40% of the value of the subject then we considered it too scattered and have no reliability in the estimate.

5.3 Statistical Analysis

To create the membership functions for the five characteristics, which are illustrated in Figure 17, we ran our system on 7,293 properties from Contra Costa county in California. The predicted sales price of each property was calculated and compared with its actual sales price[3] to derive the estimate's error. The percentage error and its five reliability characteristics were calculated each subject. Figure 18 shows the values calculated for a random sample of ten of the 7,293 subjects. Each row is a different subject. The columns show the estimate error, the five characteristics calculated along with the estimate, and the reliability value obtained by taking the minimum of the evaluation of the membership functions of Figure 17 using the estimate's five characteristics.

Error	Comps Found	Simil.	Atyp.	Comps Dev.	Comps Span	Conf. Value
-9.8	3	0.63	1.42	2.02	6.32	0.15
-2	35	0.94	0.38	2.24	8.57	1.00
17.3	11	0.71	0.94	5.67	19	0.70
0.5	24	0.85	0.66	2.05	7.24	1.00
-1.6	14	0.95	0.29	2.89	9.33	1.00
5.2	15	0.90	0.73	3.24	12	1.00
5.2	12	0.74	0.17	4.5	18	0.80
3.1	19	0.74	0.81	2.83	8.11	0.80
-13.9	12	0.82	1.97	3.85	15	0.00
7.8	11	0.77	1.34	4.24	13	0.32

Figure 18: Sample of test run

---

[3] Although the actual sale price was known, it was never used in the estimate's computation.

Then we analyzed the conditional distributions of the estimate error, given each of its five reliability characteristics, and try to predict the error. For instance, Figure 19 shows that the estimate error (in percentage) decreases as the number of comparables found in the initial retrieval increases. Therefore, we can use this number as a filter to predict the expect expected error.

We used C4.5 [16] to create rules predicting the error from the system's characteristics. Then we validated these rules via data visualization. Finally, the rules were manually transformed into the membership functions illustrated in Figure 17. The estimate's reliability value is the conjunctive evaluation of all the rules.

At our customer's request, the reliability value generated by the rules was subdivided into three groupings (*good, fair,* and *poor*). The reliability measure should then produce the largest good set with the lowest error. Of the 7,293 subjects, we could classify our reliability in 63% as *good*. The *good* set has a medium absolute error of **5.4%**, an error which is satisfactory for the intended application. Of the remaining subjects, 24% were classified as *fair*, and 13% as *poor*. The fair set has a medium error of **7.7%**, and the poor set has a median error of **11.8%**.

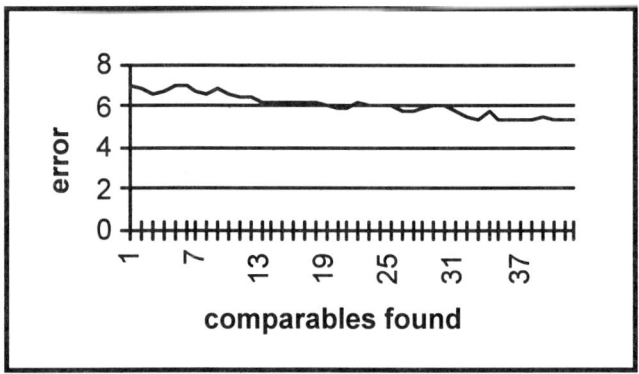

Figure 19: Median error as a function of number of comparables found

The system can also be used in validation mode to support a sales price, or to determine the reliability value in a sales price. The sales price could either be given or supplied by another estimator. In this mode, the system can find comparables to validate such a price. This feature is needed because appraisals are required to be supported by evidence of current market conditions. Using the actual sales price as a target, we were able to find comparables supporting a sales price with a median absolute difference from the actual sales price of **0.5%**. Clearly, when the system is used in this mode it yields different results than when it is used to estimate the property's market value. In validation mode, the search for comparables is *biased* by the sales price. Since this price is also used to evaluate the results, error statistics show a large reduction in the median of the absolute error (from 5.4% to 0.5%). Note that median error for Human Appraisers is generally agreed to be equal to 3%. These statistics were derived from the trade literature and include a large number of cases in which the sales price was available to the appraiser. On the other hand, not all sales price are necessarily originated from *bona-fide* transactions, so results obtained from the *unbiased* search are actually more reliable.

6. Fusion

The final step in obtaining an ARPV estimate is to combine the outputs of the three estimators described in the preceding sections, namely, LOCVAL, AIGEN, and AICOMP. These three estimators provide independent estimates of the same target quantity (property value) using different methodologies.

This fusion of several estimates to give a combined answer has several advantages:

- the fusion process provides an indication of the reliability or trust in the final estimate,
- if reliability is high, the fused estimate is more accurate than any of the individual ones, if reliability is limited, the system generates an explanation in human terms, and
- the fused estimate is more robust.

These characteristics allow the user to determine the suitability of the estimate within the given business application context. Knowledge-based rules are used for constructing this fusion of technologies at a supervisory level.

6.1 Related Work

Combining forecasts and estimates has been extensively studied in disciplines such as econometrics and market research [5,7,8,10,12,15]. A common fusion technique is to use a weighted average where the weights are related to some measure of reliability in the individual forecasts. This is essentially the approach we have taken in this work. On the other hand, we believe the method we have used to obtain a combined reliability is unique.

6.2 Approach to Fusion

Our approach is broken down into four steps:

1. Assess the reliability or "goodness" of each individual estimate.
2. Develop an algorithm for combining the three values produced by the individual estimators into a fused value.
3. Develop a rule-base which determines the overall quality of the fused estimate -- this is referred to as the fusion of the reliabilities.
4. Generate explanatory messages to the user when the overall quality is limited. These messages enable the user to understand why the best possible estimate cannot be produced. Further information by the user may then enable the system to improve its results.

We will refer to the overall system as ARPV (Automated Residential Property Valuation). The final output of the system will be referred to as the ESTIMATEARPV. The accompanying measure of reliability is called the QUALITY of the ESTIMATE.

6.3 Fusion Rules

As seen in Figure 2, LOCVAL is used as an input to AIGEN, and AICOMP and AIGEN both use property descriptions to produce the answers. These two are then combined to produce the final ARPV ESTIMATE of property value and an overall measure of reliability or QUALITY. Finally, ARPV provides a description of circumstances for the data, property, and environment that may have led to a limited value of QUALITY.

The precise manner of their combination depends on the relative strengths of the two individual reliabilities, and the amount of disagreement between the two estimator values. Each reliability is a number in [0,1] The amount of disagreement is measured by **contention** between the two values v_{AIG} (produced by AIGEN), and v_{AIC} (produced by AICOMP). Contention is

$$(v_{AIG} - v_{AIC}) / ((v_{AIG} + v_{AIC}) / 2)$$

and is defined only when both estimators have produced a valid answer.

Rules for computing the fused ESTIMATE and QUALITY are described below.

6.3.1 Case 1

If both AIGEN and AICOMP estimates are known, then ESTIMATE is set to the mean of the two estimates, weighted by their respective normalized reliabilities. This is given by

$$(v_{AIG} * r_{AIG} + v_{AIC} * r_{AIC}) / (v_{AIG} + v_{AIC})$$

where v denotes estimates, and r denotes the respective estimator reliabilities.

QUALITY is obtained by the following rules :

- If contention is low, and the reliability of one of the estimates is high, and the reliability of the other estimator is not low then the Quality of the fused estimate is EXCELLENT.
- If contention is high, or the reliabilities of both estimators are low then Quality is set to UNRELIABLE.
- In all remaining cases, Quality is set to INDICATIVE.

Initially, the definitions of the terms *low, medium, and high* for contention as well as the reliabilities have been numerically set so as to create a conservative system. These sets are currently crisp, and not fuzzy. However, both these characteristics can be suitably changed to suit the needs of a specific business application.

6.3.2 Case 2

If one of AIGEN and AICOMP is known but the other is not, then no combination is possible. In this case, ESTIMATE is set to the value of the available estimator and QUALITY is conservatively deemed UNRELIABLE. (As a further refinement of the methodology there are certain circumstances within this case where QUALITY could be upgraded to INDICATIVE.)

6.3.3 Case 3

If both AIGEN and AICOMP are unknown, then no combination is possible. In such cases where the property can be geocoded and the living area is known, ESTIMATE is set equal to LOCVAL. Otherwise, ESTIMATE is set to a simple average such as for the 5-digit ZIP or the county. QUALITY is deemed UNRELIABLE. These three cases cover all the possibilities and are encoded as rules. The final outputs are the fused ESTIMATE and QUALITY.

Recapitulating, QUALITY is a measure of the reliability of the fused ARPV estimate and takes one of three values:

- EXCELLENT -- All essential data is available, reliability for the independent estimators is high, and the independent estimators agree.
- INDICATIVE -- All essential data is available, reliability of one or more estimators is not high due to somewhat unusual property and/or local market characteristics, and/or the estimators disagree.
- UNRELIABLE -- Some essential data may be missing, and/or reliability in one or more estimators is low due to very unusual property and/or local market characteristics, and/or the estimators disagree markedly.

In addition, if the QUALITY is not EXCELLENT, two kinds of explanatory messages are produced:

The **first message** explains why one or more of the estimators were not able to produce an estimate. As this is due to missing or unusual attributes, they will be listed.

The **second message** explains why QUALITY may be less than EXCELLENT. The message may have the following three parts, each of which is explained using an example:

- Contention = 0.5 --- indicates amount of disagreement between AIGEN and AICOMP
- AIGConf not HI (TotalRooms=5) --- indicates that AIGEN reliability was not HIGH because the property has a significantly smaller total room count than the typical house.
- AICConf not HI (CompsFnd=8) --- indicates that AICOMP reliability was not HIGH because the first phase of comparable searches found only 8 candidate comparable houses within a year and a mile.

7 Conclusions

We have considered the important and difficult problem of residential property valuation and shown that techniques based on Soft Computing can successfully attack it. A multitude of approaches using Fuzzy Logic, Case-based reasoning, and Neural networks was shown to be useful in this regard. Moreover, the reliability computation and the fusion process increases the robustness and human usefulness of the system. It has been shown to achieve good accuracy and be scaleable for thousands of automated transactions. This makes it a transparent, interpretable, fast, and inexpensive choice for bulk estimates of residential property value for a variety of financial applications.

Acknowledgments

The work described herein was part of a larger project band we are indebted to contributions from other members of the team. In particular, Mel Simmons developed the LOCVAL methodology. Barbara Vivier led the effort to acquire and analyze the data. Cheryl Wiebe and Lewis Alan provided knowledge on the mortgage industry and appraisal practice. Other contributors were Jeanette Bruno, Mike Hartman, Margaret Kelliher, Joe Leva, Carolyn Morgan, Lorinda Opsahl-Ong, Lianne Schroeder, and Jeff Wisnewski.

References

[1] Appraisal Institute, *Appraising Residential Properties, Part VI*, Chicago IL, 1994.
[2] Bonissone, P.P. and Ayub, S. "Similarity Measures for Case-based Reasoning Systems", Proc. of the Fourth Intl. Conf. on Information Processing and Management of Uncertainty (IPMU-92) in Knowledge-Based Systems, pp. 483-487, Palma, Spain, 1992.
[3] Bonissone, P.P. and Cheetham W., Financial Applications of Fuzzy Case-Based Reasoning to Residential Property Valuation, *FUZZ-IEEE'97*, pp. 37-44, Barcelona, Spain, July 1997
[4] Breiman, Friedman, Olshen & Stone, *Classification and Regression Trees*, Monterey, CA: Wadsworth and Brooks, 1985
[5] Bunn D., Combining Forecasts, *European Journal of Operations Research*, 33, 223-229, 1988
[6] Case K.E. and Shiler R.J., Prices of Single-Family Homes since 1970: New Indexes for Four Cities, *New England Economic Review*, Sept./Oct. 1987
[6] Clemen R. T., Combining Forecasts: A review and Annotated Bibliography, *International Journal of Forecasting*, 4, 559-584, 1989
[7] Granger C.W.J. and Ramanathan R., Improved Methods of Combining Forecasts, *Journal of Forecasting*, 3: 197-204, 1984
[8] Gonzalez, A. J. "A Case-Based Reasoning Approach to Real Estate Property Appraisal," *Expert Systems with Applications,* Vol. 4, pp. 229-246, 1992.
[9] Hoch S.J., Experts and Models in Combination, *in The Marketing Information Revolution,*
[10] Jang, J.S.R. ANFIS: Adaptive-Network-Based Fuzzy Inference System, *IEEE Trans. Systems, Man, Cybernetics,* 23(5/6):665-685, 1993

[11] Kacapyr E., Consensus Forecasts, in *Economic Forecasting: The State of the Art*, M. E. Sharpe, Inc., 1996

[12] Klir, G. and Folger, *Fuzzy Sets, Uncertainty, and Information*, Prentice Hall, 1988.

[13] Kolodner, J. *Case-based Reasoning*. Morgan Kaufmann, 1993.

[14] McNees S. K., Consensus Forecasts: Tyranny of the Majority, *New England Economic Review* November-December: 14-21, 1987

[16] Quinlan, J.R. *C4.5: Programs for Machine Learning*. Morgan Kaufmann, San Mateo, CA, 1993.

[17] Saaty, T.L. *The Analytic Hierarchy Process*, McGraw-Hill, 1980.

[18] Takagi, T. and Sugeno, M., Fuzzy Identification of Systems and Its Application to Modeling and Control, *IEEE Transactions on Systems, Man, and Cybernetics* 15(1):116-132, 1985

[19] Zadeh, L. A. Fuzzy Sets, *Information and Control* 8:338-353, 1965.

6

AUDITING AND REPORTING

Theoretical Investigation of Belief Revisions in Auditing

Saurav K. Dutta [1] and Rajendra P. Srivastava [2]

[1] Graduate School of Management
Rutgers University
Newark, Newark, NJ
[2] Ernst & Young Centre for Auditing Research and Advanced Technology
School of Business
University of Kansas, Lawrence, KS 66045, USA

Abstract. In this paper we examine the empirical findings of belief revision under two alternatives: the Bayesian framework and the Dempster-Shafer theory of belief functions. Bayesian theory is very stringent in its requirement that the probability of mutually exclusive and collectively exhaustive events sum to one. It requires that the belief be increased in light of supporting evidence, and be decreased in light of conflicting evidence. These results are consistent with the empirical findings. However, the Bayesian analysis entails the largest increase (decrease) in belief for medium priors in light of supporting (conflicting) evidence. This is contrary to empirical findings. The largest increase was observed for smallest priors when presented with supporting evidence. The largest decrease was observed for highest priors when presented with conflicting evidence. Further, Bayesian theory fails to explain the 'recency' and the 'dilution' effects. In the belief-function formalism, the belief in a proposition increases in light of supporting (positive) evidence. Further, the largest increase is for the lowest priors. This is consistent with the empirical findings. The belief in a proposition decreases in light of conflicting (negative) evidence and the largest decrease is for medium priors. This is not totally consistent with the empirical findings. However, with discounting we can attain the largest decrease for the highest prior, consistent with the empirical findings. By incorporating discounting in belief functions, we are able to model the 'recency' and the 'dilution' effects.

Key Words: Belief Functions, Bayesian, Audit Evidence, Aggregation, Belief Revision.

1. INTRODUCTION

The purpose of this paper is to investigate theoretically the belief revision process in auditing using two approaches, Bayes' theorem and the Dempster-Shafer theory of *belief-function*[1], and to compare and contrast the findings with the empirical results of Ashton and Ashton (1988) and Tubbs et al. (1990). Both the approaches considered here are based on the mathematical theory of probability. Bayesian formalism is based on additive probabilities, whereas the *belief-function* formalism is based on non-additive *beliefs* (see Shafer 1976; and Shafer and Srivastava 1990 for details).

Recent studies on auditors' behavior in aggregating evidence have furnished some very interesting results (Ashton and Ashton 1988; Tubbs et al. 1990). First, in the case of positive evidence, auditors revise their belief the most for the lowest prior (anchor). Second, in the case of conflicting evidence, auditors revise their belief the most for the highest prior. Third, in the case of mixed evidence, auditors put more credence on the recent piece of evidence. Fourth, for a given set of evidence, an auditor's belief revision varies with how the items of evidence are processed, i.e., there is a significant difference between the belief revisions when the items of evidence are presented simultaneously versus sequentially.

The Bayesian approach fails to model some of the empirical findings. In contrast, the Dempster-Shafer theory of *belief* functions models most of the findings. The Bayesian theory suggests that the belief be increased in light of positive evidence, and be decreased in light of conflicting evidence. This is consistent with the empirical findings. However, the Bayesian analysis entails the largest increase (decrease) in belief for medium priors in light of supporting (conflicting) evidence. This is contrary to the empirical findings: The largest increase (decrease) was observed for the smallest (highest) priors when presented with supporting (conflicting) evidence. Also, in the Bayesian analysis, the extent of belief revision is independent of the order in which the evidence is presented. Thus, the Bayesian formalism is unable to model the recency effect. The mode of presentation of evidence, sequential versus simultaneous, does not affect the extent of belief revision in Bayesian formalism. Thus, the dilution effect cannot be explained by Bayesian formalism.

The *belief*-function formalism, on the other hand, is able to model the behavior of auditors. In *belief* functions, the *belief* in a proposition increases in light of supporting (positive) evidence. Further, the largest increase is for the lowest priors. This is consistent with the empirical findings. The *belief* decreases when a conflicting item of evidence is presented. The decrease in *belief* is the most for the medium prior. This is inconsistent with the empirical findings. However, with discounted *belief* functions, the largest decrease for the highest priors can be attained.

In this paper, the concept of discounted *belief* functions is applied to model an auditor's behavior in aggregating evidence. Belief functions have previously been employed in an audit setting to aggregate audit evidence (Srivastava 1995; Srivastava, Dutta and Johns 1996). However, there has not been any empirical justification provided that the auditor's revision of beliefs are in accordance to the prescription of *belief* functions. Though, auditors belief revision process has been studied, no attempt has been made to analyze these findings on the basis of

---

[1] The word „belief" in italics means the level of support in belief-function formalism, otherwise it represents the generic meaning as used by Ashton and Ashton (1988).

normative theories of belief revision. Here we are attempting to model the belief revision proces using *belief* functions.

As mentioned earlier, our objective here is to make an attempt to model the empirical findings regarding the auditor's behavior in aggregating evidence by using Bayes' theorem and the *belief*-function framework. We will assume here that the reader has basic familiarity with the Bayesian and *belief*-function formalisms (for details see Shafer 1976; Shafer and Srivastava 1990).

The rest of the paper is divided into five sections. Section II presents belief revisions with positive and negative items of evidence using both the Bayesian and the belief -function formalisms. In Section III, belief revisions with mixed evidence are discussed using discounted belief functions. A discussion on simultaneous versus sequential aggregation of evidence is presented in Section IV. Summary and conclusions are presented in Section V.

2. EFFECT OF PRIOR BELIEF ON BELIEF REVISION

2.1 Belief Revision with Consistent Positive Items of Evidence

Ashton and Ashton (1988) found that belief increases with additional positive evidence. Furthermore, the study showed that the maximum increase was for the lowest priors. That is, when presented with positive evidence, the subjects who had lower anchors (smaller priors) revised their beliefs the most. Their study also showed that there was no order effect with consistent positive evidence, i.e., changing the order of presentation of the same set of evidence had no effect on the extent of revision. In this section we will analyze these findings from both, the Bayesian as well as the belief function perspectives.

Bayesian Perspective

In Bayesian formalism, the prior belief, $P(A)$, in an event A is updated when an evidence E is obtained. This updated belief is called the posterior belief and is represented by $P(A|E)$. Bayes' theorem is used to determine the posterior belief:

$$P(A|E) = P(E|A)P(A)/[P(E|A)P(A) + P(E|{\sim}A)P({\sim}A)] \qquad (1)$$

The likelihood, $P(E|A)$, is the probability of an observation E, given that the event A has occurred. The likelihoods, $P(E|A)$ and $P(E|{\sim}A)$, depend on the audit procedure and should be known to the auditor. The likelihoods are independent of the population characteristics, whereas the prior belief or anchor $P(A)$ depends on the population and is an estimate of the auditor.

An item of evidence is positive if our belief in A increases after we have observed E, i.e., when $P(A|E) > P(A)$ (Toba, 1975; Kissinger, 1977). This was shown to be equivalent to $P(E|A) > P(E|{\sim}A)$ (Dutta and Srivastava 1993). And, an item of evidence is negative if our belief in A decreases after we have observed E, i.e., when

$P(A|E) < P(A)$, or equivalently $P(E|A) < P(E|{\sim}A)$. If we observe E and if E implies A then we are sure that A is true, that is, if E implies A then $P(A|E) = 1$ and $P({\sim}A|E) = 0$. This type of evidence is known as categorical positive evidence (Dutta and Srivastava 1996). Similarly, if E is a categorical negative evidence, that is, if E implies ${\sim}A$ and if we observe E then A is false, i.e., $P(A|E) = 0$ and $P({\sim}A|E) = 1$. Thus, it is obvious that for categorical positive evidence, the lower the prior the more the increase. And similarly, for categorical negative evidence, the higher the prior the more the decrease.

Table 1. Bayesian Probability Revision

Prior	Evidence E1		Posterior	Evidence E2		Posterior	Increase
(Anchor)	$P(E1|A)$	$P(E1|{\sim}A)$	$P(A|E1)$	$P(E2|A)$	$P(E2|{\sim}A)$	$P(A|E1\&E2)$	Probability
0.2	0.6	0.10	0.600	0.800	0.10	0.923	0.723
0.5	0.6	0.10	0.857	0.800	0.10	0.980	0.480
0.8	0.6	0.10	0.960	0.800	0.10	0.995	0.195
0.2	0.8	0.10	0.667	0.600	0.10	0.923	0.723
0.5	0.8	0.10	0.889	0.600	0.10	0.980	0.480
0.8	0.8	0.10	0.970	0.600	0.10	0.995	0.195
0.2	0.4	0.30	0.250	0.600	0.40	0.333	0.133
0.5	0.4	0.30	0.571	0.600	0.40	0.667	0.167
0.8	0.4	0.30	0.842	0.600	0.40	0.889	0.089
0.2	0.6	0.40	0.273	0.400	0.30	0.333	0.133
0.5	0.6	0.40	0.600	0.400	0.30	0.667	0.167
0.8	0.6	0.40	0.857	0.400	0.30	0.889	0.089

Empirical studies have focused on the amount of increase (decrease) in belief for different priors given the same item of evidence. The results of combining the same items of evidence with different priors are shown in Table 1. These items of evidence are all positive because the posterior probabilities for A in the two cases are greater than the prior probabilities for A. We have used three different priors, 0.2, 0.5 and 0.8, representing weak, moderate and strong priors, respectively, in our calculation. It is observed that the largest increase in belief is for the lowest prior (see rows 1 and 4 in Table 1). Also, the increase in the posterior belief is larger for the stronger evidence as seen from comparing rows 1 and 7 of Table 1. These results are consistent with the findings of Ashton and Ashton (1988). Further, the ordering of the evidence has no effect on the extent of belief revision as evident from comparing rows 1-3 with row 4-6 in Table 1. This finding is also consistent with the empirical results.

However, it is interesting to find that the increase in the revised belief peaks at an intermediate value of the prior under Bayesian formalism as seen from Figure 1 and also from rows 8 and 11 of Table 1. The peak occurs at a prior[2]:

$$P(A)_{max} = [\{P(E|A).P(E|\sim A)\}^{1/2} - P(E|\sim A)]/[P(E|A) - P(E|\sim A)] \qquad (2)$$

As evident from Equation (2), $P(A)_{max}$ value depends on the strength of evidence, $[P(E|A) - P(E|\sim A)]$. For example, for a strong positive evidence, i.e., for a large value of $[P(E|A) - P(E|\sim A)]$, the increase in the prior belief is the highest at a low value of $P(A)$ as seen from Case 3 in Figure 1. Whereas, for a weak evidence, i.e., for a small value of $[P(E|A) - P(E|\sim A)]$, the peak occurs at a medium value of $P(A)$ as seen from Case 1 in Figure 1. Such a phenomenon has not been observed empirically.

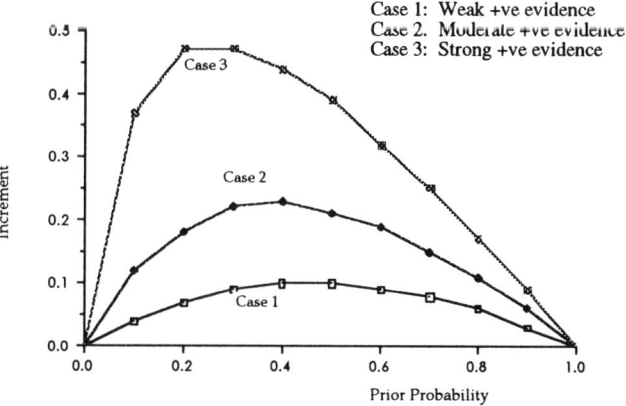

Figure 1. The difference between posterior and prior probabilities, $P(A|E) - P(A)$, as a function of prior probability, $P(A)$. Case 1: $P(E|A) = .6$ and $P(E|\sim A) = .4$. Case 2: $P(E|A) = .5$ and $P(E|\sim A) = .2$. Case 3: $P(E|A) = .8$ and $P(E|\sim A) = .1$.

Belief Function Perspective

In *belief-function* formalism two items of evidence are combined using Dempster's rule (Shafer 1976). Here, a general case of combining corroborating evidence is illustrated.

---

[2] The increase in the posterior can be written as:

$$P(A|E) - P(A) = P(E|A)P(A)/[P(E|A)P(A) + P(E|\sim A)P(\sim A)] - P(A).$$

The value of $P(A)$ for which the above increase in the prior is maximum is obtained by differentiating the increase with respect to $P(A)$ and equating the resulting expression to zero.

Without loss of generality, let m_0 be the prior *belief*[3] in proposition A, i.e., $\mathbf{Bel_0}[A] = m_0$, and assume that no prior is assigned to ~A, i.e., $\mathbf{Bel_0}[\sim A] = 0$. Also, let m_1 be the *belief* obtained from the new piece of evidence, i.e., $\mathbf{Bel_1}[A] = m_1$, and no *belief* for negation of proposition A, i.e., $\mathbf{Bel_1}[\sim A] = 0$. The combined *belief* in A using Dempster's rule is $\mathbf{Bel}[A] = m_0 + m_1 - m_0 m_1$. Thus, the increase in *belief* due to the new item of evidence is given by:

$$\mathbf{Bel}[A] - \mathbf{Bel_0}[A] = (m_0 + m_1 - m_0 m_1) - m_0 = m_1(1 - m_0)$$

From the above expression it can be seen that the increase in the revised *belief* is higher for lower prior *belief*s. This is consistent with the empirical findings of Ashton and Ashton (1988). Table 2 and Figure 2 both clearly show this effect.

Table 2. Belief Revision with Positive Evidence

Prior Belief in A (Anchor) $\mathbf{Bel_0}[A]$	Support for A from 1st Evidence $\mathbf{Bel_1}[A]$	Revised Belief in A	Support for A from 2nd Evidence $\mathbf{Bel_2}[A]$	Revised Belief in A	Support for A from 3rd Evidence $\mathbf{Bel_3}[A]$	Revised Belief in A	Support for A from 4th Evidence $\mathbf{Bel_4}[A]$	Revised Belief in A	Total increase in Belief in A
0.2	0.3	0.44	0.4	0.66	0.6	0.87	0.7	0.96	0.760
0.5	0.3	0.65	0.4	0.79	0.6	0.92	0.7	0.97	0.475
0.8	0.3	0.86	0.4	0.92	0.6	0.97	0.7	0.99	0.190
0.2	0.7	0.76	0.6	0.90	0.4	0.94	0.3	0.96	0.760
0.5	0.7	0.85	0.6	0.94	0.4	0.96	0.3	0.97	0.475
0.8	0.7	0.94	0.6	0.98	0.4	0.99	0.3	0.99	0.190
0.2	0.7	0.76	0.3	0.83	0.4	0.90	0.6	0.96	0.760
0.5	0.7	0.85	0.3	0.90	0.4	0.94	0.6	0.97	0.475
0.8	0.7	0.94	0.3	0.96	0.4	0.97	0.6	0.99	0.190

Table 2 presents the computations for belief revision employing *belief-function* formalism with three priors, 0.2, 0.5 and 0.8 representing low, medium, and high anchors, respectively. Figure 2 represents a plot of rows 1-3 of Table 2. As one can see from comparing rows 1, 2, and 3, as well as, rows 7, 8 and 9 of Table 2 that the greatest revision is observed for the lowest prior. Also, the order in which different items of evidence are aggregated does not affect the revised *belief* as seen by comparing rows 1-3 with rows 4-6, and rows 7-9 with rows 10-12 in Table 2. These

---

[3] For the sake of exposition the degree of support is represented as an **m**-function. Here all the examples consist of only two possible states, say A and ~A, thus the **m**-value for any proposition is also equal to the **Bel**-function for the proposition. For example, $\mathbf{Bel}(A) = \mathbf{m}(A)$ and $\mathbf{Bel}(\sim A) = \mathbf{m}(\sim A)$. By definition $\mathbf{Bel}(\varnothing) = 0$ where $\varnothing$ is an empty set, and $\mathbf{Bel}(A,\sim A) = 1$.

results are in full agreement with Ashton and Ashton's findings. However, the results using the Bayesian formalism were not in full agreement with the empirical findings.

2.2 Belief Revision with Consistent Negative Items of Evidence

The empirical findings indicate that the subjects decreased their belief when they were furnished with a negative (conflicting) item of evidence. Furthermore, in light of negative evidence the largest anchors were affected the most, i.e., the decrease in

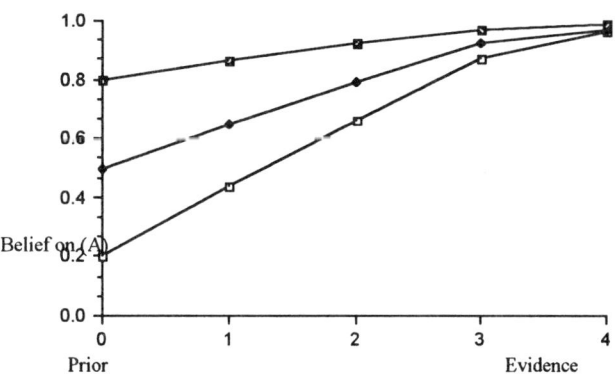

Figure 2. Belief revision with consistent positive evidence using *belief-function* formalism for three priors, $\mathbf{Bel}_0(A) = 0.2, 0.5$ and 0.8. The **m**-values for the four items evidence are: $\mathbf{m}_1(A) = 0.3$, and $\mathbf{m}_1(\sim A) = 0$; $\mathbf{m}_2(A) = 0.4$, and $\mathbf{m}_2(\sim A)=0$; $\mathbf{m}_3(A)= 0.6$, and $\mathbf{m}_3(\sim A) = 0$; and $\mathbf{m}_4(A) = 0.7$ and $\mathbf{m}_4(\sim A)=0$.

belief was the highest for the highest prior belief. The order of presentation of the evidence again had no effect on the extent of revision as observed in the case of consistent positive evidence. Again, we will analyze these findings from both the Bayesian as well as the *belief-function* perspectives.

Bayesian Perspective

In Bayesian formalism, an item of evidence is negative if $\mathbf{P}(A|E) < \mathbf{P}(A)$. The decrease in belief, $\mathbf{P}(A|E) - \mathbf{P}(A)$, is plotted in Figure 3 against the prior belief $\mathbf{P}(A)$. It shows that the decrease in belief peaks at an intermediate value of the prior belief which is similar to the result obtained earlier for a positive item of evidence under Bayesian formalism.

490

It is clear from Figure 3 that the decrease in belief is the highest for the medium prior belief using Bayesian formalism, contrary to the empirical findings (Ashton & Ashton 1988). However, it can be easily shown that the order of presentation of the evidence under Bayesian formalism will not have any effect on the extent of revision. This result is in agreement with the empirical findings of Ashton & Ashton.

Belief Function Perspective

In general, the largest decrease in the revised belief is not for the highest prior but for a certain intermediate value of the prior *belief*. This value depends on the strength of evidence. For a weak evidence, i.e., for a small value of $m_1[\sim A]$, the largest decrease in the revised belief occurs around a prior *belief* of 50%.

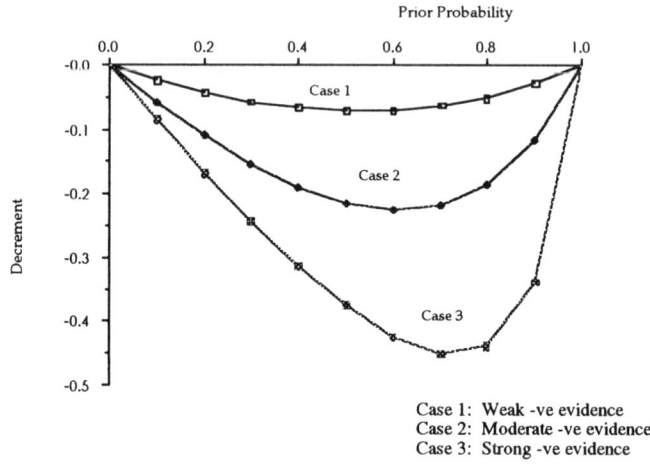

Figure 3. Belief revision with negative evidence using Bayesian formalism. Difference between posterior and prior probabilities, $P(A|E) - P(A)$, as a function of prior probability, $P(A)$. Case 1: $P(E|A) = .3$ and $P(E|\sim A) = .4$. Case 2: $P(E|A) = .2$ and $P(E|\sim A) = .5$. Case 3: $P(E|A) = .1$ and $P(E|\sim A) = .6$.

Whereas, for a strong negative evidence, i.e., for a large value of $m_1[\sim A]$, the decrease in *belief* peaks at a large value of the prior *belief*. In fact, one can obtain an analytical expression[4] for which the decrease is the largest at a prior *belief*:

---

[4] The decrease in the revised *belief* in A can be written as:

$$Bel_0[A] - Bel[A] = m_0 - m_0(1-m_1)/(1 - m_0m_1).$$

The value of the prior belief, m_0, at which the decrease is maximum is obtained by differentiating the decrease with respect to m_0 and equating the resulting expression to zero.

$$\text{Bel}_0[A] = [\{1 - (1 - m_1(\sim A))^{0.5}\}/m_1(\sim A)]. \tag{3}$$

Thus, it is seen that like Bayesian formalism, *belief-function* formalism does not explain the empirical findings regarding belief revision under consistent negative items of evidence.

Table 3. Belief rvision with negative evidence using discounting

Prior Belief in A	Evidence 1: Support for ~A	Level of Conflict*	Discounted Prior in A	Revised Belief in A	in ~A	Decrease in Belief
0.2	0.1	0.02	0.1976	0.18	0.08	0.02
0.5	0.1	0.05	0.485	0.46	0.05	0.04
0.8	0.1	0.08	0.7616	0.74	0.03	0.06
0.2	0.3	0.06	0.1928	0.14	0.26	0.06
0.5	0.3	0.15	0.455	0.37	0.19	0.13
0.8	0.3	0.24	0.6848	0.60	0.12	0.20
0.2	0.6	0.12	0.1856	0.08	0.55	0.12
0.5	0.6	0.3	0.41	0.22	0.47	0.28
0.8	0.6	0.48	0.5696	0.35	0.39	0.45

*The level of conflict is defined to be the probability mass assigned to the impossible outcome.
** A discount rate of 60% of the level of conflict is used in the table.

However, if we discount the prior *belief* as shown in Table 3, the decrease in the revised *belief* becomes the largest for the highest prior[5] as observed empirically. Thus, the Dempster-Shafer theory of *belief function* with discounting can be used to explain the empirical findings. The discounting of prior *belief* makes more intuitive sense, especially in situations with large positive priors and many negative items of evidence.

---

[5] The decrease in the revised *belief* in A can be written as:

$$\text{Bel}_0[A] - \text{Bel}[A] = m_0 - (1 - k.m_0 m_1) m_0 (1 - m_1)/(1 - (1 - k.m_0 m_1) m_0 m_1).$$

The above expression is differentiated with respect to m_0. The resulting expression is positive for all values of m_1, provided $k > 0.5$. Thus, $\text{Bel}_0[A] - \text{Bel}[A]$, is a monotonically increasing function with respect to m_0. The maximum decrease is thus attained for the highest value of m_0, provided the discount rate is not too small.

3. BELIEF REVISION WITH MIXED EVIDENCE

In this section we consider aggregation of mixed evidence. Mixed evidence implies that one item of evidence supports a hypothesis, while the other rejects the hypothesis. It is interesting to note that the order of presentation of the evidence in a mixed evidence situation affects the belief revision process. In fact, it has been observed that more weight or credence is attached by the auditor to the latest information (e.g., see Ashton & Ashton 1988; Tubbs et. al. 1990). This effect has been called the 'recency' effect in the accounting literature.

Bayesian theory cannot explain the recency effect, neither can *belief-function* formalism when applied without discounting. However, when previous items of evidence are *discounted* in light of new evidence, *belief-function* formalism does explain the recency effect.

In Table 4, we present the results of combining mixed items of evidence using *belief-function* formalism with discounting. However, we would like to discuss the essential steps involved in calculating the final *beliefs* in Table 4 in detail and provide the logical reasoning behind it. First, we assume here that the discounting rate is proportional to the probability mass assigned to the impossible state. Let us consider row one of Table 4(a) for our illustration. The prior probability mass (**m**-values) assigned to A, $\sim$A and {A,$\sim$A} for this case are: $m_0(A) = 0.2$, $m_0(\sim A) = 0$, and $m_0(\{A,\sim A\}) = 0.8$. The **m**-values obtained from the first evidence in row one and column two of Table 4(a) are: $m_1(A) = 0.4$, $m_1(\sim A) = 0$, and $m_1(\{A,\sim A\}) = 0.6$. These two items of evidence are not conflicting, i.e., when we multiply the two sets of **m**-value we do not get any non-zero product for the state (A&$\sim$A = $\varnothing$). Since we are assuming the discounting rate to be proportional to the level of conflict, the discounting rate is zero as there is no conflict.

Using Dempster's rule (Shafer 1976) to combine these two items of evidence, one obtains the following **m**-values: $m(A) = 0.52$, $m(\sim A) = 0$, and $m(\{A,\sim A\}) = 0.48$ and the corresponding *beliefs* are: **Bel**[A] = 0.52, and **Bel**[$\sim$A] = 0, **Bel**[{A,$\sim$A}] = 1. Column 3 of Table 4(a) represents the *belief* in A computed at this stage. The second item of evidence is also not conflicting to the previous two. The **m** values for the second evidence are given as: $m_2(A) = 0.6$, $m_2(\sim A) = 0$, and $m_2(\{A,\sim A\}) = 0.4$.

Table 4. Belief revision with mixed evidence: recency effect by discounting

a) Sequencing of Evidence (+,+,-,-)

Prior Belo[A]	Evidence Bel1[A]	Revised Belief	Evidence Bel2[A]	Revised Belief	Evidence Bel3[~A]	Revised Belief	Evidence Bel4[~A]	Revised Belief	Increase in Belief
0.20	0.40	0.52	0.60	0.81	0.50	0.44	0.30	0.32	0.12
0.50	0.40	0.70	0.60	0.88	0.50	0.48	0.30	0.35	-0.15
0.80	0.40	0.88	0.60	0.95	0.50	0.52	0.30	0.38	-0.42

b) Sequencing of Evidence (-,-,+,+)

Prior Belo[A]	Evidence Bel1[~A]	Revised Belief	Evidence Bel2[~A]	Revised Belief	Evidence Bel3[A]	Revised Belief	Evidence Bel4[A]	Revised Belief	Increase in Beleif
0.20	0.50	0.05	0.30	0.04	0.40	0.23	0.60	0.59	0.39
0.50	0.50	0.19	0.30	0.14	0.40	0.33	0.60	0.65	0.15
0.80	0.50	0.47	0.30	0.35	0.40	0.52	0.60	0.77	-0.03

N.B.- A discount rate of 0.6 was used in the computations.

This evidence when combined with the first two items then yields the following new set of **m**-values: $\mathbf{m}'(A) = 0.81$, $\mathbf{m}'(\sim A) = 0$, and $\mathbf{m}'(\{A,\sim A\}) = 0.19$. The **m**-values for the third evidence are: $\mathbf{m}_3(A) = 0$, $\mathbf{m}_3(\sim A) = 0.5$, and $\mathbf{m}_3(\{A,\sim A\}) = 0.5$. This evidence is conflicting to all the previous items of evidence. The level of conflict in this case is 0.405 (the level of conflict = probability mass associated with the impossible state $(A\&\sim A = \varnothing)$ which is equal to $\mathbf{m}'(A) \times \mathbf{m}_3(\sim A) = 0.81 \times 0.5 = 0.405$).

In this situation, before the the third item is combined with the previous two, the previous *beliefs* will be discounted. Just to illustrate the discounting process we assume here that the discount rate, δ, is equal to 60% of the level of conflict, i.e., in this case, $\delta = 0.6 \times 0.405 = 0.243$. The reason for making δ dependent on the level of conflict is intuitive, since the decision maker will be more prone to reevaluating the previous items of evidence if he encounters a new piece of evidence that is conflicting. The higher the conflict the bigger the concern. The discounted *beliefs*, $\mathbf{m}_\delta'$, are obtained by multiplying each **m**-values with $(1 - \delta)$ and adding δ to the **m**-value for the frame $\{A,\sim A\}$:

$\mathbf{m}_\delta'(A) = (1 - 0.243) \times 0.81 = 0.613$, $\mathbf{m}'(\sim A) = 0$, and
$\mathbf{m}'(\{A,\sim A\}) = (1 - 0.243) \times 0.19 + 0.243 = 0.387$

These discounted *beliefs* are now combined with $\mathbf{m}_3$'s resulting into a new set of **m**-values:

$\mathbf{m}''(A) = 0.442$, $\mathbf{m}''(\sim A) = 0.279$, and $\mathbf{m}''(\{A,\sim A\}) = 0.279$.

The corresponding *belief* in A is equal to 0.442 as shown in row one and column seven of Table 4(a).

The fourth item of evidence is a weak negative item for which the **m** values are given by:

$\mathbf{m}_4(A) = 0$, $\mathbf{m}_4(\sim A) = 0.3$, and $\mathbf{m}_4(\{A,\sim A\}) = 0.7$

This evidence is in conflict with the aggregate evidence evaluated so far. We will discount this aggregate evidence and then combine that with the fourth item of evidence. The level of conflict, in this case, is 0.1326 (= $\mathbf{m}''(A) \times m_4(\sim A)$ = 0.442x0.3 = 0.1326). Thus, the discount rate is 0.07956 (δ = 0.6x0.1326). The discounted *beliefs* are given in terms of **m**-values as: $\mathbf{m}'''(A) = 0.4068$, $\mathbf{m}'''(\sim A)$ = 0.2568, and $\mathbf{m}'''(\{A, \sim A\})$ = 0.3364.

Combining the above **m** functions with $\mathbf{m_4}$'s one obtains the final **m** values as:

$$\mathbf{m_f}(A) = 0.3243, \mathbf{m_f}(\sim A) = 0.4074, \text{ and } \mathbf{m_f}(\{A, \sim A\}) = 0.2683.$$

The overall *belief* in A is 0.3243 which is given in row one and column 9 of Table 4(a). Similarly, all the other numbers in Tables 4(a) and 4(b) can be calculated. The results of Table 4 are plotted in Figure 4.

The results in Table 4 and Figure 4 indicate that, in a mixed evidence situation, the extent of belief revision is dependent upon the order in which the items of evidence are presented, provided the previous evidence is discounted. Thus, it appears that the Dempster-Shafer theory of *belief function* with discounting can be used to model the recency effect.

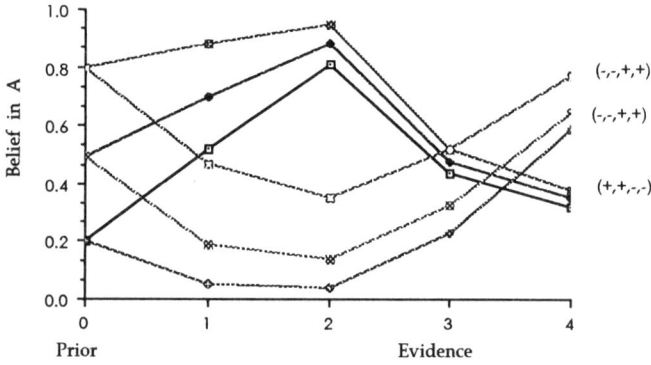

Figure 4. Belief revision under mixed items of evidence using *B\belief-function* formalism with discounting. Data used in the graph are given in Table 8.

4. SIMULTANEOUS VERSUS SEQUENTIAL AGGREGATION OF EVIDENCE

In this section, we examine the 'dilution' effect. The empirical studies revealed that the belief revisions were diluted for simultaneous processing. The simultaneous evaluation of evidence resulted in a less extreme belief change than the sequential processing of the same set of evidence. The effect was more pronounced for consistently negative evidence (Ashton & Ashton 1988).

Bayesian theory cannot explain the dilution effect, neither can *belief functions* without discounting. However, when items of evidence are discounted, in light of conflict, the *belief-function* formalism does explain the dilution effect.

In the previous section, we discussed discounting when mixed items of evidence were presented sequentially. The previous items of evidence were discounted in light of new evidence. Discounting was done in favor of the latest information.

In case of simultaneous processing, a uniform discounting of all items of evidence seems more reasonable. Unlike sequential processing, there are no previous or later items of evidence, since all items of evidence are presented simultaneously. Thus, when there is conflict between different items of evidence, all items of evidence are discounted uniformly.

The discounting methods could be different in both cases. While in the sequential processing the discount rate is biased by the last piece of evidence, there is no bias in simultaneous processing. One would expect an averaging, or uniform discounting, when conflicting items of evidence are presented simultaneously. Thus, there is no order effect and the revision of belief is less pronounced compared to sequential evaluation.

In Table 5 (a), we present the results of simultaneously combining negative items of evidence using *belief function* with discounting. Since all items of evidence are simultaneously presented, a uniform discounting is applied to all the items. Here we will illustrate with an example the mechanism of uniform discounting. Let us consider row 1 of Table 5(a) for an illustration. The prior probability mass (**m**-value) assigned to A, ~A and (A,~A) for this case are: $m_0(A) = 0.2$; $m_0(\sim A) = 0$; and $m_0(A,\sim A) = 0.8$. The **m**-values obtained from evidence 1 and 2 are, $m_1(A) = 0$, $m_1(\sim A) = 0.3$, $m_1(A,\sim A) = 0.7$, $m_2(A) = 0$, $m_2(\sim A) = 0.25$ and $m_2(A,\sim A) = 0.75$, respectively. We first compute the level of conflict of all the items of evidence. In this case the level of conflict is 0.095^6. We assume that the discounting rate, δ, is 60% of the level of conflict. Thus, $\delta = 0.6 \times 0.095 = 0.057$. The discounted **m**-values are obtained by multiplying each **m**-value by a factor $(1-\delta)$ and adding a δ degree of belief to the **m**-value for the entire frame. We thus obtain the discounted **m**-values of 0.189, 0.283 and 0.236, for the prior, evidence 1 and evidence 2, respectively. The overall revised belief in A is obtained by combining the discounted **m**-values (columns 6-8 of Table 5a) using Dempster's rule of combination. The resultant belief in A, $m(A) = \text{Bel}(A)=0.113$.

Simultaneous processing of mixed evidence results in less extreme belief changes. This can be verified by comparing the results of Table 5(b)with those of Tables 4(a) and (b). In Table 4(a) and (b), we showed that the extent of revision was dependent on the order in which the items of evidence were presented. For example, the anchor

---

[6] In general, the level of conflict $= \Sigma\{m_0(B)m_1(C)m_2(D) | B \cap C \cap D = \varnothing\}$ where B, C, and D represent subsets of the elements of the frame $\{A,\sim A\}$. The nonzero terms of the above expression yields:

Level of conflict $= m_0(A)m_1(\sim A)m_2(\sim A)+m_0(A)m_1(\sim A)m_2(\{A,\sim A\}) + m_0(A)m_1(\{A,\sim A\})m_2(\sim A) =$
$0.2 \times 0.3 \times 0.25 + 0.2 \times 0.3 \times 0.75 + 0.2 \times 0.7 \times 0.25 = 0.095$

of 0.5 was revised to 0.35 when the items of evidence were presented in +,+,-,-sequence (row 2, col. 9, Table 4a), and it was revised to 0.65 when the order of presentation was -,-,+,+ (row 2, col. 9, Table 4b). However, when the items of evidence were simultaneously presented the belief was revised to an intermediate value of 0.53 (row 2, col. 9, Table 5b).

In case of consistently positive evidence, both sequential as well as simultaneous processing attain the same degree of belief revision. There is no conflict when all items of evidence are confirming (positive). Since there is no conflict, the discount rate is zero. Hence, the items of evidence are aggregated without discounting in either case. Thus, both the processes attain the same degree of belief revision. This is consistent with the empirical findings (Footnote 9, Ashton & Ashton, 1988).

Table 5. Simultaneous aggregation of evidence with uniform discounting

a) Consistent Negative Evidence

Prior Bel0(A)	Evidence m1(~A)	Evidence m2(~A)	Conflict	Discount Rate	Discounted Prior	Evidence1	Evidence2	Revised Belief	Decrease in Belief
0.20	0.30	0.25	0.095	0.057	0.189	0.283	0.236	0.113	0.087
0.50	0.30	0.25	0.238	0.143	0.429	0.257	0.214	0.305	0.195
0.80	0.30	0.25	0.380	0.228	0.618	0.232	0.193	0.500	0.300
0.20	0.50	0.20	0.120	0.072	0.186	0.464	0.186	0.090	0.110
0.50	0.50	0.20	0.300	0.180	0.410	0.410	0.164	0.255	0.245
0.80	0.50	0.20	0.480	0.288	0.570	0.356	0.142	0.422	0.378

b) Mixed Evidence

Prior Belief	Evidence on (A)*	Evidence on (~A)**	Conflict	Discount Rate	Discounted Prior	Evidence	Evidence	Revised Belief	Change in Belief
0.20	0.76	0.65	0.525	0.315	0.137	0.521	0.445	0.440	0.240
0.50	0.76	0.65	0.572	0.343	0.328	0.499	0.427	0.531	0.031
0.80	0.76	0.65	0.619	0.371	0.503	0.478	0.409	0.628	-0.172

N.B.- A discount rate of 0.6 of the level of conflict was used.

* The number is obtained by combining two positive items of evidence in Table 4(a) (columns 2 & 4)
** The number is obtained by combining two negative items of evidence in Table 4(a) (columns 6 & 8).

To sum up, a uniform discounting of all items of evidence is appropriate when all the items are presented simultaneously. There is no difference in sequential versus simultaneous processing for confirming (positive) items of evidence. Simultaneous processing leads to dilution for mixed and negative items of evidence.

5. SUMMARY AND CONCLUSION

In this paper we examined the empirical findings under the framework of probability theory. We employed two alternatives: the Bayesian framework and the Dempster-Shafer theory of belief functions. The scope of the paper is limited to explaining the empirical results using the two approaches. This paper provides no normative prescriptions for belief revision.

The Bayesian theory of probability is unable to explain most of the empirical findings. Bayesian theory is very stringent in its requirement that the probability of mutually exclusive and collectively exhaustive events sum to one. Bayesian theory requires that the belief be increased in light of supporting evidence, and be decreased in light of conflicting evidence. This is consistent with the empirical findings. However, the Bayesian analysis entails the largest increase (decrease) in belief for medium priors in light of supporting (conflicting) evidence. This is contrary to empirical findings. The largest increase was observed for smallest priors when presented with supporting evidence. The largest decrease was observed for highest priors when presented with conflicting evidence. Further, Bayesian theory fails to explain the 'recency' and the 'dilution' effects.

Belief-function formalism, on the other hand, can model the behavior of the auditors. In belief functions, the belief in a proposition increases in light of supporting (positive) evidence. Further, the largest increase is for the lowest priors. This is consistent with the empirical findings. The belief in a proposition decreases in light of conflicting (negative) evidence and the largest decrease is for medium priors. This is not totally consistent with the empirical findings. However, with discounting we can attain the largest decrease for the highest prior, consistent with the empirical findings. By incorporating discounting in belief functions, we have explained the 'recency' and the 'dilution' effects.

With the advent of expert systems in auditing such studies have become imperative. In the construction of an expert system, the issue of how auditors combine evidence is enigmatic. Expert systems are built to emulate experts, thus the need to understand the expert's behavior is imperative. Belief function formalism seems to provide a theory which can model an expert's decision process and hence is highly viable.

The theory of evidence aggregation will ease the process of audit planning and audit risk assessments (Srivastava and Shafer 1992; Dutta, Harrison and Srivastava 1997). Once we know how auditors aggregate evidence, we can formulate an efficient way of evidence search. This would lead to more efficient audits and will subsequently reduce the cost of audits. We feel this is a very crucial and fundamental area in auditing and much research effort should be expended in understanding the evidence aggregation process.

ACKNOWLEDGMENTS

We would like to express our appreciation for the comments and suggestions provided on an earlier version of this paper by Pierre Ndilikillikesha, Glenn Shafer, Tim Shaftel, Prakash

Shenoy and Rago Srinivasan. Our thanks are also due to the participants of the accounting workshop and artificial intelligence seminar at the University of Kansas. This research has been supported in part by grant from the School of Business Research Funds of the University of Kansas.

REFERENCES

Ashton, A. H. & R. H. Ashton, 1988. „Sequential Belief Revision in Auditing". *The Accounting Review* (October): 623-41.

Dutta, S. K., and R. P. Srivastava, 1993. „Aggregation of Evidence in Auditing: A Likelihood Perspective". *Auditing: A Journal of Practice and Theory* (Supplement): 137-160.

Dutta, S. K., and R. P. Srivastava, 1996. "A Bayesian Perspective on the Strength of Evidence in Auditing," *Indian Journal of Accounting,* Vol. XXVII, (June), pp. 4-18.

Dutta, S. K., K. Harrison, and R. P. Srivastava, 1997. "The Audit Risk Model Under the Risk of Fraud," *Applications of Fuzzy Sets & The Theory of Evidence to Accounting* (forthcoming).

Kissinger, J.N., 1977. „A General Theory of Evidence as the Conceptual Foundation in Auditing Theory: Some Comments and Extensions." *The Accounting Review,* (April) pp. 322-339.

Shafer, G. 1976. *A Mathematical Theory of Evidence.* (Princeton University Press).

Shafer, G., and R. P. Srivastava. 1990. „The Bayesian and Belief-Functions Formalisms: A General Perspective For Auditing". *Auditing: A Journal of Practice and Theory* (Supplement): 110-148.

Srivastava, R. P., 1995. „A General Scheme for Aggregating Evidence in Auditing: Propagation of Beliefs in Networks," *Artificial Intelligence in Accounting and Auditing.* Vol. 3 Miklos A. Vasarhelyi, editor, Markus Wiener Publishers, Princeton, pp. 55-99.

Srivastava, R. P., S. K. Dutta, and R. Johns, 1996. "An Expert System Approach to Audit Planning and Evaluation in the Belief-Function Framework," *International Journal of Intelligent Systems in Accounting, Finance and Management,* Vol. 5, No. 3, pp. 165-183.

Srivastava, R. P., and G. Shafer. 1992. „Belief-Function Formulas for Audit Risk". *The Accounting Review* (April): 249-283.

Toba, Y. 1975. „A General Theory of Evidence as the Conceptual Foundation in Auditing Theory". *The Accounting Review* (January): 7-24.

Tubbs, R. M., W. F. Messier and R. Knechel. 1990. „Recency Effects in the Auditor's Belief Revision Process". *The Accounting Review* (April): 452-460.

Self-Organizing Fuzzy and MLP Approaches to Detecting Fraudulent Financial Reporting

Ehsan H. Feroz[1] and Taek Mu Kwon[2]

[1] Department of Accounting, School of Business and Economics, University of Minnesota, Duluth, MN 55812, USA. Email: eferoz@d.umn.edu

[2] Department of Electrical and Computer Engineering, College of Science and Engineering, University of Minnesota, Duluth, MN 55812, USA. Email: tkwon@d.umn.edu

Abstract. In this paper, we employ seven redflags which are composed of four financial redflags and three nonfinancial turn over redflags in order to detect targets of the Securities and Exchange Commission's (SEC) investigation of fraudulent financial reporting. Two prominent nonlinear approaches, i.e. artificial neural networks and fuzzy sets, are applied to detection of SEC investigation targets and compared with the conventional statistical methods.

Keywords. fraudulent financial reporting, artificial neural networks, self-organizing fuzzy controller, KNN membership function.

1. Introduction

The purpose of this study is to compare a class of neural networks and fuzzy controller approaches, more specifically, multi-layered perceptron (MLP) [1] and a self-organizing fuzzy approach [2, 3], in determining the efficacy of the selected Statement of Auditing Standard No. 53 redflags in predicting targets of the Securities and Exchange Commission (SEC) investigation [4]. The motivation for studying these two approaches is provided in part by our earlier work with conventional tools such as logit which generally lead to inferior prediction accuracy for such classification problems [5]. It is also demonstrated in the extant literature that incorrect model specification leads to poor performance since the probability distribution of estimates tends to deviate from the true underlying characteristics of the data. In contrast, the two approaches presented in this paper require minimum *a priori* knowledge regarding the data under consideration.

The rest of the paper is organized as follows. Section 2 briefly discusses the neural network approach we applied. Section 3 describes the self-organizing KNN fuzzy approach. Section 4 describes the empirical results. Section 5 concludes the paper.

2. Neural Network Approach

We selected the neural network architecture based on the following considerations. Since the present application has some known historical data based
on which of the firms had been investigated by the SEC [6], a supervised
learning on a MLP network was considered appropriate. For the learning
algorithm, we chose the basic back-propagation (BP) algorithm [1] with an
improved weight initialization technique [7]. This decision was made after
some trial and error on recent fast algorithms, in which we found that the
fast approaches did not improve generalization capability of the network as
much as a proper weight initialization. Moreover, considering that the present
application does not require any real time constraints, the speed of algorithms
was not important.

Detection of firms engaged in fraudulent financial reporting is essentially
a two-class problem, in which a network with a single output node is sufficient
i.e.

$$\phi(\boldsymbol{x}^p) > \theta \tag{2.1}$$

for treatment class, and $\phi(\boldsymbol{x}^p) \leq \theta$ for control class where θ is the threshold
level that determines the decision boundary ($0 < \theta < 1$). All nodes in the
network are the typical sigmoid neuron described by $y_j = \frac{1}{1+\exp(-\boldsymbol{w}_j^T \boldsymbol{x}_j)}$
where $\boldsymbol{w}_j$ is the weight vector of a node j and $\boldsymbol{x}_j$ is the input vector to the
same node [8].

Because of the existence of many local minima in the solution space of
MLP and search of the minima by gradient in BP algorithm, the quality of
the solution obtained by backpropagation algorithm is sensitive to the initial
weights of the network. Kwon and Cheng [7] found that the following relation
holds in general for two-layered BP networks:

$$||W|| \geq 4\sqrt{\frac{\epsilon_{output}}{\epsilon_{input}}} \tag{2.2}$$

where $||W||$ denotes l_2 norm of the weight matrix W, and ϵ_{output} and ϵ_{input}
denote the minimal distances that are required in the input patterns and the
minimum discrimination at the output, respectively.

The following observations can be made from (2.2):

1. If $||W|| \leq |\delta|$, then the network at most can detect the rate of change
in the output with respect to input change smaller than $(\delta/4)^2$.

2. If two patterns must be discriminated at the output node with ϵ_{output},
the distance between the two patterns must be larger than $\frac{16\epsilon_{output}}{||W||^2}$.

These observation lead to a specific data treatment and a weight initialization technique suggested in [7], which we adopted for this study.

3. Self-Organizing KNN Fuzzy Controller Approach

In recent years there have been many successful engineering applications of fuzzy logic controllers. These applications include welding, automobile speed control, aircraft flight control, robot control, elevator control, and train control. The design technique common to these applications follows the conventional fuzzy set formulation, which relies on the available human expert's knowledge [9]. The state variables of a controller are expressed by linguistic descriptions that are subjectively characterized by the expert through membership functions. A finite set of fuzzy rules (or IF/THEN knowledge base) is then developed to describe the desired control rule. In both steps, the expert's knowledge is essential. This classical approach presents several problems. First, if the expert's knowledge is not available, the system cannot be designed. Second, frequently the expert's knowledge is incomplete or incorrect. Moreover, if a fuzzy system receives an unexpected input signal which was not prescribed by IF/THEN fuzzy rules, the system responds with a "don't know state" instead of some approximation. Finally, the fuzzy rules constructed by the expert do not usually cover all possible combinations of input variables due to the large dimensionality of the variable space.

The problem studied in this paper is very difficult to formulate with the conventional fuzzy IF/THEN rule-base which must be defined by an expert or experts. The rule base regarding detection of fraudulent financial report is mostly unknown. Only a small subset out of the very large solution space is suggested by some experts. Consequently, direct application of the conventional fuzzy controllers to the present domain is not possible.

To overcome the stated problem, we resorted to employing a trainable fuzzy controller which estimates the expert's knowledge through some form of adaptive process. We adopted the self-organizing fuzzy controller developed by Kwon and Zervakis [2, 3], which are rooted to the well known KNN pattern classification technique. The rules are automatically created by the cluster centers of the structural information contained in the data. From a theoretical point of view, this approach is well supported by the radial-basis-functions (RBFs) in function-approximation problems as analyzed in [2].

3.1 The Basic Controller Structure

Since it is assumed that the expert's knowledge needed to construct the membership functions and the fuzzy rule-base are not available, the fuzzy system is estimated from the ordered pairs of training set that consists of observed-input and desired-output vectors:

$$(\boldsymbol{x}^{(1)}; \boldsymbol{y}^{(1)}), (\boldsymbol{x}^{(2)}; \boldsymbol{y}^{(2)}), (\boldsymbol{x}^{(3)}; \boldsymbol{y}^{(3)}), \cdots \qquad (3.1)$$

where $\boldsymbol{x}^{(i)} = (x_1^{(i)}, \cdots, x_n^{(i)})$ is the ith input vector and $\boldsymbol{y}^{(i)} = (y_1^{(i)}, \cdots, y_m^{(i)})$ is the ith desired output vector. The goal of the controller is to determine a close functional approximation to the mapping relation $\{f : X \rightarrow Y\}$ reflected by the finite samples in the training set. We first introduce a new membership function called the K-nearest-neighbor (KNN) membership function, which forms the basis for the operation of controller. Suppose that N clusters $\{C_1, C_2, \cdots, C_N\}$ have been identified in the input space, then the KNN membership measure is defined as:

$$\mu_{C_i}(\boldsymbol{x}) = \frac{1}{d_i} / \sum_{j=1}^{K} \frac{1}{d_j}. \tag{3.2}$$

Notice from (3.2) that as the distance from the unknown data to a cluster gets smaller, the membership value for the class gets bigger. If an input pattern exactly matches one of the center vectors, then the membership for the cluster becomes one while others are zeros. Also notice that the summation of all membership values is equal to one. Since this membership function directly provides the degree to which a pattern belongs to a class, the estimated output $\boldsymbol{y}^*$ for the input $\boldsymbol{x}$ is simply given by

$$\boldsymbol{y}^* = \frac{\sum_{i \in N_K} \mu_{C_i}(\boldsymbol{x}) \boldsymbol{z}_i}{\sum_{i \in N_K} \mu_{C_i}(\boldsymbol{x})} = \sum_{i \in N_K} \mu_{C_i}(\boldsymbol{x}) \boldsymbol{z}_i \tag{3.3}$$

where N_K denotes the set of the K-nearest neighboring clusters and $\boldsymbol{z}_i$ is the output values corresponding to the center of the input cluster i. This method utilizes the idea of centroid defuzzification in that if a pattern is similar to K-neighboring patterns with different degree of membership, the estimated output (crisp) is computed by finding the centroid of the corresponding K output patterns.

In the above formulation, there are no steps requiring the construction of fuzzy rules or specifying membership functions as in conventional fuzzy controllers. In essence, the fuzzy rules of the above controller can be seen embedded into the clusters that determine the membership values in (3.2) by considering that each cluster represents an approximation of a local set of data specified by one or more fuzzy rules. Hence, the fuzzy rules in the above model are indeed self-organized. In the next sub-section we describe a clustering algorithm that effectively allocates clusters based on a set of training data.

3.2 Pattern Clustering and Fine-Tuning of Center Vectors

In order to apply the above algorithm, the center vector of each cluster must be found and allocated for the data base for KNN membership. For this task, we utilize a simple distance-based clustering technique which was used in the RBF estimation [10]. A new center vector is allocated, if

$$||\boldsymbol{x} - \boldsymbol{m}_{nearest}|| > \delta(t) \tag{3.4}$$

where $m_{nearest}$ is the nearest vector to x among the center vectors already assigned. The function $\delta(t)$ represents a monotonically decreasing function of time to gradually increase the density of the center vectors. In addition, the distance from the output vector y to the current estimate y^* in (3.3) is evaluated. A new center vector is allocated, if

$$||y - y^*|| > \epsilon(t) \qquad (3.5)$$

where $\epsilon(t)$ is a measure of prediction accuracy that is monotonically decreased with time. In actual implementation, a new center vector is allocated by copying the pair of input and output vectors to the cluster data base.

This procedure is continued until $\delta(t)$ and $\epsilon(t)$ are decreased down to the predetermined stopping criterion. Initially, $\delta(t)$ and $\epsilon(t)$ are large, thus the system has a coarse representation of the desired function. However, as $\delta(t)$ and $\epsilon(t)$ are decreased, more and more center vectors are allocated and the accuracy of the representation increases. The number of passes of the above algorithm through the data is finite with maximum number of clusters allocated equal to the finite data in the training set. As more data are available to the controller, the above clustering algorithm can adaptively allocate new clusters.

4. Empirical Results

The firms used in this study is a subset of firms listed in the SEC's Accounting and Auditing Enforcement Releases (AAER) 1 through 244 [6]. The firms included are distributed among various industry sectors such as food, publishing, chemical, electronic, insurance, hospital, etc. Each firm is classified into one of two groups: the treatment and the control [8]. A firm in the treatment group refers to a firm that was investigated by the SEC on the grounds of fraudulent financial reporting. The control group consists of those firms that match the treatment group by industry type and size, but were not investigated. For each firm, we collected five years of information i.e. from the year of the SEC investigation (treatment firm) to four years preceding the investigated year. Similarly for each treatment-control pair, the control firm's years need to match the treatment years for consistency. For each firm, we tried to collect information on nineteen financial and non-financial variables which are considered independent. Unfortunately, many firms did not have information on the seven red flags. During the computation of redflags as explained in [8], if an item in the denominator of any reflag is missing and replaced with zero, the redflag became infinity. This problem was overcome by replacing the missing items by K-nearest neighbor estimate that minimizes the bias of the pattern. After the bias-minimizing interpolation was done, there were a total of 70 firms, 35 treatment-control matched pairs, from which seven redflags are constructed. The seven reflags are categorized into two groups financial and non-financial. The financial redflags are: Profitability, Sensitivity, Difficult to Audit, and Going Concern ratios which are computed from the Compustat data base. using the formulae shown in [8]. The non-financial redflags are the turnover redflags (change of CEOs, CFOs, and auditors), which were hand collected from the Moody's Industrial Manuals.

The changes in the four financial redflags and the three turnover redflags are the input items used for our empirical study. The data set containing the 70 firms is randomly partitioned into a Training-Test Set Pairs (TTSPs). The training set contains 55 firms (79%) and the test set contains the remaining 15 firms (21%). Six different partitions were used in order to derive an average cross-validation performance [11] that would give less biased information than the performance obtained solely from a single partitioned data set.

The MSE criterion (the mean of the squares of the difference between the actual output of the network and the target value for each input pattern) was used as the basic error measure. Two different MSE values were used, the training set MSE and the test set MSE. The training set MSE is the MSE calculated while the network is in the training phase. The test set MSE is the MSE calculated for the test set after completion of the training.

The MLP architectures used in this study were 3-layered feedforward networks with a 7-x-1 architecture where x is the number of hidden units determined based on the best generalization performance and 7 corresponds to the seven redflags. Table 4.1 as in [8] shows empirically optimized results of the network architecture on different partitions of TTSP. The average classification accuracy was 87.8%.

The performance of self-organizing fuzzy controller approach applied to the same data set pairs is summarized in Table 4.2. The equivalent count of epoch in this case is the epoch needed for the clustering process (since after clustering the computational model is already constructed). Notice that the solutions are always obtained instantly. The average classification accuracy was 71%.

Table 4.1. Classification of training-test set pairs by the MLP approach

TTSP Number	Epochs	Hidden Nodes	Learning Rate	Training Set MSE	Test Set MSE	Classification Accuracy
1	48535	8	0.4	0.03214	0.02596	86.7%
2	49060	3	0.4	0.03488	0.01247	100.0%
3	49833	8	0.4	0.02648	0.03667	86.7%
4	8852	4	0.4	0.02760	0.03023	80.0%
5	40916	4	0.4	0.02521	0.02096	93.3%
6	39657	8	0.4	0.02124	0.03382	80.0%

source: [8]

Finally, we compare the MLP and fuzzy controller results with one of the conventional nonlinear regression tools, logit [5] which has been popularly used as a prediction tool. The same 70 firm data was run by logit avail-

Table 4.2. Classification of training-test set pairs by the self-organizing fuzzy controller approach

TTSP Number	Epochs	Training Set MSE	Test Set MSE	Classification Accuracy
1	4	0.01122	0.1158	73.3%
2	5	0.00258	0.1326	66.7%
3	6	0.00114	0.1189	73.3%
4	7	0.00656	0.0841	60.0%
5	7	0.00310	0.1129	73.3%
6	13	0.00039	0.1012	80.0%

able in SAS, and the classification accuracy is summarized in Table 4.3. The classification accuracy of logit was around 50% in all categories, which is significantly inferior to the result of the MLP or fuzzy approach. Since the detection of fraudulent financial reporting is a two-class problem, the logit regression result is about the same as randomly drawing a number out of two numbers. In comparison between MLP and self-organizing fuzzy approach, MLP was superior in the classification performance, while the self-organizing fuzzy approach works much faster than the MLP in computational speed. We believe that the MLP's superior performance is due to the fine tuning of the model through many repeated learning steps. Thus, the self-organizing fuzzy approach is also expected to improve its classification performance if cluster-centers are fine-tuned using the method such as the one suggested in [2].

Table 4.3. Performance comparison

Method	Classification Accuracy
Logit	47.1%
Neural Network	87.8%
Fuzzy Controller	71.2%

5. Conclusions

The main contribution of this paper is to compare the MLP and fuzzy controller approaches in predicting the targets of SEC investigation. In direct comparison of the performance on the present SEC investigation problem, the MLP network outperformed both the logit and fuzzy approaches. We believe that the performance of the fuzzy approach can be significantly improved if the center vectors are fine-tuned using some adaptive algorithms. Our empirical results demonstrate that both MLP and fuzzy approaches can be powerful tools, especially in the pattern classification or detection problems, such as those related to fraudulent financial reporting.

References

1. D.E. Rumelhart, G.E. Hinton, and R.J. Williams, "Learning internal representations by error propagation," in *Parallel Distributed Processing*, vol. 1, D.E. Rumelhart, J.L. McClelland, and PDP research group, Eds., Cambridge, Mass: MIT press, pp. 318-362, 1986.
2. T. M. Kwon and M. E. Zervakis, "A Self-Organizing KNN-Fuzzy Controller and Its Neural Network Structure," *International Journal of Adaptive Control and Signal Processing*, vol. 8, pp. 407-431, Jul.-Aug., 1994.
3. T. M. Kwon, M. E. Zervakis, and A. N. Venetsanopoulos, "Design and Analysis of a Class of Self-Organizing and Trainable Fuzzy Controllers," *Journal of Intelligent and Robotic Systems*, vol. 12, pp. 1-15, 1995.
4. American Institute of Certified Accountants, *Statement on Auditing Standards No. 53. The Auditor's Responsibility to Detect and Report Errors and Irregularities*, New York: AICPA, 1988.
5. J. H. Aldrich and F. D. Nelson, *Linear Probability, Logit, and Probit Models*, London: SAGE Publication Ltd, 1984.
6. E. H. Feroz, K. Park, and V. Pastena, " The Financial and Market Effects of the SEC Accounting and Auditing Enforcement Releases," *Journal of Accounting Research*, vol. 29, pp. 107-142, Supplement, Spring 1991.
7. T. Kwon and H. Cheng, "Contrast enhancement for back-propagation," *IEEE Trans. on Neural Networks*, vol. 7, no. 2, pp. 515 - 524, Mar. 1996.
8. T. M. Kwon and E. Feroz, "A Multi-layered Perceptron Approach to Prediction of the SEC's Investigation Targets," *IEEE Trans. on Neural Networks*, vol. 7, no. 5, pp. 1286 - 1290, Sep. 1996.
9. L. A. Zadeh, "Fuzzy logic," *IEEE Comput. Mag.*, pp. 83-93, Apr. 1988.
10. J. C. Platt, "Learning by combining memorization and gradient descent," in *NIPS-3*, eds., by R.P. Lippmann, J.E. Moody, and D.S. Touretzky, pp.714-720, San Mateo, CA: Morgan Kaufmann, 1991.
11. M. Stone, "Cross-validation: A Review," *Mathematische Operationsforschung Statistischen, Serie Statistics*, vol. 9, pp. 127-139, 1978.

Studies in Fuzziness and Soft Computing

Vol. 25. J. Buckley and Th. Feuring
Fuzzy and Neural, 1999
ISBN 3-7908-1170-X

Vol. 26. A. Yazici and R. George
Fuzzy Database Modeling, 1999
ISBN 3-7908-1171-8

Vol. 27. M. Zaus
Crisp and Soft Computing
with Hypercubical Calculus, 1999
ISBN 3-7908-1172-6

Springer
and the
environment

At Springer we firmly believe that an international science publisher has a special obligation to the environment, and our corporate policies consistently reflect this conviction.

We also expect our business partners – paper mills, printers, packaging manufacturers, etc. – to commit themselves to using materials and production processes that do not harm the environment. The paper in this book is made from low- or no-chlorine pulp and is acid free, in conformance with international standards for paper permanency.

Springer

Printing: Weihert-Druck GmbH, Darmstadt
Binding: Buchbinderei Schäffer, Grünstadt